Evangelos Karakasis
T. Calpurnius Siculus

Trends in Classics –
Supplementary Volumes

Edited by
Franco Montanari and Antonios Rengakos

Scientific Committee
Alberto Bernabé · Margarethe Billerbeck
Claude Calame · Philip R. Hardie · Stephen J. Harrison
Stephen Hinds · Richard Hunter · Christina Kraus
Giuseppe Mastromarco · Gregory Nagy
Theodore D. Papanghelis · Giusto Picone
Kurt Raaflaub · Bernhard Zimmermann

Volume 35

Evangelos Karakasis
T. Calpurnius Siculus

A Pastoral Poet in Neronian Rome

DE GRUYTER

ISBN 978-3-11-061171-7
e-ISBN (PDF) 978-3-11-047325-4
e-ISBN (EPUB) 978-3-11-047269-1
ISSN 1868-4785

Library of Congress Cataloging-in-Publication Data
A CIP catalog record for this book has been applied for at the Library of Congress.

Bibliographic information published by the Deutsche Nationalbibliothek
The Deutsche Nationalbibliothek lists this publication in the Deutsche Nationalbibliografie;
detailed bibliographic data are available on the Internet at http://dnb.dnb.de.

© 2018 Walter de Gruyter GmbH, Berlin/Boston
This volume is text- and page-identical with the hardback published in 2016.
Logo: Christopher Schneider, Laufen
Printing and binding: CPI books GmbH, Leck
♾ Printed on acid-free paper
Printed in Germany
www.degruyter.com

Preface – Acknowledgments

Recent years have witnessed a growing interest in post–Vergilian Roman pastoral, especially in Calpurnius Siculus, with several important commentaries and individual papers focusing on various aspects of his bucolic poems. In terms of this revival of interest, the main aim of this book is to offer a systematic reading of Calpurnian poetics from the viewpoint of 'generic evolution' and within the historical context of the Neronian period. Some of the material included in this book has already been published as separate papers on individual poems; however, it has been revised in the light of new research and bibliographic data, and has been enriched and incorporated into a book exploring Calpurnian poetics as a whole.

I would like here to express my deepest thanks to friends and colleagues who have helped me during the preparation of this book: first, I would like to thank the two anonymous readers for their valuable remarks overall and in points of detail. Many thanks are also due to Prof. R. L. Hunter (University of Cambridge) who has kindly discussed with me several thorny 'pastoral issues' and given me his insightful feedback. A special debt of gratitude goes to Prof. T. D. Papanghelis (University of Thessaloniki and Academy of Athens), who proved once again a bucolic Mentor, helping me decisively in forming my ideas on the 'generic evolution' of Calpurnian pastoral and its historical contextualisation; his continuous help, thought–provoking remarks and invaluable criticism made me re–assess several problems and bring this book to its completion. Last but not least, I would like to warmly thank Prof. A. Rengakos (University of Thessaloniki and Academy of Athens); his constant interest in the progress of my work, his strong willingness for help and assistance, his unfailing eagerness to include this book in the *Trends in Classics–Series* make him yet again worthy of many special and cordial thanks.

Contents

Introduction —— 1
    The Poet (Dating and Origin) —— 1
    The Poems —— 3
    This is the Plot of the Calpurnian eclogues: —— 4
    Aims / Objectives of the Present Study —— 5
    Generic 'Self-Consciousness' / Generic 'Tradition and Originality' —— 7
    Politics and Poetics —— 9

Part A: The Political Eclogues 1, 4, 7

Calpurnius 1 —— 15
    The Bucolic Frame —— 15
    The *Antrum* as a Scene of Bucolic Narration —— 19
    The Prophecy —— 22
    Epic / Tragic Intertexts and Bucolic / Elegiac Models —— 24
    Panegyric in the Years of the *Quinquennium Neronis* The Comet of 54 AD and its 'Poetics' —— 36
    The Epilogue of the Pastoral Narrative —— 41
    Linguistic Novelty and 'Generic Transgression' —— 43
    Conclusion —— 45

Calpurnius 4 —— 48
    The Introductory Narrative —— 48
    The Song-Exchange —— 67
    Reception of the *laudes principis* – Closure —— 78
    Diction and 'Generic Novelty' —— 83
    Conclusion —— 85

Calpurnius 7 —— 87
    Framing Introduction —— 87
    The Ecphrasis —— 97
    The Reception of Corydon's Account —— 108
    Criticism of the Neronian Regime or not? —— 110
    Inverting Scenes of Poetic Initiation? —— 113
    The Language of the 'Generic Evolution' —— 115
    Conclusion —— 117

Part B: Pastoral, Elegy, Comedy and the Georgics

Elegy and Comedy

Calpurnius 3 — 123
    Methodological Remarks: Pastoral vs. Elegy — 123
    The Introductory Narrative — 125
    Lycidas' Account of his Erotic Plight; Iollas' Reaction — 131
    Lycidas' Song — 137
    Werbung — 139
    Musical Excellence — 140
    Beauty — 141
    Wealth — 142
    Repentance — 144
    Gifts — 145
    Threats for Suicide — 147
    The Concluding Narrative — 149
    Menander's *Perikeiromene* — 150
    Conclusions — 152

Georgics

Calpurnius 5 — 157
    Methodological Remarks and Caveats: the Notion of the Didactic Genre and Mode — 158
    'Didactic Intent' – 'Teacher–Student Constellation' — 161
    'Didactic Intent' – 'Teacher–Student Constellation' and Calp. 5 — 166
    The Spring Manual — 168
    The Summer Manual — 172
    The Autumn and Winter Manual — 177
    Didactic Style and Arrangement-Patterns — 179
    'Poetic Self-Consciousness' – 'Poetic Simultaneity' — 182
    'Poetic Self-Consciousness' – 'Poetic Simultaneity' and Calp. 5 — 185
    Pastoral Framings and Georgics Framed — 186
    A *Dichterweihe*-Setting? — 189
    Conclusion — 191

Elegy and Georgics

Calpurnius 2 —— 195
    The Prerequisites —— 195
    The Singing Match —— 202
    The Draw —— 216
    Linguistic Realism —— 217
    Conclusion —— 219

Part C: Challenging the Very Structure of the Singing Match...

Calpurnius 6 —— 223
    A Singing Match off Stage —— 224
    Past – 'Generic Tradition' vs. Present – 'Generic Novelty' —— 226
    Bickering – Part One —— 227
    The Stakes and their Ecphrases —— 235
    The Location of the Singing Match —— 239
    Bickering – Part Two —— 244
    Closure Devices —— 248
    Conclusion —— 249

General Conclusions —— 251

Bibliography —— 255

Index Locorum —— 273

General Index —— 307

Introduction

The Poet (Dating and Origin)

The dating of Calpurnius' life and works still remains a hotly debated issue. Suggestions include the late first century, after Statius, the reign of Domitian, the period of Severus Alexander, in the third century AD, or the end of the third, sometimes even the fourth century. It has also been proposed that the poet, although of a later date, chose to set his bucolics in the Neronian years[1]. But the consensus view, since Haupt 1875, 1.358–406, is that Calpurnius should be considered a Neronian poet and that his poems, in all likelihood written in praise of the Neronian regime, should be dated to the Neronian period[2], and in particular to the

---

[1] Cf. Champlin 1978, 95–110; 1986, 104–12 (in the time of Severus Alexander; the scholar constructs his argument on the basis of several alleged historical allusions in the Calpurnian text, which he mistakenly contextualises in the Severan period (namely, vv. 1.45, 49, 77–81, 4.39–42, 87, 7.48ff., 65–6). For a compelling refutation of his thesis, cf. especially Townend 1980, 166–74, Vinchesi 2014, 17–8; see also Mayer 1980, 175–6, Wiseman 1982, 57–67; cf. also Kraffert 1883, 151); Armstrong 1986, 113–36 (rejection of the Neronian chronology, based mainly on linguistic, stylistic and metrical criteria; for a refutation of this thesis with some justification, cf. mainly Schröder 1991, 17 and n. 7, Horsfall 1997, 166–96, Mayer 2006, 455, Vinchesi 2014, 18 and the literature cited there), see also Armstrong–Champlin 1986, 137 – a post–script to the previous discussion; Ostrand 1984 (Domitian's reign vs. Verdière 1993, 349–55); Courtney 1987, 148–57 (late first century, after Statius), cf. also 2004, 426–7. On account of several similarities between Calpurnius Siculus, on the one hand, and Martial, Statius and Silius Italicus, on the other, Courtney comes to the conclusion that Calpurnius, a minor poet, is the imitator; see, however, the convincing reservations expressed by Vinchesi 2014, 18–9; Horsfall 1993, 269–70; 1997, 166–96 (indeterminably later than the Neronian period; yet Calpurnius shows a particular taste for this phase), see also Coleman 2006, 85 and n. 5 for a dating of the eclogues to the third century, despite the fact that the poems 'are set in the reign of Nero', Edmondson 1996, 89–90 and n. 90 for a poet (Calpurnius) writing sometime after the Flavian era, though choosing to set his poems in the Neronian period, Feeney 2007, 136–7; Baldwin 1995, 157–67 (third century AD). Cf. also Keene 1912, 96 for a dating of Calpurnius in the age of Commodus as claimed by T. Maguire, Garnett 1888, 216 opting for Gordian III (a date also accepted by Fuxa and Chindemi, cf. Spadaro 1969, 5 and n. 2, Gagliardi 1984, 12–3 and n. 15, Di Salvo 1990, 23 and n. 27), Jennison 1922, 73 postulating a chronology from Gordian I onwards (see also 1937, 70–1, 188–9), Raynaud 1931, 34 claiming a date in Probus' years; see also Burckhardt 1954, 112 for a date in Numerianus' time and Chastagnol 1976, 81–2 (end of the third / fourth century).

[2] Haupt 1875, 358–406, Skutsch 1897, 1401–6, Postgate 1902, 38–40, Ferrara 1905, 15 ff., Butler 1909, 151–2, Summers 1920, 90–1, Chiavola 1921, 7 ff., Cesareo 1931, 7–8, Wendel 1933, 35, De Sipio 1935, 7 ff., Manni 1938, 113–4, Bardon 1968, 226; 1972, 9–10, Toynbee 1942, 87, 90, Giarratano 1943, V, Momigliano 1944, 97–9, Levi 1949, 76, Rogers 1953, 241,

so-called *quinquennium Neronis*, 54–9 AD. The poet's origin is equally obscure, as the *cognomen* Siculus does not necessarily refer to the poet's place of birth, but may point to his 'generic identity' as a representative of Sicilian (that is, pastoral) poetry[3]. Even for his name, T.(itus) Calpurnius Siculus, there is no consensus in the transmission, with some manuscripts giving a different *praenomen* or abbreviation thereof, namely C., L., Lucil., Theocritus, C. Titus, whereas the

---

243, Verdière 1954, 15; 1985, 1849–50; 1992, 34; 1993, 349–98, Theiler 1956, 568–70, Duff 1960, 264–5, Grant 1965, 71, Lana 1998, 823–7, Cizek 1968, 147–8; 1972, 371, Rosenmeyer 1969, 20, 123, Spadaro 1969, 5, Scheda 1969, 60–5, Korzeniewski 1971, 1ff., Cupaiuolo 1973, 191–2, Fuchs 1973, 228, Leach 1973, 53, Joly 1974, 42, Gnilka 1974, 124, Messina 1975, 8, 14, Bartalucci 1976, 85–6, Friedrich 1976, 8, Perutelli 1976, 781, Cooper 1977, 4, Kettemann 1977, 99, Grimal 1978, 163, Williams 1978, 276, 299, Narducci 1979, 26, Mayer 1980, 175–6; 2005, 234; 2005a, 67; 2006, 454–6, Townend 1980, 166–74, Casaceli 1982, 85–103, Wiseman 1982, 57–67, Gagliardi 1984, 10–2, Griffin 1984, 37, 272 and n. 2, Küppers 1985, 341, Sullivan 1985, 51–2 and n. 63, Amat 1988, 75; 1991, vii-viii, xix-xxiv; 1998, 193, Effe-Binder 1989, 113, Mackie 1989, 9, Coleman 1990, 52 and n. 69, Di Salvo 1990, 21–2, Langholf 1990, 355, Kegel-Brinkgreve 1990, 151, Pearce 1990, 11, Schröder 1991, 17 and n. 7, Krautter 1992, 188–201 (cf. especially p. 189), Fugmann 1992, 202–7, Vinchesi 1992, 151; 1996, 5–6, 12–3; 2002, 139 and n. 2; 2009a, 572 and n. 7; 2014, 15–20, Fear 1993, 43; 1994, 269 and n. 3, Dihle 1994, 108, Vozza 1994, 76 and n. 22, Römer 1994, 98, Slater 1994, http://, Beato 1995, 626; 2003, 83, Esposito 1996, 32–4; 2009, 33, Fantham 1996, 161, Keene 1996, 2–14, Martin 1996, 18; 2003, 73 and n. 2, Paschalis 1996, 135, Schubert 1998, 44ff., Merfeld 1999, 71–2 and *passim*, Schäfer 2001, 139, Newlands 2002, 143 and n. 89, Ruggeri 2002, 201–43, Fey-Wickert 2002, 11, Di Lorenzo-Pellegrino 2008, 7, Shotter 2008, 192, Monella 2009, 77 and n. 26, Becker 2012, 17, Delbey 2013, 302, Henderson 2013, 176–85, Hutchinson 2013, 178. For a good account of the various views on the chronology of individual Calpurnian eclogues, cf. also Morford 1985, 2027–8, Di Salvo 1990, 21–4, Schröder 1991, 17 and n. 7, Verdière 1993, 349, Esposito 2009, 30 and n. 37; see also Gowers 1994, 145: 'it will always be tempting to claim Calpurnius for a Neronian'.
3 Cf. Glaeser 1842, 2–3, Haupt 1875, 377, Cesareo 1931, 8–13, Verdière 1954, 16, Korzeniewski 1971, 1, Leach 1973, 88, Gagliardi 1984, 9, Mackie 1989, 9, Amat 1991, viii-ix, Vinchesi 1996, 7, Lana 1998, 823, Fey-Wickert 2002, 11, Mayer 2006, 454 and n. 6. Verdière (cf. 1954, 17, 247 vs. Verdière 1985, 1856), not so compellingly, points to a probable Iberian origin of the poet (cf. also Bardon 1968, 222, Casaceli 1982, 102 and n. 28), on the basis of both Calp. 4.39ff. and epigraphic evidence, namely on the name Cabedus Sicculus – CIL 2.2863, whereby Sicculus may be an erroneous form of Siculus; yet for a compelling refutation of this thesis, cf. Luiselli 1960, 139ff. observing that the form Sicculus may be explained as the diminutive of *siccus*; see also Gagliardi 1984, 9 and n. 2, Vinchesi 1996, 8 and n. 6 (also for an alleged association of the poet with the *gens Calpurnia*). For the thesis that the *cognomen* Siculus may point to a Sicilian origin of Calpurnius, cf. Skutsch 1897, 1405, Hubaux 1930, 173–4, Giarratano 1930, 463, Cesareo 1931, 176, 194 and n. 1, Luiselli 1960, 142, Mahr 1964, 3–5, Messina 1975, 19–21, Gagliardi 1984, 13, Amat 1988, 75, 82; 1991, x-xi; 1995, 82, Di Salvo 1990, 24, Beato 2003, 83, Delbey 2013, 297; on the basis of Calp. 7.17: *Lucanae pecuaria silvae*, a Lucanian origin has also been argued for, cf. Chytil 1894, 8.

nomen gentis, Calpurnius, is also attested as Calphurnius[4]. As to his life, a sketch is usually drawn on the basis of the information provided by the Calpurnian narrative itself. One might claim that the poet was, in all likelihood, a man of small means, who was eventually adopted into the famous *gens Calpurnia*; a well-known member of this *gens* was the famous conspirator under Nero, C. Calpurnius Piso (65 AD), and thus Calpurnius' identity is inevitably linked with the equally vexed issue of whether or not the pastoral poet is also the author of the *Laus Pisonis* (see also below[5], pp. 3–4), a poetic panegyric most probably in praise of C. Calpurnius Piso.

The Poems

Modern scholarship attributes seven bucolic poems to Calpurnius, although until the 19th c. (Haupt 1875) Nemesianus' four pastoral poems were mistakenly transmitted under Calpurnius' name. The text of Calpurnius' bucolic poems is based on two manuscript families[6]. These seven poems (eclogues) can be viewed as a single pastoral book[7], with a 'concentric ring structure' (Hubbard 1998, 152)[8]. Thematically, it can be divided in two main groups: a) the so-called panegyric sub-group (eclogues 1, 4 and 7), whose subject-matter is the praise of the emperor and in which the pastoral setting only functions as a backdrop for the panegyric composition, and b) the pastoral poems proper (eclogues 2, 3, 5 and 6), the *merae bucolicae*, which more or less follow the line of Theocritean, Greek post-Theocritean and Vergilian bucolics[9]. Some scholars also attribute the *Laus Piso-*

---

4 Cf. Vinchesi 2014, 21 and nn. 45, 46.
5 Cf. Vinchesi 2014, 21–3.
6 Cf. especially Reeve 1978, 223–38; for the transmission of Calpurnius, see most recently the extensive discussion by Vinchesi 2014, 53–61.
7 Cf. especially Davis 1987, 32–8, 49–50.
8 For the arrangement of Calpurnian pastorals, cf. especially Grant 1965, 71, Cancik 1965, 22–3, Korzeniewski 1972, 214–6; 1974, 923–4, Leach 1975, 216–7, Friedrich 1976, 12–5, Vinchesi 1996, 51; 2009a, 573 and n. 11; 2014, 33, Hubbard 1998, 152–3, Lana 1998, 823–4, Fey-Wickert 2002, 14–6, Mayer 2006, 456–7. Cf. also Davis 1987, 32–8, 49–50, who reads the fourth eclogue as the structural separator of the realistic last three eclogues from the idealising Calp. 1–3; see also Schröder 1991, 9–13. As to the number (7) of the Calpurnian eclogues, Korzeniewski 1972, 216 rightly points out the Apollonian associations of the figure, crucial for the Apollo-image of the emperor Nero; cf. also Korzeniewski 1974, 924–5, Vinchesi 1996, 51; 2009a, 573 and n. 11; 2014, 33–4, Simon 2007, 44.
9 Cf. Hubbard 1998, 152; see also Vinchesi 2014, 28. For Calpurnius and the 'anxiety of Vergilian influence', Vergil being the main model (cf. Mayer 1982, 310–11) of the Neronian poet, cf. especially Slater 1994, http://; see also Soraci 1982, 114–8. For Theocritus and Calpurnius,

nis to Calpurnius Siculus, but this view is not undisputed[10], and the same can be said for the attribution of the *Einsiedeln* Eclogues to Calpurnius Siculus[11].

This is the Plot of the Calpurnian eclogues:

1. An old prophecy carved on a beech-tree speaks of the return of the Golden Age, inaugurated by the coming into power of a young divine *princeps* and characterised by the ideals of *pax, iustitia, securitas* and *Clementia*. Two herdsmen, Corydon and his brother, Ornytus, happen upon this prophecy, ascribed to Faunus, and come to a decision to set it to music, hoping it will provide access to the circles of the emperor.
2. The love of a girl, Crocale / Crotale, causes a singing match between the herdsman Idas and the gardener Astacus[12]. The song-exchange takes the form of strophic units whose subjects include appeals to gods, pastoral and agricultural occupations, love, etc. However, the contest is inconclusive as Thyrsis, the arbiter of the match, pronounces a draw.
3. The herdsman Iollas searches for his lost heifer, and encounters Lycidas, who has been abandoned by his beloved and is engaged in a lament. Lycidas composes a reconciliatory verse epistle, containing various motifs of the erotic *Werbung* of a bucolic lover: self-praise concerning his musical merit, good looks and assets, expression of repentance for unjust acts, offer of presents, threats of suicide. The lost heifer is found and returned by a secondary character, Tityrus, and the two herdsmen view this as a good sign for Lycidas' love-affair.
4. Corydon and his younger brother, Amyntas, engage in a song-exchange in front of Meliboeus (as in Calp. 1), Corydon's patron, in the hopes that Meliboeus will introduce Corydon into imperial circles. The song's themes include: invocations to divinities, georgic wealth and a feeling of security due to the benevolence of a godly emperor, eulogy of imperial legislation, bucolic celebrations, and requests in favour of the emperor. The eclogue ends (cf. also Calp. 2) with the pastoral characters returning to their everyday occupations.

---

see especially Leach 1975, 213, Messina 1975, 10, Di Salvo 1990a, 275 and n. 33, Esposito 1996, 29, Vinchesi 1996, 42–5; 2014, 36–7, Fey-Wickert 2002, 13, Mayer 2006, 462, Magnelli 2006, 468 and the reservations of both Gagliardi 1984, 13 and n. 17 and Hubbard 1998, 156 and n. 28.
10 Cf. Amat 1991, 71–6, Delbey 2013, 297–303; see also Vinchesi 2014, 21–3 and the literature cited therein.
11 Cf. the overview by Karakasis 2011, 44–5 and n. 229.
12 For song-contests in Calpurnius, cf. especially Gibson 2004, 1–14.

5. This eclogue is in fact a lesson *de grege regendo*, i.e., a set of instructions on the proper raising of sheep and goats offered by Micon to his (foster-) son, Canthus. This guide is arranged on the basis of the seasonal cycle, starting with the spring and continuing with the summer, autumn and winter.
6. Astylus and Lycidas engage in a singing match to settle their differences, after a quarrel over the former's decision to pronounce Alcon as the winner in a singing match against Nyctilus. The stakes are described in detail (Astylus' stag and Lycidas' horse) and the site for the song-exchange is eventually chosen. However, on account of the hostility between the two contestants, the singing match is cancelled, and the umpire, Mnasyllus, refuses to perform his role.
7. Corydon, recently returned from the city to the country, gives Lycotas an enthusiastic account of the amphitheatre in the city, and its shows. Lycotas expresses his envy for Corydon's good luck in experiencing such a show and in having seen the *princeps*, and the eclogue comes to its end with Corydon's portrayal of the emperor as a combination of Apollo and Mars.

Aims / Objectives of the Present Study

As observed above (cf. pp. 1–2), Calpurnius must have flourished in the first hopeful and promising years of the Neronian regime, the so-called *quinquennium Neronis*, during which the interest in the revival of the Augustan ideals (political, social and literary) was vigorous[13]; it would thus be appealing to study the ways in which Calpurnius exhibits his interest in one of the main literary concerns of the Augustan period, which were under the influence of the relevant Alexandrian criticism, namely the research on poetic genres – the so-called εἰδογραφία[14], with special reference evidently to the evolution of pastoral as an independent 'generic formation'. In other words, the book aims to examine Calpurnius' reception of his pastoral models (especially his Augustan predecessor, the bucolic Vergil), his efforts to widen the pastoral canon by incorporating features and topics formally belonging to other literary genres, his desire to spell out his 'generic transcendence' of previous pastoral as well as his occasional attempt to perpetuate 'generic tensions' already operating in earlier pastoral (as the one between elegy and pastoral as distinct forms of the Augustan Neoteric discourse, in Verg. *Ecl.* 2 and 10 for example). All this with a methodological cav-

---

[13] Cf. especially Momigliano 1960, 456, Mayer 1982, 305, Esposito 2009, 33 and n. 45.
[14] Cf. Hinds 1987, 116.

eat: it is not suggested here that pastoral is a time–free 'generic zone'; one could easily understand that Calpurnius, as a late comer, 'zooming out' the previous literary traditions and their occasional fine nuances does not always play by Vergil's 'generic rules' either in forming the 'generic profile' of his bucolic poetry or in depicting various 'generic interplays'. Nonetheless the surrounding literary milieu of Calpurnius' *floruit*, with its penchant for revival or even inversion of Augustan literary trends, may justify some of the research aims set out above (cf. above, p. 5). From this perspective, the present book aims to examine the ways in which the Calpurnian text converses with the previous pastoral tradition, and to focus on the means (themes, motifs, intertexts, language and style) that Calpurnius employs in order to suggest his 'generic ambivalence', his 'generic branching out' towards forms of non–traditional pastoral discourse. The manner in which Calpurnius' 'generic modification' is applied to well-known meta-linguistic signs related to Neoteric pastoral poetics, which permeates Vergilian pastoral, will also form an important concern of the readings to follow. A further objective of the present study is to set the poems in their social and historical contexts and, thus, to read the various formalistic changes discerned on the basis of a historicising analysis of the pastoral data.

Despite the fact that a significant part of modern 'generic theory' is somewhat reserved as to the definition of genre (cf. Harrison 2007, 11–2), the view largely adopted in this book is, according to the formulation of Harrison 2007, 11, that genre exists as a 'form which can be identified through a particular generic repertoire of external and internal features'. This of course does not mean that such a repertoire is rigid and remains unchanged with the passing of time; but basic features of the form seem always to be operating and thus often create specific expectations on the part of both the author and the model / informed reader, who, therefore, may construct meaning on the basis of his / her accumulated 'generic literary experience'. What is more, following again the terminology of Harrison 2007, 16, the term host–genre denotes here the main 'generic formation' under examination, the genre that keeps the 'dominant generic role', i.e., in the case in question, pastoral. A second 'generic formation', functioning on a secondary level within the host–genre, is designated by the term guest–genre, i.e., epic, elegy, comedy, etc. Yet another theoretical tool necessary for the analysis that is to follow is the notion of mode, as developed by Alastair Fowler 1982, 106–29, in a chapter significantly entitled 'Mode and Subgenre'. Mode is the literary situation whereby a text largely belonging to one genre avails itself of some features that can be readily recognised as the 'generic markers' of a different genre (see also Chapter 5, pp. 160–1).

A further theoretical admission follows at this juncture: despite the fact that in Theocritean scholarship doubts have been expressed as to the distinction of various sub-groups among the Theocritean idylls (cf. Halperin 1983, Alpers 1996, 66, 147), the view adopted here is that an obvious, demonstrable division does exist between poems dealing with rural life, its merits and interests, and those not set in the country-side (cf. Karakasis 2011, 2–3 and n. 9). Moreover, within the pastoral idylls themselves, there exist poems (especially Theocr. 3, 11) standing apart from the rest of the bucolic idylls in projecting several practices and values which run counter, as an exception to the rule, to standard habits and values of the pastoral community (cf. in Theocr. 11 the 'unpastoral' playing of the *syrinx*; see especially below, p. 226). It is thus not without significance if, in forming their 'generic profile', Theocritus' pastoral successors choose to imitate non-pastoral or 'less pastoral' instances of an otherwise well-known bucolic poet, whom, in addition, they regard as their 'generic forerunner'. Finally, following Martirosova 1999, 'pastoral' is in this book used interchangeably with 'bucolic' with a view to avoiding repetition; subtle sub-divisions between the notions of 'pastoral' and 'bucolic', as developed by modern criticism and its engagement with later developments of the genre in particular, do not seem applicable in antiquity, especially in Theocritus, but also in Vergil and Calpurnius Siculus (cf. also Martirosova 1999, 8–9).

A further term frequently used in this study is Callimachean–Neoteric. This term designates Callimachean poetic theory as deduced by Callimachus' extant oeuvre and practised, in Roman terms, not only by the initial circle of Roman Neoteric poets (Catullus, Calvus, Cinna, etc.) but also, although with some degree of detachment from the previous Callimachean tradition, by the Roman neo-Callimacheanism (term as mainly used by Sullivan 1985, 75–6 and *passim*) as well, namely the followers of the Neoterics, that is chiefly by the Roman love-poets as well as early Vergil, i.e., authors further influenced by Parthenius. Horace as well, for all his diversity, frequently aligns himself with Callimachean poetics, and thus may also be used, although with caution, as a further source of Roman Callimacheanism.

Before the analysis proper of the Calpurnian eclogues, a few introductory words on the basic trends of the present study (i.e., 'generic identity', poetics and politics) are in order:

Generic 'Self-Consciousness' / Generic 'Tradition and Originality'

Calpurnius clearly views himself as part of a broader 'generic tradition' in Vergil's footsteps. As befits his pastoral heritage, Calpurnius takes special care to include in his bucolics a number of pastoral 'generic markers' known, in most cases, as early as Theocritus. Typical examples are: the pastoral shade (Calp. 1.6, 8–12, 19, 2.5, 12, 21, 3.16, 27, 4.2, 16, 37, 133, 5.2, 20, 59, 6.2, 61), bucolic flora (e.g. pine-tree, beech, Calp. 1.9–10, 11–2, 20–1, 2.59, 4.16, 35, 7.5[15]) and fauna (e.g. goats and sheep, Calp. 2.13, 37, 4.168, 5.29, 40, 73, 84 (*ovis*) / 2.37, 62–3, 68, 4.102, 5.15, 37, 48 (*agna/us*) / 2.18, 3.1–2, 15–7, 64, 98, 4.60, 7.3 (*iuvenca, taurus*) / 3.63, 4.166, 6.3, 7.10, 14 (*haedus*) / 5.5, 14, 29 (*capella*) / 5.23, 68 (*hircus*), etc.), mountain and forest-scenery (Calp. 1.8–10, 4.38, 88, 95–8, 110–11, 133, 136, 153, 6.78, 7.2, 8, 30–2), song-exchange (Calp. 2, 6, 7.13–5), basic pastoral occupations (e.g. making of a pipe (Calp. 1.17–8, 3.26–7, 4.19–20), the rustic pantheon (Faunus, Pan, Satyrs, Nymphs, Silvanus, *pastoralis* Apollo, etc.), pathetic fallacy (Calp. 2.15–20, 7.2–3), the *locus amoenus* (Calp. 1.4–7, 8–12, 2.4–7, 57–9, 4.1–4, 6.60 ff.), *adynaton* (Calp. 1.87–8, 2.72–3), etc.[16].

However, an innovative current runs through Calpurnius' work with respect to his pastoral predecessors[17], expressed in terms of the familiar trend of Neronian literature to alter or to reverse Augustan literary trends ('Ästhetik der Verkehrung', cf. Castagna and Vogt-Spira 2002; see also Mayer 2006, 460–2). Whereas Tityrus of Verg. *Ecl.* 1 goes to Rome with the purpose of securing the continuation of his pastoral existence through the involvement of a divine young man (Octavian), and, accordingly, is only too glad to come back to his bucolic location, Corydon of Calp. 7 is so charmed by the urban grandeur that he returns to the country-side with lack of enthusiasm (see Chapter 3, pp. 87–119)[18]. 'Generic interaction' is in operation in all the Calpurnian bucolics: the political eclogues adopt clear panegyric discourses[19], absent from pre-Calpurnian pastoral (see also below – 'politics', pp. 9–11). This panegyric outlook is frequently combined with epic allusions in terms of themes, motifs, intertexts, language and style. For example, in Calp. 1 the *impia* Bellona offering her hands to be tied (vv. 46–7) brings to mind the Vergilian *impius Furor* (*A.* 1.291–6) (see Chapter 1, pp. 25–6). A 'generic movement' towards epos is also evident in the ecphrastic narratives of Calp. 6, unusually lengthy in relation to the pastoral tradition (see Chapter 7, pp. 235–9). As to the rest of the *merae bucolicae*, 'generic interaction' is detectable mainly with respect to elegy and the georgics: part of Calp. 3 is fashioned as an erotic epistle and incorporates a number of elegiac motifs, such as the character type of the *exclusus amator*, signs of *eros* (sleepless-

---

[15] The flora that appears in both Calpurnius and Nemesianus does not present the varied gamut of the previous literary tradition; cf. especially Grant 2004, 125–34, in particular p. 131.
[16] Cf. especially Karakasis 2011, 39–40 and the following chapters, *passim*.
[17] Cf. especially Magnelli 2006, 467–77; Friedrich 1976 is still invaluable.
[18] Cf. e.g. Vinchesi 2010, 142.
[19] Cf. especially Merfeld 1999, 71–101.

ness), etc.[20], see Chapter 4, pp. 123–54). Calp. 5 is a didactic lesson largely modelled on Verg. G. 3; see Chapter 5, pp. 157–91. Both georgic and elegiac features occur in Calp. 2; basic agricultural information (husbandry, planting, etc.) as well as elegiac motifs (e.g. the festival of *Parilia*) and catch-words (*urere*, v. 56) are found throughout the poem (see Chapter 6, pp. 195–219).

'Generic evolution' is also evident on the linguistic level. Calpurnius' language includes various features of Post-Classical Latin (PC), on the level of morphology, syntax and lexicon. To a certain point, this can be attributed to the historical evolution of Latin. However, there are indications that Post-Classical language is used in some parts of an eclogue and thus functions as a means for revealing Calpurnian 'generic innovation'. For example, Post-Classical Latin features abound in the prophecy of Calp. 1 and the ecphrasis of the amphitheatre in Calp. 7; both represent the Neronian sub-generic formation of the 'bucolic panegyric' (see below, pp. 43–5, 115–7).

Politics and Poetics

If Calpurnius is indeed a Neronian poet, several data of his political eclogues tally quite well with the icon of the *princeps* as promoted by the imperial propaganda. For example, in Calp. 1 the divine youth destined to re-establish the *Aetas Aurea* is presented, like Nero, as the one who will restore *pax*, secure the feeling of public security and the enforcement of justice and law, as the personification of imperial *Clementia* (see Chapter 1, pp. 15–47). It has also been reasonably argued that the ecphrasis in Calp. 7 is about the wooden amphitheatre Nero built in 57 AD at the Campus Martius and the *munus* of the same year[21]; see Chapter 3, pp. 97–108[22].

According to earlier studies on Calpurnius' work[23], the 'masquerade bucolique' is an integral part of Calpurnian poetics, with the Calpurnian characters functioning as bucolic masks for historical persons: Ornytus of Calp. 1 has, for example, been identified with Calpurnius Statura (cf. Chapter 1, p. 18 and n. 17[24]), etc. Although this hermeneutic line has long been abandoned[25], Corydon

---

20 Cf. especially Friedrich 1976, 59–104, Vinchesi 1991, 259–76, Fey-Wickert 2002, 22–9, 143–235 *passim*.
21 Cf. e.g. Green 2009, 55 and n. 1.
22 Cf. also Vinchesi 1996, 159.
23 Cf. especially Herrmann 1952, 27–44, Verdière 1954, 49–65.
24 Cf. Herrmann 1952, 35–6, Verdière 1985, 1854.
25 For a criticism of this practice, cf. especially Davis 1987, 53 and n. 36, Vinchesi 1996, 11–2.

is still read by most scholars as a persona of the pastoral poet (cf. Chapter 2, pp. 52–4 and n. 27); Simichidas (Theocr. 7) or Tityrus similarly have been understood as symbols of Theocritus and Vergil respectively[26].

Several scholars (cf. below, pp. 39–40 and n. 119, 50–1 and n. 13, 110–3) have interpreted some details of the Calpurnian poems or the choice of some Calpurnian intertexts as an oblique disapproval of the Neronian rule, a sense of 'disillusionment', and have therefore argued against the view of Calpurnius as a servile adulator of the emperor (Garson 1974, 668)[27]. However, the position adopted here is that, at the outset of the Neronian regime, the emperor's administration generated hopes for progress with respect to Claudian rule. An extreme praise of Nero is justified both by the historical setting and the 'generic identity' of the panegyric[28].

The notion of politics and of political panegyric is fully integrated into Calpurnius' political eclogues, to an extent unknown in pre–Calpurnian, not only Theocritean but also Vergilian, pastoral (cf. especially Mayer 2006, 457). The characters of the political eclogues openly and unequivocally express their eagerness to distance themselves from the pastoral tradition (cf. Calp. 4.5–6), and the assets of the pre–Calpurnian 'green cabinet'[29], such as the echoing nature, are now unenthusiastically perceived[30]. The Calpurnian corpus contains a number of catch–words of the Neoteric movement, which experiences a revival and which the emperor himself embraces[31]. However, the political march of events by now demands the unambiguous encomium of the *princeps* and, con-

---

26 Cf. e.g. Fantuzzi 2006, 253–4.
27 Cf. especially Leach 1973, 85–7; 1975, 204–30, Newlands 1987, 218–31, Davis 1987, 32–54 (speaking of 'a record of frustration and disillusionment' on p. 49), Vozza 1993, 282–308; 1994, 71–92, Martin 2003, 73–90, Green 2009, 55–67, Monella 2009, 81–3 and his helpful survey of various relevant arguments; for a criticism of this thesis, cf. especially Fear 1994, 269–77, Vinchesi 1996, 27 and n. 39; 2014, 478–9, Mayer 2006, 457–8, who points out that the early years of Nero's dominion were up to a point 'satisfactory'; see also Verdière 1966, 164, Morford 1985, 2006, 2009 further stressing the 'revival of Augustan [literary] patronage' in Nero's days, Vinchesi 1996, 5, Magnelli 2006, 471.
28 Cf. also Fear 1994, 269–77, Mayer 2006, 453–4, 457–8.
29 For the term, cf. Rosenmeyer 1969.
30 Cf. especially Damon 1973, 292–4, Mayer 2006, 460.
31 Cf. Sullivan 1985, 91, 102, 104.

sequently, Callimachean–Neoteric meta–language, previously employed for poetry of non–political colouring, is now used with reference to poetic forms assimilating clear panegyric and epic discourses (cf. especially pp. 232, 239, 249–51)[32].

---

32 Previous versions / drafts of Chapters of this book were published as follows: Chapter 1 as 'Βουκολική Ποιητική και Πανηγυρική Ρητορική στα Χρόνια του Νέρωνα: Ποιμενική Παράδοση και Νεοτερικότητα στην Πρώτη Εκλογή του Καλπουρνίου του Σικελού', in: *Dodone: Philologia* 42 (2013), 468–513 (in Greek), Chapters 2 and 6 as chapters 7 and 6 respectively of E. Karakasis, *Song Exchange in Roman Pastoral*, Berlin and New York (2011), 213–79, Chapter 3 as 'Αποχαιρετώντας το Βουκολικό Είδος. Ο Καλπούρνιος Σικελός και η έβδομη Εκλογή του', in: D. Z. Nikitas (ed.), *Laus et Gratia in memoriam Κωνσταντίνου Γρόλλιου*, Thessaloniki (2012), 23–38 (in Greek), Chapter 4 as 'Comedy and Elegy in Calpurnian Pastoral: 'Generic Interplays' in Calp. 3', in: T. D. Papanghelis, S. J. Harrison, and S. Frangoulidis (eds.), *Generic Interfaces in Latin Literature. Encounters, Interactions and Transformations*, Berlin and New York (2013), 231–64, Chapter 5 as 'The Poetics of Latin *didaxis*: A Reading of Calpurnius Siculus' Fifth Eclogue', in: E. Karakasis (ed.), *Singing in the Shadow... Pastoral Encounters in Post–Vergilian Poetry* (TCS 4.1), Berlin and New York (2012), 153–96, Chapter 7 as 'The (Singing) Game is not Afoot' – Calpurnius Siculus' Sixth Eclogue', in: *TCS* 2.1 (2010), 175–206. The Introduction includes information which may also be found in the Introduction on Calpurnius Siculus in: E. Karakasis, *Song Exchange in Roman Pastoral*, Berlin and New York (2011), 36–44, and in my lemma on Calpurnius Siculus, electronically published in The *Literary Encyclopedia* (Uploaded 29.8.2013).

Part A: **The Political Eclogues 1, 4, 7**

Calpurnius 1

Two shepherds, Ornytus and Corydon, in an attempt to protect themselves from the hot rays of the sun[1], enter, according to the bucolic norm, a shadowy place, dedicated, in the first Calpurnian eclogue, to the god Faunus, *nemus, antra… Fauni* (vv. 8–9, 19). At the same time, the narrator of the bucolic scenario also describes a typical pastoral scene: that of a herd insouciantly enjoying the good weather under the shade of some broom-trees, their soft flanks sprawling out under the thick shade (vv. 4–5, cf. Verg. *Ecl.* 6.53[2]). Ornytus, the elder and taller of the two brothers, notices that the prophecy of the god is etched onto the bark of a beech-tree (v. 20), the sacred tree of Faunus (cf. Ov. *Fast.* 4.653 ff.[3]), who, like Apollo in Seneca's *Apocolocyntosis* (4)[4], reveals the return of the Golden Age, as the result of the accession of a young, divine emperor to the imperial throne, vv. 33–88. Having carefully gone trough the content of the prophecy, the two shepherds eventually decide to set this to music with the accompaniment of a reed-pipe, in the hope that, as typical pauper-poets seeking the support of a noble patron, their song may at some point reach the ears of the emperor, vv. 92–4. The aim of this first chapter is, thus, to highlight the ways in which Calpurnius Siculus endeavours to distance himself from the preceding pastoral tradition in his first programmatic political eclogue, and, in doing so, to become, at least to some extent, the father of the 'bucolic panegyric'.

The Bucolic Frame

The dramatic scenario of the eclogue, as is common in pastoral poetry, is set at hot noon (cf. Theocr. 1.15, 6.4, 7.21, Verg. *Ecl.* 2.8–13), when the heat of the sun forces shepherds to seek the coolness of a *locus amoenus*. But, whereas earlier bucolic poetry places this hot noon in the heart of a typical summer, here, in Siculus' first programmatic eclogue, the action unfolds during the vintage, namely the end of summer or the beginning of autumn, when the intensely hot days have not yet abated, cf. vv. 1–3[5]. On a meta-poetic level, this time-shift has been con-

---

1 Cf. Karakasis 2011, 16, 18, 29, 32, 39, 45, 49.
2 Cf. Verdière 1954, 125, Korzeniewski 1971, 10, Di Lorenzo-Pellegrino 2008, 143.
3 Cf. Schubert 1998, 55 and n. 30.
4 Cf. Friedrich 1976, 135, 147.
5 Cf. e.g. Pearce 1990, 24, Fugmann 1992, 203, Schubert 1998, 48, Vinchesi 2014, 101–2. For Verdière 1966, 164 (cf. also 1968, 534–9) the bucolic scenario of the poem is associated with

vincingly read as denoting the epigonic nature of Siculus' bucolic production (cf. Hubbard 1998, 154–5[6]). If the noon of a typical summer symbolises Theocritean and / or Vergilian pastoral poetry, late summer or autumn–settings represent, instead, bucolic poetry that succeeds the Theocritean / Vergilian summer, namely Calpurnius Siculus' eclogues[7]. From this perspective, the use of the term *tradere*, which does not merely mean 'bequeath', but may also imply 'poetic succession' as a poetological term, is interesting enough, as Hubbard *loc. cit.* again notes for v. 4: *cernis ut ecce pater quas tradidit, Ornyte, vaccae*.

Consequently, within the framework of a *Dichterweihe* (poetic initiation) scene, the *vaccae*, which also constitute an easily–deciphered and familiar meta–poetic indication of pastoral poetry (cf. Verg. *Ecl.* 3.84–5)[8], depicted here in a typically pastoral reclining position (vv. 4–5, cf. Verg. *Ecl.* 6.53)[9], are presented as having been handed down from the father to the brothers in the eclogue, i.e., from the bucolic model (Theocritus, Vergil) to the pastoral epigone (Siculus). Within the context of this poetological reading, of interest is the flora in the description of the *locus amoenus* in the introduction of the poem, which includes two tree–symbols of earlier pastoral production, namely the Theocritean pine (*pinus*) and the Vergilian beech (*fagus*), vv. 9, 11. The presence of these two sym-

---

11th October, namely the festival of *Meditrinalia* (vs. Friedrich 1976, 128–9). For others, autumn specifically recalls the accession of Nero to the throne, after the death of Claudius on October 13, 54 AD; cf. Paladini 1956, 345, Townend 1980, 168, Mackie 1989, 9, Vinchesi 2002, 141; 2014, 29, 100. Hubaux 1927, 603–16; 1930, 194; 1930a, 454 ff., falsely claimed that the first three lines of the first Calpurnian bucolic belong to a poem that preceded the eclogue, as, in his opinion, the narration does not begin with the name of a bucolic character according to pastoral ethics, there is a problem in attributing the verses to a speaker and difficulty in defining the location of the bucolic scenario. Verdière 1954, 123–4 is also of the opinion that these verses are not part of the introductory narration, noting a lacuna of 9 lines; for a refutation of these viewpoints that did not gain particular acceptance in the bibliography of the eclogue, cf. Herrmann 1931, 152, Luiselli 1963, 44–52, who convincingly juxtaposes the introductory lines of Calpurnius' first eclogue with Seneca's *Apocolocyntosis*, Verdière 1985, 1848, 1860· cf. also Spadaro 1969, 8–15, Friedrich 1976, 124–6, Vinchesi 2014, 99–100.

6 Vs. Vinchesi 2014, 104–5.

7 For the view that a) the time–shift of the bucolic narration from the intensely hot summer to a less hot autumn and b) the protection from the hot sun inside the *antrum* of Faunus symbolise the calm of the first period of Nero's *principatus*, after the political tension at the time of Claudius, cf. Leach 1973, 57 and Garthwaite–Martin 2009, 312. The eclogue begins with a reference to the sun (*sol*), with whom the emperor is also associated, cf. Suet. *Ner.* 6, 53; see also Schubert 1998, 54–5, Vinchesi 2014, 102.

8 See Karakasis 2011, 104–5 and n. 72.

9 Cf. also Verdière 1954, 125, Korzeniewski 1971, 10, Di Lorenzo–Pellegrino 2008, 143, Vinchesi 2014, 105.

bolic trees[10] in the idyllic scene of Siculus again demonstrates the epigonic perspective of Calpurnius, who composes his own, largely traditional, bucolic *locus amoenus* (cf. Korzeniewski 1971, 86, Davis 1987, 39) through a combination of tree–symbols of the pastoral tradition which serves as his model[11]. Indeed, the newly-constructed, mature cane reed–pipe of Corydon, i.e., of the poetic persona of Siculus (vv. 17–8: *mea fistula, quam mihi nuper / matura docilis compegit harundine Ladon*) according to the *communis opinio* (cf. below, Chapter 2, pp. 52–4 and n. 27; see also pp. 9–10), within the framework of the afore-mentioned poetological reading, could be interpreted as a meta-poetic indication which not only underlines the epigonic nature of Calpurnius' bucolic production (chronologically, it is later than that of Vergil = *nuper*) but also the wealth of all prior bucolic tradition, which informs the pastoral poetry of Siculus (poetic maturity–*matura*)[12]. From a stylistic perspective, this epigonic nature of Siculus' poetry is stressed in v. 1: *nondum solis equos declinis mitigat aestas*, with the option of a syntagm from Vergil's *Georgics*; that is to say, of an epigonic text compared to the Vergilian eclogues, in accordance with both the tradition of the *rota Vergiliana*[13] and the opinion of Siculus himself (cf. Calp. 4.160–3). This concerns the use of *nondum* at the beginning of the verse with *aestas* in the *clausula*, cf. Verg. *G*. 2.322[14].

Calpurnius seeks to go beyond the traditional boundaries of the bucolic genre, by taking advantage of primarily epic intertexts. This technique becomes evident from the introductory lines of the poetic narrative and, what is more, in the choice of names for the pastoral characters of the eclogue. As often in bucolic poetry, here we also have a pair of pastoral characters: Corydon and Ornytus. However, while the name Corydon has a distinct bucolic prehistory, occurring both in the fourth and fifth Theocritean idylls and in eclogues 2, 5, and 7 of the Vergilian bucolic corpus, Ornytus, as a pastoral *nomen*, does not appear in earlier bucolic texts, but mainly in epic passages, i.e., Apollonius' of Rhodes *Argonautica* (2.65) and Vergil's epic *Aeneid*, although not in his *Eclogues*. Specifically, the name is to be found in the eleventh book of the *Aeneid* (vv. 677–89), where Ornytus, an Etruscan ally of Aeneas, is presented as a tall huntsman, slain by the

---

10 See Karakasis 2011, 16, 29, 39, 156, 188–9, 227, 241, 253–4, 303.
11 Cf. Hubbard 1998, 155–6.
12 Cf. Fucecchi 2009, 46–7 and n. 26; see also Vinchesi 2014, 114. Unless, of course, one sees in *matura harundo* only a reference to an old, no longer green plant; cf. Vinchesi 2014, 114.
13 Cf. Hardie-Moore 2010, 4–5, Putnam 2010, 17–38.
14 Cf. Di Lorenzo-Pellegrino 2008, 142, Vinchesi 2014, 102.

Amazon Camilla[15]. The name Ornytus also occurs in the elegiac ninth *Ode* of the third book of Horace's *Carmina* (3.9.14), in which Calais, the son of Ornytus from Thurii in Lucania[16], is extolled. However, the emphasis placed by Calpurnius on Ornytus' tall physique (vv. 26–7: *nam tibi longa satis pater internodia largus / procerumque dedit mater non invida corpus*), exactly as in Vergil (*A.* 11.679–81), demonstrates the intertextual relationship between Siculus' first eclogue and Vergil's epic episode[17], as Hubbard 1998, 154 convincingly maintains. Within the context of the poetological reading attempted in this chapter, it seems not insignificant that the character, chosen to read the non-pastoral prophecy of Faunus, recalls epic forms[18] and is also presented as *ingens* (cf. vv. 26–7). Namely, he has qualities that are negatively connotated in the Roman Callimachean program, but are, instead, clearly combined with the poetic technique of the *genus grande*[19], towards which – both at a stylistic and a thematic level – Siculus obviously moves in the eclogue under study, especially in the section of the prophecy.

In fact, this move towards the *genus grande*, away from the pastoral beaten track, is also evidenced by the detail of the shepherd wearing a cap (*galerus / galerum*) to protect his suntanned face from the heat (v. 7). As already noted (cf. p. 15), the shepherds in pastoral avoid the summer heat and protect themselves from the sun by seeking the coolness of a shade. The use of *galerus*, however, derives not from the bucolic, but again from the epic work of Vergil; in book 7 of the *Aeneid*, the rustic army of Caeculus, the founder of Praeneste, namely poor farmers who take part in the war caused by Juno following the refusal of king Latinus to open the gates of war, are shown to wear similar caps of wolf-skin for headgear (*A.* 7.688). A *galerum* is also worn by the cultivator of *Moretum* (v. 120) in the *Appendix Vergiliana* and the savage warrior in Propertius, 4.1.29[20]. Moreover, the typical *locus amoenus* in vv. 8–12 is described by means of syntagms and stylistic options taken either from Vergil's epic work (the *Aeneid*) or the *Georgics* (yet again a non-bucolic work) (vv. 9–10: *pinea*

---

15 Cf. Cesareo 1931, 124, Messina 1975, 64, Keene 1996, 51, Vinchesi 1996, 64, Hubbard 1998, 154.
16 Cf. Friedrich 1976, 130, Di Lorenzo–Pellegrino 2008, 141, Vinchesi 2014, 105.
17 According to Herrmann 1952, 35–6, this specific mention of the tall physique of Ornytus refers to Calpurnius Statura; cf. also Verdière 1985, 1854, Vinchesi 2014, 118, Henderson 2013, 181.
18 Cf. Hubbard 1998, 157–8; see also Henderson 2013, 181.
19 Cf. Karakasis 2011, 76–8.
20 Cf. Fordyce 2001, 185, Di Lorenzo–Pellegrino 2008, 143, Vinchesi 2014, 107. For a reference here to Nero's disguise by means of a *galerus* and his nocturnal escapades (Suet. *Ner.* 26.1), cf. Verdière 1954, 233.

silva = Verg. *A.* 9.85, v. 10: *rapidus sol* = Verg. *G.* 1.92, 424, cf. also 4.425[21]), or the panegyric discourse of the Catullan corpus. V. 12: *ramis errantibus implicat umbras*, namely the combination of *implicare* and *errare*, in the description of the shade of the tree, derives from Catullus' c. 61[22]. Here, in vv. 34–5: *ut tenax hedera huc et huc / arborem implicat errans*, Catullus compares the bride of the epithalamion to ivy, within the praise for his friend, Manlius Torquatus, and his bride, Junia Aurunculeia (cf. Tromaras 2001, 421). A further linguistic allusion of v. 8 to [Ov.] *Epist. Sapph.* 137 (*antra nemusque peto*; Calp. 1.8: *nemus, antra petamus*[23]) also testifies to this movement of the Calpurnian poem towards the *genus grande*; although belonging to an elegiac work, the [Ovidian] line in question crucially belongs to a passage (cf. especially vv. 137–40), where the elegiac heroine (Sappho), as if maddened by the martial goddess Enyo, abandons herself to a frenzied, bacchic wandering, as primarily known from the tragic genre / mode (cf. Eur. *Hipp.* 215–22[24]).

The *Antrum* as a Scene of Bucolic Narration

The panegyric of the bucolic prophecy unfolds in a grove (*nemus*, v. 8) which, again according to the pastoral tradition, is chosen as the final place of action, another location having initially been suggested, which was, however, subsequently rejected by the bucolic protagonists (cf. Theocr. 5.31 ff., Verg. *Ecl.* 5.1 ff.[25]). Whereas Corydon proposes the shade of some broom-trees, under which the herd is cooling itself, Ornytus counter-proposes the nearby grove, the cave of the god Faunus (vv. 5–9). In Vergil's fifth eclogue, a similar bucolic scenario takes place: when Menalcas recommends the shade of a hazel and an elm-tree as a place to exchange bucolic songs (v. 3), Mopsus counter-proposes a cave (v. 6). Menalcas ultimately accepts Mopsus' proposal and declares in v. 19: *successimus antro*.

---

21 Cf. Korzeniewski 1971, 11, Di Lorenzo 1988, 13 and n. 44, Keene 1996, 52, Di Lorenzo-Pellegrino 2008, 144–5, Vinchesi 2014, 109–10. For the use of the word *rapidus* in v. 10 in the sense of *velox*, 'rapid', and not *ardens*, 'hot', cf. Salanitro 1975–6, 481–3.
22 Cf. Verdière 1954, 234, Paladini 1956, 526–7 and n. 1 on p. 527, Korzeniewski 1971, 11, Di Lorenzo 1988, 13, Di Lorenzo-Pellegrino 2008, 144–5, 146, Vinchesi 2014, 49, 111.
23 Cf. Verdière 1954, 233, Korzeniewski 1971, 11, Di Lorenzo-Pellegrino 2008, 143, Vinchesi 2014, 107.
24 Cf. Knox 1995, 302.
25 Cf. Vinchesi 2014, 106.

Similarly, there is the expression used by Corydon in the first eclogue of Calpurnius with which he proposes the nearby shade as the place for bucolic action, v. 6: *nos quoque vicinis cur non succedimus umbris?*, and that of Ornytus, in v. 19: *et iam captatae pariter successimus umbrae*, when he announces the entrance of the two shepherds into the grove of Faunus[26]. This linguistic choice indicates the similarity between the introductory lines of the two eclogues. However, the phrase Corydon uses in his accepting the counter-proposal for the grove, where the epic / panegyric nature of the prophecy of Faunus is to be revealed, carries epic connotations; the combination of the local *quo* with *sequi* and *vocare* in phrases of the type, v. 13: *quo me cumque vocas, sequor*, again finds parallels in the epic and not the bucolic poetry of Vergil, cf *A.* 12.677 (vs. *Ecl.* 3.49: <u>*veniam, quocumque vocaris*</u>)[27]. Therefore, also on a stylistic level, the epic parallels of Corydon's linguistic choice underline the 'generic distancing' of Siculus from the pastoral tradition, which is to reach its peak primarily in the narrative section of the prophecy.

The *antrum*, as the dramatic setting for a bucolic scenario of poetological dimensions, is to be found, prior to Siculus, in the fifth and sixth Vergilian eclogue[28]. Thus, in the fifth eclogue, the shepherds Mopsus and Menalcas, in the spirit of camaraderie, decide to share bucolic songs inside an *antrum*. As I have argued elsewhere (cf. Karakasis 2011, 153–83), it is *inside* the cave that Mopsus experiences, through Menalcas, the revelation of a 'new pastoral poetics', one which incorporates, within a bucolic context, elements of both the georgic mode and panegyric discourses. Similarly inside an *antrum*, in Vergil's sixth eclogue, Silenus reveals the history of Roman Callimachean poetry to Chromis, Mnasyllos and Aegle. Consequently, the cave constitutes a place directly related to issues of poetics, and specifically to the disclosure of a 'new pastoral poetics'[29]. Thus, in the *antra...Fauni* of Siculus' first eclogue, through a *divinum carmen* (v. 32)[30], Ornytus becomes the agent for the revelation of the new 'pastor-

---

[26] Cf. Verdière 1954, 125, Korzeniewski 1971, 10–11, 12, Messina 1975, 67 and n. 59, Friedrich 1976, 131–3, Gagliardi 1984, 53 and n. 11, Davis 1987, 39, Kegel–Brinkgreve 1990, 152, Slater 1994, http://, Di Lorenzo–Pellegrino 2008, 143, 145, 147, Vinchesi 2014, 106, 115. For an illuminating comparison between Calpurnius' first eclogue and Vergil's fifth bucolic, cf. Ahl 1984, 64–5, Paschalis 1996, 137–8; see also Hulsenboom 2013, 22.
[27] Cf. Verdière 1954, 126–7, Korzeniewski 1971, 11, Di Lorenzo–Pellegrino 2008, 146, Vinchesi 2014, 111.
[28] Cf. Hubbard 1998, 157.
[29] Vs. Hubbard 1998, 155, who maintains that the choice of a *nemus* / *antrum* by Ornytus as the place for the bucolic scenario attests to 'a lack of generic identity with the limitations of bucolic poetry'.
[30] Cf. Verdière 1993, 387, Korzeniewski 1971, 13, Di Lorenzo–Pellegrino 2008, 150.

al panegyric poetics' of the Neronian age, as the prophecy of Faunus, cloaked in a bucolic mantle, apparently serves as a panegyric of the emperor.

The selection of the *antrum* by the two characters in Vergil's fifth eclogue is accompanied by a fundamental manifestation of pastoral life: song–exchange. In the first Calpurnian eclogue, however, nothing similar occurs, although there appear several typical preconditions (meeting of two shepherds, selection of a *locus amoenus*, typical pastoral exhortations for the start of a singing match (vv. 16–8, cf. Theocr. 5.78, Verg. *Ecl.* 3.52[31]) that could lead to a bucolic ἀμοιβαῖον, with the flute and reed-pipe accompaniment of the two shepherds, vv. 16–7: *prome igitur calamos et si qua recondita servas. / nec tibi defuerit mea fistula*. Ladon, presented as the manufacturer of Corydon's reed-pipe, has a name that carries epic connotations. Siculus apparently drew inspiration, for the choice of this name, from Ovid's *Metamorphoses*; in the first book (vv. 1689– 712) and in the context of an elegiac narrative incorporated into the myth of Argus (vv. 1664–723), Hermes narrates the story of the beautiful Naiad, Syrinx, whom the Nymphs of the river Ladon (cf. also Ov. *Fast*. 2.274, 5.89) help to transform into the bucolic musical instrument (lat. *fistula*) to elude the love of Pan. However, by attributing the name Ladon to a man, Siculus also seems to be alluding to the epic work of Vergil, since the name Ladon, as a *nomen hominis*, occurs in the tenth book of the *Aeneid*, v. 413[32], as the name of one of the companions of Pallas, killed by Halesus. The handing down / gifting of the reed-pipe from one bucolic character to another is a familiar meta–poetic sign of the pastoral tradition and is associated with the transfer of pastoral poetics from a more experienced shepherd-poet to one with less experience (cf. Verg. *Ecl.* 2.36–8 (Damoetas and Corydon), 5.85 (Menalcas and Mopsus), 6.67–73 (Linus, acting as representative of the Muses, and Gallus), Calp. 4.59–63 (Tityrus, Iollas and Corydon))[33]. Corydon, however, is presented here as a pastoral poetic apprentice with a teacher whose name carries explicit intertextual connotations of the *genus grande*, although this *magister* is also characterised as *docilis* (v. 18), namely *doctus*[34]; therefore, he possesses the poetological qualities of Roman Callimachean poetics (cf. e.g. Catul. 35.17) into which Latin pastoral poetry is incorporated – in any case, up until Vergil[35]. These epic undertones of the name Ladon are further enhanced by the very prophecy that follows, in which it is

---

31 Cf. Vinchesi 2014, 113.
32 Cf. Friedrich 1976, 130, Di Lorenzo–Pellegrino 2008, 147, Vinchesi 2014, 114. In Ovid's *Met.* 3.216, in terms of the story of Actaeon, Ladon is the name of a hound.
33 Cf. Papanghelis 1995, 156–7.
34 Cf. Di Lorenzo–Pellegrino 2008, 147, Vinchesi 2014, 114.
35 Cf. Karakasis 2011, 107, 292.

clearly stated that it does not have bucolic qualities and characteristics and is not the creation of a shepherd (vv. 28–9: *non pastor, non haec triviali more viator*[36], */ sed deus ipse canit*); it does not, in any way, reflect a pastoral setting (v. 29: *nihil armentale resultat*) and is not structured on the basis of the incantation technique, popular in pastoral poetry (v. 30: *nec montana sacros distinguunt iubila versus*[37]).

The Prophecy

The use of epic intertexts as a means of approaching the *genus grande* becomes particularly evident in the narrative section of the prophecy, which is presented as having been recently carved into the bark of a beech-tree by the god Faunus himself, vv. 20–3, 29. Of interest here is the syntagm *properanti falce* – 'with a hurried scythe' – used by Ornytus in v. 21 (cf. vv. 20–1: *sed quaenam sacra descripta est pagina fago, / quam modo nescio quis properanti falce notavit?*) when describing the image of the carved *vaticinium*. Although, in terms of the god's iconography, the scythe is a typical item in the equipment of Pan = Faunus[38], Mayer 2006, 462–3, rightly notes the paradox of using a scythe to carve letters into the bark of a tree. In addition, the presence of a prophetic text of 56 verses is inconsistent with the sense of haste, resulting from the use of the participle *properanti*. The linguistic syntagm occurs once again in Latin literature, in v. 59: *stipes acernus eram, properanti falce dolatus* of Propertius 4.2, which appears to serve as an intertext of this eclogue[39]. Prop. 4.2 presents motifs in common with the first eclogue of Calpurnius, as in both cases one comes across, through a carved text[40], the revelation to a passer-by of the word of an essentially bucolic / rural god (Vertumnus (cf. Prop. 4.2.11–8, 41–6), Faunus). The statue of Vertum-

---

[36] In the Vergilian eclogues too (cf. also Verdière 1954, 128, Korzeniewski 1971, 12, Di Lorenzo–Pellegrino 2008, 149, Vinchesi 2014, 119), song of low quality is associated with street music, namely Damoetas' *triviale carmen* in Verg. *Ecl.* 3.26–7: *non tu in triviis, indocte, solebas / stridenti miserum stipula disperdere carmen?*; a distinction between pastoral of higher and lower standards is thus drawn by Menalcas. Damoetas' song, notwithstanding its poor quality, remains pastoral throughout. In the Calpurnian instance, however, this sign of music of poor value is significantly associated with pastoral song in general.
[37] For a possible allusion here, through *montana...iubila*, to the anti-Neronian Curtius Montanus' *detestanda carmina* (cf. Tac. *Ann.* 16.28), cf. Hubaux 1930, 237–8; see also Verdière 1954, 235.
[38] Cf. Korzeniewski 1971, 87, Fucecchi 2009, 49, Vinchesi 2014, 108–9.
[39] Cf. Esposito 2009, 21–2, Fucecchi 2009, 49 and n. 35, Vinchesi 2014, 50, 116.
[40] Cf. Hutchinson 2006, 87–8.

nus, however, reveals the aretalogy of the god, the αἴτιον of his name, but also the history of both the god himself and his *statua*; therefore, from a 'generic perspective', it functions within the context of a Callimachean aetiological elegy of the *genus tenue*[41]. In Calpurnius, on the other hand, Faunus apparently moves towards a panegyric of mainly epic intertexts, towards the *genus grande*. Consequently, the similarity of motifs, within the framework of the familiar Neronian technique of the 'aesthetics of deviation' ('Ästhetik der Verkehrung', cf. Maes 2008, 317 and n. 14, Karakasis 2011, 40; see also Introduction, p. 8), demonstrates the difference between the poetological orientation of the two texts.

Writing in the bucolic world occurs, prior to Calpurnius, in the fifth[42] and the tenth Vergilian eclogue[43], where it is shown to be closely related to issues of 'generic admixture' and 'consciousness'. Thus, in Vergil's fifth bucolic, the older Menalcas reveals a newer version of bucolic poetry to the younger Mopsus; the Theocritean, in essence, pastoral tradition is 'enriched' in Vergil with georgic 'generic touches' and is expanded in the direction of the panegyric (cf. above, p. 20). In this eclogue Mopsus, who has carved his own song (lyrics and melody) into the bark of the *fagus* (vv. 13–5), is the recipient of the poetological message. In addition, in the tenth Vergilian eclogue, which dramatises issues of 'generic opposition' between the bucolic and the elegiac genre in the wider context of the *genus tenue* of the Augustan age, the elegiac poet Gallus, who tries to assuage his elegiac erotic pain by becoming part of the bucolic world and embracing its values[44], is shown as being desirous of carving his loves into trees, vv. 52–4. Therefore, in the bucolic world, writing is associated with issues of 'generic consciousness' and, from this perspective, the prophecy as a written text also raises, for Siculus, issues of 'generic interaction': in this case, interfaces between, on the one hand, pastoral discourses and, on the other hand, the epic tradition, as well as a panegyric rhetoric, which also appears fundamentally to belong to the *genus grande*[45].

---

41 Cf. Camps 1965, 71, Hutchinson 2006, 87, Keith 2008, 83. However, vv. 53–4 are not without epic images, assimilated, however, in the context of a wider aetiological narration, cf. Hutchinson (*op. cit.*), 97.
42 Cf. Verdière 1954, 234, Ahl 1984, 64–5, Pearce 1990, 26, Slater 1994, http://, Vinchesi 1996, 67; 2014, 115–6, Schubert 1998, 55. Korzeniewski 1976, 249 associates the prophecy of Faunus with similar traditions (i.e., inscriptions of religious nature), such as those attested in Egypt and Eastern cultures in general; see also Vinchesi 2014, 99.
43 Cf. Joly 1974, 47, Davis 1987, 53 and n. 39, Esposito 2009, 21 and n. 14, Fucecchi 2009, 47–8.
44 Cf. Conte 1986, 100–29, Papanghelis 1995, 64–87; 1999, 57–9; 2006, 401–2, Hardie 2002, 126–7, Harrison 2007, 59–74.
45 Cf. Karakasis 2011, 8.

The carved prophecy of Faunus, the panegyric of the emperor cloaked in a bucolic mantle, is described in v. 20 as *pagina*. The word occurs in the bucolic poetry of the Romans in other two cases: in the prologue of Vergil's sixth eclogue, v. 12, the term is used within the context of poetry of praise, probably written in honour of Publius Quinctilius Varus (cf. Clausen 1994, 181), to whom the eclogue is addressed. As a *vir* of Roman *negotium*, however, the man should normally be honoured with compositions of the *genus grande*, as Vergil states in the *recusatio* of the introductory verses (vv. 6–8). In any case, poetry that praises Varus is shown to touch Phoebus (the god of the *genus tenue*) to the highest degree (vv. 11–2: *nec Phoebo gratior ulla est / quam sibi quae Vari praescripsit pagina nomen*). In Siculus' fourth eclogue (v. 52: *vis, hodierna tua subigatur pagina lima?*), the word is again associated with the production of written poetry, the songs of Corydon / Siculus, which the latter asks Meliboeus to read and review. The poetry of Corydon, however, about which Meliboeus is asked to give his opinion, clearly inclines towards the panegyric (see Chapter 2, pp. 48–86), as is expressly stated by Corydon himself in vv. 5–6: *carmina iam dudum, non quae nemorale resultent, / volvimus*. In both cases, the term *pagina* demonstrates poetological fluidity, not 'generic partiality'. As a result, on a meta-poetic level, through the word *pagina*, Calpurnius appears to be emphasising the poetic nature of the prophecy of Faunus, which, indeed, as a poetic text, adopts higher tones that raise it beyond traditional pastoral poetry. This is an example of the new panegyric pastoral poetry in the Neronian age. A joyous Faunus (vv. 34–7) will voice these *laudes principis* in hexameters; in line with the image of another happy divinity also foretelling Nero's *laudes*, namely a joyful Apollo predicting Nero's blessed *imperium* in the hexameters of Sen. *Apoc.* 4.1.15–32[46].

Epic / Tragic Intertexts and Bucolic / Elegiac Models

This 'generic inclination' of Calpurnius towards the *genus grande* is also assisted by the selection of specific epic models[47], aiming at an intertextual enhancement of the panegyric of the emperor. Typical bucolic interests and common concerns of the pastoral tradition now lose their significance in the first political eclogue of Siculus, as they also do in the fourth and the seventh bucolic of the Neronian

---

46 Cf. also Verdière 1954, 129, Di Lorenzo–Pellegrino 2008, 150, Vinchesi 2014, 123.
47 Messina 1975, 75 characterises the first eclogue of Siculus as 'epica bucolica'; cf. also Cesareo 1931, 155.

poet (see Chapters 2 and 3, pp. 48–119). Corydon, as with many other heroes of the pastoral tradition, experiences the lack of sexual response, since his beloved Leuce denies him the sexual pleasures of the night (vv. 13–5). The erotic misery, however, is no longer the focal point of the bucolic narrative[48], as happens, for example, in the third or the sixth and the eleventh Theocritean idylls (where Polyphemus complains about the sexual indifference of his own (λευκή), milk-white Galatea), the second, the eighth or the tenth Vergilian eclogues or the third *merum bucolicum* of Siculus himself (cf. Chapter 4, pp. 123–54).

On the contrary, in the eclogue in question, the lack of sexual interest on the part of the bucolic *puella* is presented in a positive light, as it ensures the necessary sexual purity of Corydon (cf. Tib. 1.3.25–6[49]), which will allow him to enter the sanctuary of the god and, thus, become a party to the divine word: namely, a prophecy in which the traditional pastimes of the bucolic world give way to the panegyric of the emperor through, primarily, epic allusive references. A further breach with the pre-Calpurnian pastoral production is also evidenced by the fact that the two shepherds enter the cave and become recipients of the prophecy of Faunus, without, however, having previously assigned the care of their animals to another shepherd, according to the pre-Calpurnian bucolic convention (cf. Theocr. 1.12–4, 3.1–5, Verg. *Ecl.* 5.12, 9.23–5).

The image of *impia* Bellona, the goddess of war in general and civil wars in particular, who, having been defeated, allows her hands to be tied behind her back (vv. 46–7), has been noted by many scholars[50] to recall, even on the level of a linguistic *imitatio*, the famous passage from the first book of the *Aeneid* (vv. 291–6), where the *impius* Furor of war is similarly described with his hands tied behind his back, *post tergum*. This syntagm occurs in both poets (Vergil, Calpurnius) in the same metrical *sedes*, at the beginning of the verse (Calp. 1.47 = Verg. *A.* 1.296); indeed, the adjective *impia / impius*, attributed to Bellona and Furor respectively, covers the dactyl of the fifth foot of the two hexameters (Calp. 1.46 = Verg. *A.* 1.294). This Vergilian passage constitutes part of the Jupiter's prophecy to Venus on the fate of Aeneas (vv. 1.254–96), when the father of the gods reveals to the goddess of love the successful outcome of the adventures

---

48 Cf. Leach 1973, 57, Martin 1996, 20.
49 Cf. Vinchesi 2014, 112.
50 Cf. Cesareo 1931, 139 and n. 2, Verdière 1954, 236, Paladini 1956, 331, Korzeniewski 1971, 14, Leach 1973, 60, Joly 1974, 49, Messina 1975, 71, Friedrich 1976, 138, Gagliardi 1984, 55, Kegel-Brinkgreve 1990, 153 and n. 8, Krautter 1992, 190–1, Keene 1996, 57, Martin 1996, 24, Vinchesi 1996, 16; 2002, 143–4; 2014, 48, 130–1, Hubbard 1998, 158–9, Di Lorenzo-Pellegrino 2008, 152–3, Garthwaite-Martin 2009, 313, Esposito 2009, 16, Fucecchi 2009, 49 and n. 34, La Bua 2010, 242, Henderson 2013, 177.

of the Romans' leader and predicts the future glory of Rome. A milestone in this historical course is the Augustan age (v. 1.286), during which the *pax Augusta* reduces the centrifugal forces of the war-fury, when Augustus, like Nero in the first eclogue of Calpurnius, restores the Golden Age and the force of law after the bloodshed of civil wars. The image of the chained Bellona in Siculus also alludes to the defeated Bellona in the *scutum* of Aeneas, namely in the eighth book of the *Aeneid*, describing the victory of Octavian at Actium and its impact on the *urbs*, vv. 675–728. The joy that Roman people feel, following the defeat of the combined forces of Mark Antony and Cleopatra at Actium (vv. 8.717–9), resembles, to a great extent, the description of the happiness felt by the pastoral community, the *populus Romanus* and the people under the *imperium romanum*, upon the return of the Golden Age, during the reign of Nero (vv. 36–7, 74–6)[51]. The two epic intertexts enhance the panegyric of the emperor as, in terms of intertextuality, they identify him with the positively connotated figure of Augustus. As has been convincingly argued[52], Nero is presented as the new Augustus. As with the founder of the Julio-Claudian dynasty, Nero will ensure the salutary peace and the *securitas* that this entails.

The image of Bellona who, having been stripped of her weapons (v. 47: *spoliataque telis*), turns on herself and bites her own innards (v. 48: *in sua vesanos torquebit viscera morsus*) also recalls another epic text of the time, Lucan's *Bellum Civile*. In the prologue, which also probably dates back to the early months of the *quinquennium* (cf. Braund 2009, 12), in v. 3, the Roman people are similarly shown to turn their right hands against themselves due to civil conflicts, *in sua victrici conversum viscera dextra*[53]. The linguistic and metrical similarity between the two lines is evident through the dactylic syntagm *in sua*, which occupies the first *sedes* in the hexameter of both poets, the fifth dactyl of which in both cases is covered by the word *viscera*, while both verses exhibit the same metrical structure (DSSS)[54]. Moreover, both texts make mention of the paradox of the Roman triumph in a civil war. For Calpurnius, therefore, free from civil conflicts in the Neronian age, Rome will no longer achieve triumphs as a captive city

---

[51] Cf. Di Lorenzo-Pellegrino 2008, 154.
[52] For the image of Nero in the first Calpurnian eclogue, which exploits the *exemplum* of Augustus and Augustan ideology in general, cf. Küppers 1985, 340–61. Cf. also Friedrich 1976, 140–3, Davis 1987, 41, Martin 1996, 24–5, Hubbard 1998, 159, Emberger 2013, 19–31.
[53] Cf. Verdière 1954, 236; 1993, 352, Paladini 1956, 331, Korzeniewski 1971, 15, Leach 1973, 93 and n. 26, Messina 1975, 71 and n. 68, Armstrong 1986, 126, Slater 1994, http:// and n. 20, Hubbard 1998, 160–1, Vinchesi 2002, 144 and n. 21; 2014, 132, Di Lorenzo-Pellegrino 2008, 153, Garthwaite-Martin 2009, 313, Esposito 2009, 17, Henderson 2013, 177–8.
[54] Cf. Krautter 1992, 192–3.

(vv. 50–1: *nullos iam Roma Philippos / deflebit, nullos ducet captiva triumphos*), while Lucan, in the prologue of his epic for the second civil war of the late Roman *res publica*, makes mention of the involvement of the Romans in (civil) conflicts which cannot lead to a triumph (v. 12: *bella geri placuit nullos habitura triumphos?*)[55]. Of course, one cannot be absolutely sure who of the poets is imitating whom. However, in terms of the *recitationes* of the period, it is highly likely that Siculus listened to the prologue in the *Pharsalia* of Lucan (vv. 1–66) and then imitated it. This view is strengthened if one dates eclogue 1 to a few years after 54 AD; namely, if we accept a dating of Siculus' work[56] slightly after the beginning of the Neronian age. In this case, therefore, yet another epic intertext further evidences the inclination of Siculus' poetics towards the epic code. In this epic intertext by Lucan, Nero is shown as the figure who, as in the first eclogue of Calpurnius, will control the civil conflicts of the first lines, as the peacemaker monarch who restores the shaken *Concordia*[57] of the State.

In any case, both texts of the Neronian age seem to recall the phrase *in viscera vertere* that Vergil uses in similar contexts in book 6 of his epic, when, on the occasion of Aeneas' descent to the Underworld, Anchises shows him the unborn souls of famous Roman leaders of the future. There (vv. 826–31), when referring to Caesar and Pompey, the father of Aeneas makes mention of the civil conflict between the father–in–law (*socer*) and his son–in–law (*gener*) and advises that the forces of Rome should not turn against its innards, v. 833: *neu patriae validas in viscera vertite vires*[58]. Anchises reproves this attitude of Caesar and Pompey and contrasts them with the heroic figures who, on the contrary, put the interest of Rome before their self–interest (Brutus, Decii, Drusi, Torquatus, Camillus, 6.817–25)[59]. The peacekeeper Nero is again associated with positively connotated figures of the glorious Roman past, through the epic intertext of the *Aeneid*.

---

[55] Cf. Armstrong 1986, 126, Verdière 1993, 353, Esposito 2009, 30, Vinchesi 2014, 133.
[56] The dramatic period of the first Calpurnian eclogue is dated to the end of 54 AD (see also above, pp. 15–6 and n. 5), namely the period which, for many, is also the date of the composition of the poem (cf. Momigliano 1944, 98, Verdière 1954, 35; 1993, 358–9 (54/5), Scheda 1969, 67, Gagliardi 1984, 52 and n. 4, Kegel-Brinkgreve 1990, 154, Fugmann 1992, 204 (54/5), Merfeld 1999, 72 (54/5)). Cf. also n. 91 below.
[57] Here, I follow the currently prevailing tendency, and consequently, as with Dewar 1994, 199–211, I do not discern a satirical attitude towards the emperor in the prologue of the *Pharsalia*, cf. also Roche 2009, 8.
[58] Cf. Narducci 1979, 28–9, Armstrong 1986, 127, Krautter 1992, 191, Vinchesi 2002, 144; 2014, 131, Roche 2009, 99.
[59] Cf. Roche 2009, 99.

On the other hand, the image of Bellona fighting herself (vv. 49–50: *et, modo quae toto civilia distulit orbe, / secum bella geret*) appears to refer, also in terms of a linguistic imitation[60], to the negatively connoted, destructive anger of Hercules in Seneca's tragedy *Hercules Furens*, which, almost certainly, dates back to shortly before 54 AD (cf. Fitch 1987, 50–3). Thus, in the first scene, revealing her plan to punish Hercules with fury, Juno presents the hero, as with Bellona in Calpurnius, turning against himself, v. 85: *bella iam secum gerat*. If Hercules, as a king, functions in Seneca as a dramatic symbol of imperial *imperium* in general[61], then the Bellona of Calpurnius is in this passage associated with figures of State-power, which testify to the negative consequences of a *Furor*. It should be noted here that, in the literature of the *quinquennium*, it was the *principatus* of Claudius that was eminently distinguished for non-rational management of State-affairs. Last but not least, in terms of the pastoral tradition as well, the description of Bellona as *impia* (vv. 46–7) further associates her with another figure, negatively focalised in the narrative of the first Vergilian eclogue, namely the *impius miles* of Verg. *Ecl.* 1.70[62]. This is a military figure of civil strife, who creates havoc, through land confiscations after Philippi 42 BC, within the 'green cabinet' of the Vergilian bucolic and who causes Meliboeus' deplored departure from his pastoral space.

The interest shown by the new divine emperor in the culture of peace, his strong desire to end the wars (both external and civil, cf. vv. 46–57, 63–8, 82–3) justify his description as a new Numa (v. 65), as a new anti-Romulus. As mentioned in the Calpurnian eclogue in question as well, the second Etruscan king of Rome, Numa Pompilius, unlike his predecessor, who cared for the martial readiness of the Romans (cf. vv. 65–6: *ovantia caede / agmina, Romuleis et adhuc ardentia castris*), dealt extensively with works of peace, mainly legislation and worship (cf. vv. 67–8; trumpets now sound only for events of worship and are no longer used for calls to war; see also Verg. *A.* 6.809–12, Cic. *Rep.* 2.25–7, Liv. 1.18–21[63]). Romulus, on the other hand, was a familiar symbol of civil conflict for the Roman world, as he killed his brother Remus[64], and, from this perspective, Nero, as guarantor of the domestic political *Concordia*, also shaken by civil conflicts, is proclaimed to be the anti-Romulus of the period. This Calpurnian Numa-Nero, as another Atlas, or a Hercules who shoulders the latter's

---

60 Cf. Korzeniewski 1971, 15, Di Lorenzo–Pellegrino 2008, 153, Vinchesi 2014, 132.
61 Cf. Fitch 1987, 39–40.
62 Cf. Vinchesi 2014, 130.
63 Cf. Martin 1996, 26, Vinchesi 1996, 16, 73; 2014, 140.
64 Cf. Maltby 2002, 439–40.

burden⁶⁵, will hold up the heavy structure of the State (*pondera molis*), according to the standard image on coins of the emperor holding up a sphere that symbolises the earth⁶⁶; thus, he will ensure the continuity of the State, vv. 84–5: *scilicet ipse deus Romanae pondera molis / fortibus excipiet sic inconcussa lacertis*⁶⁷. However, the image of a (Nero) Numa, in direct comparison with his predecessor Romulus, lifting the weight of the Roman State suggests the imperial virtue of industry and assiduity, especially with reference to the 'burden of the empire', the emperor's φιλοπονία (cf. Ov. *Fast.* 1.616), i.e., both an Augustan (see e.g. Hor. *Epist.* 2.1.1, Tac. *Ann.* 1.11) and a Neronian quality (see e.g. Sen. *Cl.* 1.1.6)⁶⁸. Moreover, it recalls lines from another epic text, Ovid's *Metamorphoses*, vv. 15.1–4; here, Fama proposes Numa as being the most suitable of all to take on the *pondera molis* (*Romani*), after the apotheosis of Romulus / Quirinus. Indeed, this syntagm occurs in both poets in the same metrical *sedes* (at the end of a hexameter), v. 15.1: *quaeritur interea, quis tantae pondera molis*⁶⁹. Ovid's *Metamorphoses* often – within a wider, but in several cases quite unclear, epic framework – incorporate elements from other literary genres, mainly elegy, but also the bucolic *genus*⁷⁰. However, the narrative section in question from the fifteenth book has a clear epic / panegyric nature, as it is included within the context of the retelling of Roman history by Ovid in books 13–5; this text, in turn, as an intertext of the prophecy of Faunus also evidences the inclination of Calpurnius towards the epic genre. The political ideology of the Augustan age associates the emperor with figures such as those of Saturn and Numa (cf. Friedrich 1976, 142–3, Vinchesi 2014, 140)⁷¹. Thus, from this perspective, Nero, as the new Saturn–Numa, is also projected simultaneously to be the new Augustus.

---

65 Cf. Schubert 1998, 62, Martin 2003, 78. Towards the end of his life, Nero (cf. Suet. *Ner.* 53) wished to imitate Hercules. Here, it is likely that we have an allusion to the emperor's wish, which might have appeared earlier; cf. Verdière 1993, 367.
66 Cf. Schachter 1927, 69–76, Paladini 1956, 341, Alföldi 1970, 235–8, Friedrich 1976, 239 and n. 72, Küppers 1985, 359 and n. 62, Keene 1996, 63, Vinchesi 2014, 150.
67 Verdière 1985, 1849–50 (cf. also Verdière 1992, 38–9) convincingly discerns wordplay in the use of *fortibus* (v. 85), a linguistic allusion to Nero, as the *cognomen* Nero, in the Sabine dialect, meant strong and vigorous, *fortis ac strenuus* (cf. Suet. *Tib.* 1).
68 Cf. also Braund 2009, 174, Vinchesi 2014, 148–9.
69 Cf. Cesareo 1931, 152, Mahr 1964, 77–8, Korzeniewski 1971, 16–7, Leach 1973, 63, Messina 1975, 73, Verdière 1982, 174, Küppers 1985, 359 and n. 62, Keene 1996, 63, Martin 1996, 27, Di Lorenzo–Pellegrino 2008, 160, Garthwaite–Martin 2009, 314, Esposito 2009, 29, La Bua 2010, 241, Henderson 2013, 180, Vinchesi 2014, 148–9.
70 Cf. e.g. Farrell 1992, 235–68.
71 Cf. also Friedrich 1976, 147.

This Calpurnian approach to the themes and the style / language of higher literary genres is not achieved solely and exclusively through the intertextual recall of epic episodes, but also by means of the imitation of passages from Vergil's eclogues, where, however, the pastoral poet explicitly emphasises his distances from the pastoral beaten track, adopting a 'generically higher style'. This occurs, for example, in the fourth eclogue of the Vergilian bucolic corpus, where the poet declares, in a programmatic manner, that he will sing in higher tones (v. 1: *Sicelides Musae, paulo maiora canamus*), worthy of a consul (v. 3: *si canimus silvas, silvae sint consule dignae*). Therefore, in Vergil's eclogue 4, which has been convincingly argued to serve as a model of the Golden Age in the first eclogue of Siculus[72], mention is made of the prophecy of Cumae (v. 4), regarding the rising of the *gens aurea* (v. 9), the return of the kingdom of Saturn (v. 6: *redeunt Saturnia regna*), due to the birth of a divine child (v. 8). In fact, the arrival of the golden race results in the return of Virgo to earth, of Astraea–Dike, the daughter of Themis (v. 6)[73]. Despite whatsoever differences there may be with the Vergilian model[74], this basic motif, the return of the *Aetas Aurea*[75] (v. 42: *aurea secura cum pace renascitur aetas*) and, therefore, the return of Themis (vv. 42–5), the goddess–protector of law[76], due to the intervention of a juvenile figure, re–occurs here in the first eclogue of Siculus[77]. Moreover, within the framework of a divine genealogy, the Calpurnian Faunus expressly states his affinity with Saturn, v. 33: *satus aethere*[78], and predicts that the kingdom of Saturn, the grandson of Aether (cf. e.g. Cic. *N.D.* 3.17), will return to Latium through the peace of the new Caesar

---

72 Cf. Verdière 1954, 235, Cesareo 1931, 137, Paladini 1956, 336, Korzeniewski 1971, 15, Garson 1974, 668, Joly 1974, 48, Messina 1975, 63, 69–70, 72, Friedrich 1976, 122–3, Gagliardi 1984, 52, 54 and n. 16, Küppers 1985, 347, Davis 1987, 40–1, Binder 1989, 364, Kegel-Brinkgreve 1990, 152, 165, Pearce 1990, 28, Amat 1991, 100, Slater 1994, http://, Paschalis 1996, 137, Vinchesi 1996, 13; 2002, 142; 2014, 28, 126–7, Hubbard 1998, 153–4, 157, Schubert 1998, 57, Merfeld 1999, 75–7, Di Lorenzo–Pellegrino 2008, 13–4, 152, Evans 2008, 167–9, Garthwaite-Martin 2009, 313, Esposito 2009, 17, Henderson 2013, 177, Hulsenboom 2013, 21–2.
73 Cf. Friedrich 1976, 136, Keene 1996, 56.
74 Cf. Martin 1996, 29.
75 The term *Aetas Aurea* does not occur in Vergil and appears later in Ovid, cf. Ov. *Met.* 1.89, 15.96; see also Esposito 2009, 28, Vinchesi 2014, 126.
76 Cf. Martin 1996, 27–9.
77 The motif of the Golden Age, as the wider framework in which the praise for Nero is developed, is also to be found in Siculus' fourth political eclogue, cf. Karakasis 2011, 41 and below, Chapter 2, pp. 48–86.
78 Cf. Martin 1996, 21, 35 and n. 11; 2003, 77 and n. 11, Fucecchi 2009, 59–60. The syntagm may be deemed to refer to Stoic concepts of aether, the supreme deity of the Stoics, cf. Korzeniewski 1971, 87, Amat 1991, 99, Vinchesi 1996, 69; 2014, 122, Fucecchi 2009, *loc. cit.*

(v. 64: *altera Saturni referet Latialia regna*)⁷⁹. Therefore, Calpurnius appears to imitate those passages of the bucolic work of Vergil in which the latter consciously and self-referentially chooses to be 'less bucolic'.

Combinatorial references to the Golden Age and the return of the kingdom of Saturn (cf. Calp. 1.42, 64; also see *Eins.* 2.22–3) can be found not only in Vergil's eclogues, but also in the *Aeneid*. In the eighth book (vv. 319–27)⁸⁰, within the context of Evander's narration of the early history of his country, the golden Saturn is shown as a guarantor of peaceful life and legislation, as is the case with Nero in the Calpurnian eclogue in question. In addition, in the sixth book (vv. 792–4), again regarding Anchises' speech in the Underworld, where he informs his son, Aeneas, about the glory of his Roman descendants, it is revealed that the person who is to bring the *aurea saecula* to Latium, being among the lands that once were under the rule of Saturnus, is Augustus. Augustus is presented as the founder of Rome's Golden Age (vv. 6.792–3), *Augustus Caesar, divi genus, aurea condet / saecula*⁸¹. Therefore, from this perspective, the Calpurnian Nero, the bearer of the Neronian Golden Age and the kingdom of Saturn of the period, is again identified with Augustus of Vergil's *Aeneid* (cf. Friedrich 1976, 140–1), who is also responsible for the return of Italy to the Golden Age of Saturn. This identification is also evident from the intertext of Verg. *Ecl.* 4. It is true that no consensus has been achieved among scholars about the identity of the golden *puer* in the eclogue, which is dated to 40 BC⁸². The *divinus puer* was variously interpreted as a pastoral symbolism of the expected son of Scribonia and Octavian, the awaited son of Octavia and Mark Antony after the treaty of Brundisium, Asinius Gallus, the son of Pollio, the Greek *Aeon*, the Messiah, etc. However, some scholars⁸³ have argued that the divine child could constitute the bucolic mask of Octavian. In accordance with the political propaganda of the *quinquennium* (cf. also Calp. 4.5–8, 137–41, 7.74–5), similar expectations were engendered from the assumption of power by Nero, as is eminently evident from the image of Lachesis in Seneca's *Apocolocyntosis* (4.1). Fate, significantly

---

79 Cf. Martin 2003, 76 and n. 8.
80 Cf. Martin 1996, 26, Di Lorenzo–Pellegrino 2008, 156.
81 Cf. Korzeniewski 1971, 15, Joly 1974, 52, Ahl 1984, 62, Küppers 1985, 347–8, Davis 1987, 42, Vinchesi 1996, 16; 2002, 143; 2014, 28, 126, Di Lorenzo–Pellegrino 2008, 14, 156, Esposito 2009, 18.
82 Cf. Clausen 1994, 119, 121, Cucchiarelli 2012, 237.
83 For an enlightening discussion of the relevant literature, cf. Papanghelis 1995, 262–5, 346 and n. 44.

in epic hexameters, is shown to spin the golden thread (the destiny of Nero) that portends the *aurea saecula* of Nero's reign[84]. Symptoms of the Golden Age (lack of danger for the herd, lack of hunting) are also ascertained in the song of Menalcas in Vergil's eclogue 5 (vv. 60–1: *nec lupus insidias pecori nec retia cervis / ulla dolum meditantur*)[85], the theme of which is the deified Daphnis and the miraculous effect the latter has over nature. This god, as with the *puer* in Vergil's eclogue 4, can be interpreted as an easily–deciphered allegory of a political figure; namely, the deified Julius Caesar within the context of a bucolic song of praise. Once again, Calpurnius chooses to imitate the bucolic work of Vergil, but wherever the latter inclines towards panegyric, albeit in a quite Callimachean / allusive manner.

Alternatively, transgression of traditional 'generic boundaries' is achieved not only through the de–pastoralisation of typical pastoral motifs / characters, but also through the de–bucolisation of individual bucolic intertexts of the Calpurnian eclogue into account. Faunus, for example, is a known member of the pastoral pantheon, identified, at least to some extent, with the Greek god Pan (cf. Verg. *Ecl.* 2.33)[86]. However, in the eclogue in question, Faunus is not presented as the typical pastoral god of herds, but as a deity with the gift of prophecy, namely in a function which again does not recall a bucolic work, but rather the epic work of Vergil (*A.* 7.81–106)[87]. In the *Aeneid*, *fatidicus / Fatuus Faunus*, upon a request of his son, king Latinus, predicts the marriage of Lavinia to a foreign bridegroom, Aeneas, and the completion of the epic mission of the latter, i.e., the foundation of the globally–dominant power, Rome, in the years of his descendants. Thus, the Vergilian Faunus indirectly refers to the glory of the Augustan age, while the Calpurnian Faunus speaks of the glory of another age, the Neronian age. Consequently, from this perspective, Nero, a descendant of *pius Aeneas* through the *Iulia gens* of his mother (cf. Tac. *Ann.* 12.58), is again intertextually identified with Augustus, also a descendant of Aeneas. As a prophetic deity, Faunus also appears in a further significant passage, namely in the fourth

---

[84] Cf. Verdière 1954, 129, Paladini 1956, 336, Eden 1984, 76–7, Küppers 1985, 349–50, Braund 2009, 14–5.
[85] Cf. Friedrich 1976, 135–7, Papanghelis 1995, 236–7.
[86] See below, Chapter 6, p. 199.
[87] Cf. Verdière 1954, 234, Leach 1973, 58, Friedrich 1976, 134–5, Davis 1987, 40, Pearce 1990, 25, Amat 1991, 3, Slater 1994, http://, Vinchesi 1996, 14, 69; 2014, 122, Hubbard 1998, 157, Magnelli 2006, 468, Esposito 2009, 15–6, Henderson 2013, 178. In Ennius' epic, 206–7 Skutsch: *scripsere alii rem / vorsibus quos olim Faunei vatesque canebant*, the Fauni are associated with the *vates*, namely the prophet, as the word in Ennius has not yet taken the meaning of 'poet' (see Skutsch 1985, 372); cf. also Verdière 1966, 161–2, Di Lorenzo 1988, 7 and n. 11, Fucecchi 2009, 61 and n. 60.

book of Ovid's *Fasti* (vv. 629–76)[88], in the description of the festival of the *Fordicidia*, the αἴτιον for which goes back to the prophecy that Numa receives from Faunus, due to the tribulations that infested the flora and fauna of the kingdom of Pompilius. Indeed, this episode by Ovid is modelled on the oracle of Faunus in the *Aeneid* (cf. Fantham 1998, 213, 215). The offer of a pregnant cow in sacrifice, namely the solution to the problem, to which the second king of Rome is led through the intervention of his wife, the Nymph Egeria, forms the historical beginning of *Fordicidia*. The festival, held on 15th April, is again associated with Augustus by Ovid. At the end of his aetiological narrative, the poet makes mention of Cytherea Aphrodite (vv. 4.673–6), the deity–ancestor of the Julian dynasty, who wishes for the following day – 16th April – to come soon, as this is the day on which Octavian was given the title *Imperator*, due to his successful resistance against the forces of Mark Antony at the battle of Mutina in 43 BC[89]. Once again, Faunus is combined with the panegyric of a Caesar.

Nero, as is often the case with Augustus (cf. e.g. Prop. 4.11.60[90]), is in Calp. 1 presented as a god on earth (cf. v. 46, Chapter 2, pp. 48–86). What is more, this appropriation of Augustus' public image by Nero is also achieved through the characterisation of the emperor as *deus iuvenis* (vv. 44, 46, cf. also Calp. 4.137, 7.6). Therefore, this description of Nero as a divine youth, descendant of the *Iulia gens* (v. 45: *maternis causam qui vicit Iulis*[91]), recalls Vergil's first eclogue, where again young Octavian (v. 42, cf. also Verg. G. 1.500) is described as *deus*, vv. 6–10, 40–5[92]. However, in the case of Vergil's first eclogue, the divine

---

[88] Cf. Korzeniewski 1971, 86, Martin 1996, 21, Esposito 2009, 26–7, Vinchesi 2014, 122.
[89] Cf. Boyle–Woodard 2004, 248.
[90] Cf. Vinchesi 2014, 130.
[91] The *communis opinio* (vs. Champlin 1978, 98–100, Wiseman 1982, 57–8, Merfeld 1999, 79 and n. 1) is that, in v. 45: *maternis causam qui vicit Iulis*, Nero is praised, because, in the presence of Claudius, he delivered a speech in Greek with which he successfully defended the inhabitants of Troy in 53 AD (cf. Tac. Ann. 12.58; see also Suet. Ner. 7). The latter are explicitly described as *materni*, as relatives of his mother, belonging to the *Iulia gens*. Consequently, the eclogue must have been published before 59 AD, the year of the murder of Agrippina the Younger and the proclamation of her birthday as a *dies nefastus* (cf. Tac. Ann. 14.12); cf. also Cesareo 1931, 137 and n. 1, Verdière 1954, 35–6; 1966, 162, Paladini 1956, 338, Joly 1974, 50, Messina 1975, 70, Friedrich 1976, 136, Townend 1980, 168–9, Küppers 1985, 355–7, Pearce 1990, 29, Amat 1991, xxi–xxii, Martin 1996, 23, Vinchesi 1996, 14–5, 70; 2002, 142 and n. 15; 2014, 128–30, Schubert 1998, 49, 58–9, Di Lorenzo–Pellegrino 2008, 152; see also Armstrong 1986, 128, Horsfall 1997, 167, Henderson 2013, 178.
[92] Cf. Verdière 1954, 129; 1966, 162, Joly 1974, 50–1, Friedrich 1976, 136, 143, Davis 1987, 41, Effe–Binder 1989, 118, Kegel–Brinkgreve 1990, 152 and n. 7, Pearce 1990, 29, Slater 1994, http://, Keene 1996, 56–7, Vinchesi 1996, 15; 2002, 143, Hubbard 1998, 159, Merfeld 1999,

young emperor intervenes in order to ensure the 'pastoral permanence' of Tityrus and, thus, the latter's bucolic world as well. This basic pastoral dimension of divine intervention in Vergil's first eclogue is weakened in Calpurnius, as the 'pastoral continuity' is not part of the political program of the emperor, who is merely praised as the guarantor of political calm, a smooth operation and the peace of the State.

Basic intertexts of the prophecy section also come from Tibullan elegies, panegyric in nature, where, as in the first Calpurnian eclogue, a 'generic interaction' operates between panegyric / epic and bucolic discourses. The syntagm *gaudete coloni* in v. 36 recalls v. 83 of Tibullus' 2.5, where the farmers of the elegiac narrative are saluted in a similar manner and in a similar metrical position (at the end of the hexameter), *laurus ubi bona signa dedit, gaudete, coloni*[93]. The elegy, for which there is a convincing argument that it converses with the epic *Aeneid* (cf. Maltby 2002, 431), functions, among other things (kletic hymn, foundation narrative of a city–κτίσις πόλεως)[94], as a work in praise of the eldest son of Messalla, Valerius Messallinus, on the occasion of the election of the latter to the class of *quindecimviri sacris faciundis*, namely the officials who were commissioned to safeguard and interpret the Sibylline books. Tibullus calls on the farmers – *coloni* – to rejoice because, after the harrowing experience of the civil wars (vv. 65–78), their future is foreseen to be favourable, with enhanced agricultural and livestock production and their animals out of harm (vv. 83–90). The contrast between the image of a past tarnished by wars and the *pax* of the new *princeps*, bringing with it agricultural *securitas*, also runs through the prophecy of Faunus in the first eclogue of the Neronian bucolic corpus (vv. 36–42, 46–59, 63–8). In Tibullus' elegy, the god Apollo, in his capacity as a singer and guitar player (v. 2: *huc, age, cum cithara carminibusque veni*), is called on both to support Messallinus in his mission (vv. 1–18) and to mediate in order to ensure a happy year for the farmers (vv. 79–82). On the other hand, in Calpurnius' eclogue, agricultural regeneration occurs as a result of the intervention of another god: the divine emperor, Nero. Nero, however, is often presented in the literature of the period as a new Apollo, since his identification with Apollo as the god of music is combined with the artistic interests of the emperor[95]. Through this intertextual reading, Nero appropriates the image of the singer and guitar player Apollo, and thus Si-

---

78, Di Lorenzo–Pellegrino 2008, 152, Braund 2009, 13 and n. 40; see also Küppers 1985, 353 and n. 37, Henderson 2013, 177, Hulsenboom 2013, 21–2.
93 Cf. Korzeniewski 1971, 13, Di Lorenzo–Pellegrino 2008, 150, Esposito 2009, 23–4, Vinchesi 2014, 123–4.
94 Cf. Maltby 2002, 431.
95 Cf. Friedrich 1976, 147.

culus yet again promotes the public image of the *princeps*, at the level of intertextual allusion. Indeed, this Apollo of Tibullus – with whom the Nero of Siculus is intertextually identified – is presented, as the god of prophecy and, consequently, protector of the Sibylline oracles, also serving as helper of Aeneas (vv. 19–22), the ancestor of the *Iulia gens* according to Augustan ideology, i.e., ultimately Augustus himself. Once again, one comes across a political correlation, albeit indirect in this case: that of Nero with Augustus.

What is more, the image of the secure, wandering animals as a result of the peaceful new Neronian era along with the extended celebration of the ruler (Calp. 1.37–9, 74–6) may also bring to mind similar motifs of Theocr. 16 (vv. 88–97, 99–100), i.e., an encomium of a further acclaimed sovereign, Hieron II of Syracuse (cf. Hutchinson 2013, 310–11). If so, the encomiastic character of the sub-text further increases the panegyric outlook of the recipient Calpurnian passage.

From a 'generic perspective', of interest is the use of the term *coloni* in v. 36 to hail the inhabitants of the 'geen cabinet' of the first Calpurnian eclogue. The address recalls Vergil's ninth eclogue[96], where in v. 4: '*haec mea sunt; veteres migrate coloni*' the veteran soldier, a stranger to the pastoral community and responsible for the eviction of Moeris from his pastoral world, uses the term *coloni* to address the shepherds whom he himself forces to leave from their bucolic paradise. The term is used to describe the shepherds in Vergil when their pastoral community is lost and when, on a meta–poetic level, they deviate from the Neoteric–Callimachean pastoral poetry, opting for poetic discourses of the *genus grande*[97]. These 'generic meta–poetic connotations' of the term in Vergil are heightened in the eclogue of Siculus, where the branching out of the bucolic towards the panegyric becomes more apparent.

Finally, the syntagm *candida pax* in v. 54 refers to the same linguistic syntagm of v. 45 in elegy 1.10 of Tibullus[98], in which, as with elegy 2.5, one can discern the presence of several bucolic motifs (rural simplicity, for example, mainly of the early years), incorporated into the wider framework of the elegiac narra-

---

96 Cf. Paladini 1956, 340 and n. 4, Vinchesi 2014, 123.
97 Cf. Papanghelis 1995, 204–21, Karakasis 2011, 184–212.
98 Cf. Verdière 1954, 236, Paladini 1956, 332, Korzeniewski 1971, 15, Joly 1974, 51, Messina 1975, 71, Di Lorenzo–Pellegrino 2008, 154–5, Esposito 2009, 24–6, Fucecchi 2009, 61 and n. 61, Vinchesi 2012, 715; 2014, 40, 134, Henderson 2013, 177. The linguistic syntagm appears once more in the third book of Ovid's *Ars Amatoria* (v. 502). Although it is included in the elegiac discourse of the poet, i.e., the advice of a *praeceptor amoris* to his Amazons regarding the *vitium* of *iracundia*, the syntagm recalls the Golden Age, as also happens in Tibullus and Calpurnius; cf. Gibson 2003, 301.

tive of the poem. Indeed, the fundamental contrast in the elegy between, on the one hand, the negatively connotated war, the result of human greed, which the poet renounces (vv. 1–10, 29–32), and, on the other hand, the peace, an indication of the Golden Age (vv. 7–10) leading to agricultural wealth and rural regeneration (vv. 45–50), also occurs, as I have already elaborated (cf. p. 34), in Siculus' first eclogue. The *candida pax* that the Calpurnian Nero secures for Rome is intertextually associated with the 'white' peace of Augustus (the closing of the gates of Janus' temple in 29 BC), as hailed in the afore-mentioned elegy of Tibullus[99]. Indeed, this peace, as the *founder* of agriculture (vv. 45–6), also appears to have basic characteristics of Ceres (cf. Verg. *G.* 1.147–9), again[100] according to the Augustan ideology.

Panegyric in the Years of the *Quinquennium Neronis* The Comet of 54 AD and its 'Poetics'

As I have set out above (cf. pp. 24–36), a branching out towards the panegyric is accomplished through the dimension of praise for the emperor in some of the intertexts of the first Calpurnian eclogue. However, this inclination towards the *genus grande* is also ensured through the adoption of laudatory discourse, (panegyric) elements that form the public image of the emperor during this early period of Nero's imperial reign. These features significantly appear in texts contemporary to Calpurnius, i.e., of the first years of Nero's *principatus*[101], such as Seneca's *Apocolocyntosis* (October – December 54 AD[102]) or *De Clementia* (December 55 – December 56 AD[103]) and the prologue in Lucan's *Bellum Civile*[104] which, in my opinion, is in praise of the emperor.

---

99 Cf. Cairns 1999, 230.
100 Cf. Maltby 2002, 351–2.
101 Cf. Paladini 1956, 337–8, Luiselli 1963, 44–52, Messina 1975, 72, Casaceli 1982, 88–93, Wiseman 1982, 57–67, Küppers 1985, 352–3, 358–9, Amat 1991, xx, Vinchesi 1996, 17, Di Lorenzo-Pellegrino 2008, 150, 152, 154–7, 160, Braund 2009, 171, 351, 363–4, 386–7.
102 Cf. Eden 1984, 4–5.
103 The *communis opinio*, cf. Braund 2009, 16. On the contrary, Champlin 2003, 276–83, mainly for reasons of iconography, believes that the prophetic song of Apollo (*Apoc.* 4) is a later addition, after the death of Agrippina.
104 The similarity in motifs that is often observed in works dating back to *quinquennium Neronis* may also be due to the fact that these texts have influenced one another. However, chronology problems do not always allow for the exact determination of which poet was imitating whom. Thus, Luiselli 1963, 44–52, for example, attributes the thematic similarity between

As in contemporary political texts of the early years of Nero's reign, in the first Calpurnian eclogue the emperor is also shown as:

1) a peacemaker monarch, one who ensures the Neronian (and Augustan[105]) ideal of *pax* (vv. 42–59, 63–8, 84–8, cf. Sen. *Cl.* 1.1.2, 1.19.8, Luc. 1.33–45; and also Suet. *Ner.* 13),

2) a guarantor, like Augustus (cf. e.g. especially Hor. *Carm.* 4.5.16–40, *C.S.* 53–68[106]), of justice and public security, of the imperial ideals of *iustitia*, *securitas* and public *felicitas* (vv. 36–42, 58–62, 69–73, cf. Sen. *Cl.* 1.1.3, 5, 7–8, 1.8.2, 1.19.8, 1.26.5, *Apoc.* 4.1; and also Tac. *Ann.* 13.4–5, 28–9, 31–2, 51, 14.28, Suet. *Ner.* 10–11, 15–7, 19),

3) incarnation of the imperial *Clementia* (vv. 58–9, cf. the whole of Seneca's *De Clementia* and specifically Sen. *Cl.* 1.1.1, 4, 7–9, 1.3.3, 1.5.1–2, 4; see also Tac. *Ann.* 13.11, 14.48).

All these positive attributes of the emperor are presented in terms of his favourable comparison with his predecessor Claudius (cf. also Sen. *Cl.* 1.1.5, 1.23, 2.1.4, *Apoc.* 4.1–3; cf. also later Tac. *Ann.* 14.55). During Claudius' *principatus*, neither external nor civil wars are absent (vv. 46–57) – such as, for example, Claudius' expedition against Britain in 43 AD[107] or the movement of Lucius Arruntius Camillus Scribonianus in 42 AD[108] – nor is the domestic political calm of the State always secured (vv. 55–7 (Claudian 'palace trials'), 58–62 (Claudius' soldiers, frightening the civilians, divided cohorts, murder of senators), 69–73 (corruption, vacant, bribed offices); see especially Wiseman 1982, 64–6); cf. also Sen. *Apoc.* 7.4, 8.2, 10.3–11.2, 11.5, 12.2–3, 13.4–14.2[109]. Finally, Nero is presented as a true offspring of the *Iulia gens*, through his mother Agrippina the Younger, who was a direct descendant of Augustus (v. 45), in contrast to Clau-

---

the work of Calpurnius and Seneca's *Apocolocyntosis* to the influence of the latter on the former (cf. also Friedrich 1976, 126), while Vallet 1956, 10 (cf. also Toynbee 1942, 83–4, Amat 1991, 2 and n. 3) maintains exactly the opposite. Moreover, one should not overlook the importance of the *recitationes*. Namely, a poet / author could draw on material he listened to within the context of these recitations, without actually having come in contact with the final, published form of a text.

105 Cf. Friedrich 1976, 141–2.
106 Cf. Vinchesi 2014, 124, 127.
107 Cf. Duff and Duff 1934, 223, Paladini 1956, 337, Amat 1991, 9 vs. Wiseman 1982, 64.
108 Cf. Wiseman 1982, 59.
109 Cf. also Suet. *Cl.* 13, 29, Tac. *Ann.* 11.35, 12.42, 13.4; see also Verdière 1954, 237–8, Paladini 1956, 337, Korzeniewski 1971, 88, Friedrich 1976, 139, Amat 1991, 100–1, Ventura 2006, 121–43, Di Lorenzo–Pellegrino 2008, 153, 155–7, Vinchesi 2014, especially 28, 101, 124–8, 132, 134–43, 146–50. For *melior deus* in v. 73 as referring to Nero's title ἀγαθὸς δαίμων (*POxy* 7, 1021), cf. Verdière 1993, 358.

dius, who was not, in any way, related to the *Iulia gens* of the Julio-Claudian dynasty; this is a shortfall of Claudius which is also commented on in the literature of the *quinquennium* (cf. Sen. *Apoc.* 5.4 – 6.1).

The narrative section of the prophecy concludes with a reference to a comet, vv. 77 – 83, the brightness of which as well as its lack of any blood red shades testify to its benign character (cf. Plin. *Nat.* 2.89[110]). Here, Calpurnius makes mention of the comet of 54 AD, which was interpreted as an *omen* of Claudius' end and the accession of Nero to the throne (cf. Sen. *N.Q.* 7.17.2, Suet. *Cl.* 46, Plin. *Nat.* 2.23.92, D.C. 60.35.1)[111]. Thus, this comet is contrasted with another 'known' comet in the bucolic poetry, the *sidus Iulium / Caesaris astrum*, which appeared after the assassination of Julius Caesar and was associated with his apotheosis. This star is linked to the bloody civil war (vv. 82 – 3) following the Ides of March in 44 BC, i.e., the conflict between, on the one hand, the Republicans Cassius and Brutus, and, on the other hand, Mark Antony and Octavian, which ended with the victory of the pro-Caesarian forces at the battle of Philippi in 42 BC.

This comet occurs in the fifth (vv. 56 – 80) and the ninth (vv. 46 – 50) eclogue of the Vergilian bucolic corpus, where, however, in contrast with Calpurnius, it has positive connotations[112]; it is shown to lead into the agricultural *securitas* and the Golden Age (vv. 5.60 – 61), to regenerate the pastoral world in general (vv. 9.48 – 9) and, consequently, the bucolic genre as well[113]. It is hailed, indirectly but clearly, as, among other things, leading to Octavian Augustus (cf. Plin. *Nat.* 2.23.93 – 4; see also Hor. *Carm.* 1.12.46 – 8), who is, according to Vergil's first eclogue, at least to some extent, the guarantor of the continuity of the pastoral world, since he ensures that Tityrus remains in the 'green cabinet' (cf. above, pp. 8, 33 – 4).

---

110 Cf. Di Lorenzo–Pellegrino 2008, 159, Vinchesi 2014, 146 – 7.
111 Cf. Postgate 1902, 38 – 40, Herrmann 1931, 145 – 53, Momigliano 1944, 97, Theiler 1956, 568 – 70, Verdière 1954, 34, 238; 1985, 1856 – 7, Mahr 1964, 8 – 9, Spadaro 1969, 26, Korzeniewski 1971, 2 – 3, 89, Cizek 1972, 87, 89, Joly 1974, 53, Friedrich 1976, 127, Gagliardi 1984, 56 – 7, Sullivan 1985, 52 and n. 63, Mackie 1989, 9, Pearce 1990, 31, Amat 1991, xx–xxi, 101, Slater 1994, http://, Vinchesi 1996, 74; 2002, 145 and n. 26; 2014, 145, Lana 1998, 824, Schubert 1998, 61, Merfeld 1999, 76, Di Lorenzo–Pellegrino 2008, 158, Garthwaite–Martin 2009, 308, Bechtold 2011, 207. However, some of the scholars who accept the Neronian dating of the poet maintain that the comet of Calpurnius is that of 60 AD (cf. Sen. *N.Q.* 7.21.3, 7.29.2 – 3; see also Hubaux 1930, 208 – 11, Toynbee 1942, 90 – 3, Rogers 1953, 237, Luiselli 1960, 146 – 8, Bardon 1968, 226, Bicknell 1969, 1074 – 5). For a convincing refutation of this position, cf. Spadaro 1969, 18 – 27, Verdière 1966, 162 – 3.
112 Cf. Hubbard 1998, 162.
113 Cf. Karakasis 2011, 201 – 2.

More reserved in his opinion towards the *sidus Iulium* is Vergil in his *Georgics*, vv. 1.463–514, as here, just as in Calpurnius, the comet is associated with the civil war following the assassination of Julius Caesar and the great amount of Roman blood spilled in the fields of civil strife (vv. 1.487–92); a similar association appears in Manilius, cf. 1.905–26, who follows Vergil in this[114]. In Ovid's *Metamorphoses*, vv. 15.787–8[115], which also imitate the Vergilian passage[116], the comet is also negatively presented, as a *praesagium* of the assassination of Caesar. Calpurnius again deviates from the earlier pastoral tradition, as he does not present the *sidus Iulium* in a positive light but, following the intertext of the *Georgics* and probably of Manilius and of Ovid's *Metamorphoses*, he stresses the bloodshed that the appearance of *Caesaris astrum* entails, and, therefore, contrasts it with the star of 54 AD (vv. 77–83), which, on the other hand, is positively depicted. Contrary to the rise of Augustus to power, the *translatio imperii* in the case of the assumption of the *principatus* by Nero takes place silently, almost imperceptibly, as Calpurnius explicitly states in vv. 84–8: the noise and clamour of power changing hands will not resound at all, v. 86: *ut neque translati sonitu fragor intonet orbis*. Indeed, the feeling of security consequently felt by the Roman people is indicated through a figure popular in bucolic poetry, the *adynaton*, now astronomical in nature, in accordance with the literary norms of the time (cf. Dutoit 1936, 131–3)[117], which, in turn, is associated with the panegyric of the emperor; in vv. 87–8, it is stated that Rome will consider the *penates publici / maiores* to have been derelict in their duty to protect the *urbs* (*nec prius ex meritis defunctos Roma penates / censeat*)[118], only in the highly unlikely event that East meets West, v. 88: *occasus nisi cum respexerit ortus*[119]. However, in

---

114 Cf. Goold 1997, 77 and n. d, Vinchesi 2014, 148; for the influence of Manilius on Calpurnius, see also Costanza 1984, 26–48.
115 Cf. Paladini 1956, 335–6, Messina 1975, 71, Friedrich 1976, 127–8, Küppers 1985, 354 and n. 42, Amat 1991, 101, Keene 1996, 62, Vinchesi 1996, 74; 2002, 145; 2014, 40, Di Lorenzo–Pellegrino 2008, 158–60, Esposito 2009, 19.
116 Cf. Hill 2000, 227.
117 Cf. Hubaux 1930, 212, Paladini 1956, 344, Korzeniewski 1971, 89, Friedrich 1976, 144–5, Vinchesi 1996, 75; 2014, 151, Schubert 1998, 63, Di Lorenzo–Pellegrino 2008, 161.
118 A good number of scholars are of the opinion that the line refers to the apotheosis of the Caesars (cf. Hubaux 1930, 212, Verdière 1954, 135, Paladini 1956, 343 and n. 5, Pearce 1990, 32, Lee (in: Boyle–Sullivan) 1991, 43, Keene 1996, 62, Schubert 1998, 62–3, Esposito 2009, 36). The apotheosis, however, of the emperors is not associated with the *penates*; for a convincing refutation of this position, cf. Vinchesi 1996, 75; 2014, 150–1, Di Lorenzo–Pellegrino 2008, 161; see also Leach 1973, 63–4.
119 For some scholars, the verse indicates a shift in dynastic power, cf. Duff and Duff 1934, 225, De Sipio 1935, 61, Verdière 1954, 239; 1982, 188–9, Vallet 1956, 113 and n. 14, Joly 1974, 64 and n. 81, Friedrich 1976, 145, Küppers 1985, 360–1, Pearce 1990, 33, Amat

vv. 84–6 (*scilicet ipse deus Romanae pondera molis / fortibus excipiet sic inconcussa lacertis, / ut neque translati sonitu fragor intonet orbis*) the image of the universe that remains unshaken by the change in the rule of the *principatus* is, also[120] on a linguistic level, reminiscent of vv. 5–6 from the prologue of Lucan's epic (*certatum totis concussi viribus orbis / in commune nefas*), where, on the contrary, the world is shown to be deeply shocked by the civil conflicts, which are expected to be reduced by the divine Nero (vv. 60–2). In both texts, Nero is depicted as the divine State-ruler who puts an end to the sufferings of a *bellum civile*.

With regard to the forming of the emperor's public image, of interest is the justification of the negative presentation of *Caesaris astrum* in the first Calpurnian eclogue. This *sidus* is associated with the rise to power of Augustus, but following the large-scale bloodshed of the third civil war of the late Roman Republic. On the other hand, the rise to power of Nero, which, in turn, is assumed to be portended by the appearance of another *astrum*, the comet of 54 AD, is accomplished peacefully and without bloodshed. Thus, from this perspective and again according to the political ideology of the period, Nero is shown to have surpassed the *exemplum* set by Augustus[121]. The sources offer ample evidence of Nero's wish to appear as an extender of Augustus, cf. e.g. Suet. *Ner.* 10, where the sovereign declares his zealotry for the politics of his predecessor, *ex Augusti praescripto imperaturum se professus* (10.1; cf. also Suet. *Ner.* 12, 25)[122]. In some cases, however, as with Siculus' first eclogue, Nero appears to surpass Augustus. The reason why Nero overshadows Augustus is often the bloodless *Clementia* of the former (cf. Braund 2009, 61–4, 262–3, 290), mention of which is also made

---

1991, 102, Keene 1996, 62, Romano 2002, 91–6, Esposito 2009, 36; however, for a refutation of such positions, cf. Schubert 1998, 63 and nn. 66, 67. According to Garthwaite–Martin 2009, 314–5 the lines allude to a political concern of Calpurnius; i.e., that perhaps the new era of Nero's *principatus* (*ortus*) seeks *exempla* (*respexerit*) in the past (*occasus*), cf. also Davis 1987, 43. These scholars belong to the 'school' (see also Leach 1973, 56–64, cf. also Ahl 1984, 64, Davis 1987, 38–43, Martin 2003, 77–9) which discerns a kind of allusive and hidden criticism of the emperor or, at any rate, a feeling of unease and uncertainty (cf. also Hubbard 1998, 160–1, 163), in the political eclogues of Calpurnius. However, for a convincing refutation of such positions, which do not appear to take thoroughly into account the optimism of the early years of Nero's rule, cf. mainly Sullivan 1985, 54 and n. 65, Mayer 2006, 457–8, Introduction, p. 10.
120 Cf. Armstrong 1986, 126, Verdière 1993, 352–3.
121 Cf. Joly 1974, 50, Friedrich 1976, 147, Küppers 1985, 353, Martin 1996, 24, 26, Vinchesi 1996, 18–9; 2002, 144, Schubert 1998, 57–9 and n. 39 on p. 58, 61, Merfeld 1999, 80.
122 Cf. Friedrich 1976, 147, Martin 2003, 75 and n. 7, Esposito 2009, 33–4 and n. 46 on p. 33.

in the Calpurnian bucolic text in question. Augustus appears to embrace the imperial virtue of *Clementia* only during the period of his *principatus*, having demonstrated violent cruelty during the democratic period, when he leads the friends of his youth, Hirtius and Pansa, to death in Mutina in 43 BC, resorts to proscriptions during the second Triumvirate (43–2 BC), barbarously attacks Sextus Pompey in Sicily (38–6 BC) and kills 300 Roman senators and equestrians after the destruction of Perusia (40 BC), cf. Sen. *Cl.* 1.9.1–1.11.3. In contrast to Augustus' *lassa crudelitas*, Nero's inherent virtue is *vera Clementia* (cf. Sen. *Cl.* 1.11.2), as his policy never leads to civil bloodshed (cf. also Calp. 1.50–1: *nullos iam Roma Philippos / deflebit*, 84–6). This virtue of Nero, who rises to power without spilling a single drop of blood, is later also praised in pseudo–Seneca's *Octavia*. Seneca, now as a dramatic character, stresses, in the presence of Nero, the *incruenta* accession of the latter to power (v. 482, cf. Sen. *Cl.* 1.11.3), in contrast to the conflicts that led to Augustus' *principatus* (vv. 472–91, cf. also Sen. *Br.* 4.5, Tac. *Ann.* 13.4, 14.55)[123].

The Epilogue of the Pastoral Narrative

The eclogue does not end in the traditional Vergilian way, namely with the advent of evening and / or return of the bucolic characters to typical rural and stock farming activities (cf. Verg. *Ecl.* 1.82–3, 2.66–7, 6.85–6, 10.77; see also 9.63, Theocr. 11.12–5)[124]. Ornytus proposes to his brother that they set the prophecy of Faunus to music, vv. 92–3. However, they have no interest in establishing this song within the pastoral community, as the main concern of the two brothers is no longer the pleasure of the inhabitants of the 'green cabinet'. Instead, Corydon's wish is to have this song carried by Meliboeus[125], most likely his patron, to the emperor, cf. v. 94: *forsitan **augustas** feret haec Meliboeus ad aures*. The function of Meliboeus here is similar to the role of Meliboeus in Calpurnius' fourth eclogue, in which the pastoral character behaves as the *patronus* of Corydon and his brother, Amyntas (cf. Chapter 2, p. 48). The linguistic formulation of Corydon's wish in v. 94 recalls v. 73 of the third Vergilian eclogue: **divum** *referatis ad auris*[126], where, within the context of a typical bucolic song–contest, Damoe-

---

123 Cf. Vinchesi 1996, 19 and n. 23; 2014, 28, 101, 126, 132–3, 135, 148.
124 This also occurs in the fourth political eclogue, where the bucolic narrative again does not end with the advent of evening, but at noon, vv. 168–9; see Chapter 2, p. 82.
125 For the last line of the eclogue as an indication of the poet's wish for his poetic work to be included in the library of the emperor, cf. Korzeniewski 1976, 250.
126 Cf. Korzeniewski 1971, 17, Vinchesi 2014, 153.

tas requests that the winds carry his amorous words for his beloved to the gods, who will thus become witnesses to this love. The shepherd in Vergil focuses on a standard and common interest of the pastoral world, i.e., happiness in love; however, through the *oppositio in imitando* of the verses in question, the shepherds in the first Calpurnian eclogue again evidence the change of interests in panegyric Neronian bucolic poetry. The god in the first eclogue of Calpurnius is now the divine emperor, and the wish that the words / songs of the inhabitants of the pastoral space reach his ears is no longer associated with the traditional pastoral ideal of happiness in love, but with ensuring imperial protection.

The linguistic syntagm used by Ornytus to propose to his brother that they set to music this novel, in 'generic terms', 'bucolic panegyric', v. 93: *teretique sonum modulemur avena*, recalls the one adopted by Gallus in Vergil's tenth eclogue, when he decides, albeit temporarily, to include his elegiac poetic identity in the pastoral world and its poetic values (cf. above, p. 23), Verg. *Ecl.* 10.51: *carmina pastoris Siculi modulabor avena*[127]. This particular linguistic option has in Vergil clear 'generic connotations' and is adopted in a case of a significant 'generic interaction'; this syntagm appears to have a similar function in Calpurnius, as it is used, in a similar manner, to denote the production of panegyric poetry in bucolic settings.

This new pastoral poetry with epic intertextual associations, which branches out towards the *genus grande*, is described by a catch-word (*teres*)[128] that suggests the Callimachean–Neoteric poetics of the pastoral *genus tenue* prior to Calpurnius. Moreover, Corydon's *avena*, which is to be used to set a 'bucolic panegyric' to music, appears to have been made by a certain Ladon, who is characterised as *docilis*, i.e., *doctus* (v. 18); namely, he is described through a technical term denoting the Neoteric *homo / poeta*, according to the Neoteric idiolect. The use of these signs to describe the panegyric bucolic poetry in Siculus' first eclogue demonstrates the differentiation between Calpurnian meta–poetics and the Vergilian poetic meta-language of the *genus tenue*; terms of Neoteric meta–poetics are now adopted to indicate 'generic options' moving towards the *genus grande*, as is apparent in the poetic production of Calpurnius[129] as a whole. And while the Golden Age in the fourth Vergilian eclogue signals, as T. D. Papanghelis, 1995, 257–307, has convincingly demonstrated, the prevalence of Callimachean–Neoteric poetics within the framework of the New Age that the divine *puer* promises, nothing similar is observed in the case of the *Aetas Aurea*

---

[127] Cf. Verdière 1954, 240, Korzeniewski 1971, 17, Di Lorenzo–Pellegrino 2008, 162.
[128] Cf. Karakasis 2011, 131–2.
[129] Cf. Karakasis 2011, 43–4. For the term Post–Classical Latin, cf. also Karakasis 2005, 16.

in Siculus' first eclogue. Many of the finest poetological nuances and ambiguities of Vergilian bucolic meta-poetics appear to be less prevalent in the pastoral poetry of the Neronian age.

Linguistic Novelty and 'Generic Transgression'

It seems that, in some cases, Calpurnius adopts Post-Classical Latin linguistic options to emphasise, also on a linguistic / stylistic level, the 'generic novelty' / 'epigonism' of his bucolic poetry. Certainly, here one could argue that the presence of Post-Classical linguistic options in Siculus' work is justified by the historical evolution of Latin. This, to some extent, is of course correct; nevertheless, in this case, namely if one interprets the presence of Post-Classical Latin in the work of Calpurnius only as an indication of linguistic evolution, one would more or less expect an equal distribution of Post-Classical linguistic phenomena throughout the narrative of an eclogue. However, the presence of a relatively large number of these elements at only one point in the bucolic narrative, and their relative absence from the rest of the poem, also testifies, beyond any historical evolution of language, to the existence of specific stylistic criteria, on the part of the pastoral poet, that justify this unequal distribution. Thus, in Siculus' fourth political eclogue, Post-Classical Latin is detected mainly in the speech of Corydon and Meliboeus, who act as the prime agents and representatives of 'generic evolution' within the narrative of the fourth bucolic, while, in the seventh political bucolic, the neoteric ecphrasis of Nero's wooden amphitheatre of 57 AD includes the largest number of Post-Classical linguistic elements in the poem (see below, pp. 83–5, 115–7).

In Calpurnius' first eclogue, the prophecy of Faunus, which constitutes the main part of the bucolic narrative, demonstrates, to a much greater extent than both the introductory and the last lines of the poem, the new trends of pastoral poetry in the Neronian age; i.e., the panegyric of the emperor in pastoral contexts and in an intertextual dialogue with both epic texts and texts with epic 'generic colouring' in general. Therefore, this primarily 'generically neoteric' part of the narrative includes a sufficient number of Post-Classical linguistic uses, highlighting, on a linguistic level, the observed 'generic change' and 'epigonism'.

The elements of Post-Classical Latin found in vv. 33–88 are as follows:
Syntax
1. vv. 46–7: *dabit impia victas / post tergum Bellona manus*. In the lines in question, the preposition *post* after the verb *dare* does not merely denote the place, but specifically the motion towards a place, located behind something /

someone. In Classical Latin, this adverbial relationship is expressed by the simple dative or the prepositional complement *ad* + accusative. In the Calpurnian case, however, one comes across the usual Post–Classical use of *post* in place of *ad* (cf. also Phaedr. 4.10.2, Sen. *Tr.* 153, *Phoen.* 577)[130].

2. v. 66: *agmina, Romuleis et adhuc ardentia castris*. The syntax of *ardere* with the ablative (of an object) denoting external cause is also chiefly a Post–Classical usage, in contrast with the ablative of the internal cause (e. g. *ira*) occurring as a complement of the verb from Terence onwards or the ablative of a person (from Horace onwards) used as a complement of the external cause[131].

Vocabulary

1. v. 57: *publica diffudit tacito discordia ferro*. Here, the noun *discordia*, as correctly noted by Merone 1967, 9–10, belongs to the 'heteroclita eademque heterogenea' nouns. This is the plural accusative case of the unattested type *discordium* and is a *hapax legomenon* in the poetry of Calpurnius (cf. ThLL V 1340, 30; 1341, 70), which may be found again in an inscription of 367 AD, D. Inscr. christ., Rossi I, p. 94 (a.367)[132].

2. v. 85: *fortibus excipiet sic inconcussa lacertis*. The word *inconcussus* is often found in Seneca (cf. *H.O.* 1741) and re–occurs, during the Neronian age, in Lucan's epic (cf. 2.248, ThLL VII 1 999, 34, OLD *s.v.*). According to Mahr, 1964, 163–4, the presence of the adjective in Calpurnius is a result of Seneca's influence[133].

There follows a reference to some linguistic options which, although not exclusive to Post–Classical Latin, however prove particularly popular in the Post–Classical period, and therefore gradually replace the Classical Latin alternative options. These linguistic options complete the picture described above and enhance the linguistic novelty of the narrative section of the prophecy.

1. vv. 37–9: *licet omne vagetur / securo custode pecus nocturnaque pastor / claudere fraxinea nolit praesepia crate*. The extensive use of *licet* as an introductory subordinate conjunction of clauses of concession in place of *quamvis*, etc. is a Post–Classical Latin option (mainly of the language of Martial and Juvenal). In

---

[130] Cf. Mahr 1964, 94–5.
[131] Cf. Mahr 1964, 92–3.
[132] Cf. Mahr 1964, 175–80, who offers a detailed review of different opinions with regard to the grammatical determination of the noun *discordia*, Korzeniewski 1971, 88, Friedrich 1976, 237, Messina 1975, 108, Pearce 1990, 30, Keene 1996, 58, Di Lorenzo–Pellegrino 2008, 155, Vinchesi 2014, 136–7. For the possibility that this type is the nominalised plural of the neutral form of *discors, -rdis*, cf. also Novelli 1980, 93.
[133] Cf. Novelli 1980, 36, Horsfall 1997, 179; see also Vinchesi 2014, 149.

Calpurnius, *licet* occurs in 4 cases (1.37–9, 4.12–3, 5.107–9[134], 7.13–4), while *quamvis*, as a concessive conjunction, occurs 5 times (2.76, 3.18, 25, 5.113, 6.34)[135].

2. v. 55: *quae libera Marte professo*. The use of the past participle of deponent verbs, in a passive sense, is mainly found in texts after the Classical period, although, in some cases, this phenomenon is also observed in Pre-Classical Latin, Cicero's letters, Livy and the poets of the Augustan age[136].

3. vv. 80–1: *numquid utrumque polum, sicut solet, igne cruento / spargit et ardenti scintillat sanguine lampas?* The use of *numquid* in place of *num* is a feature of Post-Classical, but also of Vulgar Latin (for example, it is more often found in text-sources of the *sermo plebeius*, such as comedy, Horace's *Satires*, etc.). This introductory particle is also found in Calp. 3.1, while *num* is used by Siculus in 2.84[137].

Conclusion

The intention Siculus has of transcending the 'generic boundaries' of the pastoral tradition, towards the *genus grande* and panegyric discourses in particular, is evident from his very first programmatic eclogue. Calpurnius apparently distances himself significantly from earlier pastoral poetry, and this is primarily achieved through the following techniques, evident not only in the first eclogue but also in the rest of his eclogues, especially in those that do not belong in the category of the *merae bucolicae* (2, 3, 5, 6): a) intertextual references to epic texts, primarily Vergil's *Aeneid*, but also Ovid's *Metamorphoses* and, quite probably, the *Bellum Civile* by his contemporary, Lucan; b) allusive references

---

134 *licet horrida* (cf. Mahr 1964, 104) vs. *ne torrida* (v. 5.107) adopted by Duff and Duff 1934, 268.
135 Cf. Mahr 1964, 104–5. As is convincingly maintained by Mahr 1964, 105: 'Auch hier lassen sich also früh-nachklassische Merkmale im Sprachgebrauch des Calpurnius feststellen'.
136 Cf. Mahr 1964, 83–4.
137 Cf. Mahr 1964, 116–7. The only Post-Classical linguistic option which occurs in the remaining section of the first eclogue, with the exception of that of the prophecy, (38 verses vs. 56 verses of *vaticinium*) is the noun *iubilum* in v. 30. After Calpurnius, the word occurs in Silius Italicus, 14.475, Marcus Aurelius, Aur. *Fro.* 1.p.180(68N), with the meaning of 'pastoral song'. However, the verb *iubilare*, which derives from *iubilum*, is already found in Varro, *L.* 6.68; cf. Mahr 1964, 167, Merone 1967, 20–1, Novelli 1980, 35–6, Vinchesi 1992, 150–1; 2014, 120, Horsfall 1997, 182. The noun *internodium* (v. 26) is not a linguistic innovation of Calpurnius (cf. Merone 1967, 29, Messina 1975, 108); the word with the meaning of 'internode', as is the case hereof, already occurs in Varro, *rust.* 2.9.4 (cf. OLD *s.v.* a; see also Ov. *Met.* 11.793: *longa internodia crurum*, Novelli 1980, 28, Horsfall 1997, 186, Vinchesi 2014, 118).

to non-epic texts, panegyric in nature (e.g. Tibullus' elegies, laudatory in tone and style); c) allusions to Vergil's bucolics, where, however, the pastoral poet self-referentially declares his intention to transcend the 'generic boundaries' of bucolic poetry towards the *genus grande* (fourth eclogue), but also to Vergilian pastoral passages where the narrative focuses on issues of 'generic interaction' (e.g. Vergil's fifth and tenth eclogue). The imitation of pastoral passages from the Vergilian corpus, where an intention for transcending 'generic boundaries' is observed, is accompanied by an intertextual recall of lines not only from Vergil's epic but also his *Georgics*; d) adoption of bucolic motifs and pastoral stylistic / linguistic options in contexts and ways that lead to their de-pastoralisation (the god Faunus with prophetic status, the closing of the bucolic narrative, etc.). Siculus' exploitation of earlier (Vergil, Tibullus) and contemporary (Lucan) literary production also serves the poet in his promotion of the image of Nero as Apollo and as a new ('improved') Augustus in terms of intertextuality, according to the communication politics of the emperor, as revealed by contemporary (Seneca) but also later (Tacitus, Suetonius) sources. The Calpurnian bucolic poetics is consequently the poetics of 'panegyric / laudatory intertextuality', namely the production of laudatory discourse through intertextual references of epic connotations.

In terms of meta-poetics, traditional catch-words of Neoteric-Callimachean poetry, which, in Vergil's bucolic poetry, demonstrate the poetological inclusion of the poet in the neo-Neoteric literary movement of the *genus tenue* (*docilis, teres*), have a different poetological function in Calpurnius' first eclogue. They are used to indicate the new 'generic preferences' of the Neronian pastoral poetry which, in the political eclogues, inclines towards the epic and laudatory discourse of the *genus grande*. As is evident from the preserved fragments of his poetry[138], Nero was an advocate of the neo-Neoteric / Callimachean poetological program, which was experiencing a kind of rebirth during the Neronian years. However, the times, probably more than ever before, are less permissive of the poetic *recusationes* of the Neoteric 'school'. They demand the panegyric of the *princeps*, clear laudatory references and explicit praise of the emperor for his political and military achievements; i.e., poetic discourses traditionally associated with options of the *genus grande* and not – to a great extent – those of an apolitical *genus tenue*. Therefore, statements of the type: *Caesaris arma canant alii: nos Caesaris aras* (Ov. *Fast.* 1.13)[139] are no longer acceptable. Thus, a broadening

---

138 Cf. Sullivan 1985, 91, 102, 104.
139 From this perspective, the viewpoint of Casaceli 1982, 92, namely that there is an ambiguity in the use of word *deus* in v. 92: *carmina, quae nobis deus obtulit ipse canenda*, is very interesting. On the one hand, the term may denote the god Faunus, who reveals his political prophecy

of the Neoteric poetic meta-language to encompass poetic options of higher literary genres also seems to result from the new political circumstances. In any case, the wealth of the Vergilian pastoral meta-linguistic ambiguity appears to be significantly restricted in Calpurnius, as shown in, among other things, the non-metapoetic exploitation of the Neoteric poetological connotations of the Golden Age-motif.

Finally, as in the remaining two programmatic eclogues of Siculus, the 'generic novelty' also appears to be suggested on a linguistic / stylistic level. The *vaticinium Fauni* section, which reveals and exemplifies the new panegyric bucolic poetics of the Neronian age and its preferences, is also characterised by the presence of a sufficient number of Post-Classical linguistic options.

---

to the two shepherds, and, on the other hand, the divine emperor, the *deus iuvenis* (cf. vv. 44, 46; see also Vozza 1993, 283), who commissions the bucolic poet Calpurnius (under the pastoral guise of Corydon), within a 'pastoral generic context', to sing his political program, which is largely a creation of Seneca (cf. Momigliano 1944, 97, Verdière 1992, 34); see also Monella 2009, 81 and n. 37.

Calpurnius 4

A song–exchange, though not of an agonistic character, lies at the heart of the central eclogue of the Calpurnian bucolic corpus, the programmatic fourth eclogue[1]. Two brothers, Corydon and Amyntas, engage in a friendly song–exchange in front of Meliboeus, Corydon's patron, hoping to persuade him to present Corydon to the imperial circles. The songs are not performed until v. 82, with the previous lines dedicated to the relevant prerequisites and the setting up of the background[2].

The Introductory Narrative

The poet's 'generically transcending' disposition becomes evident from the very beginning, as features of the 'green cabinet', usually appreciated in the pastoral space of the pre–Calpurnian tradition, are negatively viewed or at least put in doubt. The generic *locus amoenus*[3], constituting a basic feature of the earlier pastoral genre, is in the Calpurnian text atypical; the coolness of the breeze alleviating the heat of the day, an otherwise pastoral *desideratum*, is presented with uncertainty as to the pleasantness of its effect (vv. 3–4); besides, further default pastoral values of the past are also less enthusiastically presented: the generic pastoral shade (v. 2: *quidve sub hac platano*) and the generic coolness and natural sound of the waters (v. 2: *quam garrulus adstrepit umor*) are viewed as *insue-*

---

[1] As for the dating of the present eclogue, the view adopted in this study is that Calp. 4 chronologically follows Calp. 1, as also accepted by Leach 1973, 53–97 in the analysis of Calpurnius' political eclogues vs. Schenkl 1885, xii, Chytil 1894, 8–9, Ferrara 1905, 19–20, Chiavola 1921, 37ff., Marchiò 1957, 313, Spadaro 1969, 28–9, 41, Casaceli 1982, 90–3, 101. For a refutation of this latter thesis, cf. mainly Verdière 1954, 32, 36–8; 1985, 1869, Luiselli 1960, 152, Mahr 1964, 11–3, 17, Scheda 1969, 61, Korzeniewski 1972, 214, Cupaiuolo 1973, 191, Messina 1975, 76, Friedrich 1976, 11, Gagliardi 1984, 88 and n. 14, Schröder 1991, 20 and n. 15, Amat 1991, 31, Vinchesi 1996, 19–20; 2009a, 573–4 and n. 12; 2014, 29, Merfeld 1999, 72, 84, Lana 1998, 825–6, Di Lorenzo–Pellegrino 2008, 10–11; see also Di Salvo 1990, 26–7, Davis 1987, 32–3.
[2] For the lengthiness of the introduction as a technical flaw, cf. Verdière 1966, 165; see also Gagliardi 1984, 62, Simon 2007, 43–4.
[3] For Calp. 4.1–4 as depicting a *locus amoenus*, cf. also Amat 1991, 31, Simon 2007, 58, Di Lorenzo–Pellegrino 2008, 201; see also Martin 2003, 80, Chinnici 2009, 133–4.

ta (v. 3)⁴ with quite negative undertones. It seems that a contrast developed between the choice of a *locus amoenus*, i.e., of a staple 'generic location' for producing pastoral song, and Corydon's aspirations for composing songs which *non nemorale resultent* (v. 5), as well as the eventual fulfillment of this artistic objective, may account for the above 'generically surprising' designation, *insueta*. This qualification not only points to Corydon's and Meliboeus' estrangement from a traditional pastoral world⁵, but also testifies to their 'aberration' from the pre-Calpurnian pastoral genre and its poetics; the notion of unfamiliarity, of 'the unknown' may be here associated with anti-Neoteric, un-Callimachean poetic attitudes, as mainly evidenced from the prologue of the *Aetia*, where 'the distant', 'the unfamiliar' is identified with images against the poetological orientation of the *genus tenue*, to which pastoral, at least up to its Vergilian form, belongs (cf. Karakasis 2011, 139 – 40).

Corydon's situation, in the present Calpurnian poem, may thus be viewed as an inversion of Tityrus' programmatic bliss in Verg. *Ecl.* 1.51– 2⁶, which, on the contrary, is secured among familiar (*nota*)⁷ streams, in the well-appreciated generic cooling shadow (*flumina nota...frigus captabis opacum*), also implying, as Papanghelis 1995, 187– 91 has shown, the meta-linguistic Callimachean orthodoxy of Vergilian pastoral poetics Tityrus manages to hold on to. This novel, from a 'generic point of view', Calpurnian situation, i.e., the negative depiction of a distinctly pastoral 'generic marker', the *locus amoenus* and its main features⁸, is reflected on the linguistic level as well: it is introduced by a Post-Classical expression, namely the formation *adstrepere*, cf. also Sen. *Phaedr.* 1026, employed in a transitive construction with an accusative complement, v. 2: *quam*

---

4 Vs. Keene 1996, 93, who prefers the variant *infesta*. For a refutation of this reading, cf. Vozza 1994, 87 – 8 and n. 60; see also Schröder 1991, 73, Chinnici 2009, 134 and n. 20, Vinchesi 2014, 295. In any case, both readings suggest an alienation from 'traditional generic pleasures'.
5 Cf. also Leach 1973, 66; 1975, 208, 227 and n. 14, Davis 1987, 44, Schröder 1991, 73 – 4, Vozza 1994, 86 – 8, Paschalis 1996, 145 – 6, Esposito 1996, 14 – 5, Hubbard 1998, 165, Newlands 2002, 143 – 4, 147, Garthwaite-Martin 2009, 315, Vinchesi 2014, 293, 295, Baraz 2015, 105 – 7.
6 For the passage as an echo of Verg. *Ecl.* 1.51 ff., see Korzeniewski 1971, 35, Esposito 1996, 15 – 6, Vinchesi 2002, 146; 2014, 295, Di Lorenzo-Pellegrino 2008, 202.
7 For *nosco* and its derivative formations as 'reflexive annotations' in Vergilian pastoral, cf. also Papanghelis 2006, 372 and n. 10. While the Vergilian *nota* 'may be reflexively nodding to all those familiar with the Theocritean intertext' (Papanghelis *loc. cit.*), the Calpurnian *insueta*, equally reflexively, may suggest a distance from and disapproval of an accumulated pastoral textual experience.
8 Cf. also Kegel-Brinkgreve 1990, 167.

garrulus adstrepit umor[9]. This is a first indication of Meliboeus' penchant for Post-Classical diction, which probably mirrors his novel 'generic aspirations' on the level of his diction as well (this point is further elaborated below, pp. 83–4).

Interestingly enough, the generic cool shade is not provided here by the traditional pine of Theocritean pastoral, the pastoral beech of Vergilian bucolics or any other pastoral shady tree (e.g. oaks, elms, hazels, ilexes, etc.)[10], but by a newcomer in the genre, the plane-tree. Shady plane-trees, on the other hand, appear for the first time, in the Latin literature before Calpurnius, as part of the old man's from Tarentum idyllic landscape and not of a pastoral *locus amoenus*, cf. Verg. *G.* 4.146 (see also Hor. *Carm.* 2.11.13–7)[11]; this may be read here as a hint about the significant 'generic alteration' that the passage displays. A shady plane-tree as part of a *locus amoenus* appears, on the other hand, in a Greek bucolic poet, Moschus fr. 1.11–3[12], but in a fragment without particular pastoral pretensions: a character is complaining of the perilous raging sea as compared to a calm rustic *locus amoenus*-setting. Moschus' excerpt seems thus to be about a *mariner* or, in any case, a character who appears to be 'reading' the generic bucolic *locus amoenus* rather unsuccessfully, showing himself rather unknowledgeable as to the flora of the pastoral tradition.

This sense of 'generic dislocation' is reinforced by the image of the silent Corydon in v. 1: *quid tacitus, Corydon?*[13]. Several modern critics have discussed

---

[9] Cf. also Tac. *Ann.* 2.12.12, *Hist.* 4.49.20; see also Mahr 1964, 122, Messina 1975, 76–7, 108, Novelli 1980, 45, Gagliardi 1984, 58–9 and n. 31, Schröder 1991, 73, Di Lorenzo-Pellegrino 2008, 201, Vinchesi 2014, 294.
[10] Cf. Hubbard 1998, 165 and n. 39; see also Paschalis 1996, 146–7. Plane-trees are incorporated in the pastoral tradition mainly after Calpurnius, cf. also Nemes. 1.72, 2.18. See also Vozza 1994, 81–2: 'I tratti tipici del *locus amoenus* in 4, 1 ss. sono piuttosto scarsi rispetto alla ricchezza descrittiva del genere bucolico', and 84–6 concerning the choice of the plane shade, which is attributed to Corydon's leaning towards the epic genre.
[11] Cf. Korzeniewski 1971, 35, Leach 1975, 227 and n. 14, Schröder 1991, 72.
[12] Cf. Esposito 1996, 16–8, Vinchesi 2002, 146–7; 2014, 294, Simon 2007, 58, Di Lorenzo-Pellegrino 2008, 201, Chinnici 2009, 134 and n. 18.
[13] Cf. also Vozza 1994, 72, 77. Yet Vozza *op. cit.*, 72–7 tries to examine Corydon's silence on the basis of political and religious criteria. In general Vozza's reading does not focus on 'generic issues' but tries instead to establish an association between Calp. 4.1–4 and the so-called 'literature of opposition' in the Neronian period (cf. also Introduction, p. 10; see also p. 40 and 119), and to reveal 'the difficulty the intellectual [(Corydon / Calpurnius)] meets to integrate in the Neronian socio-political system' (cf. p. 92). Similarly Martin 2003, 82–3 also reads here a latent irony and criticism of the Neronian *Aurea Aetas*, based chiefly on the intertexts of these lines, namely Cic. *Div.* 2.30.63, Verg. *Ecl.* 9 and *A.* 7.475–510, i.e., contexts with ominous associations; this underlying disapproval of the Neronian regime is, according to the schol-

the difficult issue of the relationship of this passage with *Eins.* 2.1[14]: *quid tacitus, Mystes?*, and no consensus has been reached as to whether the similarity is due to Calpurnius' imitation of the *Einsiedeln* poet or vice versa. The issue is, of course, closely connected with the equally vexed question of the chronological precedence of one poem over the other[15]. However, the most important facet of the line, under the present analysis, is the silence–motif and its running counter to the bucolic value of a pre–Calpurnian loud and resonant pastoral space. This motif had already been exploited by Vergil in the ninth eclogue (cf. Karakasis 2011, 199), where a *tacitus* Moeris (v. 37)[16] betrayed through his silence his deviation from the Vergilian pastoral norm. In a similar vein, Corydon's silence also seems to testify here to his alienation from earlier pastoral ideals. This hush becomes more evident in the lines to follow: Corydon confesses that, for quite a long time, he has been pondering lines without woodland resonances (v. 5: *carmina...non quae nemorale resultent*), and draws a distinction between pastoral poetry, on the one hand, and poetry fit for praising the *aurea saecula* and the god presiding over nations and cities, securing peace (vv. 5–8), on the other. In terms of pastoral history, Corydon with his explicit 'generic anxieties' thus partly resembles Vergil of the fourth eclogue[17], where, in a similar 'generic con-

---

ar, cf. also pp. 84–7, detectable in the intertexts of vv. 12, 31–2, 52, 94 as well. Vinchesi 2002, 146; 2014, 293, on the other hand, associates Corydon's posture with poetic inspiration.
14 Cf. Verdière 1954, 157, Pearce 1990, 92, Vozza 1994, 71 and n. 1, Amat 1998, 196, Henderson 2013, 177, Baraz 2015, 105 and n. 41.
15 For Calpurnius' posteriority to the *Eins.* 2 poet, cf. Skutsch 1905, 2115, Momigliano 1944, 98, Schmid 1953, 95–6, Hubbard 1998, 165; for the opposite view, cf. Paladini 1956, 521–3, Theiler 1956, 568–71, Verdière 1966, 174, Scheda 1969, 49–56, Sullivan 1985, 56, Courtney 1987, 156–7, Di Salvo 1990, 35, Vinchesi 1996, 6 and n. 2; 2002, 147; 2014, 47, 293, Amat 1997, 218; 1998, 197, 199, Merfeld 1999, 143 and n. 1, Simon 2007, 59. For an overview of the subject, cf. also Schröder 1991, 69–71.
16 Cf. also Schmid 1953, 94–6, Paladini 1956, 521–2, Messina 1975, 76, Schröder 1991, 69–70, Vozza 1994, 71 and n. 1, Merfeld 1999, 85 and n. 4, Vinchesi 2002, 147; 2014, 293, Di Lorenzo-Pellegrino 2008, 200, Chinnici 2009, 133 and n. 17, Baraz 2015, 106 and n. 44.
17 Cf. also Paladini 1956, 522, Rosenmeyer 1969, 221, Langholf 1990, 366, Esposito 1996, 18–9; 2009, 18, Hubbard 1998, 166, Amat 1998, 196, Merfeld 1999, 85 and n. 2, Gibson 2004, 2, Vinchesi 2014, 297. Despite the fact that the Golden Age–motif is central in Neronian panegyric (cf. also Martin 1996, 31, Esposito 2009, 17 and n. 9), within the pastoral genre Calpurnius' immediate predecessor is Vergil's fourth eclogue, cf. also Gatz 1967, 135, Küppers 1985, 347 and n. 23, Schröder 1991, 76–7.

templative disposition', he celebrates the Golden Age associated with the birth of a redeemer child[18].

Vergil's voice acknowledges a 'generic tension' between humble pastoral poetry, symbolised by the image of vineyards and low tamarisks (v. 2: *non omnis arbusta iuvant humilesque myricae*), and a loftier genre. But in opposition to Corydon, Vergil only desires subject-matters[19] that are *paulo maiora* (v. 1: *Sicelides Musae, paulo maiora canamus*); he simply decides on bucolic strains of a loftier colour, v. 3: *si canimus silvas, silvae sint consule dignae*. Corydon, on the other hand, is ready for a more radical re-evaluation of his poetic orientation: his songs should have no woodland ring (v. 5), nothing reminiscent of the herd's sound, cf. also Calp. 1.29: *nihil armentale resultat*[20], Chapter 1, pp. 21–2. The wording of the expression used for denoting Corydon's distance from long-established pastoral has significantly an Ovidian ring, as *nemoralis*, employed here for denoting the pastoral genre instead of the common Vergilian and Calpurnian adjectives qualifying the bucolic *genus*, namely *silvestris* (Calp. 4.12, see also Verg. *Ecl.* 6.1–2) and *rusticus* (Verg. *Ecl.* 3.84, Calp. 4.147), appears for the first time in Ovid, cf. *Am.* 3.1.5; see also 2.6.57[21]. Corydon / Calpurnius (cf. Introduction, pp. 9–10) thus chooses to express his transcending of traditional (mainly Vergilian) pastoral by means of an Ovidian wording and intertext; this

---

18 One might counter with some justification that if pastoral is, among other things, about *loca amoena*, peaceful and idyllic settings as well as song, Vergil's fourth eclogue does aspire to exactly this condition, for it pastoralises, i.e., de-historicises, the historical landscape; this is a major pastoral gesture and aspiration. Nonetheless, the political panegyrical symbolisms operating not only in *Ecl.* 4 but also in *Ecl.* 5 of the Vergilian bucolic corpus (cf. also Karakasis 2011, 168–79) are of a loftier tone compared to the main issues dealt with in all other Vergilian eclogues (see also Hubbard 1998, 76–99, Schmidt 1998–9, 235). One should, however, discern here that, in opposition to Calpurnius Siculus, panegyric in Vergil (*Ecl.* 4 and also 5) is still subordinate to the overall pastoral setting, imagery and register (cf. also Monella 2009, 76 and n. 25), very subtly and to the point of absorbing the hard edge of the panegyric tone. This delicate balance is not retained in Calpurnius, since here panegyric seems to take precedence over pastoral, to the point of making the bucolic *genus* just a frame for the *laudes principis*. These are the novel panegyrical demands of the imperial period and, from this new perspective, the function and the idea of the song-contest mechanism are thoroughly undermined.
19 I do not see a particular colloquial nuance in the *paulo*-syntagm in question, crucially occurring also in Lucretius (cf. Van Sickle 1992, 66–7), at least to the extent of agreeing with Gotoff 1967, 67–9, who reads the whole line as ironic.
20 Cf. also Verdière 1954, 246, Paladini 1956, 528, Spadaro 1969, 28, Davis 1987, 44, Amat 1991, 107, Horsfall 1997, 188; see also Simon 2007, 57, Di Lorenzo-Pellegrino 2008, 202, Vinchesi 2014, 296–7, Baraz 2015, 107–8.
21 Cf. also Schröder 1991, 76, McKeown 1998, 142, Vinchesi 2014, 297. For similar terms as designations of pastoral poetry, see also Schmidt 1972, 243.

process of substituting the pastoral Vergil with Ovid as his poetic model is apparent throughout the eclogue, and the usage of the expression *nemoralis* here may be read as being part of this process. The above (generically) novel procedure seems to be reflected on the linguistic level once again; Corydon's / Calpurnius' inventive 'generic aspirations' are thus conveyed by way of an innovative / Post-Classical construction, namely the transitive usage of *resultare* with the neuter accusative as its direct complement (v. 5: *non quae nemorale resultent*), a syntagm later appearing in Apul. *Met.* 5.7.5 and Mart. Cap. 1.2 as well[22].

Following the pattern of the fourth Vergilian eclogue and its Golden Age analogies, the Vergilian intertext of the *deus ipse* topic of the Calpurnian lines under discussion further suggests a kind of divorce with the pastoral tradition: Calp. 4.7–8 seems to be modelled on the first Vergilian eclogue, 1.6–7, 18[23], and is in line with the tendency of Neronian literature to associate the emperor with a divine figure[24]. However, the Vergilian pastoral god is presented as securing the continuation of the pastoral space, at least for Tityrus, as a guarantor of the 'green cabinet' and its bucolic genre; this is not the case in Calpurnius: the god is simply praised as a ruler of the Roman *imperium* not associated in any particular way with the bucolic world (cf. also above, pp. 8, 33–4, 38). What is more, the wording by means of which this god is described (v. 8: *qui populos urbesque regit pacemque togatam*) alludes to epic texts[25] (cf. Verg. *A.* 1.282, 6.851, 8.325, see also Cic. *Div.* 1.21.8 (*poet.* 6.67)[26]) and thus confirms Corydon's (equated with Calpurnius[27]) endeavours for 'generic transcendence'[28].

---

22 Cf. also Merone 1967, 14, Messina 1975, 111, Gagliardi 1984, 71, Schröder 1991, 76, Di Lorenzo–Pellegrino 2008, 202; see also Vinchesi 2014, 297.
23 Cf. also Schröder 1991, 78.
24 Cf. also Bardon 1972, 12. For the various divine attributes of the deified Nero in the present eclogue, cf. also Schröder 1991, 18–9 and n. 12.
25 Cf. also Joly 1974, 46–7, Kegel-Brinkgreve 1990, 157 and n. 25, Schröder 1991, 78: 'Dieser Ausdruck...hat episches Gepräge', Di Lorenzo–Pellegrino 2008, 203: 'il nesso del linguaggio epico e solenne', Vinchesi 2014, 297–8: 'nessi epici'.
26 Cf. Cesareo 1931, 167, Verdière 1954, 246, Korzeniewski 1971, 36, Messina 1975, 77, Pearce 1990, 92, Amat 1991, 107.
27 For Corydon as the literary persona of Calpurnius, cf. also Skutsch 1897, 1403, Wendel 1901, 58–9, Morelli 1914, 120, Hubaux 1930, 174, Cesareo 1931, 158, Herrmann 1952, 34–5, Duff 1960, 266, Verdière 1966, 165, Rosenmeyer 1969, 341 and n. 55, Cizek 1972, 372, Schmidt 1972, 122–4, Joly 1974, 42, Friedrich 1976, 129, Grimal 1978, 165, Casaceli 1982, 86, Castagna 1982, 159, Küppers 1989, 39, Langholf 1990, 357, Kegel-Brinkgreve 1990, 160, 164, Schröder 1991, 22–5, Amat 1991, xxv, Vozza 1993, 287, Vinchesi 1996, 9; 2002, 140, Hubbard 1998, 154, Schubert 1998, 64, Beato 2003, 93, Martin 2003, 75, Magnelli 2006, 469–70, Simon 2007, 43–98, especially 51, Monella 2009, 75 and n. 23. For a more

Meliboeus reacts to Corydon's novel 'generic demands' by affirming the latter's traditionally pastoral and in consequence Neoteric poetic orientation, at least up to their encounter, as described in the present eclogue. Corydon's poetic production, as known to Meliboeus, is thus described as *dulce*, a poetological catch-word constituting a basic 'generic marker' of Callimachean pastoral (cf. Theocr. 1.1–3, Verg. *Ecl.* 5.47 ; see also Calp. 2.6, 4.55, 61, 150, 160, 7.20, Nemes. 1.22, 82, 2.15, 83, 4.13)[29]. He complements this claim of his with the image of Apollo casting a not unfavourable glance on the singer, vv. 9–10: *nec te diversus Apollo / despicit*. It is a common trend of Neronian literature, pastoral included, to associate or even to identify the emperor with Apollo (cf. *Eins.* 1.22–4, 27, 32–3, 2.38)[30]; from the viewpoint of pastoral poetics, however, Apollo is also the god of the *dulce* poetic trend: in the coda of Callimachus' hymn to Apollo (vv. 108 ff.), it is *Apollo* himself who, as the god of poetic inspiration, urges for poetry composed κατὰ λεπτὸν and against poetry of many lines, symbolised by the Assyrian river (cf. also *Aet.* 1.22–8 Pf.). In Roman pastoral, i.e., in Verg. *Ecl.* 6.1 ff., it is Apollo again who admonishes Vergil for a *deductum carmen*[31], cf. also Hor. *Carm.* 4.15.1–4, Prop. 3.3.13–26, 4.1b.73–4, 133–4, Ov. *Ars* 2.493– 508. Thus if Apollo were to look favourably upon Corydon, it would be for the opposite poetic orientation than the one Meliboeus expects of the pastoral singer for the future. The poetological associations of Meliboeus' *magnae numina Romae*, v. 10 (*magnus* as a catch-word opposing 'slender sensibilities' and combined with a preference for the *urbs* vs. *rus*[32]), would justify Apollo's intervention. But things change, and even gods may alter their poetic preferences: Apollo / (Nero) now accepts Corydon's poetological aspirations towards a loftier poetic style (cf. also vv. 70–2)[33], and so Meliboeus insists that Corydon will prove himself competent at singing about Rome's *numina* in a quite different manner than

---

critical approach, cf. Leach 1973, 86, Davis 1987, 39, Newlands 1987, 227–9, Effe–Binder 1989, 117–8.
28 Garson 1974, 669 speaks about a 'disparagement' of the bucolic in the case of the fourth Calpurnian eclogue.
29 Cf. also Schmidt 1972, 29 and n. 64, Schröder 1991, 79, Vinchesi 2014, 171, 298.
30 Cf. also Verdière 1954, 247, Griffin 1984, 120, Vinchesi 1996, 22–3, 103; 2014, 298, Champlin 2003, 276–83.
31 Cf. also Hubbard 1998, 166, Di Lorenzo–Pellegrino 2008, 203.
32 For Calpurnius' preference for *urbs* over *rus*, cf. especially Perutelli 1976, 781 ff.
33 Cf. also Hubbard 1998, 166; I do not see with Hubbard *ad loc.* a reversal of the prologue in Verg. *Ecl.* 6, but rather a modification. The god of the *genus tenue* here simply does not disapprove of loftier poetic inspirations, but does not advocate them.

the one adopted for his previous pastoral compositions (v. 11: *ut ovile Menalcae*[34]).

Corydon accepts Meliboeus' criticism, and tries to make allowances for the pastoral colouring Meliboeus has been exposed to, prior to their encounter in the present eclogue, i.e., before the song-exchange that follows. He thus acknowledges the traditional, sylvan character of his work (vv. 12–3: *silvestre licet videatur acutis / auribus*), crucially further describing his poetic production by means of the technical term *rusticitas* (v. 14), which, in its turn, has parallels in the previous pastoral tradition as a 'self-reflexive generic term'[35]. The expression thus alludes both to Verg. *Ecl.* 2.56[36], where Corydon self-referentially so acknowledges his adhesion to the pastoral world and the bucolic genre (cf. also vv. 60–1), and to Verg. *Ecl.* 3.84: *Pollio amat nostram, quamvis est rustica, Musam*[37], where one of the contestants, Damoetas, uses a similar qualification for describing his pastoral Muse. A sense of time-honoured pastoral colouring is further evoked by an unequivocally pastoral image: a herdsman, Corydon's brother Amyntas, sings in the shade of a pine-tree (vv. 16–8, cf. the use of the verb *meditatur* in v. 17 in the sense of 'to produce pastoral song' having its parallels in the Vergilian corpus, cf. 1.2: *silvestrem tenui musam meditaris avena*[38], 6.8; see also 6.82).

However, the Calpurnian passage is again not free from signs pointing to Calpurnius' 'generic diversification': whereas in the Vergilian intertexts the term *rusticus* simply denotes the pastoral character of the herdsmen's song and is not related to issues of poetic skill, Calpurnius' Corydon uses it to characterise his lack of artistic polish (vv. 14–5: *si non valet arte polita / carminis*)[39].

---

[34] Cf. also Ahl 1984, 66. Commenting on the use of *ovile* in the line, Schröder 1991, 81 convincingly remarks: 'bezeichnet den Gegenstandsbereich der reinen Bukolik und damit diese selbst'; see also Schmidt 1969, 192, Vozza 1993, 293. Vinchesi 1996, 46 too reads the line as constituting along with vv. 74–5 an 'emblema della tenue poesia pastorale'; see also 2014, 39, 299. For an association of the passage with Verg. *Ecl.* 4.1–4, see Verdière 1985, 1869.
[35] Cf. also Schmidt 1972, 26–7. For *rusticitas* denoting pastoral poetry as well, cf. Vinchesi 1996, 29, Magnelli 2006, 472; see also Correa 1977, 152. *Rusticitas* functions as an obstacle to the poet's urban aspirations in Calp. 7 as well, cf. vv. 40–2, 79: *o utinam nobis non rustica vestis inesset!*; see also Vozza 1993, 300–1, Chapter 3, pp. 111–3.
[36] Cf. Davis 1987, 44, Gibson 2004, 3.
[37] Cf. also Schröder 1991, 84, Vozza 1993, 291–2, Di Lorenzo-Pellegrino 2008, 204, Vinchesi 2014, 300–1.
[38] Cf. also Verdière 1971, 378, Kegel-Brinkgreve 1990, 157 and n. 25, Pearce 1990, 93.
[39] In the second Vergilian eclogue, Corydon's lays are described as *incondita* (v. 4), i.e., artless; however this aesthetic judgment comes not from Corydon himself but from the voice of the external narrator in the framing introduction (vv. 1–5). More importantly, it is not the rustic / pas-

As a result, in Calpurnius the term is not simply a 'generic characterisation', but is further semantically loaded with undertones relating to the well-known dichotomy of *rusticitas – urbanitas*[40], this time in terms of poetic proficiency. Pastoral song is certainly of rustic thematic, but not less polished in poetic style because of its *rusticitas*. Singing excellence is the highest qualification of the rustic 'green cabinet', coveted by the rustic inhabitants of the pastoral space[41]; so Corydon's self-deprecatory remarks on the quality of his traditionally pastoral / rustic poetry seem quite out of place in a pastoral work, deviating as they do from the acknowledged and positively viewed Callimachean poetological orientation of pastoral / rustic 'poetic slenderness', as suggested by the previous pastoral tradition. It is perhaps the case that pastoral has here fallen victim to the requirements of panegyric; thus it seems that any kind of non-panegyric verse, as required from the Neronian period onwards at least, is bound to be thought of as 'unpolished', i.e., not worthy of the emperor. Hence if pastoral is not undervalued *per se*, pastoral forms of no explicit imperial panegyric colouring, and as a consequence pre-Calpurnian bucolics for that matter as well, are largely rated too low.

Corydon's desire for his loyalty to be recognised (v. 15: *at certe valeat pietate probari*) constitutes one more step away from the earlier pastoral canon: although up to a point associated with the Roman *rus* (cf. e. g. Tib. 1.1.11 ff.[42]), *pietas* is primarily an epic value, ideally exemplified by *pius* Aeneas[43] and is by no means a crucial asset in the pre-Calpurnian pastoral value system. Accusations

---

toral production of Corydon that is so qualified, but rather the elegising discourse that Corydon addresses to Alexis, and, what is more, in a setting comprising as it does a lone singer (v. 4: *solus*), recalling the also counter-pastoral disposition of the lone singer in both the eleventh Theocritean idyll and the ninth Vergilian eclogue (cf. in particular Karakasis 2011, 201). This discourse of Corydon's has led scholars to label *Ecl.* 2 as an 'anti-Eclogue' (cf. Galinsky 1965, 175), as the 'most elegiac of pastorals' (cf. Coleman 1977, 108; see also Cucchiarelli 2012, 172–3).

40 Cf. also Calp. 7.40–2, Di Salvo 1990, 42. Vinchesi 1996, 20 discerns here a form of the so-called 'formula di modestia' of the kind known mainly from panegyrical *incipits* and dedicatory parts of heroic / panegyric compositions of the later imperial period; see also 2014, 301.

41 The very expression *valet arte* points to Callimachean–Neoteric poetic directions; its intertext is the poetological Elegy – σφραγίς 1.15 of the Ovidian *Amores*, cf. also Schröder 1991, 84, Fucecchi 2009, 44 and n. 16, Vinchesi 2014, 301. Callimachean poetry (bucolic poetry included) is characterised by *ars* in opposition to Corydon's remarks.

42 Cf. also Schröder 1991, 85, Vinchesi 2014, 301.

43 Cf. also Cizek 1972, 374, Vozza 1993, 294. Amat 1991, 107 reads the term as equivalent to 'l'attachement à la cité, le patriotisme que pousse Corydon à se réjouir de la paix'. For the political and religious undertones of the term however, cf. Vozza 1993, 293: 'devozione religiosa all' imperatore'; see also Vinchesi 2014, 301.

of poetic incompetence together with appeals to ideals related to *pietas* move the reader once again away from the pastoral tradition, thus reinforcing an overall yearning for transcending pre-Calpurnian pastoral as a 'generic system', evidenced from vv. 5ff. onwards. Similar poetological aspirations are to be discerned in the poetic production of Corydon's brother, Amyntas, who composes pastoral song assimilating the poetic quality of his brother's novel production (v. 17: *haec eadem nobis frater meditatur Amyntas*). The setting of Amyntas' diversified pastoral production about to be disclosed is, however, given once again by means of long-established, common pastoral images, that of a rocky-setting (v. 16: *rupe sub hac*, cf. also [Theocr.] 8.55, Verg, *Ecl*. 1.56) and a pine tree-scenery (v. 16: *proxima pinus*, cf. also Theocr. 1.1, Verg. *Ecl*. 1.38, 7.24, 65, 68, 8.22, Calp. 1.9 – 10[44]) securing the omnipresent pastoral shade; conventional pastoral signs are thus mingled with 'generically deviating' markers further blurring the 'generic outlook' of the poem.

In vv. 19ff., a distinction is drawn between the past, exhibiting a hostile attitude towards poetry, vs. a more favourable present[45], a division common in panegyric contexts[46]: Corydon is presented as prohibiting his brother Amyntas from joining the reeds of his pastoral flute and from producing pastoral music (vv. 19 – 21). Emphasis is given not only to the fact that Corydon tries to eliminate pastoral poetry but also to his doing away with the Callimachean-Neoteric character of this 'slender' bucolic poetic production. The lines under question contain several catch-words of poetological import, such as the hemlock stems which are described as *leves* (v. 20: *levibus...cicutis*), and the piping which is phrased by means of the verb *ludere* (v. 21: *ludere conantem vetuisti*)[47]. Corydon thus functions in just the opposite way of the *praesens deus*[48] of the first Vergilian eclogue to whom Calpurnius intertextually refers. Whereas the urban god intervenes in order to secure Tityrus' enjoyment of the woodland 'slender Muse' (Verg. *Ecl*. 1.10[49]: *ludere quae vellem calamo permisit agresti*; note here again the presence of the Neoteric term *ludere*, cf. also Verg. *Ecl*. 6.1, 7.17), Corydon urges the elimination of the Callimachean pastoral song. His attitude, opposing

---

44 For the references, cf. also Schröder 1991, 85 – 6, Di Lorenzo-Pellegrino 2008, 204, Vinchesi 2014, 302.
45 Cf. also Schubert 1998, 64 – 5.
46 Cf. also Schröder 1991, 181, Vinchesi 2014, 346.
47 For the Callimachean-Neoteric character of the terms in Vergilian pastoral, cf. also Schröder 1991, 90.
48 For the motif as typical of the Augustan period, cf. also Simon 2007, 80.
49 For vv. 20f. alluding to Verg. *Ecl*. 1.10, see also Verdière 1954, 159, Korzeniewski 1971, 37, Di Lorenzo-Pellegrino 2008, 205, Vinchesi 2014, 304.

as it does crucial aesthetic preferences of the bucolic tradition, is enhanced by the frown of an angry father (*fronte paterna*, v. 21), which he adopts when admonishing his brother, Amyntas, against his *cicuta*-playing. Angry fathers are not a feature of the pastoral tradition, appearing chiefly in other literary genres such as comedy and mime; their occasional presence in pastoral (e.g. [Theocr.] 8 and Verg. *Ecl.* 3) may be interpreted as a comic or mimic influence, and are often complemented with other 'generic comic characteristics' (cf. Karakasis 2011, 107–9). In any case the father–figure, apprehensive of property-loss in the two pre-Calpurnian pastoral intertexts, is here associated with the abolition of the highest value of the pastoral tradition.

The pursuit proposed by Corydon is that Amyntas should assuage his hunger, which the Muses cannot alleviate, a crucial 'materialistic concern' alien to Theocritean, Greek post–Theocritean and Vergilian pastoral idealism (vv. 26–7: *quid enim tibi fistula reddet, / quo tutere famem?*). The topic of the poor poet, the 'intellektuelle Proletarier'[50], threatened by hunger has no parallels in pre-Calpurnian pastoral[51] and, what is more, is here connected with the promotion of georgic interests[52] in place of default concerns of the pastoral tradition (v. 23: *frange...calamos*[53]), as a means of escape from hunger[54], exemplified mainly by the milking imagery in vv. 25–6 (cf. also Verg. *G.* 3.177, 309, 400–2, etc.[55]). Hunger, to make things worse, forces the herdsman to abandon the pastoral space for the *urbs*, in order to sell his milk (vv. 25–6: *lac venale per urbem... porta*). The herdsman is thus presented as being interested in profit (*venale*), a 'materialistic concern' commonly associated with georgic ideals[56]. As Rosenmey-

---

50 Cf. Simon 2007, 63.
51 Cf. also Schröder 1991, 91 speaking of the motif of 'brotlosen Kunst'. The motif points to other genres, cf. Ov. *Trist.* 4.10.21–3, Mart. 5.56.
52 For the influence the georgic *genus* has upon the fourth Calpurnian pastoral in general, cf. also Schröder 1991, 26–9, Schubert 1998, 64.
53 For the image common in both Juvenal and Martial, cf. Verdière 1954, 159, Korzeniewski 1971, 37, Townend 1973, 150, Mayer 1980, 176, Armstrong 1986, 128–9, Courtney 1987, 153–4, Braund 1988, 39, 210 and n. 40, Amat 1991, 107, Schröder 1991, 90–1, Vozza 1993, 294–5 and n. 45, Keene 1996, 96, Vinchesi 1996, 30; 2014, 304–5, Hubbard 1998, 167, Simon 2007, 66.
54 The image of destitution is further underlined by Corydon's advising his brother to gather acorns and red cornel cherries (v. 24: *i, potius glandes rubicundaque collige corna*), i.e., a type of food that the Romans thought fit for men only in ancient times, but was associated in historical period with situations of extreme poverty, cf. also Schröder 1991, 92, Vinchesi 1996, 104; 2014, 305–6.
55 Cf. also Korzeniewski 1971, 37, Vinchesi 2014, 306.
56 Cf. especially Davis 1987, 37.

er 1969, 102 observes: 'the pastoral herdsman does not look upon his flock as chattel, and instruments of profit, but as associates in pleasure and happiness'. This ideal pastoralism has no place in Corydon's exhortations to his brother. What is more, the motif of the materialistic interests of a pastoral inhabitant further harks back to Verg. *Ecl.* 1.34[57], where Tityrus complains that his spendthrift ex-wife, Galatea, was responsible for his poor financial situation, despite the large number of his flocks (v. 33) and the amount of cheese he produces (*pinguis...premeretur caseus urbi*). This passage constitutes a characteristic case of deviation from pastoral ideals, containing several non-pastoral features, such as is the notion of *libertas* (v. 32), Tityrus' *peculium* (v. 32) and the comic-related image of the wasteful wife[58]. The image of this 'dislocation' from the pastoral tradition towards different 'generic ideals' is in the Calpurnian eclogue complemented by the motif of the echo (vv. 27–8): the herdsman complains that nobody is repeating his song apart from the wind-sped echo; but the effect of the repetitive echo, simply functioning as a foil to Corydon's grievance here, constitutes one of the basic 'generic markers' of earlier pastoral, pointing to the close bond between man and nature (cf. Verg. *Ecl.* 1.5, 6.84, 10.8, see also Nemes. 1.72–4). The somewhat negative depiction of the echo-motif here betrays once again a movement away from time-honoured pastoral values[59].

However, things have changed under the influence of the new god, Nero, and his new, Augustan maecenatism[60], v. 30: *non eadem nobis sunt tempora, non deus idem*; pastoral order seems to be restored and pastoral song appears to be reborn. A series of customary pastoral 'generic markers' and allusions to the programmatic first Vergilian eclogue testify to this: the sense of relaxation under the shadow of a tree (v. 37), the enjoyment of Amaryllis' woods[61] (v.

---

[57] Cf. also Pearce 1990, 93, Schröder 1991, 93, Di Lorenzo–Pellegrino 2008, 206, Vinchesi 2014, 306.
[58] Cf. Coleman 1977, 78, Papanghelis 1995, 193–4, Cucchiarelli 2012, 151–2.
[59] Cf. Leach 1973, 68, Schröder 1991, 94–5; see also Simon 2007, 61, Baraz 2015, 108. Calpurnius in general seems to avoid the sonorous nature of pre-Calpurnian pastoral, cf. especially Damon 1973, 292–4; see also Rosenmeyer 1969, 186, Vinchesi 2014, 307, Baraz 2015, 91–120, especially 99–114 and *passim* in the present study, especially pp. 240–1.
[60] Cf. Pearce 1990, 94, Amat 1991, 108, Monella 2009, 67, Vinchesi 2014, 291–2; Hubaux 1930, 183 thinks that the qualification simply refers to an eminent member of the imperial court. For a distinction made between Claudius' *principatus* and Nero's ascension, cf. Cesareo 1931, 171, Verdière 1954, 247, Vozza 1993, 286 and n. 12, Keene 1996, 97, Vinchesi 1996, 30–1, 105; 2002, 139, 147–8, Merfeld 1999, 86, Martin 2003, 75, Simon 2007, 61, Di Lorenzo–Pellegrino 2008, 207; see also Spadaro 1969, 38–9, Joly 1974, 53.
[61] Cf. Kegel-Brinkgreve 1990, 157 and n. 25. Verdière 1954, 247 reads the image as a reference to pastoral poetry, see also Schröder 1991, 102–3, Amat 1991, 108, Vinchesi 2012, 720 and n.

38), Corydon's departure from his familiar pastoral environment and his exile[62], prevented by Meliboeus' intervention (vv. 39–49)[63], have their parallels in the Vergilian bucolics. These include: Tityrus lying *lentus in umbra* in *Ecl.* 1.4 (cf. also 1.1, Theocr. 7.88–9), Amaryllis resounding in the woods in *Ecl.* 1.5, and Meliboeus setting off for the world's extremities in *Ecl.* 1.64–6[64]. However, in the Vergilian case a poetological reading may suggest the association of Tityrus' permanence in the pastoral world with his continuing adhesion to the Callimachean pastoral poetry, whereas Meliboeus' forced departure may be read, on the basis of the imagery of 'the distant', 'the remote' in Callimachus' *Aetia* (1.13–6 ff. Pf.), as an indication of his alienation from the purity of Neoteric pastoral song (cf. Papanghelis 1995, 194–7; see also above, pp. 49, 57). Such poetological preoccupations seem to be absent from the Calpurnian text. Corydon is enthusiastic over the satisfaction of his hunger and blesses himself for staying in his familiar pastoral space, which contrasts with the hostile and war–like Iberian landscape[65], for otherwise it would be very difficult to move the imperial ears with his songs (of a loftier poetic calibre) and thus to integrate himself into the imperial circles. No one would have paid attention to his music in the midst of the thorn bushes of his exile (vv. 46–7: *nec quisquam nostras inter dumeta Camenas / respiceret*), believes Corydon. Note here the term that he employs for his singing

---

79; 2014, 312; see also p. 39 (*otium* pastorale); for Amaryllis as a metonymy for Rome or a simple realistic reference to a shepherdess' name, cf. also Langholf 1990, 358 and n. 25, Schröder 1991, 102, Keene 1996, 98.

62 The syntagm *extremo...in orbe iacere* is appropriate in the diction of exile (Ovidian poetry included); the same holds true for the adjectives *ultimus* (cf. vv. 38–41), *obnoxius* (v. 40) and *trux* (v. 40) as well as for the motif of the poet deploring his lack of contact with Rome (vv. 43–9), also occurring in Ovidian exile poetry, cf. Schröder 1991, 107, Vinchesi 2012, 720–1 and nn. 80, 81, 82, 83; 2014, 42–3, 314.

63 Verdière 1954, 15 sees here autobiographical allusions that point to the Iberian origin of the poet, see also De Sipio 1935, 13–4, Amat 1991, ix, 32; yet cf. Mahr 1964, 3–5, Messina 1975, 79 and n. 81, Schröder 1991, 104. Ahl 1984, 67, on the other hand, detects here a scathing indirect allusion to the many prominent Spaniards during the Neronian period ('Romans' are thus seen as 'being replaced by provincials'); but irrespective of the potential biographical / historical allusions, the key–element of this passage is its undoubted Vergilian intertext, that of the first eclogue.

64 Cf. also Cesareo 1931, 170–1, Verdière 1954, 247; 1966, 165, Paladini 1956, 522–3, Korzeniewski 1971, 38, Leach 1973, 68–9, Joly 1974, 64 and n. 86, Messina 1975, 78, Friedrich 1976, 152–3, Davis 1987, 44–5, Langholf 1990, 358–9, Pearce 1990, 94, Schröder 1991, 100–1, 103, Vinchesi 1996, 32–3, 107; 2012, 720–1; 2014, 311–2, Hubbard 1998, 168, Schubert 1998, 65, Simon 2007, 55, Di Lorenzo–Pellegrino 2008, 208–9.

65 For an association of the passage with contemporary history, namely the death of the king of Mauritania (40 AD) and the subsequent riot, cf. Verdière 1954, 247, Vinchesi 1996, 107; 2014, 313, Simon 2007, 53 and n. 46.

production, *Camenas*, i.e., the equivalent of the Muses. As already remarked (cf. Karakasis 2011, 8), a basic feature of pastoral is the close association of the genre with the Nymphs rather than the Muses; the use of this term may also point to the 'generic transcending aspirations' of Calpurnian pastoralism.

Corydon, one may conclude on the basis of the symbolism he makes use of, is not interested in having a traditional pastoral voice restored. First of all, he declares himself pleased for no longer having to live on the glands of the beech, v. 35, the emblematic tree of Vergilian pastoral poetry[66]. Instead, Meliboeus has him fed with grain (v. 33), out of pity for his meager means and docile young age (v. 34: *tu nostras miseratus opes docilemque iuventam*)[67]. This last quality is again of no particular importance in pastoral tradition, and is not attributed to any Theocritean or Vergilian herdsmen. It therefore indicates the adoption of a different value system, rather belonging to other literary genres of a more panegyric outlook, cf. Hor. *C.S.* 45, *Serm.* 2.2.52[68]. This alienation from traditional pastoral may also be read in the negative presentation of the strawberries and the green mallow in vv. 31–2: *ne fraga rubosque / colligerem viridique famem solarer hibisco*, as opposed to their positive connotations in the rest of Latin literature[69]. Strawberries have their place in Vergilian pastoral, cf. *Ecl.* 3.92[70], where they constitute an element of the pastoral landscape against the 'unpastoral' disposition of a lurking snake (for the symbolism of the image, see Karakasis 2011, 118–9). The case of the *hibiscum* is more significant, since it occurs in programmatic instances within the Vergilian corpus: in

---

[66] Cf. Hubbard 1998, 167.
[67] One should notice here with Sauter 1934, 14 the hymnic / religious character of Corydon's appeal to Meliboeus, as chiefly evidenced by the 'Du-style' of vv. 33 ff.; see also Vinchesi 2014, 308–11. Thus, it is not only the emperor, who is perceived as a god, but also the go-between Meliboeus, who seems to be credited with divine properties as well. Ritual / hymnic – prayer features do appear in the appeals to the divine Nero too, especially the 'Er-style' of vv. 88–9, 122–6, 127–8; see La Bua 1999, 294–6, Vinchesi 2009a, 571–88. Further hymnic / ritual features include: the hymnical structure of the song-exchange (i.e., the *laudes principis*), the proemium and invocation (vv. 82 ff.), the aretalogy (vv. 97 ff.), the prayer and requests (vv. 137 ff; see also v. 86), the so-called *Relativ Stil* (cf. vv. 84–6), the ritual epiclesis (e.g. *parens*, v. 93), the duplication (cf. v. 100), the epanalepsis and polyptoton (vv. 144–5); see especially Vinchesi 2014, 291, 331, 336, 339–40, 357. Hymnic / ritual style is also occasionally employed in the presentation of Tityrus: note the 'Er-style' and the polyptoton of the relative pronoun in vv. 65 ff.; cf. Vinchesi 2014, 30, 323–4.
[68] Cf. Korzeniewski 1971, 38, Schröder 1991, 100, Di Lorenzo-Pellegrino 2008, 208, Vinchesi 2014, 310.
[69] Cf. Schröder 1991, 98 with his text-references.
[70] Cf. Di Lorenzo-Pellegrino 2008, 207, Vinchesi 2014, 309.

Ecl. 2.30[71] Corydon, the representative of the Vergilian 'green cabinet', invites Alexis, his urban beloved, to join him in several pastoral activities including flock–driving with a green *hibiscum*–switch (*haedorumque gregem viridi compellere hibisco*). This attribute of the Vergilian pastoral space re–appears in the programmatic tenth eclogue as well (v. 71), where the pastoral poet is presented as weaving a basket of 'slender *hibiscum*' (*gracili fiscellam texit hibisco*), i.e., an obvious poetological image of the Callimachean character of pastoral poetry[72]. Vergil thus seems to depict himself as a pastoral poet of Callimachean aspirations before embarking on loftier poetic genres[73]. Corydon's negative depiction of the green mallow, the strawberry and the emblematic beech–tree betrays not only his drifting apart from pastoral life[74] but also a certain degree of 'generic alienation' from earlier Vergilian pastoral. Besides, this feeling of a 'generic estrangement from the pastoral tradition' seems to be further evidenced on the linguistic level as well; namely, by Corydon's inserting in the pastoral host–text a *iunctura* of a clear modal georgic colouring, fashioned after Verg. *G.* 1.159[75], i.e., *famem solarer*, v. 32.

Corydon desires something loftier than Vergil's bucolic poetry, and thus appeals to the criticism of Meliboeus, who significantly is not a renowned pastoral singer, like Menalcas in the ninth Vergilian eclogue for example, but a poet of greater aspirations, who exhibits a wider poetic gamut, ranging from lyric poetry to tragedy. He has astronomical and georgic interests (didactic poetry), as suggested by his knowledge of weather signs, i.e., the rain storms to come (vv. 53–4, for this didactic concern, cf. Cic. *Div.* 1.13–5 (Arat. 909–87), Verg. *G.* 1.351–92) and the quality of sunrises and sunsets (vv. 54–5, cf. also Verg. *G.* 1.441–64)[76]. The bacchic ivy clusters and the apolline laurel, on the other hand, may symbolise his engagement with both tragedy and lyric poetry[77]. The

---

71 Cf. also Messina 1975, 78 and n. 80, Vinchesi 1996, 105; 2014, 309, Mayer 2006, 463, Di Lorenzo–Pellegrino 2008, 207.
72 For the poetological character of the scene, cf. also Schröder 1991, 98.
73 Cf. Hubbard 1998, 138.
74 Cf. Schröder 1991, 98: 'Corydons Entfremdung vom Hirtenleben'.
75 Cf. Di Lorenzo–Pellegrino 2008, 207, Vinchesi 2014, 309.
76 Cf. also Korzeniewski 1971, 97, Bartalucci 1976, 93, Schröder 1991, 114–6, Vinchesi 2014, 318. See also Morford 1985, 2009 and n. 33, who also reads here a reference to a didactic work by Meliboeus; he also understands the image in vv. 53–7 as figuratively referring to Nero himself, on the basis of *sol aureus* and *pulcher...Apollo* imagery in vv. 54, 57 respectively.
77 Cf. Duff and Duff 1934, 248, Bartalucci 1976, 93, Amat 1991, 109, Keene 1996, 100, Vinchesi 1996, 108; 2014, 319–20. Even if one does not accept Duff's reading, since Bacchus is often depicted in Latin literature as presiding over poetry in general, cf. Schröder 1991, 118, what matters here is that Meliboeus is never presented as a professional pastoral poet (or a

combination of ivy and laurel appears once in Vergilian pastoral, in *Ecl.* 8.13[78]; in this passage it appears significantly in the *recusatio*, it is associated with the political figure of the poem (cf. Karakasis 2011, 126–30) and is related to the conquering / epic outlook of the eclogue's cryptic figure (*inter victricis hederam tibi serpere lauros*).

Corydon will perform on the reeds of Tityrus, symbolising in all probability, by means of the common in Latin literature *primus / princeps*-motif, Vergil himself[79] as the first Roman pastoral poet (vv. 62–3: *cecinit qui primus in istis /*

---

herdsman). For the allegorical reading of Meliboeus, two main contemporary figures have been proposed in the relevant bibliography: Seneca the younger (cf. Sarpe 1819, 34, Ferrara 1905, 36–7, Morelli 1914, 120–5, Luiselli 1960, 149, Duff 1960, 265–6, Bardon 1968, 222, Messina 1975, 79 and n. 81, Friedrich 1976, 148, Casaceli 1982, 86, Ahl 1984, 67, Gagliardi 1984, 59 and n. 32, Keene 1996, 12, 100, Simon 2007, 51; see also Mayer 1982, 315–6) and C. Calpurnius Piso (cf. Haupt 1875, 392, Schenkl 1885, xi, Skutsch 1897, 1404–5, Wendel 1901, 58, Butler 1909, 152, Chiavola 1921, 27, Salvatore 1949, 188, Herrmann 1952, 28–9, Bickel 1954, 197, Verdière 1954, 50–1; 1977, 15–21, Mahr 1964, 23–5, Lana 1965, 118; 1998, 826, Cizek 1972, 372–3, Grimal 1978, 164, Sullivan 1985, 48 and n. 61, Di Lorenzo-Pellegrino 2008, 9, Delbey 2013, 302; see also Beato 1995, 619 and n. 8 and the reservations of Cesareo 1931, 160–4 and n. 2). Less likely candidates include Messalla, cf. Hubaux 1930, 176 (for a refutation of this thesis, see Bardon 1968, 221–2), Columella, cf. Chytil 1894, 6, Bartalucci 1976, 93, 112 and n. 27, and Nero, cf. Horsfall 1997, 167. For a different association in the period of Severus Alexander, cf. also Champlin 1978, 108–9 (L. Marius Maximus); see also Díaz-Cíntora 1989, x (Iunius Tiberianus). For Meliboeus as a 'Präfiguration Neros', cf. Schubert 1998, 66, whereas for Leach 1973, 65 Meliboeus might be 'a purely imaginative patron, a figure to typify the urban world'. Schröder 1991, 113 rightly does not see a reference to a particular work of a contemporary literary figure here; cf. also 30–4, Korzeniewski 1971, 97, Merfeld 1999, 84 and n. 2. In a similar vein, Vinchesi 1996, 11–2 remains sceptical and cautious and, thus, advises against any identification; see also Summers 1920, 91, Correa 1977, 149, Baldwin 1995, 166–7, Mayer 2006, 458–9 and n. 13, Monella 2009, 75 and n. 23.

78 Cf. also Verdière 1954, 163, Korzeniewski 1971, 39, Di Lorenzo-Pellegrino 2008, 211, Vinchesi 2014, 319.

79 Cf. Wendel 1901, 58, Hubaux 1930, 176, Cesareo 1931, 159–60, Wendel 1933, 38–9, Verdière 1954, 51–3; 1966, 165; 1971, 377, Theiler 1956, 566, Cizek 1968, 149; 1972, 372, 374, Rosenmeyer 1969, 341 and n. 55, Pearce 1970, 336, Korzeniewski 1971, 97, Schmidt 1972, 122, Cupaiuolo 1973, 105, Messina 1975, 79, Friedrich 1976, 67–8, Griffin 1984, 148, Walter 1988, 30, Davis 1987, 45–6, Díaz-Cíntora 1989, xxv, Mackie 1989, 10, Kegel-Brinkgreve 1990, 158, Pearce 1990, 96, Schröder 1991, 22, 119, 121–2, Amat 1991, xxv-xxvi, 32, Vozza 1993, 287–90, Esposito 1996, 24, 31–2, Keene 1996, 100, Vinchesi 1996, 9, 108; 2002, 148; 2012, 717 and n. 59; 2014, 39, 321–2, Cupaiuolo 1997, 122, Hubbard 1998, 168 and n. 42, Schubert 1998, 64, Gibson 2004, 3, 12, Di Lorenzo-Pellegrino 2008, 212, Garthwaite-Martin 2009, 317, Monella 2009, 75 and n. 23, Hutchinson 2013, 178. A less convincing candidate is Lucan, cf. Herrmann 1952, 33–4, Casaceli 1982, 103 and n. 29. While admitting that Tityrus of the fourth Calpurnian eclogue is most probably a mask of Vergil, Hubaux

montibus, see also Verg. *Ecl.* 6.1)[80]. However, the readers' expectations for a bucolic performance in imitation of Vergil[81] prove unfounded in the end, despite the fact that several hallmarks of the genre, as shaped chiefly by Vergil, are repeated throughout Corydon's lines. These include: the sweet (cf. v. 61: *dulcisssima*) Hyblean[82] quality of Vergil's pipe, handed down by Iollas[83] in a gesture of a 'poetic succession' / initiation[84], vv. 59 ff., the combination of *modulabile carmen* with *avena* (v. 63) harking back to Verg. *Ecl.* 10.51[85], i.e., in a programmatic context, where *avena* is used to denote traditional pastoral[86], and the motif of the orphic syndrome in vv. 60–1 (the appeasing of wild bulls[87]), as a result of Vergil's pastoral *avena*, which possesses the properties of the orphic lyre (vv. 65–6: *qui posset avena / praesonuisse chelyn*[88]), closely associated with the impact of

---

1930, 179 ff. also envisages the possibility of a second Tityrus, a contemporary of the Neronian poet, as the mask of Tityrus of the third Calpurnian eclogue; see also the reservations by Hulsenboom 2013, 23 and n. 9.

80 At least in opinion of the post–Vergilian ancient criticism, cf. Mart. 8.55.7–12, on the basis of Verg. *Ecl.* 6.3–5.

81 Cf. Schetter 1975, 6.

82 A further catch-word of Callimachean poetological undertones. For the poetological undertones of *Hyblaeus*, cf. also Korzeniewski 1971, 97, Pearce 1990, 96, Schröder 1991, 123. For *Hyblaea avena* as a metonymy for bucolic poetry, cf. Verdière 1954, 248; see also Di Lorenzo–Pellegrino 2008, 212, Hutchinson 2013, 178.

83 For Iollas as a pastoral mask, cf. (Annaeus Cornutus) Herrmann 1952, 38–9, Verdière 1954, 58, Messina 1975, 79; for an account of older views, cf. Cesareo 1931, 174, Vinchesi 2014, 321.

84 See also Korzeniewski 1971, 41, 97, Cizek 1972, 374, Thill 1979, 50–2, 490–4, Pearce 1990, 95–6, Schröder 1991, 120, Vozza 1993, 288, Esposito 1996, 23, Vinchesi 1996, 108; 2002, 148 and n. 39; 2014, 321, Hubbard 1998, 169 and n. 43, Gibson 2004, 3–4, Simon 2007, 55–6, Di Lorenzo–Pellegrino 2008, 212.

85 Cf. Amat 1991, 109, Di Lorenzo–Pellegrino 2008, 212.

86 Meliboeus acknowledges the pastoral and the Callimachean–Neoteric character of Tityrus' 'slender poetics' with the words *silvestrem tenui musam meditaris avena* (Verg. *Ecl.* 1.2), and the elegiac Gallus (Verg. *Ecl.* 10.51) expresses his willingness to adhere to pastoral 'generic rules', as a means for alleviating his elegiac distress, by declaring *carmina pastoris Siculi modulabor avena*.

87 But note here with Schröder 1991, 121 and Vinchesi 2014, 321 the Ovidian and not Vergilian wording of *truces...tauros*, *Met.* 7.111, 8.297, 9.80–1, also suggesting a movement away from Vergilian pastoral wording, as observed elsewhere as well (cf. pp. 52–3). Cf. also Ahl 1984, 67: 'Corydon and his brother have sung...an Ovidian song in praise of the Golden Age'.

88 Quite imaginative and rather inconclusive is Verdière's 1985, 1893 reading of *chelyn* as symbolising epic poetry, the *Aeneid* in particular, or Lucan's epic poetry. *Chelys* is a musical instrument frequently associated with Apollo (cf. e.g. [Ov.] *Epist. Sapph.* 181); for a refutation of Verdière with some justification, cf. Schröder 1991, 127–8.

pastoral song and Vergil as a pastoral poet (cf. Verg. *Ecl.* 3.46, 4.55 – 7, 6.27 – 30, 69 – 71, 8.2 – 4[89]).

The readers' expectations for a song of traditional pastoral thematic and 'Callimachean slenderness' are further falsified by Meliboeus' subsequent remarks. His imagery of a Naias, a pastoral Nymph, adorning the bucolic poet[90] (vv. 68 – 9) with red acanthus, a plant also having the sanction of pre–Calpurnian pastoral (Theocr. 1.55, Verg. *Ecl.* 3.45, 4.20, see also Nemes. 2.5), goes back to Verg. *Ecl.* 6.21 – 2[91], where another Nymph, Aegle, v. 21: *Naiadum pulcherrima*, paints Silenus' face and brows with mulberry crimson. Similarly, the pathetic fallacy–motif of the submissive beasts and a halted oak (vv. 66 – 7)[92] constitutes a further long–established pastoral 'generic marker'. Nevertheless, Meliboeus qualifies Vergil, whom Corydon aspires to imitate[93], as *vates*, v. 65, a term having poetological associations beyond pastoral, denoting the poet who is involved in the political arena of the Augustan period[94]. Lycidas in the ninth Vergilian eclogue, despite having lost his pastoral memory, has not yet grown so distanced from the pastoral ideal as to claim this title for himself (cf. Karakasis 2011, 199)[95]. In Corydon's case however this aspiration becomes more explicit and is further seconded by Meliboeus' v. 64: *magna petis*, where the adjective *magnus* arguably alludes to Corydon's aspirations towards the *genus grande*.

The syntagm at the beginning of the line as here (v. 64: *magna petis*) has several Ovidian parallels, as it plausibly comes from instances such as Ov. *Met.* 2.54, see also 14.108, *Fast.* 3.313[96]. The Ovidian expression (two out three instances come from the Ovidian epic) seems to suggest, on a stylistic level, a movement away from earlier pastoral forms, which will take firmer hold further down. Me-

---

89 Cf. also Verdière 1954, 249, Langholf 1990, 362, Pearce 1990, 97, Schröder 1991, 129, Hubbard 1998, 169 and n. 44, Di Lorenzo–Pellegrino 2008, 212 – 3, Vinchesi 2014, 321.
90 Schröder 1991, 130 sees here an instance of 'bukolische Dichterweihe'.
91 Cf. also Korzeniewski 1971, 41, Vinchesi 1996, 46 – 7; 2014, 39, 325, Simon 2007, 50, Di Lorenzo–Pellegrino 2008, 214.
92 For a version of the orphic syndrome here, cf. also Amat 1991, 39 and n. 80, Esposito 1996, 25 – 6, Vinchesi 2014, 324.
93 Note in v. 64 the verb *laboras*, suggesting a relatively long–term and careful poetic process, aspiring to Callimachean 'slender ideals', not unknown to pastoral (Theocr. 7.51, Verg. *Ecl.* 10.1); see also Vinchesi 2014, 323.
94 Vozza 1993, 289 remarks: 'e simbolo del potere della poesia...incarna l' esigenza augustea di una poesia civile e morale'.
95 For the poet as *vates*, cf. mainly Newman 1967, *passim*. See also Esposito 1996, 25 and n. 11, Simon 2007, 65 – 6.
96 Cf. also Verdière 1954, 165, Schröder 1991, 124, Esposito 1996, 25 and n. 10, Di Lorenzo–Pellegrino 2008, 212, Fucecchi 2009, 45, Vinchesi 2014, 322.

liboeus' remarks in vv. 73 ff., concerning the quality of Corydon's imminent song, also indicate this feeling of a 'generic transcendence': Corydon's pastoral song (v. 74: *fistula*) should not be *fragilis* (= delicate[97], v. 74: *fragili...buxo*), as it is when the subject–matter of his lyrics is Alexis. Corydon's *past* poetic production and its motifs (pastoral love)[98] is described here by means of the well-known *fragilis*-catch word denoting 'poetic slenderness' of the Callimachean persuasion. Instead, Corydon's *future* poetic quality should be worthy of a consul (vv. 76–7: *canales / exprime qui dignas cecinerunt consule silvas*), an allusion to Verg. *Ecl.* 4.3: *si canimus silvas, silvae sint consule dignae*, i.e., an intertext[99] also suggesting a wish for 'generic re-evaluation', a movement away from traditional pastoral towards more elevated poetic trends (cf. above, pp. 30, 46, 51–2). A linguistic tell-tale sign of innovation is that in his description of a new panegyric pastoral genre, Meliboeus uses a πρῶτον λεγόμενον (for pastoral) in order to refer to the musical instrument which accompanies this new genre, namely *canales*[100] in vv. 76–7, and the equally unknown, in pre-Calpurnian bucolics, *respirare* instead of *resonare* in v. 74[101] in order to describe the playing of the pastoral instrument.

---

97 Cf. Schröder 1991, 133, who reads the adjective in the sense of "zarten', 'kraftlosen' Ton'.
98 Cf. also Hubaux 1930, 223, Korzeniewski 1971, 97. See also Amat 1991, 109–10, who also sees here a particular 'référence amusée à la deuxième bucolique de Vergile', and Verdière 1954, 165; 1966, 165, Davis 1987, 46, Keene 1996, 102, Vinchesi 1996, 111; 2014, 39, 327, Paschalis 1996, 143, Martin 2003, 80, Gibson 2004, 2, 4, Vallat 2006, http://, Simon 2007, 56–7, Di Lorenzo-Pellegrino 2008, 215. Schmidt 1969, 192 draws a distinction, within pastoral boundaries, 'zwischen höherer und niedrigerer Bukolik'; thus Verg. *Ecl.* 2 represents the latter variant, whereas Verg. *Ecl.* 4 exemplifies the higher form of bucolic song. More plausibly Leach 1973, 70 draws a distinction between 'the fragile, personal art of pastoral love song' and an 'elevated, historically oriented mode'.
99 Cf. also Cesareo 1931, 178, Verdière 1954, 36, 165; 1966, 165, Korzeniewski 1971, 41, Joly 1974, 42–3, Messina 1975, 80, Friedrich 1976, 149, 154, Correa 1977, 153, Gagliardi 1984, 60 and n. 38, Davis 1987, 46, Mackie 1989, 10, Kegel-Brinkgreve 1990, 159 and n. 31, Pearce 1990, 97–8, Schröder 1991, 136, Amat 1991, 110, Keene 1996, 102, Paschalis 1996, 143, Vinchesi 1996, 46, 111; 2014, 39, 328, Hubbard 1998, 169, Martin 2003, 76 and n. 8, 80, Gibson 2004, 5, Di Lorenzo-Pellegrino 2008, 215. Cf. also Clausen 1994, 126, Hubbard 1998, 76–86 for the 'generic ambivalence' of the fourth Vergilian eclogue.
100 For this Calpurnian *hapax*, see also Merone 1967, 27, Korzeniewski 1971, 97, Messina 1975, 108, Novelli 1980, 31, Gagliardi 1984, 60 and n. 38, Armstrong 1986, 120, Schröder 1991, 134–5, Keene 1996, 102, Di Lorenzo-Pellegrino 2008, 215, Vinchesi 2014, 328 and further down, pp. 83–4.
101 Cf. especially Novelli 1980, 31, Di Lorenzo-Pellegrino 2008, 214–5, Vinchesi 2014, 51, 327 and further below, p. 83.

The Song–Exchange

According to the typical pattern of a singing match, Meliboeus, assuming the role of an umpire, establishes the succession of song–performances, with Corydon singing first and his brother, Amyntas, following[102]. Corydon begins by an invocation to the inspiring god, a common gambit in ancient literature. However, his invocation has strong undertones of 'generic transcendence', as it refers first to Jupiter, v. 82: *ab Iove principium*; in the case of the third Vergilian eclogue (cf. Karakasis 2011, 111–2), it was shown that this appeal derives mainly from Theocritus' encomium of Ptolemy (Theocr. 17)[103], and, more importantly, appeals to a god not closely related to the pantheon of the pastoral tradition. Corydon draws a distinction between his output, on the one hand, and astronomical / didactic poetry on the other, suggested by his reference to the signs of the sky and Atlas' Olympian load (vv. 82–3)[104], and thus dissociates his work from a genre entitled to the invocation of Jupiter. Nevertheless, he does not invoke a distinct pastoral

---

[102] The song–exchange presents several textual problems, mainly as to the attribution of the exchanged strophes and the alleged loss of a strophe; the allocation followed here is that of Duff and Duff 1934. For a comprehensive discussion of the relevant textual issues in the Calpurnian bibliography, cf. especially Schröder 1991, 139–45. See also Korzeniewski 1971, 98–9, Fuchs 1973, 229 and n. 3, Friedrich 1976, 150, Castagna 1982, 159–69, p. 165 in particular, Pearce 1990, 99, Amat 1991, 33, Simon 2007, 79 and n. 145, Di Lorenzo–Pellegrino 2008, 15, 219–20, Vinchesi 2009a, 581–2; 2014, 290–1. Boswell 1994, 67 and n. 74, based on the term *frater* (cf. Calp. 1.8 and 4.17, 78), believes that Corydon and Amyntas are not brothers but homosexual lovers; for a refutation of his unconvincing argument, see Hubbard 1998, 164 and n. 38. For *frater* as possibly simply denoting friendship between the pastoral figures of the eclogue, cf. Cesareo 1931, 159, Messina 1975, 78 and n. 78; see also Vinchesi 2014, 25–6.
[103] Cf. also Cic. *Leg.* 2.7.13 (= Arat. 1, see also Hubbard 1998, 171), Germ. *Arat.* 1, V. Max. 1.pr.1.17, Quint. *Inst.* 10.1.46, Gibson 2006, 94, Simon 2007, 80 and n. 147, 81–2, Vinchesi 2014, 35. For v. 82 also alluding to Verg. *Ecl.* 3.60, see also Cesareo 1931, 180 and n. 1, Verdière 1954, 249, Paladini 1956, 531 and n. 2, Korzeniewski 1971, 41, Leach 1973, 71, Joly 1974, 54, 64 and n. 85, Messina 1975, 81, Friedrich 1976, 150, Gagliardi 1984, 60 and n. 40, Pearce 1990, 98, Amat 1991, 110, Keene 1996, 103, Vinchesi 1996, 23 and n. 31; 2009a, 575; 2014, 330, Gibson 2004, 5–6 (his view of a closer association with Germ. *Arat.* 1–2 is more plausible, as both texts (Calp. 4 and Germ.) replace Jupiter with the emperor / a political figure as a song–inspirer; see also La Bua 1999, 294–5), Simon 2007, 80 and n. 146, Di Lorenzo–Pellegrino 2008, 217. Castagna 1982, 161–2 also convincingly associates the present tag mainly with Theocr. 17 (a not bucolic idyll) and Verg. *Ecl.* 3 (for the 'generically inovative' character of the herdsmen in this eclogue, cf. Karakasis 2011, 87–124), as the Calpurnian instance shares with its first intertext a *recusatio*, after Jupiter's mention, for proceeding with the very encomium and with its second intertext a combination of Jupiter with Apollo.
[104] For the suggestion of an astronomical didactic poem here, cf. Schröder 1991, 146; see also Vinchesi 2014, 331.

god of the established pastoral pantheon, but the imperial god (vv. 84–6); Corydon's request, v. 86: *laetus et augusto felix arrideat ore* in particular, contains adjectives having unmistakable political undertones with reference to Corydon's god, as *augustus* and *felix* are often used to qualify the *princeps* as well[105]. Corydon's political god is also characterised by his *praesenti numine* (v. 84), alluding to Tityrus' *praesentis...divos* of the first Vergilian eclogue again (v. 41)[106]; yet, as already observed (cf. pp. 8, 33–4, 38, 53, 57), whereas in Vergil the divine imperial figure is credited with ensuring Tityrus' permanence in the pastoral realm, no preoccupation with the restoration of pastoral order appears in Calpurnius' case. Corydon instead focuses on the political power of this divine youth (cf. also Calp. 1.44, 4.137, 7.6) and his ability to secure eternal peace (v. 85: *perpetuamque regit iuvenili robore*[107] *pacem*), in line with Neronian propaganda (cf. Chapter 1, pp. 15–47). Crucially, similar concerns for peace also appear in the Vergilian corpus, but only in the fourth eclogue, 4.17: *pacatumque reget patriis virtutibus orbem*, i.e., in the least pastoral poem, something which suggests again, as often remarked (cf. above, p. 66), the transgression of traditional pastoral[108].

Amyntas resumes the 'generically transcending' drift of Corydon's invocation with a second appeal to the emperor as inspiring deity, but this time with Apollo as his comrade (vv. 87–8: *comitatus Apolline Caesar / respiciat*), resorting to another well-known motif of chiefly the Neronian period[109]. He invites the political god not to look down on hills that even Phoebus and Jupiter appreciate (vv. 88–9), thus resembling Corydon of the second Vergilian eclogue, who tried to entice his beloved Alexis by referring to the gods who had deigned to

---

[105] Cf. Wistrand 1987, 63 ff., Di Lorenzo–Pellegrino 2008, 217, Keene 1996, 103, Vinchesi 2014, 332–3.

[106] For *praesens* here possibly in the sense of ἐπιφανής, cf. Sauter 1934, 52–3, Gibson 2006, 93–4. See also Korzeniewski 1971, 42, Pearce 1990, 98, Keene 1996, 103, Di Lorenzo–Pellegrino 2008, 217, Vinchesi 2009a, 576–7; 2014, 332.

[107] Verdière 1987, 137–8 plausibly reads in *robore* an allusion to the notion of *fortis* suggested by the name of Nero; see also Schubert 1998, 67, Vinchesi 2014, 332, Chapter 1, p. 29 and n. 67.

[108] The motif is common, on the other hand, in Neronian pastoral, cf. also Calp. 1.42, *Eins.* 2.21–34, Schröder 1991, 148; see also Vinchesi 2014, 332.

[109] Cf. Vinchesi 2002, 148–9; 2014, 333; see also Verdière 1992, 35, Rosati 2002, 238–49. For a further association of the eclogue's political god (i.e., Nero) with Phoebus, cf. also vv. 158–9, where Nero's residence is crucially identified with the sacred inner temple of the Palatine Apollo, *sacra Palatini penetralia...Phoebi*, v. 159; cf. also Verdière 1954, 254–5, Amat 1991, 114, Schröder 1991, 212, Vinchesi 1996, 122; 2014, 363, Keene 1996, 115, Di Lorenzo–Pellegrino 2008, 229–30.

dwell in the woods (v. 60: *habitarunt di quoque silvas*[110]). Vergil's Corydon did not specify which gods he meant, but Calpurnius' Amyntas specifically mentions Phoebus and Jupiter, although the latter has no particular association, as elaborated in Karakasis 2011, 111–2, with pre-Calpurnian pastoral space and pastoral as a genre (see also above, pp. 67–8). Also, in Amyntas' lines the 'green cabinet' is not praised for the usual bucolic delights it offers (a *locus amoenus*, the pleasure of song, etc.), but for the fact that laurel and its companion tree (vv. 90–1) grow there. Laurel is crucially presented in its relation to the imperial triumph (v. 90: *visuraque saepe triumphos*)[111], an association belonging to the contemporary military reality, to the epic code and its poetry, rather than to traditional pastoral. The laurel's companion tree should be either the oak or the myrtle[112]; yet both are often used in epic / panegyric contexts, as the myrtle is associated with the *ovatio*, while the laurel is used in *triumph* and, in its combination with the oak, for the celebrations of the emperor (cf. Ov. *Fast.* 4.953–4)[113], something which may account for their selection here. Laurel with myrtle also appear in the Vergilian intertext of the second eclogue, vv. 54–5[114]; but whereas in the Vergilian precedent the trees function simply as love–tokens, gifts that the *rusticus* Corydon bestows on his urban love, Alexis, in order to entice him in the bucolic realm, the same combination of trees in the Calpurnian eclogue exhibits clear epic nuances unrelated to the traditional pastoral codes. The epic colouring of the Calpurnian lines under discussion is further increased, on a stylistic level, by a common epic linguistic marker, the use of the joining couplet, *que...que...* (vv. 90–1: *visuraque...vicinaque*)[115].

---

110 Cf. also Schröder 1991, 151, Vinchesi 2014, 334.
111 Cf. also Leach 1973, 72, Friedrich 1976, 11, Vinchesi 1996, 113; 2009a, 579, Schubert 1998, 67.
112 Cf. Cesareo 1931, 183, Korzeniewski 1971, 98, Pearce 1990, 99, Amat 1991, 110, Keene 1996, 104–5, Simon 2007, 94–5, Vinchesi 2009a, 580. For an extensive account of the (far from unanimous) relevant literature concerning the identification of this plant, cf. especially Schröder 1991, 152–4.
113 Cf. Verdière 1954, 249, Schröder 1991, 153, Vinchesi 2009a, 580 and n. 50; 2014, 335–6. For a hint, in these lines, to an agreement with the Parthians (55 AD), cf. Vinchesi 2014, 29.
114 Cf. also Verdière 1954, 249, Paladini 1956, 523–4, Korzeniewski 1971, 43, Langholf 1990, 368, Vinchesi 1996, 113; 2014, 335, Di Lorenzo-Pellegrino 2008, 218. See also Nemes. 2.49.
115 For the epic character of the combination, see also Schubert 1998, 67. An epic, elevated colouring may also be observed in Corydon's previous reference to Jupiter (vv. 82 ff.), as both *aether* in v. 82 and *pondus molitur* (v. 83) are favourites of epic diction, cf. Di Lorenzo-Pellegrino 2008, 19, 216; see also Vinchesi 2009a, 577–8; 2014, 330–1. Thus, apart from their thematic affinity, the two first strophes of the opening song–exchange are further combined on the basis

This association of Caesar with Jupiter, fashionable in the literature of the period and in various depictions in coins[116], continues in Corydon's following lines, where Jupiter is depicted in his traditional[117] function of presiding over the heavens (v. 92: *polos etiam qui temperat igne geluque*, cf. also Sen. *Ep.* 107.11); in a role, however, of no pastoral parallels. Pastoral space (and by implication pastoral as a genre as well[118]) is nonetheless defended here thanks to the account of Zeus' visits to the Cretan meadows (v. 95: *Cresia rura*). In imitation of the well-known Augustan image of both Zeus and the emperor holding his thunderbolt[119], the god is here depicted as laying down his thunderbolt (v. 94: *posito paulisper fulmine*), also a symbol of epic poetry (cf. Call. *Aet.* 1.20 Pf., Ov. *Am.* 2.1.15), in order to recline in a lush grotto (v. 95: *viridique reclinis in antro*), i.e., in a typical pastoral landscape calling to mind Tityrus' programmatic *lentus in umbra* (Verg. *Ecl.* 1.4, cf. also v. 75: *viridi proiectus in antro*, Nemes. 3.26)[120] of the first Vergilian eclogue and the *antrum*-setting, the place of pastoral poetry exchange, in the fifth Vergilian eclogue (5.6, 19, see also Karakasis 2011, 154–5).

Despite all these *bona fide* signs of the pastoral tradition, the lay that Jupiter listens to is not associated with time-honoured qualities of pastoral song, but instead once again points to the epic code: it is about a war dance that the Kouretes danced in order to cover Jupiter's cries as a baby, according to Call. *Hymn to Zeus*, 52ff., probably the model of the line, v. 96[121]. Amyntas continues with the motif of the calming of the wind as a result of a divine epiphany / intervention (cf. also in a similar vein Eur. *Bacch.* 1084–5, Theocr. 22.19, Hor. *Carm.* 1.12.30, Verg. *G.* 1.27, etc.[122]), also confirmed by the resonance of Pan's reeds, v. 101:

---

of their epic linguistic diction as well, suggesting, on the stylistic level as well, a 'generic redirection' towards loftier poetic trends of the *genus grande*.
116 Cf. Vinchesi 2014, 336.
117 Cf. Schröder 1991, 155–6, Vinchesi 2014, 336.
118 Cf. also Castagna 1982, 162.
119 Cf. Schröder 1991, 158, Gibson 2006, 127, 228, Vinchesi 2014, 337.
120 Cf. also Korzeniewski 1971, 43, Pearce 1990, 101, Schröder 1991, 159, Di Lorenzo-Pellegrino 2008, 219, Vinchesi 2009a, 581 and n. 55; 2014, 337; see also Leach 1973, 72, 94 and n. 44.
121 Cf. Hubaux 1930, 200, Verdière 1954, 168–9, Korzeniewski 1971, 98, Díaz-Cíntora 1989, xxv-vi, Amat 1991, 110, Schröder 1991, 159. The Kouretes, young men from Crete, danced this war-like dance every year on Mt. Ida calling on Jupiter to bless the year to come, cf. Nisetich 2001, 202; see also Cesareo 1931, 183–4, Keene 1996, 105, Vinchesi 1996, 113; 2009a, 580–1 and n. 51; 2014, 338.
122 Cf. also Korzeniewski 1971, 99, Castagna 1982, 165, Schröder 1991, 164, Simon 2007, 89–90, Vinchesi 2009a, 582; 2014, 338–9. For an association of the motif with the elimination of political turmoil, cf. also Verdière 1954, 37; 1985, 1853. On the basis of a similarity discerned among Matt. 8.23–7, Marc. 4.35–41, Lu. 8.22–5, on the one hand, and Calp. 4.97–

*nec mora; Parrhasiae sonuerunt sibila cannae*¹²³. However, this motif, in all probability a variant on the panegyric *topos* of 'the emperor's command over nature'¹²⁴, is here associated with the elimination of a pre–Calpurnian pastoral 'generic marker', that of a loud nature with echoing effects and whispering trees (cf. above, pp. 10, 48–9, 59 and n. 59): the woods are muted at Caesar's name, the grove's boughs are at peace (vv. 97–101, cf. also Baraz 2015, 109–10).

In the following exchanges an intertextual association with the fourth and the fifth Vergilian eclogue emerges; this is not without significance, since, as discussed in Karakasis 2011, 168–79, *Ecl.* 5 concerns the elaboration of a new pastoral which also incorporates panegyric, while eclogue 4, the least pastoral of Vergil's eclogues, is often read as a mode of 'generic transcendence' (cf. above, p. 68). Therefore, the association of the following strophes with these Vergilian intertexts is a sign of the changing 'generic character' of the Calpurnian pastoral poem under discussion. As an instance of this, Corydon (vv. 102–6) describes an image of cattle fertility / prosperity as the outcome of Caesar's arrival, equated to the advent of the rustic goddess Pales¹²⁵. Both main images of the Calpurnian *Aurea Aetas*, the sheep loaded with abundant milk (v. 103) and the wonderful re-growth of their fleece after a recent shearing (v. 104), have their parallels in the Golden Age-imagery of the fourth Vergilian eclogue¹²⁶ (vv. 21–2: *ipsae lacte domum referent distenta capellae / ubera*, and 43–4: *aries…mutabit vellera*¹²⁷, as the result of the divine baby's birth) and significantly are not connected with the milk profusion picture of pre–Vergilian pastoral, which is associated with the pastoral bliss caused by the presence of the pastoral lover, cf. [Theocr.] 8.41–2.

101, on the other, Verdière 1956–7, 89–92 reads here a messianic rumour current in Nero's time; see also Spadaro 1969, 34–5, 39–40, Messina 1975, 83, Verdière 1985, 1852–3.
123 The reading *Pharsaliae*, as offered by the manuscript tradition, is not accepted here (cf. also Postgate 1905, 257–60) as 'utterly alien to the immediate context', according to Heslin's 1997, 590–1 (the quotation comes from p. 590) compelling remarks. I hereby follow the emendation of Heinsius to *Parrhasiae* vs. Bardon 1968, 227, Messina 1975, 82 and n. 87, Amat 1991, 111 claiming an allusion to the image of the peacemaker prince (cf. also Calp. 1.58f., Vinchesi 1996, 115; 2009a, 583; 2014, 340); yet for a refutation of this thesis, cf. Heslin *op. cit.* and n. 11. See also Mackie 1989, 10, Di Salvo 1990a, 278–9; 1991, 311, Chinnici 2009, 136 and n. 27.
124 For this motif, cf. also Coleman 2006, 112, 201, 206, Vinchesi 2014, 340.
125 Castagna 1982, 165 speaks about: 'prodigi dell' apparizione di Nerone come quelli di un dio Nomios'; see also Simon 2007, 87–8, Vinchesi 2014, 341.
126 Cf. also Leach 1973, 73, Merfeld 1999, 90, Vinchesi 2014, 341.
127 Cf. also Messina 1975, 84, Langholf 1990, 367, Schröder 1991, 169–70, Di Lorenzo-Pellegrino 2008, 221, Vinchesi 2009a, 584.

Further down (vv. 112–6), in describing the agricultural prosperity as being due to Caesar's influence, Corydon draws the image of crops free from the choking caused by infertile tare or barren oats; both the image and its wording (vv. 115–6: *nec praefocata malignum / messis habet lolium nec inertibus albet avenis*) allude again to Verg. *Ecl.* 5[128], namely v. 37: *infelix lolium et steriles nascuntur avenae*, where this reversal of pastoral and georgic order (cf. also Verg. *G.* 1.154[129]) is due to Pales' leaving the fields because of Daphnis', the archetypical pastoral singer's, death, v. 35: *ipsa Pales agros atque ipse reliquit Apollo*[130]. The particular motif (a combination of *lolium* and *avena*), however, that Calpurnius incorporates in his panegyric strophes here is associated with pastoral values of no specific panegyric undertones, drawn as it is on Mopsus' song describing Daphnis' passing away instead of Menalcas' panegyric singing account of the *sidus Iulium* (cf. Karakasis 2011, 153–83). Calpurnius thus reverses the Vergilian imagery: whereas the Vergilian Pales leaves the rustic country-side as a sign of mourning over the loss of the highest pastoral value, thus causing severe damage to the harvest, the Calpurnian Caesar, as if he were Pales (cf. v. 106), brings with his presence a restored agricultural bliss, as it happens in the Vergilian intertext with the deified Daphnis, i.e., Julius Caesar, of Menalcas' and not Mopsus' song, an intertext functioning in its turn as the model for the georgic abundance of vv. 112ff.[131], a rich harvest as the result of a divine effect. Whereas, however, the Pales-image is associated in Vergil with the loss of the pre-Calpurnian pastoral value par excellence, that is pastoral song, as the result of Daphnis' death, in the Calpurnian re-fashioning everything simply works towards the praise of the emperor. Additionally, the imagery as well as the wording of the passage appears to be influenced by Vergil's *Georgics* (vv. 114–5: *legumina plenis / vix resonant siliquis*, cf. Verg. *G.* 1.74: *unde prius laetum siliqua quassante legumen*[132]), something further enhancing a sense of 'generic alteration'.

Amyntas too displays in his lines (107–11) motifs evoking the Vergilian eclogues: the efflorescence, the bloom he describes as a natural reaction to the sound of Caesar's name has its parallel in Verg. *Ecl.* 7.53–6, where junipers

---

[128] Cf. also Verdière 1954, 171, Korzeniewski 1971, 45, Leach 1973, 73–4, Schröder 1991, 180, Hubbard 1998, 171–2, Simon 2007, 88–9.
[129] Cf. Verdière 1954, 171, Keene 1996, 108, Di Lorenzo–Pellegrino 2008, 223, Chinnici 2009, 137–8, Vinchesi 2014, 345.
[130] Cf. also Schröder 1991, 171.
[131] Cf. also Schröder 1991, 177.
[132] Cf. also Verdière 1954, 171, Paladini 1956, 334, Joly 1974, 64 and n. 84, Messina 1975, 84, Korzeniewski 1971, 45, Keene 1996, 108, Di Lorenzo–Pellegrino 2008, 222, Chinnici 2009, 137, Vinchesi 2014, 345.

and chestnuts bloom, fruits are in abundance and all nature cheers because of Alexis' presence. But in the Vergilian intertext emphasis is given on the pastoral ideal of blissful love (cf. also [Theocr.] 8.41–8), secured by the presence of the beloved[133], while in the Calpurnian treatment this idealised pastoral moment simply functions as a foil to the emperor's panegyric again; what is more, the image of the sluggish earth warming to life and blossoming with flowers (vv. 109–10) alludes to a similar image in Verg. *Ecl.* 4.18–20: *nullo munuscula cultu / errantis hederas passim cum baccare tellus /...fundet*[134], thus bringing Amyntas' lines too even closer to the pastoral 'generic innovation' of the fourth Vergilian eclogue. Furthermore, the motif of the mute worshipper, represented by the picture of an arbutus-tree[135] paying silent respect to the deified emperor (vv. 108–9: *quem sic taciturna verentur / arbuta*), also found in other literary genres (cf. Hor. *Carm.* 3.1.2, Prop. 4.6.1, Ov. *Met.* 3.18, Sen. *Ep.* 115.4[136]), stands here in direct opposition to the highest pre-Calpurnian pastoral value of the sonorous nature, as often remarked, cf. above, p. 71[137]. Finally, a sense of departing from traditional pastoral is also imparted by the image of the spellbound tree coming into bloom as the result of the divine intervention of the political god again, v. 111: *stupefacta regerminat arbos*. This motif of the spellbound nature also appears in the Vergilian eclogues, but only as a result of the power that poetry possesses, cf. Verg. *Ecl.* 8.3: *quorum stupefactae carmine lynces*[138]; thus an asset associated in Vergilian pastoral with the highest pastoral value is in Calpurnian pastoral once more connected to the panegyric praise of the emperor.

---

133 Cf. Hubbard 1998, 172 and n. 47.
134 *Iners* may be here equivalent to *incultus*. Cf. also Korzeniewski 1971, 100 vs. Schröder 1991, 173–4.
135 Merone 1967, 40–1 reads here *arbuta* as equivalent to *arbores*; cf. also Korzeniewski 1971, 45 'die Bäume', Schröder 1991, 172–3, Vinchesi 2014, 343.
136 Cf. also Schröder 1991, 172, Nisbet-Rudd 2004, 7, Vinchesi 2014, 342–3.
137 Cf. also Baraz 2015, 110.
138 For a compelling reading of *stupefacta* as 'spellbound because of the divine epiphany', cf. also Spadaro 1969, 35, Friedrich 1976, 186 and n. 57, Schröder 1991, 176–7; see also Keene 1996, 107: 'awe-struck by the emperor's presence', Vinchesi 2014, 343. For a reading of the participle as equivalent to 'barren', 'withered', cf. especially Merone 1967, 36, Champlin 1978, 106 and n. 48: 'a tree dormant for the winter'. Haupt 1875, 387, Hubaux-Hicter 1949, 428–9, Verdière 1954, 250, Townend 1980, 167 and n. 7, Keene 1996, 4 relate the term with the *ficus Ruminalis* (cf. Tac. *Ann.* 13.58); see also Spadaro 1969, 30. For an association of the image with spring-time, cf. Gustin 1947, 324–5, Di Lorenzo-Pellegrino 2008, 222; see also Gagliardi 1984, 70. Shackleton-Bailey 1978, 320 emends in *stipesque*; for a convincing refutation of the emendation, see Schröder 1991, 177.

The emperor's panegyric continues with a reference to a new legislation passed under Nero's reign, which enabled a ploughman, here described by means of the georgic term *fossor*[139] (v. 118), to keep for himself any treasure he discovered while working in his field, as were also the previsions with the *Leges Iulia* and *Papia* in the age of Augustus[140]. A further association between Nero and his imperial model, Augustus, is thus brought forward here. Once more, the bucolic disguise is put aside: Amyntas gives a wealth of legalistic information, normally alien to the concerns of the pastoral tradition. It is true that even in Vergil one may come across legal details, such as the *peculium* and the related urban issues of the first Vergilian eclogue (cf. above, p. 59); but these instances of legalistic terminology have often been interpreted as 'unpastoral' in character, betraying an urban intrusion onto traditional bucolic values (cf. also relevant remarks in Karakasis 2011, 134–5; see also pp. 100 and n. 56, 186–7) within Vergilian pastoral. Calpurnius thus once again imitates Vergil on points where the latter transcends the pastoral tradition, incorporating alien matters in the pastoral register, which seem to function in the Vergilian pastoral corpus as well as a foil to pure bucolic idealism. What is more, the very image of a ploughman (*fossor*: v. 118, cf. Verg. *G.* 2.264, *arator*: v. 119) turning up his field with his plough (vv. 119–21, *presso...aratro* – v. 121) further indicates, on the level of linguistic assimilation as well, georgic interests[141], cf. Verg. *G.* 1.45; see also 119, 213 and the georgic sensibilities of the *Corpus Tibullianum*, 3.7.161.

Corydon retorts by describing pastoral festivals establishing the Neronian notion of *securitas* against the menace of an external war[142]. He relates a feast of Ceres (vv. 122–3), a ritual of Bacchus (vv. 123–4: *Vindemia* or *Liberalia*) and

---

139 Cf. Schröder 1991, 185: 'unbukolische Berufsbezeichnung'; see also Vinchesi 2014, 347.
140 For a legal reference here, cf. Bonfante 1912, 123–42, Hubaux–Hicter 1949, 425–37, Verdière 1954, 37–8, 251–2, Momigliano 1944, 98, Scheda 1969, 62, Spadaro 1969, 36–7 (for a good overview of the issue, cf. also pp. 31–5), Korzeniewski 1971, 100, Friedrich 1976, 11–2, Amat 1991, xxiii, 34, 111–2, Vinchesi 1996, 25, 116–7; 2009a, 585; 2014, 346–7, Schubert 1998, 69 and n. 85, Simon 2007, 96, Chinnici 2009, 138; see also Bartalucci 1976, 94, Horsfall 1997, 170, Di Lorenzo–Pellegrino 2008, 223, Garthwaite–Martin 2009, 317. Castagna 1982, 167, Braund 1983, 67–8 and Schröder 1991, 183 do not read the lines as necessarily symbolising the passing of a new legislation but as suggesting the feeling of *securitas* in the Neronian age; see also Merfeld 1999, 90 and n. 3. For a refutation of this view, cf. also Schubert 1998, 69 and n. 85.
141 For a general georgic colouring, cf. also Schubert 1998, 69, though without much detail. See also Merfeld 1999, 91 and n. 2, Di Lorenzo–Pellegrino 2008, 224, Vinchesi 2014, 347–8.
142 Cf. Vinchesi 2014, 348.

finally in vv. 125–6 the *Compitalia*[143], as evidenced by the image of games held at the crossroads, i.e., a celebration current also in the Augustan period and often associated with the *genius Augusti*[144]. Although the combination of Bacchus and Ceres seems to be the norm in Latin literature (cf. Lucr. 5.14–5, Var. *rust.* 1.1.5, Verg. *G.* 1.7, etc.), appearing in the Vergilian pastoral as well, cf. Verg. *Ecl.* 5.79, this Calpurnian passage displays the image of religious festivals as a means for recreation with song and games. However, these are settings generically not sanctioned by earlier pastoral (yet, cf. later *Eins.* 2.15 ff.), but appearing in other literary genres, mainly in the Vergilian *Georgics* (cf. 1.338–50, 2.380–96, 527–31[145]). Thus once again an initial anticipation for a pastoral song of traditional colouring seems to be materialised as deviation rather towards georgic trends within a panegyric setting.

Amyntas follows up by recounting the beneficial effects of the Augustan peace on the restored musical order of the pastoral space (v. 127: *meis... montibus*[146]). This motif, i.e., music restored / secured due to the intervention of a political god, significantly has its pastoral parallel in the first programmatic Vergilian eclogue[147], where (vv. 9–10) Tityrus still enjoys producing pastoral song thanks to a similar divine interference: *ille meas errare boves, ut cernis, et ipsum / ludere quae vellem calamo permisit agresti*. The 'generic identity' of the restored song is clear enough in the Vergilian eclogue; it is Callimachean–Neoteric pastoral: this is evident from the use of the term *agrestis* qualifying the flute and of the verb *ludere* pointing to poetic production of the *genus tenue* with Neoteric–Callimachean aspirations. In the Calpurnian setting, however, matters are no longer clear. Amyntas does not refer exclusively to the re-established pastoral song, symbolised here chiefly by the image of the reed–pipes (v. 131: *calamos*, a bucolic musical instrument), which are immune to destructive effect of war-trumpets. Cf. also the picture of a song preserved on the bark of a tree[148] (vv. 130–1, for such inscriptions of pastoral songs, cf. also Verg. *Ecl.* 5.13–4, Calp. 1.22–3, 3.43–4, Nemes. 1.28–9). Yet Amyntas is also concerned with iambic and choral song (vv. 128–9: *ter pede lenta ferire / gramina* and v. 129:

---

143 Cf. Verdière 1954, 37, 173, Korzeniewski 1971, 101, Bartalucci 1976, 97, Schröder 1991, 187, 189–90, Amat 1991, 112, Keene 1996, 109–10, Vinchesi 1996, 25, 119; 2009a, 585; 2014, 348–50.
144 Cf. Keene 1996, 109–10, Vinchesi 2014, 350.
145 Cf. also Castagna 1982, 167, Schröder 1991, 187. See also Paladini 1956, 334–5, Korzeniewski 1971, 45–6, Vinchesi 1996, 25; 2014, 348–50, Di Lorenzo–Pellegrino 2008, 225; see also Verg. *A.* 8.717, Hor. *Epist.* 1.1.49, Ov. *Fast.* 1.669.
146 For *mons* as a term denoting pastoral space, cf. also vv. 63, 88 with Schröder 1991, 190.
147 Cf. also Schröder 1991, 190–1, Vinchesi 2014, 351.
148 Cf. also Slater 1994, http://, Hubbard 1998, 151 and n. 18, Vinchesi 2014, 352.

licet et cantare choreis)[149], further underlying the sense of 'generic fluidity' which can be felt throughout the poem.

Corydon's following lines (vv. 132–6) are more traditionally pastoral in character, dealing as they do with the feeling of safety that even pastoral gods experience under the divine protection of the new emperor[150]. What is more, the image of an Oread who no loger runs the risk of treading on human blood (*humanum non calcatura cruorem*, v. 135) may further allude to Nero's *vera / incruenta Clementia* (cf. Chapter 1, pp. 40–1). Pan, Faunus and Nymphs are distinct members of the pantheon of the pastoral tradition (cf. Karakasis 2011, 18–9, 157–60); Faunus, in particular, is depicted in a typical pastoral location, reclining in the shade of a *locus amoenus* (vv. 133–4, reminiscent of a similar scene with Tityrus lying *sub tegmine fagi*, *lentus in umbra* (Verg. *Ecl.* 1.1, 4))[151]. But the very motif of a god (Pan) returning to his natural milieu as a sign of the *Aurea Aetas*, vv. 132–3, brings us back to the fourth Vergilian eclogue, Verg. *Ecl.* 4.6[152], where Vergil, as often remarked (cf. above, p. 71), sets out to transcend the pastoral code; pastoral tradition is once more combined with markers pointing to 'generic transcendence'.

The pretence at traditional bucolic poetry, as elaborated until the Neronian panegyric pastoral literature, is totally given up in the final strophic exchange: Amyntas concentrates in his part on several features of the panegyric style[153], such as wishes for long life and apotheosis (vv. 137–41, cf. also Hor. *Carm.* 1.2.45, Ov. *Met.* 15.868–70, *Trist.* 2.57, 5.2.52, 5.5.61, 5.11.25–6, Sen. *Dial.* 11.12.5, Luc. 1.46, Sil. 3.626–7, Stat. *Silv.* 1.1.105–7, 4.2.22, Mart. 5.65.15–6, 13.4.1[154]), the motif of a deity sent from heaven (vv. 137–8, as in Verg.

---

149 Korzeniewski 1971, 101 speaks of a dance 'im Dreitakt nach der Art der Salier'; see also Verdière 1954, 173. Cf. also Schubert 1998, 70; he also reads, rather unconvincingly, *cantare* as symbolising bucolic or lyric poetry, although the verb is by no means strictly restricted to these genres only. For a possible (lyric) Horatian influence, especially Hor. *Carm.* 1.37.1–4, 3.18.15–6, cf. Paladini 1956, 335, Messina 1975, 85, Vinchesi 2014, 351.
150 Cf. also Vinchesi 2014, 350–1.
151 Cf. also Schröder 1991, 101. For Calp. 4.132–4 harking back to Hor. *Carm.* 1.17.1–3, cf. Kegel-Brinkgreve 1990, 159 and n. 29.
152 Cf. also Schröder 1991, 161, Schubert 1998, 68, Gibson 2006, 225–6, Vinchesi 2014, 353. See also Calp. 1.43–4, *Eins.* 2.23.
153 Cf. also Simon 2007, 83–6.
154 Cf. Hubaux 1930, 203, Cesareo 1931, 197 and n. 1, Verdière 1954, 252–3; 1966, 166 and n. 38, Nisbet-Hubbard 1970, 37, Korzeniewski 1971, 47, Schröder 1991, 194–5, Keene 1996, 111–2, Merfeld 1999, 92 and nn. 1, 2, Di Lorenzo-Pellegrino 2008, 227, Vinchesi 2009a, 586 and n. 70; 2014, 355. For panegyrical wishes for longevity, cf. Coleman 1988, 100; see also Henderson 2013, 179, Vinchesi 2014, 355.

Ecl. 4.7[155]: *iam nova progenies caelo demittitur alto* also not of a so pastoral provenance) and the wish for the emperor not to exchange his palace for the sky (v. 141, for this image of a celestial abode, cf. also Verg. *G.* 1.503–4, Luc. 1.45–6, Stat. *Silv.* 1.1.106)[156]. The same also holds true for Corydon's verses, where one comes across the following: the motif of a god disguised in the form of someone else (vv. 142–4), modelled in all probability on Hor. *Carm.* 1.2.41–3[157], the qualification of the divine emperor as *aeternus* (v. 145, cf. also Ov. *Fast.* 3.421–2, *Pont.* 2.2.48, Stat. *Th.* 1.23–4[158]) and *pater* (v. 146, cf. e.g Suet. *Aug.* 58[159]), the *regere orbem / populos regere*-syntagm / motif (vv. 144–5, Hor. *Carm.* 1.12.57, [Sen.] *Octav.* 489[160]), and finally the appeal to a god not to give up the peace he first established (vv. 145–6, cf. also Ov. *Fast.* 1.287–8[161]). All these motifs, as can be inferred from the (selected) citations above, elsewhere appear in several literary genres but not in pastoral. The only pastoral parallels come from Verg. *Ecl.* 4, namely 4.15: the apotheosis-motif (*ille deum vitam accipiet*), 4.17: the *regere orbem*-formulation and 4.46–7: the *Parcae*-motif, where the goddesses are depicted as holding the thread of men's lives; cf. also Calp. 4.139–40: *vel potius mortale resolvite pensum / et date perpetuo caelestia fila metallo*, although in the Calpurnian passage the image of the life-threads is associated with an appeal to the gods in general and not to the *Parcae* in particular[162]. The intertexts thus direct the reader once again to the least pastoral Vergilian eclogue, where (see also above, p. 76) the authorial voice self-referentially acknowledges his 'generic movement' away from the earlier pastoral tradition.

---

155 Cf. also Langholf 1990, 367, Vinchesi 2014, 355.
156 For the panegyric character of these features, cf. also Schröder 1991, 194–7, Men. Rh. 2.377. See also Cesareo 1931, 195–6, Verdière 1954, 253, Joly 1974, 55, 64 and nn. 88, 89, Schubert 1998, 70, Di Lorenzo-Pellegrino 2008, 228, Vinchesi 2014, 356.
157 Cf. Verdière 1954, 253, Paladini 1956, 524, Nisbet-Hubbard 1970, 33, Messina 1975, 87, Schröder 1991, 198–9, Keene 1996, 112–3, Merfeld 1999, 93 and n. 1, Di Lorenzo-Pellegrino 2008, 228, Vinchesi 2009a, 587; 2014, 356–7.
158 Cf. Schröder 1991, 200, Vinchesi 2009a, 587; 2014, 357.
159 Cf. Keene 1996, 112–3, Vinchesi 2014, 358.
160 Cf. Schröder 1991, 200, Vinchesi 2009a, 587; 2014, 357. For *populos regere* as an epic tag, see Schröder 1991, 78–9, Vinchesi 2009a, 574 and n. 14.
161 Cf. Schröder 1991, 200, Vinchesi 2014, 357–8.
162 Cf. also Küppers 1985, 349–50. See also Paladini 1956, 336, Langholf 1990, 367, Merfeld 1999, 92, Vinchesi 2014, 355–7.

Reception of the *laudes principis* – Closure

Despite an initial expectation for a traditional bucolic song, based on Corydon's alleged association with Tityrus–Vergil (vv. 60–3), Meliboeus' verdict also judges the two singing performances as untypical specimens of (traditional) pastoral, since (traditional) pastoral song is presented by him in negative colours: rustic lays are fit for cloddish ears only (v. 148: *obesis auribus apta*). Once again, the highest value of the pre-Calpurnian 'green cabinet', the basic feature of a time-honoured pastoral identity is deconstructed; thus poetic qualities often associated with the pastoral tradition, such as purity and sweetness (v. 150: *tam liquidum, tam dulce*)[163], which also constitute, especially the second, poetological markers of the pre-Calpurnian bucolic genre, are transferred to songs not aspiring to traditional pastoral aesthetic choices but deviating towards other literary genres[164]. Thus Corydon is not associated with the father of the Roman pastoral, Vergil, whose pastoral reed he opted to make use of (vv. 60–3), but with Ovid, as suggested by the image of the Pelignian swarms in v. 151: *quod Paeligna solent examina lambere nectar*[165]. Therefore, a certain confusion is discernible in traditional poetological attitudes and conceptions: traditional pastoral poetic production is presented in a negative instead of a positive light, and the pastoral poet is compared to Ovid instead of his 'generically default model', i.e., Vergil. Yet it is true that, especially in the last exchange, most of the topics hark back more to Ovid than to Vergil and, what is more, to a 'less pastoral' Vergil.

Corydon accepts the poetic quality of his song, as evaluated by Meliboeus; he crucially describes his lyrics as *tereti…versu* (v. 152), where the adjective qual-

---

163 *Liquidus* often qualifies poetry / song in Latin literature, cf. also Nisbet–Hubbard 1970, 283, Vinchesi 2014, 359; in the Calpurnian instance the term seems to suggest the 'clear' / 'unblemished' character of the song (cf. Duff and Duff 1934, 257), as derived from *liquere*; it is thus about a basic asset of Callimachean poetics (of the pastoral genre as well) associated with the clean, unpolluted water of the sacred spring in opposition to the filthy Assyrian river, cf. above, p. 54; see also Karakasis 2011, 84.
164 In a similar vein, Lycotas of Calp. 7 describes Corydon's panegyric poetic account of the amphitheatre as *dulce*, vv. 20–2; cf. also Vozza 1993, 303–4, Chapter 3, p. 95.
165 Cf. Duff and Duff 1934, 257, Verdière 1954, 254; 1966, 166; 1992, 37, Korzeniewski 1971, 102, Messina 1975, 87, Bartalucci 1976, 99, 115 and n. 44, Kegel-Brinkgreve 1990, 159, Pearce 1990, 103, Schröder 1991, 204–6, Amat 1991, 113, Keene 1996, 113, Vinchesi 1996, 122; 2012, 716–7; 2014, 43, 359, Hubbard 1998, 173, Martin 2003, 79, Simon 2007, 64, Di Lorenzo–Pellegrino 2008, 228, Garthwaite–Martin 2009, 318, Fucecchi 2009, 43–4. For the significant influence of Ovidian poetry on Calpurnius Siculus, cf. especially Vinchesi 1996, 47, Magnelli 2006, 467, Fucecchi 2009, 41–65.

ifying 'verse' constitutes a further catch-word of Callimachean–Neoteric sensibilities of the *genus tenue*[166] (cf. also Karakasis 2011, 131–2; see also Chapter 1, pp. 42, 46). However, this poetic quality, associated with traditional pastoral song as well, is here transferred, as in the case of the equally Neoteric terms *liquidus et dulcis*, to Corydon's recent singing performance in front of Meliboeus, i.e., to poetry transcending long-established bucolic trends in the direction of a panegyric with several non-pastoral intertexts (cf. also Calp. 1.93). This confusion of well-established poetological signs continues with the subsequent images: the appeal to the intervention of a political god in the hopes of securing pastoral fortune and, as a consequence, pastoral poetic production, cf. vv. 152–5, recalls once again the first Vergilian eclogue; the divine politician intervenes and thus secures Tityrus' pastoral holdings and the continuation of his pastoral poetry (cf. above, pp. 68, 75). Similarly, Corydon asks Meliboeus to ensure for him, thanks to his association with a *divine* emperor, a homestead and private pastures (the 'material reward' of an 'imperial patronage'; cf. also Hor. *Serm.* 2.6 and the Sabine estate granted to the poet by his patron, Maecenas[167]), so that his songs can resonate on the mountains; but the quality of the pastoral song to resound is no longer associated with the traditional, pastoral 'generic form' of the first Vergilian eclogue and, what is more, whereas the *deus* of Verg. *Ecl.* 1 simply restores pastoral order after the confiscations, Corydon's appeal is associated with the well-known panegyric request for materialistic assistance[168], cf. e.g. *Laus Pis.* 216–9.

The inversion of established poetological imagery occurs in the following picture as well, vv. 155ff.: as elaborated above (cf. p. 54), one of the most well-known poetological settings in Roman literature has Apollo, as a god of poetic inspiration of the *genus tenue*, admonish against deviations towards the *genus grande* (cf. especially Verg. *Ecl.* 6.3–5 to which the present passage harks back[169]). Calpurnius substitutes Apollo with a personified *Paupertas*. Pov-

---

[166] Cf. also Duff and Duff 1934, 257, Keene 1996, 114, who also associates *teres* with *tenuis* and *deductum* as poetological catch-words; see also Bartalucci 1976, 95–6 vs. Korzeniewski 1971, 47 and Schröder 1991, 208, who read the adjective in the sense of 'geglätteten', 'wohlgeschliffenen'; see also Vinchesi 2014, 360–1: 'fluido, privo di scabrosità del ritmo'. However, the above translations also show the 'slender poetic quality' of Corydon's songs.
[167] Cf. Martin 2003, 82, Garthwaite-Martin 2009, 318, Vinchesi 2014, 45, 361, Henderson 2013, 181.
[168] Cf. also Leach 1973, 77.
[169] Cf. also Cesareo 1931, 198–9, Verdière 1954, 254, Paladini 1956, 524, Korzeniewski 1971, 48, Messina 1975, 87–8, Friedrich 1976, 153, Davis 1987, 47, Pearce 1990, 103, Vozza 1993, 290 and n. 30, Keene 1996, 115, Vinchesi 1996, 34 and n. 53; 2014, 361, Gibson 2004, 6, Di Lorenzo-Pellegrino 2008, 229.

erty has of course Callimachean associations, betrayed by the *topos* of 'a poet of small means', according to which Callimachus fashions himself, especially in his *Iambs*. Besides, the Callimachean lover too is normally poor, cf. πλούτου κενεαὶ χέρες (cf. *Ep.* 32.1 Pf.)[170]. Nevertheless *Paupertas* is crucially associated here with the anti-Callimachean – anti-Neoteric *invidia*[171]; and so whereas Apollo warns against the *genus grande*, the Calpurnian poverty necessitates Corydon's occupation with *ovilia* (v. 156). In other words, instead of a Callimachean–Neoteric Apollo urging towards the *genus tenue* as opposed to an eschewed *genus grande*, in the Calpurnian scenery it is poverty of anti-Callimachean – anti-Neoteric attitude that makes the poet occupy himself with bucolic space and bucolic poetry[172] instead of poetic trends of a loftier tone. This constitutes a complete inversion of this traditional poetological sign, complementing the poetological semiotic reversal already observed in the previous lines.

Corydon asks Meliboeus to introduce him in the imperial circles (vv. 158–9, cf. also Calp. 1.94 where Ornytus similarly remarks: *forsitan augustas feret haec Meliboeus ad aures*[173]) and to function as Vergil's patron did[174], that is having en-

---

[170] Cf. also Karakasis 2005a, 100.
[171] Cf. also Wimmel 1970, 294, Vinchesi 1996, 34 and n. 56; 2014, 361–2. For poverty and not Apollo as the agent of the poetological command, cf. Hor. *Epist.* 2.2.51–2, where *Paupertas* has a similar function; for a contamination of this latter passage with the opening of Verg. *Ecl.* 6, cf. also Kegel-Brinkgreve 1990, 159, Vinchesi 1996, 34 and n. 55; 2014, 45, 361, Simon 2007, 67.
[172] For the poetological undertones of *ovilia*, cf. also Wimmel 1970, 296, Vozza 1993, 290 and n. 30, Simon 2007, 67 vs. Paladini 1956, 524–5, Bartalucci 1976, 111 and n. 25, Davis 1987, 47, Gibson 2004, 6; see also Friedrich 1976, 184 and n. 48, Schröder 1991, 211, Vinchesi 2014, 362. Cf. also *ovile* in v. 162 describing Vergil's pastoral poetry as a foil to his *Georgics* and the *Aeneid*. See also v. 11: *ovile Menalcae*, where the syntagm suggests the pastoral subject–matter of traditional bucolics, as opposed to poetry of higher aspirations dealing with the great divinities of the mighty city, Rome. It is, therefore, unclear why in this distinct poetological setting evoking programmatic texts, *ovilia* should have only a literal meaning. My reading of the line, however, differs from Leach 1973, 76, who sees poverty as 'spur[ring] the poet's longings for communication with the great world' against pastoral purity. For the *paupertas*-motif in the Neronian age as well as for Corydon's / Calpurnius' small means, cf. especially Gagliardi 1984, 9–10, Vozza 1993, 305 and n. 76; see also Beato 1995, 617–27, Simon 2007, 66–8.
[173] Cf. also Verdière 1954, 175, Vozza 1993, 287, Vinchesi 2014, 362.
[174] Probably Maecenas, cf. Cesareo 1931, 200, Verdière 1954, 255, Wimmel 1970, 296, Pearce 1970, 337, Messina 1975, 88, Friedrich 1976, 10, 152, Sullivan 1985, 56, Kegel-Brinkgreve 1990, 159, Pearce 1990, 104, Schröder 1991, 213, Amat 1991, 44 and n. 12, Vozza 1993, 287, Vinchesi 1996, 31–2 and n. 48; 2002, 149; 2014, 363, Gibson 2004, 6, Garthwaite-Martin 2009, 318, Monella 2009, 75 and n. 23, Hulsenboom 2013, 23 vs. Asinius Pollio, cf. Hubaux 1930, 184, Korzeniewski 1971, 102. Cf. also Cizek 1972, 372, Friedrich 1976, 184 and n. 47, Küppers 1989, 40–1 and n. 39, Schubert 1998, 72–4.

abled the transformation of Tityrus–Vergil from a pastoral poet to the poet of the *Georgics* (v. 163: *rura prius*) as well as of an epic, the *Aeneid* (v. 163: *post cantabimus arma*)[175]. Significantly, this process of 'generic transition' from the *genus tenue* to the *genus grande* is conveyed in the Calpurnian instance by means of the verb *deducere*: *e silvis dominam deduxit in urbem* (v. 161); *deducere* is the verb that forms the participle *deductum* qualifying the *genus tenue* (cf. Verg. *Ecl.* 6.5: *deductum dicere carmen*), and so a movement towards the *genus grande* is described by means of a verb suggesting the very opposite 'generic development'.

Within the above poetological setting of inversed traditional pastoral motifs and catch-words, Amyntas' offering to the deified Caesar in v. 166: *tenerum... headum* may also be read as further establishing this inversion of poetological symbolism: the tender kid as a ritual offering to a political god may derive again from Verg. *Ecl.* 1.8[176], where Tityrus offers to his deified *iuvenis*[177] *tener nostris ab ovilibus...agnus*, but it may also possess further poetological meaning within a passage redolent with issues of poetics. As already observed (cf. pp. 54, 79), in the prologue to Callimachus' *Aetia* (1.22–4 Pf.) Apollo, the inspiring god of Callimachean poetics, makes a clear distinction between the 'slender character' of Callimachus' Muse (τὴν Μοῦσαν δ' ὠγαθὲ λεπταλέην) and a fattened animal offer (τὸ μὲν θύος ὅττι πάχιστον, cf. also Verg. *Ecl.* 6.4–5, where a similar opposition is developed between a *pinguis...ovis* and a *deductum...carmen*[178]). Calpurnius thus reverses the Callimachean 'slender poetic tradition' by changing the sacrificial animal from a fattened to a soft and delicate one.

The eclogue closes with the well-known Vergilian motif of the return to everyday pastoral menial tasks (cf. also Verg. *Ecl.* 2.66–7, 70–2, 3.111, 9.66, 10.77 as well as Calp. 2.93–4, 96–7[179]), as Meliboeus asks the two herdsmen to bring

---

[175] Cf. also Verdière 1954, 255, Korzeniewski 1971, 102, Casaceli 1982, 86–7, Küppers 1989, 39–40, Mackie 1989, 10, Pearce 1990, 104, Schröder 1991, 22, 214–6, Amat 1991, 44 and n. 112, Vozza 1993, 289–90, Beato 1995, 622, Keene 1996, 115, Hubbard 1998, 174, Esposito 1996, 27–8, Fey-Wickert 2002, 12 and n. 12, Byrne 2004, 255, 257, Gibson 2004, 6–7, Simon 2007, 74–5, Di Lorenzo-Pellegrino 2008, 230, Vinchesi 2014, 364, Baraz 2015, 108–9.
[176] Cf. also Schröder 1991, 217, Di Lorenzo-Pellegrino 2008, 230, Vinchesi 2014, 365; for the image of Calpurnius' *deus* associated with the deified *iuvenis* of Verg. *Ecl.* 1, cf. also Langholf 1990, 359–61.
[177] For an allegory of Octavian, cf. especially Du Quesnay 1981, 35, 40–4, 133–4.
[178] Cf. also Ross 1975, 26–7.
[179] Cf. also Schröder 1991, 218, Vinchesi 2014, 366. Hubbard 1998, 174 sees in Meliboeus' *deducite* as well as in the lowering of position implied meta-linguistic signs suggesting the *genus tenue*; cf. also Simon 2007, 76: '*deducite* weist auf das vergilische Vorbild', i.e., Verg. *Ecl.* 6.3–5. These remarks of Meliboeus' have also been read in the relevant bibliography as

their sheep by the river (v. 168: *nunc ad flumen oves deducite*). The shadow–motif in the last line (v. 169: *iam sol contractas pedibus magis admovet umbras*) has its Vergilian intertexts, namely *Ecl.* 1.83[180] and 2.67; but in both these instances the motif is associated with the coming of the evening, i.e., a further Vergilian closure–motif, occasionally linked to the above mentioned return to everyday pastoral activities. Despite the initial pastoral Vergilian impression, this sense of a return to the typical / traditional bucolic order is put again in question, as, instead of the arrival of evening, the short shadow suggests noontide[181], i.e., usually a time for starting to sing[182], cf. Verg. *Ecl.* 2.7–13, rather than to bring a song–exchange to its end. Moreover, this alienation from the expected pastoral norm is also suggested by the wording of the phrase, the combination *contractas* (*contrahere*) ...*umbras* (v. 169) originating in Ovid[183]. The reversal of Vergilian pastoral order is thus further complemented with a wording not having the sanction of earlier pastoral but significantly coming instead from Ovid, the poet who functions as the model Corydon appears as aiming to surpass (vv. 147 ff.) in preference to his default generic pastoral predecessor, Vergil[184].

---

the latter's advice against the urban aspirations of Corydon, cf. also Verdière 1966, 165, Schröder 1991, 219 vs. Vinchesi 2014, 366.

180 For an association of this closure with the ending of the first Vergilian eclogue, cf. also Cesareo 1931, 201, Balzert 1971, 29, Simon 2007, 76; yet, see also Messina 1975, 88, Novelli 1980, 79.

181 Cf. also Verdière 1954, 255, Korzeniewski 1971, 102, Messina 1975, 88, Ahl 1984, 68, Schröder 1991, 218–20, Amat 1995, 80, Hubbard 1998, 174, Keene 1996, 116, Gibson 2004, 7–8, Vinchesi 2014, 366.

182 Cf. also Leach 1975, 208, Keene 1996, 39.

183 Gagliardi 1984, 62 and n. 45 reads the end of the eclogue as a 'tecnica combinatoria' by means of which Calpurnius brings forward his two main models, namely Vergil and Ovid. See also Ov. *Ars* 3.723, *Met.* 3.144, Korzeniewski 1971, 49, Schröder 1991, 220, Di Lorenzo–Pellegrino 2008, 231, Vinchesi 2014, 366.

184 Even in the domain of metre, despite being a pastoral poet, Calpurnius in several cases patterns his dactylic hexameter not after his standard 'generic model', Vergil, but after Ovid, with whom Corydon of Calp. 4 is significantly associated, as underlined by the image of the Pelignian swarms in v. 151. For example, Calpurnius shows a penchant for hexametric combinations of a dactylic prevalence as favoured by Ovid (e.g. DDDS, DDSD, cf. Di Lorenzo–Pellegrino 2008, 24–5), while his use of the caesura also brings him close to Ovidian metrical practices, cf. Di Lorenzo–Pellegrino 2008, 28; for Calpurnian metre, cf. especially Duckworth 1969, 96–8, Verdière 1971, Korzeniowski 1998, especially 98–114, 146–54, 192–210, 237–95, 319–21.

Diction and 'Generic Novelty'

As previously remarked, Meliboeus' diction exhibits a predilection for Post-Classical usages that can be read as a further, linguistic, sign of his novel 'generic orientation' and of the Post-Classical development of the genre[185]. Apart from the transitive usage of *adstrepere* in v. 2, in Meliboeus' diction one comes across the following Post-Classical linguistic features as well: in vv. 19–20: *iam puerum calamos et odorae vincula cerae / iungere non cohibes*, the construction of *cohibere* with the a.c.i. (cf. also Plin. *Nat.* 20.147, Dict. Cret. 3.4)[186]; the transitive usage of *remurmuro* in vv. 27–8: *mea carmina...ventosa remurmurat echo* (cf. also Fr. *Ep. ad Am.* 2.7.1 p. 192 N)[187], possibly the use of *fragilis* instead of *fractus* of the weakness of a tone (v. 74), which first appears here and later re-emerges in Fulg. *Myth. praef.* p. 7.1, 12.21 Helm[188], and finally in v. 168: *iam fremit aestas*, the use of *fremere* with reference to the heat (*de rebus fervidis* – ThLL VI I, 1285, 64–7, cf. also V. Fl. 7.66–7) rather than in its normal usage for hearing effects[189]. Finally one may mention two *hapax* usages: in v. 66: *praesonuisse chelyn*, the transitive use of *praesonare* in the sense of 'play better than' instead of its Classical meaning of 'sound before / earlier than' (cf. Ov. *Am.* 3.13.11) is a usage unique in Calpurnius[190], and so is *respirare* in the sense of *resonare*[191] in v. 74: *tinnula tam fragili respiret fistula buxo* as well as *canales* with the meaning of *fis-*

---

[185] It could also be counter-argued here that Post-Classical diction may easily be an indication of date and not a sign of 'generic deviation'. However, as already remarked, in this case one might expect an even distribution of such linguistic features in the narrative of a specific eclogue as well as in the speech of the various bucolic figures involved; thus the uneven spread of the phenomena in Calp. 1, 2, 4 and 7 should not be read as accidental. This asymmetrical distribution is to be otherwise justified and thus 'generic novelty' may account for the allocation of the linguistic features in question; see also Chapters 1, 3, 6, pp. 43–5, 115–7, 217–8.
[186] Cf. Mahr 1964, 135, Merone 1967, 18, Novelli 1980, 45, Gagliardi 1984, 71, Armstrong 1986, 124, Schröder 1991, 89, Horsfall 1997, 185, 189, Vinchesi 2014, 303.
[187] Cf. Merone 1967, 13–4, 32–3, Messina 1975, 108, Novelli 1980, 94, Gagliardi 1984, 75 and n. 23, Armstrong 1986, 119, Schröder 1991, 95, Horsfall 1997, 185, Vinchesi 2014, 51, 308.
[188] Cf. Novelli 1980, 58, Schröder 1991, 133, Horsfall 1997, 191, Vinchesi 2014, 327.
[189] Cf. Novelli 1980, 60, Schröder 1991, 219–20, Horsfall 1997, 181, Vinchesi 2014, 51, 366.
[190] Cf. Mahr 1964, 124, 160–1, Merone 1967, 12–3, Messina 1975, 108, 115 and n. 18, Novelli 1980, 85, 98, Armstrong 1986, 119–20, Schröder 1991, 127, Horsfall 1997, 191, Di Lorenzo-Pellegrino 2008, 213, Vinchesi 2014, 324.
[191] Cf. Merone 1967, 33–4, Messina 1975, 108, Novelli 1980, 31, 98, Armstrong 1986, 123, Schröder 1991, 133, Horsfall 1997, 188, Vinchesi 2014, 327.

tula pastoralis in vv. 76–7: *canales / exprime*[192]. The list may be extended with a further linguistic feature that, although not absent from Classical speech, seems to characterise Post–Classical Latin as far as its productivity is concerned: the use of *praeter* instead of *praeterquam* in the sense of *nisi* after a preceding negative word, vv. 27–8: *certe mea carmina nemo / praeter ab his scopulis ventosa remurmurat echo*. This usage belongs to the colloquial register in Classical Latin, but in Post–Classical Latin it is present in all stylistic registers[193] and, as Mahr 1964, 109 claims, it is 'als eine nachklassische Erscheinung zu werten'.

It is probably not a coincidence, therefore, that Corydon, who tries to follow Meliboeus' 'generic and stylistic orientation', also incorporates in his poetic diction several Post–Classical features of the kind that Meliboeus' diction favours. Meliboeus' final positive reaction to Corydon's performance may thus be due not only to the latter's adoption of several topics aspiring to a loftier poetic style but to Corydon's linguistic usage as well. Thus, apart from the transitive construction of *resulto* in v. 5 (see above, p. 53), one may also point out the following innovative linguistic usages in Corydon's lines: The unique construction of *attribuere* with the dative and the infinitive occurs in vv. 53–5: *nam tibi...dicere...attribuere dei*[194], and the use of *modulabile* as a qualifying adjective of *carmen* (probably on the basis of the common expression *carmen modulari*, Tib. 2.1.53–4, etc.), also found later in Paul. Nol. *Carm*. 27.79 and Cassiod. *Inst. Div. Litt*. 2.5.10, comes in v. 63[195]. In v. 83 one comes across the formation *Atlantiacus* in place of the more common *Atlanticus / Atlanteus* (see Schröder 1991, 147), cf. also Sil. 13.200, Aus. *Mos*. 144[196] and a similar formation, *Cureticus* for *Curetis* (cf. Ov. *Met*. 8.153), in v. 96 (cf. also Sil. 15.308)[197]. *Exundare* in the sense of 'to abound' of the wool of an animal in v. 104 also occurs in Post–Classical authors as well, Colum. (cf. 9.9.1), Luc. (cf. 9.619), Sil. (cf. 3.316), Stat. *Th*. (cf. 10.535), etc.[198], *praefocata* in v. 115 occurs in a figurative sense for the first time

---

192 Cf. Merone 1967, 27, Novelli 1980, 31, Armstrong 1986, 120, Schröder 1991, 134–5, Horsfall 1997, 186, Vinchesi 2014, 51, 328.
193 Cf. Mahr 1964, 108–9, Schröder 1991, 94, Vinchesi 2014, 307.
194 Cf. Merone 1967, 17, Messina 1975, 108, Armstrong 1986, 124, Schröder 1991, 116–7, Horsfall 1997, 187, 189, Di Lorenzo–Pellegrino 2008, 211, Vinchesi 2014, 319.
195 Cf. Merone 1967, 22, Novelli 1980, 36, 57–8, Armstrong 1986, 119, Schröder 1991, 123–4, Horsfall 1997, 191, Vinchesi 2014, 322.
196 Cf. Schröder 1991, 147, Horsfall 1997, 181, Vinchesi 2014, 331. Armstrong 1986, 120 wrongly believes that the form is 'unique in Latin'.
197 Cf. Merone 1967, 20, Messina 1975, 109, 111, Novelli 1980, 36, 98, Schröder 1991, 160, Horsfall 1997, 181, Di Lorenzo–Pellegrino 2008, 219, Vinchesi 2014, 338.
198 Cf. Horsfall 1997, 179, Vinchesi 2014, 51, 341.

here[199], *calcator* in v. 124 is a further Post–Classical formation later to re-appear in Zeno (e. g. *Tract.* 2.27.2) and Jerome (*In Isa.* 16.9 f.)[200]. Finally, the use of a future participle in a conditional sequence of the unreal in vv. 39–40: *nisi tu... fuisses ultima visuri*[201] is an option which, despite its occasional occurrence in Classical Latin, constitutes a further distinct linguistic marker of the Post–Classical language.

Conclusion

The fourth Calpurnian eclogue is obviously also about the formation of a 'generically modified' Neronian pastoral, as Calpurnius is moving away from traditional (Theocritean, Greek post–Theocritean and Vergilian) pastoral towards other

---

199 Cf. Merone 1967, 30–1, Messina 1975, 108, Novelli 1980, 85, Armstrong 1986, 123, Schröder 1991, 180, Horsfall 1997, 188, Vinchesi 2014, 345.
200 Cf. Mahr 1964, 173–4, Armstrong 1986, 121, Schröder 1991, 188–9, Horsfall 1997, 183; see also Vinchesi 1992, 155; 2014, 349. Post–Classical formations appear in Amyntas' speech as well; but what matters again is the relative accumulation of the features in question in the speech of a specific character and their relative absence from the diction of another, different pastoral figure. In most cases, the Post–Classical features in Amyntas' diction, as claimed in the relevant bibliography, are textually doubtful or demonstrably not Post–Classical; thus in v. 91 *fructificare* is textually doubtful, cf. also Schröder 1991, 154. The variant *fruticare* (Haupt, Schenkl, Leo) is a Classical formation also found in Cic. *Att.* 15.4.2. In v. 111, I would read *densat odora* (Ulitius, Haupt, Shackleton–Bailey, see also Horsfall 1997, 188) instead of the alleged Post–Classical ablative construction *densat odore* (vs. Armstrong 1986, 120–1); in any case Armstrong's claim as to the Frontonian character of the ablative construction is only an impression without any solid argumentation, cf. also Schröder 1991, 175, Vinchesi 2014, 343. The neuter plural *arbuta* (cf. Armstrong 1986, 123: 'rare or late'; see also Horsfall 1997, 189) in v. 109 seems to refer, as in Classical Latin, to the tree (cf. also Verg. *G.* 3.301, 4.181. See also Novelli 1980, 66, Schröder 1991, 172, Keene 1996, 107, Vinchesi 2014, 343); *turbidus* in v. 131 (cf. Novelli 1980, 60, Horsfall 1997, 188), although used of sound, appears in its Classical meaning 'in a state of turmoil, confused, disordered', cf. OLD *s.v.* 4b. As for *nullus* for *nemo* in v. 129, it occurs, as Armstrong 1986, 121 himself remarks, even in Plautus; see also Vinchesi 2014, 351–2. Thus the only Post–Classical formations that appear in Amyntas' speech are *regerminare* in v. 111, also found in Plin. *Nat.* 16.141, 19.122 (cf. also Novelli 1980, 38, Gagliardi 1984, 69–70 and n. 1, Armstrong 1986, 121, Schröder 1991, 177, Horsfall 1997, 185–6, Vinchesi 2014, 344), and *surdare* in v. 131, found only in Calpurnius (cf. Mahr 1964, 185, Merone 1967, 25, Messina 1975, 108, Novelli 1980, 94, Gagliardi 1984, 71, Armstrong 1986, 121, Schröder 1991, 192–3, Vinchesi 2014, 352), but this latter case seems to be a plebeian formation (cf. Armstrong 1986, 121), which imparts a colloquial / rustic linguistic colour to Amyntas' diction when singing of rustic fests.
201 Cf. Mahr 1964, 87: 'eine ausgesprochen nachklassische Eigentümlichkeit', Schröder 1991, 105.

'generic directions', always in the use of an imperial panegyric. This is achieved mainly by incorporating motifs and stylistic features or wording unknown in previous pastoral, associated instead with other literary genres, often the georgics (e.g. plane-trees as the 'generic marker' of a georgic *locus amoenus* in Roman literature, the milking interests of Amyntas, the georgic tasks of a *fossor* finding a treasure, etc.) or the Ovidian corpus (e.g. the qualification of the emperor as *aeternus*), by handling traditional bucolic markers in a novel manner (e.g. the negative depiction of a generic *locus amoenus*, the motif of the spellbound nature connected in previous pastoral with poetic power, but associated in the Calpurnian eclogue with an appeal to Caesar) or even by choosing topics which have a precedent in the previous pastoral corpus, yet suggesting, even in this latter case, a deviation from the traditional pastoral norm (e.g. the silence-motif in Corydon's case, the legalistic interests in vv. 117 ff.).

The present eclogue's connection with the fourth and the fifth Vergilian eclogues is especially strong (e.g. the *Aurea Aetas*-imagery, the georgic blooming resulting from the beneficial influence of a deified political figure). These two eclogues also attempted a 'generic re-evaluation' of pastoral in the panegyrical direction, thus foreshadowing the similar trend of the Neronian period.

This 'generic re-assessment' becomes evident in the case of the poetological meta-language of the eclogue as well: traditional 'generic signs, catch-words and motifs' suggesting the *genus tenue* of the pastoral kind are here transformed and often inversed or express opposite 'generic sensibilities' (e.g. the image of Apollo, the inspiring god of the *genus tenue*, accepting Corydon's aspirations as to loftier poetic genres). Corydon sacrifices the 'generic tradition' for the sake of the emperor's encomium: therefore he often employs motifs related to the praise of the emperor (as is for example the association of Jupiter with Apollo, specific effects associated with the appearance of a divine figure, etc.) which repeatedly oppose or even eliminate basic pre-Calpurnian pastoral values or attributes (e.g. the blemished traditional pastoral pantheon, the silence of natural sounds, etc.). Without claiming that evidence of post-Augustan linguistic usage should always be seen as a further sign of a 'generic re-orientation', I believe that the 'generic novelty' of the present poem is finally mirrored by a certain degree of linguistic innovation, especially in the speech of Meliboeus and Corydon, who adopt several linguistic peculiarities of Post-Classical Latin.

Calpurnius 7

In the seventh and last eclogue of the Calpurnian pastoral corpus[1], Corydon is presented as reluctantly leaving the city and returning to the 'green cabinet', where he gives the elder herdsman, Lycotas, a dithyrambic account of the Roman amphitheatre and its mechanisms, so favoured by Nero himself[2], and of the various shows it hosts.

Framing Introduction

Verg. *Ecl.* 1 has long been claimed as one of the principal intertexts of Calp. 7[3], mainly due to the fact that the two poems, structured in the form of a dialogue between two pastoral figures[4], share the same narrative pattern: a journey to Rome of a principal pastoral figure and the sympathetic reaction of other pastoral characters and / or of the bucolic landscape to the absence of the main bucolic hero. A further basic narrative detail connecting the two bucolic poems has to do with the crucial presence of a *iuvenis* – divine *princeps*[5], who in both instances appears to be the ultimate cause of the journey. Tityrus of the first Vergilian eclogue goes to Rome in order to meet the young prince (cf. vv. 6–10, 40–5) and thus to secure his *libertas* and his permanence within the precinct of the 'green cabinet' (vv. 27 ff., cf. Chapter 2, p. 79). His temporary absence causes sorrow in humans and the empathy of pastoral life in vv. 36–9: a sad Amaryllis is calling on the gods, as a sign for her mourning over Tityrus' absence to the *urbs*, and, indifferent to everyday menial pastoral activities, is letting the apples hang on

---

1 For Calp. 7 as a 'farewell to pastoral', cf. Magnelli 2006, 476; see also Friedrich 1976, 158, Effe–Binder 1989, 130, Vinchesi 1996, 29, Hubbard 1998, 177–8, Monella 2009, 85 and n. 51. For Spencer 2005, 46–7 (see also pp. 48–9), Calp. 7 may also be read as 'an elegy for pastoral' – p. 47; in the extravagant Neronian world, as symbolised by the sumptuous wooden amphitheatre, pastoral poetry can no longer survive.
2 Cf. Di Salvo 1990, 110. See also Suet. *Ner.* 31.2.
3 Cf. Cesareo 1931, 98, Duff 1960, 267, Grant 1965, 73, Verdière 1966, 167–8, Leach 1973, 77–9, Gnilka 1974, 130 and n. 4, Friedrich 1976, 157, Ahl 1984, 68, Gagliardi 1984, 63, Davis 1987, 48, Newlands 1987, 219–22, Effe–Binder 1989, 125–7, Schubert 1998, 80–1, Kegel-Brinkgreve 1990, 162, Pearce 1990, 142, Vozza 1993, 297–8, Fear 1994, 274–5, Hubbard 1998, 175–6, Merfeld 1999, 94–6, Vinchesi 2002, 149–50 and n. 44; 2010, 142; 2012, 718; 2014, 477, Mayer 2006, 460–1, Fucecchi 2009, 51, Taliercio 2010, 52–74, Baraz 2015, 113.
4 Cf. also Green 2009, 55.
5 Cf. Di Salvo 1990, 76–7, Vinchesi 1996, 26; 2010, 142, Di Lorenzo–Pellegrino 2008, 271.

the trees, whereas constituent elements of the generic pastoral *locus amoenus*, such as pine-trees, springs and orchards, are also longing for the absent Tityrus[6]. In a similar vein, Corydon of the last Calpurnian poem is also presented as coming back to the pastoral space after a trip to Rome, where he experienced a taste of the amphitheatre and its shows, established by another young divine figure (cf. v. 6: *iuvenis deus*; see also v. 80), namely Nero. And just as Amaryllis and the inanimate nature of the first Vergilian eclogue respond with sadness to Tityrus' absence, the forests of the seventh Calpurnian eclogue are similarly presented, again in terms of the well-known bucolic motif of the pathetic fallacy, as longing for the renowned pastoral singer (v. 2: *ut nostrae cupiunt te cernere silvae*) and the bulls as saddened, waiting for his yodellings (v. 3: *ut tua maerentes exspectant iubila tauri*). A similar instance of animals experiencing grief for an absent pastoral figure appears in the fourth bucolic Theocritean idyll, where Aegon's cows experience love-symptoms (lowing denoting their longing, loss of appetite, vv. 12–4[7]) as a result of Aegon's leaving the 'green cabinet', in order to follow Milon to the Olympic games[8]; this particular intertext further increases a sense of traditional pastoralism in the introductory lines of the Calpurnian eclogue. Last but not least, both Tityrus (Verg. *Ecl.* 1, vv. 19–25) and Corydon (Calp. 7, vv. 37 ff.) seem to have no previous knowledge of the city and its ways and so both feel amazed at the new sight, although this is clearly more evident in the case of the Calpurnian Corydon.

On a linguistic level, a feeling of a time-honoured pastoralism is further created by the colloquial idiom, a staple feature of rustic diction in earlier bucolic poetry that the old sylvan figure, Lycotas, makes use of. In v. 2: *ut nostrae cupiunt te cernere silvae*, *ut* functions as equivalent to *ex quo* or *cum* in a temporal meaning ('since'); such a linguistic option appears randomly in Early Latin (cf. Plaut. *Stich.* 29–30), is avoided by the purism of Classical Latin with the exception of less strict literary genres, as is the case with the epistology (cf. Cic. *Att.* 1.15.2), whereas in Post-Classical Latin it either appears in the archaising

---

[6] Cf. also Cesareo 1931, 97 and n. 1, Verdière 1954, 262, Korzeniewski 1971, 66, Newlands 1987, 226, Pearce 1990, 142, Hubbard 1998, 175–6, Di Lorenzo-Pellegrino 2008, 269–70, Vinchesi 2010, 145; 2012, 717 and n. 60; 2014, 481.
[7] Cf. Hunter 1999, 134. The feelings of *eros* experienced by Aegon's cows in Theocr. 4 are here brought to the fore through the elegiac undertones of syntagms consisting of *lentus* + *abesse* (cf. v. 11), occasionally used of the estranged lover of Roman elegy (cf. Ov. *Epist.* 1.66, 2.23, Verdière 1954, 263, Korzeniewski 1971, 67–8, Di Salvo 1990, 82, Di Lorenzo-Pellegrino 2008, 272–3, Vinchesi 2012, 718–9 and nn. 69, 70; 2014, 50, 480). Corydon is thus presented as the cruel lover, whose absence is deplored by the pastoral space and for whom the 'green cabinet' longs.
[8] Cf. Verdière 1954, 262, Korzeniewski 1971, 66, Messina 1975, 90 and n. 98, Di Salvo 1990, 74, Di Lorenzo-Pellegrino 2008, 270, Vinchesi 2012, 717 and n. 60; 2014, 481.

register as a conscious archaism (cf. Tac. *Ann.* 14.53) or creeps up as a colloquialism in less formal literary genres (e. g. satire, Mart. 10.103.7–8)[9]. This twofold linguistic identity of the construction in Post–Classical Latin (both archaic and popular, as often in the case of the conservative Latin colloquial idiom) seems to account for its presence here, namely in the diction of an aged rustic character.

This traditional pastoral colouring of the first lines of the eclogue, largely secured by its demonstrably bucolic intertexts, is undermined by the model of Lycotas' formulation in vv. 1–2, concerning Corydon's non-presence in the 'green cabinet' for twenty days, *vicesima certe / nox fuit*[10]. As frequently and compellingly observed[11], the line is modelled on Theocr. 12.1: ἤλυθες, ὦ φίλε κοῦρε, τρίτῃ σὺν νυκτὶ καὶ ἠοῖ. This non–bucolic Theocritean idyll, which functions as the model of the Calpurnian formulation, seems to signal a Calpurnian 'generic deviation' from the earlier pastoral norm, since one of the principal means Calpurnius employs in order to suggest his 'generic transcendence' consists in intertextual references to non–pastoral poems of an otherwise well–known pastoral poet; this is the case here, since the pederastic *Id.* 12 does not belong to the close circle of the Theocritean bucolic poems. This non–pastoral intertextual reference is followed in Calp. 7 by several 'generically transcending turns' of the narrative plot.

Thus, whereas Corydon's intertextual double, Tityrus, comes back to the 'green cabinet' in order to continue his earlier pastoral life-style, with a sense of relief and gratitude for the divine youth to whom he owes his 'pastoral permanence' (cf. vv. 40–5), Corydon of Calp. 7 does not return gladly to his bucolic home, for he clearly rates his earlier rustic life too low in comparison to citylife and its spectacles. This is a clear inversion of Tityrus' objectives in the first Vergilian eclogue, where 'pastoral continuance' constitutes the *desideratum* of the main bucolic figure's endeavours, whereas the city is by no means sought after, but simply functions as the means for Tityrus to safeguard his bucolic identity, his immovability from the 'green cabinet'. Linguistic and stylistic similarities between Verg. *Ecl.* 1 and Calp. 7 further underline the above inversion of pre–Calpurnian pastoral values in the Calpurnian poem in question[12]. The adjective *lentus* introducing the Calpurnian eclogue (v. 1: *lentus ab urbe venis, Corydon*) is used in the sense of 'slow', *serus* (cf. Calp. 6.1: *serus ades, Lycida*, Mahr 1964, 42) denoting Corydon's reluctant return to his pastoral dwelling after spending

---

9 Cf. Kühner–Stegmann 1962, 362, Mahr 1964, 120, Vinchesi 2014, 481.
10 For a possible numerical symbolism here, cf. Vozza 1993, 297 and n. 50.
11 Cf. Korzeniewski 1971, 66, Di Salvo 1990, 72.
12 Cf. Garthwaite–Martin 2009, 311, 319.

twenty nights in Rome (vv. 1–2), whereas in the first Vergilian eclogue the adjective suggests typical pastoral values, i.e., describes Tityrus' ease in a distinct pastoral situation, i.e., when occupying himself with the bucolic occupation par excellence, the composition of pastoral song beneath the 'generic pastoral shade' (vv. 4–5: *tu, Tityre, lentus in umbra / formosam resonare doces Amaryllida silvas*)[13]. Both the wording and the image of the Calpurnian line in question (i.e., the picture of a rustic figure returning late to his pastoral home after a visit to the city) call to mind a Tibullan passage, namely 1.7.61–2: *te canet agricola, a magna cum venerit urbe / serus*[14]. But this Tibullan intertext constitutes a quasi–hymnic representation of Tibullus' patron, Messalla, and his accomplishments, on the occasion of his birthday. The narrative part in question deals with Messalla's funding of the restoration of a section of the *via Latina* from the Aquitanian triumph wealth[15]. Besides, the very motif of a journey to Rome to enjoy its pleasures has an obvious panegyric colouring, recalling as it does Prop. 4.1[16], where, as in Calp. 7, a distinction is drawn between the sumptuosity of the *urbs* Rome, on the one hand, and a poor pastoral landscape, on the other. Both these panegyric intertexts further build up the praising dimension of the Calpurnian account under discussion. This is also the case with yet another panegyric intertext, namely Prop. 2.31[17], where the poet is similarly presented as being delayed due to his prolonged stay in admiration of a splendid architectural construction of the emperor, the golden portico of Palatine Apollo; the poet has significantly attended its opening by Augustus (cf. vv. 1–2). Once again Nero and his amphitheatre are intertextually associated with Augustus and his imposing buildings.

Up to a point, the implications of the adjective *patulus* are similar; in Verg. *Ecl.* 1.1: *Tityre, tu patulae recubans sub tegmine fagi*[18], the word confirms once again time–honoured pastoral values, referring to the 'generic pastoral shade' and, what is more, to the hospitable shadow cast by the *fagus*, the emblematic tree of Vergilian bucolics, under which Tityrus engages in a characteristic pastoral occupation, namely lying at ease and enjoying the *otium*, the prerequisite for pastoral production of the Neoteric kind, the *otium poeticum* of the Neoteric va-

---

13 Cf. Newlands 1987, 219–20, Di Salvo 1990, 71, Martin 2003, 87–8, Mayer 2006, 460–1, Di Lorenzo–Pellegrino 2008, 269, Vinchesi 2010, 142–3; 2012, 718; 2014, 480.
14 Cf. Verdière 1954, 201, Korzeniewski 1971, 66, Di Salvo 1990, 71, Vinchesi 2014, 480–1.
15 Cf. Murgatroyd 1991, 208.
16 Cf. Di Salvo 1990, 99, Di Lorenzo–Pellegrino 2008, 280.
17 Cf. Vinchesi 2010, 141; 2014, 40–1.
18 Cf. Friedrich 1976, 249 and n. 25, Newlands 1987, 222, Di Salvo 1990, 77, Di Lorenzo–Pellegrino 2008, 271, Vinchesi 2010, 143; 2012, 718 and n. 67; 2014, 483.

cuus. At Calp. 7.6: *quae patula iuvenis deus edit harena, patulus* is, instead, used of the spacious arena of the city, extolling urban values which, furthermore, cause Tityrus' depreciation of his earlier pastoral life. What is more, the linguistic formulation (*quae tanta* + form of the verb *esse* + possessive dative + *causa* + genitive of the gerund complement) by means of which Tityrus is asked for the reason of his short visit to Rome (Verg. *Ecl.* 1.26: *et quae tanta fuit Romam tibi causa videndi?*) is in Calp. 7 associated with Corydon's intentional delay in the city, v. 7: *quae tanta foret tibi causa morandi*[19].

In vv. 4–6 Corydon reacts to Lycotas' initial remarks concerning his delayed return (vv. 1–3) and, without showing the proper respect a younger member ought to have shown towards an elder pastoral figure, at least according to the ethics of the earlier 'green cabinet' (cf. Verg. *Ecl.* 5.54–5)[20], he censures his interlocutor for preferring *veteres fagos* to the *nova spectacula* founded by the divine youth in the amphitheatre, i.e., for valuing traditional pastoral life above urban ideals and sights. On a poetological level, *veteres fagos* may produce further meaning in meta-poetic terms: apart from being a constituent feature of the pastoral landscape (cf. also Verg. *Ecl.* 3.12: *ad veteres fagos*[21]), *fagus* may also denote pastoral poetry of the Vergilian kind, for *fagus* is, as elsewhere demonstrated in detail (cf. Karakasis 2011, 189; see also Uden 2010, 211–2), a well-known symbol of Vergilian pastoral poetics. What is more, the adjective *vetus* qualifying the beech-tree (Calp. 7.5) may also function as a meta-linguistic term emphasising hallowed and long-established bucolic poetics of the Vergilian kind; in Verg. *Ecl.* 9.9[22] the adjective appears to have similar meta-poetic semantic properties, as *veteres fagos* once again, with broken tops in this case, also seem to stand for traditional pastoral poetics of the bucolic ἀσυχία deconstructed by the intrusion, in the case of Roman pastoral, of contemporary history in the otherwise literary discourse of the largely a-historical Greek pastoral. Thus *veteres fagos* may also

---

19 Cesareo 1931, 99 and n. 1 reads here (v. 7: *mirabar, quae tanta foret tibi causa morandi*) a contamination of Verg. *Ecl.* 1.36: *mirabar, quid...* with Verg. *Ecl.* 1.26: *et quae tanta fuit Romam tibi causa videndi?*; see also Verdière 1954, 262, Korzeniewski 1971, 67, Messina 1975, 91, Friedrich 1976, 248 and n. 23, Hubbard 1998, 176, Di Lorenzo-Pellegrino 2008, 271–2. Yet the construction of *mirari* with an indirect question as its complement is a common enough syntactical option (cf. OLD s.v. 2c) and, therefore, may not necessarily be modelled on the Vergilian instance adduced.
20 Cf. Newlands 1987, 220, Vinchesi 2012, 717–8 and n. 62.
21 Cf. Verdière 1954, 201, Korzeniewski 1971, 67, Newlands 1987, 221, Di Salvo 1990, 76, Keene 1996, 145, Vinchesi 1996, 26 and n. 38; 2010, 143; 2014, 482, Hubbard 1998, 176, Mayer 2006, 461, Di Lorenzo-Pellegrino 2008, 271.
22 Cf. also Leach 1973, 78, Newlands 1987, 221, Martin 2003, 88, Vinchesi 2010, 143; 2012, 718 and n. 65; 2014, 482.

suggest in the Calpurnian instance earlier pastoral poetry, in opposition to its Neronian evolution with its clear panegyric colouring, as evidenced by Calp. 7 as well, with its praise of the emperor and his public shows[23]. This polarity between old and new with perceptible poetological dimensions may also be found in the ninth Vergilian eclogue (cf. Karakasis 2011, 202–3): in the fragmented song of vv. 46–50, Daphnis is asked to turn a blind eye to the ancient stars (v. 46: *antiquos signorum…ortus*) symbolising the old pastoral ways, in favour of the new star of the deified Caesar (v. 47: *Dionaei…Caesaris astrum*), which stands for a new diversified Roman pastoral intermingled with georgics and politics, much more than the earlier Greek pastoral production. Similarly, Calpurnius is in Calp. 7 distancing himself from older pastoral models, as symbolised by the *veteres fagos*, and is following new poetic directions, as suggested by the *nova spectacula*, by adopting the new pastoral trends imposed by the period and its main marker, the panegyric of the emperor; the strong metrical position of *nova* after the caesura in v. 5, as Newlands 1987, 221 compellingly claims[24], also points to the importance of the new poetic discourse to be followed.

Thus Lycotas, i.e., the defender of the earlier 'green cabinet' and its virtues, the promoter of traditional pastoral poetry, that is of a poetic *genus* aspiring to Callimachean–Neoteric poetological ideals, at least up to the Neronian period, is credited by Corydon with anti-Neoteric / non-Callimachean meta-linguistic properties: he is characterised as unbending (*non mollis*), as a hard (*durus*) axle (v. 4: *o duro non mollior axe, Lycota*). In a striking reversal, the blame attributed to Lycotas for preferring, according to Corydon's initial impression anyway, traditional pastoralism, and for rating the spectacles of the arena and, within the poetological context in question, also the rather non-Neoteric poetic discourse praising such urban events, lower than the pastoral community and its Neoteric poetry is expressed by means of non-Callimachean catch-words. Once again this points to the blurred use of Callimachean meta-linguistic signs in post-Vergilian pastoral and further complements the sense of inversion of earlier bucolic trends and directions in accordance with the poetic taste of the Neronian era (cf. above, pp. 6, 10–11, 42–3, 46, 78–81, 86).

A series of counter-bucolic situations resulting from Corydon's tarrying in the city and his absence from the pastoral landscape are described in vv. 7 ff. Corydon's *fistula* is crucially described as idle (v. 8: *cur tua cessaret…fistula*), evoking Aegon's pastoral pipe in the fourth Theocritean idyll, which is spotted with mil-

---

[23] Cf. also Friedrich 1976, 157–8; see also Vinchesi 2014, 482.
[24] Cf. also Vinchesi 2002, 150 and n. 46; 2012, 718 and n. 66; 2014, 482.

dew (vv. 26–8), also due to lack of use[25], for Aegon had similarly deserted the pastoral space and its activities for the spectacles of Olympic games. In other words, the pre-Calpurnian pastoral occupation par excellence is, in Calp. 7, rejected in favour of Rome's *spectacula* and the equally time-honoured pastoral pleasure of *listening to* bucolic song is replaced by the urban delight of practically *viewing* the rich amphitheatre, as earlier pastoral simplicity and frugality gives way to urban opulence. The woods, accordingly, become silent (v. 8: *taciturnis... silvis*), contrasting with the 'generic prerequisite' of the pre-Calpurnian sonorous bucolic landscape, full of natural noises and song (cf. Chapter 2, p. 73). As already pointed out elsewhere (cf. Karakasis 2011, 199), silence, even in Vergilian pastoral, is associated with situations eliminating traditional pastoral voice, as is for example the case of the ninth Vergilian eclogue (cf. v. 37), where land confiscations bring about a blemished pastoral landscape, loss of pastoral memory and customary pastoral song as well as changed circumstances as far as the production of bucolic song is concerned. In a similar vein, as also demonstrated in detail in the previous Chapter (cf. pp. 50–1), analogous instances of a silent pastoral landscape have been read as disruptions of traditional pastoral order in the Calpurnian corpus as well, as signs of the pastoral poet's 'generic distanciation' from standards of the earlier bucolic tradition and its penchant for a resonant nature, cf. Calp. 4.1–4, 97–8, 108, 111[26], etc. The image of the lone singer Stimicon in v. 9 (*et solus Stimicon caneret pallente corymbo*) constitutes a further contravention of earlier pastoral habits. Pastoral song, as again already observed elsewhere (cf. Karakasis 2011, 18; see also Chapter 2, pp. 55–6 and n. 39), is usually the outcome of 'convening', that is of the coming together of two or more pastoral singers, in terms of either an agonistic or simply a friendly exchange. Instances of lone singers, as the goatherd and the Cyclops in the third and the eleventh Theocritean idyll respectively as well as Corydon and Moeris in the second and the ninth Vergilian eclogue, have long been read as deviations from the pastoral norm[27]. Because of Corydon's trip to Rome, Stimicon cannot engage in a singing match with a prominent pastoral singer, like the one Corydon appears to be, and thus, due to lack of a competent rival, Stimicon is offered the prizes of the bucolic contest, namely a tender kid (vv. 9–10)[28]. In this way, the typology of a long-established song-exchange, a key-element of traditional bucolic song, is

---

25 Cf. Di Salvo 1990, 78.
26 Cf. Di Salvo 1990, 78–9.
27 Cf. Karakasis 2011, 200–1; see also Hunter 1999, 234.
28 Cf. also Di Salvo 1990, 79, Di Lorenzo-Pellegrino 2008, 272, Hulsenboom 2013, 25, Vinchesi 2014, 484.

totally deconstructed. Stimicon is also described as decked with pale ivy, v. 9: *pallente corymbo*, i.e., by means of a linguistic syntagm associated in pre-Calpurnian bucolics with the ecphrasis of the marvellous cup of Theocr. 1 (cf. vv. 29–31) and the *fagina pocula* in Verg. *Ecl.* 3 (cf. v. 39: *diffusos hedera vestit pallente corymbos*)[29], namely with the pastoral artifacts symbolising and objectifying the quality of pastoral poetic production. This linguistic combination associated with emblematic values of the 'green cabinet' is, in the Calpurnian instance, attributed to the non-pastoral situation of the lone singer Stimicon. All these situations brought about by Corydon's urban preferences are moreover given as a foil to a pure traditional pastoral image, further emphasising Corydon's transcending the long-established pastoral beaten track; the counterpoint is Tityrus' agricultural and pastoral occupations, i.e., the purification of the pen (*lustratio*) and the young herdsmen's bucolic singing matches (vv. 11–2)[30]. The term used for describing Corydon's period of absence, during which Tityrus' bucolic tasks went on, is crucially once again *lentus* (v. 11: *dum lentus abes*), but without the semantic load of the pastoral ease as in the case of Tityrus of the first Vergilian eclogue (cf. v. 4). Similarity of diction once again signals the changed circumstances of the Calpurnian eclogue.

Despite Lycotas' remarks concerning Corydon's bucolic competitor, Stimicon, and the latter's pastoral victory, in an effort to awaken Corydon's competitiveness, a well-known technique in the traditional pastoral community (cf. e.g. Theocr. 5, Verg. *Ecl.* 3, 5, 7), Corydon is so deeply affected by what he has experienced in the city (v. 18: *quae spectavimus urbe*) that his outlook towards the basic values of the bucolic world is disdainful. He appears indifferent to his rival's pastoral victories and the wealth of the prizes won, were it even as much as the whole of the pens purified by Thyrsis or the herds of proverbial quality from the Lucanian woods (vv. 13–8, cf. also Hor. *Epod.* 1.27–8, *Epist.* 2.2.177–8[31]). Pastoral wealth holds no charm for him; he is instead ecstatic in the face of urban imperial affluence. A further detail attesting to Corydon's 'flawed pastoral identity', as the result of the influence of the *urbs* and its attractions, comes from the

---

[29] Cf. Cesareo 1931, 100 and n. 2, Verdière 1954, 263, Castiglioni 1955, 21, Korzeniewski 1971, 67, Di Salvo 1990, 80, Amat 1991, 119, Keene 1996, 145, Di Lorenzo–Pellegrino 2008, 272, Hulsenboom 2013, 25, Vinchesi 2014, 484.

[30] For a reference to the *Parilia / Palilia* here, cf. Duff and Duff 1934, 278, Verdière 1966, 167, Friedrich 1976, 248 and n. 19, Champlin 1978, 107 (of 224 AD), Newlands 1987, 227, Di Salvo 1990, 82, Kegel-Brinkgreve 1990, 163, Amat 1991, 61, 119, Keene 1996, 146, Vinchesi 1996, 149; 2010, 146; 2014, 485.

[31] Cf. Di Salvo 1990, 83–4, Vinchesi 1996, 151; 2014, 486, Di Lorenzo–Pellegrino 2008, 274. For a cryptic reference here to the *Silvae* of Lucan, cf. Herrmann 1952, 35, Verdière 1954, 202, Ahl 1984, 68.

use of *dives* in vv. 13–4: *praemia dives auferat*. The pastoral singer of the bucolic tradition is certainly interested in the quality and the quantity of the pledges he wins in a bucolic song, but only as tokens of his singing / piping excellence and not as means of growing rich. This last concern constitutes an obvious materialistic value, and profit of this kind is either unknown to earlier pastoral or has been rightly read as a sign of 'generic deviation' towards other literary genres (e.g. Tityrus' comic interest for securing money, an objective not fulfilled due to the spendthrift Galatea in Verg. *Ecl.* 1 (vv. 31–5), or even Corydon's rather georgic concern for profit, opposing the utmost pastoral value, i.e., producing pastoral song, in Calp. 4.23–8; see Chapter 2, pp. 58–9). In this case, Corydon's pregnant use of the adjective with reference to his rival, Stimicon, although in negative statements proving Corydon's lack of interest in his rival's wealth, also betrays a diversified pastoral value system in the bucolic world of Calp. 7.

Even Lycotas, the representative of old time pastoral ideals, is eager to listen to Corydon's panegyrical poetic account of the Neronian amphitheatre and its shows, i.e., not to a usual pastoral narrative, but to an account associated with the city and its poetic discourses. However, this agent of traditional pastoralism does not refrain from assigning customary Callimachean–Neoteric metalinguistic signs and catch-words of the earlier, pre-Calpurnian pastoral norm to the expected panegyrical poetic account related to the *urbs* and its interests. Corydon's narrative is thus anticipated to be sweet (v. 20: *mihi dulce loquere*), i.e., to possess the well-known Callimachean–Neoteric poetological attribute of sweetness, characterising the Callimachean profile of pastoral poetry from Theocritus onwards (cf. e.g. Theocr. 1.1–3, 7.51, Bion fr. 3, Verg. *Ecl.* 5.47)[32]; this quality is, however, here crucially transferred to a non-Callimachean panegyric account. What is more, the sweetness of this panegyric is equated with the *dulcitas* one may experience from listening to traditional pastoral song, i.e., the bucolic songs performed during ritual ceremonies, where invocations to two distinct pastoral deities, namely *pastoralis* / νόμιος Apollo and Pales, take place ((vv. 20–2), cf. also Verg. *Ecl.* 5.35)[33]. What is more, Lycotas notably asks Corydon not to be envious, i.e., not possess the very meta-linguistic attribute of non-Callimachean poetic production, and thus to continue with his epic-style account of un-Callimachean properties (vv. 19–20: *nec nostras invidus aures / despice*, see also below, pp. 108–10). The singer is thus asked to be freed from meta-poetic qualities which characterise the poetic norm in which he is about to perform.

---

[32] Cf. also Di Salvo 1990, 86–7, Di Lorenzo–Pellegrino 2008, 274.
[33] Cf. Verdière 1954, 203, Korzeniewski 1971, 68–9, 108, Di Salvo 1990, 87–8, Vinchesi 1996, 151; 2014, 487, Di Lorenzo–Pellegrino 2008, 274–5.

Theocr. 15 is yet another basic intertext of Calp. 7. The panegyric colouring of the poem is thus further enhanced by its intertextual association with the similar panegyric narrative of the fifteenth Theocritean urban mime (for Theocr. 15 as an intertext of Calp. 7, cf. also Newlands 1987, 228–9, Kegel-Brinkgreve 1990, 163, Amat 1991, xxxi, Magnelli 2006, 467, Monella 2009, 83–4, Hutchinson 2013, 311 and n. 37); several narrative patterns and details clearly witness the intertextual relationship between the two texts. In both cases there is a movement from periphery to centre; in the case of Theocr. 15 it is about the transfer of Gorgo and Praxinoa from Syracuse to the town of Alexandria, whereas a similar progress also occurs in the case of Corydon in Calp. 7, who travels from *rus* to *urbs*. Furthermore, in both instances a spectacle gives the characters of the narrative the opportunity to spend some days off; thus in Theocr. 15, the two ladies visit the royal residence, where an Adonis festival is staged by Arsinoe in honour of her mother, Berenice. Similarly Corydon has his twenty days off in the city in order to enjoy the amphitheatre shows. A contrast between the 'straitened circumstances' (a term of Hunter, adopted from Verity (Hunter) 2002, 104) of the Syracusan women and Corydon, on the one hand, and the sumptuous royal palace and the lavish amphitheatre, on the other, is a further common feature in both encomiastic narratives. Another common feature is the fact that an ecphasis of a work of art constitutes the focus of both accounts, of the amphitheatre and its spectacles in Calp. 7 and of the tapestries in Theocr. 15. The narrative device of the 'figure interrupting the characters' state of astonishment' constitutes a further link between the texts; in Calp. 7 (vv. 40–6) it is the urban old man who comments upon Corydon's amazement and informs him of the continuous improvement of the imperial show industry, which has the power to amaze even experienced city residents, while in Theocritus it is the unidentified figure reprimanding the Syracusans' prolixity in vv. 87–8. Finally, the two works share the common feature of emphasis on a piece of clothing, a brooch in the case of Corydon (vv. 81–2) and a pleated garment with agraffes in the case of Praxinoa (vv. 34–5). As already remarked (cf. p. 89), Calpurnius occasionally suggests his 'generic transcendence' towards non-pastoral discourses by imitating the non-bucolic works of an otherwise pastoral poet. This technique is followed here through the intertext of the non-pastoral Theocritean idyll 15.

The Ecphrasis

The ecphrasis begins in v. 23. This is the longest ecphrastic piece in Roman pastoral, running for 50 lines, namely vv. 23–72. It is divided in two main parts[34], a *descriptio loci* in vv. 23–56, where an account of the wooden amphitheatre erected by Nero in 57 AD at Campus Martius (cf. also Suet. *Ner.* 12.2, Tac. *Ann.* 13.31.1) is given[35], and a report of the amphitheatre shows (including the animal exhibition), in all probability the *munus* of 57 AD, at vv. 57–72 (cf. Suet. *Ner.* 12.1)[36]. Ecphrastic pieces of this kind and length are not characteristic of the pastoral genre, but belong instead to the epic and / or epicising 'generic tradition'; when occurring in pre-Calpurnian pastoral, ecphrases (e.g. the κισσύβιον of the first Theocritean idyll (vv. 27–56, out of 152 lines) or the *fagina pocula* of the third Vergilian eclogue (vv. 36–47, out of 111 verses)) cover much shorter textual space than in Calp. 7, where the narrative segment in question covers 50 out of 84 lines in total[37]. This narrative device rather belongs to the *genus grande*[38]

---

34 Cf. Di Lorenzo–Pellegrino 2008, 275, Vinchesi 2010, 148; 2014, 477–8.
35 Cf. e.g. Duff and Duff 1934, 280, Di Lorenzo–Pellegrino 2008, 276, Vinchesi 2012, 718 and n. 68; 2014, 487 vs. Baldwin 1995, 160–2.
36 Cf. Gnilka 1974, 124, Messina 1975, 89–90, Townend 1980, 169–73, Fugmann 1992, 204, Fear 1993, 43, Fantham 1996, 161, Keene 1996, 197–203, Schubert 1998, 75, Spencer 2005, 46, Green 2009, 55 and n. 2. Verdière 1966, 166–7 (see also 1954, 39), Di Salvo 1990, 29, 32, 130–3 are of the view that the spectacles described are of a slightly later date, suggesting the spring of 58 AD – probably as part of the *Ludi Florales*, as Di Salvo argues in some detail; see also Romano 1980–1, 245–6, Kegel-Brinkgreve 1990, 163 (*Palilia* of 59 AD), Vinchesi 1996, 25 and n. 36; 2014, 30, 480, Mayer 2006, 456 and n. 11. On the basis of vv. 26–9 and Tac. *Ann.* 15.32 (cf. also Suet. *Ner.* 11.1, Plin. *Nat.* 8.21) speaking of Nero's assigning different seats to the knights and the plebs in 63 AD, it has been proposed a date after 63 AD, cf. Latte 1932, 268, Luiselli 1960, 152, Bardon 1968, 243; see also Hubaux 1930, 29–30, Champlin 1986, 110–11, Horsfall 1997, 169. However, for a criticism of this thesis with some justification (Calp. 7 a) refers to non-reserved posts (*libera...loca*, vv. 28–9) and b) mentions the amphitheatre and not the circus unlike Tacitus, cf. *apud circum*, *Ann.* 15.32.3), cf. especially Momigliano 1944, 97–9, Verdière 1954, 39; see also Mahr 1964, 14–6, Scheda 1969, 62–5, Spadaro 1969, 41–7, Amat 1991, 119–20, Fugmann 1992, 206, Mayer 2006, 455, Vinchesi 2014, 490–1. A suggestion for a third century show (cf. Champlin 1978, 107) is not compelling, nor are there any conclusive grounds for viewing this amphitheatre as the Colosseum (cf. Chastagnol 1976, 82); for the Flavian Colosseum here, cf. also Hubbard 1998, 176 and n. 55, whereas for a show in the period of Gordian I, a claim based on the lack of evidence, in the age of Nero, for exhibitions of polar animals, as suggested by vv. 65–6 referring to the *ursus maritimus*, cf. Jennison 1922, 73.
37 Cf. also Effe–Binder 1989, 125.
38 Cf. also Küppers 1989, 42 and n. 29, Vozza 1993, 299 and n. 58.

and thus proves once again the branching out of Calpurnian pastoral towards alternative poetic discourses.

Several traditional pastoral 'generic constituents' / 'cornerstones' are consequently inverted in the narrative part under discussion as well; as already seen above (cf. pp. 90–1), the pathetic fallacy–motif is, in the present eclogue, used as a means for stressing Corydon's desire to prolong his visit to the city, charmed by its attractions (cf. vv. 1–3). In a similar vein, other 'generic cornerstones' of the bucolic tradition as well are associated with situations opposing earlier pastoral habits, values and qualities. A distinct pre–Calpurnian pastoral marker is the construction of a *locus amoenus* (shadowy trees, cool waters, and natural sounds) as the place of a harmonious interaction between man and nature, as the location where pastoral song is produced, also attesting, by its supreme poetic quality, to the pleasures of this pastoral landscape, functioning, in its turn, as the prerequisite for the genesis of bucolic song. This generic *locus amoenus*, from which pastoral inhabitants derive pleasure, has been substituted in Calp. 7 by the very urban amphitheatre and its games[39]; the latter fascinate Corydon and lead him to the composition of a panegyric poetic account of these urban delights, having nothing to do with both earlier pastoral enjoyment and bucolic poetic norm. However, this urban amphitheatre – *locus amoenus* is crucially described by means of bucolic similes, whereby the wooden edifice and its features are related to common pastoral images, showing, in part at least, Corydon's inadequacy to cope with his new urban experience, but more importantly further inverting traditional pastoral features by means of their association with distinct urban qualities. Thus the curve of the amphitheatre, surrounding the level ground, is compared to a valley, which develops into an ample circuit and, by coiling at the side, extends its hollow curve among a continuous succession of hills (vv. 30–3). The image of the contiguous woods completes this pastoral imagery (v. 31: *resupinis undique silvis*). What is more, the amphitheatre is compared to an egg (v. 34), while the tusks, upon which the gold wire nets of the amphitheatre hang, are also described as longer than the agricultural plough (vv. 53–6, cf. v. 56 in particular: *nostro dens longior omnis aratro*); last but not least, the rustic narrator also describes the huge construction with reference to inclines and slopes (v. 25: *gradus et clivos lene iacentes*)[40].

---

39 Cf. also Hubbard 1998, 176.
40 Cf. also Cesareo 1931, 104, Verdière 1954, 207, Korzeniewski 1971, 109, Leach 1973, 80, Gnilka 1974, 131, Messina 1975, 93, Davis 1987, 48–9, Newlands 1987, 221–2, Di Salvo 1990, 33, 95–7, 114, Amat 1991, 62, Vinchesi 1992, 160–1; 1996, 27; 2010, 148, 150–2; 2014, 501, Keene 1996, 151, Green 2009, 59, Henderson 2013, 180, Baraz 2015, 113. Al-

The earlier, chiefly domestic pastoral fauna is substituted in Calp. 7 by the rare and wild animals of the arena, in line with the literary zoological interests of the period (cf. Lucan; see also Martial's *De Spectaculis*[41]); these wild animals, however, are referred to by means of familiar animal names and common animal qualifications of the traditional pastoral landscape[42]. This exotic fauna, materialising the Neronian aesthetic preferences for the so-called *locus horridus* (cf. Perutelli 1976, 785, 787, Gagliardi 1984, 66), provoking fear and inverting the Augustan *locus amoenus* (e.g. Erichtho's abode in Lucan, cf. 6.507 ff.[43]), includes: the *lepus variabilis* or *timidus* with its white skin (v. 58, cf. Var. *rust.* 3.12.6, Plin. *Nat.* 8.217, Ov. *Fast.* 5.371–2), here qualified as *niveus*, that is by means of an adjective normally qualifying 'pastoral' sheep (cf. Calp. 5.37; see also Tib. 2.5.38, etc.) and only here hare of this alpine kind[44], the *sus babirussa*[45], the 'African wart-hogs'[46] or even, less probably, the rhinoceros[47], animals unknown to earlier bucolic tradition, and alluded to here by means of a common pastoral designation, i.e., as boars equipped with horns (v. 58), the elk, i.e., a rare species of the pastoral deer (v. 59)[48], the humped bull, that is the zebu, the *bos Indicus* also described by way of a further pastoral qualification, *taurus* (vv. 60–1)[49], the shaggy *tauri*, namely the bison (vv. 61–3; cf. Mart. *Sp.* 23.4)[50],

---

though the last qualification, namely *clivus*, is a technical term as well (cf. ThLL III, 1357, 80), it also adds to the overall pastoral colouring of the presentation.
41 Cf. also Di Salvo 1990, 36–7.
42 Cf. also Messina 1975, 94, Perutelli 1976, 784, Gagliardi 1984, 66 and n. 58, Amat 1988, 85, Vinchesi 1996, 27; 2014, 478, Henderson 2013, 180.
43 Cf. also Castagna 2002, xvi; Vinchesi 2014, 478.
44 Cf. Verdière 1954, 264, Korzeniewski 1971, 109, Di Salvo 1990, 115, Amat 1991, 120, Keene 1996, 152, Vinchesi 1996, 155; 2014, 501.
45 Cf. Keller 1963, 405.
46 Cf. Toynbee 1973, 134; Di Salvo 1990, 116, Vinchesi 2014, 502.
47 Cf. De Sipio 1935, 217, Messina 1975, 94, Gagliardi 1984, 66 and n. 58; see also Di Salvo 1990, 115–6, Vinchesi 1996, 155; 2002, 150.
48 Cf. also Di Lorenzo-Pellegrino 2008, 282. Gnilka 1974, 124–47 is of the view that *hic raram...alcen* in v. 59 is the result of an interpolation, already in the archetype, for the original *mantichoram...alcen;* for a refutation of this thesis, cf. Korzeniewski 1976, 252–3; see also Verdière 1985, 1916–7, Di Salvo 1990, 116.
49 Cf. Verdière 1954, 207, Korzeniewski 1971, 110, Toynbee 1973, 148–9, Di Salvo 1990, 117, Vinchesi 2002, 151; 2014, 503.
50 Cf. Di Salvo 1990, 118, Coleman 2006, 192. De Sipio 1935, 217 reads in vv. 60–3 a range of bison species; see also Messina 1975, 94, Gagliardi 1984, 66 and n. 58, whereas Verdière 1954, 207, 264 is of the view that in the lines in question there is a reference to three different animals, namely the zebu (vv. 60–1), the Indian *bubalus* or alternative the urus (vv. 61–2), and the European bison (*bison bonasus*, vv. 62–3) and, in a similar vein, Amat 1991, 120–1 reads in the lines in question a mention of the zebu or the buffalo, the urus and the European

completing the list of the forest animals, crucially described as *monstra* (v. 64). This designation notably points to the rift between man and nature, uncharacteristic of the earlier pastoral tradition, for which pastoral animals are part of the everyday bucolic experience and can by no means described as monsters, i.e., by means of a qualification suggesting lack of familiarity[51].

The animal exhibition continues with marine fauna, probably in the context of a *naumachia*[52], beginning with the seal, normally rendered in Latin either as *phocae* or *vituli marini* (cf. Plin. *Nat.* 9.19)[53]; Calpurnius, following the naming pattern previously applied to woodland animals, employs a slight variation of the second designation which includes the pastoral term *vituli*, namely *aequorei vituli* (v. 65). The enumeration goes on with the polar bear (in all probability[54]), i.e., one more unknown species of an otherwise pastoral animal (cf. Theocr. 1.115, 11.41), which feeds on seals (vv. 65–6), and the hippopotamus (vv. 66–8)[55] also

---

bison vs. Toynbee 1973, 148–9, Korzeniewski 1971, 110 (*bos bison*), Di Salvo 1990, 118–9, Vinchesi 1996, 155; 2002, 151; 2014, 502–3, who see in vv. 61–3 the mention of the same animal, namely a bison. Duff and Duff 1934, 283 understand the humped bulls as standing for the buffalo, whereas the hairy ones as a circumlocution for the urus; see also Keene 1996, 152.

51 Cf. also Di Salvo 1990, 119.
52 Cf. Leach 1973, 83.
53 Cf. also Verdière 1954, 264, Keller 1963, 408 (*Phoca monachus*), Gnilka 1974, 134, Messina 1975, 94, Di Salvo 1990, 120, Amat 1991, 67, Fear 1993, 43–4, Keene 1996, 153, Vinchesi 1996, 156; 2014, 504. For the possible image of a walrus here, cf. Gnilka 1974, 135 and n. 10. Leach 1973, 81 is not right in claiming an *adynaton* in the above image of the *vituli* of the sea and the *equi* of the river.
54 Cf. Jennison 1922, 73; 1937, 188, Duff and Duff 1934, 283, Toynbee 1973, 94, Coleman 2006, 89 and n. 8; see also Keene 1996, 153 vs. Keller 1963, 180, who claims that polar bears were unknown in Roman antiquity and, therefore, appear for the first time in the work of the German medieval chronicler (11th century) Adamus Bremensis. Gnilka 1974, 134 sees here bears of the Lucanian woods, Townend 1980, 171 speaks of an African or Asian bear species forced to swim in the interests of a spectacle, while Di Salvo 1990, 30–1, 120–1, who offers a helpful overview of the *status quaestionis*, also argues that, if these were polar bears, the author would have not missed the opportunity to comment upon their white fur, as he does with the white hares of v. 58. Fear 1993, 43–5 also rules out the possibility of polar bears known in ancient Roman world; cf. also Fear 1994, 272 and n. 20, Vinchesi 2014, 505. But the issue here is not so much the species of the bear, as the image of the bear hunting the seal, i.e., a deconstruction, in urban terms, of one more activity of the pastoral tradition. Di Salvo 1990, 121 is of the view that the preposition *cum* in *cum certantibus ursis* (v. 65) is equivalent to *et*, et sim., as occasionally in enumerations (cf. also ThLL IV, 1377, 42, Vinchesi 2014, 504–5). *Cum*, however, seems to be used here in terms of the above image of a preying bear.
55 Cf. Cesareo 1931, 112, Verdière 1954, 209, Korzeniewski 1971, 110, Gnilka 1974, 134–5, Messina 1975, 94, Díaz–Cíntora 1989, xxvi, Di Salvo 1990, 122, Pearce 1990, 145, Amat 1991, 67, Keene 1996, 153, Vinchesi 1996, 156; 2002, 150–1; 2014, 505.

rendered, according to the naming pattern already pointed out (cf. pp. 98–100), as *equorum nomine dictum, sed deforme pecus* (vv. 66–7). Lastly, unspecified wild animals also form part of the amphitheatric show, vv. 69–71; however, whereas the *ferae* of the Vergilian pastoral world are well-integrated in the pastoral value system, enjoying the best thing this world has to offer, namely pastoral song (cf. Verg. *Ecl.* 6.27–8), in the present eclogue they simply function as elements of the panegyric discourse, i.e., of the emperor's encomium. They are presented as emerging out of a hole from the *hypogeum*[56], artificially brought onto the ground of the arena in order to astonish the spectators and add to the glorification of the emperor (vv. 69–71). The image seems to be modelled on Lucr. 5.780–820 (cf. Leach 1973, 82, 95–6 and n. 56), where in a similar way the first animate life is presented as emerging from the bowels of the earth; thus Lucretian allusions, frequently functioning as a marker of the Callimachean Neotericism of the *genus tenue*, at least in the meta-poetic discourse of the late Republican and the Augustan poetic production (cf. Karakasis 2011, 72), are also used here as part of Corydon's praising account. If what is in general described here is a *venatio* and not simply an enumeration or exhibition of wild and exotic animal life[57], we are faced with one more pastoral activity, i.e., an occupation sanctioned by earlier bucolics (cf. Verg. *Ecl.* 3.74–5), reduced to an amphitheatre show.

What is more, the artificial flora of the arena also seems to substitute the natural growth of the earlier 'green cabinet'; the arbutus, a common pastoral tree (cf. Theocr. 5.129, [Theocr.] 9.11, Verg. *Ecl.* 3.82), is now golden[58] as part of a fake garden constructed for the enjoyment of the audience (vv. 71–2), and, in line with the tastes of the period for collapsible stage mechanisms (cf. Sen. *Epist.* 88.22), it is brought onto the arena, in the midst of a saffron (in all probability[59]) fountain spray[60] (cf. also Mart. *Sp.* 21.3–4), most likely a *sparsio*

---

56 Cf. Coleman 1990, 52.
57 As argued by Di Salvo 1990, 131; 1991, 313; see also Gnilka 1974, 145. For Nero honoured as πότνιος θηρῶν, cf. Korzeniewski 1976, 251–2.
58 Cf. Duff and Duff 1934, 285, Leach 1973, 82, Newlands 1987, 223, Mackie 1989, 14, Di Salvo 1990, 128, Pearce 1990, 141, 145, Amat 1991, 67, Vinchesi 1996, 157; for *arbuta* (v. 72) as arbutus-trees with golden fruits in particular, cf. Verdière 1954, 209, Novelli 1980, 66. For an image of golden trees in general, cf. Korzeniewski 1971, 71, Messina 1975, 94, Champlin 1986, 110, whereas for trees with golden fruits, cf. Merone 1967, 40–3. For Newlands 1987, 223, the passage in question, and rightly so, may be seen as 'almost a parody of the idealized description of the rural setting that is conventional in pastoral poetry', i.e., again the *locus amoenus* with its basic constituent features, namely the shade of a tree and cool waters; see also Leach 1975, 222.
59 Cf. Horsfall 1997, 171, Vinchesi 2014, 507–8; see also Luck 1983, 234.

with a deodorant liquid, cf. e.g. Suet. *Ner.* 31.2, Sen. *Epist.* 90.15[61]. The artificial aspects of the urban landscape (as against the constitutional naturalness of the country-side) also align well with the 'artificiality cult', fashionable with visual arts in imperial Rome (artificial gardens, painted landscapes, grottoes like the one in Calp. 6; see Chapter 7, pp. 241–2); Ovidian poetry, a main model of the Calpurnian bucolics (cf. Chapter 2, p. 78), is also influenced by this artistic trend[62] and, thus, signs of an 'artificiality cult' in Calpurnius may also be read as the result of Ovidian influence.

Both the image of the golden arbutus-trees and the sense of an automatism suggested by the quasi-magic springing up of the artificial garden may evoke the gifts of a Golden Age (cf. Newlands 1987, 222–3 and n. 14); this impression is strengthened by the golden constructions of the amphitheatre (cf. vv. 41, 47–8, 53–4, 72)[63]. However, whereas the imagery of the *Aetas Aurea* is associated in the Vergilian meta-language with the poetological supremacy of 'New Poetry' (cf. Papanghelis 1995, 257–307, Chapter 1, pp. 42–3, 47), in Calp. 7, yet again, this pastoral motif is inverted and thus linked with forms of poetic composition, not derived from the Callimachean-Neoteric poetics and aestheticism. Pastoral meta-poetics is normally about the art of bucolic poetic discourse; Calp. 7, however, is about the art of the amphitheatre (its construction as well as the various *munera* it abounds in) and, consequently, about the poetic art of such panegyric accounts.

A further deconstructed signpost of the earlier bucolic *genus* has to do with its competitive character; as already remarked (cf. Karakasis 2011), singing matches belong to the heart of the bucolic tradition (cf. Theocr. 5, 6, 7, [Theocr.] 8, 9, Verg. *Ecl.* 3, 5, 7, 8, Calp. 2, 4, 6) and, what is more, in several cases a harsh initial hostility is eventually resolved through a song-exchange (cf. Theocr. 5, Verg. *Ecl.* 3). This sense of competing is in the present Calpurnian eclogue, as already noted in the case of the framing introduction (cf. pp. 92–4), either presented simply as a foil to Corydon's indifference to long-established standards of pastoral life or incompletely functioning in the case of the lone singer Stimicon without Corydon as his singing rival (cf. vv. 9–12). This notion of competing also appears in the narrative segment of the amphitheatre description; but this time, it is no longer the pleasure of *listening* to pastoral song that matters, but the joy of *viewing* the magnificence of the amphitheatre's furnishings (cf. p. 93). The gemmed belt vies in luminosity with the arcade covered with gold (vv. 47–8);

---

60 Cf. Duff and Duff 1934, 285, Newlands 1987, 222, Di Salvo 1990, 129–30.
61 Cf. also Di Salvo 1990, 129–30; 1991, 314, Vinchesi 2014, 507–8.
62 Cf. Barchiesi 2005, CLI-CLVI, Vinchesi 2014, 460.
63 Cf. also Ahl 1984, 69, Fugmann 1992, 204–6, Schubert 1998, 81, Merfeld 1999, 98, 100.

note also that it is the very adverb *certatim* (v. 48: *certatim radiant*) that signals this competition, i.e., a cognate word of the verb *certare* denoting, as a technical term, the singing match of the bucolic genre (cf. e.g. Calp. 2.19)⁶⁴. Another time-honoured pastoral characteristic consists in the use of proverbial expressions involving competing animals, in order to suggest difference in musical or poetic qualities, cf. Verg. *Ecl*. 8.55: *certent et cycnis ululae*. In Calp. 7 seals are presented as competing with polar bears, vv. 65–6, but no poetological dimension is to be discerned here. The bears are simply preying on the seals (cf. vv. 65–6: *aequoreos ego cum certantibus ursis / spectavi vitulos* – note here once again the *terminus technicus certare*) in the spirit of the bloodthirsty customs of the arena, despite the fact that it is at the very shows of 57 AD that Nero explicitly forbade cruelties resulting in the murder of humans (cf. Suet. *Ner*. 12.1), as far as the *gladiatorum munus* of the event (57 AD) is concerned⁶⁵.

What is more, the agonistic or friendly song-exchange of the pastoral tradition, a central bucolic 'generic motif', is, as already mentioned (cf. p. 93), the outcome of the 'convening process', i.e., the coming together of two pastoral figures, resulting in either a pastoral conversation or a bucolic song-exchange (cf. Theocr. 5, Verg. *Ecl*. 1). 'Convening' is again here employed as a panegyric means; an elder figure (cf. vv. 43–4: *en ego iam tremulus iam vertice canus et ista / factus in urbe senex stupeo tamen omnia*), as often one of the 'convening' pastoral characters (cf. also Verg. *Ecl*. 5.4), interacts in vv. 40–6⁶⁶ with the younger Corydon, in a form of a conversation without any particular bucolic connotations. Instead the elder urban figure stresses here the magnificence of the Neronian amphitheatre and its shows, by comparing it with all similar experiences he has had in the past. Thus the astonishment a pastoral figure experiences is further backed up by the amazement an experienced urban figure feels in front of the Neronian accomplishment⁶⁷. A parallel situation seems to develop at Ov. *Fast*. 4.377–

---

64 Cf. Di Salvo 1990, 82.
65 The lack of any description of the gladiatorial games in Calp. 7 may be read as a conscious choice on Calpurnius' part, in order to ephasise imperial clemency (cf. also Chapter 1, pp. 37, 40–1); see also Fear 1994, 270.
66 Cf. Duff and Duff 1934, 280, Vozza 1993, 300, Vinchesi 2014, 496. Gnilka 1974, 132 and Schubert 1998, 78 claim that the speech of the urban elder figure ends with line 55a, whereas Verdière 1954, 204 and Korzeniewski 1971, 68 are of the view that the part of the *senex* ends with v. 44 after *certe*, whereas Di Salvo 1990, 58 (see also pp. 102–3; 1991, 313–4) makes the speech of the elder character end in v. 44 after *tamen omnia*, constructing *certe* in enjambment with the following *vidimus* (v. 46).
67 Cf. also Gnilka 1974, 132, Vozza 1993, 300.

86[68]; once again an old man, a veteran military tribune under Ceasar's command, sitting next to the poet during a festival, namely at the circus games for the *Ludi Megalenses*, embarks on a panegyric account, i.e., Caesar's victory at Thapsus (46 BC); the celebratory character of the intertext further increases the panegyric nature of the receiving Calpurnian passage, intertextually associating Nero with the adoptive father of his imperial model, Augustus. Pastoral techniques and intertextual poetics are once more put into the service of the imperial panegyrics (cf. Chapters 1, 2, pp. 15–86).

Linguistic assimilation of the *genus grande* further enhances the 'generic deviation' from the earlier pastoral norm and a branching out towards non–pastoral discourses; thus the syntagm *aperto...caelo* in v. 28 has a Vergilian epic colour (cf. *A.* 1.155, 8.523)[69], and so does the intransitive *sufficere* construed with the infinitive in the sense of 'to have sufficient capacity' in vv. 35–6 (*suffecimus...spectare*, cf. *A.* 5.21–2, OLD s.v. B. 4b; see also Luc. 5.153–5, Stat. *Th.* 7.379–80[70]), the combination of *balteus* and *gemma*, in v. 47 (cf. *A.* 5.312–3)[71], and of *torus* with *cervix* (vv. 60–1) as in both Verg. *A.* 12.6–7 and Luc. 2.604–5[72]; the syntagm *mento / barba iacet* in vv. 62–3 also recalls Verg. *A.* 6.299–300: *cui plurima mento / canities inculta iacet*[73]. Moreover, the *iunctura* consisting in *nomine* and forms of the verb *dicere*, *dictum* in v. 66, as a final *clausula*, also has an epic ring, appearing several times in both the Vergilian epic (cf. *A.* 3.210, 6.441, 7.607, 9.387) and in the 'generically flexible', but epic hosting account of the Ovidian *Metamorphoses* (cf. e.g. *Met.* 1.447, 2.840, 5.411, 10.644)[74]. Epic is also the model for the description of the valley in vv. 30–4, fashioned, in all probability, after Verg. *A.* 5.286–9, 11.522–9[75].

On the level of poetic meta–language, traditional terms, notions and catchwords denoting aesthetic and poetological sensibilities of the *genus grande* are

---

68 Cf. Verdière 1954, 205, Korzeniewski 1971, 69, Di Salvo 1990, 99, Keene 1996, 149, Di Lorenzo–Pellegrino 2008, 280, Fucecchi 2009, 53, La Bua 2010, 244 and. n. 30, Vinchesi 2010, 153; 2012, 719–20; 2014, 41–2, 494.
69 Cf. Di Lorenzo–Pellegrino 2008, 277, Vinchesi 2014, 490.
70 Cf. Di Salvo 1990, 98, Keene 1996, 148, Di Lorenzo–Pellegrino 2008, 279, Vinchesi 2014, 493.
71 Cf. Di Lorenzo–Pellegrino 2008, 281, Vinchesi 2014, 497.
72 Cf. also Di Salvo 1990, 118, Vinchesi 2014, 503.
73 Cf. Korzeniewski 1971, 71, Martin 2003, 89, Di Lorenzo–Pellegrino 2008, 282, Vinchesi 2014, 504.
74 Cf. Korzeniewski 1971, 71, Di Salvo 1990, 122, Di Lorenzo–Pellegrino 2008, 283, Vinchesi 2014, 505.
75 Cf. Korzeniewski 1971, 69, Di Lorenzo –Pellegrino 2008, 278, Green 2009, 59–60, Vinchesi 2014, 491.

in Calp. 7 positively presented; poetic meta-language is used to stress both the quality of the amphitheatre's construction and, consequently, of the poetry praising such architectural excellence. So the weaving imagery, as suggested by the verb *texere* in v. 23, emphasises the quality of the construction and – in self-reflexive terms – Corydon's panegyric poetic account; on the contrary, in the earlier pastoral tradition such meta-poetic signs are used for suggesting, on the level of poetics, the production of Callimachean–Neoteric pastoral poetry (cf. e.g. the image of the boy weaving cricket traps in the κισσύβιον of the first Theocritean idyll (vv. 52–4), standing as an emblem of the pastoral poet himself and its pastoral poetic art, or the poet weaving a basket of supple willow, that is yet again bucolic poetry of Callimachean orientation, at the end of Vergil's tenth eclogue, v. 71: *gracili fiscellam texit hibisco*; cf. also Nemes. 1.1–8). In the same vein, another meta-linguistic catch term, found elsewhere in pastoral, *teres* (cf. Verg. *Ecl.* 8.16, Karakasis 2011, 131–2; see also above pp. 42, 46, 78–9 and n. 166), is, in Calp. 7, simply used of an axle, upon which a cylinder slides, as part of a mechanism preventing the animals of the arena from assaulting the audience (vv. 51–3)[76], and significantly so, in narrative terms, as part of the poetic discourse having as its aim to secure the emperor's praise. What is more, the notion of 'big', 'large', plainly censured by Callimachean poetics and negatively presented in the meta-poetic discourse of Neoteric poetry (cf. Karakasis 2011, 76–7), is in Calp. 7 positively coloured: the amphitheatre rises to the sky and hence nearly looks down on the Tarpeian peak (the top of the Capitoline, vv. 23–4); the vast size of the structure is brought to the fore through a bird's eye view, favoured in painting, hence also in Ovid[77]; the height of the amphitheatre is thus given through a glance from its peak down to the top of the Capitoline. What is more the steps of the auditorium are immense (v. 25)[78], the wooden

---

[76] Cf. also Townend 1980, 171 ff. vs. Chastagnol 1976, 81–2 and Champlin 1978, 96–7, who understand the mechanism as *cochleae*, used in the *venationes* of the amphitheatre for the protection of the *bestiarii*, from the second half of the fourth century; see also Luck 1983, 234, Di Salvo 1990, 111–2, Pearce 1990, 145, Keene 1996, 150, Vinchesi 2014, 498–9.
[77] Cf. Barchiesi 2005, CLIII.
[78] I accept here the reading *immensosque*, i.e., the one given by the codd. and not *emensique*, i.e., Schrader's correction, also accepted by Duff and Duff 1934, 280. The reading of the transmission does not present any linguistic or metrical problems, nor is it problematic as to the hermeneutics of the passage and, therefore, I do not see any reason for rejecting it. Cf. also Korzeniewski 1971, 109, Di Salvo 1990, 91, Keene 1996, 147, Di Lorenzo-Pellegrino 2008, 276, Vinchesi 2010, 150; 2014, 488–9. The adjective does not occur in the Vergilian pastoral; it is found, however, in both Vergil's *Georgics* (cf. 1.29, 49, etc.) and the *Aeneid* (cf. 2.185, 3.672, etc.). Thus, its appearance here may also be read as a further linguistic sign of Calpurnius' 'generic orientation' towards the *genus grande*.

structure is an oval formation enclosed by two *moles* (cf. also Tac. *Ann.* 13.31.1), denoting the largeness of a bulky construction (v. 34)[79], etc. As a general rule, emphasis is laid throughout the ecphrasis on both the enormity of the construction and its wealth (cf. also the specific mention here of precious stones and gold – v. 47, marble – v. 49 and ivory – v. 50). Therefore, as already pointed out above (cf. pp. 93, 102), the interest shifts from the *listening* delights of the pastoral song to the *viewing* pleasures of the amphitheatre and the shows it offers and, accordingly, an emphasis on vision is manifest in the poem under discussion, where a series of verbs of viewing (*videre* – vv. 23, 46, 57, 60, 70, 80, *cernere* – vv. 2, 6, 64, 76, *mirari* – v. 38, *spectare* – vv. 18, 27, 36, 46, 66, *notare* – v. 77, *conspicere* – v. 82)[80] testifies to this change of tastes.

Green 2009, 60–3 is right in highlighting Calpurnius' description of the amphitheatre in terms of snake imagery. This impression is cumulatively created through an emphasis on the twisting character of the construction and on the notions of snake-like sliding, binding and shifting (vv. 30–4, 48–53), the intertext of v. 34, i.e., the imagery of the embracing serpents in Laocoon's episode (Verg. *A.* 2.203ff.), and the use of linguistic terms common in descriptions of snakes, as is the case with combinations of *sinuare* with *orbis* (vv. 30–1, cf. also Ov. *Met.* 9.64, *Aetn.* 46–7), *(al)ligare* (v. 34, cf. also Verg. *A.* 2.217), *moles* (v. 34), a designation of gigantic snakes (cf. also Liv. 21.22.8–9, etc.), *lubricus* (v. 51), a further common qualification for *angues* (cf. Verg. *A.* 2.474; see also Serv. ad 2.474: *lubricum dicitur et quod labitur, dum tenetur, ut piscis, serpens*). Crucially, the snake constitutes a further common meta-poetic sign suggesting anti-Callimachean aestheticism and poetics. The image of the venomous snake with its poetological implications occurs elsewhere in pastoral, in the third (v. 93) and the eighth Vergilian eclogue (v. 71), whereas the venom the snakes also possess has developed into an anti-Callimachean sign of the Roman Neoteric jargon (cf. Catul. 14a.19, 44.10–5; see also Papanghelis 1995, 273ff.[81]). Serpentine meta-language comes thus as a sign of the 'generic re-evaluation' of Calpurnian pastoral, which proclaims its clear panegyric preferences over traditional pastoral poetry of Callimachean–Neoteric poetological background.

Pastoral ecphrastic pieces frequently serve as meta-poetic symbolisms of pastoral poetics; this is, for example, the case of the cup in the first Theocritean

---

[79] Cf. also Coleman 2006, 30, Vinchesi 2014, 493.
[80] Cf. Di Lorenzo–Pellegrino 2008, 275; see also Gnilka 1974, 135, Davis 1987, 48, Vozza 1993, 299–300, Paschalis 1996, 138, Schubert 1998, 78, 81, Chinnici 2009, 140, Vinchesi 2010, 144; 2014, 487.
[81] Cf. also Karakasis 2011, 118–9.

idyll, with the bucolic poetological symbolism of the boy weaving cricket cages as a foil to the general poetic interests represented by the icon of the fisherman and the erotic triangle imagery, and the *pocula* in the third Vergilian eclogue, with their themes and decoration also attesting to the Callimachean–Neoteric sensibilities of the pastoral *genus tenue*, as elsewhere elaborated in detail (cf. Karakasis 2011, 13–4, 88–95; see also above, pp. 104–5). Accordingly, the ecphrasis of the Calpurnian eclogue in question, associated with urban values, namely the amphitheatre's construction and its shows, and availing itself of meta–poetic signs denoting elevated literary *genera*, also implies, as a meta–poetic account, the shift of Neronian pastoral literary interests and the branching out of Calpurnian pastoral towards poetic discourses devoid of the rustic element and in favour of panegyric narratives and urban aestheticism. After the experience of the amphitheatre and its poetic praise, Corydon can no longer remain a composer of *iubila* (v. 3), as his previous poetic production, until his novel experiences in Rome, is crucially described. Lycotas makes use of this particular term for referring to Corydon's pastoral poetry, longed for by the distressed bulls in the pathetic fallacy–setting of v. 3: *ut tua maerentes exspectant iubila tauri*. Significantly, this designation has a clear rural colouring, cognate as it is with the verb *iubilare*, the rustic character of which both Var. *L.* 6.68: *ut quiritare urbanorum, sic iubilare rusticorum* and Paul. *Fest.* p. 92.2.3 L: *iubilare: rustica voce inclamare* testify[82]. The term is, however, used with negative connotations in the programmatic first Calpurnian eclogue[83], with reference to the rustic poetic production to which Faunus' prophecy, a declaration of the new poetic objectives, is clearly opposed; the poetic excellence of Faunus' divination is, as plainly stated, due to the fact that *nihil armentale resultat, / nec montana sacros distinguunt iubila versus* (vv. 29–30, cf. Chapter 1, pp. 21–2). After the experience of the arena, Corydon cannot return to poetry no longer esteemed, considered of low quality in the changed political and poetological circumstances, but has to move on to poetry of a loftier style (as is the ecphrasis of Calp. 7) along the lines traced by Faunus' prophecy in the first Calpurnian eclogue.

Whereas Tityrus of the first Vergilian eclogue, to whom, as frequently observed, Corydon of Calp. 7 intertextually alludes, makes his journey to the city in order to secure his 'bucolic permanence' and, on a second, meta–poetic, level, the retention of the Neoteric character of the pastoral *genus*, as evidenced by the poetic meta–language of Verg. *Ecl.* 1 (cf. Papanghelis 1995, 187–91; see also Chapter 2, pp. 49, 57, 60, 75), this is not the case with the Calpurnian Cory-

---

[82] Cf. Vinchesi 1992, 150–1; see also Mahr 1964, 167.
[83] Cf. also Newlands 1987, 227.

don, whose visit to city results in the loss of his traditional pastoral identity, and in a novel preference for elevated 'generic poetic forms', not closely associated with traditional Callimachean–Neoteric discourse[84]. Corydon seems to willingly put himself in the shoes of Meliboeus[85] away from the 'pastoral permanence'; Meliboeus pities himself for having to move away from the *flumina nota* of Verg. *Ecl.* 1.51 (one should not miss here the demonstrably self-reflexive / self-referential function of the term), i.e., the well-known pastoral space and, accordingly, its pastoral poetics as well. Corydon of Calp. 7, on the other hand, experiences guilt and frustration for just the opposite reason, i.e., for his, reluctant as it is, 'pastoral permanence'. Not only does Corydon of Calp. 7 function as a foil to the Vergilian Tityrus (Verg. *Ecl.* 1), but also to Moeris of Verg. *Ecl.* 9, who also travels to the city. In the case of the Vergilian Moeris, his 'pastoral dislocation' and the concomitant, on the meta-poetic level, deviation towards poetics opposing earlier Callimachean–Neoteric trends, is negatively perceived (cf. Karakasis 2011, 184–212); in the Calpurnian instance this movement towards the city and its poetic discourses is, as already suggested (cf. pp. 104–5), presented in positive colours. What is more, in the wake of the elegiac poet Gallus of the Vergilian tenth eclogue, who, after his short-lived experience into the pastoral world and the bucolic host-genre (cf. above, pp. 23, 42, 64 and n. 86), comes to realise at the end the strength of his elegiac identity and, therefore, does not eventually merge himself in the pastoral host-genre, Corydon of Calp. 7 is also presented as experiencing the urban world and its poetics within a pastoral host-genre and as finally becoming conscious of his 'generic rift' from the assets of the hosting bucolic poetics, at least as known from the pastoral tradition up to the Neronian period, in the direction of the hosted mode.

The Reception of Corydon's Account

On the basis of the cumulative evidence for communality between the first Vergilian pastoral and the Calpurnian eclogue under discussion, Lycotas' *o felix Corydon* in v. 73 may also be perceived as an intertextual allusion to Meliboeus' *fortunate senex* in Verg. *Ecl.* 1.46, 51[86]. But, whereas Tityrus of the first Vergilian eclogue is blessed by his pastoral interlocutor for having managed to secure

---

[84] Cf. also Friedrich 1976, 157–8, Di Salvo 1990, 86.
[85] Cf. also Vozza 1993, 306.
[86] Cf. Effe-Binder 1989, 128, Di Salvo 1990, 133, Vinchesi 2002, 151; 2014, 508. For a μακαρισμός of the pleasure a *mystes* experiences upon viewing (ἐποπτεία) his mystic god, cf. Korzeniewski 1976, 250–1; see also Merfeld 1999, 97 and n. 1, Di Salvo 1990, 133.

his 'pastoral continuity', after having listened to Corydon's account for 50 lines, Lycotas of Calp. 7 blesses his younger interlocutor's good luck (μακαρισμός), i.e., Corydon's young age during the first years of the emperor's regime, which enables him to visit the city, experience its attractions and see the emperor; for Lycotas is impeded by his old age from doing so (vv. 73–5). The change of preferences towards the direction of urban enjoyments and aestheticism is once again self-evident. Not only is Corydon allured by the *urbs* but it is also the very spokesman of earlier pastoral tradition who is presented as succumbing to the appeals of the city, crucially brought to his knowledge by means of Corydon's poetic description. Judging from the positive reaction of Lycotas, Corydon's panegyric had the expected effect upon its recipient within the fiction of Calp. 7[87], and a similar reaction, admiration of the emperor and his accomplishments, is expected from the reader of this encomiastic text (Lycotas may thus be read as representing the recipient or the target group of the Calpurnian panegyric narrative). This conversion of the old herdsman had already been foreshadowed, as previously noted, by his positive remarks concerning the awaited narrative of Corydon (vv. 19–22), i.e., before v. 23. Thus, in imitation of Meliboeus in the first Vergilian eclogue, v. 18: *sed tamen, iste deus qui sit, da, Tityre, nobis*[88] (an intertextual reference stressing yet again, as elaborated above (cf. p. 108), the altered circumstances of the seventh Calpurnian poem), Lycotas asks about the countenance of the divine youth, v. 78: *dic age dic, Corydon, quae sit mihi forma deorum*. Although hindered by his rustic appearance from getting a close look at the emperor (he was probably dressed in the rustic *tunica* instead of a *toga*, as required in the presence of the emperor during the time of various public shows, cf. also Suet. *Aug.* 40.5, Mart. 2.29.4, Iuv. 11.204)[89], Corydon replies that the divine *princeps* looks like both Apollo and Mars. In this way, a modification of a further 'generic constituent' takes place at this juncture of the narrative, an expansion of the bucolic pantheon. Apollo, namely Apollo *pastoralis*, belongs to the pastoral pantheon from Theocritus onwards (cf. Karakasis 2011, 18–9, 32), but this is not the case with Mars, the god of war, and consequently, in poetological terms, of genres favouring war-like narratives, namely epic. It is a trend of the Neronian

---

[87] Cf. also Schubert 1998, 77 and n. 116, Vinchesi 2014, 496.
[88] Cf. Korzeniewski 1971, 72, Di Salvo 1990, 135, Di Lorenzo–Pellegrino 2008, 284, Vinchesi 2014, 510.
[89] Cf. Di Salvo 1990, 136; see also Edmondson 1996, 89, Vinchesi 1996, 153; 2010, 158–9; 2014, 27, 478, 510. The mention of the *fibula* in v. 81 is a further sign of pastoral small means as well as an evidence of the fact that Corydon is dressed with the tunic and not the *toga*, as the latter is worn without a clasp; cf. also Korzeniewski 1971, 110; 1973, 499–500, Di Salvo 1990, 138.

period to associate the emperor, who shows a particular interest in literature and the arts, with Apollo, the god of these artistic pursuits (cf. above, pp. 3 and n. 8, 34–5, 46, 54, 62 and n. 76, 68)[90]. However, although associating Nero with Augustus, whose divine profile also included Apollo (*Palatinus*) and Mars (*Ultor*)[91], Nero's likeness with Mars, probably due to the retreat of the Parthians from Armenia in 55 AD, as a result of which the emperor was offered a statue in the temple of *Mars Ultor* (cf. Tac. *Ann.* 13.8.1)[92], moves the informed reader once again away from earlier pastoral trends. What is more, this 'generic transcending' towards the epic mode is further highlighted, as often in Calpurnian pastoral, by an epic linguistic reminiscence in v. 81: *adunco...morsu*, slightly varying Verg. *A.* 1.169: *unco morsu*[93].

Criticism of the Neronian Regime or not?

The present poem has also been read by some critics as an implicit criticism of the Neronian regime. Leach 1973, 77–89, in particular, reads the extravagant luxury of the amphitheatre and the reversed natural order which reigns there as a conscious desire of Calpurnius to distance himself from the praise of the emperor, constructing a couched censure[94] to be appreciated by a mystic circle around the satirist Persius, opposing the emperor. However, both wealth and admiration of wealth constitute basic 'generic features' of encomiastic narratives from Pindar onwards and[95], what is more, as Fear 1994, 270–3 rightly observes, lavish constructions and shows constitute a typical feature of imperial Rome, of the Neronian period espe-

---

[90] Cf. also Di Salvo 1990, 139.
[91] Cf. Friedrich 1976, 249 and n. 26, Fear 1994, 276, Schubert 1998, 76–7, Merfeld 1999, 99 and n. 1.
[92] Cf. Verdière 1954, 264; 1966, 167; 1992, 37–8, Amat 1991, 121, Vinchesi 1996, 159; 2014, 512; see also Di Salvo 1990, 31, 139–40, Di Lorenzo-Pellegrino 2008, 284. For Romano 1980–1, 246–7 the reference to Mars indicates a chronology of the eclogue after 63 AD (the year of the Parthian defeat). Martin 2003, 89–90 reads in the reference to Mars a probable allusion to the Sabine descent of the *gens Claudia*, whereas for a possible allusion here to the emperor's policy in Britain (57 AD), cf. Fear 1994, 276.
[93] Cf. Verdière 1954, 264, Korzeniewski 1971, 72, Di Salvo 1990, 138, Di Lorenzo-Pellegrino 2008, 284, Vinchesi 2014, 511.
[94] Cf. also Martin 2003, 89–90, who is of the view that Nero's likeness with Mars might be read as a sign of the emperor's 'potentially dangerous' disposition.
[95] Cf. also Hunter 1996, 117.

cially (cf. also Mayer 2006, 458)⁹⁶, as evidenced by both literary (cf. Martial's *Liber Spectaculorum*) and epigraphic evidence. More recently Green 2009, 55–67 has also detected in Calp. 7 a pessimistic criticism of the Neronian regime, on the basis of the eclogue's intertextual references to the second book of Vergil's *Aeneid*, namely the episode of the Trojan horse and Laocoon's snakes. The gloomy undertones of such an intertextual association are read as constituting a concealed disapproval of the progress of the Neronian regime, around the end of the so-called *quinquenniun Neronis*. However, the intertexts, if right, may simply further increase the impression of a pastoral branching out towards poetic discourses of the *genus grande*, as frequently suggested by the various epic linguistic reminiscences of the Calpurnian pastoral (cf. above, p. 104).

Davis 1987, 48–9 is more reserved in discerning a sense of 'frustration and disillusionment' concerning Corydon's failure to integrate into the imperial circle⁹⁷; Corydon does not gain access to the emperor because of a feeling of embarrassment about his rustic identity. Newlands 1987, 218–31 offers a similar criticism of the eclogue: the poet criticises the fact that only 'wealth and prestige' are well-appreciated and thus secure right of entry to the imperial circle (cf. also similarly Vozza 1993, 304–5). The poet consequently complains about his inability to ensure patronage (see also Spadaro 1969, 46–7, Messina 1975, 95–6, Casaceli 1982, 93–4, Gagliardi 1984, 26–7, Amat 1991, 63, Vozza 1993, 299, Hulsenboom 2013, 25–6). Seeking of patronage, however, is an issue of the other two Calpurnian political eclogues, namely 1 and 4, where the figure of Meliboeus is expected to introduce the poet to the Neronian circle (cf. Fear 1994, 273–5). This objective is nowhere stated in the fiction of the present eclogue.

It is therefore a matter of whether one reads these three eclogues as a strictly continuous narrative or not; even in the latter case, however, it is legitimate to detect (cf. also Green 2009, 56, Henderson 2013, 180) a sense of 'frustration' on Corydon's part caused by the sitting arrangements in the amphitheatre, with the lower classes piled up in the upper zones, which did not allow him, because of his poverty, to behold the emperor but from afar (vv. 79–84). Although this seems not to

---

96 Cf. Coleman 2006, lxxiv; see also Di Salvo 1990, 98, Di Lorenzo–Pellegrino 2008, 279. For a criticism of Leach's views concerning anti-Neronianism in Calp. 7, cf. also Friedrich 1976, 249–50, Korzeniewski 1976, 252 and n. 27, Schröder 1991, 35–8 and n. 17 on p. 36, Vinchesi 1996, 27 and n. 39; 2014, 478–9, Schubert 1998, 75–6, Magnelli 2006, 475–6; see also Sullivan 1985, 54 and n. 65.
97 Kegel-Brinkgreve 1990, 163, on the other hand, considers the possibility of a not serious 'disillusionment' and reads the present high-flown encomium of the emperor as 'yet another bid for social success'.

constitute a criticism of the Neronian regime[98], Corydon obviously resents this distant viewing of the *princeps*, when exclaiming (vv. 79–80: *o utinam nobis non rustica vestis inesset: / vidissem propria mea numina!*[99]). It is true, as Newlands 1987, 230 observes, that in the parallel first Vergilian eclogue Tityrus' humble slave status did not prevent him from meeting with the emperor and thus securing his 'pastoral permanence' as well as his liberty; but, as Fear 1994, 274–5 pertinently notes in his counter-argument, Vergil's Tityrus is compelled to go to Rome, where he eventually sees the divine youth, whereas this urge is never explicitly stated for Corydon in Calp. 7, who appears to be travelling to Rome, as many other country people must have done, for the shows of 57 AD. He is thus obliged to view, due to his social status, the emperor and the shows from a distance, due to the strict sitting arrangements of the Roman amphitheatre[100].

What matters more here is that once again one comes across a variation upon a Callimachean and traditional pastoral motif, put to use in a panegyric narrative: the image of the poor poet, of the poet of small means, is a common literary motif, in the Callimachean register as well. This poverty deprives the Callimachean poet of his beloved, who eventually accepts the favours of a rich rival (cf. especially *Iamb* 3; see also *Iamb* 12, Karakasis 2005a, 99–100), whereas rusticity is a reason for erotic rejection in the bucolic world as well: [Theocr.] 20 is an anonymous herdsman's account of his rebuff by the urban figure Eunica (cf. also [Theocr.] 8.52), while the second Vergilian eclogue is similarly about Corydon's losing, also due to his rusticity, the affections of the urban Alexis, although the Vergilian Corydon, unlike his Calpurnian namesake in Calp. 7, eventually ac-

---

[98] The fact that Nero, although viewed from far away, is perceived as a combined image of Apollo and Mars (vv. 83–4, see also further below, p. 118) may be read, according to Fear 1994, 276, not as a criticism of the emperor, but instead as an unambiguous acknowledgement of Nero's divine looks. In this context, Schubert 1998, 76–7 proposes the impersonal construction *esse putatur* instead of *esse putavi* for the closure of the eclogue (v. 84), which, in his view, would suggest an objective judgment concerning Nero's divine appearance vs. Vinchesi 2014, 512.

[99] *numina* is simply a plural *maiestatis*, common in Latin literature, when referring to a divinity, cf. e.g. Verg. *A.* 1.666, Hor. *Epod.* 17.3 with Cesareo 1931, 120 and n. 1, Di Salvo 1990, 137. Cf. also Calp. 1.91, 4.112.

[100] For a possible veiled criticism of Nero, cf. also Messina 1975, 95–6; the poet seems to be giving up the idea of a career as a court-poet. However, the argument that Corydon returns to the country, because, after the intrigues of the court, 'solo in essa poteva trovarsi a suo agio' – p. 95, and that the main pastoral character of the eclogue's fiction keeps praising Nero, because he simply had to, does not seem compelling. It is quite evident that Corydon comes back to his pastoral residence reluctantly and, in the case of the σύγκρισις ἀγροῦ καὶ πόλεως, it is clearly the city that emerges as the winner in Calp. 7; cf. also Korzeniewski 1971, 108, Gnilka 1974, 130, Vinchesi 2010, 138.

knowledges his rustic identity and plainly declares that the woods constitute his main pleasure, Verg. *Ecl.* 2.62: *nobis placeant ante omnia silvae* (cf. also Calp. 2.60–1, Nemes. 2.70–1, where Alcon rationalises his separation from Donace, also finding fault with his rustic identity)[101]. The motif of *rusticitas* combined with the topic of small means is in Calp. 7 used in terms of a new clear panegyric narrative; the object of the poet's affection, lost because of his poverty / rustic identity, is no longer a sweet-heart but the emperor, who thus functions as the highest value of a pastoral figure. The situation here is analogous to Calp. 4, where *Paupertas* is the reason for Corydon's need to continue his occupation with his *ovilia*, i.e., with the bucolic life and, on a meta-linguistic level, with pastoral poetry instead of poetic compositions of a more elevated poetic register (vv. 155–6; see also Chapter 2, pp. 79–80)[102]. In a similar vein, the lack of sufficient wealth, which prevents the poet from sitting in the seats of the tribunes or the knights close to the emperor (cf. vv. 28–9), accounts for Corydon's forced return to the 'pastoral cabinet' and, consequently, to its activities, bucolic poetry included, despite his reluctance.

Inverting Scenes of Poetic Initiation?

A typical feature of pastoral poetics has to do with scenes of poetic initiation; an elder pastoral figure reveals to a younger member of the pastoral community a new form of poetic discourse and / or gives to the younger character a token of his poetic art. The Theocritean *Thalysia* appear to construct a clear discourse on the pastoral initiation of the younger Simichidas (cf. Theocr. 7.43–4) by the elder semi-divine figure, Lycidas, who presides over pastoral poetry and space. Obvious parallels occur in both Vergil and Calpurnius, where the passing on of a bucolic pipe, above all, functions as a clear sign of pastoral succession, cf. Verg. *Ecl.* 2.36–8 (Damoetas and Corydon), 5.85 (Menalcas and Mopsus), 6.67–9 (Linus, as the deputy of the Muses, and Gallus), Calp. 4.59–63 (Tityrus, Iollas and Corydon); see also Chapter 1, p. 21. More to the point, in Verg. *Ecl.* 5, the elder Menalcas reveals to the younger Mopsus a new form of Roman diversified pastoral, in which traditional bucolic poetics are intermingled with georgic and panegyric features (cf. Karakasis 2011, 153–83, Chapter 1, pp. 20, 23); a similar revelation of a new reformed pastoral norm, the one favoured by the Neronian period with its penchant for the encomiastic and almost hymnic presenta-

---

[101] Cf. also Di Salvo 1990, 99–100; see also Vinchesi 2010, 139–40.
[102] Cf. also Di Salvo 1990, 137.

tion of the emperor, seems to function as the meta-poetical background of the present Calpurnian poem.

However, it is regularly the older figure who bequeaths his poetic legacy to the younger character; in Calp. 7 this pattern is once again inversed. Lycotas is explicitly presented as an old man in opposition to Corydon, not yet held back by a quivering old age (vv. 73 – 4: *o felix Corydon, quem non tremebunda senectus / impedit!*). What is more, Corydon is blessed by his elder interlocutor for living his early years in the period of the divine *princeps* (vv. 74 – 5: *primos... annos*). Thus the pastoral figure to reveal the new panegyric bucolics, as evidenced by Corydon's poetic account of the Neronian praise, is the younger bucolic character, whereas the recipient of the poetological message, accepting in advance this reformed pastoral form as also belonging to the poetological register of the *dulce*-style, in the line of earlier pastoral production (v. 20), is the elder Lycotas. What is more, an intertextual allusion of vv. 80 – 1 to Theocr. 7.15 – 8 establishes a direct association of the Calpurnian Corydon with the Thalysian Lycidas, i.e., the pastoral initiator par excellence, through the image of the two herdsmen dressed in a rustic garment with an emphasis both on its filthiness (cf. Theocr. 7.16: ποτόσδον, Calp. 7.80 – 1: *sordes / pullaque paupertas*) and its manner of being fastened (cf. Theocr. 7.17 – 8: ἐσφίγγετο...ζωστῆρι, Calp. 7.81: *adunco fibula morsu*)[103]. In this way Corydon, intertextually, further acquires the status of a pastoral figure of a clear poetological import. But, whereas Theocr. 7 is clearly about the bucolisation of an urban poet, Simichidas, Calp. 7 functions in just the opposite direction, evidencing the de-bucolisation of the pastoral poet Corydon[104]. A further inversion of earlier pastoral habits has to do with the names of the bucolic figures of the eclogue; in Verg. *Ecl.* 5 it is the elder and more experienced figure who is credited with a name of special pastoral history (Menalcas), whereas the younger bucolic character, the recipient of the new pastoral, is named Mopsus, i.e., is given a name without 'pastoral pedigree'. In Calp. 7 the changed circumstances are also reflected in the allocation of names; it is the elder figure who is now offered a name with no special pastoral history (Lycotas only appears once before, in Calp. 6[105]), whereas the younger

---

[103] Cf. Di Salvo 1990, 138, Vinchesi 2014, 511.
[104] Cf. also Di Salvo 1990, 85.
[105] As often in post-Vergilian pastoral, in the case of Calp. 7 as well, the pastoral figures involved have been read as bucolic masks of contemporary historical figures. Apart from Corydon, commonly viewed as standing for the pastoral poet Calpurnius himself (cf. above, pp. 9 – 10, 52, 53 – 4 and n. 27), Lycotas has also been perceived as a symbolism, standing for the poet C. Caesius Bassus (cf. Herrmann 1952, 43, Verdière 1954, 60, Messina 1975, 90, Di Salvo 1990, 75 vs.

member of the 'green cabinet', but the one to reveal alternative pastoral poetic forms, is called Corydon, i.e., is given a name found as early as Theocritean bucolics (cf. Theocr. 4; see also Verg. *Ecl.* 2, 7)[106].

The Language of the 'Generic Evolution'

Calpurnius' ability to make use of linguistic means in order to suggest both age and status of a speaking character has already been pointed out above (cf. pp. 88–9). It has also been claimed in detail (cf. Chapters 1 and 2, pp. 43–5, 83–5; see also Chapter 6, pp. 217–8) that Post-Classical diction also belongs to Calpurnius' linguistic register, as a means for emphasising, in terms of diction, his novel 'generic aspirations'. Although, as already pointed out (cf. pp. 43, 83 and n. 185), it is not possible to associate Post-Classical diction with every instance of 'generic deviation' from the earlier pastoral norm, in cases where Post-Classical features are not evenly distributed within the text of a specific eclogue, then one is entitled to look for other reasons other than the linguistic evolution of Latin, in order to account for the specific allocation of the features in question. In this case, although the textual length of the present eclogue is almost equally divided between the mime-like narrative part (cf. also Novelli 1980, 18–9), which consists of the conversation between various characters (Corydon, Lycotas and the unnamed urban elder figure, vv. 1–22, vv. 40–6, vv. 73–84 = 41 lines), and the ecphrasis (vv. 23–72 with the exception of vv. 40–6 = 43 lines), all Post-Classical features significantly occur in the ecphrasis and play their part in materialising Corydon's novel 'generic endeavours' towards ecphrastic pieces of clear panegyric identity and poetic function.

The Post-Classical features occurring in the ecphrasis of Calp. 7 are the following:

Morphology
Gender variation: the masculine accusative *rotulum* instead of the more common feminine form, *rotulam* (cf. Plaut. *Pers.* 443, Colum. 11.3.52), occurs at Calp. 7.51 with reference to a small wheel (cf. OLD *s.v.*) or a cylinder[107].

Gagliardi 1984, 63 and n. 50, Vinchesi 2014, 482). As already remarked (cf. pp. 9–10, 62–3 and n. 77), such associations are beyond the scope of the present analysis.
106 Cf. Di Salvo 1990, 71–2, 75.
107 Cf. also Merone 1967, 24, Novelli 1980, 93, Di Salvo 1990, 108–9, Vinchesi 2014, 499.

Syntax
1. verbal syntax: i) *se alligare* construed with the *accusativus effectus* (term as used by Mahr 1964, 124–8), i.e., with a kind of inner accusative, appears in v. 34: *et geminis medium se molibus alligat ovum*. In the instance in question the construction is equivalent to *se alligando medium ovum efficit*, cf. also Sen. *Med.* 98, Mart. 8.50.7[108]; ii) the construction of *eminere* with the *ablativus separativus* in v. 61: *deformis scapulis torus eminet* is a further Post–Classical usage (cf. also Curt. 4.2.21), to be accounted for by the penchant of Post–Classical diction for such ablative syntagms[109]; iii) the construction of verbs of seeing, namely *videre*, with a perfect infinitive not referring to the past in vv. 69–71: *sola discedentis harenae / vidimus in partes, ruptaque voragine terrae / emersisse feras*[110].
2. prepositional syntax: i) *concedere in* + accusative in v. 30: *qualiter haec patulum concedit vallis in orbem*, where the verb is used in the sense of 'to expand into', is a *hapax* construction in Calpurnius, formed on the analogy of a further chiefly Post–Classical prepositional syntagm, namely *coire in* + accusative (*aliquid*); a similar case is *discedere in partes* in vv. 69–70: *a! trepidi, quotiens sola discedentis harenae / vidimus in partes* (cf. also Sen. *Ep.* 73.8)[111]; ii) the use of *per* in a distributive function in vv. 35–6: *quae vix suffecimus ipsi / per partes spectare suas?* (for the phrase *per partes*, cf. also Colum. 1.4.5, 4.24.4, Plin. *Ep.* 2.5.10)[112]; iii) the construction of *exstare* in the sense of *eminere* with a prepositional complement realised by *in* + accusative in v. 54: *totis in harenam dentibus exstant* (cf. also Sol. 33.11, ThLL V 2, 1928, 71 ff.)[113].
3. coordination: the asyndetic construction of a clause following a sentence introduced with *nec solum*; cf. vv. 64–6: *nec solum nobis silvestria cernere monstra / contigit: aequoreos ego cum certantibus ursis / spectavi vitulos...* The second clause would normally have begun with a *sed etiam* or even *verum* (as in vv. 14–5, i.e., not in the ecphrasis segment)[114].

---

[108] Cf. Mahr 1964, 124–8.
[109] Cf. Mahr 1964, 91–2.
[110] Cf. Mahr 1964, 134–5; for this construction as a syntactic Hellenism, cf. also Traglia 1950, 230, Di Salvo 1990, 127. I accept here the reading *in partes* (cf. Mahr 1964, 133) vs. *inverti* (cf. Duff and Duff 1934, 284).
[111] Cf. Mahr 1964, 96, 133.
[112] Cf. Mahr 1964, 93.
[113] Cf. also Di Salvo 1990, 113.
[114] Cf. Mahr 1964, 101–2. For the non–inclusion of *iubilum* in the lexical Post–Classical features of Calpurnian language, see Chapter 1, p. 45 and n. 137.

Lexicon
1. particles of comparison: in vv. 30–3 the two members of the comparison are introduced by *qualiter* and *sic* respectively, as in Mart. *Sp.* 7.1–3, V. Fl. 5.304–9, Plin. *Nat.* 18.61[115].
2. individual lexemes: *balteus* in v. 47 as a probable synonym of *praecintio*, cf. also Tert. *Spect.* 3[116].

Conclusion

Corydon's narrative of the urban show in Calpurnius 7 symbolises a departure from the established traditions of pastoral poetry towards panegyric. Vergil's *Ecl.* 10 provides an obvious parallel of a closing pastoral poem, which also engages in detail with a non–pastoral genre (Gallan love–elegy); in both cases the employment of another type of poetry is a closing gesture wrapping up a pastoral collection. Calp. 7 may thus be read as an account of Calpurnius' transcending earlier pastoral trends in the direction of panegyric poetic discourses, not endorsed by Theocritean pastoral production, as the founder of the bucolic genre largely keeps his pastoral and panegyric production quite distinct. A panegyric element does occasionally appear in the Vergilian bucolics (cf. Verg. *Ecl.* 1, 3, 4, 5, 6, 8, 9), but Vergil manages to absorb the sharp panegyric edge into the overall demands of the pastoral setting. This is not the case in Calpurnius, where the panegyric dimension gains the upper hand in all programmatic eclogues, namely Calp. 1, 4 and 7. By an intertextual conversation with the first Vergilian eclogue above all, which marked the foundation of the pastoral genre in Rome, Calpurnius inverts several 'generic constituents' as known from the pastoral tradition, and reveals his 'generic orientation' towards the explicit encomium of the emperor, albeit in a bucolic framing[117]. The pleasure of *listening* to bucolic song is replaced by the *viewing* delight one experiences upon looking at the sumptuous amphitheatre and its shows, the arena takes over the 'generic function' of the pastoral *locus amoenus*, exotic fauna and artificial flora substitute common pastoral animal life and vegetation as known from bucolics from Theocritus onwards, the games of the arena take over various activities of the pastoral tradi-

---

115 Cf. Novelli 1980, 86, Di Salvo 1990, 95, Coleman 2006, 85, Vinchesi 2014, 491–2.
116 Cf. also Di Salvo 1990, 103–4, Di Lorenzo-Pellegrino 2008, 281, Vinchesi 2014, 497; see also OLD *s.v.* 7.
117 Monella 2009, 82–5, on the other hand, reads the present eclogue as a failure of Nero's bucolisation, of a process aiming at incorporating the divine emperor into the 'green cabinet'; the balance between panegyric and bucolic poetry is no longer feasible.

tion (e.g. the *venatio* substitutes pastoral hunting, song–contests give way to contests between the animals of the amphitheatre as well as to the figurative competition of various parts of the Neronian construction in terms of wealth and external appearance), the pastoral pantheon is extended in order to include the martial god as well (Mars), the uppermost value of the pre–Calpurmian bucolic space, namely the production of pastoral song, is presented as cancelled, the typology of a set singing match is seriously altered with the image of the lone singer–competitor, the picture of the silent nature deconstructs earlier pastoral settings of sonorous bucolic landscapes, the pastoral character shows lack of interest in pastoral wealth, 'convening' does not result in pastoral conversation and / or bucolic song–exchange, the motif of the 'frustrated pastoral love' due to the lover's rusticity is crucially replaced by a situation where small means stop the rustic character not from rejoicing in his pastoral lover but from viewing the emperor from a close distance, etc.

Everything functions in the service of Nero's encomium and a close intertextual association with the fifteenth Theocritean idyll, a panegyric discourse on the Ptolemies, further enhances the novel 'generic interests and aims' of the present 'pastoral' narrative. On the meta–poetic level, a positive attitude towards notions and catch–words associated with poetic production opposed to Callimachean–Neoteric trends (the concept of 'big', the image of the serpent, etc.) further suggests the 'generic re–orientation' that Calpurnian pastoral exhibits towards discourses approximating poetic sensibilities of the *genus grande*. This movement is further complemented by the various epic and / or panegyric intertexts evoked by the lines of Calp. 7 (e.g. a passage from the second book of Vergil's *Aeneid*, the encomiastic models from Roman elegy (i.e., both Tibullus – 1.7 and Propertius – 4.1)) as well as by the choice of a non–pastoral work of an otherwise pastoral poet also as a model for Calpurnius' text (cf. Theocr. 12, 15). Finally, the 'generic novelty' of a panegyric poetic account, the *laudes Neronis*, as chiefly evidenced by the ecphrasis of the poem in question, is further emphasised by the novel Post–Classical diction Calpurnius uses, crucially only in this particular narrative segment of the eclogue.

Nero seems to have attached great importance to a program of public constructions and this architectual zeal of the *princeps* is often viewed in a positive light (cf. e.g. Suet. *Ner.* 16, 32). The emperor was obviously guided by the precepts of Vitruvius' school of thought, for whom architectural excellence was a crucial facet of human culture. Nero was also very interested in technological progress and placed great importance on the usefulness of various technical devices (cf. e.g. Suet. *Ner.* 31.3). Inevitably, the panegyric of the period could not overlook these views of the *princeps*, nor his glorious constructions themselves, which now function as a *spectaculum*; thus in this celebratory eclogue one comes across a dithyrambic account of several of the emperor's favourites, as presented in various historical and biographical accounts of the emperor, often with reference to the *Domus Aurea*; namely spectacles (vv. 5–6; cf. Suet. *Ner.* 11.1), huge, lavish and splendid structures, rare and precious stones and gold (vv. 36–7, 41, 47–8, 53–4, 71–2; cf. Tac. *Ann.* 15.42.1, Suet. *Ner.* 11.2, 30.3, 31), porticoes in particular (v. 47, cf. Tac. *Ann.* 15.43.1–2, Suet. *Ner.* 31.1), cylindrical mechanisms (vv. 50–3, cf. Suet. *Ner.* 31.2), *sparsiones*, hydraulic devices and the 'mechanically ingenious' (Bradley 1978, 179) in general (vv. 71–2, cf. Suet. *Ner.* 31.2). What is more, common key-words and ideas of imperial propaganda, like the Apollonian beauty of the divine emperor (vv. 83–4, cf. Sen. *Apoc.* 4.1.22 ff.) and the slogan of Neronian *felicitas* (v. 73; see also above, pp. 36–7, 68) have also found their way into the pastoral narrative[118].

The *Domus Aurea* is probably the culmination of Nero's building policy. This palace also constitutes Nero's attempt to decompose, on the architectural level, i.e., through art (cf. Tac. *Ann.* 15.42), by means of technical equipment and a rich artificial decoration, different well-established contrasts, e.g. between public and private life, *urbs* and *orbis*, and, what is more important, between town and country (cf. mainly Malamud 2009, 303–6); this house is treated by the emperor as a kind of a rural habitat, as a bucolic *locus amoenus* in the city. This Neronian trend for undermining traditional dichotomies, on the poetological level, is evident in Calpurnius' poetry, especially in his seventh political eclogue; in a text that is to say, which, although it generically belongs to the pastoral genre, significantly praises urban life and its joys. Pastoral thus functions as a framing mechanism of the *laudes principis*. The big question now is which new genre, if any, is, up to a point, represented by the amphitheatre-ecphrasis of Calp. 7. The description of prestige imperial building projects and festivals in Rome belongs to the occasional hexameter verse exemplified later in Statius' *Silvae*, of which, however, there were surely lost Neronian instances. What is more, poems in which arena animals are discussed may function as another point of contact. Such poems are found later in Martial's *De Spectaculis*, and again such a genre may well have existed in the Neronian period (in the sense that the very shows that Corydon describes may have elicited such poetry).

---

[118] Cf. Vinchesi 2014, 482–3, 494, 497–8, 500, 508, 510.

Part B: **Pastoral, Elegy, Comedy and the Georgics**

Elegy and Comedy

Calpurnius 3

The third eclogue of the Calpurnian pastoral corpus has long been convincingly read as a narrative, where the host–pastoral text interacts with elegy as the guest–genre (cf. especially Friedrich 1976, 59–104, Vinchesi 1991, 259–76; 2012, 706–12; 2014, 32, 227–74 *passim*, Fey-Wickert 2002, 22–9, 143–235 *passim*)[1]. The present chapter aims to build on this established 'generic interaction' and argue for complex 'generic interfaces' operating in the text of Calp. 3, beyond simple elegiac intrusions. In particular, I shall argue for a multifaceted patterning of systematic and standardised intertextual allusions, forming the 'transcending generic profile' of the eclogue: non-bucolic Theocritean intertexts or pastoral intertexts of 'ambiguous bucolic generic character', combined with instances of obvious elegiac intrusions within the pastoral text of the Vergilian bucolics. These are further complemented by motifs and stylistic / linguistic options either de-pastoralised towards 'elegiac generic trends' or drawn from the Roman elegiac register as a conscious authorial choice. The 'generic association' of the poem with the comic genre, particularly New Comedy, will also form a significant part of the analysis.

Methodological Remarks: Pastoral vs. Elegy

Before embarking on the analysis proper of the 'generic identity' of Calp. 3, some initial remarks concerning the 'generic interfaces' of pastoral with elegy are in order[2]: 'generic interaction' and / or 'confrontation', especially between pastoral and elegiac discourses, lies at the heart of the pastoral genre, as early as the Vergilian eclogues. Roman elegy and pastoral, both belong to the Neoteric discourse of the Augustan *genus tenue*, capitalising on the Callimachean poetological model, although pastoral seems to be a more refined and disinterested version of the Callimachean–Neoteric paradigm – a 'song about songs', as opposed to the fiction of elegy's alleged practical usefulness (*Nützlichkeit*) in matters of love. Thus in Verg. *Ecl.* 10, Gallus has persuasively been read as the incarnation of a failed 'generic process'; Gallus, the exemplary elegiac lover / poet, strives, unsuccessfully, to alleviate his erotic predicament by immersing himself in the 'green cabinet' and its poetry, despite the fact that he eventually comes to realise

---

[1] Cf. also Grimal 1978, 165, Davis 1987, 34–5, Hubbard 1998, 153 and n. 20, Magnelli 2006, 467–8, Di Lorenzo-Pellegrino 2008, 15.
[2] Cf. also Karakasis 2011, 1–11.

the impracticality of this 'generic plan' (cf. especially Conte 1986, 100–29, Papanghelis 1995, 64–87; 1999, 57–9; 2006, 401–2, Hardie 2002, 126–7, Harrison 2007, 59–74; see also above, pp. 23, 42, 64 and n. 86, 108). Equally compelling readings have been put forward in favour of an elegising attitude and rhetoric on Corydon's part in the second Vergilian bucolic (cf. Papanghelis 1995, 43–63; see also Kenney 1983, 48–52, Papanghelis 1999, 47–50; 2006, 400–1, Hardie 2002, 125; see also Chapter 2, pp. 55–6 and n. 39) as well as for the elegiac 'break of faith' experienced by Damon's unnamed goatherd and Alphesiboeus' sorceress in the eighth Vergilian pastoral poem (cf. Papanghelis 1995, 87–100; see also Kenney 1983, 52–7, Papanghelis 1999, 50–7, Karakasis 2011, 125–52).

For an epigonal poet, however, as Calpurnius Siculus is, one might, with some justification, claim instead a 'zooming out' of the earlier literary production and the fine 'generic nuances' between various literary genres, a blurred 'telescoping' of earlier 'generic demarcations'. Be that as it may, it is of essence, I think, that Calpurnius' *floruit* should, in all probability, be dated in the age of Nero, i.e., when a clear and close interaction between the literature of the period and the Augustan culture is observable, and, what is more, often in terms of the so-called 'aesthetics of deviation'[3]; i.e., the emulation as well as the inversion of Augustan literary trends (cf. Introduction, p. 8). From this perspective, Calpurnius' penchant for incorporating into his 'generically transcending' aesthetics and poetics an imitation of Vergilian passages where an obvious elegiac 'generic intrusion' is observed should not be read as accidental, especially when the bucolic poet himself draws attention to them through self-reflexive and meta-poetic comments. Vergilian emulation combined with the adoption of well-established elegiac topics and stylistic / linguistic options, as known primarily from their regular presence as *topoi* in the elegiac corpus in opposition to their random occurrences in other 'generic formations', seem crucial for the construction of the Calpurnian transcending poetics, significantly branching out towards 'generic discourses' not sanctioned by earlier 'pastoral generic norms'. In this frame of mind, the association of the narrative of Calp. 3 with the comic genre, as known from Roman New Comedy, also seems interesting to examine, especially if one takes into account the close association of Roman elegy with the Roman comic genre, which foreshadows, in several instances, later elegiac 'generic favourites'[4].

The aim of the present chapter is, accordingly, to examine how such a patterning of complex intertextual allusions (non pastoral–'idyllic', comic and ele-

---

[3] Cf. Maes 2008, 317 and n. 14, Karakasis 2011, 40.
[4] Cf. Barsby 1999, 90–1; see also Martirosova 1999, 20, James 2012, 253–68.

giac / elegising) may produce meaning both in terms of the closed narrative of Calp. 3 as well as within the Calpurnian poetological program as a whole.

The Introductory Narrative

The dialogue (vv. 1–44), framing, as in the programmatic Theocr. 1[5], the only song of the eclogue's plot, Lycidas' reconciliatory verse epistle, begins with time-honoured 'pastoral generic constituents' harking back to previous bucolic texts. This, however, is done with a view to 'generically twisting' the pastoral story towards 'generic interests' of the elegiac *genus*. The fortuitous meeting (cf. also Verg. *Ecl.* 7.1–2; see also Calp. 2.4–6, 5.1–2[6]) of pastoral figures, aptly labelled 'convening' by Alpers 1996, occurs in the first lines of the eclogue; two figures bearing names sanctioned by the earlier pastoral tradition, Iollas (cf. Verg. *Ecl.* 2, 3) and Lycidas (cf. Theocr. 7, Bion fr. 9.10, [Bion] 2, Verg. *Ecl.* 7, 9)[7], meet, when the former is involved in the staple pastoral occupation of looking for a lost heifer (vv. 1–6). However, as already pointed out (cf. Chapter 3, pp. 93, 103, 118), whereas 'convening' in earlier pastoral is followed by an exchange of bucolic songs (cf. especially Theocr. 5, 7) or a conversation of traditional pastoral import (cf. Verg. *Ecl.* 1), in Calp. 3 this meeting simply functions as the prerequisite for the construction of an elegiac discourse, namely Lycidas' amatory epistle (cf. Prop. 4.3), which aspires to put an end to his *discidium* with Phyllis, a sweet-heart significantly bearing a name of clear erotic associations in Latin literature (cf. especially Ov. *Epist.* 2, Phyllis to Demophoon), almost exclusively occurring in earlier pastoral in amatory contexts of the Vergilian bucolics (cf. Verg. *Ecl.* 3.76, 78, 107, 5.10, 7.14, 59, 63, 10.37, 41)[8].

The motif of the animal lost from the herd has its parallel in the seventh Vergilian eclogue, where Meliboeus' he-goat is similarly presented as having strayed (v. 7: *vir gregis ipse caper deerraverat*)[9]. But, whereas, in the Vergilian model, this situation is only a way for establishing Daphnis' divine status (cf. vv. 7–9), in Calp. 3 the motif is crucially associated with the poem's erotic discourse. It triggers the unfolding of the plot and functions as the 'dramatic

---

5 Cf. also Fey-Wickert 2002, 144; see also Friedrich 1976, 64.
6 Cf. Friedrich 1976, 76.
7 Cf. Vinchesi 1991, 260 and nn. 4, 5; 2014, 229, 232, Di Lorenzo-Pellegrino 2008, 185.
8 Cf. Friedrich 1976, 66, Vinchesi 1991, 261 and n. 9, Fey-Wickert 2002, 153–4; see also Vinchesi 2014, 232–3.
9 Cf. Mahr 1964, 21, Friedrich 1976, 71–2, Kegel-Brinkgreve 1990, 156 and n. 21, Vinchesi 1991, 260; 2014, 36, 229, Fey-Wickert 2002, 144, 146.

means' for Iollas to learn about Lycidas' erotic plight and thus to undertake the elegising mission of a *praeceptor amoris*.

Iollas tells of the length of his search (v. 3: *et iam paene duas, dum quaeritur, eximit horas*) and the adversity of the landscape, whose rough butcher's broom and bramble thickets cause his feet to bleed (vv. 4–6). Harmful thorns similarly appear in the fourth bucolic Theocritean idyll, in vv. 50–3[10], where Battus complains about being pierced by a thorn in the ankle when dealing with a heifer, as in the Calpurnian instance. The motif, however, significantly occurs in the non-bucolic thirteenth idyll of the Theocritean corpus as well, where Hercules is similarly depicted as running through thorns, forlorn because of his erotic passion for the vanished Hylas (vv. 64–5)[11]; taking into account Calpurnius' regular usage of various non-bucolic models of the Theocritean corpus for suggesting his willingness for 'generic transcendence', 're-evaluation', the above distribution of the topic may also be significant as to the construction of the 'generic outlook' of these lines. What is more, the Calpurnian detailed account with its references to excessive blood-loss, crucially absent from the Theocritean instances, seems to incorporate within the pastoral narrative the so-called *locus horridus*, favoured, as previously remarked (cf. Chapter 3, p. 99), by Neronian literature, substituting here the pastoral 'generic constituent' of the *locus amoenus*.

Lycidas' erotic passion accounts for his inability to help Iollas with his missing animal; the pastoral lover is so bewildered by his erotic plight that he has no time for anything else, Iollas' heifer included, v. 7: *non satis attendi: nec enim vacat*. Lycidas thus gives notice of his frustration as a lover and, accordingly, develops in his narrative a series of chiefly elegiac but also comic 'generic markers': the well-known erotic triangle consisting of a lover, his beloved, and a rival *amator* (Lycidas – Phyllis – Mopsus, cf. Tib. 1.6.5–6, Prop. 1.8a.3–4, 1.15.1–2, Ov. *Am.* 3.4.1–8 and most of Roman Comedy plots)[12], the extreme pain the lover has to bear (vv. 7–8, cf. Tib. 2.5.109–10, Prop. 2.1.57–8, Ov. *Epist.* 12.57–8, Plaut. *Asin.* 591ff.)[13], the loved one's ingratitude, especially after having received many gifts (vv. 8–9, cf. Prop. 2.8.11, Ov. *Epist.* 2.107–10, 7.27[14]). This 'generic inclination' is further evidenced on the linguistic / stylistic

---

[10] Cf. Messina 1975, 42, Friedrich 1976, 76, Kegel-Brinkgreve 1990, 156 and n. 21, 165, Vinchesi 1991, 260 and n. 6, Keene 1996, 81.
[11] Cf. Verdière 1954, 243, Korzeniewski 1971, 27, Fey-Wickert 2002, 148, Vinchesi 2014, 230.
[12] Cf. Friedrich 1976, 59–60, Fey-Wickert 2002, 183; see also Fedeli 1980, 209, Vinchesi 2014, 227–8.
[13] Cf. Murgatroyd 1994, 230–1.
[14] Cf. Vinchesi 1991, 262; 2014, 234, Fey-Wickert 2002, 25, 156, Di Lorenzo-Pellegrino 2008, 187; see also Fedeli 2005, 251.

level, as suggested by the chiefly elegiac use of *uror* for denoting the burning of love (vv. 2–3, cf. Tib. 2.4.6–7, [Tib.] 4.13.19–20, Ov. *Am.* 2.4.12) and, what is more, in a repeated syntagm, *uror, Iolla, uror*, in the line of the Ovidian Phaedra (cf. *Epist.* 4.19–20: *urimur intus; / urimur*)[15], the designation of the erotic rival as a *novus* (v. 9: *novum...Mopsum*, cf. Prop. 1.15.8, Ov. *Epist.* 5.1, 12.25[16]; see also Plaut. *Cas.* 782, 859) and the equally chiefly elegising use of *ingratus* for denoting the unthankful beloved of the elegiac *genus* (vv. 8–9, cf. also Catul. 76.9, [Tib.] 3.6.41–2, Prop. 1.6.9–10, 4.7.31, Ov. *Epist.* 12.21, 124, 206[17]; see also Plaut. *Pers.* 228, Ter. *Andr.* 278) as well as the use of *immodice* (v. 8) denoting the intensity of the elegiac passion (cf. also Prop. 2.15.29–30, Ov. *Fast.* 2.585)[18]. The same elegising discourse resounds in Iollas' responding lines, which contain the topic of the elegiac lover's, especially the *puella*'s, fickleness (v. 10: *mobilior ventis o femina!*, cf. Prop. 2.9a.31–6, 2.16.25–6, Ov. *Am.* 2.16.45–6, *Epist.* 5.109–10, Hor. *Carm.* 2.8.5–8; see also Plaut. *Amph.* 836, *Mil.* 185–94, Ter. *Hec.* 312) and of the untrustworthiness of a lover's oath, (vv. 10–2, cf. Catul. 70.3–4, Tib. 1.4.21–6, 1.9.1–2, Prop. 1.15.25, Ov. *Am.* 1.8.85–6, *Ars* 1.631–6; see also Plaut. *Cist.* 472)[19].

Most of the above elegiac / comic markers, however, have a pastoral parallel as well, but drawn from settings where a 'pastoral dislocation' towards the elegiac mode is observable; Calpurnius thus seems to deliberately opt for pastoral intertexts adding to his 'generically innovative' pastoral discourse. The situation where a lover deplores his alienation from his darling due to the intervention of a rival alludes first and foremost to Gallus' erotic plight of the 'generically diversifying' tenth Vergilian eclogue (see above, pp. 123–4)[20].

The 'generic tension' of this Vergilian model seems to be operating in the present Calpurnian eclogue as well, for Lycidas too is trying to overcome his pas-

---

15 Cf. Pichon 1966, 301, Korzeniewski 1971, 27, Pearce 1990, 66, Vinchesi 1991, 261; 2014, 232, Fey–Wickert 2002, 26, 152, Di Lorenzo–Pellegrino 2008, 186; see also Maltby 2002, 418.
16 Cf. Pichon 1966, 216, Korzeniewski 1971, 93, Vinchesi 1991, 261; 2014, 234, Fey–Wickert 2002, 26, 154–5; see also Fedeli 1980, 341.
17 Cf. Pichon 1966, 169, Vinchesi 1991, 261; 2014, 233–4, Fey–Wickert 2002, 26, 153; see also Fedeli 1980, 175, Navarro–Antolín 1996, 506–7, Bessone 1997, 92.
18 Cf. Vinchesi 1991, 261; 2014, 232, Fey–Wickert 2002, 24, 152–3; see also Fedeli 2005, 458.
19 Cf. Verdière 1954, 243–4, Otto 1964, 231–2, Messina 1975, 43, Friedrich 1976, 77–8, 214, Gagliardi 1984, 38 and n. 36, Amat 1991, 105, Fey–Wickert 2002, 24, 156–9, Di Lorenzo–Pellegrino 2008, 187, Vinchesi 2014, 234–6; see also Nisbet–Hubbard 1978, 122–3, Fedeli 1980, 353; 2005, 295, Hollis 1977, 131–2, McKeown 1989, 245; 1998, 362–3, Murgatroyd 1991, 139, 259, Maltby 2002, 221–2, Perrelli 2002, 136.
20 Cf. also Friedrich 1976, 62, Di Lorenzo–Pellegrino 2008, 187.

sion by means of an elegising song (like Gallus' Lycoris–elegy, cf. Verg. *Ecl.* 10.44–9) within a bucolic (textual) setting. This elegiac inclination of Calp. 3 further alludes to both Damon's and Alphesiboeus' song-topics in the eighth Vergilian eclogue, whose elegiac undertones have been detected by previous scholarship (see above, p. 124), where, respectively, a goatherd loses his beloved Nysa to a rival Mopsus, and a pastoral sorceress is faced with her pastoral husband's adultery with an urban lady[21]. Moreover, the image of a lover on fire, as evoked by *uror*, harks back to yet another pastoral intertext of 'elegiac generic propensities', the elegiac discourse of Corydon in the second Vergilian eclogue, when, before returning to the pastoral norm of the last lines, he acknowledges his elegiac behaviour, v. 68: *me tamen urit amor; quis enim modus adsit amori?*[22]. The question of the line, namely the reference to the lack of erotic *modus* with reference to Corydon's infatuation, further evokes the notion of a strong erotic passion, that both the elegiac (see above, p. 127) and the Calpurnian *immodice* (cf. Calp. 3.8) also imply. The Calpurnian formulation by means of the adverb *immodice* significantly alludes to the elegiac disposition of Gallus in Verg. *Ecl.* 10 as well; Pan, a characteristic pastoral god, pays the elegiac poet a visit, when the latter is pining away with non–reciprocated elegiac love (cf. v. 10), and similarly asks of Gallus' elegiac fascination for Lycoris, *ecquis erit modus?* (v. 28)[23]. Last but not least, the image of a lady distraught on account of her lover's absence, as suggested in the case of Phyllis (vv. 10–2), also has a pastoral intertext of a 'generically ambivalent character'; it alludes to Amaryllis in the first Vergilian eclogue[24], who is similarly depicted as saddened, because of Tityrus' absence, as well as indifferent to every day agricultural activities (vv. 36–8). This image crucially belongs to a narrative part where the eclogue seems again to move away from the pastoral beaten track, towards the comic and the elegiac 'generic realm', as suggested by the figure of the squanderer spouse Galatea, the notion of *libertas* and a slave's *peculium* (vv. 30–5; cf. also Chapter 2, pp. 59, 74)[25].

Lycidas promises his pastoral fellow to let him know of his erotic troubles, when not preoccupied with the loss of the animal and, accordingly, bids him search for it so that later he can listen in leisure to Lycidas' quandaries (vv. 13–4); the landscape where this pursuit of the animal should take place,

---

[21] Cf. also Friedrich 1976, 66, Fey-Wickert 2002, 156, 166, Di Lorenzo–Pellegrino 2008, 187.
[22] Cf. Davis 1987, 34.
[23] Cf. also Vinchesi 1991, 261; 2014, 232, Fey-Wickert 2002, 152.
[24] Cf. also Vinchesi 1991, 263 and n. 16, Fey-Wickert 2002, 159.
[25] Cf. also Coleman 1977, 78–9, Papanghelis 1995, 193–4, Martirosova 1999, 74–5, Hardie 2002, 125 and n. 36, Karakasis 2011, 134–5, Cucchiarelli 2012, 151–2.

however, with its common pastoral trees, the willows and the elms (v. 14: *has pete nunc salices et laevas flecte sub ulmos*), and the shady coolness of a summer hot day (vv. 15–6) calls to mind the typical pastoral *locus amoenus* often functioning as the dramatic setting for the pastoral activity par excellence, singing (cf. e.g. Theocr. 5.31–4, Verg. *Ecl.* 7.9–13; see also above, pp. 49, 98). The setting is here associated with Lycidas' bull in rest, the object of the lost heifer's affection, stretching out in the cool shadow and masticating his cud (vv. 15–7), an image recalling another Vergilian pastoral passage, with alternative 'generic tendencies', namely Verg. *Ecl.* 6.53–4[26], where Pasiphae's darling is similarly presented as reclining on supple hyacinths, in the shadow of an ilex, and chewing his grass (*ille latus niveum molli fultus hyacintho / ilice sub nigra pallentis ruminat herbas*). The Vergilian parallel, however, drawn from a narrative segment dealing with Pasiphae's story, popular in Roman elegy, and replete with stylistic markers of the epylliac style (tale within a tale narrative structure (vv. 45ff.), apostrophe introduced by the interjectional *a!* (v. 52), etc.) also adds, because of its peculiar 'generic character', to the 'generic diversity' of the Calpurnian recipient text[27]. What is more, the image of the reclining bull also appears in Ovid's *Remedia Amoris*, cf. v. 421, whereas the picture, within an erotic context, of the animal chewing grass further alludes to Ov. *Am.* 3.5.17[28], where the bull of the poet's dream, standing for the elegiac poet / lover himself, is also presented as masticating his food; this elegiac image is supplemented by the elegiac syntagm *spatiare in umbra* (cf. Calp. 3.16: *spatiosus in umbra*) occurring in Prop. 4.8.75 and Ov. *Ars* 1.67[29]. The overall elegiac colouring of this narrative section is further enhanced by the staple elegiac use of *queror* in the sense of 'to bemoan an erotic loss' in v. 13: *altius ista querar* (cf. Tib. 2.6.34, Prop. 2.20.4, Ov. *Rem.* 644[30]). *Querella* and *queri* are also significantly 'generic descriptive terms' denoting the elegiac genre and the composition of elegy respectively (cf. Prop. 1.7.8)[31].

Iollas is so interested in Lycidas' erotic quarrel with Phyllis that he delegates the task of looking for the vanished animal to his helper, Tityrus (vv. 18–23), and gives him typical pastoral orders, such as the punishment of a badly behaving an-

---

[26] Cf. Cesareo 1931, 18–9 and n. 1, Verdière 1954, 244, Vinchesi 1991, 263; 2014, 237, Amat 1995, 81, Fey-Wickert 2002, 160, Di Lorenzo–Pellegrino 2008, 188.
[27] Cf. Papanghelis 1995, 148–51.
[28] Cf. Verdière 1954, 244, Friedrich 1976, 78, Vinchesi 1991, 263; 2014, 230, 237, Keene 1996, 82, Di Lorenzo–Pellegrino 2008, 188.
[29] Cf. Verdière 1954, 244, Vinchesi 1991, 263, Fey-Wickert 2002, 161; see also Hutchinson 2006, 203.
[30] Cf. also Pichon 1966, 248–9, Vinchesi 2014, 236.
[31] Cf. Karakasis 2011, 133.

imal (vv. 20–1[32]). Leaving menial tasks to a pastoral assistant is a further common motif of the bucolic tradition (cf. Theocr. 3.2–5, Verg. *Ecl.* 5.12, 9.23–5[33]), creating the sense of a time-honoured 'generic pastoral surface', further complemented by the detail of driving the animal back to the flock with a crook (vv. 20–1), which alludes to a similar situation in the bucolic Theocr. 4.45–9[34], where Corydon is similarly presented as wishing to drive his animals up the hill with the poke of a curved stick. However, the assignment of pastoral everyday activities to a third person functions in pre-Calpurnian pastoral as a means for alleviating the pastoral singer from his menial burden so that he can devote himself to the pastoral occupation par excellence, i.e., bucolic singing. On the contrary, in Calp. 3, it is simply a means for Iollas to adopt the elegiac stance of a *praeceptor amoris*, consulting the distressed lover as to the way the latter should act for winning back his sweet-heart. What is more, Iollas' advice will bring about an elegising song in letter form (*Werbende Dichtung* fashioned as an erotic epistle, where the name of both the sender and of the recipient are given as well as the distraught lover's predicament, in the line of the Ovidian *Heroines*[35]), meant to appease Phyllis' wrath and lead to the couple's reunion. Another element of Iollas' elegising 'generic profile' is his repetition of a well-known motif of the elegiac discourse, that of holding a god accountable for the separation of a couple in love, v. 23: *quis vestro deus intervenit amori?*, cf. also Tib. 1.5.19–20, Prop. 1.12.9, Ov. *Epist.* 5.5, 7.4[36]. The use of *iurgia* in vv. 22–3: *quae noxam magna tulere / iurgia?* further points to the elegiac 'generic preferences' of Calp. 3; at Verg. *Ecl.* 5.10–11 *iurgia Codri* along with *Phyllidis ignes* and *Alconis laudes* are presented as the conventional pastoral subject-matters that Menalcas chooses as song-topics for a friendly song-exchange with his fellow-pastoral singer Mopsus. Besides, bickering between pastoral characters forms part of the pastoral narrative framing the very bucolic song or functions as topic of the pastoral song itself (cf. Theocr. 5, Verg. *Ecl.* 3, Calp. 6); the term here, however, applies to the erotic quarrel of a couple in a consummated love-affair, of the

---

32 Cf. Fey-Wickert 2002, 163, Vinchesi 1991, 263–4; 2014, 238–9.
33 Cf. Paladini 1956, 531 and n. 2, Korzeniewski 1971, 93, Messina 1975, 44, Friedrich 1976, 72, 213, Kegel-Brinkgreve 1990, 156 and n. 22, Pearce 1990, 67, Amat 1991, 27, Keene 1996, 82, Fey-Wickert 2002, 145, Vinchesi 2014, 238.
34 Cf. Leach 1975, 213, Vinchesi 1991, 263–4; 2014, 238–9, Fey-Wickert 2002, 163.
35 Cf. Korzeniewski 1971, 93–4; 1972, 215 and n. 5, Friedrich 1976, 87, Effe-Binder 1989, 113, Kegel-Brinkgreve 1990, 157, Vinchesi 1991, 268–9; 1996, 38; 2014, 228, 251, Fey-Wickert 2002, 186–7, Simon 2007a, 172.
36 Cf. also Vinchesi 1991, 264; 2014, 239, Fey-Wickert 2002, 24, 165, Di Lorenzo-Pellegrino 2008, 189.

kind marking the Roman elegiac genre[37]. From this 'generic perspective', Lycidas' earlier use of a distinct Neoteric term, *vacare* (v. 13: *si forte vacabis*), seems to be significant as far as the meta-poetics of the passage in question is concerned. Lycidas promises his interlocutor to reveal his elegiac plight, when in leisure; in other words he undertakes an elegiac poetic discourse, when, on a meta-poetic level, the *otium poeticum*, indispensable for the production of Neoteric poetic discourse, is also secured.

Lycidas' Account of his Erotic Plight; Iollas' Reaction

The 'generic outlook' of this narrative piece (vv. 24 ff.) is also construed by means of elegiac topics and style as well as through the medium of pastoral texts exhibiting a certain pastoral alienation towards the elegiac 'generic code'. The 'diversifying generic status' of the lines is further complemented by allusions to pastoral texts of a particular 'generic status' like Theocr. 3, which functions as a rustic version of an urban topic, the *komos*, with clear comic implications (cf. Hunter 1999, 110, Karakasis 2011, 194–5) or the eleventh Theocritean idyll, also standing out of the main bucolic Theocritean pastoral production, both due to its language and metre (e.g. rare Dorisms, frequent breaches of Callimachean metrical rules) and the rather 'unpastoral' situations it describes (e.g. the playing of the *syrinx* by Polyphemus in the night, cf. Hunter 1999, 217–8, 234, Karakasis 2011, 200–1; see also above, pp. 7, 55–6 and n. 39, 93). The 'generic patterning' of the passage is complemented by non-bucolic intertexts of an otherwise pastoral model author (Theocritus).

Lycidas starts with the motif of the elegiac contentment with the love of one beloved only, v. 24: *Phyllide contentus sola*. This topic of erotic and sexual exclusivity is for the most part favoured by the elegiac Neoteric discourse of the *genus tenue*, in opposition to pre-Calpurnian pastoral, which, as a rule, prefers a looser attitude towards sex[38]. The linguistic means for expressing this erotic exclusiveness, namely *contentus*, comes again chiefly from elegiac (and up to a point comic) diction, cf. Catul. 68.135, Prop. 2.30b.23, 4.11.91, Ov. *Epist.* 5.9–10; see also Plaut. *Merc.* 824, Afran. *tog.* 117 Ribb.³, Ter. *Eun.* 122[39]. The mention of a rejected erotic rival's name, as is the case of the spurned Callirhoe here (v. 25: *Callirhoen sprevi*), also appears in the 'generically peculiar' third Theocritean

---
[37] Cf. also Vinchesi 2014, 247.
[38] Cf. Karakasis 2011, 216.
[39] Cf. Pichon 1966, 112, Fey-Wickert 2002, 25, 168, Di Lorenzo-Pellegrino 2008, 189, Vinchesi 2014, 240; see also Hutchinson 2006, 247.

idyll, cf. Theocr. 3.34–6, where the anonymous goatherd tries to intimidate Amaryllis by bringing up Mermnon's slave-girl, willing to accept his affectionate gifts. This rhetorical device notably also appears in the elegiac discourse of the love-struck Corydon of the second Vergilian eclogue, when in vv. 14–6, 40–4 the elegising pastoral lover sets out to inflame Alexis' erotic jealousy by referring to a certain Amaryllis, a dark Menalcas, and a Thestylis, keen to receive his love-gifts[40]. What is more, the representation of the erotic competitor, Callirhoe, as an *uxor dotata* (cf. v. 25: *quamvis cum dote rogaret*[41]) also brings the narrative close to the 'generic interests' not only of the elegiac genre, as the Ovidian elegiac heroines occasionally raise the issue of their dowry (cf. Ov. *Epist.* 3.55, 6.117–8, 7.149; see also Prop. 1.8b.35[42]), but also of comedy, where women with considerable fortune are stock 'generic characters' (e.g. in Plautus' *Asinaria*, *Casina*, *Menaechmi* or in Terence's *Phormio*[43]). The elegiac colouring is linguistically increased by the use of *spernere* of erotic scorn (cf. Tib. 1.4.77, 1.8.55, Prop. 2.18a.7, Ov. *Am.* 3.6.65, *Epist.* 4.168, *Fast.* 3.553; see also Hor. *Carm.* 1.9.15–6, Plaut. *Mil.* 1050[44]) as well as of *rogare* in the sense of 'to solicit for favours', 'make overtures to' in v. 25, cf. OLD s.v. 7c, Catul. 8.13–4, Tib. 1.4.55, Prop. 2.4.2, Ov. *Am.* 1.8.43–4, *Ars* 1.708[45]. The picture of Phyllis making a wax-joined pipe and singing under a typically pastoral shady oak (cf. Theocr. 5.44–5, 60–1, 7.88–9, Calp. 2.12) with Mopsus as her company in song (vv. 26–7) brings to mind once again the elegiac discourse of Verg. *Ecl.* 2, where, in vv. 28 ff.[46], Corydon tries to convince his darling boy, Alexis, to dwell in the woods and to entice him by talking about the quality of their prospective joined song in the 'green cabinet', able to rival a pastoral divinity of musical attributes, Pan (v. 31: *mecum una in silvis imitabere Pana canendo*).

What is more, pastoral apprenticeship, which lies at the heart of pastoral poetics, as evidenced by the regular pastoral focus on the relationship between a bucolic teacher and his pupil (Verg. *Ecl.* 2.36–8 (Damoetas and Corydon); see also 5.85 (Menalcas and Mopsus), Calp. 4.59–63 (Tityrus, Iollas and Corydon),

---

[40] Cf. also Vinchesi 1991, 264; 2014, 240–1, Fey-Wickert 2002, 169.
[41] Cf. also Messina 1975, 44 and n. 19, Friedrich 1976, 207–8, Vinchesi 1996, 92; 2014, 241.
[42] Cf. also Vinchesi 1991, 264; 2014, 241, Di Lorenzo-Pellegrino 2008, 189, Fey-Wickert 2002, 170; see also Piazzi 2007, 259.
[43] Cf. Duckworth 1952, 283.
[44] Cf. Pichon 1966, 267, Vinchesi 1991, 264 and n. 22; 2014, 240, Fey-Wickert 2002, 26, 169; see also Murgatroyd 1991, 157, Perrelli 2002, 258–9.
[45] Cf. Fey-Wickert 2002, 170, Vinchesi 2014, 241; see also Pichon 1966, 254, McKeown 1989, 223, Fedeli 2005, 160–1.
[46] Cf. Fey-Wickert 2002, 172, Vinchesi 2012, 709; 2014, 242.

above, pp. 21, 113)⁴⁷, is here used as a means for courting an engaged lady, that is for the construction of an elegiac situation par excellence, the elegiac triangle, which also brings to mind elegiac inclinations of the Vergilian pastoral corpus, such as the liaison between Gallus, Lycoris and her soldier lover of the 'generically semantic' tenth Vergilian eclogue⁴⁸. Mopsus is teaching Phyllis how to join the pipe-reeds with wax, that is they engage in a major pastoral occupation (vv. 26–7, cf. Theocr. 1.128–9, [Theocr.] 8.18–9, Verg. Ecl. 2.32–3, 3.25–6⁴⁹), which eventually leads to an elegiac situation. This is the first instance in pastoral tradition of a female character playing the pastoral pipe, with the exception of Bucaeus' darling, Polybotas' daughter, in the agricultural and not pastoral tenth Theocritean idyll, vv. 15–6⁵⁰. 'Music' (flute, lute) girls do not regularly belong to the traditional 'green cabinet' but are, instead, stock characters of the comic genre as female figures of easy virtue (cf. Plaut. Epid. 403, Ter. Eun. 457, 985, Ad. 476)⁵¹. Thus the perception, on Lycidas' part, of Phyllis' apprenticeship in pastoral music under the teaching of Mopsus, who helps Phyllis join reeds with wax (cf. Duff and Duff 1934, 237), i.e., of a pastoral liaison par excellence, as evidence of a love-affair leading to comic or elegiac situations, may also be due to Lycidas' viewing the liaison between Phyllis and Mopsus through the 'generic lens' of the comic mode, especially when no signs of flirting or love-making between these two bucolic figures are reported, not even by Lycidas himself when describing the disturbing incident (vv. 26–30). Thus Lycidas, out of jealousy / erotic sorrow, an emotion conveyed through the common elegiac use of *ardere*⁵² (v. 28, cf. Ov. *Rem.* 287–8, *Ars* 2.377–8; see also Ter. *Eun.* 72), also found in the urban mime of Theocr. 2.40 (καταίθομαι) as well as in the elegiac rhetoric of Verg. Ecl. 2.1, experiences a further reaction not sanctioned by the pastoral tradition, when he attacks his beloved, tears open her garments and strikes her uncovered breast (vv. 28–30). Violence of this type is associated with both comic and elegiac love (cf. Menander's *Perikeiromene*, *Rhapizomene*, Plaut. *Bacch.* 859–60, *Cist.* 522ff., *Truc.* 926–7, Ter. *Ad.* 120–1, *Eun.* 646; as for elegy, cf. also Tib. 1.1.73–4, 1.6.73–4, 1.10.59–66, Prop. 2.5.21–4, 2.15.18–20,

---

47 Cf. Papanghelis 1995, 156–7.
48 Cf. also Fey-Wickert 2002, 166–7. 'Pastoral apprenticeship' associated with a love-story later occurs in Longus' *Daphnis and Chloe* (cf. 1.24.4); see Vinchesi 1991, 265 and n. 24.
49 Cf. Fey-Wickert 2002, 171.
50 Cf. also Vinchesi 1991, 265; 2014, 249.
51 Cf. also Ireland 1992, 87, Rosivach 1998, 179 and nn. 9, 10, 11, 12, Traill 2008, 39; see also Habrotonon of the *Epitrepontes*, Men. *Per.* 340, Arnott 1996, 405.
52 Cf. Friedrich 1976, 79, 215, Fey-Wickert 2002, 25, 173, Vinchesi 2014, 243; see also Pichon 1966, 89, Pinotti 1993, 179.

3.8.8, 4.5.31, Ov. *Am.* 1.7.47–50, *Ars* 2.169–71, 3.567–70; see also Hor. *Carm.* 1.17.25–8)[53].

The motif is also attested in the Theocritean corpus, significantly, however, in the non–bucolic mime of Theocr. 14[54], i.e., a non–pastoral idyll, owing much to the 'generic favourites' of comedy (e.g. the motif of a military service far off, as an antidote to a broken love–affair[55]). Aeschinas there similarly attacks his beloved Cynisca, because the latter has feelings for a rival, Lycos, an act of violence which results in the ending of Aeschinas' love–affair and to Cynisca's also leaving their shared home (vv. 35–6). The fashioning of Calp. 3 after Theocr. 14 is further evidenced by the fact that in both instances it is a song that leads to the lover's aggressive behaviour, namely Phyllis' singing along with Mopsus in Calp. 3 and the song of Lycos in Theocr. 14, as well as by the cow / bull simile applied to both victimised girls (cf. Calp. 3.1–9, 96–8, Theocr. 14.43). The elegiac inclination of the Calpurnian lines in question is also underscored by the typical elegiac imagery of the *exclusus amator* in vv. 33–4, where Lycidas expresses his fear that Phyllis will deny him entry into her dwelling (cf. also Tib. 1.2.31, Prop. 1.16.23–4, Ov. *Am.* 1.6.17–8; see also [Theocr.] 23.17)[56]; the situation appears in comedy as well (cf. Plaut. *Curc.* 147–57, Ter. *Eun.* 771–816, *Ad.* 120). The elegiac use of *improbus* in vv. 31–2: 'relicto, improbe, te, Lycida, Mopsum tua Phyllis amabit', i.e., with the meaning of 'cruel, hard lover' (cf. Prop. 2.8.14, Ov. *Epist.* 18.41[57]), complements the 'generic picture' of this narrative segment.

Iollas adopts the typical stance of the elegiac *praeceptor amoris* and gives his pastoral interlocutor a piece of advice, elsewhere attested in elegy (cf. Ov.

---

53 Cf. McKeown 1989, 162, Korzeniewski 1971, 93, Friedrich 1976, 79–80, 215, Vinchesi 1991, 266; 1996, 93; 2012, 707 and n. 7; 2014, 243, Keene 1996, 84, Fey-Wickert 2002, 24, 174–5, Di Lorenzo-Pellegrino 2008, 189–90; see also Nisbet-Hubbard 1970, 226, Murgatroyd 1991, 204, 293, Maltby 2002, 277, Fedeli 2005, 185–6, 452–3, Hutchinson 2006, 144, Mayer 2012, 95.
54 Cf. Schenkl 1885, xxii, Cesareo 1931, 22–3, Verdière 1954, 244; 1966, 169 and n. 58, Mahr 1964, 20–1, Messina 1975, 41, 44, Friedrich 1976, 73–4, 79, Kegel-Brinkgreve 1990, 157, Amat 1991, 105, Keene 1996, 84, Fey-Wickert 2002, 175, Magnelli 2006, 467, 468, Di Lorenzo-Pellegrino 2008, 189–90, Hutchinson 2013, 311–2, 343 vs. Wendel 1901, 54, Hubaux 1930, 222–3; see also Leach 1975, 213, 228 and n. 24, Vinchesi 2014, 243–4; for a reserved view, cf. Vinchesi 1991, 259: 'benché si sia in qualche caso esagerato, io credo, nel voler individuare un rapporto diretto, esclusivo, fra Calpurnio e Teocrito', 266.
55 Cf. Verity (Hunter) 2002, 103.
56 Cf. also Friedrich 1976, 83–4, Fey-Wickert 2002, 184–5, Vinchesi 2014, 228; see also McKeown 1989, 132.
57 Cf. Pichon 1966, 172, Vinchesi 1991, 266; 2012, 708 and n. 19; 2014, 245.

Am. 3.4.43–6), namely indulgence to a lady's demands, especially when Lycidas is to be blamed for starting the quarrel with her (vv. 36–9). This guidance is crucially formulated here by way of the well-known elegiac imagery of the surrendered hands (v. 37: *victas tende manus; decet indulgere puellae*, cf. also [Tib.] 3.4.64, Ov. *Am.* 1.2.19–20, 1.7.28, *Ars* 1.462, *Epist.* 4.14, 17.260, 21.240, *Fast.* 3.688[58]), pointing in its turn to the familiar, in both comedy and elegy, topic of the *militia amoris* (cf. Plaut. *Pers.* 231–2, Caec. *com.* 66–7 Ribb.³, Ter. *Eun.* 59–61; see also Catul. 66.13–4, Tib. 1.1.75–6, 1.10.53–6, Prop. 3.8.29–32, Ov. *Am.* 1.9, *Epist.* 17.253–60[59]) as well as through the use of *nocere* (v. 38: *vel cum prima nocet*) also denoting the culpability, the erotic fault of a lover in Roman love-elegy, cf. Ov. *Am.* 1.7.59, 2.19.14, *Ars* 2.412, *Epist.* 7.61[60]. He additionally presents himself as eager to take on the elegiac role of the go-between, also appearing in the second Theocritean urban mine, 94 ff.[61] (cf. Tib. 2.6.45–6, Prop. 3.6.5, Ov. *Am.* 1.11.7–8, *Ars* 1.383–5, 3.621–6) and thus to help with the reconciliation of the estranged couple, i.e., by bringing a poem-letter of Lycidas to Phyllis (vv. 3, 8–9). The elegiac *iunctura sedulus...aures* (v. 39), also occurring in Ov. *Ars* 3.699–700[62], reinforces the elegiac character of the lines.

Such a mission, however, constitutes one of the main dramatic undertakings of a slave character, more often than not of the *servus callidus*, in Roman New Comedy as well, who is often called upon to assist his young master, when erotically distressed (cf. Ter. *Haut.* 300–1). The situation in question is also developed, as earlier remarked, in the second Theocritean non-pastoral idyll, cf. vv. 94–103, where Thestylis is similarly asked by Simaetha to function as a mediator between herself and her beloved Delphis. The means for securing Phyllis' favours again will thus be a poem / song, as elsewhere in elegy (cf. Ov. *Ars* 2.281–6[63]), for, according to Lycidas, his sweet-heart much appreciates his poetic production, v. 42: *et solet illa meas ad sidera ferre Camenas*, an elegising situation approximating e.g. Prop. 2.24.21–2, where Cynthia, also enjoying the love

---

58 Cf. Verdière 1954, 245, Friedrich 1976, 95, Vinchesi 1991, 267; 1996, 38 and n. 62; 2014, 248, Fey-Wickert 2002, 25, 179, Di Lorenzo-Pellegrino 2008, 190, 195; see also McKeown 1989, 44, Michalopoulos 2006, 354–5.
59 Cf. McKeown 1989, 257–9, Murgatroyd 1991, 69, Maltby 2002, 149, Perrelli 2002, 42, Michalopoulos 2006, 353, Heyworth-Morwood 2011, 174.
60 Cf. Pichon 1966, 214, Vinchesi 1991, 267; 2012, 707 and n. 12; 2014, 248, Fey-Wickert 2002, 26, 180.
61 Cf. Friedrich 1976, 80, Fey-Wickert 2002, 24, 184, Vinchesi 2012, 709 and n. 22; 2014, 248; see also McKeown 1989, 308–9, Maltby 2002, 478.
62 Cf. Verdière 1954, 151, Korzeniewski 1971, 30, Fey-Wickert 2002, 180, Di Lorenzo-Pellegrino 2008, 191, Vinchesi 2014, 248–9.
63 Cf. Vinchesi 1991, 268; 2012, 710; 2014, 251.

of a rival lover, is similarly depicted as having been praising the quality of the poet's lyrics in the recent past[64]. Phyllis is thus presented as a *docta puella* of Roman Neoteric poetry, who appreciates good poetry and is also able to express judgement (cf. also Catul. 35, Prop. 2.13.11–2[65]). The designation of his poetry through the term *Camenas*, a term without poetological specialisation, instead of the Nymphs, i.e., the pastoral goddesses par excellence who preside, in preference to the Muses, over traditional pastoral space and poetry[66] (cf. Chapter 2, pp. 60–1), may also be read as a 'generic sign' for the 'generic movement' of Lycidas' reconciliatory poetry away from long-established pastoral 'generic preferences'.

The way Iollas is willing to bring Lycidas' erotic letter to Phyllis further hints to the elegiac 'generic propensities' of the lines under consideration, as this task is associated with the motif of writing in the pastoral world, a key-topic always pointing to various 'generic interactions' operating within the pastoral host-text. Iollas will carve Lycidas' lyrics on the bark of a cherry-tree, cut away the carved part and bring it to Phyllis (vv. 43–4). As already remarked (cf. Chapter 1, p. 23), in pre-Calpurnian pastoral, writing appears once in the non-pastoral eighteenth Theocritean idyll, vv. 47–8, where a tree-inscription is meant to honour Helen, and twice in the Vergilian eclogues: once in the fifth pastoral, where Mopsus marks the words and the tunes of his lyrics on a green beech-bark (vv. 13–5), that is within a poem dealing, as elsewhere shown (cf. Karakasis 2011, 153–83), with the 'generic interaction' of pastoral and panegyric poetics and the genesis of a new reformed Roman pastoral tradition, where traditional pastoralism is blended with, clear enough, touches of political encomium. In Calp. 1 as well the *omen* of Faunus, also heralding a new bucolic tradition of a clearly panegyric colouring, is similarly carved on a beech-tree[67]. But the motif of writing in erotic settings has its parallel in the tenth Vergilian eclogue, where Gallus, according to the elegiac ethos once again, is presented as willing to carve his love-poems on the bark of trees (vv. 53–4). The writing-motif, drawn from the Acontius and Cydippe story of Callimachus' *Aetia*, the elegiac poem par excellence for the Romans, and frequently occurring in the elegiac register of Roman poetry (cf. Prop. 1.18.22, Ov. *Epist.* 5.21–5[68]) further underscores the 'elegiac generic tenden-

---

[64] Cf. Vinchesi 1991, 265; 1996, 38 and n. 61; see also 2014, 249.
[65] Cf. Vinchesi 2012, 708–9 and n. 20; 2014, 249.
[66] Cf. Fantuzzi-Hunter 2004, 153–7, Karakasis 2011, 18–9.
[67] Cf. Friedrich 1976, 80–1, Kegel-Brinkgreve 1990, 156 and n. 23, Fey-Wickert 2002, 181.
[68] Cf. Messina 1975, 46, Vinchesi 1991, 268; 1996, 95; 2012, 709–10 and n. 24; 2014, 250; see also Fedeli 1980, 434, Knox 1995, 146–7, Papanghelis 1995, 80–2, Hubbard 1998, 151 and n. 18. For a reference, in vv. 43–4: *nam cerasi tua cortice verba notabo / et decisa feram*

cies' of the Calpurnian passage, although in the Calpurnian version it is not the lover who carves the love-song but his erotic counsellor.

Lycidas' Song

From v. 45 Lycidas' song begins[69], and up to v. 55 one reads various complaints of the deserted lover: in this case as well the largely elegiac / comic motifs and stylistic / linguistic options incorporated in the narrative are combined with various pastoral intertexts further suggesting the 'generic ambivalence' of the poem in question: i.e., yet again pastoral models exhibiting 'generic transgression' towards the elegiac 'generic code' (e.g. Verg. *Ecl.* 2, 10, etc.; see above, pp. 123–4), pastoral intertexts of a rather shaky pastoral calibre, as is the case with Theocr. 3 and 11 (see above, p. 131)[70], non-bucolic poems of an otherwise pastoral poet like Theocritus (cf. also above, p. 131), as well as various other model texts, where a 'generic interaction' builds their 'generic profile', eventually affecting the 'generic outlook' of the Calpurnian lines as well. This happens for example with Ov. *Met.* 13.719 ff., i.e., the story of Polyphemus, Galatea and Acis, where a range of 'generic interfaces' between pastoral, elegy and epic are at the heart of the passage's poetics (cf. Farrell 1992, 235–68). Alternatively several motifs associated in the earlier pastoral tradition with situations sanctioned by the pre-Calpurnian bucolic norm are here transferred in an elegiac state of affairs, also pointing to the changed Calpurnian 'generic preferences'.

Lycidas starts off with the elegiac topic of the lover's sleeplessness (cf. Catul. 68.5–8, Tib. 1.8.64, Prop. 1.16.39–40, 4.3.29 ff., Ov. *Am.* 1.2.3, *Epist.* 8.107–10, 11.29, 12.57–8, 169–70; see also Plaut. *Merc.* 24–5, Ter. *Eun.* 219, Hor. *Carm.* 3.7.7–8[71]), presenting his reconciliatory song as being performed during a forlorn (*miser*, v. 46; cf. Catul. 76.19, Tib. 1.6.9, Prop. 1.3.40, Ov. *Rem.* 601[72]), betrayed lover's wakeful night (vv. 45–7), up to a point in line with Ovid's *vigilatum*

---

rutilanti carmina libro, to the red colour in the margins of a papyrus roll or red coloured incised letters, cf. Korzeniewski 1971, 93, Vinchesi 1991, 268; see also 1996, 95; 2012, 710; 2014, 250–1, Fey-Wickert 2002, 182.
69 For the structure of Lycidas' song, cf. especially Friedrich 1976, 85–7, Fey-Wickert 2002, 182–5.
70 Cf. also Friedrich 1976, 82.
71 Cf. also Friedrich 1976, 88, 218, Fey-Wickert 2002, 24, 186, 188, 189–90, Vinchesi 2014, 252; see also McKeown 1989, 34–5, Murgatroyd 1991, 251, Knox 1995, 264, Nisbet-Rudd 2004, 117.
72 Cf. Pichon 1966, 202, Fey-Wickert 2002, 26, 188, Vinchesi 1991, 269–70; 2012, 710 and n. 28; 2014, 252.

carmen (cf. *Ars* 2.285[73]). However, according to the traditional pastoral norm, singing is regularly the outcome of the 'convening' of two or more pastoral figures whiling away the heat of a summer noontide, while the song of a lone performer and, what is more, during the night, recalls the 'unpastoral' night-time playing of the *syrinx* by Cyclops in Theocr. 11.38–40, a fact accounting, as already remarked, along with other thematic and stylistic / metrical reasons, uncommon in pastoral (e.g. the unusual animal mixture in vv. 40–1; see above, p. 131), for its standing outside the main Theocritean pastoral tradition. The sadness the lover experiences due to his alienation from his beloved (vv. 46–7) recalls Corydon's similar feelings, voiced as part of the elegiac discourse he constructs for winning the favours of the urban *puer* Alexis, at Verg. *Ecl.* 2.6 ff. As for the wakefulness of the lover (v. 47: *et excluso disperdit lumina somno*), the immediate 'idyllic' model comes from a non-pastoral Theocritean poem, namely the agriculture mime of Theocr. 10[74], where in v. 10 Bucaeus asks his fellow-reaper, Milon, whether he has ever experienced a sleepless night out of love. The tears of an *exclusus amator*, a further elegiac stock topic (cf. Prop. 1.16.47–8, 3.25.9, Ov. *Am.* 1.6.17–8, *Rem.* 36), as suggested by the *exclusus* Lycidas' weeping, because of his separation from his beloved (v. 47: *dum flet*), recalls yet another non-pastoral idyll, namely the crying of the homoerotic scorned lover of [Theocr.] 23 (cf. vv. 17 ff.)[75]. The image of these tears of love as harmful to the lover's eyes (v. 47: *dum flet et excluso disperdit lumina somno*) also has an elegiac record (cf. Catul. 68.55–6, Tib. 1.8.68, Prop. 1.18.15–6)[76].

What is more, the animal and plant comparisons of the following lines (vv. 48–9 including the image of a thrust and a stripped olive-tree, on the one hand, as well as a hare and a gleaner, on the other), in the priamel form, both being stylistic markers of earlier pastoral[77], are yet again associated here with the elegiac topic of the aimless wanderings of a lover (v. 50: *ut Lycidas domina sine Phyllide tabidus erro*), occurring in pastoral, but significantly in the elegising Pasiphae-narrative of the sixth Vergilian eclogue, v. 52: *a, virgo infelix, tu nunc in montibus erras*[78], i.e., in the narrative segment also adopting, as already previously remarked (cf. p. 129), several 'generic markers' of the epyllion. This rather elegiac setting is completed with the *topos*-imagery of the erotic pallor

---

73 Cf. Vinchesi 1991, 269; 2012, 711; 2014, 252.
74 Cf. also Vinchesi 1991, 269, Fey-Wickert 2002, 189.
75 Cf. also Fey-Wickert 2002, 189; see also pp. 24, 25, 186, McKeown 1989, 132.
76 Cf. Vinchesi 1991, 269; 2012, 711 and n. 30; 2014, 252–3, Fey-Wickert 2002, 188–9; see also Theocr. *Ep.* 6.1–2, Verdière 1954, 151, Korzeniewski 1971, 30.
77 Cf. Karakasis 2011, 19–20, 24, 32, 160, 329; see also Vinchesi 2014, 253.
78 Cf. also Fey-Wickert 2002, 193, Vinchesi 2014, 254.

(v. 45: *iam pallidus*), also common in the elegiac register (cf. Prop. 2.5.30 combined with the penitence-motif as here, 3.8.28, Ov. *Am.* 3.6.25–6, *Ars* 1.729, Hor. *Carm.* 3.10.14[79]), but absent from the pre-Calpurnian pastoral tradition, although it appears in the non-bucolic second Theocritean idyll (v. 88), the designation of Phyllis as *domina* (v. 50, cf. Catul. 68.68, Tib. 1.1.46, 1.5.40, 2.3.83, Prop. 1.1.21, Ov. *Am.* 2.17.5, 2.18.17, *Epist.* 18.118, 164, *Ars* 1.504[80]), suggesting the elegiac and comic notion of the *servitium amoris* (cf. Tib. 1.1.55–6, 2.4.1–4, [Tib.] 3.4.66, Prop. 1.4.1–4, 2.8.15, Ov. *Am.* 1.2.18; see also Men. *Mis.* fr. 4 Arnott, 791 K–A, Ter. *Eun.* 1026–7, *Phorm.* 144[81]), the also elegiac use of *tabidus* of a worn lover (v. 50, cf. also Prop. 3.6.23, Ov. *Epist.* 21.60[82]) and, lastly, the motif of a distraught elegiac lover's failure to properly appreciate his surroundings, because of his beloved's absence (cf. Ov. *Am.* 2.16.33–40[83]), as in the case of Lycidas here, who is unable, because of his broken heart, to see the white colour of the lilies or to taste the fountains and the wine, but only when his Phyllis comes back into his sight (vv. 51–4).

Werbung

It is from v. 55 that the *Werbung* commences, primarily fashioned on Polyphemus' rhetoric to win over Galatea in the 'generically peculiar' eleventh Theocritean idyll as well as on its primary Roman adaptation, i.e., Corydon's elegiac narrative in the second Vergilian eclogue, composed in the hope of securing the erotic favours of Alexis.

---

[79] Cf. also Vinchesi 1991, 269; 2012, 710 and n. 27; 2014, 251, Fey-Wickert 2002, 24, 187–8, Di Lorenzo-Pellegrino 2008, 192; see also Pichon 1966, 224–5, Hollis 1977, 143, Nisbet-Rudd 2004, 146.
[80] Cf. Pichon 1966, 134, Korzeniewski 1971, 94, Messina 1975, 47 and n. 23, Friedrich 1976, 89, Vinchesi 1991, 265, 271; 1996, 37–8; 2012, 708; 2014, 50, 254, Keene 1996, 86, Fey-Wickert 2002, 25, 192, Di Lorenzo-Pellegrino 2008, 193; see also Murgatroyd 1991, 62, Maltby 2002, 138, Perrelli 2002, 31.
[81] Cf. Murgatroyd 1994, 126, Navarro-Antolín 1996, 371–2, Maltby 2002, 142, 417; for the motif in Vergilian pastoral, see especially Martirosova 1999, 71–93.
[82] Cf. Pichon 1966, 273, Vinchesi 1991, 270–1; 2012, 708; 2014, 50, 254, Friedrich 1976, 88–9, Fey-Wickert 2002, 186, 192–3; see also Fedeli 1985, 216.
[83] Cf. Fey-Wickert 2002, 193–4, Vinchesi 2014, 255; see also McKeown 1998, 355. In terms of this chiefly elegiac motif the distressed lover is unable to appreciate his surroundings; thus I do not share the view that the Calpurnian lines in question are modelled on [Theocr.] 8.41–8 and Verg. *Ecl.* 7.53–60 (cf. e.g. Messina 1975, 47, Pearce 1990, 71), both depicting the changes nature undergoes because of a beloved's presence / absence.

Musical Excellence

First comes, in vv. 55–60, the topic of the musical excellence of the lover, recalling both Theocr. 11.38–40 and Verg. *Ecl.* 2.23–4[84], where, respectively, Polyphemus is supposed to outshine all other Cyclops in the playing of the bucolic *syrinx*, and Corydon calls attention to his musical distinction by comparing himself with mythological figures, like the legendary singer Amphion. What is more, the idea of a loving couple enjoying pastoral music together, as suggested by the imagery of a joyful Phyllis deriving pleasure from Lycidas' singing (vv. 55–6), also alludes to the second Vergilian eclogue, namely to v. 31, where, as already previously observed (cf. p. 132), Corydon invites his beloved boy to enjoy their love and practise music together in the woods[85]. The motif of a lovers' kiss harks back to the 'generically awry' third and eleventh Theocritean idylls, where, however, the kisses are, according to pre-Calpurnian pastoral ethics, only sought after but never granted; thus, whereas for both the anonymous goatherd of Theocr. 3 and the Cyclops of Theocr. 11, a kiss from their sweet-hearts, Amaryllis (vv. 19–20) and Galatea (vv. 55–6), is simply a wish, Phyllis is presented as interrupting with her kisses the musical performance of her lover (vv. 56–8)[86], thus adopting a further elegiac *topos*, namely kisses breaking off a lover's speech or song (cf. Ov. *Am.* 2.4.26, *Epist.* 13.119–20, 15.44)[87].

The narrative continues with Lycidas accusing his erotic rival of musical incompetence; Mopsus' coarse voice, his unmoving song and the screech of his discordant pipe do not give, according to Lycidas, Phyllis good reasons for staying with the former (vv. 59–60), especially after she has experienced his own musical expertise (cf. vv. 55–6). Pastoral song is the highest value of the 'green cabinet', coveted by all its members, and thus Mopsus' lack of musical abilities, possibly also suggested by *anhelus* in v. 35: *Mopso...anhelo*, if read as an adjective in the sense of 'musically deficient'[88], should have made Phyllis reject him. Mopsus' voice is crucially described as *torrida* (vv. 59–60), i.e., as the

---

[84] Cf. Fey-Wickert 2002, 197.
[85] Cf. Friedrich 1976, 90, Fey-Wickert 2002, 197.
[86] Cf. Fey-Wickert 2002, 197.
[87] Cf. Verdière 1954, 245; 1966, 170 and n. 64, Korzeniewski 1971, 31, Friedrich 1976, 90–1, Amat 1991, 29, Vinchesi 1991, 271; 2012, 709 and n. 21; 2014, 257, Fey-Wickert 2002, 25, 198, Di Lorenzo-Pellegrino 2008, 193–4; see also McKeown 1998, 75–6, Reeson 2001, 184.
[88] Cf. Amat 1991, 106, Keene 1996, 84, Fey-Wickert 2002, 177–8; for *anhelus* as an adjective with obscene associations, cf. Korzeniewski 1971, 93, for the formation as equivalent to *anhelans propter amorem*, cf. Vinchesi 2014, 246–7, whereas for a verbal form here – *anhelo*, see Pearce 1990, 69, Coronati 1995–8, 393–404.

opposite of *liquidus*[89] denoting Callimachean aestheticism and its notion of poetic purity, of 'the unblemished' (cf. Chapter 2, pp. 78–9 and n. 163); Lycidas' rival is thus depicted not only as musically deficient, but also as opposing Callimachean–Neoteric sensibilities, which may make Phyllis' leaving Lycidas for the un–Callimachean Mopsus more reprehensible. Blaming a pastoral character for lack of musical skill has its bucolic precedents in both Theocr. 5.5–7, where Comatas gives Lacon the advice to stick to playing a simple reed in a duet with Corydon, for he is not worth of playing the *syrinx*, and Verg. *Ecl.* 3.26–7[90], where Menalcas accuses Damoetas of producing a miser tune on a scrannel straw. Whereas, however, in the above cases, as in Calp. 6.17ff., where Astylus also makes fun of Lycidas' alleged musical incompetence, thus causing the latter's irate reaction (cf. Chapter 7, pp. 232–3), the blames function only as part of a bickering, framing the song–exchange that follows or is expected to happen next, and are simply intended as a means of embarrassing the pastoral opponent, in Calp. 3 they are instead integrated within the elegising *Werbung* of the lover–Lycidas.

Beauty

There follows the motif of the lover's handsomeness (vv. 61–2), again harking back to the elegiac discourse of Verg. *Ecl.* 2, namely to vv. 25–7[91], where, in imitation of the Cyclops at Theocr. 6.34–40, Corydon too, as part of his elegiac *Werbung* to charm Alexis away from Iollas, is presented as in no doubt about his beauty, on the basis of his reflection on the calm waters of the sea. What is more, just as Lycidas is, in Calp. 3, compared, in terms of external appearance, with another pastoral figure, Mopsus, Corydon of Verg. *Ecl.* 2 is also weighed against the good looks of another bucolic character, the handsome Daphnis, whom the Vergilian pastoral lover believes to outshine (vv. 26–7). However, in both these instances, the lover is self-assured about his good looks, whereas in the Calpurnian lines (vv. 61–2) the lover is described as more comely than his erotic rival, on the basis of the relevant claims of a different character, namely Phyllis, and not himself. This last detail crucially transposes the 'idyllic' allu-

---

[89] Cf. Gagliardi 1984, 40 and n. 47, Keene 1996, 87, Fey–Wickert 2002, 200, Vinchesi 2014, 258.
[90] Cf. Korzeniewski 1971, 31, Leach 1975, 215, 228 and n. 27, Friedrich 1976, 91, Vinchesi 1991, 271–2; 2014, 259, Fey–Wickert 2002, 201, Di Lorenzo–Pellegrino 2008, 194.
[91] Cf. Korzeniewski 1971, 31, Messina 1975, 48, Friedrich 1976, 93, Fey–Wickert 2002, 201, Vinchesi 2014, 259.

sions to the non–Theocritean eighth idyll, where (vv. 72–3) Daphnis' beauty is similarly affirmed by a young pastoral girl as well as to the non–pastoral second urban mime, Theocr. 2.125, where Simaetha's darling, the handsome Delphis, maintains that his friends call him handsome, and to the non–Theocritean twentieth pastoral, v. 30, when the herdsman of the idyll similarly asserts the admiration all the women of his pastoral region show for his looks[92]. This combination of pastoral idylls (though not of Theocritean paternity) with a non–pastoral poem of the Theocritean corpus may also be significant as to the 'generically diversifying' character of the present Calpurnian eclogue, taking once again under consideration the use on Calpurnius' part of several non–pastoral Theocritean models as a means of going beyond more or less established pastoral 'generic norms'. The combined use of *sequi* and *fugere* in v. 60: *quem sequeris? quem, Phylli, fugis?*, in the sense of 'to be in the pursuit of' and of 'to flee from' a beloved respectively, seem to complete the elegising 'generic picture' of the lines developing the beauty–motif; the verbs also appear in this sense at Theocr. 6.17: καὶ **φεύγει** φιλέοντα καὶ οὐ φιλέοντα **διώκει** and 11.75: τί τὸν **φεύγοντα διώκεις;**, when the Cyclops eventually understands his 'pastoral dislocation' and consequently urges himself not to pursue a fleeing lady. The second verb is also found in the elegiac register of Corydon in Verg. *Ecl*. 2.60: *quem fugis, a! demens?*[93], where, in his protreptic to rustic life, the pastoral lover invites his darling to dwell in the woods with him. These pastoral intertexts with their peculiar 'generic profile' also add to the 'generic ambivalence' of the lines; this 'generic feeling' is enhanced by the *clausula iurare solebas* (v. 62), harking back to the elegiac narrative of Ov. *Fast*. 3.485, namely the story of Ariadne, betrayed by both Theseus and Bacchus[94].

Wealth

Vv. 63–7 cover the topic of the pastoral lover's wealth, also alluding to the two chief intertexts of Lycidas' love–poem, namely Theocr. 11.34–7, where Polyphemus similarly advertises his thousand animals, his milk, his cheese and his al-

---

92 Cf. also Fey-Wickert 2002, 201–2.
93 Cf. Cesareo 1931, 29, Verdière 1954, 152, Korzeniewski 1971, 31, Messina 1975, 48, Friedrich 1976, 92, Gagliardi 1984, 40 and n. 48, Vinchesi 1991, 272; 2014, 259, Fey-Wickert 2002, 26, 202–3, Di Lorenzo–Pellegrino 2008, 194.
94 Cf. Verdière 1954, 153, Korzeniewski 1971, 32, Fey-Wickert 2002, 204, Di Lorenzo–Pellegrino 2008, 195, Vinchesi 1991, 272; 2014, 260.

ways loaded racks, and to Verg. *Ecl.* 2.19–22[95], i.e., to Corydon's elegiac *Werbung* yet again presenting the lover's pastoral property, i.e., a thousand lambs and a constant milk supply. The lines are complemented with two additional motifs, which, although associated with typical bucolic circumstances in the previous pastoral tradition, are included here by Lycidas in his rhetoric with a view to persuading his former companion to abandon her new lover, i.e., function as part of an elegiac rather than a traditionally pastoral state of affairs. The motif of the evening count of one's animals, instantiated in v. 64: *quot nostri numerantur vespere tauri*, with the reckoning of Lycidas' bulls at even-tide, has its parallels in [Theocr.] 8.15–6, where Menalcas declares his inability to pledge a lamb, out of fear for his parents, who count their flock every evening, and Verg. *Ecl.* 3.32–4, where likewise Menalcas does not wager animals from his flock, because of his stern father and step-mother, who count their flock twice a day[96]. This is a typical pastoral activity concluding the pastoral doings of the day and bringing, on the level of poetics, the pastoral narrative to its closure, as in Verg. *Ecl.* 6.85–6[97]. However, the topic is in the afore-mentioned instances associated with typical activities of the pastoral tradition, namely the pledging of stakes, of prizes for a forthcoming bucolic singing match and the driving of the flock back to its stalls, in opposition to Calp. 3, where it operates as part of Lycidas' *Werbende Dichtung* over a lost sweet-heart. What is more, the *terminus technicus certare*, used in earlier pastoral of an agonistic singing match (cf. Chapter 3, pp. 102–3), is here associated with the image of two lovers competing for the love of a lady in an erotic triangle, vv. 63–4: *certaverit ille tot haedos / pascere quod nostri numerantur vespere tauri*. Similar is the 'generic transposition' of the motif of a productive animal, indicated by the image of the over-milked and fertile heifers of vv. 65–7. The prolific goat of the programmatic first Theocritean idyll, cf. Theocr. 1.25–6, as well as the cow of Verg. *Ecl.* 3.29–30[98], milked twice a day and suckling two younglings, function again as the trophy for a pastoral singer and do not belong to a discourse aiming to comfort a separated lover. Although modelled on the Theocritean and Vergilian passages mentioned above, the wealth-motif here significantly alludes, in its details, to a third model text, after which the present narrative seems to be primarily fashioned. In opposition to both the Theocritean and the Vergilian intertext, in the Calpurnian in-

---

95 Cf. Cesareo 1931, 30, Verdière 1954, 153, Friedrich 1976, 93, Amat 1991, 106, Vinchesi 1991, 272; 2014, 260, Fey-Wickert 2002, 205.
96 Cf. also Verdière 1954, 153, Korzeniewski 1971, 32, Vinchesi 1991, 272; 2014, 260, Fey-Wickert 2002, 207–8, Di Lorenzo-Pellegrino 2008, 195.
97 Cf. also Pearce 1990, 72, Keene 1996, 87, Fey-Wickert 2002, 207, Vinchesi 2014, 260.
98 Cf. also Vinchesi 1991, 272, Fey-Wickert 2002, 208.

stance there is no mention of the exact number of the animals the pastoral lover has in his possession; this, along with the lady's knowledge of her lover's riches (v. 65: *scis, optima Phylli*) and the mention of curdled milk (v. 69), point to Ov. *Met.* 13.821–30 as the immediate model; but this text[99], availing itself of a clear 'generic interaction' between elegy, pastoral and epic (see above, p. 137), further underscores the 'transcending generic anxieties' of the present passage as well. The *clausula ubera natos* in v. 67, found, although in a slight different form, in the same metrical position twice in the Vergilian epic as well[100], cf. *A.* 3.392: *ubera nati*, 5.285: *ubere nati*, may also be read as adding to the 'generic ambivalence' of the passage.

Repentance

The next theme to be developed is that of the lover's penitence, vv. 70–5. Because of the erotic predicament he finds himself in, Lycidas refrains from every day menial activities of the pastoral space, such as basket weaving and milk curdling (vv. 68–9). This abstention from bucolic occupations as a result of the pastoral lover's distress over his erotic plight has its parallels yet again in Theocr. 11.72ff, when the Cyclops exhorts himself to return to basket weaving and other bucolic tasks, once he has realised his earlier 'pastoral dislocation' and reinstated himself in the pastoral tradition and the sexual looseness of the 'green cabinet'. The same happens with Corydon of the second Vergilian eclogue; he ceases abstaining from pastoral works, when he decides to 'mend' his elegiac propensities and return to the pastoral norm; he thus similarly urges himself to undertake vine pruning and plaiting once again (vv. 69–73)[101], to scorn Alexis and look for another lover, according to pastoral rules concerning sexuality; see also above, p. 128.

In both these cases the non-participation in bucolic occupations is viewed as rather 'unpastoral' in character and a similar movement away from traditional pastoral norms is similarly evidenced by Lycidas' abstention. Lycidas feels such guilt that he offers his hands to be bound behind his back with osier and vine-twig, securing a sense of a pertinent traditional pastoralism, lest Phyllis becomes afraid of his blows (vv. 70–2, cf. also Tib. 1.6.73, Ov. *Am.* 1.7.1, 28)[102]. This is the

---

99 Cf. also Friedrich 1976, 93–5, Vinchesi 1991, 272, Fey-Wickert 2002, 206.
100 Cf. Korzeniewski 1971, 32, Vinchesi 2014, 261.
101 Cf. Friedrich 1976, 94, Vinchesi 1991, 272; 2014, 261–2, Fey-Wickert 2002, 209.
102 Cf. Verdière 1954, 155, Fey-Wickert 2002, 25, 211–3, Vinchesi 2014, 263; see also McKeown 1989, 165.

way, however, he adds, the night robber Mopsus was punished by another pastoral figure, Tityrus, within the classic pastoral setting of a sheep-fold (vv. 73–4). But, for all the typical bucolic accessories of the incident, the motif is not part of the earlier pastoral tradition. Accusations of theft appear in the pre-Calpurnian pastoral tradition, mostly as a part of a bickering scene leading to a song-exchange, and relate to the pastoral motif of 'the belittlement of the pastoral opponent'. Thus in Theocr. 5.1ff. Comatas blames Lacon for having pilfered his lamb-skin and Lacon counter-accuses Comatas of stealing his pipe, whereas in Verg. *Ecl.* 3.3ff. Menalcas accuses Damoetas of over-milking Aegon's sheep and stealing Damon's goat[103]. Such accusations of theft, however, are used in Calp. 3 as a means for Lycidas to deride his erotic opponent and thus win back his former girlfriend; they are, in other words, again associated with an erotic triangle of the type favoured in the elegiac and elegising register.

The image of the 'slender basket' Lycidas refrains from weaving (vv. 68–9: *sed mihi nec gracilis sine te fiscella salicto / texitur*) has clear meta-poetological connotations, for in earlier pastoral this activity is related to the production of pastoral poetry itself; in the programmatic tenth Vergilian eclogue the pastoral poet himself is also depicted as plaiting a basket with 'slender *hibiscum*', v. 71: *dum sedet et gracili fiscellam texit hibisco*[104], an image suggesting, by means of the well-known poetological catch-word *gracilis*, the Neoteric-Callimachean persuasion of the Vergilian bucolics[105] (cf. also above, pp. 61–2, 104–5). The rejection of this programmatic meta-poetic occupation is here associated with Lycidas' erotic troubles, in other words, as far as poetics are concerned, with his 'elegiac generic leaning'. Non-Callimachean / anti-Neoteric imagery is again associated, as elsewhere in Calpurnian pastoral, with instances of 'pastoral dislocation', of a 'generic transcending' from the earlier pastoral 'generic rules'.

Gifts

In vv. 76–85 Lycidas develops the topic of the erotic gifts[106], once more as part of a lover's attempt to regain his beloved; the distressed lover reminds Phyllis of the presents he has showered upon her during their affair, namely animals (turtle

---

103 Cf. also Fey-Wickert 2002, 214, Vinchesi 2014, 263–4.
104 Cf. Verdière 1954, 155, Korzeniewski 1971, 32–3, Friedrich 1976, 94, Pearce 1990, 72, Vinchesi 1991, 272; 2014, 262, Keene 1996, 88, Fey-Wickert 2002, 209, Di Lorenzo-Pellegrino 2008, 195.
105 Cf. Karakasis 2011, 34.
106 Cf. Friedrich 1976, 95–6.

doves and a new born hare), flowers (lilies and roses) and a wreath (vv. 76–80). The motif of the presents aiming to lure the beloved once again alludes to Theocr. 11.40–1, where Polyphemus offers his sweet-heart eleven fawns and four bear cubs as well as to vv. 56–9, where lilies and poppies are again bestowed upon Galatea as a gift. A similar situation is developed in Verg. *Ecl.* 2.40–55, where Corydon presents his beloved boy Alexis with similar gifts; Alexis is also given lilies and many other plants, fruits and flowers (violets, poppies, narcissus, fennel flower, cassia, sweet herbs, hyacinth, marigold, quinces, chestnuts, plums, laurel, myrtle)[107]. As far as the animal offers are concerned, doves as love-gifts appear as the song-topic of a singing match in Theocr. 5.96–7, 133 and Verg. *Ecl.* 3.68–9[108]. But the very combination of the turtle doves with a hare points to the model of Ov. *Met.* 13.831–9[109], the Ovidian version of Polyphemus' bucolic love, where a similar grouping of gifts also appears. Once again the 'generically diversifying' intertext underlines the 'generic ambivalence' of the present passage, as already earlier pointed out in the case of the wealth-motif (cf. pp. 142–4). As far as the flowers are concerned, whereas lilies occur as love-gifts in Theocr. 11.56 and Verg. *Ecl.* 2.45–6, and roses in the non-pastoral Theocr. 10.34, this particular Calpurnian grouping of lilies with roses, also suggesting the white / rose colouring of an elegiac *puella*'s complexion, have no pastoral precedents[110], in contrast to their regular attestation in the elegiac genre (cf. Ov. *Am.* 2.5.34–42, 3.3.5–6; see also Catul. 61.194–5)[111]. Lastly, the offering of a wreath as a love-gift, an action with a good elegiac precedent (cf. Tib. 1.2.14, Prop. 1.16.7–8, Ov. *Am.* 1.6.67–8, *Ars* 2.528, *Rem.* 32[112]), testifying to the lover's vigil, does not have a pastoral parallel; it seems that in Theocr. 3.21–3 the wreath does not function as a present but rather belongs to the typical accessories of a komast, who threatens to tear it up in pieces, because of his erotic grief over his non-reciprocated love for Amaryllis.

---

[107] Cf. Cesareo 1931, 32 and n. 2, Fey-Wickert 2002, 217, Vinchesi 2014, 265.
[108] Cf. Korzeniewski 1971, 94, Vinchesi 1991, 273; 2014, 265, Fey-Wickert 2002, 218.
[109] Cf. Cesareo 1931, 32 and n. 2, Verdière 1954, 155, Korzeniewski 1971, 33, Friedrich 1976, 96, Vinchesi 1991, 273; 2014, 265, Keene 1996, 89, Fey-Wickert 2002, 218, 219, Di Lorenzo-Pellegrino 2008, 196.
[110] Cf. Friedrich 1976, 96; see also Vinchesi 2014, 266.
[111] Cf. Vinchesi 1991, 273; 2014, 266, Fey-Wickert 2002, 219; see also McKeown 1998, 95–6.
[112] Cf. also Korzeniewski 1971, 94, Fey-Wickert 2002, 221; see also Fedeli 1980, 374, McKeown 1989, 158, Murgatroyd 1991, 78, Janka 1997, 388, Maltby 2002, 159.

The motif of the erotic gifts is in vv. 81–5 associated with a second round of the wealth topic. A well-off Lycidas is opposed to a Mopsus of small means, unable to offer Phyllis any valuable gifts (v. 81: *aurea sed forsan mendax tibi munera iactat*), but only false promises. Mopsus is accordingly described as gathering lupines, as boiling beans, being short of bread, as well as as grinding barley of low quality with his hand-mill, all suggesting the image of an individual in abject poverty (vv. 82–5, cf. Colum. 2.9.14, 2.10.1, *Moret.* 21–9), reminiscent, up to a point, of the fishermen's deprivation in the non-bucolic Theocr. 21[113]. The opposition between a *dives amator* and his impoverished erotic rival / a less well-to-do *rivalis*, however, is typical of the comic and the elegiac code (cf. Tib. 1.9.53, Prop. 4.5, Ov. *Am.* 1.8.31–2 and the function of the *miles gloriosus* in Roman Comedy). References to a pastoral figure's poverty are found elsewhere in earlier pastoral yet again in the quarrel framing the song-exchange of Theocr. 5 and Verg. *Ecl.* 3[114]. The Theocritean Comatas claims (vv. 5–7) that Lacon's slave status of small means does not allow him to own a pipe, and likewise for Lacon Comatas could never have been the owner of a skin, not afforded even by his master Evmaras (vv. 8–10); in a similar vein, Menalcas in Verg. *Ecl.* 3.25–6 claims that his hard-up pastoral opponent could never have owned a wax-jointed pipe. As with several other motifs, this poverty topic as well, used in the earlier pastoral tradition as a means for disparaging the pastoral antagonist, is here yet again incorporated in Lycidas' *Werbende Dichtung* and in his effort, as commonly in the case of the elegiac lover (cf. especially the Ovidian heroines; see also Ov. *Am.* 1.4), to devalue his erotic opponent[115].

Threats for Suicide

Last but not least comes the motif of a suffering lover's threats of suicide, vv. 86–91. Lycidas threatens to hang himself from an oak-tree, in his effort to make Phyllis come back to him. A similar resolution to die comes from the anonymous goatherd of Theocr. 3.9, 24–7, 52–4[116]; yet the lover's attempts at suicide (hanging, plunging into the sea, being eaten by lions) are here presented as giving

---

113 Cf. also Verdière 1954, 246, Korzeniewski 1971, 95, Leach 1975, 215, Friedrich 1976, 221–2, Amat 1991, 30, 107, Vinchesi 1991, 274; 1996, 99; 2014, 268–9, Keene 1996, 89–90, Fey-Wickert 2002, 216–7, 222–4.
114 Cf. Friedrich 1976, 97, Fey-Wickert 2002, 216.
115 Cf. Vinchesi 1991, 273.
116 Cf. Korzeniewski 1971, 34, Garson 1974, 672, Messina 1975, 41, Friedrich 1976, 83, 98, Vinchesi 1991, 274; 2014, 270, Keene 1996, 90, Fey-Wickert 2002, 226.

pleasure to his dearest, not reciprocating the love of the herdsman, and thus has been compellingly read as tongue in cheek[117]. The lover's suicidal disposition links the passage in question with Verg. *Ecl.* 8.58–60, where the anonymous goatherd of Damon's song drowns himself at the end, as a result of the nasty situation he experiences, namely the loss of his beloved Nysa to a rival lover, significantly named Mopsus[118], within a contextual setting evoking several elegiac ideals and situations along with an elimination of traditional pastoral assets and norms (cf. Karakasis 2011, 133–44). Threats for suicide do also belong to the discourse of the elegiac lover (cf. also Tib. 2.6.19–20, Prop. 1.6.27–8, 2.8.17 ff., Ov. *Rem.* 17 ff., 601 ff.). In elegy, the lover contemplates committing suicide according to a standard 'generic trend' as is also the case with the *adulescens* in love of the comic genre (e.g. Ter. *Phorm.* 551 f.[119]).

What is more, in Calp. 3 the hanging–motif is coupled with the inscription of a sepulchral epigram, for Lycidas asks for an epigram to be affixed on the oak upon which he will hang himself, holding Phyllis responsible for his death and, accordingly, warning the young shepherds away from female fickleness (vv. 89–90). The motif of self-inflicted death in conjunction with a sepulchral epigram, bearing witness to a lover's cruelty, as here, points yet again to a non-pastoral idyll as the more plausible direct 'idyllic' model of the lines, namely [Theocr.] 23.20–1[120], 46–8, where a lover's voluntary death, although yet again intended to function, as in Theocr. 3, as a gift to the cruel beloved, is evidenced by an inscription testifying to the erotic heartlessness of an indifferent lover. Similar inscribed texts associated with the distress of a lover do come about in elegy, especially in the Ovidian *Heroines*, where in *Epist.* 2.145–8 and 7.195–6, just as here, the epigram at the end of an epistolary narrative discloses the names of the lovers and puts blame on the pitiless lover (cf. also [Tib.] 3.2.29–30, Prop. 2.1.78, 2.13.35–6)[121].

The only other instance of an epigram in pre-Calpurnian pastoral comes from Verg. *Ecl.* 5, where Daphnis asks the following epigram to be inscribed on his tomb, vv. 43–4: '*Daphnis ego in silvis, hinc usque ad sidera notus, / formosi*

---

[117] Cf. Otis 1964, 111, Papanghelis 1995, 95, Karakasis 2011, 142 and n. 73.
[118] Cf. Cesareo 1931, 35, Friedrich 1976, 66, Pearce 1990, 74, Vinchesi 1991, 274, Fey-Wickert 2002, 226.
[119] Cf. Duckworth 1952, 239 and n. 5.
[120] Cf. De Sipio 1935, 108, Messina 1975, 50, Hutchinson 2013, 343, Vinchesi 2014, 271.
[121] Cf. also Korzeniewski 1971, 34, Friedrich 1976, 98–100, Vinchesi 1991, 274; 1996, 39 and nn. 63, 64, 65; 2012, 711–2; 2014, 271–2, Fey-Wickert 2002, 226–7, 229–30; see also Di Lorenzo-Pellegrino 2008, 197, 198, Barchiesi 1992, 180–2, Knox 1995, 139, 233, Fedeli 2005, 103–5, 395–6, Piazzi 2007, 303–5.

pectoris custos, formosior ipse'. Although the epigram also suggests the 'generic diversifying' character of a new Roman pastoral of Vergil's *Eclogues* in relation to the Greek pastoral tradition, interacting as it does to a much greater extent than Theocritean and post–Theocritean Greek bucolic poetry with politics and contemporary history (see also above, p. 136), the erotic nature of the Calpurnian lines in question indicates [Theocr.] 23 as the primary 'idyllic' model of the passage, a tell–tale, due to its 'unpastoral' plot, of a Neronian transcending of the earlier bucolic norm in keeping with Calpurnius' poetics. Finally, the designation of Phyllis' affair with Mopsus as *turpis* (v. 86, cf. Prop. 2.16.36, 3.21.33, Ov. *Am.* 3.11a.2[122]), the elegiac wording in *nostros...violavit amores* (v. 88, cf. Tib. 1.3.81, 1.9.19[123]) as well as the motif of the *levitas* of young women (v. 90, cf. Tib. 1.9.40, Prop. 1.15.1, 2.1.49, 2.24.18, Ov. *Am.* 3.1.41[124]) also increase, due to their elegiac parallels, the elegising character of the Calpurnian passage.

The Concluding Narrative

Iollas will sing Lycidas' lyrics to Phyllis; emphasis is crucially given to the harmonious musical performance of Lycidas' song by Iollas in front of Phyllis (v. 93). This testifies yet again to the high value of song within the precincts of the pastoral community, put here in the service of Lycidas' erotic endeavours. During Iollas' performance, Lycidas will, out of fear, conceal himself with a thorny reed–grass or hide beneath a garden enclose (vv. 94–5). A similar setting at Verg. *Ecl.* 3.20[125] is associated with the motif of the thief–pastoral opponent as part of an *altercatio* leading to a song–exchange; Damoetas is thus charged with hiding behind the rushes, after Menalcas realises the stealing of Damon's goat (vv. 16–20). The topic is here, as commonly in Calp. 3, incorporated into Lycidas' elegising situation.

---

122 Cf. Fey–Wickert 2002, 25, 227, Di Lorenzo–Pellegrino 2008, 197, Vinchesi 2014, 270.
123 Cf. Verdière 1954, 157, Paladini 1956, 524, Korzeniewski 1971, 34, Messina 1975, 50, Amat 1991, 30, Di Lorenzo–Pellegrino 2008, 198, Vinchesi 2012, 711 and n. 33; 2014, 50, 271.
124 Cf. Vinchesi 1991, 274; 2012, 711 and n. 34; 2014, 271–2, Fey–Wickert 2002, 24, 230, Di Lorenzo–Pellegrino 2008, 198; see also Fedeli 2005, 87, 688.
125 Cf. also Verdière 1954, 246, Korzeniewski 1971, 35, Leach 1975, 216, 228 and n. 30, Vinchesi 1991, 275; 2014, 273, Amat 1995, 81, Keene 1996, 91, Fey–Wickert 2002, 233.

Tityrus brings Iollas' lost cow back, an event which is viewed by the latter as a good *omen*, predicting a happy end to Lycidas' erotic troubles (vv. 96–8)[126]. The association of Phyllis with a cow alludes to the eighth Vergilian eclogue, where in Alphesiboeus' song (vv. 85–9), recounting Daphnis' elegiac breaking of his earlier pastoral affair, the unnamed sorceress, in the elegiac state of mind of a *dura puella*, wishes that her former lover will suffer like a worn out heifer looking for her mate. The association of Phyllis with a cow and Mopsus with a bull alludes to Ov. *Am.* 3.5, where, as already previously remarked (cf. p. 129), in his dream the poet views his sweet-heart in the form of a cow and himself as a bull[127]. Be that as it may, the image of a girl as a cow occurs in the elegiac register (cf. Ov. *Epist.* 5.117, 124; see also Hor. *Carm.* 2.5.5–9) and is also found in Theocr. 11.21, where Galatea is described as more playful than a calf[128].

Menander's *Perikeiromene*[129]

It has been previously argued that the presence in Calp. 3 of several common motifs of the comic genre (e.g. the function of Iollas as a kind of *servus fallax*, helping the *adulescens in amore* Lycidas with his love-affair, the presence of a dowry-wife and a flute-girl, the motif of a rich erotic rival, military imagery with erotic connotations, the unbearable pain of the comic lover, the female erotic fickleness, the *exclusus amator*-motif, the topic of the *servitium amoris* and the male erotic violence, of the erotic sleeplessness as well as various stylistic options, as is for example the designation of the erotic rival as *novus*, the use of *contentus* for erotic exclusivity) constitute a modal intrusion of the comic *genus* into a pastoral host–text. However, in a note of his *MH* 29, 1972 paper (p. 215 and n. 5), entitled *Die Eklogen des Calpurnius Siculus als Gedichtbuch*, D. Korzeniewski compellingly suggested, though in passing without particular elaboration, an influence of Menander's *Shorn Girl* on the third eclogue of Cal-

---

[126] Cf. also Rosenmeyer 1969, 143, 279, Korzeniewski 1971, 92–3, Garson 1974, 670, Messina 1975, 51, Friedrich 1976, 70, Kegel-Brinkgreve 1990, 156, Pearce 1990, 75, Vinchesi 1996, 101; 2014, 230, 274, Keene 1996, 91, Fey-Wickert 2002, 231–2, Di Lorenzo-Pellegrino 2008, 199, Henderson 2013, 183.
[127] Cf. also Friedrich 1976, 70, 74, Vinchesi 1991, 275; 2014, 229–30, Fey-Wickert 2002, 24, 147, 161, 232. For the question whether *Am.* 3.5 is an Ovidian poem or an Ovidian imitation of an elegiac successor, cf. the concise discussion in Antoniadis 2006, 274–5 and the relevant bibliography given there.
[128] Cf. Korzeniewski 1971, 92, 95, Vinchesi 1991, 275, Fey-Wickert 2002, 235; see also Nisbet-Hubbard 1978, 82.
[129] I follow the text of Arnott 1996.

purnius Siculus. This Menandrian comedy seems to have had a widespread distribution, as evidenced by its being mentioned by Philostratus (*Epist.* 16) and Ovid (*Am.* 1.7)[130], and thus may have been directly available to Calpurnius and not through the intermediacy of another author.

A basic detail of its narrative brings Calp. 3 close to *Perikeiromene*'s plot, namely the remorse of a lover at having acted unfairly and attacked his sweet–heart out of jealousy for a rival, and the concomitant sojourn of the lady, who abandons her aggressive lover, with another female character, a detail notably not appearing in the attack incident of Theocr. 14, which also functions as a model for Calp. 3. Thus in Menander, Polemon abuses his sweet–heart, Glykera, and cuts off her hair, because he suspects her, on shaky grounds as in Calp. 3[131], of having an affair with Moschion, whose embraces the young lady does not resist, only out of affection for her twin brother (vv. 155–7)[132]. After the incident of the attack, the molested girl finds refuge in the house of her neighbour, Myrrhine. Similarly, in Calp. 3, Phyllis abandons her lover, Lycidas, because the latter assaults her for having entered, as he believes, an erotic relationship with Mopsus, and finds shelter in the dwelling of another pastoral female figure, Alcippe (v. 33). This is a sequence of events that the Menandrian comedy and the Calpurnian eclogue significantly share, although the combination of Phyllis with Alcippe has a pastoral precedent, coming from Verg. *Ecl.* 7.14, where the two women are also presented in common, as Meliboeus' partners and helpers[133]. This basic plot–detail is also complemented by the following similarities in the contextual setting of the two narratives: both lovers, Polemon and Lycidas, rely on the help of a mediator (not only Sosias, cf. *Per.* 177 ff., 354 ff., but also Pataikos in *Per.*, cf. vv. 504 ff.[134], and Iollas in Calp. 3 for patching things up with their beloved), for they are both unwilling to face their ill–treated lady themselves. What is more, both frustrated lovers threaten, according to the comic / elegiac ethos, to commit suicide[135] (cf. *Per.* 504 ff., 976 ff.[136]), and just as Lycidas brings up the gifts he bestowed upon his beloved in the past, Polemon as well appears to be proud of the jewelry

---

130 Cf. McKeown 1989, 162–4.
131 Cf. Verdière 1954, 149.
132 Cf. Fortenbaugh 1974, 430, Lamagna 1994, 174, Konstan 1995, 107.
133 Cf. Friedrich 1976, 65–6, Pearce 1990, 69, Vinchesi 1996, 91, Fey–Wickert 2002, 176.
134 Cf. also Goldberg 1980, 46, 47, Ireland 1992, 85, 91, Lamagna 1994, 219, Traill 2008, 34.
135 Cf. also Korzeniewski 1972, 215 and n. 5: 'die Geliebte sucht bei einer Freundin Zuflucht; ein Freund des Liebhabers übernimmt die Versöhnung; der Liebhaber droht mit Selbstmord'.
136 Cf. also Gomme–Sandbach 1973, 526, Goldberg 1980, 52, Lamagna 1994, 248–9, Konstan 1995, 113, Lape 2004, 181 and n. 34.

and the clothes he provided his darling with (vv. 512 ff.[137]). This association of Calp. 3 with Menander's *Perikeiromene* further increases the comic colouring of the pastoral narrative and enhances, to a greater extent, the comic modal intrusion, also suggested by the appearance of several other comic motifs in general within the pastoral plot of Calp. 3.

Conclusions

Calp. 3 displays a multifaceted 'generic profile' with the elegiac and the comic mode often entering into an otherwise pastoral host–text; elegiac as well as comic motifs and linguistic / stylistic favourites are coupled with intertexts drawn from pastoral texts where the bucolic poet suggests his 'generic movement' away from earlier established bucolic norms, chiefly towards the elegiac and comic 'generic code', as well as pastoral models of a somewhat 'generically awry' character, as Theocr. 11 appears to be, standing out, as it does, of the main Theocritean pastoral tradition. This 'generic patterning' is crucially complemented with 'idyllic' reminiscences from non–pastoral Theocritean idylls.

Delegating the care of the flock from one bucolic figure to another has been convincingly read in the case of the Calpurnian pastoral as a meta–poetic sign suggesting an interaction between various pastoral poets (cf. Hubbard 1998, 155 and n. 25); thus Calp. 1.4: *ecce pater quas tradidit, Ornyte, vaccae* may be plausibly viewed as a meta–linguistic reference to pastoral succession, from Vergil (the father) to Calpurnius (Corydon and Ornytus; cf. Chapter 1, p. 16). Tityrus is similarly here charged by Iollas with traditional bucolic activities, namely with taking care of the flock (vv. 19–21), while Iollas adopts a rather comic / elegiac 'generic function', that of an adviser in love–matters; taking into account the well established denomination of Vergil as Tityrus in the Neronian period as well, elsewhere also occurring in Calp. 4.62, 64, 161, 163[138], Tityrus of Calp. 3

---

[137] Cf. also Gomme–Sandbach 1973, 508, Ireland 1992, 84, Lamagna 1994, 251–2, Lape 2004, 184–5, Traill 2008, 44–5.
[138] Cf. also Friedrich 1976, 67–8, Fey–Wickert 2002, 163–4. As often in post–Vergilian pastoral, in the case of Calp. 3 as well the pastoral figures involved have been read as the bucolic masks of contemporary historical figures. Apart from Tityrus, plausibly viewed as standing for Vergil (vs. Herrmann 1952, 33–4 (Lucan), Hubaux 1930, 179 ff. envisaging the possibility of a second Tityrus, a contemporary of the Neronian poet, as the mask of Tityrus of Calp. 3; cf. Chapter 2, pp. 63–4 and n. 79), Lycidas, Iollas and Mopsus have also been perceived as symbolisms, mostly standing for Persius or Phaedrus, Annaeus Cornutus and Annaeus Serenus respectively (cf. Herrmann 1952, 37–8, 43, Verdière 1954, 55–7, 58, 60, Messina 1975, 41, 43

may also be read as a mask of Vergil, to whom traditional pastoral topics are assigned, whereas Iollas may, on the other hand, be read as the novel pastoral poet engaging, demonstrably to a much greater extent than his Roman predecessor, with the 'generic interaction' of pastoral with comedy and elegy.

In opposition to Vergil, where pastoral and elegy do not merge, in the Calpurnian text the 'generic boundaries' seem to collapse[139] and instances of a 'generic enrichment' (the term as used by Harrison 2007) are made clear enough. The elegiac discourse of Corydon in the second Vergilian eclogue gives way to the pastoral norm of the last lines, when the bucolic lover resumes time-honoured activities of the 'green cabinet' and comforts himself with the sexual liberty, coveted by the inhabitants of the pastoral space; a similar reinstatement of pastoral order appears in Alphesiboeus' song in Verg. Ecl. 8, where the deserter of pastoral space and its values, Daphnis, abandons his urban, elegiac, love-affair to be reunited with his pastoral lover[140]. Similarly the elegiac leaning of the contestants of the third Vergilian bucolic poem accounts for their being unworthy of receiving Alcimedon's cups as a prize, symbolising the utmost value of the pastoral tradition, namely pastoral poetry itself and its poetic assets, whereas the 'pastoral dislocation' of Verg. Ecl. 8 results in the goatherd of Damon's song drowning himself (cf. Karakasis 2011, 87–152). As for the tenth Vergilian eclogue, it has also been convincingly claimed that Gallus eventually comes to realise his elegiac disposition, and to resist merging with his temporary identity of a pastoral guest. In Calpurnian pastoral, on the other hand, the elegiac and comic intrusions appear to be functioning as a means for 'enriching' the pastoral host-text, for these 'generic codes' seem here to interact and not to oppose each other. Elegiac and comic turns are ultimately a means for 'enriching' the established pastoral norm, for pastoral order, as known from the pre-Calpurnian bucolics, does not seem to be eventually restored in the Calpurnian world.

As often argued, Ovidian imitation constitutes an important means in the service of the 'generic re-orientation' and 'diversification' to which Calpurnian poetics aspire; in the fourth bucolic the poet is crucially associated with Ovid, whose poetry thus becomes a criterion for literary criticism (4.150–1, cf. Chapter 2, p. 78). Calp. 3, largely fashioned as an Ovidian epistle, availing itself of several elegiac markers (also Ovidian), should be read as part of this Calpurnian po-

---

and n. 17). Yet, as frequently remarked, such associations are beyond the scope of my reading here; cf. also above, pp. 9–10, 62–3 and n. 77, 114–5 and n. 105.
139 Cf. also Fey-Wickert 2002, 27–9.
140 Cf. also Clausen 1994, 239 and n. 27; vs. views claiming an open-endedness in the closure of Verg. Ecl. 8 as to the eventual return of the pastoral lover (cf. e.g. Breed 2006, 40, Saunders 2008, 53); see also Karakasis 2011, 150 and n. 108, Cucchiarelli 2012, 405.

etological mechanism for transcending traditional pastoral forms through Ovidian techniques.

Georgics

Calpurnius 5

The fifth eclogue of the Calpurnian bucolic corpus is mainly about the practical precepts that an aged bucolic figure, Micon, gives to his (foster-) son, Canthus, *de grege regendo*, i.e., regarding the taking care of the flock. This particular increase of the georgic interest in Calpurnius may be combined with the large estates of the period; hence the regeneration of the technical–georgic literature, as evidenced mainly by the work of Columella[1]. The poem has often been read in the relevant bibliography as an attempt of Calpurnius to shift to the didactic genre[2], although one also comes across some more reserved views, aiming to incorporate the present eclogue within the Calpurnian pastoral program[3]. The objective of the present chapter is to investigate the means through which the poet imparts a didactic colouring to his eclogue and eventually to re–address the issue of the 'generic standing' of the Calpurnian poem in question, by examining the manner in which various 'generic constituents' of the didactic *genus* operate within the eclogue. Therefore I shall first briefly look into the function of these

---

[1] Cf. Reitz 2013, 283.
[2] Cf. Hubaux 1930, 223–4, Verdière 1954, 256; 1966, 171, Marchiò 1957, 301–14, Mahr 1964, 153, Cizek 1968, 150; 1972, 375, Friedrich 1976, 105, Di Salvo 1990, 26, Keene 1996, 117. More reserved seem, on the other hand, the views of Davis 1987, 35, Amat 1991, 45, Vinchesi 1992, 156; 1996, 39, who speak of a more georgic than bucolic eclogue; see also Ferrara 1905, 21, Cesareo 1931, 14, Duff 1960, 267, Perutelli 1976, 782, Grimal 1978, 166, Dehon 1993, 208.
[3] Cf. Messina 1975, 97 and n. 108: 'l' ispirazione bucolica non manca e il georgico sembra servire al bucolico', Kegel–Brinkgreve 1990, 160, 165 speaking of an 'incorporation' of the 'didactic epic' into 'bucolics'; see also Korzeniewski 1971, 102: 'Mit dieser Ekloge hat Calpurnius das Element des Lehrgedichtes in die bukolische Dichtung eingefürt'; 1972, 215: 'das fünfte ist ein bukolisches Lehrgedicht', Gnilka 1974, 148, Kettemann 1977, 109, Di Lorenzo 1987, 17, Effe–Binder 1989, 113–4, Di Lorenzo–Pellegrino 2008, 16, Magnelli 2006, 474–5 understanding a 'bucolicization' of georgics and in a similar vein Landolfi 2009, 90, Becker 2012, 19–20. Fuxa 1831, 262 reads in the case of Calp. 5 the genesis of a new 'generic formation', both pastoral and didactic at the same time; see also Cesareo 1931, 61, Grant 1965, 72–3, Messina 1975, 106, Gagliardi 1984, 43, 48, 86–7, Verdière 1985, 1855. Mayer 2005, 234, within a sub–chapter crucially entitled 'Didactic mode in non–didactic poetry', views Calp. 5 as 'a bucolic epos', 'cast into the form of didactic', whereas Mayer 2006, 461 only goes so far as to speak of a 'didactic character' discerned in Calp. 5; see also Amatucci 1947, 60. According to Leach 1975, 217, on the other hand: '*Eclogue* 5 can hardly be taken for a serious essay into didactic poetry'. More to the point Hubbard 1998, 153 remarks: 'Calp. 5 unquestionably evokes the georgic / didactic mode', without, however, any further elaboration. For an overview of the issue, cf. also Magnelli 2006, 474–5 and nn. 32, 33, Landolfi 2009, 89–90.

'generic markers' of the didactic *genus* within the body of Roman didactic poetry with a view to a parallel examination of the way these features function within Calp. 5, and thus eventually determine its 'generic status'.

Methodological Remarks and Caveats: the Notion of the Didactic Genre and Mode

The very notion of a distinct didactic genre, in itself a debated issue in terms of 'generic literary criticism', requires a discussion of the problem at this juncture[4]. It is true that ancient literary criticism is for its most part agnostic enough towards didactic poetry as a distinct poetic genre, for it either considers such didactic compositions as non–mimetic, that is non–poetic works (cf. Arist. *Poet.* 1447^{b}19–20), or groups them together, because of the hexameter line in which they are usually composed (with the exception of Ovid's *Ars Amatoria* and *Remedia Amoris*), under the vast 'generic category' of epic without any further sub–distinctions, along with Homer, Apollonius, etc., even Theocritus (cf. Quint. *Inst.* 10.1.46–57, 85–8). However, two influential theoretical texts based on Hellenistic theoretical literary trends come as a reaction to this afore–mentioned 'homogenisation' of epos, establishing the realisation, on the part of the Hellenistic literary thought, which was so formative for the subsequent Roman literary production, that the didactic *genus* is firstly a poetic genre and secondly quite different from epic as known e.g. from Homer. These two theoretic texts, capitalising respectively on Aristotelian and Platonic literary theoretical traditions, are the *Tractatus Coislinianus*, based on a relevant Hellenistic Peripatetic discourse[5], and the *Ars Grammatica* of Diomedes, whose views on didactic poetry are plausibly dated to the early Hellenistic period[6]. The *Tractatus Coislinianus* characterises didactic poetry, significantly called ποίησις παιδευτική, as non–mimetical, against 'mimetic poetry' comprising dramas and narratives. This ποίησις παιδευτική is further sub–divided into ὑφηγητική (practical subject–matter like the georgic information of Vergil's didactic poem[7] and the art

---

[4] For a distinct didactic genre and its typology, cf. especially Effe 1977, Toohey 1996; see also Pöhlmann 1973, 813–901, Dalzell 1996, Batstone 1997, 129 for Latin didactic poetry in particular.
[5] Cf. Volk 2002, 32; see also Janko 1984, 43.
[6] Cf. Dahlmann 1953, 158 and n. 1, Pöhlmann 1973, 830, Volk 2002, 33.
[7] Although contemporary literary criticism is largely of the view that the *G.* does not primarily intend to teach the students–farmers agriculture, but is carrier of larger meanings and symbolisms; cf. e.g. Thomas 1988, 1.24, Hardie 1998, 28–9; *G.* seems to belong to the 'transparenter

of love, i.e., the subject of the Ovidian didactic poems) and θεωρητική (theoretical knowledge like the Epicurean physics of Lucretius or even Manilius' astrology). Diomedes, on the other hand, speaks of three *poematos genera* (cf. *GL* 1.482.14 Keil); the second kind of enunciation, the *exegeticon...vel enarrativum in quo poeta ipse loquitur sine ullius personae interlocutione* (20–1) is further sub-categorised into the *angeltice*, the *historice* and the *didascalice* (31–2), i.e., the didactic *genus*, outlined along these lines (483.1–3): *didascalice est qua conprehenditur philosophia Empedoclis et Lucreti, item astrologia, ut phaenomena Aratu et Ciceronis, et georgica Vergilii et his similia*[8]. All the above show that, despite a general theoretical lack regarding the 'generic definition' of didactic poetry, literary criticism of the Hellenistic period, decisively influencing later Roman theoretical and literary pursuits, viewed the didactic *genus* as a distinct poetic trend.

What is more, apart from the theoretical testimony itself, there is a clear sense in some didactic poets that their work belongs to a distinct 'generic norm', revealed by the mention of their eminent literary predecessors or models; Lucretius, for example, applauds Empedocles' poetic brilliance, cf. 1.716–33[9], whereas Vergil evidently aligns his *Georgics* with Hesiodic epic, cf. *G.* 2.176[10]. Vergil suggests his 'generic allegiance' with the didactic Lucretius as well, when, at *G.* 2.490–3, he juxtaposes himself – *fortunatus et ille, deos qui novit agrestis* (v. 493) to his didactic predecessor, Lucretius – *felix, qui potuit rerum cognoscere causas* (v. 490)[11], whereas intertextual references mainly to Aratus (chiefly in the first book of the *G.*) and Lucretius (on the linguistic level for the most part) complete the picture of the didactic Vergil's 'generic allegiances'[12]. Mani-

---

Typus' of the didactic poetic production (cf. Effe 1977, 80–97), the real intent of which is different from the aim it professes to fulfil. For a good review of various relevant arguments, cf. Volk 2002, 120–1; 2008, 6–7. For *G.* as didactic poetry, cf. also Wilkinson 1969, 56–65, Kromer 1979, 7–21, Farrell 1991.
8 Cf. Volk 2002, 25–34, 41.
9 For the influence of Empedocles on Lucretius, cf. especially Bollack 1959, 656–86, Furley 1970, 55–64, Gale 1994, 59–75; 2007, 11, Campbell 2003, 2–4, 101–9, Garani 2007, Tatum 2007, 132–45, Trépanier 2007, 243–82, Hardie 2009, 142–4. For Lucretius and Cleanthes / Aratus, on the other hand, cf. Asmis 2007, 88–103.
10 Cf. Volk 2002, 62–3, Gale 2009, 9, Thibodeau 2011, 8; see also Hardie 1998, 29–30.
11 Cf. Volk 2009, 196–7, Thibodeau 2011, 8–9; see also Clay 1976, 232–45, Barchiesi 1982, 41–86, Hardie 1986, 33–51, Kronenberg 2000, 341–60, Nelis 2004, 73–107.
12 Cf. Thomas 1988, 1.3–4, 6–7; see also pp. 8–9 for the influence of Varro of Atax on the didactic Vergil. For the Lucretian influence on the *G.*, cf. especially Bailey 1931, 21–39, Paratore 1939, 177–202, Farrington 1963, 87–94, Nethercut 1973, 41–52, Hardie 1986, 158–67; 1998, 30–1; 2009, 237–9, Freudenburg 1987, 59–74, Schäfer 1996, Gale 2000; for Hesiod, Aratus, Callimachus and Lucretius in Vergil's didactic production, cf. especially Farrell 1991,

lius especially resorts to several intertextual references to his primary didactic models, namely Aratus, Lucretius and Vergil, thus making particular use of intertextuality as a means for revealing his 'generic adhesion'[13]. What is more, by copying phrases from Lucretius and Vergil's *Georgics*, Ovid manages in a way to reconstruct the linguistic archaism of the Hesiodic 'didactic protomodel' and the Greek didactic poetic production in general[14]. Besides, the very reading of the canon of works written in the line of the Hesiodic epic reveals several common 'generic features'. In her seminal work entitled *The Poetics of Latin Didactic – Lucretius, Vergil, Ovid, Manilius*, Oxford 2002, Katharina Volk has persuasively drawn attention to four basic features of ancient poetic *didaxis*. By singling out various typical and recurring features of the didactic *genus*, deducible through an attentive, heuristic and close reading of didactic poetry itself, suggesting in its turn a sense of a 'standardised coherence', a 'systematisation' of didactic poetry, Volk pointed out the following 'didactic generic standards / cornerstones': a) the 'explicit didactic intent', b) the 'teacher–student constellation', c) 'poetic self–consciousness', and d) 'poetic simultaneity'[15]. It goes without saying, as is also evident from the above, that the subject–matter of didactic poetry is not only 'instructional' but also quite often 'technical and detailed', cf. Toohey 1996, 4.

A further theoretic admission at this point has to do with the notion of the didactic mode along the theoretical framework of *mode* as developed by Alastair

---

whereas for the relationship between the *G.* and Hesiod, see principally Bayet 1930, 128–50, 227–47, La Penna 1962, 225–47, Nelson 1998; for Vergil and Nicander, cf. Harrison 2004, 109–23, whereas for Aratus in Vergil, cf. Jermyn 1951, 26–37, 46–59. For technical treatises in the georgic Vergil, further enhancing the didactic character of his work, cf. especially Jermyn 1949, 49–69, Leach 1981, 35–48, Thomas 1987, 229–60.

13 Cf. Volk 2009, 8, 34–40, 47–8, 120 and n. 138, 144–5, 162–3, 167, 184–97, 217, 248–9, 259, 260; see pp. 196, 260 in particular. For Lucretius in Manilius, cf. also especially Landolfi 1990, 27–37, Flores 1996, 895–908, La Penna 1997, 107–8, Abry 1999, 111–28, Volk 2002, 219, 239–40, 242, Gale 2005, 111–2. For the Vergilian influence on Manilius, see also Effe 1971, 393–9, Di Giovine 1978, 398–402, Montanari-Caldini 1981, 71–114, Wilson 1985, 289–92, Scarcia 1993, 127–45, Hübner 2006, 137–48.

14 Cf. Hollis 1977, xviii; for Ovid's didactic, intertextual references, see also pp. 34, 104–8, 118, 148, 149. For the didactic character of the *Ars* and the influence didactic Lucretius and Vergil have exercised upon it, cf. also Kenney 1958, 201–9, Leach 1964, 142–54, Hollis 1973, 89–94, Küppers 1981, 2507–51, Steudel 1992, Gibson 2003, 7–21, Hardie 2007, 116–7.

15 I am particularly indebted to and informed by Volk's seminal work (2002), cited throughout this chapter, especially in the following theoretical sub-chapters: 'Methodological Remarks and Caveats: the Notion of the Didactic Genre and Mode', "Didactic Intent' – 'Teacher-Student Constellation", "Poetic Self-Consciousness' – 'Poetic Simultaneity".

Fowler, cf. especially 1982, 56, 106–11; see also Introduction, p. 6. All four criteria, as mentioned above, should be met in the case of poetic works belonging to the didactic genre; the appearance, however, of a number of them even in alternative forms and situations (cf. further down, pp. 161–6, 182–4, where all these 'generic key-stones' are elaborated in detail) may suggest the presence of a didactic mode[16] evoking (Fowler's term) the didactic genre. This is especially the case with Ovid's *Fasti*. The poem has a specific technical content (the Roman calendar) and is characterised by both 'didactic poetic self-consciousness' and 'didactic poetic simultaneity'; but its 'didactic intent' is not explicit enough (the poetic persona merely wants to sing and not to teach), and the addresses to the anonymous students are quite random, intermingled with further addresses to other figures / characters[17]. Thus I shall suggest that in Calp. 5 the poet avails himself of the didactic mode only to evoke the poetic didactic genre but not to adopt all its 'generic assets'; instead Calp. 5 should rather be read as an instance of didactic mode framed by the bucolic poet within a clear 'pastoral generic framing'.

'Didactic Intent' – 'Teacher–Student Constellation'

The 'didactic intent' is usually concomitant with the 'teacher–student liaison' and is secured when the first-person speaker (the teacher) within the didactic text, i.e., an 'intra-textual persona'[18], is talking to another textual figure, the addressee[19] (the student) with explicit instructional aims. Such a relationship is different from the bond developed between an author and his readers and thus the question whether the author really intended to instruct his readers or alternatively whether the readers read a didactic poem with a sincere view to being – comprehensively or not – instructed (cf. Sen. *Ep.* 86.15) is irrelevant to the 'generic demarcation' of a didactic poetic oeuvre[20]. Starting from Hesiod's *Works and Days* both the 'explicit didactic intent' and the 'teacher–student constellation' are recurrent issues of the didactic poetry; cf. *WD* 10: ἐγὼ δέ κε Πέρσῃ ἐτήτυμα μυθησαίμην. Hesiod's, Empedocles', Aratus' and Nicander's first-person poetic persona can easily be read as assuming the role of the didactic teacher, whereas Perses (*Works and Days*), Pausanias (*On Nature*), Aratus' unnamed addressee (*Phaenomena*), the dedicatees Hermesianax (*Theriaca*) and Protagoras

---

16 Cf. Volk 2002, 42–3.
17 Cf. Volk 1997, 287–313; 2002, 42; see also Miller 1992, 11–31.
18 Cf. Clay 1983, 212–6, Volk 2002, 37.
19 Cf. Schiesaro-Mitsis-Clay 1993; see also Effe 1977, 23, 30–2, Dalzell 1996.
20 Cf. also Volk 2002, 36–9, 246–7; 2009, 176, 180–1.

(*Alexipharmaca*) respectively can easily be labelled as the recipients of the didactic instruction, the didactic students within an imagined 'intra–textual dramatic setting'.

These two 'generic features' appear in the main Roman poetic didactic tradition as well. In the *De Rerum Natura*[21] Lucretius acknowledges his function as a teacher (cf. e.g. the use of *docere*, see 1.539, 4.26, etc.[22]), and addresses the 'not so attentive', 'stupid child–like' 'student–figure' Memmius[23], in all probability Gaius Memmius, Lucius' son, either by name (11 times) or in the second singular[24], with an explicit 'didactic intent', i.e., to instruct him on the Epicurean physics. The 'speaker' of the *Georgics*, i.e., a poet self–admittedly aligning himself to the Hesiodic (cf. 2.176: *Ascraeumque cano Romana per oppida carmen)* and the Nicandrean (because of the title Γεωργικά)[25] Greek didactic tradition, similarly qualifies his narrative as instructive course, a lesson, as evidenced by the use of verbs such as *docere* (3.440), *discere* (2.35), *edicere* (3.295) and syntagms like *praecepta referre* (1.176) with reference to his teaching, in poetic from, of tillage, viticulture, cattle–breeding and bee–keeping (cf. *G*. 1.1–5). These lectures of the poet–teacher are addressed to the farmers, who thus function as the students in the 'teacher–student generic constellation' and are, accordingly, addressed as *agricolae, viri, coloni* (cf. 1.101, 2.36, / 1.210, / 3.288; see also *pastor* – 3.420)[26]. Servius himself, Vergil's scholiast, also acknowledged both the 'didactic intent' (*libri didascalici, praeceptum et doctoris*) and the 'teacher–pupil relationship' (*doctoris, discipuli personam*) as formalistic components of didactic literature to which Vergil's *Georgics* also belong; cf. *Praef. ad G.* 129.9–12 Thilo: *hi libri didascalici sunt, unde necesse est, ut ad aliquem scribantur; nam praeceptum et doctoris et*

---

[21] The view adopted here is that Lucretius' Epicurean poem properly belongs to the didactic genre in contrast to scholarship that views *DRN* as an example of the epic *genus*, cf. Murley 1947, 336–46, Mayer 1990, 35–43; see also Hardie 1986, 193–219, Gale 1994, 99–128; 2000, 235–8. Effe 1977, 66–79 crucially understands the Lucretian poem as a specimen of the kind of didactic poetry that is serious about transmitting knowledge, i.e., of the 'sachbezogener Typ', a kind of didactic poetry to which Manilius' *Astronomica* also belong (cf. Effe 1977, 106–26); see also Volk 2002, 69–70, Gale 2007, 5.
[22] Cf. also Kenney 2007, 92.
[23] Cf. Keen 1985, 1–4, Mitsis 1993, 123–8, Volk 2002, 80–2; see also Fowler 2002, 217–8.
[24] Contra Townend 1978, 267–83, who, unconvincingly, argues for different categories of Lucretian addresses in the second person; for a refutation of this thesis, cf. Volk 2002, 74–5, who rightly understands all second–person addresses as referring to the student of the didactic work in question, i.e., Memmius.
[25] Cf. Volk 2002, 122; 2009, 183.
[26] Cf. Volk 2002, 123; see also Rutherford 1995, 19–29.

discipuli personam requirit. unde ad Maecenatem scribit, sicut Hesiodus ad Persen, Lucretius ad Memmium[27].

An explicit 'didactic intent' is discernible in Ovid's didactic poems as well, i.e., *Ars Amatoria* and *Remedia Amoris*[28]. The basic aim of the *Ars* is, as evidenced from the poem's first two lines, to teach, *docere*, the poet regularly refers to poetic instruction not only by means of the verb *docere* (cf. *Ars* 3.43, 195, *Rem.* 9, 298, etc.; for the passive *discere*, cf. *Rem.* 43[29]) but also through its synonym *praecipere* (cf. *Ars* 1.264, 2.273, *Rem.* 803), the didactic poems themselves are significantly designated as *praecepta* (cf. *Ars* 2.745, 3.57, *Rem.* 41), when the 'didactic speaker' too fashions himself as a *praeceptor* (cf. *Ars* 1.17, etc.) and *magister* (cf. *Ars* 2.173, *Rem.* 55, etc.)[30]. As to the students, both *iuvenes* repeatedly addressed in the first two books of *Ars Amatoria* and the *puellae* of its third book seem to adopt this 'didactic generic role'. It is primarily young men but also women (cf. *Rem.* 49–52, 607–8, 813–4) who form the student–audience in the *Remedia Amoris* as well[31]. A similar pattern may also be discerned in the last main Roman didactic poem, Manilius' *Astronomica*[32], i.e., the account of a universe governed by the Stoic συμπάθεια: description of the didactic poetic composition by way of *docere* (cf. 2.751, 3.39, 4.119, etc.; see especially the poet's deliberation on his teaching methods in 2.749–87), as well as the presence of the student–figure, belatedly brought to the reader's notice (after 1.194), probably in imitation of the model *Phaenomena* of Aratus[33].

---

27 For the view that Maecenas only functions as a simple addressee and the dedicatee of *Georgics* in opposition to the farmers who have the function of the student, cf. the convincing remarks of Volk 2002, 129–39 and her plausible analysis of Maecenas as a kind of meta-audience, i.e., an addressee receiving information chiefly on matters of poetics and the progress of the poet's ongoing didactic oeuvre; see also Perkell 1989, 26. For the various addressees of the Vergilian *didaxis* (Octavian, Maecenas, the anonymous farmer), cf. especially Schiesaro 1993, 129–47 and the comprehensive review of the subject by Fyntikoglou 2007, 28ff.
28 The not so serious character of both *Ars* and *Rem.* (cf. Effe 1977, 238) as well as the view that love is not teachable are the two main arguments against the categorisation of these two Ovidian poems as didactic poetry; for a convincing refutation of this view, cf. especially Volk 2002, 157–9.
29 Cf. Pinotti 1993, 100.
30 Cf. Gibson 2003, 105.
31 Cf. Volk 2002, 159–61, Gibson 2003, 35–6. For the technical material of the Ovidian *Ars*, a further criterion of the didactic *genus*, cf. Gibson 2003, 11–3.
32 For the didactic character of Manilius' *Astronomica*, cf. also Calcante 2002, Green–Volk 2011, 7–9.
33 Cf. Reeh 1973, 41–53, Romano 1978, 115–25, Neuburg 1993, 257–82, Volk 2002, 198–9; see also Abry 2006, 296–305. As to the presence of Caesar in the Manilian text, I

As a result of this 'didactic intent' and the 'teacher–student constellation' various didactic techniques are developed, in order to facilitate the transmission of knowledge from the teacher to the student, for didactic or pedagogical reasons:
- addresses by name or in the second person, with a view either to securing the student's attention (cf. Lucr. 1.51) or to making him accept the truth of the transmitted information (cf. *fateare necessest*-formulas in Lucretius, cf. 1.399). Use of various formulas–'calls for attention' in general, cf. Lucr. 1.50–1, 2.1023, Verg. *G.* 2.35, Ov. *Ars* 1.1–2, 267, 3.57–8, *Rem.* 41, Man. 3.36 ff.[34],
- repetition of various phrases or small passages (cf. Lucr. 2.55–61 = 3.87–93 = 6.35–41)[35],
- the use of the first plural of verbs and pronouns, consolidating the relationship between the didactic teacher and his student and reinforcing the idea of a 'joint pursuit' (cf. Lucr. 1.127–8, Verg. *G.* 2.393–6, Ov. *Ars* 1.772),
- the use of the ethical dative creating a sense of 'personal involvement' / 'empathy' on the part of the teacher or the student (cf. Lucr. 1.673, Verg. *G.* 1.43–6),
- cross-references (cf. Lucr. 1.539) and summary / recapitulation of the teaching topics (cf. Lucr. 1.54–61, 3.31 ff., Verg. *G.* 1.1–5, 2.1, Ov. *Ars* 1.35–40, 263–5, Man. 3.160 ff.)[36],
- exhortations to the addressee to work out an argument on the basis of previously given instruction (cf. Lucr. 1.402–3),
- orders in the imperative, mainly present singular forms, but plural as well[37] (cf. Lucr. 1.269, Verg. *G.* 1.100, Ov. *Ars.* 3.129–30, Man. 4.818), in the jussive subjunctive, chiefly of the third person, (singular or plural) active[38] (cf. Lucr. 1.956, Verg. *G.* 1.45–6, Ov. *Ars* 3.315–6), by means of gerundives (cf. Lucr. 1.205, Verg. *G.* 1.204–5, Ov. *Ars* 2.717, Man. 1.120) as well as in the indicative mood, mainly second person and third person, (both active and passive) forms (cf. Lucr. 1.450, Verg. *G.* 1.167, 169–75, 3.100–1, 157–8, Ov. *Ars*

---

would agree with Volk 2002, 201 that he assimilates the function Maecenas has in Vergil's *Georgics*; see also pp. 200, 202.
34 Cf. Gibson 2003, 110.
35 Cf. also Ingalls 1971, 227–36, Clay 1983, 176–85, Schiesaro 1994, 98–100.
36 Cf. also Fowler 2002, 176.
37 For statistics concerning the use of singular and plural imperative by didactic poets, cf. Gibson 2003, 146. Future imperatives in *–to* are as a rule infrequent in didactic poetic language, cf. Gibson 2003, 180–1.
38 Cf. Gibson 1997, 82–3; 2003, 203–4, 225.

1.503, 3.163–4[39]) for various purposes (e. g. *aspice* set-phrases for directing the addressee's attention, cf. Verg. *G.* 2.114, Ov. *Ars* 2.433, *Rem.* 175, Man. 1.373[40]). All the above imperativals are regular features of didactic poetry dealing with practical issues instead of theoretical knowledge[41],

- the motif of 'the manifold preparation before undertaking a main task' (cf. Lucr. 5.110 ff., Verg. *G.* 1.50 ff., Ov. *Ars* 1.50, Man. 1.809 ff.),
- the use of the *superesse*-formula for denoting transition either within the same didactic project or not (cf. Lucr. 1.50–1, Verg. *G.* 2.346, 354, 4.51, Ov. *Ars* 3.1–2)[42]; self-reflexive questions also denote transition between various subject-matters (cf. Verg. *G.* 1.104, Ov. *Ars* 1.253 ff.[43]). Other didactic set-phrases / words include e. g. *nunc age*, cf. Lucr. 2.62, Verg. *G.* 4.149, Man. 2.939 (see also Emp. B 62.1–3[44]), *nec mora*, cf. Lucr. 4.227, Verg. *G.* 3.110, Ov. *Ars* 1.146; see also Ov. *Fast.* 1.278, Grat. *Cyn.* 461[45], *qua ratione*, favoured in Lucretius (13 instances), cf. Lucr. 1.77, Ov. *Ars* 3.611, Man. 3.204[46],
- the use of *memor* and its cognates in explicitly instructional contexts (cf. Lucr. 2.66, Verg. *G.* 1.167, Ov. *Ars* 2.201, 3.59–60, *Rem.* 217) as well as the use of *video*-formulas (and of similar syntagms) imparting a sense of 'authority' / 'personal experience' (cf. Lucr. 4.577, Verg. *G.* 1.193, Ov. *Ars* 3.67, *Rem.* 101–2[47]),
- breaking-off / rounding-off of lists by way of diverse devices (cf. Lucr. 4.1170, Verg. *G.* 2.103 ff., Ov. *Ars* 1.253–6, *Rem.* 461[48]),
- emphasis on the notion of utility, chiefly by means of *prodesse, iuvare, nocere* and *utilis*-syntagms (cf. Lucr. 1.131, Verg. *G.* 1.84, Ov. *Ars* 1.161, 2.105, *Rem.* 131, Man. 2.761[49]),
- inquiring the readers by means of questions formed with the verb *dubitare* (cf. Lucr. 2.53, 3.582, 603, Verg. *G.* 2.433, Ov. *Ars* 3.349–50[50]). Rapid questioning-patterns do also function as a means a didactic poet might make use of

---

39 Cf. Gibson 2003, 160, 177–8, 275; see also p. 203, Risselada 1993, 168–78. For first-person imperativals, rather uncommon, in the didactic tradition, cf. Gibson 2003, 185, 192.
40 Cf. Kenney 1958, 203, Gibson 2003, 136–7.
41 Cf. also Gibson 1997, 67–98; 2003, 10–11.
42 Cf. Gibson 2003, 87.
43 Cf. Gibson 2003, 164.
44 Cf. Fowler 2002, 147, Landolfi 2009, 119 and n. 113.
45 Cf. Landolfi 2009, 101 and n. 58.
46 Cf. Landolfi 2009, 119–20 and n. 115.
47 Cf. Pinotti 1993, 159, Gibson 2003, 112, 114; see also p. 304.
48 Cf. Gibson 2003, 155.
49 Cf. Pinotti 1993, 335, Gibson 2003, 217–8.
50 Cf. Gibson 2003, 241.

in order to refute the views of his adversary (cf. Lucr. 1.377 ff., Ov. *Ars* 3.83 – 98[51]).

A further 'generic standard' of didactic poetry is the continuous monologue of the first-person speaker of the didactic text; although the student's reaction and remarks may be anticipated by the poet or may be reported (cf. Lucr. 5.1091, Verg. *G.* 2.288, Ov. *Ars* 1.375, 3.749 – 50, *Rem.* 487, Man. 3.203 – 5), the monologue never develops in a real dialogue, cf. also Diom. *GL* 1.482.20 – 1 Keil: *poeta ipse loquitur sine ullius personae interlocutione*[52].

'Didactic Intent' – 'Teacher–Student Constellation' and Calp. 5

Both these basic 'generic criteria' of the poetic didactic *genus* are met with in Calp. 5. First of all, Canthus is significantly described as Micon's *alumnus* (v. 1: *Micon senior Canthusque, Miconis alumnus*, cf. also v. 3). Although the word is often used in the sense of '(foster–) son' or 'child' (cf. OLD *s.v.* 1), it also denotes the 'teacher–student relationship', as it also properly refers to 'the pupils or followers of philosophers, orators etc.' (cf. OLD *s.v.* 4, Cic. *Fin.* 4.72, Vell. 2.36.2)[53]. What is more, the very counsel Micon gives to Canthus as to the taking care of the flock is also critically described as *praecepta* (cf. v. 3: *cum iuveni senior praecepta daturus alumno*), i.e., by means of a term meaning 'teaching', 'precept' (OLD *s.v.* 1) also used of the didactic lessons both Vergil's *Georgics* and Ovid's

---

51 Cf. Gibson 2003, 120.
52 Cf. also Volk 2002, 40, 74, 76 – 82, 123 – 4, 126, 180, 206; 2009, 177; see also Hollis 1977, 39, 42, 89, Thomas 1988, 1.76, 138, 231 – 2; 2.119, Gibson 2003, 381.
53 Cf. Duff 1960, 267: 'young pupil Canthus', Mahr 1964, 153: 'ein alter Hirte seinem Schüler Anweisungen...gibt', Amat 1991, 45: 'Micon à son élève'; see also Becker 2012, 69, Vinchesi 2014, 379. On the basis of Canthus' qualification as *alumnus* (v. 1; see also v. 3), also used of Nero in *Eins.* 1.41, as well as because of v. 4, which may evoke Suetonius' (*Cl.* 30.2) and Seneca's (*Apoc.* 5.2, 5.3, 6.2, 7.4) descriptions of Claudius, Verdière 1954, 256 has suggested, as frequently in the case of post-Vergilian pastoral, that the younger pastoral figure functions as a mask, namely of the emperor Nero, whereas Micon also has associations with contemporary history and politics, i.e., symbolises Claudius; see also Messina 1975, 98 and n. 111, Amat 1991, xxxvii and n. 85, 45, Marchiò 1957, 314 and n. 12, Vinchesi 2014, 381 – 2 for a criticism of this view. For Herrmann 1952, 41 – 2, on the other hand, Micon and Canthus represent Seneca and Columella respectively; see also Verdière 1954, 60 and both Messina 1975, 97 – 8 and Gagliardi 1984, 43 and nn. 57, 58 for a refutation of this thesis. For a dismissal of such allegorical readings of Calp. 5 altogether, see also Friedrich 1976, 106, 225 and n. 4, Landolfi 2009, 91 and n. 13; see also Chapter 4, pp. 152 – 3 and n. 138.

didactic corpus aim to offer (cf. above, pp. 162–3)[54]. The use of the verb *percipere* (v. 16), and, what is more, in the second singular imperative form, as commonly found in didactic texts (especially Lucretius, the didactic Ovid and Manilius), aiming at the instruction of Canthus as to how he will gain control over goats and sheep (vv. 12–6), further augments the 'didactic intent' of the eclogue[55]. Note also the use of *moneo* introducing a georgic precept in the parenthesis of v. 78: *providus (hoc moneo)...* (cf. also Verg. G. 1.167[56]). The 'didactic intent' is also evidenced by the strict technical character of Micon's precepts drawn, as they are, from both ὑφηγητικὴ poetry of the didactic *genus* and technical treatises of georgic–didactic propensities (Vergil, Varro, etc.)[57]. This didactic outlook is thus chiefly achieved in the Calpurnian eclogue by:

a) intertexts properly belonging to the 'didactic generic code', as is the case with the chief representatives of Latin didactic poetry, as developed above (cf. pp. 158–66), or intertexts exhibiting signs of the so-called didactic mode, as happens, for example, with Ovid's *Fasti*. Most of the lines of this Calpurnian eclogue display models found in didactic texts either exclusively or in majority.

b) intertexts capitalising on the 'generic tension' between didactic poetry and pastoral – as seems also to hold true for the present Calpurnian eclogue or, in any case, intertexts appearing in earlier pastoral poetry, while at the same time also having a very good 'didactic pedigree'.

c) stylistic features and linguistic options mostly associated with didactic speech, as the ones described in the table above (cf. pp. 164–6), as well as favourites of 'technical diction', and

d) wording drawn from texts of a clear didactic character.

What is more, Micon structures his 'manual of the good herdsman' by means of the seasons–cycle,[58] a further distinct didactic structural pattern from Hesiod onwards, cf. *WD* 383ff.[59].

---

54 Cf. Di Lorenzo–Pellegrino 2008, 232, Becker 2012, 70, Vinchesi 2014, 380–1. Another instance of the father ('teacher') – son ('student') constellation, where the instruction given is also about herding, appears elsewhere in pastoral literature only in Longus' roman, *Daphnis and Chloe* (1.8.2f.); see also Korzeniewski 1971, 102, Kettemann 1977, 108 and n. 35, Becker 2012, 26–8, Cyrus A.P. 9.136.
55 Cf. also Landolfi 2009, 91 and n. 15, Vinchesi 2014, 378, 386.
56 Cf. Vinchesi 2014, 410.
57 Cf. especially Becker 2012, 21–6, 28–30; see also Vinchesi 2014, 377.
58 Various scholars have different views as to the allocation of lines according to the *tempora anni*. Cf. Hubaux 1930, 97: vv. 16–48 – spring, vv. 49–94 – summer, vv. 95–105 – fall, vv. 106–18 – winter and so Kettemann 1977, 108, Grant 1965, 72: vv. 14–48 – spring, vv. 49–65 – summer, vv. 66–94 – autumn, vv. 95–118 – winter, Korzeniewski 1971, 102: vv. 14–48 – spring, vv. 49–65 – summer, vv. 66–103 – fall, vv. 104–18 – winter. As main-

The Spring Manual

Micon begins his georgic lesson with the spring tasks a herdsman has to carry out, vv. 16–48. The narrative segment in question starts off with the imagery of birds twittering as well as with the picture of the swallow that comes back from warmer places and covers its nest with mud (vv. 16–7); both images suggest the coming of the spring and thus signal the time to let the flock out of its winter-fold (v. 18). The announcement of spring by means of the swallow imagery and the picture of the bird daubing its nest have a good 'didactic, georgic pedigree' occurring in Vergil's *Georgics* (4.307: *garrula quam tignis nidum suspendat hirundo*, a line also modelled on yet another didactic text, Hes. *WD* 568[60], see also Columella 10.80: *veris et adventum nidis cantabit hirundo*) as well as in texts exhibiting a didactic mode as is Ovid's *Fasti*, cf. 1.157–8: *ignotaque prodit hirundo / et luteum celsa sub trabe figit opus*, 2.853: *veris praenuntia venit hirundo*[61]. A similar 'generic origin' may be assumed in the case of the motif of 'driving out the herd' also found in the didactic third book of the Vergilian *Georgics* (cf. 3.322–3: *at vero Zephyris cum laeta vocantibus aestas / in saltus utrumque gregem atque in pascua mittet*)[62]. Further down (vv. 22–3) one comes across a further distinct 'didactic generic motif', namely the image of the coming of the spring as a cause for the feelings of love manifested in nature, animals included; the motif appears in didactic poetry as early as Lucretius, cf. 1.10 ff., and is later found both in the georgic Vergil (cf. 2.323 ff.) and in Ovid's didactic

---

tained by Friedrich 1976, 110, the lines should be divided as follows: vv. 16–85 – spring, vv. 86–94 – summer, vv. 95–101 – fall, vv. 102–18 – winter, whereas Leach 1975, 217 gives the following classification: vv. 16–48 – spring-time, vv. 49–95 – summer, vv. 96–125 – autumn and winter to come. Similarly to Leach, Dehon 1993, 208: vv. 16–48 – spring, vv. 49–94 – summer, vv. 95–118 – fall and winter. See also Becker 2012, 76–111: vv. 16–48 – spring, vv. 49–101 – summer (vv. 49–65 – summer, vv. 66–101 – late summer), vv. 102–18 – winter.

59 Cf. Rosenmeyer 1969, 21, Kettemann 1977, 109 and n. 38, Landolfi 2009, 90–1 and n. 16 on p. 91.
60 Cf. Landolfi 2009, 93.
61 Cf. Verdière 1954, 179, Paladini 1956, 525, Marchiò 1957, 303, Friedrich 1976, 108, Kettemann 1977, 109, Di Lorenzo 1987, 21 and n. 40, Vinchesi 1992, 156–7; 2014, 388, Keene 1996, 119, Di Lorenzo-Pellegrino 2008, 234–5, Landolfi 2009, 93–4 and n. 23, Becker 2012, 76–7, Esposito 2012, 57 and n. 19; see also Green 2004, 89–90.
62 Cf. also Keene 1996, 119. In the Vergilian model, the didactic poet understands *aestas* as equivalent to 'time that cannot be characterized as *hiems*'; it is Calpurnius' innovation to add a *vere novo* period before the commencement of the *aestas*, cf. also Mynors 2003, 231, Erren 2003, 699. For Calpurnius' innovative use of Vergil and his other literary models, especially with reference to the spring section, cf. also the excellent discussion of Esposito 2012, 48–72.

mode of the *Fasti*, cf. 4.125⁶³. Besides, the use of the qualification *salientes* for the male goats in v. 23: *lascivumque pecus salientes accipit hircos* also complements the 'didactic generic feeling' that the motif of love creates, since the participle and the verb it derives from are again well-attested in this sexual sense in the technical language of both didactic poetry (cf. Lucr. 4.1200, Ov. *Ars* 2.485) and georgic-didactic prose, (cf. Var. *rust.* 2.2.14, 2.4.8, 3.10.3) only⁶⁴. Apart from the *salientes*-syntagm, in terms of language / style dynamics, the above 'generic pattern' is further suggested by the combination of *tinnire* with *volucres* in v. 16, modelled in all probability on the didactic mode of Ov. *Fast.* 3.741: *ecce novae coeunt volucres tinnitibus actae*⁶⁵, as well as by the use of the verb *lutare* (v. 17) in the sense of 'to cover with mud or clay / daub', which also appears, before the Calpurnian instance, only in the *R.R.*, namely Cato *agr.* 92, see also 128 (cf. OLD *s.v.* a, see also Pallad. 11.14.10)⁶⁶. *Pullare* in vv. 19–20: *vernanti germine silva / pullat* is a further georgic term, also found in Colum. 3.18.4⁶⁷; what is more, the syntagm including a use of the participle *vernans* in the function of an adjective has its parallel once again in didactic poetry, cf. Man. 5.259⁶⁸. To finish, v. 21: *tunc florent silvae*⁶⁹, seems to be calqued on a pastoral model, cf. Verg. *Ecl.* 3.57: *nunc frondent silvae*; however, the syntagm also testifies to a 'didactic intertextual leaning' in the Calpurnian case in question, as similar combinations appear elsewhere in didactic poetry, cf. Lucr. 1.256: *frondiferas...silvas* (see also Grat. *Cyn.* 141: *frondosas...silvas*)⁷⁰. As to the second hemiepes of v. 21: *viridisque renascitur annus*, suggesting as it does the beginning of the year in spring-time in-

---

63 Cf. Cesareo 1931, 63–6, Korzeniewski 1971, 51, Marchiò 1957, 303, Friedrich 1976, 108, 225 and n. 8, Kettemann 1977, 109, Novelli 1980, 61, Gagliardi 1984, 44 and n. 60, Di Lorenzo 1987, 21 and n. 40, Amat 1991, 45, 114, Di Lorenzo–Pellegrino 2008, 235–6, Landolfi 2009, 94–5, Becker 2012, 78, Esposito 2012, 56–7 and n. 15, Vinchesi 2014, 390; see also Thomas 1988, 1.215–6; 2.93, Fantham 1998, 113, Mynors 2003, 140.
64 Cf. Novelli 1980, 61, Vinchesi 2014, 391.
65 Cf. also Landolfi 2009, 92–3, Vinchesi 2014, 387.
66 Cf. also ThLL VII 2, 1897, 70 ff., Mahr 1964, 199–200, 204, Vinchesi 1992, 157; 2014, 388, Di Lorenzo–Pellegrino 2008, 235, Landolfi 2009, 94 and n. 28, Esposito 2012, 59. Var. *Men.* 100 probably constitutes a pun on *luo*, cf. OLD *s.v.* a.
67 Cf. also later Drac. *Rom.* 4.*tit.*, Vinchesi 1992, 157; 2014, 389. Merone 1967, 23 and Armstrong 1986, 121 wrongly believe that the verb is a Calpurnian *hapax*; see also Mahr 1964, 185.
68 Cf. Landolfi 2009, 95–6, Vinchesi 2014, 388–9.
69 *Silvae* is the reading of the codd. vs. *saltus* adopted by both Baehrens and Duff and Duff; see Duff and Duff 1934, 260.
70 Cf. Landolfi 2009, 95–6; see also Cesareo 1931, 65, Marchiò 1957, 303, Friedrich 1976, 108, Novelli 1980, 61, Vinchesi 2014, 390.

stead of winter (cf. also Plin. *Nat.* 16.95.1–3[71]), it has also been plausibly assigned, by Landolfi 2009, 96–7, to the didactic mode of Ov. *Fast.* 1.149–50.

In vv. 24–5 the herdsman is advised not to send the flocks to the meadows, before a ritual in honour of Pales takes place. Pastoral motifs and figures are thus intermingled with information of a rather didactic character; Pales is both a pastoral (cf. Verg. *Ecl.* 5.35, Calp. 2.36, 4.102–6, 5.24–5, 7.21–2, Nemes. 1.68, 2.55) and a georgic deity (cf. Verg. *G.* 3.1, 294). The ritual, as described in vv. 25–8, namely the setting up of an altar of fresh grass, the invocation, with salted meal, of the divine spirit of the place along with Faunus and Lares (also belonging to the traditional pastoral pantheon; see also above, pp. 8, 32, 76), the sacrifice of a victim and its procession around the pen, while still alive (a *lustratio*), also having the sanction of earlier pastoral, cf. Verg. *Ecl.* 1.7 ff., 5.75 (see also Calp. 2.67), call to mind similarly detailed rituals, as described in the didactic mode of Ovid's *Fasti*, cf. especially 4.721 ff.; see also 1.321, 3.284 and Tib. 1.1.35–6[72]. In addition, the image of the knives stained with the blood of the sacrificial victim (vv. 27–8) increases the didactic impression, as it appears once again in both the georgic Vergil (cf. *G.* 3.492) and the didactic Ovid. 'Linguistic generic reminiscences' complete the 'didactic generic picture', as v. 24: *sed non ante greges in pascua mitte* is in all probability modelled on Verg. *G.* 3.323: *gregem...in pascua mittet*, whereas vv. 29–30: *tunc campos ovibus, dumeta capellis / orto sole dabis* also rephrase Verg. *G* 3.323–5: *in saltus utrumque gregem atque in pascua mittet, / Luciferi primo cum sidere frigida rura / carpamus* and similarly elaborate on the georgic precept concerning a basic task of the herdsman, i.e., to let the flock out on the fields as soon as the sun has risen[73].

Micon continues (vv. 32–42) with the following georgic orders regarding milking, cheese making and taking care of the sheep: he speaks about a) the morning milk filling up the milking-pails (vv. 32–4), b) the evening milk pressed for cheese making in the next morning (vv. 34–5), c) taking care that the younglings are not deprived of the milk they need, because of the shepherd's 'materialistic concern' to produce cheese for financial profit (vv. 36–8)[74], d) the shep-

---

[71] Cf. Landolfi 2009, 96–7, Vinchesi 2014, 390.
[72] Cf. Verdière 1954, 179–80, 256, Novelli 1980, 62, Amat 1991, 114, Landolfi 2009, 98–101, Becker 2012, 79, 82, Vinchesi 2014, 391–2, Esposito 2012, 60–1. Vinchesi 1996, 128 understands here a ritual of the *Ambarvalia*.
[73] Cf. Verdière 1954, 256, Korzeniewski 1971, 51, Marchiò 1957, 304, Messina 1975, 100, Friedrich 1976, 111, Kettemann 1977, 109, Mynors 2003, 231, Di Lorenzo–Pellegrino 2008, 237, Landolfi 2009, 99, Becker 2012, 79, Vinchesi 2014, 391–2.
[74] Trading, and more specifically milk / cheese selling for profit, functions as a sign of deviation from the pastoral tradition both in Vergil and in Calpurnius: in Verg. *Ecl.* 1.34 cheese selling

herd's duty to carry on his shoulders an enfeebled ewe, which has recently given birth, as well as to take in his arms the lambs that are not yet able to stand on their own (vv. 39–42). VV. 32–5 remind of Verg. *G.* 3.309–10, 400–3 on cheese making (cf. also Var. *rust.* 2.11.3–4, Colum. 7.8, Pallad. 6.9[75]), the counsel not to over-milk the ewes which have just given birth alludes to Verg. *G.*, cf. 3.176 ff., (see also Var. *rust.* 2.2.17[76]), as also does the precept to look after the younglings, cf. *G.* 3.74; see also 3.308–10[77]. Typical linguistic features of technical language, favoured by the didactic diction, as are substantives in *-ura* (cf. *mulsura*, v. 35), accompanied by wording drawn on georgic / didactic texts (cf. v. 33: *spumantia mulctra* most likely modelled on Verg. *G.* 3.309: *exhausto spumaverit ubere mulctra*, vv. 41–2: *natos...ferre sinu* alluding to Ov. *Fast.* 2.469, 3.218) further increase the didactic appeal of the passage[78]. Crucially, the image of the herdsman taking care of the ewe, feckless because of her recent lambing, chiefly alludes to

---

is associated with the *urbs* in opposition to the pastoral landscape of the 'green cabinet' and, what is more, with the rather comic / satiric figure of the spendthrift Galatea, whose manner of life did not allow Tityrus to secure a *peculium* for ransoming his *libertas*; for the 'unpastoral' character of the squanderer wife as well as of notions like *peculium* and *libertas*, cf. Papanghelis 1995, 193–4; see also above, pp. 59, 74, 128. Moreover, in Calp. 4 food shortage forces the herdsman to abandon the pastoral community for the city, in order to put up his milk for sale (vv. 25–6: *lac venale per urbem...porta*). The herdsman is thus presented as being interested in profit (*venale*), not the uppermost value of the traditional pastoral space, i.e., bucolic song, but instead a quality of the georgic community, although, in opposition to the agrarian literature in general, profit in the Vergilian *Georgics* does not seem to have a clear monetary viewpoint (cf. Thibodeau 2011, 64–5); see also above, pp. 58–9, 95. The profit-motif in Calp. 5 is yet again associated with information of georgic import; see also Davis 1987, 37, Garthwaite-Martin 2009, 310, 322.

75 Cf. Mynors 2003, 240, Becker 2012, 84–5, Vinchesi 2014, 394; see also Erren 2003, 725–6, Esposito 2012, 63 and nn. 46, 47.
76 Cf. also Becker 2012, 86, Esposito 2012, 64. In the pastoral tradition, on the other hand, a goat (Theocr. 1.25–6) and a heifer (Verg. *Ecl.* 3.29–30), recently having given birth, are positively presented as milked three times or twice a day respectively (cf. also Chapter 4, p. 143); the animals are thus viewed as the materialistic equivalent to Thyrsis' and Damoetas'– Menalcas' pastoral art, i.e., pastoral song.
77 Cf. also Verdière 1954, 257, Marchiò 1957, 305–6, Korzeniewski 1971, 102, 52–3, Amat 1991, 114–5, Keene 1996, 121, Di Lorenzo-Pellegrino 2008, 239, Landolfi 2009, 104, Becker 2012, 86, Vinchesi 1996, 129; 2014, 395.
78 Cf. Cesareo 1931, 68, Verdière 1954, 181, 257, Marchiò 1957, 304–6, Mahr 1964, 184–5, Korzeniewski 1971, 52–3, Messina 1975, 100–1 and n. 114, Friedrich 1976, 111, Kettemann 1977, 109, Novelli 1980, 37, 79–80, Gagliardi 1984, 69–70 and n. 1, Armstrong 1986, 121, Di Lorenzo 1987, 21 and n. 33, Thomas 1988, 2.73, Amat 1991, 114–5, Keene 1996, 121, Vinchesi 1996, 129; 2014, 394–5, Horsfall 1997, 183–4, Di Lorenzo-Pellegrino 2008, 238–40, Landolfi 2009, 102–3, Becker 2012, 84, Esposito 2012, 63–4.

Tib. 1.1.31ff.[79], i.e., to yet another text operating on the 'generic interaction' between pastoral, georgics and elegy (a combination of an amatory narrative (vv. 53ff.) with references to both pastoral relaxation (vv. 11–24) and georgic occupations (vv. 33–44)[80]), thus further emphasising the 'generic interplay' of the present Calpurnian poem; yet see also Var. *rust.* 2.2.15[81]. The last georgic order associated with spring-time has to do with the fickleness of spring weather, which should deter herdsmen from looking for remote pasturage for their flocks, vv. 43–8. A similar georgic advice to secure the flock in its pen in the case of dangerous weather conditions also comes from the georgic Vergil, namely from *G.* 1.355: *agricolae propius stabulis armenta tenerent*[82]. What is more, the final picture of the rain clouds and the attendant fog (vv. 47–8) seems to allude to Verg. *G.* 2.308–9, as also evidenced by the collocation *caligine nimbos*, appearing as *caligine nubem* in the Vergilian text[83]. As for didactic linguistic reminiscences, one should mention the syntagm *vernum…tempus* (v. 45), also occurring in Lucretius, cf. 5.802, 6.369, and the didactic mode of Hor. *Ars* 302[84].

The Summer Manual

The next main narrative segment is all but a herdsman's guide for the summer. Micon offers the following guidance: a) flocks should be driven to the woods, to distant pasturages in general, only in summer-time, when stable weather conditions permit it (vv. 49–52), b) as to the time of pasturage, the flock should be let out of the pen early in the morning, when the humid air renders the animal's food sweet, the night-dew still covers the cool fields, and when dazzling

---

79 Cf. Cesareo 1931, 68–70, Verdière 1954, 181; 1966, 171 and n. 70, Marchiò 1957, 306–7, Korzeniewski 1971, 53, Messina 1975, 101, Friedrich 1976, 111, Gagliardi 1984, 44–5 and n. 62, Di Salvo 1990a, 280, Amat 1991, 115, Keene 1996, 121, Vinchesi 1996, 40–1; 2012, 715; 2014, 44–5, 395–6, Maltby 2002, 133, Di Lorenzo-Pellegrino 2008, 239, Landolfi 2009, 104–5, Becker 2012, 88, Esposito 2012, 65–6.
80 Cf. Murgatroyd 1991, 48; see also Maltby 2002, 115–51, Thibodeau 2011, 210–2.
81 Cf. Hubaux 1930, 225 vs. Marchiò 1957, 306 and n. 5; see also Verdière 1966, 171 and nn. 69, 70, Friedrich 1976, 226 and n. 15, Kettemann 1977, 109 and n. 36, Landolfi 2009, 104 and n. 69, Becker 2012, 87. Friedrich's view, *loc. cit.*, regarding an influence of Verg. *Ecl.* 1.12ff. here does not seem conclusive enough.
82 Cf. Verdière 1954, 181, Korzeniewski 1971, 53, Kettemann 1977, 109, Keene 1996, 121, Becker 2012, 88, Esposito 2012, 66–7, Vinchesi 2014, 397. For a possible influence of Verg. *G.* 3.318ff. here, cf. Cesareo 1931, 70–1, Marchiò 1957, 307.
83 Cf. Di Lorenzo-Pellegrino 2008, 241.
84 Cf. also Landolfi 2009, 105–6, Vinchesi 2014, 398, Esposito 2012, 67.

drops are still found on the meadows (vv. 52–5), c) during the hot hours of the noon, the flocks should in all cases be watered; they also should not be let exposed under the scorching sun, but instead they ought to be protected by the spreading shade of an oak (vv. 56–9), d) with the cooling of the heat, the flock should be sent for a last grazing (vv. 60–2), e) the flock should not be driven back to its summer pen until the birds chirp their plaints and think of slumber (vv. 63–5). Such guidance on the herdsman's summer day has its parallels in the didactic prose, i.e., Var. *rust*. 2.2.10 ff. (see also Colum. 7.3.23–4, Pallad. 12.13), i.e., a technical treatise, once more underlining the 'generic didactic intent' of Calp. 5[85]. With respect to didactic poetry in particular, vv. 49–55 (precepts a and b – see above, pp. 172–3) once again closely follow Vergil's *Georgics*, namely 3.322–6[86], which also deal with the proper pasturing-time during summer; of the same 'georgic generic origin' is also the motif of thirst in summer heat of v. 49: *at cum longa dies sitientes afferet aestus*, modelled on Verg. *G*. 3.327[87], whereas the image of the chilly grass drenched with the night-dew (v. 54) has its parallels not only in the pastoral Vergil (cf. Verg. *Ecl*. 8.14–5) but also in the didactic mode of Ov. *Fast*. 1.311–2[88]. What is more, the picture of the gleaming morning dew on the lawn (v. 55) also has a previous didactic, both Lucretian and Vergilian, 'generic history', cf. Lucr. 2.319, 5.461 ff., Verg. *G*. 3.322–6[89]. VV. 56–62 (precepts c and d – see above) follow the *Georgics* of Vergil too, namely 3.327–38[90]. A didactic origin may again be traced in the case of the motif of the 'shrill cicada setting out to sing when the heat of the day increases' (v. 56); the theme has its bucolic parallels (cf. Theocr. 7.138–9, Verg. *Ecl*. 2.12–3), and, furthermore, appears in didactic poetry (cf. Hes. *WD* 582 ff., Verg. *G*. 3.327 ff.)[91]. As to the motif of the pastoral shade (v. 59), although it is a distinct 'bucolic generic theme', it appears in

---

[85] Cf. Korzeniewski 1971, 104, Kettemann 1977, 109 and n. 36, Thomas 1988, 2.102–3, Becker 2012, 92.
[86] Cf. Cesareo 1931, 71–2, Marchiò 1957, 307–8, Messina 1975, 101–2, Friedrich 1976, 112, Kettemann 1977, 109, Gagliardi 1984, 87, Di Lorenzo 1987, 21 and n. 41, Landolfi 2009, 107, Becker 2012, 91, Vinchesi 2014, 400.
[87] Cf. Verdière 1954, 183, Korzeniewski 1971, 53, Kettemann 1977, 109, Di Lorenzo–Pellegrino 2008, 241, Becker 2012, 90, Vinchesi 2014, 399.
[88] Cf. Di Lorenzo–Pellegrino 2008, 242, Vinchesi 2014, 400–1.
[89] Cf. Verdière 1954, 257, Korzeniewski 1971, 53, Novelli 1980, 62, Amat 1991, 115, Fowler 2002, 394, Di Lorenzo–Pellegrino 2008, 242, Landolfi 2009, 107–8, Vinchesi 2014, 401.
[90] Cf. Cesareo 1931, 72, Verdière 1954, 183, Marchiò 1957, 308, Friedrich 1976, 112, Di Lorenzo–Pellegrino 2008, 242, Landolfi 2009, 108–9, Becker 2012, 92, Vinchesi 2014, 401–3.
[91] Cf. Korzeniewski 1971, 53–5, 104, Messina 1975, 102, Novelli 1980, 80, Di Lorenzo 1988, 19, Keene 1996, 122–3, Mynors 2003, 232, Di Lorenzo–Pellegrino 2008, 242, Landolfi 2009, 108–9, Becker 2012, 92, Vinchesi 2014, 401–2.

the present passage in the image of a shadowy oak screening the flock from the sun, i.e., a picture of a clear georgic colouring, cf. Verg. *G.* 3.332–3: *antiquo robore quercus / ingentis tendat ramos*[92]. Georgic is also the image of the sweet evening air in vv. 60–1, fashioned after Verg. *G.* 3.336–7: *cum frigidus aera vesper / temperat*[93]. As to vv. 62–5, one may read an allusion to Verg. *G.* 3.335ff[94]. On the level of linguistic borrowing as well, one may easily discern an intertextual 'didactic generic allegiance': the syntagm *sitientes...aestus* (v. 49) is an alternative combination for *sitis aestatis* (cf. Colum. 11.3.9) or *aestatem sitientem* (Man. 2.183). In vv. 52–3, *dulces..cibos* seems to be a loan *iunctura* from Verg. *G.* 2.216, *rursus pasce* in v. 62 comes from Verg. *G.* 3.335: *et pascere rursus*, whereas *somnos captare* (v. 64) is a variant of the also georgic *carpere somnos*, cf. Verg. *G.* 3.435[95], i.e., a crucial passage from a 'generic point of view', where the traditional pastoral assets of the sweet sleep and of bucolic reclining in a typical pastoral landscape, cf. also Theocr. 5.50–1, Verg. *Ecl.* 1.1, 4, 7.45, are only brought up to be rejected[96].

Micon continues with the following georgic topics: a) shearing of the flock including branding and penning together animals of similar fleece quality, thus facilitating the bundling of the wool (vv. 66–71), b) looking after a wounded animal after shearing; use of native sulphur, the head of a sea–leek, bitumen, and Bruttian pitch for medical reasons (vv. 72–82), c) stamping the name of the owner on the animals with quicksilver in honey and sticky pitch so as to avoid legal disputes (vv. 82–5), d) driving away the snakes, especially when the ground is dry, by burning yellowish gum–resin and by way of the smoke of a burned deer's horn (vv. 86–94). VV. 66–71 (precept a, see above) is drawn again on didactic texts; the shearing of the flock occurs as a topic in Varro's didactic prose, cf. Var. *rust.* 2.11.6ff.[97], while the trimming of a he–goat as a georgic concern (v. 68) also has its parallel in the third book of the *Georgics*,

---

[92] Cf. Korzeniewski 1971, 55, Kettemann 1977, 109, Di Lorenzo–Pellegrino 2008, 243, Landolfi 2009, 109, Vinchesi 2014, 403; see also Paladini 1956, 526, Becker 2012, 93.
[93] Cf. Di Lorenzo–Pellegrino 2008, 243, Vinchesi 2014, 403.
[94] Cf. Mazzarino 1983, 407–11, Becker 2012, 93, Vinchesi 2014, 404.
[95] Cf. Marchiò 1957, 308, Korzeniewski 1971, 55, Kettemann 1977, 109, Novelli 1980, 72 and n. 60, Mazzarino 1983, 407, Di Lorenzo–Pellegrino 2008, 242–4, Landolfi 2009, 107, 109, Becker 2012, 93.
[96] Cf. Thomas 1988, 2.123.
[97] Cf. Korzeniewski 1971, 104, Friedrich 1976, 113, Keene 1996, 124, Vinchesi 1992, 158; 1996, 131; 2014, 405–6, Di Lorenzo–Pellegrino 2008, 244, Landolfi 2009, 111, Becker 2012, 94–5.

namely Verg. *G.* 3.311 ff., although Vergil places it in the winter[98], and the same is valid for the georgic concern of not mingling animals growing wool of different quality and colour as evidenced in vv. 69–71, cf. also similarly Verg. *G.* 3.384 ff., 387–90[99]. The presence of technical terms like *demere* (v. 66) and *sucida…vellera* (v. 67) enhances the didactic character of the passage[100]. Wool shearing as well as an interest in wool quality appears in the pre-Calpurnian pastoral tradition as well, cf. Theocr. 5.98–9; see also Verg. *Ecl.* 3.95[101]; yet the motif simply functions as a song-exchange topic, and, what is more, in the Theocritean instance it is associated with the equally traditional pastoral motif of a present to one's beloved. The distinct technical information given here is not to be met with anywhere else in the bucolic world apart from Calp. 2.78–9, also branching out, as Calp. 5, towards the georgic genre / mode (cf. Chapter 6, pp. 195–219).

In the same vein, vv. 72–82 (precept b, see above, p. 174) follow part of Vergil's section on the diseases of animals, *G.* 3.440 ff., 448–54 in particular (see also Var. *rust.* 2.1.21–3[102]), although Vergil deals with a wider range of animal afflictions and infections than Calpurnius, who focuses on the skin hurt caused by shearing, capable of causing a lethal infection[103]. Besides, the detail of the malicious infection covered beneath the wound (vv. 74–6; see also here the technical terms *pustula* (v. 74) of an 'inflamed sore', 'blister', 'pustule', cf. also Cels. 5.26.31, 5.28.15.$_B$, OLD s.v. 1, and *forpex* of 'shears' (v. 74), cf. Cat. *agr.* 10.3, 11.4, OLD s.v.[104]) alludes to both Verg. *G.* 3.453–4, a passage crucially referring in its turn to the didactic Lucr. 4.1068[105], and the didactic prose; cf. Var. *rust.* 2.11.7; see also Colum. 7.5.10, 16, Pallad. 6.8[106]. The medical ingredients mentioned above (sulphur, sea-leek, bitumen and pitch) have the same thera-

---

98 Cf. Verdière 1954, 185, Marchiò 1957, 309, Korzeniewski 1971, 55, Amat 1991, 115, Vinchesi 1992, 158; 1996, 131; 2014, 406, Di Lorenzo-Pellegrino 2008, 244–5, Landolfi 2009, 111–2, Becker 2012, 95.
99 Cf. Marchiò 1957, 309, Vinchesi 1992, 158; 2014, 406–7, Di Lorenzo-Pellegrino 2008, 245; see also Cesareo 1931, 73, Friedrich 1976, 113, Becker 2012, 95–6.
100 Cf. Vinchesi 1992, 158; 2014, 405–6.
101 Cf. Friedrich 1976, 105.
102 Cf. Thomas 1988, 2.123.
103 Cf. Cesareo 1931, 73–4, Marchiò 1957, 309–10, Friedrich 1976, 113, Vinchesi 1992, 159; 1996, 132; 2014, 407, Di Lorenzo-Pellegrino 2008, 245, Landolfi 2009, 112–3, Becker 2012, 97.
104 Cf. De Meo 1983, 40, Vinchesi 1992, 159; 2014, 408, Landolfi 2009, 112 and n. 91.
105 Cf. Thomas 1988, 2.126, Erren 2003, 744, Vinchesi 2014, 408–9.
106 Cf. Verdière 1954, 257–8, Marchiò 1957, 310, Korzeniewski 1971, 55, 105, Friedrich 1976, 113, Kettemann 1977, 109, Keene 1996, 125, Vinchesi 1996, 132; 2014, 408, Di Lorenzo-Pellegrino 2008, 245, Landolfi 2009, 113–4 and n. 93, Becker 2012, 97–8.

peutic properties against the disease caused by shearing in Vergil (cf. *G.* 3.448 ff., with the difference that the Calpurnian pitch from Brutium in Vergil comes instead mainly from Ida – see also *G.* 4.41) and a similar medication is recommended by Columella, 6.32.2–3[107]. What is more, σκίλλα (v. 79) is a technical term, also found in several technical, didactic treatises as in Var. *rust.* 2.7.8, Colum. 12.33, Plin. *Nat.* 19.93.3, etc., and so is *bitumen* (v. 79, cf. Plin. *Nat.* 7.65) and *pix* (v. 81, cf. Plin. *Nat.* 16.53), further adding to the didactic colouring of the passage[108]. The branding of the flock (precept c – see above, p. 174) has its georgic intertexts in Verg. *G.* 1.263, 3.158; see also Colum. 7.9.12, 11.2.14, Pallad. 2.16[109], while the use of *galbanum* (also a technical term – v. 89) for chasing off serpents is also commended in Verg. *G.* 3.414–5 (see also Nic. *Ther.* 51–4) as well as in didactic prose, cf. Colum. 7.4.6, 8.5.18, Plin. *Nat.* 12.126, 24.22, Pallad. 1.35.11[110]. The use of the hart's horn as a source of ammonia against snakes (v. 90) is also commended in Var. *rust.* 3.9.14, Colum. 7.4.6, 8.5.18, Plin. *Nat.* 8.118, 10.195, Pallad. 1.35.11[111]. Verg. *G.*, namely vv. 3.420–4, fashioned in its turn after the didactic Nic. *Ther.* 179–80[112], is the model for the image of the disarmed snake in vv. 92–4[113]. The summer-setting of vv. 86–8 with an emphasis on the dry parched fields has its parallels both in Vergil's eclogues (cf. 7.56) and in his georgic work, cf. *G.* 1.107[114], whereas various linguistic reminiscences (v. 77: *contrahet*

---

107 Cf. Korzeniewski 1971, 55, 104–5, Messina 1975, 102, Kettemann 1977, 109, Di Lorenzo 1987, 20 and n. 24, Amat 1991, 115–6, Vinchesi 1992, 159; 1996, 132; 2014, 410, Mynors 2003, 247, Di Lorenzo-Pellegrino 2008, 246–7, Landolfi 2009, 115, Becker 2012, 99.
108 Cf. Verdière 1954, 258–9, Korzeniewski 1971, 105, Vinchesi 1992, 159; 1996, 132; 2014, 410–11, Di Lorenzo-Pellegrino 2008, 246; see also Erren 2003, 743.
109 Cf. Verdière 1954, 186, Marchiò 1957, 310–11, Korzeniewski 1971, 57, 105, Kettemann 1977, 109, Thomas 1988, 1.113; 2.71, Keene 1996, 127, Vinchesi 1996, 133; 2014, 412–3, Di Lorenzo-Pellegrino 2008, 247, Landolfi 2009, 115–6 and n. 103 on p. 115, Becker 2012, 101–2.
110 Cf. Cesareo 1931, 76–7 and n. 1 on p. 76, Verdière 1954, 187, Marchiò 1957, 311–2, Korzeniewski 1971, 57, 105, Messina 1975, 102–3, Friedrich 1976, 113–4, Kettemann 1977, 109, Gagliardi 1984, 47 and n. 70, Thomas 1988, 2.119, Amat 1991, 116, Keene 1996, 127, Vinchesi 1992, 159; 1996, 133; 2014, 413–4, Di Lorenzo-Pellegrino 2008, 248, Landolfi 2009, 117; see also Mynors 2003, 244, Erren 2003, 730, Becker 2012, 102–3.
111 Cf. Korzeniewski 1971, 105, Pearce 1990, 117, Amat 1991, 116, Vinchesi 1992, 159; 1996, 133; 2014, 414–5, Di Lorenzo-Pellegrino 2008, 248, Landolfi 2009, 118, Becker 2012, 103.
112 Cf. Thomas 1988, 2.120.
113 Cf. Di Lorenzo-Pellegrino 2008, 249; see also Kettemann 1977, 109, Becker 2012, 104–5.
114 Cf. Di Lorenzo-Pellegrino 2008, 248.

ossa = Verg. *G.* 3.484–5, v. 78: *viventia sulphura* = Verg. *G.* 3.449, v. 92: *serpentum cecidisse minas* inverting the Vergilian *tollentemque minas* also used of a serpent at *G.* 3.421[115]) as well as technical terms such as *pulverare* (v. 88: *fragiles nimium sol pulverat herbas*, approximating here the semantic load of *occare*, cf. also Colum. 11.2.60, Pallad. 4.7.1)[116], further underline the clear georgic outlook of the lines under consideration.

The Autumn and Winter Manual

The georgic lesson ends with guidelines for the herdsman when winter approaches, i.e., a) pruning of the wood, a kind of a *frondatio*; in particular lopping off of the tender twigs on the tree-top, while still unwithered and not blown off by the winds, storage of fresh leaves for feeding them to the animals during winter, when bad weather conditions would prevent the herdsman from looking for such stuff in the woods (vv. 95–115), b) use of straw and fallen leaves to cover the chilly ground for warming up the animals (vv. 116–8). As to vv. 95–115 (precept a, see above), Calpurnius makes use of the following individual motifs, also alluding to texts of didactic, mainly georgic interest: i) the practice of using a cutter / trimmer for lopping branches and cutting leaves (v. 99) appears in Verg. *Ecl.* 3.11; but as in several cases where the Calpurnian lines involve a Vergilian pastoral intertext, this passage also alludes to several georgic contexts, appearing in the georgic Vergil (cf. *G.* 1.157, 2.365–6, 400ff.) as well as in texts of the didactic mode, cf. Ov. *Fast.* 4.753–4; see also Colum. 4.17.3, 4.27.5[117], ii) the practice of storing food, leaves in particular, in the haylofts for the winter, in order to feed the flocks (vv. 102–3) is a practice occurring in Verg. *G.* 3.320–1; see also Cat. *agr.* 30, Colum. 7.3.21[118]. The farmer should in addition mingle dray with humid green stuff, so that moisture is preserved for quenching the thirst of the animals during winter (vv. 106–7, 111–2)[119]. Furthermore the imagery of branches and leafage blown off by the wind (v. 101) seems to be reworking sim-

---

[115] Cf. Marchiò 1957, 310, Messina 1975, 102, Gagliardi 1984, 46 and n. 69, Amat 1991, 47, Keene 1996, 125–6, 127–8, Di Lorenzo–Pellegrino 2008, 246, 249, Becker 2012, 99, 104, Vinchesi 2014, 409–10.
[116] Cf. Vinchesi 1992, 159–60; see also Bruno 1969, 239, Armstrong 1986, 121.
[117] Cf. Di Lorenzo–Pellegrino 2008, 250; see also Mynors 2003, 32, 152–3.
[118] Cf. Korzeniewski 1971, 105–6, Friedrich 1976, 114, Dehon 1993, 208, Keene 1996, 129, Di Lorenzo–Pellegrino 2008, 250, Landolfi 2009, 119, 121–2, Becker 2012, 107–8, Vinchesi 2014, 417–8.
[119] Verdière 1954, 189 reads here a reference to grafting techniques; see also Verg. *G.* 2.73–82, Amat 1991, 47, 52 and n. 134. For a refutation of this view, cf. Dehon 1993, 209 and n. 31.

ilar pictures frequently found – although by no means exclusively – in didactic texts, i.e., Verg. *G.* 2.404 (a line drawn, according to Servius, on Varro of Atax[120]) and Ov. *Ars* 3.162; see also Cic. *Arat.* 119[121]. VV. 116–8 (precept b, see above, p. 177) are similarly drawn from the *Georgics:* in particular the motif of strewing the floor with leaves (fern in the Vergilian model) and straw, and thus prevent the animals from catching a cold is found in Verg. *G.* 3.297 ff.; the motif has some parallels in the didactic prose as well, cf. Cat. *agr.* 5.7, Var. *rust.* 2.5.14, Colum. 7.3.8[122]. What is more, cold as an animal disease is found in Verg. *G.* 3.298–9 and 441–3[123]. Importantly, Verg. *G.* 3.298–9: **glacies ne frigida laedat / molle pecus scabiemque ferat turpisque podagras** alludes in its turn to yet another 'generically ambivalent case', namely Verg. *Ecl.* 10.48–9: *a, te ne **frigora** laedant! / a, tibi ne teneras **glacies** secet aspera plantas!*[124], where the elegiac poet Gallus expresses his fear lest the legs of his beloved suffer because of the cold. Both the idea of the cold as harmful to the feet and the wording of the two texts point to their intertextual relationship. However, the line of the eclogue–intertext clearly operates, as already remarked (cf. above, pp. 23, 42, 64 and n. 86, 108, 123–4, 127, 132–3, 136, 153), on the 'generic interaction' of pastoral with elegy, as it refers to the well-known elegiac affair of Gallus with Lycoris, which the poet unsuccessfully tries to overcome by his 'generic intrusion' into the pastoral world and genre, for a short time[125]. Thus this 'generic ambivalence' of the pastoral intertext may further underline the 'generic diversity' of the present Calpurnian eclogue as well. Linguistic appropriation of the georgic diction of Vergil's *Georgics* yet again points to the georgic propensities of the verses: v. 104: *labor hic* = Verg. *G.* 3.288 (cf. also 2.401–2[126]), v. 116: *fronde caduca* as a *clausula* = Verg. *G.* 1.368, v. 113 – the syntax of *positus* with a bare *ablativus loci* complement (*ingenti positus...strue*), cf. also Verg. *G.* 3.135[127].

---

120 Cf. Thomas 1988, 1.231.
121 Cf. Korzeniewski 1971, 57, Di Lorenzo–Pellegrino 2008, 250, Landolfi 2009, 121, Vinchesi 2014, 418; see also Gibson 2003, 159, Verg. *A.* 4.441 ff., Ov. *Met.* 3.729–30.
122 Cf. Verdière 1954, 259, Marchiò 1957, 312, Korzeniewski 1971, 58–9, Friedrich 1976, 114, Kettemann 1977, 109 and n. 36, Di Lorenzo 1987, 21 and n. 42, Dehon 1993, 210 and n. 40, Keene 1996, 130, Vinchesi 1996, 135, Di Lorenzo–Pellegrino 2008, 251, Landolfi 2009, 123–4; see also Mynors 2003, 227, Erren 2003, 691–2, 740, Becker 2012, 111.
123 Cf. Di Lorenzo–Pellegrino 2008, 252, Becker 2012, 111, Vinchesi 2014, 422.
124 Cf. Thomas 1988, 2.99, Erren 2003, 691.
125 Cf. Conte 1986, 100–29, Papanghelis 1995, 64–87.
126 Cf. Vinchesi 2014, 419.
127 Cf. Keene 1996, 130, Marchiò 1957, 312, Kettemann 1977, 109, Horsfall 1997, 187, Di Lorenzo–Pellegrino 2008, 250, 251–2, Becker 2012, 107, Vinchesi 2014, 419, 422.

Didactic Style and Arrangement—Patterns

The 'didactic intent', generically imposed, is thus largely achieved by means of the didactic, mostly georgic, intertexts and the technical diction / precepts found throughout Micon's monologue[128]; nevertheless, one often also comes across several distinct 'didactic generic markers / tropes', like the ones accumulated in the relevant table above, pp. 164–6:

- first of all, Micon's georgic lesson is a continuous monologue, according to the 'generic precepts' of the didactic *genus*, whereas Canthus is also presented, by 'generic convention' as well, as the 'mute listener–student[129].
- various addresses in the second singular (either mentioning the name of Canthus or not) try to secure the student's attention as well as his appropriation of the information / technical knowledge given, cf. v. 7: *Canthe puer*, v. 112: *Canthe*; see also vv. 5, 8, 10, 11, 12, 14, 16, 18, 24, 26, 27, 28, 30, 32, 36, 38, 39 ff., 44, 51, 52, 57, 58, 62, 69, 70, 73, 79, 80–1, 81–2, 83, 89–90, 91, 95–6, 98, 102–3, 104, 106 ff., 111, 117[130].
- use of the plural of the personal pronoun creating a sense of 'personal empathy', a distinct personal bond between the teacher and the student, cf. vv. 12–3: *adspicis ut nobis aetas iam mille querellas / afferat*, where *nobis* is used instead of *mihi*; see also v. 104.
- use of the ethical dative stressing the 'personal involvement' of the student, cf. vv. 72–3: *sed tibi cum vacuas posito velamine costas / denudavit ovis*.
- the didactic topic of a comprehensive preparation before embarking upon the main task / mission occurs in the following instances: in vv. 24 ff., where a complex ritual with all its details should take place, before the cattle is let free for grazing, in vv. 66 ff., where the shearing of the flock is accomplished only after the animals are branded and separated according to the length, the smoothness and the colour of the wool, and in vv. 98 ff., where the feeding of moist green stuff to the animals during the winter presupposes the farmer's lopping of tender twigs and leafage before the coming of cold *hiems*.
- stress on the notion of *utilitas* by means of the *conveniet*–syntagm[131] in vv. 89 ff.; see also v. 102.

---

128 Cf. Vinchesi 1992, 156–60; 1996, 40; see also Paladini 1956, 527–8 (*praesaepia*, v. 43), Mahr 1964, 203–4, Di Lorenzo 1987, 22 (*mulctra*, v. 33, *compendia*, v. 36), Horsfall 1997, 183 (*circitor*, v. 97), 183–4.
129 Cf. Friedrich 1976, 106, Kettemann 1977, 109; see also Correa 1977, 150.
130 Cf. also Di Lorenzo 1987, 22.
131 Cf. also Di Lorenzo–Pellegrino 2008, 113.

- use of various formulas like *superesse*–syntagms, cf. v. 119: *nam plura supersunt* in terms of a *praeteritio* (cf. also Verg. G. 1.176: *possum multa tibi veterum praecepta referre*[132]), as well as various transitional set–phrases, like the *nunc age*–*iunctura*, common in the didactic register[133], cf. v. 95 marking the narrative transition from the summer tasks to the farmer's chores for the period close to winter–time; cf. also *nec mora* in v. 29[134], *qua ratione* in v. 96[135].
- use of *memini* forms in instructional contexts, cf. vv. 81–2: *tu liquido picis unguine terga memento, / si sint rasa, linas*; see also v. 119: *plura quidem meminisse velim* once again of didactic information that the student is spared of in terms of the rhetorical *praeteritio*[136]. What is more, the use of *ipse videbis* in v. 91, cf. vv. 91–2: *ispe videbis / serpentum cecidisse minas*, also enhances, as often in didactic texts, the sense of 'personal authority / experience' as to the results of a previous didactic, georgic order concerning the driving away of the snakes and the elimination of their poisonous attacks.
- various didactic imperativals / directive expressions[137].
  - present imperatives: Calpurnius makes use of such imperativals in didactic contexts, frequently at the beginning of a line (cf. vv. 10, 16, 26, 36, 52, 117) or in the *clausula* (cf. vv. 24, 28, 62 – imperatival + accusative complements) and less often before the *semiquinaria* (cf. v. 27) or between the *semiquinaria* and the bucolic *diaeresis* (cf. vv. 73, 95)[138],
  - future imperatives, commonly found in the three first books of Vergil's *Georgics* as well as in both Cato and Varro[139], cf. v. 83: *coquito*; see also the imperative of *memini*, v. 81: *memento*, also reinforced by the deictic *tu*,
  - gerundives of purpose, as commonly in the second book of Vergil's *Georgics* as well as in Varro's *De Re Rustica*[140], cf. vv. 9–10: *ipse tuendos /*

---

132 Cf. Marchiò 1957, 312.
133 Cf. Landolfi 2009, 119, Vinchesi 2014, 416.
134 Cf. Landolfi 2009, 101.
135 Cf. Landolfi 2009, 119–20.
136 Cf. also Di Lorenzo–Pellegrino 2008, 252.
137 Cf. also Davis 1987, 36, Di Lorenzo 1987, 19–21, Di Lorenzo–Pellegrino 2008, 233–4, 235, 237, 238, 239, 240, 241, 243, 246, 247.
138 Cf. Di Lorenzo 1987, 19–20 and nn. 17, 18, 19, 20 on p. 20. For such imperatives before the *semiseptenaria*, cf. also Calp. 5.51, 57, 58, 69, 70.
139 Cf. also Di Lorenzo 1987, 20, Di Lorenzo–Pellegrino 2008, 246, Thibodeau 2011, 44.
140 Cf. also Di Lorenzo 1987, 21 and n. 36, Di Lorenzo–Pellegrino 2008, 240, Thibodeau 2011, 45, Vinchesi 2014, 398.

accipe (probably in imitation of Verg. *G.* 3.305: *hae quoque non cura nobis leviore tuendae*[141]), v. 46: *dubitanda fides*, v. 104: *hac tibi nitendum est*, v. 111: *sitis est pensanda tuorum*,
- independent clause – future active indicatives in imperatival function, as common in both didactic prose and the first two books of Vergil's *Georgics*[142], cf. v. 18: *movebis*, v. 30: *dabis*, v. 91: *videbis*, v. 111: *premes* yet again reinforced by the deictic *tu* (v. 110); for third-person imperatival future indicatives, cf. v. 89: *conveniet*, v. 102: *conveniet*,
- future passive indicatives in a jussive function, less common than equivalent future active formations, cf. v. 34: *premetur*, v. 38: *coletur*[143],
- active *coniuctivus iussivus*, favoured in Verg. *G.* 1, 3, and 4 as well as in the rustic prose of Cato[144], cf. v. 28: *imbuat*, v. 36: *ne sint*, v. 39: *pudeat*, v. 52: *exeat*, v. 58: *protegat*, v. 79: *portes*[145], v. 80: *desit*, v. 106: *ne pigeat*, v. 113: *prosit*,
- passive jussive conjunctive, unusual in Vergil's *Georgics*[146], cf. v. 63: *includatur*.

One should also note here that didactic imperatival forms common in didactic literature, as is for example the case of the present imperatives, are frequent in Micon's georgic lesson in Calp. 5 as well and, what is more, in metrical positions favoured by the Vergilian, georgic metrical practice. On the contrary, jussive formations not particularly favoured by didactic diction in general and / or Vergil's didactic poetry in particular, as holds true for the future passive indicative forms or the passive *coniuctivus iussivus* for example, are also less frequently found in the didactic narrative of the fifth Calpurnian eclogue.

Most of the didactic stylistic features, as elaborated above, pp. 164–6, the result of a comparative heuristic analysis of the didactic style, are to be found in the Calpurnian eclogue under examination as well; those that do not appear are 1) either not particularly favoured by the georgic-didactic poetry of Vergil, which functions as the primary model of the Calpurnian poem (the use of questions as a narrative means for refuting the opponent's views, repetition of passages, tests

---

141 Cf. also Di Lorenzo–Pellegrino 2008, 233.
142 Cf. also Korzeniewski 1971, 102–3, Di Lorenzo 1987, 20–1, Di Lorenzo–Pellegrino 2008, 235, Becker 2012, 77, Vinchesi 2014, 388.
143 Cf. Mahr 1964, 153, Vinchesi 2014, 394.
144 Cf. also Di Lorenzo 1987, 20 and nn. 25, 26, 27, 28, 29, Di Lorenzo–Pellegrino 2008, 243, Vinchesi 2014, 392.
145 Cf. also Mahr 1964, 155.
146 Cf. also Di Lorenzo 1987, 20, Di Lorenzo–Pellegrino 2008, 243.

concerning the reconstruction of a didactic argument on the basis of knowledge / information having already previously been given to the student), or 2) due to the small number of the lines the didactic narrative of Micon consists of, vv. 16–119 (104 lines), when compared to the larger didactic poems. Cross-references, recapitulation and summary techniques, long lists rounded off, as well as repetitions and tests examining the degree to which the student has absorbed what he has been taught (see above 1) seem to serve a particular didactic aim in larger texts, where their presence facilitates the student's power of comprehension.

To conclude: in terms of the first two 'generic criteria' regarding the didactic character of a particular text, Calp. 5 adheres to the didactic pattern, as elaborated above (pp. 166–82), with remarkable consistency. The focus now moves onto the 'poetic consciousnesses' of the present Calpurnian poem. At this point, some further methodological remarks are in order.

'Poetic Self-Consciousness' – 'Poetic Simultaneity'

The other two typical 'generic features' of the poetic didactic *genus*, namely 'poetic self-consciousness' and 'poetic simultaneity'[147], i.e., the self-reflexive presentation of the didactic teacher as a poet and of didactic teaching as poetry as well as the attendant illusion of a 'lecture in progress', of a poem 'coming into being' right away, evoking the ongoing denouement of the poetic composition itself and its various phases (beginning, end, etc.)[148], are an equally necessary prerequisite of didactic poetry. Thus at the start of a poem, the poetic composition may be viewed as either about to start or as a future product, at the end of the poem the poet may self-reflexively comment on the accomplishment of his poetic work, while in the course of the poem the poet may also comment on the ongoing progress of the poetic composition; various images, especially journey-imagery (cf. Hes. *WD* 659), may occasionally complement this self-referential process[149]. In the *Works and Days* the Hesiodic persona invokes the inspiring Muses, as also does Aratus (cf. *Phaen.* 16–8), and describes himself as a poet (cf. vv. 1–2, 654–62), Empedocles' *On Nature* clearly refers to itself as poetry (cf. B 3, B 4, B 23.11, B 35.1–3, B 131), whereas in the σφραγὶς of the *Theriaca* and *Alexipharmaca* the didactic persona is also clearly referred to as a poet. As for the 'poetic simultaneity' discerned in Greek didactic literature, one may

---

147 Cf. Volk 2002, 247.
148 Cf. Volk 2002, 9–24, 39–40 and *passim*.
149 Cf. Volk 2002, 13–4, 20–4.

in passing refer to several lines self-reflexively commenting upon the process of teaching–poetic composition, cf. Hes. *WD* 10, 106–7, 286, Emp. B 8.1, B 17.1, 16, B 38.1, Arat. *Phaen.* 1, 1–18, 460–1, 1036–7[150].

These poetological features have been handed down to Roman didactic poetry as well: Rome's first serious didactic poet[151] is a clear teacher–poet, according to the 'generic demands' of the poetic didactic *genus*, and thus repeatedly acknowledges the poetic character of his didactic, Epicurean teaching, when referring to his words either as *versus* (cf. 1.24, 137, 2.529, 3.36, 4.24, 6.83, etc.) or *carmen* (1.143, 3.420, 4.9, 5.1, 6.937, etc.) as well as when describing his poetic *didaxis* by means of the verb *canere* (cf. 5.509, 6.84), all plainly suggesting a certain degree of 'poetic self-consciousness' as described above[152]. What is more, in 1.921–50, Lucretius' first-person speaker appears to be seeking fame as a poet, stresses the novelty of his poetic work by means of the well-known poetological *primus*-motif, elaborates on the Callimachean poetic program he is following[153] and, last but not least, makes use of the didactic journey-imagery commonly used within the Roman didactic poetic corpus with reference either to the poet's didactic, teaching–poetic composition or the student's learning process (1.926–7; cf. also 1.80–2, 1.370–1, 6.92–5, etc.)[154]. 'Poetic simultaneity' is also achieved by means of the image of Lucretius' poetic production as a future accomplishment (cf. 1.24–6, 149), i.e., as not yet perfected but 'coming into being' right now, once again according to the 'didactic generic illusion' of poetry fashioned in the act of training, as well as by the various self-referential remarks concerning the development of the poetic instruction, cf. 4.26, 29–30, 6.43 ff., 92–5, etc.[155].

'Poetic self-consciousness' characterises Vergil's *Georgics* as well, especially in the poet's address to Maecenas. In the line of Lucretius, Vergil calls attention to the poetic character of his didactic instructions and, accordingly, describes the process of his didactic, poetic production by means of the verb *canere*, cf. *G.* 1.5: *hinc canere incipiam*. He also presents the Callimachean poetic program of the didactic *genus tenue* (country issues vs. natural philosophy in particular) he plans to follow (cf. *G.* 2.39–46; see also 2.483–6, 3.40–2[156]) and finally he

---

150 Cf. Volk 2002, 39, 44–57.
151 Cf. Conte 1994, 160.
152 Cf. Volk 2002, 84.
153 For Lucretius and Callimachus, cf. also Brown 2007, 328–50; see also Gale 2007a, 70–2.
154 Cf. Volk 2002, 86–92; 2009, 200.
155 Cf. Volk 2002, 75–6, 84, 104–5.
156 Cf. also Thomas 1988, 1.1–3 and *passim*; see also Thomas 1983, 92–113; 1985, 61–73; 1993, 197–215; 1998, 99–120.

also employs the distinctively didactic journey–metaphor, when imploring Maecenas, *G.* 2.39: *inceptumque una decurre laborem* (see also *G.* 1.40–2. 3.291–3). 'Poetic simultaneity' markers are not missing from the *Georgics* either, as Vergil often comments upon the ongoing process of his didactic poetic composition (e.g. announcement of the changing subject–matter of the didactic narrative, cf. *G.* 2.1–2, 3.1–2, 284–6, 294, 4.1–2, reference to restraints of time preventing the teacher–poet from a lesson–poem on gardening, cf. *G.* 4.116–48)[157].

Similar 'didactic generic features' are to be found in the rest of the main Latin poetic didactic tradition, i.e., in Ovidian didactic poetry, namely the *Ars Amatoria* and the *Remedia Amoris,* and Manilius' *Astronomica,* also preceding the Neronian Calpurnius. The Ovidian *praeceptor amoris* also refers to himself as *poeta* or *vates* (cf. *Ars* 1.29, 2.11, *Rem.* 3, 77, 398, etc.), and in a similar vein Manilius views himself as a *vates* (cf. 1.23, 2.142, 3.41, 4.121). Both didactic poets identify their didactic teaching as *carmen* (cf. Ov. *Ars* 1.2, 2.3, 3.342, *Rem.* 252, etc. / Man. 1.1, 2.137, 3.4, 4.430, etc.), and finally describe the composition–process of the didactic material they instruct as poetry, i.e., once again by means of the verb *canere* (cf. Ov. *Ars* 1.30, 2.493, 3.790, *Rem.* 703, 715, etc. / Man. 1.10, 2.767, 3.93, 5.27, etc.). Passages revealing the poetological orientation of the *genus tenue* also preferred by the elegiac teacher (cf. *Rem.* 361–98) and divine–epiphany scenes influencing the course of the didactic poem (cf. *Ars* 2.493–4) further complement the sense of 'generic poetic self–consciousness' of the elegiac, didactic poetry. This seems also to hold true for Manilius' poetological principles based on Callimachus' 'poetic slenderness', his 'untrodden paths' (cf. *Aet.* 1.25–8 Pf.), cf. 2.8–11, 49–59, 137–40[158]. As to 'poetic simultaneity', this is achieved once again by well–known –by now– 'didactic generic techniques': the didactic teaching–poem is about to commence (cf. Ov. *Ars* 1.30–3 / Man. 1.4, 113–7), enumeration of the various subject–matters as well as comments / reflections on the change of didactic topic / sub–topic, the course and the various stages of the didactic, poetic composition (cf. Ov. *Ars* 1.35–40, 253–4, 263–6, 771–2, 3.667–72, *Rem.* 407, etc. / Man. 5.1–11), the use of the *primus*–motif suggesting poetic novelty (cf. Man. 1.4–6, 113–4; see also 2.53–9), the also familiar journey–metaphors self–reflexively dealing with the progress of the teaching–poem (cf. Ov. *Ars* 1.772, 2.9–10 / Man. 1.13–9, 117, etc.)[159].

---

157 Cf. Volk 2002, 124–5, 131–9, 144, 156.
158 Cf. Dams 1970, 15–37, Volk 2002, 161–3, 183, 193–4, 204, 208–9, 212–3 and n. 32, 215, 227; 2003, 628–33; 2009, 176, 197–205, 260.
159 Cf. also Volk 2001, 85–117; 2002, 173–88, 209–19, 225–34; 2003, 628–33; 2004, 34–46; 2009, 200, 205, 208, 212; see also Landolfi 1999, 151–65, Abry 2002, 65–73.

'Poetic Self-Consciousness' – 'Poetic Simultaneity' and Calp. 5

Nowhere, within the didactic 'intra-textual drama' (term of Volk 2002, 17, 37) of Calp. 5, is a view of Micon as a poet and of his lesson as a poem to be found. It is certainly a poetic narrative in the sense that the tutorial assumes the textual form of written dactylic hexameters, i.e., the didactic metre par excellence; however a 'generic prerequisite' of didactic poetry is the illusion of the didactic instruction *qua* poetry on the part of both the teacher and the student of the afore-mentioned 'intra-textual drama' of the didactic scenario. Although a clear awareness of the poetical character of the instructional, didactic speech on the literary level is generically demanded in the case of didactic poetry, the poetic dimension of Micon's instructions is not acknowledged not even in terms of the poetological meta-language, of which the 'host-generic formation', i.e., pastoral, frequently avails itself, with the exception of a possible meta-poetic reading of Micon's bequeathing his livestock to Canthus (see below, pp. 189– 90). Easily-decipherable ideas, motifs and catch-words of Callimachean-Neoteric meta-language do not seem to produce meaning on the poetological level in the present eclogue[160]; nor does one meet any poetological settings suggesting the poetological orientation of Calpurnian Callimachean poetics, as happens with the rest of the Latin didactics. As to 'poetic simultaneity', although the didactic narrative is clearly structured according to the annual season cycle and the various georgic precepts propounded to Canthus evidently suggest the process of the didactic course and its phases, there is no implication of 'a lesson-poem on the go'.

---

160 Cf. v. 32: *vaces* (= 'to have leisure', cf. Duff and Duff 1934, 261, Davis 1987, 36–7), v. 49: *longa* dies of the long summer days (cf. Korzeniewski 1971, 103), v. 64: *levibus* nidis of the frail bird nests, v. 67: *tereti...iunco* of the rush to be used for the binding of the fleeces, vv. 70–1: *longa minutis, mollia...duris* of the animals with long and smooth wool, which should not be penned with those of short and rough fleece, v. 72: *vacuas...costas* of the uncovered sides of an animal after being shorn, v. 88: *fragiles...herbas* of the fragile herbs that a strong sun turns to dust, v. 99: *teneras...virgas* of the juicy twigs to be lopped off as winter fodder of the livestock, v. 110: *leves* hederas aut *molle* sallictum of the ivy and the willow useable as green foodstuff instead of other trees, in case the herdsman is impeded by frost or snow from locating the necessary green stuff, v. 113: *ingenti...strue* of the pile of withered greenery useless for noshing the animals.

Pastoral Framings and Georgics Framed

The lines framing Micon's georgic instructions at the beginning of the poem, vv. 1–16, display 'generic features' closely associated with a long-established 'pastoral generic code', being essential 'generic markers' of the traditional bucolic *genus*, thus creating the anticipation of a pastoral song on the informed reader's part: a) 'convening', i.e., the act of coming together of various herdsmen (cf. also above, pp. 93, 103, 118, 125, 138), b) presentation of the basic characters of the eclogue's pastoral story from the very first lines of the poem, through mention of their names and age, i.e., the elder Micon and the younger Canthus (cf. vv. 1, 3–4, 7, 9, 11, 12–3), c) the pastoral shade, i.e., the shade of a tree with well-known pastoral history, a holm-oak (*ilex*) in the case under question – v. 2, protecting the bucolic characters from the harmful scorching sun, cf. v. 2: *torrentem patula vitabant ilice solem* (cf. also Introduction, p. 8), d) the image of the carefree goats wandering off through the thickets (v. 5: *quas errare vides*), calling to mind similar pastoral instances like Verg. *Ecl.* 1.9, *Eins.* 2.26[161]. What is more, the wording of the very first two lines of the eclogue recalls Verg. *Ecl.* 7.1: *forte sub arguta consederat ilice Daphnis*[162], with the crucial substitution of the Vergilian *arguta*, evoking the sonorous character of the Vergilian pastoral landscape, with the Calpurnian *patula* (yet cf. also Verg. *Ecl.* 1.1: *patulae...fagi*[163]), a replacement further suggesting the elimination of Vergilian sonorous effects within Calpurnian bucolic settings, not particularly keen, as already remarked (cf. above, pp. 10, 48–9, 59 and n. 59, 71, 73, 86, 93, 118), on natural pastoral noises[164]. Equally traditionally bucolic is also the end of Calp. 5, vv. 120–1, displaying the common Vergilian pastoral closure of the coming of the evening, which puts an end to the pastoral scenario of the individual pastoral poems, cf. Verg. *Ecl.* 1.82–3, 2.66–7, 6.85–6, 10.77, see also 9.63, also bequeathed to post-Vergilian bucolic poetry, cf. Calp. 2.93, Nemes. 1.86–7, 2.88–90, 3.67–9[165].

For all the pastoral colouring of the framing verses, the introductory framing narrative as well as the closing lines also contain signs evoking the 'georgic ge-

---

161 Cf. Verdière 1954, 256, Marchiò 1957, 302, Korzeniewski 1971, 49–50, Di Lorenzo-Pellegrino 2008, 233, Becker 2012, 71.
162 Cf. Verdière 1954, 177, Marchiò 1957, 301, Korzeniewski 1971, 49, Messina 1975, 98, Gagliardi 1984, 43 and n. 58, Di Lorenzo 1987, 18 and n. 9, Amat 1991, 114, Magnelli 2006, 474, Di Lorenzo-Pellegrino 2008, 232, Landolfi 2009, 124, Becker 2012, 68, Vinchesi 2014, 379; see also Friedrich 1976, 107.
163 Cf. Cesareo 1931, 62, Messina 1975, 98, Novelli 1980, 71, Pearce 1990, 114; see also Nemes. 3.2.
164 Cf. especially Chinnici 2009, 129–42.
165 Cf. Magnelli 2006, 474; see also Vinchesi 1996, 39–40; 2014, 423, Becker 2012, 112.

neric code', and thus build on the 'generic interaction' of pastoral and didactic, as evidenced throughout the whole of the present Calpurnian eclogue. In the initial framing, it is worth noting the following didactic reminiscences: a) the qualification of Micon's counsels as *praecepta* in v. 3 and various stylistic markers of the didactic code, such as the imperativals of vv. 9–10; see also above, pp. 166–7, 179–81, b) linguistic reminiscences of didactic poetry, cf. v. 8: the *clausula gramina campo* also appearing in Lucr. 2.660[166], v. 15: *pratis...mollibus*, see also Verg. G. 2.384, 3.520–1 (*Ecl.* 10.42 as well), Ov. *Ars* 1.279[167], c) the emphasis on the notion of *labor*, also appearing in the Vergilian pastoral corpus (cf. Verg. *Ecl.* 10.1), but with reference to poetic compositions, according to the Hellenistic / Callimachean poetological ethos (cf. also Verg. G. 2.39)[168]. However, the term, as used in Calp. 5.10: *iam certe potes insudare labori*, clearly points toward the 'georgic labour', the 'man's pursuit of toil' (Thomas 1988, 1.16; see also Garthwaite-Martin 2009, 310), a key-notion of the Vergilian *Georgics*, whose adaptation seems to be the larger part of the present Calpurnian poem, in terms of both georgic topics and didactic linguistic / stylistic features[169]. As previously remarked (cf. p. 186), the closure of the eclogue is brought about by means of the common pastoral ending provided by the motif of the coming of the evening. Yet v. 119: *plura quidem meminisse* **velim**, *nam plura supersunt* mostly alludes to the conclusion of the sixth Vergilian eclogue[170], namely v. 86: *iussit et* **invito** *processit Vesper Olympo*, both exhibiting the '(un)willingness-motif'. However, the sixth Vergilian eclogue also operates on the edge between the pastoral and the didactic 'generic code', being a lesson of Silenus (= the teacher) in front of Chromis and Mnasyllos (= the students) on Roman Callimacheanism; what is more, this lesson frequently incorporates both didactic topics and stylistic features, cf. especially the initial cosmology inspired by Lucretian *didaxis*[171].

---

166 Cf. Vinchesi 2014, 383.
167 Cf. Verdière 1954, 179, Marchiò 1957, 302, Korzeniewski 1971, 51, Kettemann 1977, 109, Novelli 1980, 79 and n. 79, Di Lorenzo-Pellegrino 2008, 234, Becker 2012, 75, Vinchesi 2014, 386.
168 Cf. Clausen 1994, 293, Cucchiarelli 2012, 482–3.
169 For the view that *labor* is here used in the sense of 'flock', cf. Horsfall 1997, 191–2.
170 Cf. Marchiò 1957, 312, Magnelli 2006, 475 and n. 34; see also Landolfi 2009, 125.
171 Cf. the use of the archaic *uti* instead of *ut*, favoured by Lucretius, in v. 31, the common Lucretian syntagm *magnum per inane* in v. 31 (cf. also Lucr. 1.1018, 1103, 2.65, 105, 109), *semina* in the sense of 'atoms', in vv. 31–2, as commonly in Lucretius (cf. also Lucr. 2.1059–60), the use of the plural *terrae* (chiefly in the genitive, accusative and ablative) with the meaning of 'earth' – v. 32, also idiolectal in Lucretius (cf. also Lucr. 5.446), *anima* as equivalent to 'air' in v. 32 (cf. also Lucr. 1.714–5), *concrescere* in v. 34, *paulatim* in v. 36, two more Lucretian linguistic favourites (18 and 23 instances respectively), Lucretian word order patterns, e.g. the po-

Thus a plausible suggestion would be to read Micon's georgic instructions as belonging to the georgic mode framed, however, by common pastoral framing-patterns, while also taking advantage of the 'generic contact' of pastoral with didactic / mainly georgic poetry. Nevertheless, the evidence examined provides no support to the interpretation of Calp. 5, proposed by some critics, as a miniature / *Verkleinerung*-form of the didactic genre. 'Poetic self-consciousness' and 'poetic simultaneity', i.e., two basic 'generic standards' of didactic poetry, as evidenced by a heuristic deconstructive analysis of the whole of ancient didactic poetic production, seem to be lacking in the present Calpurnian eclogue, despite its omnipresent 'didactic intent' also resulting in the construction of a 'didactic teacher-student' bond. Calp. 5 undoubtedly avails itself of the didactic mode, as seems to be the case with Horace's *Ars Poetica* which appears equally short of 'poetic self-consciousness' and 'poetic simultaneity'[172], but cannot properly be labelled as didactic poetry. A key-feature of Calpurnian poetics is its constant 'generic contact' with other, i.e., non-'pastoral generic formations' and 'modes' with a view to transcending traditional pastoral as handed down to the Neronian poet chiefly by Vergil, 'enriching' the 'generic boundaries' of the bequeathed pastoral, as well as further perpetuating 'generic tensions' already evidenced in pre-Calpurnian bucolic poetry (e.g. elegy vs. pastoral). It is in terms of this 'generic progress' that one should understand the 'generic identity' of the Calpurnian bucolic in question; Calp. 5 incorporates within the pastoral host-text several 'generic features' of a didactic / georgic hosted text, a situation uncommon in the Theocritean bucolic poems, but not unknown in Vergilian pastoral, although not to the extent this 'generic contact' of the pastoral and the farming-georgic world is to be observed in Calpurnian pastoral poetics (cf. also especially Calp. 2 and 4)[173].

---

sitioning of the last item of an enumeration in the following line, further qualified by an adjective in v. 33 (cf. also Lucr. 6.529–30), ablative syntagms (noun and its modifying complement) divided by a postponed *ex* also followed by another word in v. 33: *his ex omnia primis* (cf. also Lucr. 2.731–2, 3.10, 4.829), epanaleptic constructions, where the word in epanalepsis is repeated in two consecutive lines after the insertion of another word, in vv. 33–4: *omnia primis, / omnia* (cf. also Lucr. 2.955–6, 6.528–9), as well as various individual Lucretian reminiscences, cf. v. 34 = Lucr. 5.498–9, 510, v. 39 = Lucr. 2.114, v. 40 = Lucr. 2.532, 5.823–4. Cf. especially Ramorino 1986, 326–7, Clausen 1994, 189–92, Hardie 2009, 27–8, 32–3, Cucchiarelli 2012, 341–3.
172 Cf. Volk 2002, 42.
173 Cf. especially Chapters 2, 6, pp. 72, 74, 86, 195–219; see also Messina 1975, 96–7.

A *Dichterweihe*-Setting?

Taking all the above into account, one should also pay attention to the possible meta-linguistic associations of the emphasis put on Micon's old age, to the bucolic prehistory of Canthus and Micon as pastoral names as well to the imagery of cattle passed on from an older to a younger pastoral figure. Micon is described as *senior* three times (cf. vv. 1, 3, 9), in opposition to Canthus, who is addressed as *puer* (v. 7) or portrayed as *iuvenis* (vv. 3, 9; see also v. 11), and the narrator draws attention to old Micon's trembling lips when uttering his georgic precepts (v. 4); last but not least, Micon himself enlarges on the grievance of his old age as well as on his need of a leaning staff (vv. 12–3). Thus a clear distinction between an older and a younger member of the 'green cabinet' is established. What is more, whereas the aged and thus more experienced bucolic figure is given a name with a clear pastoral past, cf. Theocr. 5.112, Verg. *Ecl.* 3.10, 7.30, Calp. 6.92, the younger Canthus' name derives from the non-pastoral tradition, as it previously appears in Apollonius of Rhodes (cf. 1.77, 4.1467, 1485, 1497) to reappear in the Latin handling of the Argonautic story by Valerius Flaccus, cf. 1.166[174]. A parallel situation is developed in the fifth Vergilian eclogue, where an aged Menalcas, possessing a name of unambiguously 'pastoral pedigree', engages in a song-exchange with a younger pastoral figure, Mopsus, also addressed as *puer* (vv. 19, 49) and bearing a name without clear bucolic dimensions. In the case of Verg. *Ecl.* 5, I have elsewhere suggested that one might read a *Dichterweihe*-setting, whereby the younger Mopsus functions as the recipient of a 'new diversified pastoral norm', as elaborated by the poetic account of the elder Menalcas, where earlier bucolics are intermingled with panegyric and georgic features to an extent not observed in the pre-Vergilian pastoral tradition[175].

A similar situation is also developed in the Calpurnian eclogue in question: there is an age distinction between two bucolic characters, of which only the elder and better qualified draws his name on the 'green tradition'. *Mutatis mutandis*, just as Menalcas of Verg. *Ecl.* 5 reveals to the younger member of the 'green community' a new pastoral form, in a similar vein Canthus of Calp. 5 may be read as the beneficiary of another poetological revelation concerning a new, more diversified and 'generically ambivalent' Calpurnian pastoral, where the pastoral and the georgic mode interact on a very close level, once again to

---

[174] Cf. Friedrich 1976, 106, Di Lorenzo 1987, 19 and n. 11, Vinchesi 1996, 127, Magnelli 2006, 474, Di Lorenzo-Pellegrino 2008, 232, Esposito 2012, 53 and n. 10.
[175] Cf. Karakasis 2011, 153–83; see also above, pp. 20, 23, 113.

an extent unknown to pre-Calpurnian pastoral poetics[176]. This meta-poetic reading seems to be further backed up by the image of a father bequeathing cattle to his (foster-) son heralding Calp. 5 (vv. 5–11), also read as 'troping', in terms of Calpurnian poetics, the transmission of the pastoral poetic tradition from an older to a younger representative of the genre. As already noted before (cf. above, pp. 16, 152), Hubbard 1998, 155 and n. 25 plausibly reads Calp. 1.4: *ecce pater quas tradidit, Ornyte, vaccae* as a meta-linguistic reference to pastoral succession, suggested mainly by the use of the verb *tradere* in the sense of 'to transmit ancestral knowledge'. From this perspective, the father of the programmatic first Calpurnian eclogue bequeathing his farm animals may be Vergil, the flock may symbolise pastoral poetry, and finally the recipients of this livestock / pastoral poetry, Corydon and Ornytus, may be read as the successors of Vergil (post-Vergilian bucolics). Similarly, Micon's (the father's) cattle, which consists of both goats and sheep, i.e., characteristic animals of the Vergilian *Georgics* (cf. especially 2.380 ff., 3.300 ff., and 1.272, 3.295 ff., 441 ff. respectively, Thibodeau 2011, 121), and is entrusted to Canthus (the son) may also be read as 'troping' the passing on of the new expanded pastoral, where bucolics significantly branch out towards the georgic mode. As Leach 1975, 217 plausibly remarks, Micon's handing down of his goats and sheep to Canthus constitutes a gesture which 'is equivalent to the more poetically glorified transfer of a shepherd's pipe'[177]. This crucial remark further strengthens the poetological reading of the scene, since the passing on of the pipe, often by an older to a younger member of the 'green cabinet' as in the Calpurnian instance in question, also frequently 'tropes', on the symbolic level, the transmission of pastoral art, cf. Verg. *Ecl.* 2.36–8, 5.85, 6.67–9, Calp. 4.59–63, where, as already elaborated, the handing over of a pastoral pipe similarly appears in the background of a pastoral succession (cf. above, pp. 21, 64, 113, 132–3)[178]. Thus the 'teacher-disciple' bond, inherent as it is to pastoral, in terms, however, of a purely poetic *didaxis*, becomes in Calp. 5 more practical and professionalised; in other words, despite the demonstrable didactic element of the Calpurnian eclogue under discussion, in spite of its obvious thematic and stylistic alignment with canonical specimens of the didactic genre, one may also read here an extension of the pastoral 'teaching constellation', as mentioned above[179].

---

[176] Cf. Mackie 1989, 11 as to Calp. 5: 'the most 'Georgic' of the collection'; see also Lana 1998, 824.
[177] Cf. also Hubbard 1998, 153.
[178] For the motif of the flute as a gift and its associations with 'poetic succession', cf. also Papanghelis 1995, 156–7, Fey-Wickert 2002, 79–80.
[179] I owe this remark to Prof. T. D. Papanghelis.

Conclusion

Calp. 5 clearly benefits from the didactic / georgic mode to an extent not found in earlier bucolics; it displays an evident 'didactic intent' secured not only by common linguistic / stylistic markers of the didactic genre (e.g. the qualification of the didactic information as *praecepta*, various common didactic imperativals and formulas, etc.) but also through the technical–georgic knowledge it aims to transmit as well as the various intertexts (on the level of both topics and diction) often drawn not only from texts plainly belonging to the didactic *genus* but also from texts incorporating the didactic mode, as is for example Ovid's *Fasti*. The 'teacher–student constellation' further implements the 'didactic intent' of the eclogue.

However, the poem lacks the last two 'generic prerequisites' of the poetic didactic *genus*, namely clear cases of 'poetic self–consciousness' and 'poetic simultaneity', and thus cannot be characterised as didactic poetry. The poem seems to be rather framing a didactic mode chiefly drawing on Verg. *G.* 3 within traditional, pastoral framing lines and, what is more, by means of well-established, bucolic framing techniques. Finally, on the meta–poetic level, Micon's handing over his flock to his son, Canthus (the inexperienced younger bucolic member named after characters of no special pastoral calibre in opposition to the father-figure Micon), may be read as symbolising the transmission of a new, 'generically more varied pastoral', considerably 'enriched' by the didactic mode.

Elegy and Georgics

Calpurnius 2

The only eclogue in the pastoral group of the Calpurnian corpus that remains faithful to the agonistic song-contest structure of the pastoral tradition is eclogue 2.

The Prerequisites

Following the standard pattern, two singers meet (cf. also Verg. *Ecl.* 3.55 ff., 5.1) with a view to exchanging songs in an agonistic setting (v. 9: *magnum certamen erat*, see also Verg. *Ecl.* 7.16, 8.3[1]). From a formalistic viewpoint, the prerequisites of a bucolic song-contest, as established by the pastoral tradition preceding Calpurnius (cf. Karakasis 2011, 52–3), are largely met[2]: reference is made by the external narrator to both physical and artistic qualities of the two contestants (vv. 3–4: *formosus uterque nec impar / voce sonans*, cf. also [Theocr.] 8.3–4, Verg. *Ecl.* 7.4–5[3]), who are introduced by name from the very first line of the poem (v. 1: *puer Astacus et puer Idas*) and, what is more, in a chiastic presentation (vv. 1–2: *puer Astacus*[1] *et puer Idas*[2], */ Idas*[2] *lanigeri dominus gregis, Astacus*[1] *horti*), *reversio* also having the sanction of earlier pastoral, cf. Verg. *Ecl.* 7.2–3[4]. The youth of both singers, a further 'generic marker' of the traditional amoebaean βουκολιασμός[5], is clearly signalled in the narrative, through the so-called ἄμφω-motif. Additionally, a generically impeccable location and time for the singing match of the bucolic tradition is announced: the noontide heat of a summer day (v. 4: *cum terras gravis ureret aestas*, cf. also Theocr. 6.3–4) in the surroundings of a chilly *locus amoenus*[6] comprising a cooling spring and a shady tree, v. 5. The adherence to standard bucolic practice continues with the

---

1 Cf. also Verdière 1954, 136, Messina 1975, 53, Friedrich 1976, 32, Kettemann 1977, 100 and n. 9, Gagliardi 1984, 30, Keene 1996, 66, Schäfer 2001, 142, Vinchesi 2014, 171–2.
2 Cf. also Fey-Wickert 2002, 53, Vinchesi 2014, 165.
3 Cf. also Cesareo 1931, 39–40, Wendel 1933, 37, Verdière 1954, 240, Messina 1975, 52, Friedrich 1976, 25–9, Stanzel 1989, 186 and n. 5, Kegel-Brinkgreve 1990, 155 and n. 17, Pearce 1990, 44, Amat 1991, 11, 14 and n. 25, Vinchesi 1996, 36, 45; 2014, 169, Schäfer 2001, 141 and n. 6, Fey-Wickert 2002, 57–8, Di Lorenzo-Pellegrino 2008, 165. See also later Nemes. 2.16.
4 Cf. Keene 1996, 65, Fey-Wickert 2002, 56, Di Lorenzo-Pellegrino 2008, 164, Vinchesi 1996, 76; 2014, 168.
5 Cf. Stanzel 1989, 190, Schäfer 2001, 141; see also Friedrich 1976, 21, Vinchesi 2014, 168.
6 Cf. Friedrich 1976, 29–30, Davis 1987, 33, Vinchesi 2014, 170; see also Amat 1995, 80.

fortuitous character of the 'convening' of the two pastoral characters (v. 5: *forte*, cf. also Verg. *Ecl.* 7.1–2[7]), evaluative remarks concerning the sweetness of the songs to be performed (v. 6: *dulcique simul contendere cantu*), the fixing of prizes (vv. 7–8) and the appointment of an umpire (v. 9). Last but not least, a time-honoured pastoral scenery is complemented with the orphic syndrome of vv. 10–20[8], harking back to a Vergilian song-contest, *Ecl.* 8.1–4[9], and approximating a further 'generic pastoral motif', that of the pathetic fallacy.

However, a closer reading of the details of the setting described reveals that the pre-Calpurnian pastoral canon is being up to a point deconstructed: first of all the names ascribed to the two singers do not have any pastoral prehistory whatsoever[10]. It is true that Vergil too employs characters with names without a 'pastoral pedigree' in his pastoral work; but in his singing matches, both competing herdsmen possess a clear pastoral antecedent. In the third Vergilian eclogue, the non-Theocritean Menalcas (yet, cf. [Theocr.] 8, 9, 27.44) is coupled with the Theocritean Damoetas, impersonating Polyphemus in Theocr. 6, while in the seventh eclogue both contestants have genuine Theocritean antecedents: Corydon harks back to the cowherd in the fourth Theocritean idyll, and Thyrsis comes from Theocr. 1.19. Astacus and Idas of the second Calpurnian poem, on the contrary, have nothing to do with the earlier 'green cabinet'; instead Idas and Astacus (the latter in its patronymic form *Astacides*) show up in other literary genres, mainly in epic (cf. Verg. *A.* 9.575, Ov. *Met.* 8.305, Stat. *Th.* 8.718, 724–7, 746, see also Ov. *Ib.* 515, *Fast.* 5.699–702)[11]; Idas does appear in the Theocritean corpus, yet significantly in the non-pastoral idyll 22.137–40. Calpurnius thus breaks up the Vergilian pattern.

These two singers bearing names of no pastoral prehistory (note also that one of them has a non-bucolic profession, being a gardener (v. 2: *dominus...Astacus horti*))[12] are further involved in an elegiac triangle, whereby both young

---

7 Cf. Fey-Wickert 2002, 146, Vinchesi 2014, 171.
8 Cf. also Leach 1975, 209; see also Vinchesi 2014, 172.
9 Cf. also Cesareo 1931, 42, Friedrich 1976, 26, 36, Kettemann 1977, 100–1 and n. 10, Davis 1987, 34, Schäfer 2001, 142–3 and n. 12, Fey-Wickert 2002, 64, Di Lorenzo-Pellegrino 2008, 21, Vinchesi 2014, 172.
10 Cf. also Vinchesi 1996, 76; 2012, 712 and n. 36, Vallat 2006, http://.
11 Cf. Friedrich 1976, 22, Fey-Wickert 2002, 55–6, Di Lorenzo-Pellegrino 2008, 163, Vinchesi 2014, 165, 168.
12 Cf. also Kettemann 1977, 100, 102 (see also pp. 107–8), Gagliardi 1984, 30–1 and nn. 3 (the heightened interests of the period for gardening as an interpretation of this choice; see also Perutelli 1976, 781–2, Vinchesi 1992, 152 and n. 9; 1996, 35; 2014, 165–6, Uden 2010, 212–3 also bringing to the fore the imperial intense concern for urban gardening), 8, Stanzel

men are in love with the same *puella*, Crocale (vv. 1–3: *Crocalen puer Astacus et puer Idas…dilexere diu*[13]), crucially also bearing a name of no pastoral history[14]. This is primarily an elegiac pattern (cf. Chapter 4, pp. 126, 132–3, 145), absent from previous pastoral, with the exception of the third Vergilian eclogue, where its function as an elegiac modal intrusion into a pastoral host–text has elsewhere been demonstrated (cf. Karakasis 2011, 100–3). The only other reference in previous pastoral to such a lovers' triangle may occur in the ecphrasis of the two suitors in the κισσύβιον of the first Theocritean idyll, where, however, it is a depiction about the general world, simply functioning as a foil to the 'pastoral cabinet' of the weaving boy–imagery (cf. Chapter 3, pp. 105–7).

Crucially, the elegiac colouring of the passage is also evident by the elegiac wording of the very first line of the eclogue, functioning as a kind of programmatic declaration concerning 'generic allegiance': *intactam Crocalen puer Astacus et puer Idas…dilexere diu* (vv. 1–3) evokes Verg. *Ecl.* 2.1: *formosum pastor Corydon ardebat Alexin*[15]. This is the very eclogue where, as already remarked (cf. above, pp. 5, 55–6 and n. 39, 93, 124, 128, 132–3, 137–9, 141–4, 153), 'pastoral dislocation' looms large, with Corydon constructing an elegiac discourse in a clearly 'unpastoral' mind–set, <u>solus</u> / *montibus et silvis studio iactabat inani* (vv. 4–5), and re–assuming 'pastoral correctness', the sexual looseness which is familiar in the pastoral world[16], only at the end of the poem. The rapprochement with elegy is suggested not only by means of the intertextual reference to a 'generically dubious' eclogue, but also through the substitution of *formosum* with *intactam*. This change of wording brings the Calpurnian line significantly closer to the handling of Verg. *Ecl.* 2.1 by Propertius 2.34.73–4: *felix intactum Corydon*

1989, 191, 195, Vinchesi 1991, 276, Schäfer 2001, 140, Di Lorenzo–Pellegrino 2008, 14–5, 164.

13 For the 'unpastoral' character of the erotic triangle in question, quite peculiar within an amoebaean βουκολιασμός–setting, cf. also Stanzel 1989, 192 and n. 23, Schäfer 2001, 140: 'Die Liebe zweier Sänger zu ein– und demselben Mädchen ist ein dem antiken bukolischen Wettstreit gänzlich fremdes Motiv', Vinchesi 2012, 712.

14 Vs. Crotale, the reading of N; see also Soraci 1997, 315–21, Fey–Wickert 2002, 54–5, Di Lorenzo–Pellegrino 2008, 164, Vinchesi 2012, 712 and n. 38. For the non–pastoral character of the name Crocale, cf. Friedrich 1976, 22; see also Vinchesi 2014, 167–8.

15 Cf. also Stanzel 1989, 184, Fey–Wickert 2002, 53–4, Vinchesi 2014, 167.

16 Whereas the Vergilian eclogue, functioning as a model for Calp 2, involves two lovers, Calpurnius adds an additional elegiac touch to his piece by substituting a liaison between two lovers with the elegiac triangle, as elaborated above, pp. 196–7. For the theme of the homosexual love–affair converting to a 'straight' love–experience and for the theme of the twosome turning into a threesome, cf. also Stanzel 1989, 184–5. For Alexis as a beloved's name in Verg. *Ecl.* 2, belonging to the elegiac rather than pastoral tradition, cf. also Plato A.P. 7.100, Meleager A.P. 12.127 and Coleman 1977, 91; see also Cucchiarelli 2012, 176–7.

qui temptat Alexin / agricolae domini carpere delicias![17]. In other words, Calpurnius manages to imply his 'generic flexibility' not only by alluding to an 'elegiac' Vergilian eclogue, but also by means of an intertextual allusion to the reworking of this line in the hands of a purely elegiac poet. The construction in question is significantly repeated in a similar elegiac pattern (a *puella* besieged by two lovers) in another eclogue of elegiac character, the second eclogue of Nemesianus', vv. 1–2: *formosam Donacen puer Idas et puer Alcon / ardebant* (cf. Karakasis 2011, 298–9).

The pathetic fallacy–imagery also points to a 'generic alteration', if examined in its details: Calpurnius accumulates several markers of the motif, constructing an image which at times exhibits a formalistic completeness to a much greater extent than its Theocritean and Vergilian counterparts; this is evident e.g. in the description of the animal life reacting to the orphic power of Idas' and Astacus' song, in vv. 10–11: cattle (v. 10: *omne genus pecudum*), wild beasts (v. 10: *genus omne ferarum*) and finally birds (v. 11: *quodcumque vagis altum ferit aera pennis*). Whereas in Theocritus and Vergil wild and tamed animals often feature in relevant situations (Theocr. 1.71–5 (with Friedrich 1976, 34–5), 4.12, Verg. *Ecl.* 5.25–8, 6.27–8, 8.3, 10.16, cf. also Calp. 4.60–1, 66–7), this is not the case with the fowling–imagery of v. 11[18], which appears in pastoral, apart from this Calpurnian instance, only in [Moschus] 3.46–9. Yet, despite the over–accumulation of traditional pastoral motifs (including that of the Theocritean distinction between tame and wild animals, bequeathed to Vergil in the case of his fifth eclogue), probably as a sign of self–conscious belatedness (cf. e.g. the same procedure in Prop. 3.1[19]), the wording by means of which the *topos* of the pathetic fallacy is rendered here has clear georgic overtones: v. 10 is modelled on Verg. *G.* 3.480: *genus omne neci pecudum dedit, omne ferarum*, while v. 11 seems to be moulded on Verg. *G.* 1.406: *quacumque...aethera pennis* with a *clausula* favoured in the Ovidian epic[20]. Traditionally pastoral thematic

---

17 Cf. Stanzel 1989, 187, Fey–Wickert 2002, 54, Vinchesi 2012, 712–3; 2014, 167.
18 Cf. also Friedrich 1976, 35; Vinchesi 2014, 173.
19 When proclaiming his poetological credo, Propertius, as a late comer, similarly 'telescopes' / 'zooms out' and accumulates several intertexts of analogous poetological intentions and aspirations, namely: Hor. *Carm.* 3.30.7–8, 13–4, Verg. *G.* 3.8 ff., 17 ff., Lucr. 1.117–8, 925–30, Theocr. 16.48 ff., and finally Callimachus' prologue to the *Aetia*; see also Camps 1985, 51. For the over–accumulation of motifs in Prop. 3.1, see especially Papanghelis 1994, 198–200.
20 Cf. Friedrich 1976, 35, Perutelli 1976, 782 and n. 61, Kettemann 1977, 102 and n. 11, Fey–Wickert 2002, 64–5, Di Lorenzo–Pellegrino 2008, 21, 166; see also Verdière 1954, 240, Gagliardi 1984, 30 and n. 4. What is more the syntagm *aera /e pennis* is very common in Ovid; cf. *Met.* 1.466, 7.354, 379, 8.253, 10.159, 11.732 with Fey–Wickert 2002, 65, Vinchesi 2014, 174.

with non-pastoral, georgic and Ovidian wording (in this case): this is gradually developing as a literary tendency of the author.

In the standard generic pastoral location, the shady tree (holm-oak) (v. 12: *umbrosa...sub ilice*, cf. Theocr. 1.22–3, Verg. *Ecl.* 6.54, 7.1[21]), shepherds meet with many representatives of the bucolic pantheon: Faunus (a god often identified with Pan[22]; see also Chapter 1, pp. 22, 32), Satyrs and the Nymphs, divided here into dry-foot wood Nymphs and watery foot river Nymphs (vv. 13–4). All these deities appear separately in Theocritean (in their Greek divine equivalent of course, cf. Theocr. 1.77 ff.), post-Theocritean ([Moschus] 3.27–9, *E.A.* 19) and Vergilian pastoral (cf. *Ecl.* 5.20–3, 6.27–8, 10.21–30), in the context of pathetic fallacy-imagery. However, this combination, although giving the impression of completeness (though the absence of the pastoral Apollo is remarkable), is crucially found once more only in Ovid, *Met.* 6.392–4[23]. The Ovidian wording of the previous lines is thus complemented with the present Ovidian 'epic' imagery, crucially functioning as the backdrop for the depiction of the time-honoured pastoral pantheon in its 'generic gathering', expressing the motif of συμπάθεια τῶν ὅλων. Ov. *Met.* 6.392–4 is, however, a highly 'pastoral' passage in Ovid's Protean poem and constitutes a further instance of a 'generic interplay' between pastoral and epic, for epic hexameters and epic language (cf. e.g. the epic circumlocution *Tritoniaca...harundine* in v. 384, the epic compound *ruricolae* in v. 392, etc.[24]) are here hosting Marsyas' story, availing itself of clear bucolic markers (e.g. Marsyas' satyr identity, the presence of Minerva's pipes, challenge to a musical match, a contest between the Satyr and Apollo, lament for a lost poet[25]). This very 'generic interaction' the Ovidian model seems to operate on further underscores the 'generic ambivalence' of the Calpurnian instance as well.

Ovidian allusions are thus far from coincidental, since Ovid appears to function as a distinct and specific poetic model of reference and comparison in Calpurnian poetics, betraying the 'generic comprehensiveness' of the Calpurnian pastoral world. For example, in the fourth programmatic eclogue of the Calpurnian corpus, which deals mainly with genre-issues of pastoral as a foil to the emperor's panegyric, Corydon's (i.e. Calpurnius') and Amyntas' songs are considered by the umpire Meliboeus not simply as regular rustic lays bestowed to them as a gift by the sylvan deities (vv. 147–8), but also as a performance surpassing the sweetness (a distinct meta-linguistic term for poetics) of the

---

21 Cf. Fey-Wickert 2002, 67, Vinchesi 2014, 174.
22 Cf. also Stroh 1999, 559.
23 Cf. Fey-Wickert 2002, 67, Vinchesi 2014, 175.
24 Cf. also Anderson 1972, 202–3.
25 Cf. also Hill 1992, 183.

honey that Pelignian swarms sip (cf. v. 151). This, as already remarked, is a direct allusion to Ovid, who was born at Sulmo in the area of Peligni (cf. Chapter 2, pp. 78, 82 and n. 184; also p. 153). So pastoral performance is here evaluated by a distinguished member of the 'green cabinet' not through reference to established pastoral models, but through comparison with a poet belonging to the norms of different literary genres, chiefly elegy and epic – although of a peculiar 'generic character'.

The bucolic imagery describing nature's reaction to the sublime quality of Idas' and Astacus' performance is further enhanced by the common motif of the speeding torrents halting their courses (v. 15: *et tenuere suos properantia flumina cursus*, cf. also *Ciris* 233, [Tib.] 3.7.126 (= 4.1.126), Prop. 3.2.3 – 4, Hor. *Carm.* 1.12.9 – 10), which has the sanction of earlier pastoral, being modelled on Verg. *Ecl.* 8.4: *et mutata suos requierunt flumina cursus*, where rivers changed and stayed their flow as a reaction to Damon's and Alphesiboeus' song (cf. also Verg. *Ecl.* 9.57 – 8)[26]. The abstinence-motif in vv. 18 – 9, where bulls are indifferent to pasture and tread on it (*neglectaque pascua tauri calcabant*, cf. also Theocr. 4.14, [Moschus] 3.23 – 4, Verg. *Ecl.* 5.25 – 6, 8.2 – 3, Nemes. 2.29 – 30[27]), is another pastoral staple; but the very image of pastoral empathy to the quality of pastoral performance is complemented by activities opposed to ideals of the pastoral tradition, and adding in their turn to the feeling of 'generic fluidity' discernible throughhout the poem.

The idea of silence reigning in the hills (vv. 16 – 7), caused by the East winds (*Euri*), crucially absent from Vergil's bucolics[28] and failing to shake the foliage of the trees, stands in opposition to the resounding liveliness and verve of pastoral nature of mainly the Vergilian eclogues, cf. 8.22 – 4 (cf. also above, pp. 10, 48 – 9, 59 and n. 59, 71, 73, 86, 93, 118, 186)[29]. Negative associations with respect to the Neoteric principles of the pastoral genre are evoked through the image of the bee keeping off the nectar of the flowers, as a result of the two singers' orphic powers (vv. 19 – 20: *illis etiam certantibus ausa est / deadala nectareos apis intermittere flores*). The bee is a well-known poetological symbol of the poet, and its depiction here as a craftsman (*daedala*) further alludes to the process of poetic

---

26 Cf. also Verdière 1954, 137, Paladini 1956, 523, Messina 1975, 54, Pearce 1990, 46, Fey-Wickert 2002, 69 – 70, Di Lorenzo-Pellegrino 2008, 167 – 8, Vinchesi 2014, 176 – 7.
27 Cf. also Fey-Wickert 2002, 71 – 2, Di Lorenzo-Pellegrino 2008, 168, Vinchesi 2014, 178; see also Verdière 1954, 137.
28 Cf. Vinchesi 2014, 177.
29 Cf. also Davis 1987, 34, Papanghelis 1995, 90 – 1, Garthwaite-Martin 2009, 315, Baraz 2015, 100 – 5.

composition³⁰; furthermore, both the bee and the sweetness of the flowers are also key-words denoting poetry of Callimachean aesthetics, as evidenced by programmatic Callimachean texts (e.g. the prologue to the *Aetia* and the coda of the *Hymn to Apollo*, as elaborated in detail elsewhere – cf. especially Karakasis 2011, 66–7, 84). The dissociation of these two rather obvious Neoteric poetological symbols could be read as a move towards anti-Neoteric attitudes³¹. Last but not least, note the georgic wording evidenced by the use of the adjective *daedalus* (cf. Verg. *G.* 4.179), instead of the regular *sedulus*, to denote the constructive abilities of a bee³².

Interestingly, even the way in which the succession of performances is decided also points to unusual 'generic directions': according to the pastoral singing norm, the order of appearance, all-important as it puts the second contestant at a distinct disadvantage, obliging him to adapt and improve on the topics of the first, is also an issue in the present eclogue. By the standards of the previous pastoral tradition of the amoebaean βουκολιασμός, the choice is either made by lot (as in the case of the eighth pseudo-Theocritean idyll (8.30)) or is the result of a voluntary giving way of a singer, who lets his opponent sing first (cf. Verg. *Ecl.* 5). Elsewhere, the decision is also made on the basis of who was the first to start the altercation (Theocr. 6), or rests with the umpire or some other character of the pastoral setting (Verg. *Ecl.* 3; see also *Eins.* 1, Calp. 4 / [Theocr.] 9); twice the agent of this decision remains unspecified (Verg. *Ecl.* 7; see also Nemes. 2). In all the above cases, however, a reference to the decision-making is offered in the text, and is often coupled with the choice of pledges (cf. Karakasis 2011, 52–3).

In this eclogue, on the contrary, although the judgment is associated with the umpire's verdict, the means for this decision have no intertextual references within the bucolic corpus; thus in vv. 21 ff. the umpire, crucially called Thyrsis, a name often read as persona of Vergil as a pastoral poet, and even sitting under the generically characteristic shady tree, lays down new rules and puts forward a 'generically novel' proposal: the succession of the singers will be determined through the Roman game of *mora*³³. Similarly, the usual pledges for the contest

---

30 Cf. also Fey-Wickert 2002, 72: 'Calpurnius hingegen bezeichnet durch das Adjektiv *daedalus* den Kunstsinn der Biene; dieser richtet sich...auf die Dichtung'; see also Vinchesi 2014, 179.
31 Vs. Schröder 1991, 44, who thinks that 'Calpurnius...nicht mehr auf die Auseinandersetzung mit poetischen Grundsatzfragen verwiesen war'.
32 Cf. also Fey-Wickert 2002, 72, Vinchesi 2014, 179.
33 Cf. also Messina 1975, 54, Friedrich 1976, 41, Vinchesi 2014, 181–2. For the rather 'unpastoral' character of the *mora* decision, cf. also Schäfer 2001, 143 and n. 13.

are rejected, in favour of the abstract notions[34] of glory for the victor (v. 24: *laudem victor*), a rather epic aspiration, and of reproach for the defeated (v. 24: *opprobria victus*). Once again a traditional pastoral coating is associated with a formalistic neotericism.

The Singing Match

Idas wins in the *mora* and the singing match begins; this fluctuation between the 'generically traditional' and the 'generically novel' recurs throughout this ἀγών. In vv. 28–35 both singers invoke the god of their poetic inspiration and professional protection[35], but in both cases a clear inversion of the roles usually adopted in earlier Roman pastoral by the deities invoked is observable. Idas sings about Silvanus wreathing his temples (here with pine leaves), a gesture often associated with poetic excellence in the 'green cabinet' (cf. Verg. *Ecl.* 7.25–6, Calp. 4.56–7). More importantly, the pastoral singer creates, through the prophesying words of the god, the image of the 'slender pipe' (v. 31: *levis...fistula*) growing on a slopping reed. The scenery unequivocally symbolises poetic initiation and succession, as suggested by the motif of the god inspiring poetry (note the use of *levis*) and the image of the flute as a gift. Clear parallels occur in both Vergil and Calpurnius, where, as often remarked (cf. also above, pp. 21, 63, 113, 132–3, 190), the handing over of a pastoral pipe appears in the background of a pastoral succession, cf. Verg. *Ecl.* 2.36–8, 5.85, 6.67–9, Calp. 4.59–63[36]. *Levis*, the well-known catch-word denoting Callimachean and Neoteric sensibilities, complements the setting and thus Idas' *fistula*, a metonymy for pastoral poetry[37], is described as aspiring to the 'slender poetics' of Roman Callimacheanism, following the standards of Vergilian pastoral poetics. The beginning of v. 31: '*iam levis obliqua*', calquing in all probability the first part of Ov. *Fast.* 2.457: *iam levis obliqua subsedit Aquarius urna*[38], i.e., of a well-known Neoteric text of clear Callimachean artistic sensibilities, further adds to the Neoteric background of the image.

However, in the previous tradition, it is not Silvanus but primarily Apollo and the Muses that carry out this task in similar scenes of poetic initiation:

---

[34] Cf. Stanzel 1989, 196; see also Vinchesi 2014, 180.
[35] Cf. also Schäfer 2001, 143–4; see also Vinchesi 2014, 182.
[36] For the motif of the flute as a gift and its associations with 'poetic succession', cf. mainly Papanghelis 1995, 156–7, Fey-Wickert 2002, 79–80; see also Vinchesi 2014, 183.
[37] Cf. also Pearce 1990, 48.
[38] Cf. Vinchesi 2014, 184.

the instances of Hesiod *Th.* 22–3, cf. also Call. *Aet.* 2.1–2 Pf. (Muses), the prologue of Callimachus' *Aetia* (1.22–4 Pf.) and its reworking in the sixth Vergilian eclogue (vv. 1–12 – Apollo) easily come to mind, cf. also Theocr. 5.80–3 (an appeal to both the Muses and Apollo), Verg. *Ecl.* 3.62–3 (Apollo), 7.21–2 (Nymphs, that is the pastoral Muses). Thus it is not without significance that the linguistic syntagm Idas uses in v. 28: *me Silvanus amat*, probably modelled on Verg. *Ecl.* 3.62: *me Phoebus amat*[39], substitutes the expected deities of poetic induction by Silvanus, a god who does appear in pre–Calpurnian pastoral, but mainly as presiding over *arvorum pecorisque* (Verg. *A.* 8.601, cf. also Verg. *Ecl.* 10.24–5, Nemes. 2.56[40]), and seems thus to be rather unrelated to issues of 'poetic succession' and initiation. Note also that, whereas the flute that awaits Idas is described as 'slender', the opposite holds for the prophecy of the god himself, crucially described as of no 'slender import' (v. 30: *non leve carmen*)[41].

Idas thus seems to have intentionally committed the *faux pas* of invoking a god unrelated to poetic epiphanies of the (pastoral) tradition (cf. Chapter 2, pp. 67–8); crucially, Astacus commits exactly the reverse 'error': he appeals to a deity of rather a poetic calibre, the Nymphs, for protection in menial and georgic tasks having nothing to do with poetry. Astacus displays a rather georgic outlook and interests throughout the eclogue[42]: the Italian rustic deities Flora and Pomona sport with him (vv. 32–3) and are combined with the Nymphs, the pastoral goddesses par excellence (cf. also Verg. *Ecl.* 3.9, 5.74–5) often associated in the pastoral corpus with pastoral song, as a substitute of the Muses in their func-

---

39 Cf. Cesareo 1931, 45, Messina 1975, 54, Friedrich 1976, 42, Keene 1996, 69, Di Lorenzo–Pellegrino 2008, 169, Vinchesi 2014, 182.
40 Cf. Keene 1996, 69, Fey–Wickert 2002, 80, Vinchesi 2014, 182.
41 For a poetological colouring in the passage under discussion, see also Verdière 1954, 241, Friedrich 1976, 42–3, Davis 1987, 34, 52 and n. 19, Stanzel 1989, 190–1 and n. 17, Magnelli 2006, 472–3, Vinchesi 2009, 151; 2014, 183–4.
42 One should of course take into account that Astacus is a gardener and gardening, at least in Vergil. *G.* 4, is a marginal activity in the georgic world. Hence, from this perspective, one might argue that the above designation, georgic outlook, may here over–simplify the situation. Nonetheless, even in Vergil's *praeteritio* (*G.* 4.116–48), some scholars have detected a skeleton for a possible fifth book of the *Georgics* dealing with the art of gardening (cf. especially Thomas 1988, 2.167–8). Columella, on the other hand, taking literally Vergil's *G.* 4.148: *aliis post me memoranda relinquo*, takes over from Vergil (cf. especially 10 *praef.* 3) and treats gardening chiefly in the tenth book of his work, significantly written in dactylic hexameters, thus suggesting a sense of a 'generic sequel' to Vergilian *Georgics*, and not in prose as elsewhere in the *De re rustica*. Taking all the above caveats into consideration and despite the fact that gardening may function as a marginal aspect of the Vergilian georgic world, I still believe that horticulture is by no means a traditional pastoral pursuit but rather forms part of the georgic interests, with the reservations, of course, already expressed.

tion as deities of poetic inspiration (cf. Verg. *Ecl.* 7.21–2, 10.1; see also above, pp. 60–1, 136, 202–3). However, these deities are regarded by Astacus simply as guarantors of his professional prosperity, securing the fountains which are indispensable for watering his orchards (vv. 34–5, see also Verg. *G.* 4.32, 120, 126[43]). The impression of traditional pastoralism, secured by the appeal to the rustic pantheon (though significantly not appearing in the Vergilian bucolic oeuvre with the exception of the Nymphs), and by Flora's adorning Astacus' locks with pale green grass, a gesture reminiscent of Aegle in Verg. *Ecl.* 6.21–2[44] painting Silenus' face, is only superficial: the close association of the poetic deities (i.e., the Nymphs) with georgic tasks is to be read as a significant 'generic alteration' from the earlier pastoral norm.

The next exchange of quatrains gives a clear impression of a 'generic branching out', a movement towards a more inclusive, later development of the pastoral form, as it furnishes proof of Idas' notable georgic interests: the herdsman, the representative of traditional pastoral as opposed to the upstart, in 'generic terms', gardener Astacus, concerns himself with issues of husbandry, clearly belonging to the georgic code / mode rather than to the preoccupations of the pastoral tradition, which involve mainly pastoral song and its prerequisites and not the menial tasks of every day professional life. Idas sings about flock–breeding, and in particular about the way a lamb of varied colour testifies to the mating of a black ram with a white ewe (vv. 36–9). Script. *R.R.* abound with similar occupations (Var. *rust.* 2.2.4, Colum. 7.3.1, Plin. *Nat.* 8.189, see also Verg. *G.* 3.387–90[45]); what is more, the very term *cultum* (*gregis*) (v. 36) that the Italian goddess Pales teaches to the shepherd is a *terminus technicus* having intertextually links with texts of clear georgic interests, cf. Verg. *G.* 1.3–4, 4.559; see also Colum. 1 *praef.* 32, 6 *praef.* 3–4[46]. Pales belongs to the traditional pastoral pantheon: she appears in Verg. *Ecl.* 5.34–5 leaving the fields with Apollo, another eminent pastoral deity, as a sign of grief for Daphnis' loss; hence in Vergil Pales acts within a traditional pastoral setting, grieving over the passing away of a great pastoral singer, and she also acts in character in Nemes. 1.68, where she is shown to offer bowls of milk in the company of the pastoral pantheon again (Apollo, Fauns, Nymphs, Muses, Flora), significantly as a farewell to Meliboeus, an old and renowned member of the 'green cabinet'. In Calpurnius, on the other hand, this deity is charged with a clear georgic (cf. also Pales in Verg. *G.* 3.1,

---

43 Cf. also Friedrich 1976, 43–4, Fey–Wickert 2002, 85–6, Vinchesi 2014, 185–7.
44 Cf. Di Salvo 1990a, 273, Vinchesi 2014, 185.
45 Cf. also Keene 1996, 71, Fey–Wickert 2002, 19, Di Lorenzo–Pellegrino 2008, 172, Vinchesi 2014, 189.
46 Cf. Friedrich 1976, 45, Keene 1996, 71, Fey–Wickert 2002, 18, 87–8, Vinchesi 2014, 188.

294⁴⁷) assignment (cf. also Calp. 4.102–6, 5.24–5; above, pp. 71–2, 170). This mingling of pastoral with georgic features is meta-linguistically reflected in the imagery of the lines: Calpurnian pastoral could be likened to the varicoloured lamb born to parents of different colour, yet able to testify to both his progenitors (pastoral and georgic)[48].

A similar meta-language of poetological import may be read in the case of Astacus' grafted trees, trees growing unfamiliar leaves (*ignotas frondes*) and fruits of a different species (*non gentilia poma*, v. 41)[49]. The imagery may be understood meta-poetically as denoting a new 'generic artistic formation' (note here the iteration of *ars mea* in vv. 40, 42), suggested by the mingling of pastoral and georgic as exemplified in Astacus' lines, where several georgic technical terms and georgic concerns in general are to be met with: *induit*, v. 40, *insita*, *praecoquibus*, v. 43, cf. also Colum. 5.11.1, Plin. *Nat*. 17.102, 104, Verg. *G*. 2.33–4, 78–80, etc.[50]. The remark acquires further weight if one takes into account that the term *gentilia* < *genus* in the sense of 'belonging to different species' seems to be coined by Calpurnius as a substitute for *non sua* in Verg. *G*. 2.82: *novas frondes et non sua poma*, a line which probably functions as the model of this Calpurnian line, as Fey-Wickert 2002, 90 has convincingly remarked[51]. The word appears, according to the ThLL VI 2, 1813, 73–8, for the first time in the present Calpurnian pastoral, and alludes, by means of its etymological connections, to the 'generic quality' or divergence of Calpurnius' bucolics, especially in Calp. 2[52], where an extended association of a pre-Calpurnian pastoral form

---

47 Cf. Vinchesi 1996, 81; 2014, 188.
48 One might of course argue here that menial tasks, whether bucolic or georgic, are normally referred to in brackets; i.e., they become quoted as material, subject-matter for song, and are thus neutralised as features of the *negotium*, within a pastoral form that thematically seems to be growing more 'omnivorous', as time goes on. Be that as it may, this emphasis on material of specific technical colouring, although citational, to an extent not found in pre-Calpurnian bucolic, suggests a clear 'generic re-orientation' of the bucolic form, a re-orientation, at least, towards novel 'generic favourites'.
49 For the alternative reading *genitalia*, cf. Di Salvo 1991, 310; see also below, p. 217.
50 Cf. Verdière 1954, 140, Paladini 1956, 527, Friedrich 1976, 45–6, Kettemann 1977, 101, 104, Amat 1991, 103, Vinchesi 1992, 152 and nn. 10, 11; 1996, 81; 2014, 189–91, Keene 1996, 71–2, Fey-Wickert 2002, 18–9, 89–91, Di Lorenzo-Pellegrino 2008, 172–3. Cf. also the meta-poetic function of *nota* in Verg. *Ecl*. 1.51: *flumina nota* as a further 'reflexive annotation', 'troping allusion as recognition' (cf. Hinds 1998, 8–10, Papanghelis 2006, 372 and n. 10) of the previous familiar pastoral 'generic identity', which Tityrus manages to hold on to in opposition to the dispossessed Meliboeus.
51 Cf. also Novelli 1980, 52, Vinchesi 1992, 152, Di Lorenzo-Pellegrino 2008, 172, Uden 2010, 212 and n. 78; see also Verdière 1954, 241, Vinchesi 2014, 190.
52 Cf. also Clément-Tarantino 2006, http://.

with georgics is attempted. Another indication of the validity of this poetological reading is the use of the term *ignotas*, instead of the less evocative *novas* of the Vergilian intertext, suggesting in its turn the notion of 'the unknown', 'the alien', which has clear poetological associations in relation to the Callimachean–Neoteric poetological outlook of Roman pastoral: this impression of the estranged suggests, as elsewhere discussed (cf. especially Karakasis 2011, 139–40), anti-Neoteric deviations and thus testifies to the lapse of the new pastoral from a traditional pastoral Neoteric ideal.

A 'generically innovative' attitude combined with signs of 'poetological aberration' from Callimachean ideals is also pre-eminent in the following exchange (vv. 44–51): Astacus keeps harping on the georgic theme, singing about planting and watering (vv. 48–51, cf. e.g. Verg. *G.* 4.32, 112–5 and several georgic technical terms such as *pangitur*, v. 49 (Var. *rust.* 1.43, Colum. 3.18.1, Plin. *Nat.* 17.156), *area*, v. 49 (Cat. *agr.* 151.3, Colum. 2.10.26), *plantaria*, v. 51 (Verg. *G.* 2.27, Plin. *Nat.* 13.37, *et al.*[53])), while Idas' song is about lopping branches and feeding young flocks, once more a georgic concern (cf. also Var. *rust.* 2.2.15–7, *putare* as a *terminus technicus*, v. 44 (Cat. *agr.* 32.1, Var. *rust.* 1.36, Verg. *G.* 2.407, Colum. 11.2.41)[54], *fetura*, v. 47, also a technical term (Var. *rust.* 2.1.18[55])). Moreover, Idas sings about a *frondatio*, censured in the pastoral community as it deprives pastoral space / poetry from its basic 'generic prerequisite', shade, as elsewhere discussed in the case of the ninth Vergilian eclogue; cf. Karakasis 2011, 204–5. The *salix* (willow), a common pastoral tree (cf. Verg. *Ecl.* 1.53–4, 77–8, 3.65, 83, 5.16, 10.40, Calp. 3.14, 19, 68, 5.110, Nemes. 1.6–7), is crucially described as *tener*, v. 44, and strikingly, is presented as having its branches chopped off. Thus a *frondatio*, itself 'unpastoral' in character, is furthermore exercised upon *teneras salices*, with an intentional use of the Callimachean catchword: it is not only traditional pastoral typology that is at stake here but also the Neoteric character of the poetry that displays it.

The next two amoebaean quatrains (vv. 52–9) transport the reader to the elegiac realm: resorting to common elegiac tactics[56] (cf. e.g. [Tib.] 3.1.15ff., 3.3.1ff.), both contestants ask for divine help in order to secure Crocale's love, that is to ensure erotic bliss and reciprocated love, the elegiac value par excellence. As a response to the gods' elegiac help, Idas consecrates a grove (*nemus*) which, apart

---

[53] Cf. Messina 1975, 55, Kettemann 1977, 101, 102 and n. 11, 104, Keene 1996, 72–3, Fey-Wickert 2002, 94–6, Di Lorenzo–Pellegrino 2008, 174, Vinchesi 2014, 194–6.
[54] Cf. Friedrich 1976, 46–7, Amat 1988, 80; 1991, 12, 103, Vinchesi 1992, 154; 2014, 192–4, Fey-Wickert 2002, 19, 92–4, Di Lorenzo–Pellegrino 2008, 173–4.
[55] Cf. Di Lorenzo–Pellegrino 2008, 173, Vinchesi 2014, 194.
[56] Cf. also Di Lorenzo–Pellegrino 2008, 175, Vinchesi 2012, 713; 2014, 166, 196.

from its religious associations (cf. OLD *s.v.* 2), is closely connected with poetic inspiration, including bucolic poetry, as elaborated by Hunter 2006, 7 ff.; cf. also Karakasis 2011, 155. But this religious location of poetological import is associated here with sacral expressions not found in previous pastoral: the ritual sending away of the uninitiated within an erotic setting (v. 55: *ite procul – sacer est locus – ite profani*). On the contrary, the image complemented with the *ite procul*-syntagm appears in other literary genres, especially, yet not exclusively, in the elegiac corpus, chiefly as a parody of ritual diction (cf. Tib. 1.1.75 – 6, 2.4.15, 20, [Tib.] 3.4.3, 3.6.7, Prop. 4.6.9; cf. also Tib. 1.9.51, Ov. *Am.* 2.1.3 – 4)[57]. Accordingly the elegiac appeal to the gods is accompanied by an offer exhibiting a further common elegiac motif, thus adding to the 'generic diversification' shown by the shepherd-singer.

This elegiac appeal is traceable in Astacus' quatrain as well, where one should further take notice of the first and foremost elegiac use of *urere* in v. 56: *urimur in Crocalen*[58]; the verb in the sense of *amare et dolere*, as here, has a very good elegiac register (cf. Catul. 72.5, Tib. 2.4.6, Ov. *Am.* 2.4.12, *et al.*; see also Prop. 3.9.45, Hor. *Carm.* 1.19.5, OLD *s.v.* 6a) and is, additionally, associated in Vergilian pastoral with the elegiac discourse of Corydon in the second Vergilian eclogue, v. 68: *me tamen urit amor*, as well as the 'elegiac turn' exhibited by Daphis' urban love–affair in Verg. *Ecl.* 8.83: *Daphnis me malus urit* (cf. Karakasis 2011, 149, see also Calp. 3.7 – 8: *uror, Iolla, / uror*, of Lycidas' *amor* for Phyllis, a further instance of an elegiac intrusion in pastoral[59]). Yet, although for Idas the elegiac outlook is complemented with the sacral imagery of the shepherd's offer, Astacus' sacral offerings re–assert pastoral conventions and secure once again a contrast between pastoral tradition and 'generic novelty', as often in Calpurnian pastoral. Astacus' offering is a beechen bowl (v. 59: *faginus*)[60], a gift of

---

[57] Cf. Verdière 1954, 141, Kornzeniewski 1971, 23, Fey–Wickert 2002, 100, Di Lorenzo–Pellegrino 2008, 175, Vinchesi 2014, 197 – 8. Cf. also Mart. 14.47.1.
[58] Cf. Pichon 1966, 301, Di Lorenzo–Pellegrino 2008, 175: 'verbo tipico del *sermo amatorius*', Vinchesi 2012, 713 and n. 46. In the *Aeneid* as well the verb occurs in the also elegising love–story of the fourth book, v. 68: *uritur infelix Dido*; cf. also Karakasis 2011, 304 and n. 33.
[59] Cf. Fey–Wickert 2002, 152, Vinchesi 2014, 198, Chapter 4, pp. 126 – 8.
[60] For an account of the different readings of *faginus*, i.e., beechen bowl (*scyphus, crater, poculum*, etc.), beechen statue or beech-tree, cf. especially Armstrong 1986, 118, Horsfall 1997, 190, Fey–Wickert 2002, 103 – 5, Di Lorenzo–Pellegrino 2008, 176, Vinchesi 2014, 199 – 200. For the view adopted here, i.e., the first alterative, cf. also Theocr. 5.58 – 9, Tib. 1.10.8, Korzeniewski 1971, 91, Leach 1975, 211, Keene 1996, 74, Vinchesi 1996, 83; 2014, 199; see also Verdière 1954, 241 – 2, Amat 1991, 17 and n. 35. For *faginus* as a statue, cf. also Verdière 1954, 241, Castiglioni 1955, 19 – 20 vs. Mahr 1964, 187 ff. *Faginus* both in the sense of a bee-

programmatic importance in bucolic poetry, reminiscent of the κισσύβιον of the first programmatic Theocritean idyll, symbolising the supreme poetic quality of pastoral. What is more, this emblematic symbol is here presented as made of beech–wood, a further 'generic marker' of pastoral (cf. Karakasis 2011, 188–9), similarly to the *pocula…fagina* of the third Vergilian eclogue (vv. 36–7), which function as the prize of the bucolic song–contest of the eclogue. These bowls also suggest traditional pastoral values, which both contestants fall short of, and therefore, as shown in Karakasis 2011, 87–124, fail to acquire them. The *locus amoenus*–setting within which the bowl appears (vine-clad elms, chilly brook, lilies, vv. 57–9) in Calp. 2 completes the traditionally pastoral 'generic background' of Astacus' elegiac appeal. Crucially, this partial reinstatement of (traditional) bucolic is effected through Astacus the gardener, that is the novel character in 'generic terms', and not through the herdsman Idas, who can be seen as the representative of traditional bucolic poetry who has evidently deviated towards the elegiac realm; this points again to a sense of 'generic fluidity' sensible throughout the Calpurnian eclogue.

From v. 60 onwards it is Theocr. 11 and its Vergilian adaptation, *Ecl.* 2, that function as the primary models for Calp. 2; see also above in Calp. 3, especially pp. 139–50. All motifs appearing in these two intertexts (the appeal for sharing rustic lodgings (Theocr. 11.42–9, Verg. *Ecl.* 2.28–35), the account of goods and chattels (Theocr. 11.34–7, Verg. *Ecl.* 2.20–2), the donation of gifts (Theocr. 11.40–1, Verg. *Ecl.* 2.36–55), the self presentation–motif (Theocr. 11.31–3, Verg. *Ecl.* 2.25–7)) have their counterpart in the present Calpurnian pastoral (vv. 60–1, 68–75, 76–83, 84–91 respectively) with one exception: instead of reference to the singing excellence of the herdsman (Theocr. 11.38–40, Verg. *Ecl.* 2.23–4), Calpurnius prefers the topic of religious piety (vv. 62–7)[61], a marginal pastoral activity in comparison to singing, the ultimate pre–Calpurnian pastoral value, something which betrays once more the 'generic re–orientation' of Calpurnian pastoral. Also, the choice of 'generically doubtful' intertexts (Verg. *Ecl.* 2 exhibiting elegiac sensibility and Theocr. 11 assimilating comic markers; cf. the relevant discussion in Karakasis 2011, 200, Hunter 1999, 241, above, pp. 7, 55–6 and n. 39, 93, 131, 137–9, 152) further points to the 'generic ambivalence' of the Calpurnian pastoral song–contest.

In vv. 60 ff. Idas asserts his pastoral identity, when describing himself as a rustic (v. 61: *rusticus est…Idas*) in his apostrophe to Crocale[62]; this pastoral iden-

---

chen figure and with the meaning of the substantive *fagus* (cf. also Svennung 1935, 145 and n. 3, Pearce 1990, 50, Di Lorenzo–Pellegrino 2008, *loc. cit.*) seem less compelling options.
61 Cf. Fey–Wickert 2002, 105.
62 Cf. Cesareo 1931, 52, Friedrich 1976, 51.

tity of his is also conveyed by means of his presentation as *non...barbarus* (v. 61). Whereas *rusticus* denotes the dweller of pastoral space, *barbarus*, on the other hand, a characterisation that Idas denies, is a term qualifying the opponent of the 'green cabinet'. A clear indication of this is the first programmatic Vergilian eclogue, where the term *barbarus* is applied to the newcomer *miles*, who evicts Meliboeus and is thus responsible for the latter's alienation from the pastoral world (vv. 70 – 1[63]). Idas however chooses to establish his pastoral identity not by recurring to the traditional pastoral motif of musical excellence, but through marginal functions of the pre-Calpurnian bucolic space, namely offerings of religious piety (cf. Theocr. 5.81–3, Verg. *Ecl.* 1.7–8, 42–3, 5.65–80, 7.29–36[64]), and, what is more, in rather elegiac settings. Idas mentions the festival of Pales, *Palilia* or *Parilia* (cf. Ov. *Fast.* 4.721 ff.); although a rural celebration (cf. Ov. *Fast.* 4.723: *pastoria sacra*), the festival has no parallels in the bucolic corpus, in opposition to its presence in elegiac poetry (cf. Tib. 2.5.87–104; see also 1.1.35–6, Prop. 4.1.19–20, 4.4.73–8[65]). The leaning towards elegy is thus revealed in the intertexts that Idas chooses both when claiming (vv. 52 ff.) his beloved and when expressing his piety.

Besides, the very term *rusticus*, although aiming to affirm Idas as inhabitant of the bucolic space, appears, from a 'generic point of view', in 'generically dodgy' instances, i.e., in contexts where pastoral seems to diverge towards elegiac trends: Idas' immediate intertext is Verg. *Ecl.* 2.56: *rusticus es, Corydon*[66], an apostrophe uttered by Corydon when, in the guise of an elegiac suitor, he hankers after the favours of the urban young Alexis (cf. also Calp 2.60 < Verg. *Ecl.* 2.29[67]). What is more, the term *rusticus* has ominous connotations as to the outcome of a love-affair, as it is frequently associated with the failure of a suitor. It is used by Corydon of the second Vergilian eclogue in his self-presentation, when realising that his rural background is the main cause of his erotic frustration. Another example is [Theocr.] 20.3–4, where the kiss of a herdsman is rejected as coming from a βουκόλος, cf. also Nemes. 2.70–1 (cf. Chapter 3, p. 112). A further indication of Idas' lack of skill as a pastoral singer is his choice of sacrifice: although bloodless offerings are the order of the day in the *Parilia*

---

[63] Cf. Korzeniewski 1971, 23, Fey-Wickert 2002, 110, Di Lorenzo-Pellegrino 2008, 177, Vinchesi 2014, 200.
[64] Cf. Vinchesi 2014, 201.
[65] Cf. Fey-Wickert 2002, 111–2, Di Lorenzo-Pellegrino 2008, 177, Vinchesi 2012, 714; 2014, 44, 200.
[66] Cf. Verdière 1954, 142, Friedrich 1976, 49, Fey-Wickert 2002, 109–10, Vinchesi 2014, 44, 201. See also Messina 1975, 56–7.
[67] Cf. Di Lorenzo-Pellegrino 2008, 177, Vinchesi 2014, 200.

(cf. Sol. 1.19: *observatum deinceps, ne qua hostia Parilibus caederetur, ut dies iste a sanguine purus esset*, Ov. *Fast.* 4.743–6[68]), Idas sings about the sacrifice of a lamb (vv. 62–3), crucially having its counterpart in the Vergilian pastoral corpus, Verg. *Ecl.* 1.7–8, cf. also *Eins.* 2.15–6, but not associated with the Pales festivals[69]. Astacus responds with bloodless offerings, which have the sanction of earlier pastoral (apart from the *primitias*, v. 65, for *liba*, v. 65, cf. Verg. *Ecl.* 7.33, for *rorantes...favos, liquentia mella*, v. 66, cf. Theocr. 5.59[70]), to the Lares of the gardens as a distinct divine group and to Priapus in particular, in consequence of his profession (vv. 64–7). But although offers to Priapus, as here v. 65: *fingere liba Priapo*, do appear in Vergil (*Ecl.* 7.33[71]: *haec te liba, Priape*, albeit with negative connotations, since Thyrsis has lost the poetic contest due to his lack of clear pastoral / Neoteric outlook[72]), Lares rituals do not appear in the Vergilian pastoral but instead often come up in the pastoral elegies of Tibullus (Tib. 1.1.19–20, 1.3.34, 1.10.15, 25 ff., 2.1.60; see also 2.5.20, 42[73]). Thus a 'generically awry' pastoral intertext is here combined with the interests of pastoral elegy.

The following lines (vv. 68–75) develop the motif of a singer's pride in his possessions as a means of working upon the beloved's feelings and mind. Idas sings about his multitude of lambs and ewes providing him with fleece, and about his rich cheese, all at Crocale's disposition throughout the year (vv. 68–71), while Astacus describes the rich harvest of his garden, also destined to function as an erotic gift for Crocale (vv. 72–5). The motif appears in pastoral as early as Theocr. 11.34–7[74], where the Cyclops tries to charm Galatea by relating the number of animals as well as the dairy he has at his disposal. Yet even in the case of Polyphemus, the comic, in 'generic terms', character of the incident, drawn from Attic comedy (cf. Antiphanes fr. 131 K–A[75]), has long been recognised. Furthermore, the Roman adaptation of this scene by Vergil (the reference to *caseus* (v. 70) rather than to *lac* as in Vergil (2.20) points to a Theocritean

---

68 Cf. also Fey-Wickert 2002, 112, who thinks that Idas' sacral offering is modelled on Tib. 1.1.23: *agna cadet*, transferred from a ritual in honour of the Lares to the *Parilia*.
69 Cf. Cesareo 1931, 47–8 and n. 1, Latte 1960, 88, Fey-Wickert 2002, 112, Di Lorenzo-Pellegrino 2008, 177 vs. De Sipio 1935, 79 and n. 2 and Messina 1975, 57 accepting Calpurnius' statement at face value. See also Friedrich 1976, 50, 101 and n. 110, Vinchesi 2014, 204.
70 Cf. Keene 1996, 75, Vinchesi 2014, 202–3.
71 Cf. also Di Salvo 1990a, 276.
72 Cf. Karakasis 2011, 54–86.
73 Cf. Fey-Wickert 2002, 113, Vinchesi 2012, 714–5 and n. 49; 2014, 44, 202.
74 Cf. also Verdière 1954, 242, Pearce 1990, 51–2, Di Salvo 1990a, 275–6, Di Lorenzo-Pellegrino 2008, 179, Vinchesi 2014, 204.
75 Cf. Hunter 1999, 233.

adaptation in the Calpurnian case, Theocr. 11.35–7[76]) occurs in a setting where a movement towards elegiac erotic feelings is to be discerned: in *Ecl.* 2.19–22 again, when Corydon, as an elegiac suitor, tries to win over Alexis' affections by mentioning his fortune[77]. Finally, the refrain of this strophic unit, vv. 71, 75: *si venias, Crocale, totus tibi serviet hortus*, echoes a further 'generically diversifying model', the Polyphemus and Galatea episode in Ovid's *Metamorphoses*, demonstrably capitalising on 'generic interfaces' between elegy, pastoral and epic (cf. Chapter 4, pp. 137, 144, 146); the line seems to be modelled on Ov. *Met.* 13.820: *omnis tibi serviet arbor*[78].

Apart from their 'generically novel feel', similarly to *rusticus* above, p. 209, the two intertexts bode ill for Idas' erotic success, since in both of them the suitor is rejected. A perhaps significant variation with respect to the intertext, which may also betray a 'generic deviation' from traditional pastoral, is the fact that whereas [Theocritus]' and Vergil's flocks are Sicilian (cf. [Theocr.] 8.56, Verg. *Ecl.* 2.21: *mille meae Siculis errant in montibus agnae*), Calpurnius' ewes are qualified as Tarentine (v. 69: *Tarentinae...matres*), famous for the quality of their wool, cf. Var. *rust.* 2.2.18, Colum. 7.2.3, 7.4.4[79]. The term 'Sicilian' has strong 'generic associations', evoking as a 'generic term' Theocritean, Greek post–Theocritean and Vergilian pastoral (cf. Karakasis 2011, 11–2, 22, 25, 33). In fact, Calpurnius himself may have acquired the *cognomen* Siculus, marking him as a successor of both Theocritus and Vergil (cf. Introduction, p. 2)[80]. This change from Sicily to south Italy may be read as a further sign for Calpurnius' going away from the

---

[76] Cf. also Verdière 1966, 168, Messina 1975, 58, Friedrich 1976, 51–2, Keene 1996, 76, Vinchesi 2012, 716 and n. 54; 2014, 35–6; see further Cesareo 1931, 52, Dehon 1993, 206, Hutchinson 2013, 179–80. Paladini 1956, 529 also reads here a contamination of Verg. *Ecl.* 1.34: *pinguis...premeretur caseus* and Verg. *Ecl.* 2.22.
[77] The motif does also significantly appear in the third Calpurnian eclogue, the elegiac character of which, as already remarked, is generally acknowledged in the relevant bibliography, cf. Chapter 4, pp. 123–54. Thus Lycidas advertises his rustic possessions (bulls, heifers, calves) for the sake of his beloved Phyllis in opposition to his erotic rival, Mopsus (vv. 63–9; see also above, pp. 142–4 particular). In a similar vein, Nemes. 2.35–6 has Idas exhibit a similar elegiac sensibility, when trying to charm his beloved Donace by praising his rustic wealth (a thousand heifers, milk-pails that never run out); the lines are modelled on the elegiac intertext of Calp. 3 and are complemented with further elegiac motifs, as is the kiss in vv. 37–8, given by a lover during his musical performance (cf. Duff and Duff 1934, 466); for the elegiac character of this motif, cf. also Fey-Wickert 2002, 25, 198. See also in detail Karakasis 2011, 308–9.
[78] Cf. Verdière 1954, 143, Keene 1996, 76, Di Lorenzo-Pellegrino 2008, 179, Vinchesi 2012, 716; 2014, 36, 50, 205.
[79] Cf. also Cesareo 1931, 52 and n. 1, Pearce 1990, 52, Amat 1991, 104, Keene 1996, 75–6, Vinchesi 1996, 85; 2014, 204, Fey-Wickert 2002, 118, 120–1. See also Dalby 2000, 66.
[80] Cf. also Korzeniewski 1971, 1, Di Salvo 1990, 24.

pastoral tradition, as known mainly from Theocritus, post–Theocritean Greek pastoral and Vergil.

Astacus' topics and wording also show a tendency to approach other literary genres: as Fey-Wickert 2002, 122 has convincingly shown, lines 72–3 follow the elegiac model of Catul. 61.206–10: *ille pulveris Africi / siderumque micantium / subducat numerum prius, / qui vestri numerare volt / multa milia ludi*[81]. The motif of selecting fruits for a loved one has its pastoral intertext in Verg. *Ecl.* 2.51: *ipse ego cana legam tenera lanugine mala*[82]; but this intertext also has elegiac connotations, as it is associated with the elegiac transformation of Corydon, before his final resolution to return to the long-established pastoral norm. What is more, Astacus' intertexts are no less ill-omened concerning erotic success than Idas': Corydon, the intertext of *Ecl.* 2.51, fails to win the favours of Alexis. Thus 'generic versatility' and ominous erotic connotations are combined in Astacus' lines as well.

A similar departure from traditional pastoral is detectable in the gifts that are presented to Crocale in the following verses (vv. 76–83): Idas offers to his sweet-heart pails of curdled milk (v. 77: *sume tamen calathos nutanti lacte coactos*) and promises fleeces (v. 78: *vellera*) in the period between the spring equinox and the middle of summer (vv. 78–9). However, although fleece as an erotic gift has its parallels in pastoral (in the fifth Theocritean idyll, in the context of an amoebaean βουκολιασμὸς too, vv. 98–9, μαλακὸν πόκον is offered), the same cannot be said for the curdled milk, crucially appearing in vv. 86–7 of the idyll in question but not as a love-gift[83]. What is more, the real / traditional, pastoral erotic present, that of the fleeces, is associated in Idas' promise with georgic information, concerning the proper period for shearing according to the Script. *R.R.* (cf. also Var. *rust.* 2.11.6–9, Colum. 7.4.7, Pallad. 5.6, 6.8, 7.6[84]), thus complementing the georgic image of the parched field at the beginning of Idas' lines, v. 76[85]. Astacus (vv. 80–3) offers fruits (Chian figs, chestnuts) as

---

[81] Mainly on the basis of two linguistic parallels, namely the Calpurnian *qui numerare velit* alluding to the Catullan *qui...numerare volt* and the Calpurnian *citius numerabit* probably alluding to the Catullan *subducat numerum prius*. See also Verdière 1954, 242, Vinchesi 2014, 205–6.

[82] Cf. Verdière 1954, 242, Di Lorenzo-Pellegrino 2008, 179. Fey-Wickert 2002, 119 sees in Astacus' offerings an Ovidian influence, namely Ov. *Met.* 13.812–20.

[83] Cf. also Fey-Wickert 2002, 124–5, Vinchesi 2014, 207. For the georgic character of *coactos* as a technical term, cf. Fey-Wickert 2002, 19, Vinchesi 2014, 207.

[84] Cf. also Amat 1991, 104, Keene 1996, 76, Vinchesi 1996, 87; 2014, 207–8, Fey-Wickert 2002, 126–7.

[85] Cf. also Fey-Wickert 2002, 18–9, see also the *terminus technicus excoquere* (v. 76), Verg. *G.* 2.259–60, Colum. 11.3.13; see also Verg. *G.* 1.107, Friedrich 1976, 203 and n. 123, Vinchesi 2014, 207.

love-gifts, something which has its parallels in the pre-Calpurnian pastoral world; but the specific intertextual models, Theocr. 3.10–11 and Verg. *Ecl.* 2.51–3[86], are again instances of a 'generic leaning' towards comedy or elegy, as already shown (cf. also Karakasis 2011, 194–5 for the case of the third idyll; see also above, pp. 131–2, 140). Furthermore, chestnuts as an erotic present are a direct allusion to Verg. *Ecl.* 2.51–3, where the fruits are sanctioned as love-offers; but this intertext, apart from its elegiac disposition (being about an elegiac lover trying to persuade the urbane Alexis to accept as gifts fruits, once the delight of a rustic Amaryllis), also once again bears negative associations as to the outcome of Astacus' erotic appeal.

In the following exchange a central value of the bucolic space, *formositas*[87], with its meta-linguistic poetological implications (cf. Karakasis 2011, 166), is at stake. Bucolic singers often possess, as a standard pastoral 'generic marker', a fair countenance (cf. Theocr. 6.36, [Theocr.] 8.3–4, 72–3, 20.21ff., Verg. *Ecl.* 7.4–5, Calp. 2.3–4 and Nemes. 2.16), and Daphnis, the archetypical pastoral singer, is described as *formosus* in the fifth Vergilian eclogue (v. 44: *formosior ipse*). In addition, bucolic singers are often not only handsome but in the prime of their youth (cf. Theocr. 6.3, 11.9, [Theocr.] 8.3, 28, 29, 61, 88, 93, Verg. *Ecl.* 8.39, Nemes. 2.77). *Formositas* and youth are both doubted in Idas' lines: the herdsman asks Crocale whether she finds him uncomely (*informis*, v. 84) and aged (*gravis annis*, v. 84), a syntagm clearly modelled on Theocr. 3.8 (*videor tibi* = καταφαίνομαι) and Verg. *Ecl.* 2.25: *nec sum adeo informis*[88], i.e., in pastoral intertexts with 'alternative generic leanings', as developed above (cf. Chapter 4, pp. 131–3, 137–8; see also above, pp. 197, 208–13)[89]. Also under threat, on a meta-poetic level this time, is Idas' Neoteric quality as a singer, as evidenced by the accumulation of catch-words of Callimachean import used in the description of Idas' *formositas*, which thus are also called in question (*mollissima*, v.

---

[86] For the Vergilian intertext, cf. also Verdière 1954, 145, Amat 1991, 13, 104, Vinchesi 1992, 153; 2014, 208, Di Lorenzo-Pellegrino 2008, 181.
[87] Cf. also Stanzel 1989, 187–8.
[88] Cf. Fey-Wickert 2002, 130, Vinchesi 2014, 209–10. See also Verdière 1954, 145, Díaz-Cíntora 1989, xxv, Di Lorenzo-Pellegrino 2008, 181.
[89] The same motif appears in Calp. 3, the elegiac pastoral of the Calpurnian corpus, in vv. 61–3, where Lycidas praises himself not only as *divitior* (v. 63) but also as *formosior illo* (sc. *Mopso*), v. 61; cf. Chapter 4, pp. 141–2. The same holds true for Nemes. 2.74–81, where Alcon, in imitation of Calp. 3 and functioning within the elegiac triangle of a lover (Alcon), his *puella* (Donace) and his erotic rival (Idas), calls himself *nostro formosior Ida*, v. 78. Cf. also Karakasis 2011, 317–8.

85[90], *gracili*, v. 87). Astacus in his responding lines takes over from Idas on the subject of external beauty, with the characteristic for him georgic wording (vv. 90 – 1[91]); yet in spite of Idas' sense of uncertainty Astacus seems confident of his external appearance[92].

The singing match ends with a usual closure of pastoral narratives, the coming of evening (v. 93: *sed fugit ecce dies revocatque crepuscula vesper*), which often has this function mainly in Vergilian pastoral[93] (*Ecl*. 1.82 – 3, 2.66 – 7, 6.85 – 6, 10.77, cf. also 9.63) and is bequeathed to post-Vergilian bucolic poetry as well, cf. Calp. 5.120 – 1, Nemes. 1.86 – 7, 2.88 – 90, 3.67 – 9; see also above, pp. 41, 81 – 2, 186 – 7. Nightfall signals the return to the everyday tasks of pastoral life, and so Idas relates the driving of the flocks (v. 94) and Astacus the watering of the gardens (vv. 96 – 7), cf. also Verg. *Ecl*. 2.70 – 2, 6.85 – 6, 10.77, Calp. 4.168, Nemes. 1.87, 3.67 – 9. Such assignments are as a rule postponed for the sake of a song-exchange, but in the present eclogue's strong georgic background they appear, along with the sunset-motif, as song-topics[94]. Note that despite its pastoral antecedents, Idas' intertext for v. 92: *nec fistula cedit amori*, which brings the song-contest to its end, is Verg. *Ecl*. 10.69: *omnia vincit Amor: et nos cedamus Amori*[95], a significant line with respect to the 'generic outlook' of pastoral: it is the line uttered when the elegiac poet Gallus, after his short-lived bucolic experience, re-asserts his elegiac disposition and renounces his adhesion to the pastoral code[96]. Again, as often in this Calpurnian eclogue, traditional pastoral ideas are combined with intertextual wording bearing witness to the 'generic diversity' of the singing match, since the *fistula*, a usual metonymy for pastoral poetry, succumbs to the power of *amor*, a term also denoting elegiac love-poetry. This idea follows in the Calpurnian eclogue another maxim, that *carmina poscit amor*; it is thus about the well-known ancient view that poetry is either the

---

90 Yet the adjective is common especially with *os* denoting the first fluff of a young man or the absence of facial hair, cf. also Lucr. 5.672 – 4, Prop. 3.15.14, Vinchesi 2014, 210 – 11.
91 Cf. also Friedrich 1976, 54, Kettemann 1977, 106 and n. 25, Amat 1991, 104, Fey-Wickert 2002, 133 – 4.
92 Cf. Cesareo 1931, 56, Friedrich 1976, 54, Gagliardi 1984, 74, Stanzel 1989, 195 – 6, Vinchesi 2014, 211.
93 Cf. Rumpf 1996, 198. See also Pearce 1990, 55, Di Lorenzo–Pellegrino 2008, 182, Karakasis 2011, 201, Vinchesi 2014, 213.
94 Cf. also Friedrich 1976, 55 – 6.
95 Cf. also Verdière 1954, 243, Stanzel 1989, 193, Schäfer 2001, 148, Di Lorenzo–Pellegrino 2008, 182, Vinchesi 2014, 213. Di Salvo 1990a, 277; 1991, 310 plausibly corrects from *non...* in *ac...cedit*; see also Baehrens 1872, 186 (*et...cedit*), Shackleton-Bailey 1978, 319.
96 Cf. the relevant discussion in Papanghelis 1995, 64 – 87, especially 83 – 7, with a critical review of the relevant criticism on the subject.

symptom of or the antidote to love. This attitude towards poetry is attested in ancient pastoral, but is more common in the elegiac corpus (e.g. Prop. 2.1.4, Ov. Am. 2.17.34, 3.12.16). When appearing in pastoral, it is often a sign of a 'generic issue': it occurs in the 'generically deviant' eleventh Theocritean idyll (vv. 1–3, 17–8, 80–1)[97], it complements the elegiac discourse of the second Vergilian eclogue (vv. 3–5), and it recurs in the second eclogue of Nemesianus (Idas' and Alcon's elegiac passion for the same *puella* (Donace), for whom they engage in an amoebaean song–contest) as well as in the fourth Nemesianus' eclogue (Lycidas and Mopsus relieving their elegiac erotic plight (cf. 2.14–5, 4.19, 25))[98].

Astacus' lines also exhibit the same pattern of a traditional pastoral facade intertextually alluding to 'alternative generic trends': he speaks about the rustling of leaves (v. 95: *iam resonant frondes*) and about the georgic tasks of opening the channel and watering the garden[99] (cf. also vv. 34–5, 48–51). The natural noise produced by the rustling leaves is positively coloured in the pastoral tradition (cf. Theocr. 1.1–2, Verg. *Ecl.* 7.1, 8.22), often also constituting a basic component of a generic *locus amoenus*; however, this natural sound is here associated with the image of a forest drowning out pastoral song, i.e., eliminating the highest value of the traditional pastoral world, instead or reproducing it by means of an aiding echo. This attitude is conveyed through a Propertian wording, 4.4.4: *obstrepit arbor aquis*[100], further establishing the 'generically novel' setting. This sense of 'generic disposition' of the lines seems to be further complemented with the appearance of a character crucially bearing a name with no pastoral

---

97 Cf. also Hunter 1999, 215, 220–1. Cf. Bion fr. 3.
98 Cf. also Effe-Binder 1989, 159, Karakasis 2011, 297–338.
99 As to vv. 96–7, they are simply an inversion of Verg. *Ecl.* 3.111: *claudite iam rivos, pueri: sat prata biberunt*; whereas the intertextual model focuses on the closing of the water supply, the present lines concentrate on the opening of the channel, but the motif is basically the same. For this Vergilian intertext and its inversion here, cf. also Cesareo 1931, 56–7, Friedrich 1976, 56, Grimal 1978, 164, Pearce 1990, 55, Amat 1991, 19 and n. 44, Keene 1996, 78–9, Schäfer 2001, 148, Fey-Wickert 2002, 138, Di Lorenzo-Pellegrino 2008, 184, Vinchesi 2014, 214–5, Baraz 2015, 104–5. This intertext from the third Vergilian eclogue further underscores the 'generic fluidity' of the eclogue: for, as in the present Calpurnian poem, both contestants of the third Vergilian eclogue also prove themselves alienated, to a certain degree, from traditional pastoral values and norms of bucolic poetry, verging towards other literary genres; this also accounts, as shown in Karakasis 2011, 87–124, for their not receiving, as a prize, Alcimedon's cups, read as symbolising pastoral poetry; see also above, pp. 153, 208. The Calpurnian singer is here intertextually associated with the Vergilian contestants of the third eclogue, as both display a certain lack of '(traditional) generic awareness'.
100 For the syntagm (*obstrepo* + *arbor* + dative complement) modelled on Propertius, cf. Fey-Wickert 2002, 138.

history, Dorylas[101] (v. 96), as a foil to both Daphnis (cf. Theocr. 1, 5, 6, 7, [Theocr.] 8, 9, 27, Verg. *Ecl.* 2, 3, 5, 7, 8, 9) and Alphesiboeus (cf. Verg. *Ecl.* 5, 8, see also Ἀλφεσίβοια, Theocr. 3.45) of Idas' lines (v. 94), who in contrast have the sanction of previous bucolic poetry. On the linguistic level, the above 'generic impression' seems to be rounded off by the rather georgic syntagm *sitientes...hortos* in v. 97, cf. also Colum. 10.1.1.24[102].

The Draw

The song–contest ends with the arbiter declaring a draw, a not un–heard of outcome in pastoral (cf. also Theocr. 6.46, Verg. *Ecl.* 3.108–10[103]), but definitely an ending which should be approached here from a 'generic point of view' as well; unlike both Theocritus' and Vergil's bucolics, where no mention of the umpire's advanced age is made, Thyrsis here appears, because of his age, cf. v. 98, to be capitalising on the accumulated previous pastoral experience and tradition. The contradistinction of an aged pastoral figure, suggesting pastoral tradition, with younger bucolic characters, incarnating the continuation of pastoral as a genre, does appear in post–Vergilian pastoral, e. g. in the case of Tityrus (Vergil) in relation to Corydon (Calpurnius) in the fourth Calpurnian eclogue (vv. 62ff., cf. Chapter 2, p. 63), and in the first eclogue of Nemesianus' pastoral corpus, where the aged Tityrus represents Vergilian pastoral with respect to Timetas standing for Nemesianus' pastoral succession[104]. It is within this framework that the emphasis on Thyrsis' age should be read (v. 98: *senior cum talia Thyrsis*); significantly, the elderly umpire takes his seat under an aged tree (v. 21: *iamque sub annosa medius consederat umbra*), where the hypallage of the wording further complements the notion of a built up pastoral experience. The umpire Thyrsis, representing pastoral tradition as evidenced from his advanced age, proclaims his verdict on the new pastoral compositions (tradition vs. novelty) as follows: both singers are equal not only on the level of beauty, love and youth but also, after their respective musical performances are heard, on the level of song; this draw is justified, on the basis of the analysis above, not only in terms of musical excellence but also because of the 'generic outlook' of the songs, which both display 'generic novelty'.

---

101 Cf. Vinchesi 2014, 214. Fey–Wickert 2002, 139 draws attention to the fact that the gardener Astacus utters the name and not the herdsman Idas; see also Friedrich 1976, 22.
102 Cf. Di Lorenzo-Pellegrino 2008, 184, Vinchesi 2014, 215.
103 Cf. Fey–Wickert 2002, 140–1, Vinchesi 2014, 215.
104 Cf. also Schetter 1975, 7–8, Walter 1988, 29–31, Hubbard 1998, 169, 178.

To go one step further, the present eclogue is, to a great extent, a reading of the previous, mainly Vergilian bucolic tradition, a meditation on the pastoral genre as shaped chiefly by Vergil. In this sense, Calpurnius follows through, extends, elaborates and, no doubt, re-formulates hints, suggestions and themes already present in Vergil. Being 'belated', the eclogue thematises, in the course of the song–contest, even those parts of the pastoral scenarios which, in Vergil, remain outside the domain of song, e.g. the nightfall topic; this constitutes a clear meta–poetic, meta–generic gesture, a procedure peculiar to evolving pastoral, namely the inclusion of the world within the song–quotations. If 'real life', i.e., life conducted outside bucolic song in earlier pastoral poems, is finally inserted between song–quotes in a later specimen – this is also a generic / genetic feature of pastoral as 'song about songs', which ultimately may also be read as reducing the impact of theme as against song–activity. In any case, an eclogue that takes stock of the pastoral genre is more likely to be resolved on a non–confrontational note; hence a draw is declared. If pastoral is mainly about song, and if everything, georgic elements, elegiac mood, etc. included, can eventually become song, there is no point in declaring victory for either of the two contestants; moreover both Idas and Astacus appear to be almost equally capitalising on the novel thematic stock, to such a degree at least that there is no need for an explicit winner.

Linguistic Realism

A final remark concerning the linguistic outlook of the poem: as previously pointed out (cf. p. 196), Astacus the gardener constitutes, because of his profession, a 'generic innovation'. This 'generic novelty' of his profession seems to be reflected on his linguistic behaviour as well, since many novel / Post–Classical linguistic options are dispersed throughout his speech. An example is in v. 41 *genitalia* (if one accepts this reading vs. *gentilia*, see above, p. 205) in the sense of 'inborn', 'natural': *induit arbos ignotas frondes et non genitalia poma* (vv. 40 – 1), a meaning that appears later in [Heges.] 3.9.5, Cassiod. *var.* 7.15.3, Eustath. *Bas. hex.* 2.9 p.884^B (cf. ThLL VI 2, 1813, 73 – 8)[105]. In v. 56 the construction of *uri* with the accusative in the sense of 'to be in love with' is Post–Classical, in place of the Classical *uri* + ablative syntagms (cf. Ov. *Met.* 7.22); the construction seems to be modelled on similar *ardere* + accusative syntagms (cf. Sen. *H.O.* 369) and thus is rightly labelled by Mahr 1964, 132 – 3 as 'ein nachklassisches

---

[105] Cf. Fey–Wickert 2002, 90; see also Vinchesi 2014, 190.

Merkmal'[106]. *Faginus* in the sense of 'beechen cup' (v. 59) is a further Post-Classical usage[107] and the same also applies to *echinnus* for the chestnut-husk (v. 83), cf. also Pallad. 14.155, Serv. ad 7.53, Gloss. 5.619.20 (see ThLL V 2, 46, 51–6)[108], as well as to *lana* in v. 91: *cerea sub tenui lucere cydonia lana* of the fruit's fluff, see also Mart. 10.42.3, *et al.* (ThLL VII 2, 915, 41–50)[109]. *Praetorridus* (v. 80) in the sense of *valde torridus* is yet another Post-Classical formation, a *hapax* of Calpurnius[110].

A further relatively Post-Classical feature, although not unparalleled in Classical Latin, occurs in vv. 56–9, *si...audiat,...ponetur:* the use of the future *ponetur* in place of a *coniuctivus potentialis* as the apodosis of the *si...audiat* conditional clause, cf. also v. 75: *si venias...serviet* (see, on the other hand, Calp. 5.112–4, 7.16–8). Present indicative or future indicative tense as an apodosis in a conditional sequence expressing the possible instead of a present subjunctive is more productive in Post-Classical Latin and the above usages are again plausibly characterised by Mahr 1964, 104 as specimens of 'der früh-nachklassische Sprachgebrauch unseres Dichters'[111].

---

106 Cf. also Fey-Wickert 2002, 101, Vinchesi 2014, 198.
107 Cf. Merone 1967, 44–5, Messina 1975, 108, Armstrong 1986, 118, Horsfall 1997, 182, 190.
108 Cf. Novelli 1980, 29–30, who, however, sees here a reference 'al mallo delle noci anziché al guscio delle castagne', Armstrong 1986, 119, Vinchesi 1992, 153; 2014, 209, Horsfall 1997, 182, Fey-Wickert 2002, 128–9, Di Lorenzo-Pellegrino 2008, 181.
109 Cf. also Dalby 2000, 152, Fey-Wickert 2002, 134, Vinchesi 2014, 212.
110 Cf. Mahr 1964, 186: 'eine Schöpfung unseres Dichters', Novelli 1980, 85, Armstrong 1986, 118, Horsfall 1997, 182, Fey-Wickert 2002, 127; see also Vinchesi 2014, 208.
111 Cf. also Fey-Wickert 2002, 101, Vinchesi 2014, 198. Apart from v. 71: *si venias...serviet*, the only other Post-Classical construction that appears in Idas' speech is the *dativus auctoris* with intransitive verbs of passive meaning (*palpitare, cadere*) in vv. 62–3: *mihi...palpitat...cadit*, cf. Mahr 1964, 75, Fey-Wickert 2002, 111; but it could also be interpreted as a *dativus commodi*. *Oleastra* for *oleastri* (v. 44, cf. ThLL IX 2, 541, 19–22, Messina 1975, 108, Novelli 1980, 93, Armstrong 1986, 123, Horsfall 1997, 189), not found before Calpurnius, seems to be a poeticism, a metrical variant, see Fey-Wickert 2002, 93, Vinchesi 2014, 192–3. As to the alleged novel use of *taeda* (v. 29) in the sense of 'pine branch' (cf. also Merone 1967, 37–8, Messina 1975, 108), one could easily agree with Horsfall 1997, 186 that this linguistic option is 'not that new after Hor. *Carm.* 4.4.43, Verg. *Aen.* 4.505', where the word does also refer to pine-trees and pine-wood in particular (cf. OLD *s.v.* 1a, 3; see also Vinchesi 2014, 183). In any case what matters again is the quantity and the variety of Post-Classical features in Astacus' speech in opposition to the rather Classical colouring of Idas' diction.

Conclusion

Although the eclogue belongs to the type of amoebaean βουκολιασμός, the traditional pastoral song-contest, both Idas and Astacus appear to be 'reading' previous pastoral tradition with the intention of transcending earlier pastoral 'generic boundaries' primarily towards elegiac[112] and georgic preferences[113]. This is often evident through motif usage and wording; additionally, in most cases the intertextual models are ill-omened from the point of erotic success. What is more, not only the 'generic tradition' but also the Neoteric poetological program is at stake, as evidenced by the critical re-evaluation of relevant catch-words denoting Callimachean trends. On the level of linguistic characterisation, the 'generically novel' gardener, Astacus, often resorts to novel Post-Classical diction.

---

112 Cf. also Friedrich 1976, 48, 57, Schäfer 2001, 148–9.
113 Cf. also Kettemann 1977, 99–108, Vinchesi 1996, 36–7; see also Correa 1977, 157–8.

Part C: **Challenging the Very Structure of the Singing Match...**

Calpurnius 6

The sixth eclogue of the Calpurnian bucolic corpus has as its main subject an announced and anticipated song-contest that, nevertheless, eventually does not take place, something which goes against the traditional 'generic patterning' of a bucolic singing match, as exemplified by the pastoral practice from Theocritus onwards (cf. Theocr. 5, [Theocr.] 8, 9, Verg. *Ecl.* 3, 7, Calp. 2, *Eins.* 1)[1]. Astylus and Lycidas, the two chief pastoral figures of the poem, quarrel over the decision of Astylus, the umpire in a recent singing match between Alcon and Nyctilus[2], in which the former was declared as the winner. In accordance with a well-established 'generic bucolic ethos', on the basis of the accumulated 'generic experience', from Theocritus on, that Calpurnius too has at his disposal, this hostility between the two inhabitants of the 'green cabinet' is expected to be resolved by means of a singing match involving this time Astylus and Lycidas as the pastoral contestants. However, this expectation is never fulfilled, since the umpire himself, Mnasyllus, acting (as will be shown below, cf. pp. 234, 242–4, 248–9) as the voice of traditional, pre-Calpurnian pastoralism, faced with a 'generically

---

[1] Thus Gagliardi 1981, 44; 1984, 37 speaks of an 'antiegloga' (cf. also Rivoltella 2006, 121 and n. 1). Davis 1987, 38 as well talks about an 'anti-pastoral', in the sense that pastoral song cannot ultimately triumph over the hostility both herdsmen experience in the present eclogue; for Davis this is an indication of song's impotence. The utmost value of the pastoral world is thus presented as losing its power.

[2] As frequently in post-Vergilian bucolics, the pastoral figures of the present eclogue have also been read as a masquerade, as symbolising *per allegoriam* contemporary historical persons; thus for Astylus as a mask of Phaedrus, cf. Herrmann 1952, 39–40, Verdière 1954, 58, Messina 1975, 32–3, as an allegory for Arruntius Stella, cf. Verdière 1954, 59; see also Amat 1991, 118. Lycidas is, on the other hand, equated either with Phaedrus (cf. Verdière 1954, 55–7, 60) or with Persius (cf. Herrmann 1952, 37–8, Messina 1975, 33), whereas Mnasyllus and Stimicon stand for L. Iunius Silanus Torquatus (cf. Herrmann 1952, 41, Verdière 1954, 59) and Statius respectively (cf. Herrmann 1952, 42, Verdière 1954, 60). Mopsus represents Annaeus Serenus (cf. Herrmann 1952, 43; yet see also Verdière 1954, 60), Nyctilus functions as a pseudonym of Nero and Alcon is Britannicus' *nom de plume* (cf. Verdière 1954, 60–1; for Lucan as Alcon, a view also of Verdière, latter dropped by the scholar, cf. Verdière 1952, 799–804; see also Di Salvo 1991, 306). Last but not least, Annaeus Cornutus (cf. Herrmann 1952, 38, Verdière 1954, 58) or Seneca (cf. Hubaux 1930, 213, 230; see also Chytil 1894, 7) are the candidates for Iollas as an allegory, whereas Lycotas and Micon have been read as C. Caesius Bassus and Seneca respectively (cf. Herrmann 1952, 43, 41–2, Verdière 1954, 60). Nonetheless such symbolisms are once again beyond the scope and the objectives of this chapter; for a justifiable criticism of these views, cf. especially Gagliardi 1984, 33 and n. 16: 'siamo ben lontani da quelle forme di allegoria'; see also Vinchesi 1996, 41; 2014, 437 and Verdière himself 1966, 172: 'quête qui, aujourd' hui, m' apparaît aussi stérile que peu assurée'.

shocking' loss of temper by both prospective singers, decides, with no bucolic precedent whatsoever, to break off the singing match. The cancellation of the song–exchange and the concomitant prominence of the introductory framing narrative focusing on the wrangling between the two pastoral figures –an early editor of the poem, Filippo da Giunta (Florence, 1504), fittingly entitled it *Litigium*[3]– has led critics to believe that the textual tradition of the poem may be faulty[4]. Alternatively, the eclogue has been considered Calpurnius' youthful writing, a less carefully crafted poem, especially when compared with the poet's second eclogue, where an amoebaean singing contest does come about (cf. Chapter 6, pp. 195–219)[5].

A Singing Match off Stage

The present poem (Calp. 6) seems to operate on the basis of a dichotomy between a traditionally pastoral past, where fixed 'generic rules' of amoebaean βουκολιασμὸς hold true, and an unconventional bucolic present, which tends towards a 'generic transcendence', a distanciation from long–established and time–honoured pastoral norms[6]. The eclogue begins with Astylus' description of a narrated singing match, as e.g. the whole of the seventh Vergilian eclogue[7], where Calpurnius in general observes a sort of formalistic completeness[8]; thus

---

[3] Cf. also Simon 2007b, 58.
[4] For a brief account of this critical response to the sixth Calpurnian eclogue, cf. especially Friedrich 1976, 116, 227 and nn. 2, 3, Gagliardi 1984, 36 and n. 30, Simon 2007b, 59–60 and nn. 6, 7.
[5] Cf. especially Hubaux 1930, 226, Cesareo 1931, 93, Keene 1996, 132; see also Vinchesi 1996, 42; 2008, 544; 2014, 33, 436. Besides Cesareo 1931, 92 considers Calp. 2 as posterior to Calp. 6 (cf. also Grant 1965, 71), for the former is, according to his, outdated by now, sense of 'literarische Wertung', a more advanced / sophisticated and finish version of the singing contest–type of pastoral poetry in relation to the latter; see also similarly Messina 1975, 51. For a refutation of this thesis, however, cf. Gagliardi 1984, 37 and n. 33.
[6] For Leach 1975, 220–2, on the other hand, the narrative of the poem rather operates on the following division: a 'precious and refined' vs. a 'rough and natural' version of pastoral, respectively exemplified by the pairs Alcon–Astylus and Nyctilus–Lycidas. Indications for the former type of pastoral are Alcon's good looks and Astylus' tamed stag offered as a stake, his revulsion against the noise of the brook, as well as his homosexuality – 'an extension of the idea of his over–refinement' (cf. Leach *op. cit.*, 222), whereas signs of the latter bucolic kind are Nyctilus' rough, unrefined appearance and Lycidas' fierce and swift *equus* as a pledge. At the end, it is Lycidas who makes his opponent leave aside his preciosity and consequently resort to rudeness.
[7] Cf. Messina 1975, 34, Vinchesi 2014, 435.
[8] Cf. also Schäfer 2001, 149–50, Di Lorenzo–Pellegrino 2008, 254, Vinchesi 2014, 438–9.

the agonistic setting described comprises all the basic 'generic essentials' of a bucolic singing match (cf. Karakasis 2011, 52–3). Key-features are: (i) the 'convening', the coming together of two pastoral figures, i.e., Nyctilus and Alcon, with an eventual view to exchanging songs (vv. 1–2), (ii) the pastoral shade, that is the branches beneath which the song-exchange takes place (v. 2, cf. also e. g. Theocr. 1.21, 3.38, 5.48–9, 61, 7.8–9, 88, 138, Verg Ecl. 1.1, 4, 14, 52, 2.8–9, 5.3, 5, 40, 7.1, 10, 9.20[9]), (iii) an alternation of song-performances according to familiar and recognised amoebaean pastoral standards (v. 2, see also Theocr. 5, [Theocr.] 8, Verg. Ecl. 3, 7[10]), (iv) the young age of at least one of the contestants (v. 1: *puer Alcon*, cf. also [Theocr.] 8.3–4, Verg. Ecl. 7.4–5), (v) the presence of an umpire (v. 3, cf. also Theocr. 5, [Theocr.] 8, 9, Verg. Ecl. 3, 7), (vi) the verdict declaring a winner (Alcon – v. 5 as in Theocr. 5, [Theocr.] 8, Verg. Ecl. 7) and finally (vii) the staking of prizes (cf. also Theocr. 5.21–30, [Theocr.] 8.11–24, Verg. Ecl. 3.29–48), which the champion finally carries off (vv. 3–5).

What is more, both prizes, as is also the case with all singing matches of pre-Calpurnian pastoral, are closely related to the traditional pastoral world (cf. Theocr. 5.21–30: a billy-goat and a lamb, [Theocr.] 8.13–24: pastoral flutes, Verg. Ecl. 3.29–48: a cow): Nyctilus thus pledges goat-kids together with their mother (vv. 3–4: *haedos / iuncta matre*), i.e., a characteristic animal of the bucolic fauna, whereas Alcon, in his turn, stakes a dog protector of the pastoral flock (v. 4: *catulum...leaenae*)[11]. Last but not least, the use of traditional keywords, *termini technici* of the pastoral *genus*, further complements the sense of formalistic comprehensiveness in the narrated pastoral exchange: *certavere* in v. 2 constitutes a familiar designation of the amoebaean βουκολιασμός (cf. also Verg. Ecl. 3.31, 4.58, 5.8, 9, 15, 7.16. 8.3; see also above, pp. 102–3, 143[12]), *alternus* in the same line (v. 2: *alterno carmine*) suggests the exchange of consec-

---

[9] Cf. also Becker 2012, 115.
[10] Cf. also Keene 1996, 132: *alterno carmine = amoebaeo carmine*; see also Verdière 1954, 259, Korzeniewski 1971, 59, Pearce 1990, 130, Di Lorenzo-Pellegrino 2008, 255, Becker 2012, 115.
[11] I understand *catulum leaenae* as equivalent to a 'wolf-hound' (cf. also Ov. *Fast.* 5.177, Kegel-Brinkgreve 1990, 161 and n. 35, Keene 1996, 133) or as having the sense of 'the pup of a dog called *leaena*', according to the ancient habit of naming the dogs after wild animals – *leo, tigris*, etc. (cf. Hyg. *Fab.* 181, Iuv. 8.34–6, Verdière 1954, 259, Korzeniewski 1971, 106, Vinchesi 1996, 137; 2014, 439, Di Lorenzo-Pellegrino 2008, 255, Becker 2012, 117). Heinsius' and Giarratano's correction *Lacaenae* (cf. also Messina 1975, 34 and n. 7), also adopted by Di Salvo 1990a, 283; 1991, 313 and Pearce 1990, 130, referring to the well-known breed of the *canes Laconici*, seems therefore unnecessary; see also Amat 1991, 116, Vinchesi 2014, 440.
[12] Cf. also Clausen 1994, 99, Cucchiarelli 2012, 213, Becker 2012, 114–5, Vinchesi 2014, 438–9.

utive strophic units according to the traditional pastoral song–exchange pattern (cf. also Verg. *Ecl.* 3.59, 7.18–9), while *pignus* in v. 3 (*non sine pignore*) is also an identifiable designation of the pastoral stake (cf. also Verg. *Ecl.* 3.31[13]).

Past – 'Generic Tradition' vs. Present – 'Generic Novelty'

However, this wealth of standard motifs refers to the past, albeit recent; the reader experiences the formalistic span of vv. 1–5, the 'traditional generic fullness' of this initial reported narrative as over and done with, in opposition to the atypical and thus novel, 'generic character' of the following segment (vv. 6 ff.), which constitutes the poetical present. The non-conformist character of the present situation is emphasised by a significant detail not endorsed by previous bucolic, namely the motif of belatedness, as suggested by Astylus' (v. 1) opening remarks: *serus ades, Lycida*. The motif, which appears in Calp. 7 as well (cf. Chapter 3, pp. 89–90), has no Roman, pre-Calpurnian bucolic precedents, whereas in Theocritus it crucially appears in two of his non-bucolic idylls only, namely 14.2 and 15.1[14]. It has already often been suggested that the intrusion in post-Vergilian pastoral of (a) motifs drawn from a pastoral poet's non-bucolic works (the non-bucolic idylls of Greek pastoral for example[15]; see also above, pp. 7, 89, 96, 118, 123–6, 131, 133–9, 142, 147–9, 152, 188, 196), or (b) from a pastoral poem where 'generic tensions' are the main focus of the poem's meta-narrative (e.g. the second Vergilian eclogue stamped by Corydon's elegiac rhetoric; see also pp. 5, 55–6 and n. 39, 93, 124, 128, 132–3, 137–9, 141–4, 153, 197–8, 208–13, 215), or (c) alternatively from a bucolic poem possessing a peculiar 'generic character', as is the case with the eleventh Theocritean idyll, whose themes and narrative techniques (e.g. the 'unpastoral' practice of the *syrinx* – v. 38, the address to Nikias as a framing narrative; see also above, pp. 7, 55–6 and n. 39, 93, 131, 137–9, 152, 208, 210–11, 215) make it stand outside the main tradition of Theocritean bucolic poems[16], may function as a marker for the poet's 'novel generic aspirations', and for his desire for a 'generic re-evaluation' of traditional pastoral trends. It is therefore perhaps not coincidental that Calpurnius chooses, in a poem introducing 'new generic ethics' with a view to transcending

---

13 Cf. also Verdière 1954, 259, Korzeniewski 1971, 59, Di Lorenzo–Pellegrino 2008, 255, Becker 2012, 116.
14 Cf. Korzeniewski 1971, 59, Vinchesi 2014, 438.
15 E.g. the motif of the '*puella* gathering flowers – eventual victim of rape' in Nemes. 2.
16 Cf. Hunter 1999, 217–8. For the peculiar 'generic character' of Theocr. 11, cf. also Farrell 1992, 241–2.

well-established 'generic patterns' of the traditional amoebaean βουκολιασμός, to employ a non-bucolic motif of an otherwise bucolic poet. As will be shown later, the other two ways of expressing 'generic ambivalence' will also be endorsed in the Calpurnian narrative to follow.

On the other hand, the very notion of 'lateness' may be viewed as part of Calpurnius' self-fashioning of his 'generic identity' with respect to the previous literary tradition. Calpurnius significantly views his pastoral as coming late in relation to previous Greek and Roman pastoral, as evidenced by the image of the autumn in the incipit of the first programmatic eclogue of the Calpurnian oeuvre, which contrasts Calpurnian pastoral with its Vergilian predecessor, represented by the symbolism of the summer (cf. Chapter 1, pp. 15–6)[17]. From this perspective, Lycidas' tardiness here may also be read as suggesting, in terms of a 'literary secondariness' (term as used by Hinds 1998, 83–98)[18], the 'novel generic experience' of the Calpurnian narrative to follow, as compared with the traditional pastoral patterning of the recounted singing match of the recent past in vv. 1–5[19]. For it is significantly the late comer Lycidas' disbelief in Astylus' refereeing principles that triggers the 'generic novelty' of the following account[20].

Bickering – Part One

The formalistic comprehensiveness of the narrated singing match thus functions as a foil to the expected song-contest and its narrative framing, in which most of the traditional patterns of βουκολιασμός are significantly modified or even do not hold true at all. Topics having the sanction of the earlier bucolic tradition are hence interchangeable with themes without a particular pastoral calibre, thus suggesting the 'generic re-orientation' of Calpurnian bucolics. Following Astylus' description of Alcon's victory, in imitation of his pastoral predecessor, Menalcas of the third Vergilian eclogue (vv. 25–7), who also appears to be sceptical as to Damoetas' singing superiority over his opponent Damon[21], Lycidas expresses his strong reservations as to Alcon's victory by means of a further *topos* of the pastoral tradition, namely the use of an animal *adynaton* (cf. above, pp. 8,

---

[17] Cf. Hubbard 1998, 154–5.
[18] Cf. also Gibson 2004, 14 and n. 35.
[19] Cf. also Becker 2012, 113–4.
[20] For Gibson 2004, 13 Lycidas' criticism of Astylus' verdict also 'suggests that the construction of literary hierarchies and aesthetic judgments is in fact open to criticism'.
[21] Cf. also Di Lorenzo-Pellegrino 2008, 255.

39). The different singing quality of the contestants of a bucolic ἀγών is conveyed by means of a simile, where various animals, birds or insects symbolise the singing ability of the competitors, cf. especially Theocr. 5.136–7, where, within a setting of a singing contest as here, Lacon is compared to the less musical jay or hoopoe (κίσσας, ἔποπας) against the challenging voice of a nightingale or a swan (ἀηδόνα, κύκνοισι), to which is equated the musical competence of Comatas, see also Theocr. 1.136, 5.29, 7.41, Verg. *Ecl.* 8.55, 9.36[22]. Likewise Alcon, crucially described as 'untrained', 'inexpert' (v. 6: *cantu rudis*), could have defeated Nyctilus, if only the crow could surpass the goldfinch or the eerie owl excel over the melodious nightingale (vv. 7–8: *si vincat acanthida cornix, / vocalem superet si dirus aedona bubo*).

The pre-eminence of Nyctilus' bucolic song, when compared to Alcon's, is furthermore revealed through the style and the linguistic morphology of Lycidas' simile: whereas Alcon is compared to birds not only of untuneful voice but also rendered in the text by their Latin names (*cornix*, v. 7 for the Greek κορώνη and *bubo* for βύας[23], v. 8), Nyctilus, on the other hand, is associated with melodic animals (*acanthis*, v. 7 (cf. also Theocr. 7.141[24]), *aedon*, v. 8) that are referred to by their Greek transliterated names (vs. the proper Latin forms *carduelis* (found as early as Plin. *Nat.* 10.116) and *luscinia* (in use from Hor. *Serm.* 2.3.245 on) respectively[25]), and even with Graecising morphology, the singular accusative in –a (*acanthida, aedona*)[26], something which constitutes a learned linguistic op-

---

[22] Cf. also Paladini 1956, 530, Korzeniewski 1971, 59, Messina 1975, 34, Friedrich 1976, 119, Keene 1996, 133, Schäfer 2001, 150, Gibson 2004, 9, Di Lorenzo–Pellegrino 2008, 20, 256, Becker 2012, 118–9, Vinchesi 2014, 441.
[23] Cf. also Messina 1975, 34 and n. 8, Keene 1996, 133.
[24] Cf. also Mazzarino 1983, 409 and n. 27, Becker 2012, 117–8.
[25] Cf. also Mahr 1964, 165–6, Keene 1996, 133, Di Lorenzo–Pellegrino 2008, 20, 256–7.
[26] Cf. also Pearce 1990, 130, Di Lorenzo–Pellegrino 2008, 256–7. As to the distribution of accusative Graecising endings of proper names, however, one notices an even spread, without specific reference to individual characters: v. 6 – *Nyctilon*, v. 51 – *Petason*, v. 77 – *Acanthida* (by Lycidas), v. 18 – *Alcona* (by Astylus), v. 75 – *Petalen*, *Phyllida* (by Mnasyllus). Yet, even in this last case, one may observe that Lycidas makes use of the afore-mentioned Hellenising forms only to refer to the tuneful, as he believes, Nyctilus as well as to Acanthis, i.e., the pastoral character, who allegedly beat Astylus in a singing match on Mnasyllus' verdict (vv. 77–8). In other words, Lycidas, once again, seems to associate Graecising morphology with (singing) supremacy, whereas the also Hellenising form *Alcona* is crucially uttered by Astylus, and not Lycidas, i.e., the herdsman who believes, in opposition to Lycidas, in Alcon's both melodious voice and good looks. *Petason*, on the other hand, is spoken by Lycidas in reference to his precious horse-stake (cf. vv. 49–50: *genus est...equarum non vulgare mihi*); excellence in both external appearance and epic swiftness may account for the above designation. Greek morphology thus seems in most cases to function as a sign of distinction.

tion redolent of Alexandrian *doctrina*, favoured in the Neoteric poetic discourse of Rome. Analogous Graecising expressions as a textual marker of excellence reappear in Lycidas' speech with reference, this time, to the supremacy of Alcon's external appearance; in v. 15: *crinemque simillimus auro*, *crinem* is an accusative of respect[27], the so-called *accusativus Graecus*, a conspicuous syntactic Hellenism especially with superlative forms, also frequently used in Neoteric texts and contexts[28]. What Lycidas denies for Alcon's voice, rated as too low by the herdsman in comparison with Nyctilus', is granted for Alcon's unquestionable physical beauty. Similar Hellenising syntagms form part of the pastoral Vergil's stylistic repertoire as well[29], a crucial evidence of the Augustan poet's Neoteric interests and aspirations, and thus may be read, in terms of Calpurnian bucolic poetics, as yet another stylistic tendency having the sanction of the earlier Roman pastoral tradition.

Lycidas' disagreement with Alcon's success, not unparalleled in previous bucolic texts, his equally traditionally bucolic use of the animal *adynaton* in order to express Nyctilus' musical superiority and, finally, his Hellenising wording, as a means of suggesting the supremacy of Nyctilus' voice, also sanctioned by earlier pastoral, meet with the comparatively 'unpastoral' reaction of Astylus' (non-pastoral again in the sense of defying the horizon of expectations on the part of the model reader, who has constructed his literary competence on the basis of his previous accumulated 'generic experience'). Astylus tries to justify his verdict by offering as a pledge his love for Petale[30], v. 9: *non potiar Petale, qua nunc ego maceror una* (may I never obtain Petale, for whom only I fade away!). But exclusiveness in love-matters, as suggested by Astylus' *una* (cf. also Catul. 68b.135, Prop. 2.30b.23, Ov. *Ars* 2.399[31], Chapter 4, pp. 131, 150), as well as the winning of the beloved, i.e., erotic bliss as the ideal par excellence, project sensibilities, principles and values chiefly of the elegiac genre[32].

Pastoral, on the contrary, is characterised by a penchant for emotional and sexual liberty, whereas success in love as the *raison d' être* of the pastoral lover

---

[27] Cf. also Pearce 1990, 131.
[28] Cf. also Di Lorenzo-Pellegrino 2008, 258; see also Novelli 1980, 24–5.
[29] Cf. especially Papanghelis 1995, 126, 129.
[30] For Cesareo 1931, 81–2 and Gagliardi 1984, 33 and n. 18, an erotic rivalry between Astylus and Lycidas for Petale seems to account for their intense hostility, evident throughout the eclogue; see also Messina 1975, 34 and n. 9. Yet this is not so convincing a view, not supported by the narrative of the poem (cf. also Cesareo *op. cit.* 'nulla ci dice espressamente il poeta'); see also Di Lorenzo-Pellegrino 2008, 257.
[31] Cf. Pichon 1966, 112. See also Vinchesi 1991, 264.
[32] Cf. e.g. Lyne 2003, 65–81.

and the ideal of erotic exclusivity, both distinct elegiac values, have often been read in the relevant bibliography as modal intrusions of elegy into the 'pastoral generic landscape'. A case in point is, as already observed (cf. above, p. 226), the elegiac discourse Corydon constructs in the second Vergilian eclogue, only to abandon it in the end and reinstate himself into the pastoral value system, by renouncing his obsession with Alexis and deciding to search for another lover[33] – a stance similar to that of Polyphemus in Theocr. 11.76, who similarly adopts the proper pastoral attitude towards erotic rebuff by exclaiming: εὑρησεῖς Γαλάτειαν ἴσως καὶ καλλίον' ἄλλαν. What is more, the formulation of Astylus' statement has a clear elegiac ring; *potior* in the sense of 'win my beloved' as well as *maceror* belong to the *sermo amatorius* (cf. Ov. *Ars* 1.711, *Ars* 1.385, 737, *Fast.* 3.21, 6.126 and Hor. *Carm.* 1.13.8, *Epod.* 14.16, Ov. *Epist.* 20.125 respectively)[34]. Also, the syntagm *qua nunc ego maceror una* in the second place of the hexameter could be seen as reminiscence, through the well-known Alexandrian technique of *oppositio in imitando*, of an elegiac Ovidian verse, namely *Rem.* 283: *hic amor et pax est, in qua male vulneror una* with the substitution of *vulneror* by the equally elegiac *maceror*[35]. In other words, Astylus sets out to defend his judgment as a pastoral umpire, i.e., his function as a key-persona of the pastoral *genus*, as the guardian of both the pastoral space and the bucolic genre, by means of an appeal to elegiac ethics and, what is more, in a language evoking elegiac intertexts.

Lycidas is quick to detect this elegiac inclination of the umpire and further accuses Astylus of deviating from customary pastoral ideals regarding the tasks of a bucolic arbiter. According to Lycidas, Astylus bases his judgment not on expected pastoral precepts but on criteria of the elegiac discourse, i.e., on good looks instead of singing / musical supremacy. Whereas the bucolic prize should have been given to the tuneful Nyctilus, according to the demands of the traditional bucolic norm, it was accorded to the handsome Alcon, in accordance with elegiac principles[36]. This is clearly suggested by Lycidas' description of the external appearance of the two contestants in the singing match off stage: Nyctilus was pale with a 'beard pricklier than the bristly porcupine', v. 13 (transl. by Duff and Duff 1934, 271), whereas Astylus was fair (*candidus*), smoother than a

---

33 Cf. especially Papanghelis 1995, 61; see also 1999, 47–8; 2006, 400–1.
34 Cf. Pichon 1966, 237, Di Lorenzo–Pellegrino 2008, 257, Becker 2012, 119–20; see also Gagliardi 1984, 73.
35 Cf. also Verdière 1954, 259, Korzeniewski 1971, 59, Di Lorenzo–Pellegrino 2008, 257, Becker 2012, 120, Vinchesi 2014, 442. Note also the similarity in the *qua* syntagm in the middle of the line as well as the *una* complement at the end of the verse.
36 Cf. also Becker 2012, 120.

soft egg (*levique decentior ovo*), with laughing eyes (*ridens oculis*) and gleaming blonde hair (*crinemque simillimus auro*), an Apollo, one would say (*qui posset dici...Apollo*)[37], in terms of external beauty (vv. 14–6); but this impression could hardly be maintained, once Alcon opened his mouth to sing (v. 16: *si non cantaret*).

Nyctilus' description connects him intertextually to the unnamed goatherd of Damon's song in Vergil's eighth eclogue (cf. also above, pp. 124, 128, 148, 153, 200), who is similarly presented as having a *hirsutumque supercilium promissaque barba* (v. 34)[38]. This herdsman, now, also represents the traditional 'generic values' of the 'green cabinet' and is, therefore, despised by Nysa, his former sweet-heart, who clearly leans towards 'unpastoral' ideals and objectives: she looks down on his rustic outlook and his pastoral *fistula* (a metonymy of bucolic poetry itself, vv. 33–4) and is about to marry Mopsus, setting up an elegiac erotic triangle between herself, Damon's herdsman, and Mopsus. She hopes to legally become Mopsus' bride, *coniunx*, in a typical wedding ceremony, *deductio* (vv. 29–30), something which also lies well beyond the interests and the practices of the earlier 'green cabinet' and the pastoral *genus*, belonging instead to the epithalamion sub-generic formation of mainly lyric Neoteric poetry[39]. The melodious Nyctilus, clearly presented by Lycidas as abiding to and endorsing traditional pastoral ideals and norms, is thus intertextually equated with a further defender of the bucolic space, a pastoral figure that finally commits suicide (vv. 58–60), as a result of the violation of his pastoral world, torn by a love-affair that, although born as a blissful pastoral *eros* at first sight, later develops into a distressing liaison of rather tragic / epic associations, likened e.g. to Medea's cruel love (cf. vv. 43–50). Just before ending his life, Damon's goatherd says his final adieu to the woods, to the 'green cabinet' (*vivite silvae*, v. 58), to which he remains devoted, crying out for the reinstatement of the traditional / 'generically unblemished' earlier pastoralism. Therefore, the herdsman, wishing for the return of the Golden Age when pastoral / Neoteric singing will reign supreme[40], resorts to a sequence of *adynata* also expressing his desire for the reinstatement of a 'pure pastoral world': Tityrus, metonymically the resident of the 'green cabinet', the bucolic singer par excellence, will be equated with models of poetical

---

[37] Messina 1975, 40 detects here a comic colouring, a 'comicità'. For a '*vis comica*' in Calp. 6, cf. also Cesareo 1931, 82.
[38] Cf. also Verdière 1954, 259, Korzeniewski 1971, 60, Di Lorenzo–Pellegrino 2008, 257–8, Becker 2012, 121, Vinchesi 2014, 443.
[39] Cf. Karakasis 2011, 135.
[40] Cf. Papanghelis 1995, 257–301.

skill, i.e., with mythical figures such as Orpheus and Arion, *sit Tityrus Orpheus, / Orpheus in silvis, inter delphinas Arion*, vv. 55–6[41].

Terms like *candidus* and *levis* in reference to human beauty (Alcon's in this case) should be considered, as developed above (cf. pp. 230–1), as features of non-pastoral imagery, in the sense of being rated higher than the time-honoured pastoral value par excellence, i.e., singing supremacy. On a meta-linguistic level, however, these two terms (the second in the almost *idem sonans lĕvis* metrical form) also function, within Roman pastoral, as catch-words regularly denoting the Callimachean-Neoteric poetics of the bucolic *genus* in Rome, especially in Vergil. Curiously, this meta-poetic jargon is here associated by Lycidas not with the pleasant voice of Nyctilus, the true representative of the traditional pastoral world and its values, but with Alcon, i.e., the contestant praised for his beauty and not for the highest value of the pre-Calpurnian 'green cabinet', i.e., musical command, despite Astylus' claims for the opposite. As often remarked (cf. above, especially pp. 6, 10–11, 42–3, 46, 78–81, 86, 92, 95, 104–8, 118, 206), traditional meta-generic signs thus seem in Calpurnian pastoral to lose their Vergilian meta-poetic semantic load, suggesting once again a sense of 'generic blurriness' in post-Vergilian pastoral meta-language.

Astylus does not accept the accusations of 'generic digression from traditional pastoral', trying instead to make amends for his rather elegiac earlier behaviour by explicitly praising Alcon's good voice and not his excellent looks. He thus criticises Lycidas for lack of musical skill, which accounts, according to Astylus, for his interlocutor's inability to appreciate Alcon's performance, vv. 17–8: *si quis tibi carminis usus inesset, / tu quoque laudatum nosses Alcona probare*. As a result of this mutual exchange of accusations, a singing match is proposed in

---

41 However, it could be counter-argued here that Verg. *Ecl.* 8.52 ff. might seem a paradoxical wish for the advent of the Golden Age, since a series of *adynata*, probably to express despair, are further topped with the image of *omnia vel medium fiat mare* (v. 58), possibly playing on Theocr. 1.134; for pessimistic readings, i.e., in the line of the above frame of mind, cf. especially Hubbard 1998, 115–6, Breed 2006, 50–1. Nonetheless, one should also pay attention to both the fact that v. 58 – *omnia vel medium fiat mare* – does not belong to the same strophical unit (vv. 58–60) with the earlier *adynata* (vv. 52–6) and that the narrative focus of the various strophes in Damon's song significantly varies, is, in any case, not always the same. According to my reading, Damon's herdsman initially expresses his wish for the coming of the Golden Age (cf. also e.g. Leach 1974, 157), clearly suggested by the typical *Aetas Aurea*-imagery of wild animals fleeing before domestic fauna, the copious and unusual vegetation, and finally the picture of trees bearing golden fruits as well. After this craving of his for Golden Age assets, the unnamed lover realises once again his distancing from the pastoral norm of his past and consequently wishes (for himself) all to become mid-ocean, i.e., to drown, as he throws himself into the waves.

vv. 19–20; the proposal of a song-contest, as a means of resolving tension after a quarrelling scene, has its parallels in both the fifth Theocritean idyll and the third Vergilian eclogue, i.e., the main intertexts of the present Calpurnian poem[42], Theocr. 5.20 ff., Verg. *Ecl.* 3.25 ff, see also [Theocr.] 8.6–11. However, in this first part of the quarrel, i.e., before the ecphrases of the two stakes, there are no reproaches of thievery or unseemly sexual behaviour, which constitute, along with allegations of musical incompetence, the main focus of the bickering scenes in the Theocritean and Vergilian model. Lycidas simply insinuates that another pastoral figure, Lycotas, absent during the action of the eclogue, could also bring several censures against Astylus (vv. 25–6).

The Calpurnian instance seems, nevertheless, to be closer to the Vergilian intertext, as in both cases the ἀγών is proposed immediately after and as a result of accusations of musical incompetence, (cf. also the similarity in the wording of the song-exchange proposal, v. 19: *vis igitur...* = Verg. *Ecl.* 3.28 f.: *vis ergo...*)[43]. Thus in the Vergilian model, Menalcas doubts Damoetas' ability to defeat Damon in singing and, what is more, he charges his interlocutor with lack of musical expertise, when 'murder(ing) a sorry tune on a scrannel straw' (v. 27: *stridenti miserum stipula disperdere carmen*, – transl. by Fairclough–Goold 1999, 39; see also Chapter 4, p. 141)[44]. A parallel situation is developed in [Theocr.] 8.6–10, where Menalcas and Daphnis also appear extremely confident of their singing and piping abilities and convinced of their eventual victory over their contender. These claims of musical superiority, crucially not followed by explicit doubting of the opponent's musical skill as in the present eclogue, also lead up to the proposal of a singing match (vv. 11–2). The wording of the exhortation for the beginning of the match, with which this typical pastoral scenario normally ends, seems, once again, to suggest different 'generic trends' in this Calpurnian

---

[42] Cf. especially Friedrich 1976, 118 in particular; see also Cesareo 1931, 90, Effe-Binder 1989, 120–2 (for the Vergilian model of *Ecl.* 3), Vinchesi 1996, 41; 2008, 544; 2014, 436–7, Simon 2007b, 60, Becker 2012, 32–9, 123.

[43] Cf. also Korzeniewski 1971, 61, Friedrich 1976, 118, 228 and n. 11, Di Lorenzo–Pellegrino 2008, 258, Vinchesi 2008, 547; 2014, 445, Becker 2012, 123.

[44] Mutual accusations, on the part of both interlocutors, regarding their alleged lack of musical skill continue in vv. 19 ff. as well; hence Astylus' remarks as to Lycidas' 'dry throat' (v. 23: *aride*, crucially a *terminus technicus* of rhetorical / stylistic jargon, cf. Cic. *de Or.* 2.38.159, *R.H.* 4.16, Korzeniewski 1971, 107, Leach 1975, 229 and n. 35, Di Lorenzo–Pellegrino 2008, 24, Becker 2012, 124, Vinchesi 2014, 446), 'dribbling notes' (vv. 23–4: *qui vix stillantes...voces rumpis*) and 'squirting words forth in miserable gaps' (v. 24: *expellis male singultantia verba*) – (transl. by Duff and Duff 1934, 271) as well as his ironic doubts as to his opponent's ability to defeat anybody (v. 22: *vincere tu quemquam?*) come as a response to Lycidas' earlier ironical accusations of Astylus for musical incompetence (v. 19: *quoniam nec nobis, improbe, par es*).

case. *Conferre manum* (v. 21) is a common syntagm in the Vergilian epic (cf. Verg. *A*. 9.44, 690, 10.876, 12.345, 480, 678[45]) and has the meaning of 'to come to blows' (cf. OLD s.v. 15c), thus suggesting physical confrontation, alien to the norms of traditional, pre-Calpurnian pastoral. Lycidas' epicising challenge results in the equally epicising reaction of Astylus, as the syntagm *voces rumpere* (vv. 23–4) is also a Vergilian epic combination (cf. Verg. *A*. 2.129, 3.246, 11.377[46]).

By means of two further allusions to the intertext of the third Vergilian eclogue (cf. v. 28: *ecce venit Mnasyllus* = Verg. *Ecl*. 3.50: *vel qui venit ecce Palaemon*, v. 28: *nisi forte recusas* = Verg. *Ecl*. 3.29: *ne forte recuses*[47]), an umpire is introduced, again in the line of the Vergilian intertext, i.e., before the setting of the match location and not after, as in the case of Theocr. 5[48]. The referee is, furthermore, presented as the adventitious bystander, according to the traditional pastoral *topos* of the 'fortuitous, passer-by / bystander arbiter' (cf. also Theocr. 5.65, [Theocr.] 8.25–7, Verg. *Ecl*. 3.50–1[49]), and as also possessing the time-honoured quality of the impartial judge (v. 29: *arbiter inflatis non credulus…verbis*, cf. also Theocr. 5.68–71). What is more, in the line of the chief Theocritean intertext, i.e., Theocr. 5, Mnasyllus is in Calp. 6 presented as the eventual umpire, although another pastoral figure has been earlier proposed as the arbiter of the singing match; thus Lycidas is so confident of his victory over Astylus[50] that he does not hesitate to recommend Alcon as the pastoral judge (v. 21: *veniat licet arbiter Alcon*), i.e., the victorious singer of the reported singing match, at the beginning of the eclogue, on Astylus' verdict. Likewise, in Theocr. 5.60–5, Morson is finally chosen, although Lycopas has also been previously nominated as a ref. These long-established pastoral habits yet again are immediately followed by certain practices, once more moving away from the traditional earlier pastoral norm, namely the pledging of *pignora*.

---

[45] Cf. also Verdière 1954, 259, Korzeniewski 1971, 61, Di Lorenzo-Pellegrino 2008, 258, Becker 2012, 124, Vinchesi 2014, 445.
[46] Cf. Di Lorenzo-Pellegrino 2008, 259, Vinchesi 2014, 446.
[47] Cf. also Verdière 1954, 260, Korzeniewski 1971, 61, Messina 1975, 35, Friedrich 1976, 119, Gagliardi 1981, 40 and n. 14; 1984, 34 and n. 22, Schäfer 2001, 151, Di Lorenzo-Pellegrino 2008, 259–60, Vinchesi 2008, 549; 2014, 448.
[48] Cf. also Friedrich 1976, 118.
[49] See also Gibson 2004, 10, Becker 2012, 125–6.
[50] Cf. also Pearce 1990, 131.

The Stakes and their Ecphrases

What follows is the setting of the stakes, yet another opportunity for Calpurnius to expand a traditional bucolic motif by incorporating 'innovative generic features'. With the exception of the programmatic first Theocritean idyll and its κισσύβιον (vv. 27–56), where the images depicted also suggest the interrelation of the 'green cabinet' and its poetry with the wider world (cf. above, pp. 105–7, 197), in all previous song-exchanges the description of the stakes, when it exceeds a mere mention (cf. Theocr. 5.21, 24, 30, [Theocr.] 8.14–5, Verg. *Ecl.* 3.48), takes up much less narrative space than in the present eclogue[51]. In Calpurnius it occupies 27 out of 93 lines altogether; see, on the other hand, [Theocr.] 8.18–24 (pastoral flutes), Verg. *Ecl.* 3.29–31 (a cow coming twice a day to the milking-bucket). The ecphrasis of a pledge is also found in the case of Alcimedon's cups in the third Vergilian eclogue, where, however, it takes up only 11 lines (vv. 36–47) out of the 111 that make up the eclogue's narrative. Thus in the present Calpurnian poem there occur two ecphrastic pieces of the kind mostly associated with the epic or the epylliac *genus*; hence both ecphrases suggest a 'generic re-orientation' of Calpurnian bucolics chiefly towards the *genus grande* and further re-affirm the 'generic versatility' of Neronian pastoral poetics.

The epic colouring of the two pledges is further underscored by the epic intertexts they refer to: Astylus bets a stag dear to his beloved, Petale, v. 34: *quamvis hunc Petale mea diligat*. The deer, as a bucolic love-token / a pet for a sweetheart's pleasure, has its pastoral precedent in the eleventh Theocritean idyll, Theocr. 11.40–1[52], as part of the Cyclops' rhetoric to win over his beloved Galatea; elsewhere in pastoral the *cervus* is presented as a hunting animal / game, cf. Verg. *Ecl.* 2.29, 7.30[53] or is part of an *adynaton*-formulation (cf. Theocr. 1.135, Verg. *Ecl.* 1.59, 5.60)[54]. Despite its Theocritean counterpart, albeit of a rather 'generically deviant' idyll (cf. above, p. 226), Calpurnius' deer intertextually alludes to two epic texts, Verg. *A.* 7.483 ff. and especially Ov. *Met.* 10.110 ff.[55], i.e., to Silvia's pet,

---

51 See also Simon 2007b, 63.
52 Cf. Messina 1975, 36, Courtney 1987, 155, Keene 1996, 138, Vinchesi 1996, 141; 2014, 449, Simon 2007b, 64 and n. 22, Becker 2012, 129.
53 Cf. Friedrich 1976, 120.
54 The last case is about an *adynaton* that becomes feasible as a sign of the Golden Age after Daphnis' apotheosis; cf. also Davis 1987, 52 and n. 32.
55 Cf. Lenchantin de Gubernatis 1912, 87, Verdière 1954, 260–1; 1966, 172; 1993, 394–5, Korzeniewski 1971, 61, Messina 1975, 35–6, Friedrich 1976, 121, Bömer 1980, 54–5, 57, Effe-Binder 1989, 123, Kegel-Brinkgreve 1990, 161, Amat 1991, xl–xli, 117, Beato 1995, 624, Vinchesi 1996, 42; 2008, 550; 2014, 450, Keene 1996, 136–7, Schäfer 2001, 151 and n. 38, Gibson 2004, 10, Simon 2007b, 64–6, Di Lorenzo-Pellegrino 2008, 260, Becker

a stag accidentally shot by Ascanius, and to Cyparissus story in Ovid's *Metamorphoses*, also modelled on the *Aeneid* incident[56]; note that the two literary episodes are associated with each other and presented together by Martial as well (cf. Mart. 13.96[57]). In this Ovidian case, a stag, very dear to Cyparissus, is accidentally killed by the young boy, who is metamorphosed, because of his constant weeping, into the funeral tree cypress (cf. especially the similarity between Calpurnius' stag and the two models even in the phrasing of the following lines: v. 35 = Ov. *Met.* 10.118–9, 125, v. 36 = Verg. *A.* 7.490, v. 38 = Ov. *Met.* 10.113, v. 41 = Ov. *Met.* 10.114–5, vv. 42–3 = Verg. *A.* 7.488, Ov. *Met.* 10.123[58]). Both intertexts derive of course from epic texts, and the epic colouring is further underlined by the *clausula cingula bullas* (v. 41) in the description of Astylus' stag, which is drawn from Verg. *A.* 12.942[59]; the pastoral pet is thus associated with Pallas' belt, a crucial epic accessory and emblem. Similarly the *iunctura (non) improba...ora* (v. 36) harks back to Verg. *A.* 10.727–8 (namely to the greedy mouth of a ravening lion to which Mezentius is compared, in terms of an epic simile[60]). These allusions may suggest once again the occasional 'generic re-orientation' of Calpurnian pastoral poetics towards the *genus grande*. Most importantly, however, the two main intertexts (Silvia's pet, Cyparissus story) capitalise on the 'generic interaction' between epic and pastoral, as seems also to be the case with the present Calpurnian narrative or with Calpurnian pastoral in general, especially in the so-called political eclogues, where the 'generic interplay' between pastoral as a host-text and modal intrusions of the *genus grande* looms large (1, 4, 7)[61].

It has long been pointed out that in the *Aeneid* episode the transition from tranquility, prior to the Trojans' arrival, to war between Trojans and Rutulians following the loss of the stag, can be viewed as a 'generic transposition' from

---

2012, 39–45, 127. For a possible influence of Hor. *Carm.* 4.2.57–60 on v. 45, see Verdière 1954, 261; 1966, 172 and n. 75, Amat 1991, 117, Di Lorenzo-Pellegrino 2008, 262; nonetheless, for a convincing refutation of this view, cf. Friedrich 1976, 228 and n. 16, who plausibly claims that Calpurnius might have been influenced here by the common motif of *luna lunaticus* (cf. Verg. *A.* 1.490, Iuv. 7.192, Mart. 1.49.31).

[56] Cf. also Solodow 1988, 83, Connors 1992, 8, 12 and n. 17, Smith 1997, 115–20, Fordyce 2001, 147, Fantham 2004, 77, Simon 2007a, 168–9.

[57] Cf. Vinchesi 2014, 450.

[58] Cf. also Di Lorenzo-Pellegrino 2008, 260–2, Becker 2012, 128–9, Vinchesi 2014, 450–3.

[59] Cf. Verdière 1954, 195, Korzeniewski 1971, 62, Di Lorenzo-Pellegrino 2008, 261, Becker 2012, 129, Vinchesi 2014, 452.

[60] Cf. Novelli 1980, 81.

[61] Cf. e.g. Hubbard 1998, 158–63, Vozza 1993, 299 and n. 38; 1994, 85–6.

the bucolic, and to some extent from the georgic, to the epic code / mode[62]. Thus Alecto is presented as calling the farmers to arms using her trumpeter, crucially described as *pastorale signum* (7.513), while nature's response to the trumpet call significantly results in a parody of a traditional 'generic marker' of pastoral, the bucolic echo (7.514–8). The narrative setting is nothing else but a *locus amoenus* of the pastoral tradition (cf. above, pp. 8, 48–50, 69, 76, 86, 88, 98, 101 and n. 58, 117, 126, 129, 215)[63], while the image of the empathetic reaction of nature to human emotions (cf. vv. 7.483–510)[64] constitutes a further 'generic essential' of pastoral, namely the pathetic fallacy, συμπάθεια τῶν ὅλων-motif (cf. above, pp. 8, 65, 88, 196, 198). Furthermore, the picture of ploughs and reaping hooks giving way to swords (vv. 7.635–6) complements the process of the 'generic shift' suggested above, this time from the georgics (cf. Verg. *G.* 1.506–8) to the epic genre. Cyparissus' episode in the Ovidian epic narrative also relies on the 'generic dialogue' between bucolic and epic. The story is about a pastoral narrative set on a green field on a hill (a conventional bucolic landscape), comprising several formal typical constituents of the bucolic *genus* (the omnipresent pastoral shade, the noonday heat, the orphic syndrome, etc.), intermingled with markers of the epic genre, as for example the epic catalogue of the trees offering Orpheus their shadow to sing about the transferring of his love to tender boys, epic compounds in *–cola* (v. 96: *amnicolae*), or in *–pes* (v. 99: *flexipedes*)[65], etc.

---

[62] Cf. especially Hardie 1998, 61; see also Williams 1973, 202–3, Vance 1981, 133, Connors 1992, 11–2, Putnam 1995, 118–9, 125–6; 1995a, 125.
[63] Cf. Smith 1997, 115–6.
[64] Cf. Putnam 1995a, 125.
[65] Cf. Anderson 1972, 482–3. For the Ovidian Cyparissus–narrative as a further text generating 'generic tensions', namely a 'generic interplay' between epic and non-epic poetry, cf. especially Connors 1992, 10–2. In particular, Connors (*op. cit.*) detects in Apollo's admonition to Cyparisssus, v. 133: *ut...leviter pro materiaque doloret*, a meta-poetic dimension, chiefly based on the meta-linguistic / poetological semantic load of both *leviter* and *materia* = poetry. Thus the divine request may also be read as an instigation for Cyparissus to denounce any epic harshness (cf. also Ov. *Met.* 10.150ff.) for the sake of something 'lighter' in 'generic terms'. For Phoebus the story of Cyparissus' grief is 'light' enough and thus inappropriate for a rigid traditional epic norm. Similar 'generic tensions' seem to be generated by the *clausula redimicula collo* (v. 38), probably alluding to Ov. *Epist.* 9.71–2: *detrahat Antaeus duro redimicula collo, / ne pigeat molli succubuisse viro* (cf. Korzeniewski 1971, 62, Vinchesi 2014, 451; one should note here the contradiction between *durus* and *mollis*, namely terms also having 'generic undertones', denoting the *genus grande* and the *genus tenue* respectively); despite being part of the elegiac epistle by Deianira to Hercules, depicted as a common, cruel elegiac lover, the intertextual Ovidian lines also refer to the rather epic confrontation between Antaeus and Hercules; cf. Luc. 4.589–660.

Lycidas, on the other hand, pledges (v. 50: *ponam*[66]) a distinct epic animal, a horse, not occurring anywhere in previous pastoral[67] and often functioning as a meta–poetic symbolism of the epic *genus grande*, cf. Prop. 3.3.39–40: *contentus niveis semper vectabere cycnis, / nec te fortis equi ducet ad arma sonus*. The sense of the non–bucolic afforded by this animal, here pledged for his epic agility and fierce character (thus the name Petasos probably from πέτομαι[68], though in accordance with the earlier pastoral ethos to name animals, cf. Theocr. 4.45–6, Λέπαργος, Κυμαίθα, 5.102, Κώναρος, Κιναίθα[69]), is reinforced by the horse's description with wording drawn from Vergil's *Georgics* (for vv. 53–4, cf. *G.* 3.56–7, 72ff., especially 79–80, 88)[70]. This interaction of pastoral with epic is further underscored by the intertexts to which the last two images of the ecphrasis allude. V. 56: *viridi sic exsultavit in arvo* refers to Ov. *Met.* 2.864: *viridique exsultat in herba*[71], i.e., to 'epic' hexameters 'hosting' a quite 'bucolic' story, dramatised in an Arcadian setting, as evidenced by characteristically bucolic imagery including herds grazing on mountain pastures, the bucolic *topos* of 'driving the flock', the omnipresent pastoral tender grass, the depiction of a *puella* gathering flora through the meadows and adorning a bull with her flowers (Europa), thus suggesting the traditional pastoral 'generic prerequisite' of nature's friendly relation to man (cf. above, pp. 59, 98). What is more, the Ovidian account seems to be

---

66 See also the very same verb used of the stakes in Verg. *Ecl.* 3.36: *pocula ponan* as well; cf. also Pearce 1990, 132, Keene 1996, 139.

67 Cf. also Cesareo 1931, 85 and n. 1, Leach 1975, 221, Friedrich 1976, 121, Davis 1987, 38, Keene 1996, 138, Vinchesi 1996, 42; 2008, 551, Simon 2007b, 60, Di Lorenzo–Pellegrino 2008, 262; see also Rosenmeyer 1969, 164. In Verg. *Ecl.* 5.26, *quadrupes* does not seem to be used with its specific meaning 'horse', as frequently in Vergilian epic; the reading 'horse' is supported, if one traces here an allusion to (Suet. *Iul.* 81.2) the reaction of Caesar's horses to his demise, i.e., their refusal at Rubicon to eat before their master's death. The word, however, also denotes 'animals' in general (cf. Ter. *Andr.* 865) and, thus, appears to be simply used, in the Vergilian eclogue in question, of the animals, in general, mourning over Daphnis' death.

68 Cf. also Korzeniewski 1971, 107, Amat 1991, 117, Keene 1996, 139, Vinchesi 1996, 143; 2014, 455, Becker 2012, 132. Merkelbach 1983, 71, on the other hand, unnecessarily emends to *Petasan*.

69 Cf. also Friedrich 1976, 121, Becker 2012, 132.

70 Cf. Verdière 1954, 196, Paladini 1956, 524, Korzeniewski 1971, 63, Friedrich 1976, 121, Keene 1996, 139, Di Lorenzo–Pellegrino 2008, 22, 263–4, Becker 2012, 131. Paladini 1956, 333 and Di Lorenzo–Pellegrino 2008, 16, not so convincingly, detect in Calpurnius' use of the horse-motif an influence of Tib. 2.1.67–8.

71 Cf. also Bömer 1969, 439, Korzeniewski 1971, 63, Di Lorenzo–Pellegrino 2008, 23, 264, Becker 2012, 133, Vinchesi 2014, 457. In the case of Astylus' pet as well, the *clausula porrigit ora* (v. 36) also alludes to the Ovidian story of Europa (*Met.* 2.861; cf. Korzeniewski 1971, 61–2, Vinchesi 2014, 450) with similar 'generic implications' for the hosting Calpurnian passage.

modelled on Moschus' epyllion Εὐρώπη[72]; the interaction between the epylliac norm and the bucolic plot in Moschus' oeuvre, i.e., in a work, not formally belonging to the bucolic genre, written by a well-known bucolic poet (cf. p. 226), further highlights the 'generic tension' operating in the Ovidian and ultimately the Calpurnian narrative.

The image of Petasos, strutting across the green corn land so lightly as to only touch and not curve the slim blades (vv. 56–7), evokes, on the other hand, the clearly epic image of Camilla on her horse flying over the corn without treading on the ears (Verg. A. 7.808–9)[73], lines further calling to mind another epic reminiscence, Il. 20.226 ff., i.e., the description of Erichthonius' magic horses[74]. The epic undertones of the passage are emphasised by the *clausula ungula cornu* (v. 55), alluding to Verg. G. 3.87–8[75]; crucially, the Vergilian line harks back even further, in terms of rhythm as well, to an epic Ennian line, Enn. Ann. 263 Skutsch: *summo sonitu quatit ungula terram*[76]. On the meta-poetic level, note here the copiousness of meta-linguistic terms – catch-words suggesting Callimachean-Neoteric sensibilities and poetological aspirations (cf. *candida* – v. 33, *tereti* – v. 38, *subtiles, molles* – v. 42, *teneris* – v. 52, *fragiles* – v. 57), but within a narrative setting indicative of a 'generic dialogue' between pastoral as a host-text and epic as a modal intrusion. The presence of the Neoteric meta-language of the *genus tenue*, complementing as it does ecphrastic depictions of noticeably epic colouring, is a further indication not only of the looser usage of the Neoteric meta-poetic discourse in Calpurnian pastoral as opposed to Vergilian bucolics, but also of the very 'generic polyphony' operating in Calpurnian pastoral as a general rule.

The Location of the Singing Match

Yet another motif of pastoral origin appears later on, when the herdsmen choose the location where the singing match will take place. As in Theocr. 5.31 ff. and

---

[72] Cf. Otis 1970, 395–6.
[73] Cf. Cesareo 1931, 87, Verdière 1954, 197, Paladini 1956, 524, Korzeniewski 1971, 63, Messina 1975, 37, Friedrich 1976, 121, 229 and n. 18, Gagliardi 1981, 42 and n. 19, Keene 1996, 139, Di Lorenzo-Pellegrino 2008, 264, Vinchesi 2008, 552; 2014, 457, Becker 2012, 134.
[74] Cf. Fordyce 2001, 203; see also Vinchesi 1996, 143; 2014, 457, Simon 2007b, 66 and n. 28, Becker 2012, 134.
[75] Cf. Di Lorenzo-Pellegrino 2008, 264, Vinchesi 2014, 457.
[76] Cf. Thomas 1988, 2.54–5.

Verg. *Ecl.* 5.1 ff.[77], alternative options are available (cf. also above, p. 19 on Calp 1. 5–9): Mnasyllus, the arbiter, proposes a couch under a traditional pastoral tree, the ilex (vv. 60–1: *istic / protinus ecce torum fecere sub ilice Musae*), although in the Calpurnian case, where a bucolic piece is also expected, it is a couch made by the Muses and not by the pastoral Nymphs, the patronesses of bucolic song in the previous pastoral tradition. This could of course be attributed to Calpurnius' 'zooming out' / 'telescoping' of previous pastoral poetry, to his inattention to such points of detail. On the other hand, if one takes into account the important 'generic position' of the Nymphs within the traditional pastoral pantheon as the par excellence inspiring deities and the 'generic tensions' that the appearance of deities not belonging to the 'generic pastoral pantheon' may cause from Theocritean pastoral onwards[78] (ultimately affecting the 'generic outlook' of a pastoral performance; see also above, pp. 60–1, 136, 202–4), this substitution of the Nymphs by the Muses in the Calpurnian eclogue may also indicate a sort of estrangement of Mnasyllus himself from the previous literary norms of pastoral, to a lesser degree of course than this 'generic rift' is observed in the case of the two contestants. Finally it is the caves, the neighbouring crags that are chosen as the setting of the song–exchange, a detail that brings the Calpurnian instance closer to the intertext of Verg. *Ecl.* 5, where a cave is similarly chosen for the song–exchange between Mopsus and Menalcas[79]. Interestingly, this happens at Lycidas' instigation (v. 66: *si placet, antra magis vicinaque saxa petemus*), who seems to agree with Astylus' desire, unprecedented in the corpus of Greek and Roman earlier pastoral, to distance themselves from natural sounds perceived, as often in Calpurnian pastoral (cf. above, pp. 10, 48–9, 59 and n. 59, 71, 73, 86, 93, 118, 186, 200, 215), as disturbing and disagreeable.

Whereas the patterning of the alternative localities follows the 'generic norms' of earlier pastoral, the rejection of basic, long–established 'generic fea-

---

[77] Cf. Korzeniewski 1971, 107, Schäfer 2001, 152; see also Vinchesi 2008, 553; 2014, 459, Becker 2012, 134–5.

[78] In Theocritus, for example, invocations to Jupiter –not a member of the pastoral pantheon– are significantly uttered by pastoral figures atypical of the bucolic genre, as is Battus of the fourth idyll (4.50) characterised by his paratragic language, Lacon in the fifth idyll (5.74), the contestant who eventually loses in the song–contest of the poem, and, finally, the Cyclops in 11.29, i.e., a character of a 'generically dubious' idyll (cf. also above, p. 226). Alterations to the norm of the bucolic pantheon thus seem often to generate further 'generic meaning', cf. also Fantuzzi–Hunter 2004, 153–7, Chapter 2, pp. 67–8.

[79] Cf. also Friedrich 1976, 120. A final acknowledgment, on the part of one of the pastoral figures, of both the location chosen for song–exchange and the eventual arrival to the place opted for further brings closer Calp. 6 to its main intertext, Verg. *Ecl.* 5, cf. Calp. 6.70: *venimus et tacito sonitum mutavimus antro* = Verg. *Ecl.* 5.19: *successimus antro*, Schäfer 2001, 152.

tures' of the pastoral *locus amoenus* expressed in the present passage largely makes it differ from its intertexts: in both Greek and Roman pastoral, as already remarked (see above, p. 240), natural sounds in general and the babble of the flowing water in particular (cf. Theocr. 1.7–8, Verg. *Ecl.* 5.84) constitute a formative component of an idyllic setting; here they are presented as impeding the quality of pastoral singing, cf. Astylus' negative remarks concerning the sound of the river drowning their music and the gravel of the gurgling stream ruining the pastoral song (v. 62: *ne vicini nobis sonus obstrepat amnis*, v. 65: *obest arguti glarea rivi*). Even the bucolic echo is negatively depicted by means of the image of the water hoarsely echoing Astylus (vv. 64–5: *sub exeso raucum mihi pumice lymphae / respondent*). What is more, the syntagm *exeso...pumice* (v. 64) also calls to mind Ov. *Fast.* 4.495: *est specus exesi structura pumicis asper*[80], where a *locus horridus*, Ceres' volcanic cave with her serpents, is described; the very *locus amoenus* of the pastoral tradition, full of natural noises, is therefore here intertextually presented as a ghastly location, corresponding to the aesthetic preferences of the period (see also above, pp. 99, 126).

Mnasyllus at the end acknowledges that noise has been exchanged for the silent cave (v. 70: *venimus et tacito sonitum mutavimus antro*)[81]. The very preference for silence, however, produces further 'generic meaning' with respect to the interaction of Calpurnian poetics with contemporary politics and urban / non-rustic qualities and sensibilities. As already remarked (cf. pp. 35, 50–1, 93, 108), silence has, in earlier Vergilian bucolic, quite ominous associations and is clearly viewed, in the ninth eclogue, as a side-effect, a symptom of the destructive (from a 'generic point of view' as well) intrusion of history and politics into the apolitical milieu of Greek pastoral[82]. The silence-motif, associated in Vergil with a sense of 'pastoral dislocation', Moeris' faulty memory and his deviation from everyday practices of the 'green cabinet', as a result of politics imposing upon literature (cf. vv. 37–8: *id quidem ago et tacitus, Lycida, mecum ipse voluto, / si valeam meminisse*), is however the preferred alternative in Calpurnian pastoral, which is clearly 'generically re-oriented' towards city values and political practices, especially, but by no means exclusively, in the programmatic pieces (Calp. 1, 4, 7).

The 'generic profile' of the cave, eventually chosen by the pastoral figures of the eclogue, is also indicative of the 'generic re-orientation' of Calpurnian poetics away from traditional pre-Calpurnian bucolics, occasionally towards dis-

---

[80] Cf. Korzeniewski 1971, 63–5, Di Lorenzo-Pellegrino 2008, 265, Vinchesi 2014, 460.
[81] Cf. also Kegel-Brinkgreve 1990, 161, Pearce 1990, 133, Gibson 2004, 10, 14 and n. 32, Chinnici 2009, 134–5, Baraz 2015, 111–3; see also later Nemes. 1.1–2, 30–1.
[82] Cf. also Karakasis 2011, 199.

courses of the *genus grande*. The overhanging rocks of the Calpurnian cave (vv. 68–9) call to mind epic caves, similar epic locations, in particular the abode of epic Nymphs of Verg. *A.* 1.166–8[83]. Moreover, v. 67: *saxa, quibus viridis stillanti vellere musco*s alludes to a similar phrase in Lucr. 5.951: *umida saxa, super viridi stillantia musco*[84]; this line, which belongs to a passage where a forest spring is described (5.948–52), is part, however, of a larger narrative segment, where, in terms of the Lucretian history of early civilisation and human life (5.925–1010), traditional ideas and figures of the pastoral 'generic repertoire', such as Golden Age beliefs, deified Nymphs, etc., are rationalised or even undermined. In the Lucretian lines in question specifically, Lucretius rationalises Naiads and Dryads up to a point identifying them with simple woodland springs[85]. Such an undermining of traditional pastoral assets may also be read as a sign of Calpurnius' 'generically diversifying poetics'.

In vv. 70 ff., i.e., when the place of the song–exchange has finally been agreed upon, Mnasyllus takes up his traditional role as the passer-by pastoral umpire and advises the contestants to stop their squabbling (v. 73: *seposita... lite*), thus giving the signal for the commencement of the singing match (v. 73: *nunc mihi...reddantur carmina*). He also recommends the type of the song–exchange and the alternating order of performance: Astylus will sing first followed by Lycidas (v. 75, cf. [Theocr.] 9.1–2, 5–6, Verg. *Ecl.* 3.55–9, *Eins.* 1.19–21). Finally he proposes the song–topics, namely pastoral love (v. 74: *teneros...amores*) with Astylus singing the praises of Petale and Lycidas those of Phyllis (v. 75: *Astyle, tu Petalen, Lycida, tu Phyllida lauda*); *teneros* here might also suggest, as a metapoetic catch–word, the Callimachean–Neoteric character of the song (cf. Ov. *Trist.* 2.1.361, 4.10.1[86]) that Mnasyllus, as a representative of traditional pastoral poetics, expects.

As a marker of Mnasyllus' Neoteric poetological aspirations, one should also mention his earlier use of a major Neoteric meta–linguistic term, *vacat*, when offering himself as the judge of the match (*et vacat et vestros cantus audire iuvabit*, v. 59). The verb may be translated 'I am at leisure', but at the same time evokes the Neoteric situation of the *vacuus* and his *otium poeticum* (cf. above, pp. 90–1,

---

[83] Cf. Verdière 1954, 261, Korzeniewski 1971, 65, Amat 1991, 118, Di Lorenzo–Pellegrino 2008, 264–5, Vinchesi 2008, 555; 2014, 461.
[84] Cf. Korzeniewski 1971, 65, Di Lorenzo–Pellegrino 2008, 265, Vinchesi 2008, 555; 2014, 461.
[85] Cf. Gale 2009, 177, 180.
[86] Cf. Verdière 1954, 199, Korzeniewski 1971, 65, Di Lorenzo–Pellegrino 2008, 266, Vinchesi 2014, 462–3.

131)⁸⁷. What is more, Mnasyllus also proposes the two standard pastoral postures while singing or piping, sitting on soft grass (v. 71: *seu residere libet, dabit ecce sedilia tophus*, cf. also Theocr. 1.12, 21, 5.31–2, 6.3–4, 8, 11.17, [Moschus] *E.B.* 21, Verg. *Ecl.* 3.55, 5.3, 7.1, 10.70–1⁸⁸; see also Calp. 4.3, Nemes. 1.32–3) or lying / reclining (v. 72: *ponere seu cubitum, melior viret herba tapetis*⁸⁹, cf. also Theocr. 7.88–9, Verg. *Ecl.* 1.1). In imitation of his predecessors, Lacon and Comatas in the fifth Theocritean idyll (vv. 66–73⁹⁰), Lycidas asks for the impartiality of the umpire, which the latter was generous enough to display when acting as a judge in an ἀγών between Astylus (in all probability the loser⁹¹) and Acanthis⁹²

---

87 For *vacuus* in Neoteric poetry, see e.g. Hor. *Carm.* 1.6.17 ff., *Epist.* 1.7.44–5, Ov. *Am.* 1.1.26, *Rem.* 752, *Met.* 1.520, Prop. 1.10.30.
88 Cf. also Clausen 1994, 34, 105.
89 Rivoltella 2006, 121–2 detects in v. 72 a contrast between the pastoral *herba* symbolising the modesty of the bucolic way of life on the one hand, and the rather epic symbolism of the τάπης on the other, standing for a more sumptuous life-style. What is more (cf. Rivoltella *op. cit.*, 121–3), this opposition constitutes an Epicurean / Lucretian reminiscence (cf. fr. 207 Usener, Lucr. 2.34–6), through the medium of the Vergilian *Georgics* (cf. *G.* 2.490–542); see also Vinchesi 2014, 462.
90 Cf. Becker 2012, 140, Vinchesi 2014, 463.
91 Since they are uttered by Lycidas, these lines may also be read as a nasty remark against Astylus, perfectly in line with the mutual spiteful comments both herdsmen exchange. Thus it might be guessed that Astylus was not the winner in this recounted singing match, a view corroborated by Astylus' irate reaction to the above comments of Lycidas, vv. 79 ff., cf. also Leach 1975, 221, Friedrich 1976, 229 and n. 20, Merkelbach 1983, 70, Gagliardi 1984, 36, Pearce 1990, 133, Amat 1991, 55, Keene 1996, 141, Vinchesi 1996, 41; 2008, 543; 2014, 463, Gibson 2004, 11, Di Lorenzo –Pellegrino 2008, 266.
92 *Acanthida* in v. 77 is a Greek accusative in -*a* of a male name Acanthis, used of a herdsman rivaling with Astylus in a song–contest with Mnasyllus as the referee, cf. Di Lorenzo–Pellegrino 2008, 266; see also Keene 1996, 141, Vinchesi 1996, 137; 2014, 464, Becker 2012, 141. For Herrmann as well 1952, 41 Acanthis is a male name, but a mask of A. Furius Rufus (cf. also Verdière 1954, 58). Other views include a) Acanthis, as a female name, i.e., a shepherdess or a dangerous witch on the basis of Prop. 4.5.61 (cf. Duff and Duff 1934, 276–7, Keene 1996, 141), b) a woman with whom Astylus had sexual intercourse in the woods, with Mnasyllus as a voyeur; the disclosure of Astylus' affair with Acanthis accounts for the herdsman's anger, who thus proves erotically unreliable, for he previously expressed his love for Petale only – a reading of these Calpurnian lines on the basis of Theocr. 4.58 ff. by White 1999, 150–1; for a criticism of this thesis, not taking into account the function of the *iudex*, cf. also Gibson 2004, 14 and n. 33, Becker 2012, 140–1, Vinchesi 2014, 464, c) acanthis, i.e., a goldfinch as in v. 7 (cf. Merkelbach 1983, 70; see also Friedrich 1976, 229 and n. 20), d) a poetess of the Neronian period or e) a work of Astylus bearing this title, presented by him to Mnasyllus for criticism (cf. Verdière 1954, 58–9; see also Amat 1991, 118), both quite imaginative speculations – see Friedrich 1976, 229 and n. 20. If *Acanthida* is read as a feminine proper name, in the sense of a shepherdess engaging in a song–contest with Astylus, then this constitutes a fur-

in the bucolic forests, i.e., in 'the wood in which contests in bucolic poetry are wont to take place' (vv. 76–8)[93]. The traditional immediate prerequisites of a bucolic ἀγών are thus all in place, with remarkable thoroughness: the ideal reader would naturally be expecting the contest to begin any minute now.

Bickering – Part Two

But it never does...What happens instead is a second round of bickering[94], for Lycidas, according to his opponent, due to his reminiscence of Astylus' earlier defeat in an agonistic song-exchange, is looking for nothing else but a quarrel (*nihil nisi iurgia quaerit*, v. 80). *Iurgia* of course constitute along with *amores* and *laudes* the traditional topics of a song-exchange, as evidenced e.g. by the fifth Vergilian eclogue, where it is proposed by the elder shepherd, Menalcas, as a topic for Mopsus' song (vv. 10–11): *Phyllidis ignes, Alconis laudes, iurgia Codri*. However, in the present poem *iurgia* do not become a song-topic, do not function as quoted song, but instead inhibit the song-production itself. Astylus threatens Lycidas that he will make his evil deeds public (vv. 82–3) and Lycidas retorts with accusations of unseemly sexual behaviour[95]. Accusations of this

---

ther formalistic alteration of Calpurnian bucolics in relation to the earlier tradition of pastoral singing matches; namely a song-contest between a male and a female character as a foil to the 'generically standardised' amoebaean βουκολιασμός between two male herdsmen. But this, according to Friedrich 1976, 229 and n. 20: 'wäre sehr ungewöhnlich'.

93 Keene 1996, 142; see also Amat 1991, 118. I understand *Thalea* in v. 78 as an adjective (cf. also Vinchesi 1996, 145; 2008, 556, Di Lorenzo-Pellegrino 2008, 266, Becker 2012, 141) in the sense of 'bucolic', as Thale/ia is the Muse presiding over both comedy and pastoral poetry; for other views, i.e., a) Thalea as equivalent to 'Sicilian', because of the homonymous Nymph of Sicily (cf. Macrob. *Sat.* 5.19), or associated with the mystic boughs of *Ciris* 376, b) as a nominative complement of *iudex*, 'a very Muse of pastoral, a Thale/ia in your proficiency as umpire', c) as the Greek equivalent of the Latin *virens* (cf. Korzeniewski 1971, 108: *silva virens*), or d) as the name of the forest, cf. also Duff and Duff 1934, 276–7, Verdière 1954, 261–2, Díaz-Cíntora 1989, xxvi, Pearce 1990, 134, Keene 1996, 141–2, Di Lorenzo-Pellegrino 2008, 266–7. For Thalea as the judge of a song-contest between Astylus and a goldfinch, with Astylus as the loser, cf. Merkelbach 1983, 70, who, however, makes the unnecessary emendation of *diceris* to *dicitur*. Without any textual evidence whatsoever, Merkelbach (*op. cit.*) further claims that *acanthis* was declared winner of the singing match on the verdict of Thalea, despite Astylus' earlier courting of the female umpire.

94 Cf. also Grant 1965, 72.

95 Cf. also Correa 1977, 154; vs. Merkelbach 1983, 70 assigning vv. 84–6 (83–5 according to Merkelbach's line numbering) to Astylus and not to Lycidas. He also assigns vv. 87–8 (86–7 – according to his line numeration, cf. *loc. cit.*) to Lycidas and not to Astylus, once again against the *communis opinio*.

kind form part of the quarrel scenes in both intertexts, Theocr. 5 and Verg. *Ecl.* 3, but in these models the charges occur before the setting of the pledges and the exhortations for the singing to start. Calpurnius thus splits up the accusations framing an amoebaean βουκολιασμός, as known by earlier bucolic texts, in two segments and incorporates customary sexual allegations only in the second part of the introductory narrative, which would normally lead to the song–exchange. Lycidas hence tries to undermine his rival by bringing forward his alleged homosexuality / bisexuality[96]; he accuses Astylus of simulating the kisses of an adult man with the youthful Mopsus, crucially described as *tener*, i.e., more probably 'effeminate' (cf. also Cic. *Pis.* 89, Iuv. 12.39, OLD s.v. 7[97]) and not simply 'of tender age' – v. 86: *oscula cum tenero simulare virilia Mopso*, in order to conceal their sexual affair; the incident that took place in the shrubbery made the onlookers Stimicon and Aegon silently laugh at Astylus (vv. 84–6). At this point then, Astylus' pledge seems significant as to his bisexuality hereby (vv. 84–6) revealed. On the basis of the Calpurnian text (v. 34), Astylus' stag is a pet dear to Petale, namely Astylus' beloved in a heterosexual affair; yet the intertext of this deer, Cyparissus' *cervus*, is, on the other hand, associated with a homosexual affair, recounted as part of Orpheus' 'transferring love to tender young males'[98], Ov. *Met.* 10.83–4: *amorem / in teneros transferre mares*. Thus Astylus' eventual bisexuality may be read as already anticipated by the homosexual undertones of Petale's cherished stag[99].

However, bisexuality constitutes one of the basic characteristics of the 'green cabinet', and often functions as a marker of its 'generic identity'. A pastoral figure may, and frequently does, enjoy sexual intercourse with both sexes, expressing his feelings for or boasting of his successes with both men and women, cf. Thyrsis' reference to both a she – Phyllis and a he – Lycidas in the seventh Vergilian eclogue (vv. 59, 67). The same applies to instances of pastoral homosexuality, which is by no means disapprovingly portrayed; in the fourth Theocritean idyll, for example, Aegon is presented as having followed the athlete Milon, most probably his lover, to the Olympic games, whereas in the programmatic *Thalysia* the archetypical pastoral / poetic figure, Lycidas, sings a *propemptikon* for his beloved, Ageanax, while his opponent, the urban Simichidas, sings the

---

96 Cf. also Becker 2012, 143.
97 Cf. also Korzeniewski 1971, 108: 'unmännlich'; see also Becker 2012, 143, Vinchesi 2014, 465–6.
98 Translated by Anderson 1972, 482.
99 See also Leach 1975, 229 and n. 36.

love of his friend, Aratus, for a boy, Philinus[100]. Similarly, Bion fr. 12 recounts the homosexual love of the following male pairs: Theseus and Pirithous, Orestes and Pylades, Achilles and Patroclus[101]. Analogous themes are to be found in Vergil's eclogues as well, cf. especially Corydon's homoerotic love for Alexis, in his turn Iollas' darling, and its prominent place in the narrative of the eclogue (cf. also Verg. *Ecl.* 10.37–40[102]). In this perspective, the negative attitude towards Astylus can be seen as a transgression of earlier pastoral ethical canons, since his erotic involvement with both a woman, Petale, for whom he has previously expressed his desire (vv. 9, 34), and a man, the youngster with whom he allegedly imitated the kisses of an adult, should have had the approval of the pastoral community. In other words, according to the ethics of the 'green cabinet' as known from Theocritean, post–Theocritean and Vergilian bucolics, there was no reason either for Astylus to conceal his sexual liaison with a younger male lover or for the bystanders to make fun of a perfectly normal liaison; unless what they are laughing at is Astylus' distanciation from the values of the traditional pastoral world, i.e., the attempt at simulation and not the homosexual affair *per se*.

The negative depiction of homosexuality in previous pastoral is related to issues of sexual dominance / penetration, as evidenced by both Theocr. 5.41ff. (see also 116ff.) and Verg. *Ecl.* 3.8ff.[103]. Nonetheless, in the case of the fifth Theocritean idyll, as pointed out elsewhere (cf. Karakasis 2011, 96–7), it is not so much issues of sexual domination ('top' vs. 'bottom' sexuality) that are at stake, but rather the blameworthy, disrespectful attitude of a younger member towards an older pastoral figure within a παιδικά-type liaison. The link between Comatas and Lacon seems to be that of a pedagogue and a boy[104], since two basic requisites of this type of relationship are found in the bond under consideration, i.e., age difference and an educational relation, for Comatas was once Lacon's music teacher. Thus Comatas does not accuse his interlocutor of being less of a man because of his 'passive' sexual habits (as is the case in the third Vergilian eclogue to be discussed further down), but simply reminds him, although in quite unsophisticated terms, of the liaison that once existed between them, in view of which Lacon's bad-manners towards the older man are unjustifiable. Accusations relating to 'passive' homosexual preferences, as weakening a lover's masculinity and, what is more, viewed outside a pederastic relationship do appear, on the other hand, in the case of the third Vergilian eclogue, where

---

100 Cf. especially Effe 1992, 55–67; see also White 1999, 151.
101 Cf. also Reed 1997, 162, 175–6.
102 Cf. Becker 2012, 143–4.
103 Cf. also Verdière 1954, 199, Korzeniewski 1971, 108, Friedrich 1976, 119.
104 Cf. Prestagostini 1984, especially 138.

Damoetas accuses Menalcas of improper sexual orientation, i.e., of taking the 'female' part in homosexual intercourse. For his opponent, Menalcas is a 'passive' homosexual lover and consequently is blamed for not being a man, as Damoetas clearly implies, v. 7: *parcius ista **viris** tamen obicienda memento*. However, as pointed out elsewhere[105], the imagery of two squabbling Roman slaves, as Menalcas and Damoetas are, the criticism of improper homosexual preferences as well as the comic linguistic colouring of the relevant narrative fragment of the eclogue in question suggest a 'generic intrusion' of Roman Comedy into the pastoral host-text. This comic makeup of the main Roman pastoral intertext of Lycidas' criticism of Astylus' alleged homosexuality seems to be in tune with the equally comic depiction of Astylus' subsequent reaction to Lycidas' claims.

Astylus resorts to assault and battery, wishing that the sturdy Mnasyllus were absent, v. 87: *fortior o utinam nondum Mnasyllus adesset!*, so as not to prevent him from assaulting and disfiguring Lycidas with his fists, (v. 88: ***efficerem, ne te quisquam** tibi turpior esset*). The wording of the expression clearly alludes to a similarly phrased threat in Verg. *Ecl.* 3.51: ***efficiam**, posthac **ne quemquam** voce lacessas*[106]. Despite the pastoral intertextual wording, such slapstick / farcical threats to come to blows do not have the sanction of previous pastoral, but are instead staple 'generic features' of the comic genre, especially Roman Plautine comedy. In *Rudens*, for example, the *leno* Labrax is similarly threatened with clubs (vv. 807 ff.), as it is the blocking character of the pimp that frequently functions as the recipient of farcical threats and blows (cf. also Plaut. *Pers.* 809 ff., Ter. *Eun.* 715–6; see also Plaut. *Amph.* 374 ff., *Cas.* 404 ff., *Men.* 1007 ff.). In Terence as well, in the Sannio-scene adapted from Diphilos' Συναποθνῄσκοντες, where Terence reworks his material in a more Plautine direction[107], the *leno* Sannio likewise falls the victim of similar bullying and abuse (*Ad.* 170 ff.)[108]. Therefore Messina 1975, 39 is right in holding, albeit impressionistically and without adducing parallels, that 'il verso 88 ricorda il linguaggio dei servi nella commedia'[109].

---

105 Cf. Karakasis 2011, 87–124.
106 Cf. also Verdière 1954, 262, Korzeniewski 1971, 65, Schäfer 2001, 153 and n. 40, Di Lorenzo-Pellegrino 2008, 268, Becker 2012, 144, Vinchesi 2014, 466.
107 Cf. Karakasis 2005, 125 and n. 15.
108 Cf. also Duckworth 1952, 325.
109 In fact it is not the language that links Astylus with comic figures but the very nature of the buffoon threats he uses; Mnasyllus' abandonment of his role as an *arbiter* (vv. 90–1) also recalls comic devices (cf. Plaut. *Amph.* 1035, Vinchesi 2008, 556; 2014, 466–7, Becker 2012, 145). One may read here (vv. 90–1) an allusion to the Senecan distinction (*Ben.* 3.7.5), current in Calpurnius' time, between *arbiter* and *iudex*; whereas an *arbiter* can exercise his power with-

Closure Devices

Faced with the above comic and epic (cf. previously the setting of the stakes, pp. 235–9) 'generic tendencies' of both herdsmen, as well as with their ensuing persistence in the prerequisites of a long–awaited bucolic match, the umpire, Mnasyllus reacts: v. 89: *quid furitis, quo vos insania tendere iussit?*[110] This insistence on the preliminaries of the pastoral singing match exemplified by the two contestants brings them even closer to Lycidas of the ninth Vergilian bucolic, who, saddened by the fragmented bucolic world he inhabits, the result of history's intrusion into the realm of 'green cabinet', quotes an excerpt from the third Theocritean idyll (vv. 23–5). But instead of relating the part of the idyll which is devoted to the song itself, Lycidas merely quotes the marginal menial task of 'passing on the charge of herdsman to somebody', sticks to the narrative framing and does not recite the song that follows. The choice of the marginal framing, although, in the Calpurnian case, not as a quoted song, the narrative opening of the very pastoral song, which is negatively viewed in the case of Lycidas (as a symptom of the pastoral upheaval he experiences[111]), is, on the other hand, opted for by both contenders of the present poem, who thus do not proceed to the enjoyment of the traditional pastoral value par excellence, i.e., song–making and song–performing.

This 'generic conduct' of Astylus and Lycidas forces the judge Mnasyllus, who significantly has been portrayed, as already remarked (cf. pp. 223, 234, 242–4), with the traditional traits of a pastoral umpire and as the delegate of the long–established, traditional pastoral norm, also aspiring to the Neoteric poetological orientation of bucolic poetics, to finally refuse to function as the ref-

---

out restrictions, a *iudex* has to take into account the praetor's *formula*; see Braund 2009, 161, 420.

110 The combination of *furor* with *tendere* in two direct questions introduced by the *quis* pronoun and the *quo* adverb respectively point directly to the intertext of Verg. *A.* 5.670: *quis furor iste novus? quo nunc, quo tenditis* (cf. also Korzeniewski 1971, 65–6, Di Lorenzo–Pellegrino 2008, 268, Vinchesi 2008, 556; 2014, 466, Becker 2012, 145), where Ascanius similarly describes as *furor* the setting on fire of Aeneas' ships in Sicily by the Trojan women, and asks whether they are bound. So, the 'madness' of the two contestants, as pastoral figures possessing a degree of 'generic awareness', in going on with the quarrel, thus delaying the accomplishment of the 'generic objective' of an agonistic pastoral amoebaean, i.e., the production and the exchange of bucolic song, may be read as intertextually linked with the insanity of the Trojan women when burning the ships and thus also putting off the accomplishment of the 'generic goal' of the Roman Augustan epic, the completion of the hero's mission (in this case Aeneas') and consequently the foundation of Rome.

111 Cf. also Karakasis 2011, 195.

eree (cf. vv. 89–93). Instead, he puts forward as substitute options two other mute bucolic figures, Micon and Iollas, also chance passers-by, according to the well-established pastoral *topos* regarding the appearance of the bucolic adjudicator[112]. It seems that the arbitrator cannot judge any longer, for the time-honoured bucolic values he stands for are no longer valid. Mnasyllus thus resembles, to some extent, Palaemon of the third Vergilian eclogue; this referee, after realising the novel 'generic orientation' of Menalcas and Damoetas towards comedy (stand-up comic squabbling between slaves chiefly regarding 'bottom sexuality', the presence of the tightfisted *noverca*, the comic riddles, several linguistic reminiscences of Plautus and Terence, etc.) and their preference for song-topics occurring chiefly in the elegiac genre (elegiac erotic triangle, the motif of the 'token resistance of the beloved', barking dogs as an impediment to a lover, etc.), and for themes denying the pleasures of the idyllic pastoral landscape (the unfriendly country-side, etc.), similarly announces his reluctance to settle the contest[113], v. 108: *non nostrum inter vos tantas componere lites*. But in the Vergilian intertext, contrary to the poem under discussion, the song-exchange does take place.

Conclusion

Calp. 6 is partly designed as a pastoral narrative of the kind mostly known from Theocr. 5, [Theocr.] 8 and Verg. *Ecl.* 3, where an initial quarrel scene is followed by alternate bucolic songs; the various intertextual allusions to these models, however, underscore the 'generic novelty' of the present eclogue, disappointing the literary expectations of the ideal reader of (earlier) pastoral, for the song-exchange never occurs. This seems to be one of the ways in which Calpurnius engages with earlier pastoral tradition in order to implement his 'generic re-orientation'. Traditional pastoral motifs, as found in the long-established tradition of pre-Neronian pastoral, are constantly altered (e.g. sexual allegations after the setting of the pledges, varying the typology of previous framings of pastoral ἀγῶνες), undermined (e.g. bisexual affairs) or even outright rejected (e.g. natural sounds as part of an idyllic *locus amoenus*); they are also often intermingled with novel themes / motifs, linguistic options and meta-linguistic signs, all sug-

---

112 Cf. Becker 2012, 145.
113 Cf. also Karakasis 2011, 122–4; see also Verdière 1954, 201, Korzeniewski 1971, 66, Di Lorenzo-Pellegrino 2008, 268, Becker 2012, 145, Henderson 2013, 183, Vinchesi 2014, 467.

gesting an interaction of pastoral, as known up to Calpurnius, with various different literary genres.

Thus, elegiac sensibilities seem to be projected, when e.g. physical attractiveness is rated higher than singing excellence and, accordingly, functions as the criterion for assigning victory in a bucolic song–exchange. Both ecphrases seem, on the other hand, to operate, from a 'generic point of view', on the dichotomy pastoral vs. epic, since, although they formally belong to the pastoral host–text, they obviously exhibit a modal intrusion of the epic *genus*; besides, the intertexts to which they clearly allude also suggest a 'generic dialogue' between epic and pastoral. Intertextuality in general seems to function as a major means for Calpurnius to evoke his 'generic ambivalence', as most of the intertexts, earlier texts (pastoral or not) imply a 'generic contact' between various literary *genera* (e.g. the intertext of Nysa of Verg. *Ecl.* 3 and her elegiac / non-pastoral aspirations, Lycidas and his option for silence in Verg. *Ecl.* 9, etc.). Last but not least, the comic colouring in the slapstick stance of both herdsmen near the end of the narrative, after the setting of the stakes, complements the multifaceted 'generic contact' running through the eclogue. Mnasyllus, the umpire, depicted as a representative of traditional pastoral, faced with the 'generically modified' bucolics that both Astylus and Lycidas represent, has no option but to resign.

General Conclusions

Calpurnius Siculus exhibits, from his very first programmatic eclogue, his inclination to move away from the previous pastoral tradition of Theocritus and Vergil. Adopting epic or, at least, epicising intertexts, 'less pastoral' moments of the bucolic Vergil, but also de-pastoralising main motifs and scenes of the bucolic tradition, Calpurnius produces a panegyric of the emperor in bucolic clothing. Through 'panegyric intertextual poetics', Nero is presented as another Augustus and as a young Apollo, according to the communicative policy of the Neronian age. Meta-poetic terms of the *genus tenue* are put in the service of a bucolic panegyric, which, of course, now moves towards the *genus grande*; the ambiguity of Vergilian pastoral poetry decreases and Post-Classical Latin, finally, serves as a means of demonstrating the 'generic novelty' of the *vaticinium Fauni*. A similar pattern is developed in the following political eclogues as well: in Calp. 4, another encomium of the emperor, Calpurnius continues to de-bucolise traditional bucolic motifs, as is for example the negative presentation of the *locus amoenus* at the beginning of the eclogue. This deconstruction of the bucolic space is crucially once again underlined through catch-words of Callimachean poetics which are semantically transformed in order to express notions of the *genus grande*. Intertexuality is also instrumental to this process, as the poet often alludes to prior bucolic texts, which, however, display a branching out from the idealised image of a bucolic community or a branching towards discourses of panegyric colouring (e.g. Verg. *Ecl.* 4 and 5). The 'generic renewal' suggested by Meliboeus and adopted by Corydon seems to be reflected, once again, on the linguistic / stylistic level and the Post-Classical colouring of their speech.

Calp. 7, the last eclogue of the Calpurnian bucolic corpus, is a work which also showcases Calpurnius' artistic objectives concerning his pastoral poetics and its interaction with Neronian politics; in this respect, it is comparable to his other two political eclogues, 1 and 4, which precede it, if not chronologically, at least in terms of book structure. In this case as well Calpurnius interacts with the previous literary pastoral tradition with a view to inverting time-honoured bucolic 'generic constituents' and motifs, in line with the well-known tendency of Neronian literature for the so-called 'aesthetics of deviation'. Accordingly, traditional pastoral topics, such as the pastoral *locus amoenus*, the bucolic fauna and flora, the singing matches of the 'green cabinet', etc., are in Calp. 7 de-bucolised, when associated with urban values and assets, i.e., the arena and its games. The long-established pastoral norm gives way to the explicit panegyric of the emperor and his achievements, chiefly by means of a lengthy ecphrasis uncharacteristic of the bucolic *genus*. Stylistic choices favoured by the *genus grande*, as well as by epic / panegyric intertexts in general, seem to complement this Calpurnian 'generic branching out' towards forms of elevated poetic discourse, and the same can be claimed for novel elements of Post-Classical diction which appear in this work.

'Generic interaction' is evident in the *merae bucolicae* as well; Calpurnian scholarship has long viewed Calpurnius' relationship with his pastoral antecedents as an attempt to widen the 'generic boundaries' of the bucolic genre. In this perspective, Calp. 3 can be read as a characteristic instance of 'generic interaction' between pastoral and elegy, which aims to 'enrich' the pre-Calpurnian pastoral norm with standard elegiac traits. This is achieved not only through the adoption of language, style, and motifs of elegiac provenance but also, more interestingly, through the systematic imitation of Vergilian pastoral passages marked by clear elegiac qualities. This leaning of Calp. 3 towards non-pastoral modes of discourse is complemented by the intrusion of a number of features of arguably comic descent, as well as by intertextual allusions to Theocritean idylls which either do not belong to the pastoral cycle or are of a peculiar 'generic standing' (e.g. Theocr. 11).

In Calp. 5 an extensive interaction of pastoral with georgics is detectable; Calpurnius enhances his poem's 'didactic intent' by drawing on the previous didactic tradition of both didactic poetry and didactic prose in terms of themes / motifs and language / style as well as by stressing the 'teacher–student' relationship, i.e., a 'generic essential' of the didactic genre. However, Calp. 5 cannot be properly read as a specimen of didactic poetry in miniature, as it lacks two other essential 'generic prerequisites' of the Greek and Roman poetic didactic genre, namely 'poetic self-consciousness' and 'poetic simultaneity' (the terms are used in a specific and restricted didactic sense, after Volk 2002). For all the pastoral character of the framing introduction and the closure of the eclogue, the fifth Calpurnian poem is a case of a bucolised didactic mode within a process of 'generic enrichment' and, what is more, an instance of poetic initiation-narrative, 'troping', on a meta-poetic level, the passing down of a 'new diversified and enriched Calpurnian pastoral form' from an older to a younger member of the 'green cabinet'. Although a traditional bucolic veneer permeates poem 2 as well, both Idas and Astacus, the singers of this eclogue, combine into their bucolic song several elegiac and georgic themes and stylistic / linguistic options. What is more, the singers also remind the reader of texts which either have a clear elegiac or didactic / georgic 'generic history' and / or appear in the earlier pastoral tradition, but as individual cases of 'generic diversion' from the bucolic norm towards elegiac and didactic trends.

Last but not least, Calp. 6 constitutes a total inversion and deconstruction of the pre-Calpurnian bucolic singing match, for the much-awaited βουκολιασμός crucially never takes place, despite the formalistic completeness foreshadowing the beginning of a song-exchange; what is more, elegiac values, again, gain mastery over bucolic ethics, the epicising ecphrasis once more covers a large textual space of the poem, and the various intertexts of the poem also suggest a sense of a pervasive 'generic interaction' running through the whole of the eclogue. The arbiter symbolising traditional pastoral values and facing the significant 'generic change' operating in the eclogue can do nothing but resign.

Opposing the prioritisation of Neoteric *ludus* as against the *seria* of everyday pastoral existence in Vergil, cf. Verg. *Ecl.* 7.17: *posthabui tamen illorum mea seria ludo*, Calpurnius' poetics resort to more inclusive tactics by means of which the poet makes both pastoral and georgic *seria* part of an expanded, 'enriched' pastoral, or a quasi-pastoral, world (Calp. 2, 5). The same also holds true for elegy and its world (Calp. 2, 3). This is often achieved through Calpurnius' increase of 'citationality' – a trend highly visible already in Vergil. In the case of the panegyric eclogues, one observes a serious transposition of 'what is important', the praised *locus amoenus* included, to the urban space (Calp. 7); such a move is, in terms of 'generic development', in some way parallel to the panegyric turn. This transposition and the panegyric functionality open pastoral up towards the political space of the *urbs*, and the result may be viewed as a definite rapprochement between two entities (*rus – urbs*), which not only in Vergilian pastoral but also in much of Latin Neoteric poetry (elegy, Catullus) remain more or less antagonistic. In Vergil, *Ecl.* 2, Corydon, despite his passion for a city youth, eventually shows himself decidedly rooted in the pastoral domain. His namesake in Calpurnius 7 proclaims, in the strongest possible terms, a preference for the city over the country-side. Read on the meta-poetic level, this suggests a certain destabilisation of the 'generic *locus*' of pastoral; similar are the implications of Calpurnius' endorsement of georgic and elegiac elements in the *merae bucolicae*, which point to the same kind of destabilisation. Pastoral in the Calpurnian political poems largely loses its function as a fictional discourse that brings out the full implications of a Neoteric attitude within a broader Roman context. It is on its way to become a straightforward instrument of political (panegyric) discourse, which makes a purely formalistic use of the pastoral scenario. Vergil's pastoral is a self-sufficient discourse that subjects all panegyric discourses that come into it to some kind of pastoralisation. In Calpurnius, on the other hand, the eulogy of a political figure, explicit and devoid of the subtle Vergilian nuances, becomes a quoted song in the course of a pastoral session, while panegyric itself becomes part of a literary fiction, where the pragmatics of song-production do not gain the upper hand over the song's theme. In Vergil, in contrast, what is important is a discourse on the function, position and even merits of Neoteric pastoral singing within a certain ideological / political context; even

Ecl. 4 is pervaded by a sense of standing at the intersection of practical politics (in the sense of 'who is to rule the State'), on the one hand, and a de-historicised landscape of non-tension, on the other; Vergil manages to subordinate the panegyric element to the overall pastoralism of the eclogue. It is hard to find any of these in Calpurnius' panegyric, for Calpurnius' innovative urge affects this principle of Vergilian pastoral. In this sense, in Calpurnius pastoral largely loses its function as a fictional discourse that brings out the full implications of a Neoteric attitude within a broader Roman context. Things have changed; while in constant dialogue with previous pastoral, Calpurnius strikes out on his own and moves, among other things, in the direction of explicit panegyric; hence a serious modification of pastoral poetics in the service of the *princeps*.

Bibliography

Text-acknowledgement: Unless otherwise stated, for post-Vergilian pastoral (Calpurnius Siculus, *Eins*. Eclogues, Nemesianus), I accept the text of Duff and Duff 1934.

Abry, J. H. (1999), 'Présence de Lucrèce: Les *Astronomiques* de Manilius', in: R. Poignault (ed.), *Présence de Lucrèce*, Tours, 111–28.
— (2002), '*Inveniunt et in astra vias…* (Manilius, *Astr.*, 4, 152–161)', in: *Pallas* 59, 65–73.
— (2006), '*Sed caelo noscenda canam…*(*Astr.*, 2, 142): Poésie et Astrologie dans les *Astronomiques* de Manilius', in: C. Cusset (ed.), *Musa docta: Recherches sur la Poésie Scientifique dans l' Antiquité*, Saint-Étienne, 293–333.
Ahl, F. M. (1984), 'The Rider and the Horse: Politics and Power in Roman Poetry from Horace to Statius', in: *ANRW* 2.32.1, 40–124.
Alföldi, A. (1970), *Die monarchische Repräsentation im römischen Kaiserreich*, Darmstadt.
Alpers, P. (1996), *What is Pastoral?*, Chicago.
Amat, J. (1988), 'La Révélation d'un Artiste Méconnu. L'Imaginaire de Calpurnius Siculus', in: J. Thomas (ed.), *L'Imaginaire de l'Espace et du Temps chez les Latins*, Cahiers de l'Université de Perpignan 5, Perpignan, 75–90.
— (1991), *Calpurnius Siculus, Bucoliques. Pseudo-Calpurnius, Éloge de Pison. Texte Établi et Traduit*, Paris.
— (1995), 'L'Image Bucolique Post-Virgilienne', in: J. Thomas (ed.), *Les Imaginaires des Latins. Actes du Colloque International de Perpignan (12–13–14 Novembre 1991)*, Perpignan, 77–87.
— (1997), *Consolation à Livie, Élégies à Mécène, Bucoliques d' Einsiedeln. Texte Établi et Traduit*, Paris.
— (1998), 'Humour et Ironie dans les *Bucoliques* de Calpurnius Siculus et les Carmina Einsidlensia', in: *REL* 76, 192–9.
Amatucci, A. G. (1947), *La Letteratura di Roma Imperiale*, Bologna.
Anderson, W. S. (1972), *Ovid's Metamorphoses: Books 6–10*, Norman, Oklahoma.
Antoniadis, T. (2006), *Η Ρητορική της 'Επιγονικότητας'. Ερμηνευτικός Σχολιασμός των Amores του Οβιδίου*, Diss., Thessaloniki.
Armstrong, D. (1986), 'Stylistics and the Date of Calpurnius Siculus', in: *Philologus* 130, 113–36.
Armstrong, D. and Champlin, E. (1986), 'The Date of Calpurnius Siculus. Conclusion', in: *Philologus* 130, 137.
Arnott, W. G. (1996), *Menander* vol. II, *Heros–Perinthia*, Cambridge, Mass.
Asmis, E. (2007), 'Lucretius' Venus and Stoic Zeus', in: M. R. Gale (ed.), *Oxford Readings in Classical Studies: Lucretius*, Oxford, 88–103.
Bailey, C. (1931), 'Virgil and Lucretius', in: *PCA* 28, 21–39.
Baldwin, B. (1995), 'Better Late than Early: Reflections on the Date of Calpurnius Siculus', in: *ICS* 20, 157–67.
Balzert, M. (1971), 'Hirtensorgen im Goldenen Zeitalter. Eine Interpretation des *Carmen Einsidlense* II', in: *AU* 14.3, 24–42.

Baraz, Y. (2015), 'Sound and Silence in Calpurnius Siculus', in: *AJPh* 136, 91–120.
Barchiesi, A. (1982), 'Lettura del Secondo Libro delle *Georgiche*', in: M. Gigante (ed.), *Lecturae Vergilianae II: Le Georgiche*, Naples, 41–86.
— (1992), *P. Ovidii Nasonis Epistulae Heroidum 1–3*, Florence.
— (2005), *Ovidio Metamorfosi, Volume I, Libri I–II. A Cura di Alessandro Barchiesi. Traduzione di Ludovica Koch*, Milan.
Bardon, H. (1968), *Les Empereurs et les Lettres Latines d'Auguste à Hadrien*, Paris.
— (1972), 'Bucolique et Politique', in: *RhM* 115, 1–13.
Barsby, J. (1999), *Terence: Eunuchus*, Cambridge.
Bartalucci, A. (1976), 'Persio e i Poeti di Età Neroniana', in: *RCCM* 18, 85–116.
Batstone, W. (1997), 'Virgilian Didaxis: Value and Meaning in the *Georgics*', in: C. Martindale (ed.), *The Cambridge Companion to Virgil*, Cambridge, 125–44.
Bayet, J. (1930), 'Les Premières 'Géorgiques' de Virgile (39–37 avant J–Chr.)', in: *RPh* 4, 128–50, 227–47.
Beato, J. (1995), 'Calpúrnio Sículo: um Poeta Pobre ou um Pobre Poeta?', in: *Humanitas* 47, 617–27.
— (2003), 'Da Normalidade de Calpúrnio à Singularidade de Nemesiano', in: *Ágora* 5, 83–105.
Bechtold, C. (2011), *Gott und Gestirn als Präsenzformen des toten Kaisers: Apotheose und Katasterismos in der politischen Kommunikation der römischen Kaiserzeit und ihre Anknüpfungspunkte im Hellenismus*, Göttingen.
Becker, G. (2012), *Titus Calpurnius Siculus. Kommentar zur 5. und 6. Ekloge*, Trier.
Bessone, F. (1997), *P. Ovidii Nasonis Heroidum Epistula XII Medea Iasoni*, Florence.
Bickel, E. (1954), 'Politische Sibyllenekloge: Die Sibyllenekloge des Consularis Piso an Nero und der politische Sinn der Erwähnung des Achilles in der Sibyllenekloge Vergils', in: *RhM* 97, 193–228.
Bicknell, P. J. (1969), 'Neronian Comets and Novae', in: *Latomus* 28, 1074–5.
Binder, G. (1989), 'Hirtenlied und Herrscherlob. Von den Wandlungen der römischen Bukolik', in: *Gymnasium* 96, 363–5.
Bollack, J. (1959), 'Lukrez und Empedokles', in: *Die Neue Rundschau* 70, 656–86.
Bömer, F. (1969), *P. Ovidius Naso: Metamorphosen, Buch I–III*, Heidelberg.
— (1980), *P. Ovidius Naso: Metamorphosen, Buch X–XI*, Heidelberg.
Bonfante, P. B. (1912), 'La Vera Data di un Testo di Calpurnio Siculo e il Concetto Romano del Tesoro', in: *Mélanges P. F. Girard. Études de Droit Romain Dédiées à P. F. Girard. 1*, Paris, 123–42.
Boswell, J. (1994), *Same-Sex Unions in Premodern Europe*, New York.
Boyle, A. J. and Sullivan, J. P. (1991), *Roman Poets of the Early Empire*, London.
Boyle, A. J. and Woodard, R. D. (2004), *Ovid. Fasti*, London.
Bradley, K. R. (1978), *Suetonius' Life of Nero. An Historical Commentary*, Brussels.
Braund, D. B. (1983), 'Treasure-trove and Nero', in: *G&R* 30, 65–9.
Braund, S. H. (1988), *Beyond Anger: A Study of Juvenal's Third Book of Satires*, Cambridge.
— (2009), *Seneca, De Clementia*, Oxford.
Breed, B. W. (2006), *Pastoral Inscriptions. Reading and Writing Virgil's Eclogues*, London.
Brown, R. D. (2007), 'Lucretius and Callimachus', in: M. R. Gale (ed.), *Oxford Readings in Classical Studies: Lucretius*, Oxford, 328–50.
Bruno, M. G. (1969[repr.]), *Il Lessico Agricolo Latino*, Amsterdam.

Burckhardt, J. (1954), *Constantino il Grande e i suoi Tempi*, – Italian translation by Michelson, A., Milan.
Butler, H. E. (1909), *Post-Augustan Poetry from Seneca to Juvenal*, Oxford.
Byrne, S. N. (2004), 'Martial's Fiction: Domitius Marsus and Maecenas', in: *CQ* 54, 255–65.
Cairns, F. (1999), 'Tibullus, Messalla, and the *spica:* I 1.16; I 5.28; I 10.22; II 1.4; II 5.48', in: *Emerita* 67, 219–30.
Calcante, C. M. (2002), *Miracula rerum: Strategie Semiologiche del Genere Didascalico negli Astronomica di Manilio*, Pisa.
Campbell, G. (2003), *Lucretius on Creation and Evolution: A Commentary on De Rerum Natura 5.772–1104*, Oxford.
Camps, W. A. (1965), *Propertius. Elegies Book IV*, Cambridge.
Cancik, H. (1965), *Untersuchungen zur lyrischen Kunst des P. Papinius Statius*, Hildesheim.
Casaceli, F. (1982), 'Temi Letterari e Spunti Autobiografici nell' Opera di T. Calpurnio Siculo', in: *CCC* 3, 85–103.
Castagna, L. (1982), 'Il Carme Amebeo della IV *Ecloga* di Calpurnio Siculo', in: J. M. Croisille and P. M. Fauchère (eds.), *Neronia 1977: Actes du 2ᵉ Colloque de la Société Internationale d'Études Néroniennes*, Clermont-Ferrand, 159–69.
— (2002), 'Anticlassicismo Neroniano? Spunta per Una Verifica', in: L. Castagna and G. Vogt-Spira (eds.), *Pervertere: Ästhetik der Verkehrung. Literatur und Kultur neronischer Zeit und ihre Rezeption*, Beiträge zur Altertumskunde 151, Munich, ix–xix.
Castagna, L. and Vogt-Spira, G. (2002), (eds.), *Pervertere: Ästhetik der Verkehrung. Literatur und Kultur neronischer Zeit und ihre Rezeption*, Beiträge zur Altertumskunde 151, Munich.
Castiglioni, L. (1955), 'Due Note alle *Bucholiche* di Calpurnio e Nemesiano', in: *Studi in Onore di Gino Funaioli*, Rome, 19–22.
Cesareo, E. (1931), *La Poesia di Calpurnio Siculo*, Palermo.
Champlin, E. (1978), 'The Life and Times of Calpurnius Siculus', in: *JRS* 68, 95–110.
— (1986), 'History and the Date of Calpurnius Siculus', in: *Philologus* 130, 104–12.
— (2003), 'Nero, Apollo, and the Poets', in: *Phoenix* 57, 276–83.
Chastagnol, A. (1976), 'Trois Études sur la Vita Cari', in: *Bonner Historia-Augusta Colloquium 1972 / 1974*, Bonn, 75–90.
Chiavola, C. (1921), *Della Vita e dell' Opera di T. Calpurnio Siculo*, Ragusa.
Chinnici, V. (2009), 'La Dialettica fra Suono e Silenzio in Calpurnio Siculo', in: L. Landolfi and R. Oddo (eds.), *Fer Propius Tua Lumina; Giochi Intertestuali nella Poesia di Calpurnio Siculo*, Bologna, 129–42.
Chytil, F. (1894), 'Der Eklogendichter T. Calpurnius Siculus und seine Vorbilder', in: *Jahresbericht des k. k. Gymnasiums in Znaim*, Znaim, 3–24.
Cizek, E. (1968), 'À propos de la Littérature Classique au temps de Néron', in: *StudClas* 10, 147–57.
— (1972), *L'Époque de Néron et ses Controverses Idéologiques*, Leiden.
Clausen, W. (1994), *A Commentary on Virgil, Eclogues*, Oxford.
Clay, D. (1983), *Lucretius and Epicurus*, Ithaca, NY.
Clay, J. S. (1976), 'The Argument of the End of Vergil's Second *Georgic*', in: *Philologus* 120, 232–45.
Clément-Tarantino, S. (2006), 'La Poétique Romaine Comme Hybridation Féconde. Les Leçons de la Greffe' (Virgile, *Géorgiques*, 2, 9–82), in: *Interférences Ars Scribendi* 4 (=http://ars-scribendi.enslsh.fr/article.php3?id_article=37&var_affichage=vf).

Coleman, K. M. (1988), *Statius: Silvae IV*, Oxford.
— (1990), 'Fatal Charades: Roman Executions Staged as Mythological Enactments', in: *JRS* 80, 44–73.
— (2006), *Martial: Liber Spectaculorum*, Oxford.
Coleman, R. (1977), *Vergil: Eclogues*, Cambridge.
Connors, C. (1992), 'Seeing Cypresses in Virgil', in: *CJ* 88, 1–17.
Conte, G. B. (1986), *The Rhetoric of Imitation: Genre and Poetic Memory in Virgil and Other Latin Poets*, – English translation by Segal, C., Ithaca, NY.
— (1994), *Latin Literature: A History*, Baltimore.
Cooper, H. (1977), *Pastoral: Mediaeval into Renaissance*, Ipswich.
Coronati, L. (1995–8), '*Anhelo* in Calpurnio Siculo 3,35: un Problema di Esegesi', in: *Helikon* 35–8, 393–404.
Correa, J. A. (1977), 'Los Pastores de Calpurnio Siculo', in: *Habis* 8, 149–59.
Costanza, S. (1984), 'Appunti sulla Fortuna di M. Manilio *Astr.* I 13 in Germanico, in Calpurnio Siculo e in Tertulliano', in: *Vichiana* 13, 26–48.
Courtney, E. (1987), 'Imitation, Chronologie Littéraire et Calpurnius Siculus', in: *REL* 65, 148–57.
Cucchiarelli, A. (2012), *Publio Virgilio Marone Le Bucoliche. Introduzione e Commento di Andrea Cucchiarelli, Traduzione di Alfonso Traina*, Rome.
Cupaiuolo, F. (1973), *Itinerario della Poesia Latina nel I Secolo dell' Impero*, Naples.
Cupaiuolo, G. (1997), *Marco Aurelio Olimpio Nemesiano: Eclogae*, Naples.
Dahlmann, H. (1953), *Varros Schrift 'de poematis' und die hellenistisch–römische Poetik*, Wiesbaden.
Dalby, A. (2000), *Empire of Pleasures: Luxury and Indulgence in the Roman World*, London.
Dalzell, A. (1996), *The Criticism of Didactic Poetry: Essays on Lucretius, Virgil, and Ovid*, Toronto.
Damon, P. (1973), *Modes of Analogy in Ancient and Medieval Verse*, Berkeley and Los Angeles.
Dams, P. (1970), *Dichtungskritik bei nachaugusteischen Dichtern*, Marburg.
Davis, P. J. (1987), 'Structure and Meaning in the *Eclogues* of Calpurnius Siculus', in: *Ramus* 16, 32–54.
De Meo, C. (1983), *Lingue Tecniche del Latino*, Bologna.
De Sipio, J. (1935), *T. Calpurnii Siculi Bucolica. Testo con Introduzione, Traduzione Italiana e Note*, Catania.
Dehon, P. J. (1993), 'Calpurnius Siculus, Poète Virgilien de l'Hiver', in: *REL* 71, 203–11.
Delbey, É. (2013), 'L'Éloge de l'Orateur et l'Échec du Poète chez Calpurnius Siculus', in: H. Vial (ed.), *Poètes et Orateurs dans l'Antiquité. Mises en Scène Réciproques*, Clermont Ferrand, 297–303.
Dewar, M. (1994), 'Laying it on with a Trowel: The Proem to Lucan and Related Texts', in: *CQ* 44, 199–211.
Di Giovine, C. (1978), 'Note sulla Tecnica Imitativa di Manilio', in: *RFIC* 106, 398–406.
Di Lorenzo, E. (1987), 'Sulla Tecnica Didascalica della 5ª *Egloga* di Calpurnio Siculo', in: *Misure Critiche* 17, 17–23.
— (1988), 'Aspetti Letterari e Atteggiamenti Espressivi nelle *Egloghe* di Calpurnio Siculo', in: *Misure Critiche* 18, 5–21.
Di Lorenzo, E. and Pellegrino, B. (2008), *T. Calpurnio Siculo: Eclogae*, Naples.

Di Salvo, L. (1990), *T. Calpurnio Siculo, Ecloga VII. Introduzione, Edizione Critica, Traduzione e Commento*, Bologna.
—— (1990a), 'Alcune Osservazioni sulle *Ecloghe* di Calpurnio Siculo', in: *CCC* 11, 267–87.
—— (1991), 'Qualche Osservazione in Merito a una Recente Edizione delle *Ecloghe* di Calpurnio Siculo e della *Laus Pisonis*', in: *CCC* 12, 305–16.
Díaz-Cíntora, S. (1989), *Tito Calpurnio Sículo: Églogas*, Mexico.
Dihle, A. (1994), *Greek and Latin Literature of the Roman Empire: From Augustus to Justinian*, – English translation by Malzahn, M., London.
Du Quesnay, I. M. LeM. (1981), 'Vergil's First *Eclogue*', in: *PLLS* 3, 29–182.
Duckworth, G. E. (1952), *The Nature of Roman Comedy: A Study in Popular Entertainment*, Norman, Oklahoma.
—— (1969), *Vergil and Classical Hexameter Poetry: A Study in Metrical Variety*, Ann Arbor.
Duff, J. W. (1960), *A Literary History of Rome in the Silver Age: From Tiberius to Hadrian*, London.
Duff, J. W. and Duff, A. M. (1934), *Minor Latin Poets*, London.
Dutoit, E. (1936), *Le Thème de l'Adynaton dans la Poésie Antique*, Paris.
Eden, P. T. (1984), *Seneca. Apocolocyntosis*, Cambridge.
Edmondson, J. C. (1996), 'Dynamic Arenas: Gladiatorial Presentations in the City of Rome and the Construction of Roman Society during the Early Empire', in: W. J. Slater (ed.), *Roman Theater and Society: E. Togo Salmon Papers I*, Ann Arbor, 69–112.
Effe, B. (1971), '*Labor improbus* – ein Grundgedanke der *Georgica* in der Sicht des Manilius', in: *Gymnasium* 78, 393–9.
—— (1977), *Dichtung und Lehre: Untersuchungen zur Typologie des antiken Lehrgedichts*, Munich.
—— (1992), 'Die Homoerotik in der griechischen Bukolik', in: T. Stemmler (ed.), *Homoerotische Lyrik. 6. Kolloquium der Forschungsstelle für europäische Lyrik des Mittelalters*, Tübingen, 55–67.
Effe, B. and Binder, G. (1989), *Die antike Bukolik*, Munich.
Emberger, P. (2013), 'Von neuen Zeitaltern', in: W. Sonntagbauer and J. Klopf (eds.), *Welt, Seele, Gottheit: Festschrift für Wolfgang Speyer zum 80. Geburtstag*, Salzburg, 19–31.
Erren, M. (2003), *P. Vergilius Maro. Georgica. Band 2. Kommentar*, Heidelberg.
Esposito, P. (1996), 'Per la Storia della Ricezione di Virgilio Bucolico: l' *Ecloga* IV di Calpurnio Siculo', in: *Orpheus* 17, 13–34.
—— (2009), 'La Profezia di Fauno nella I *Ecloga* di Calpurnio Siculo', in: L. Landolfi and R. Oddo (eds.), *Fer Propius Tua Lumina; Giochi Intertestuali nella Poesia di Calpurnio Siculo*, Bologna, 13–39.
—— (2012), 'Interaction between *Bucolics* and *Georgics*: the Fifth *Eclogue* of Calpurnius Siculus', in: *TCS* 4.1, 48–72.
Evans, R. (2008), *Utopia Antiqua: Readings of the Golden Age and Decline at Rome*, London and New York.
Fairclough, H. R. and Goold, G. P. (1999), *Virgil; Eclogues, Georgics, Aeneid I–VI*, Cambridge Mass. and London.
Fantham, E. (1996), *Roman Literary Culture: From Cicero to Apuleius*, Baltimore.
—— (1998), *Ovid Fasti: Book IV*, Cambridge.
—— (2004), *Ovid's Metamorphoses*, Oxford.

Fantuzzi, M. (2006), 'Theocritus' Constructive Interpreters, and the Creation of a Bucolic Reader', in: M. Fantuzzi and Th. Papanghelis (eds.), *Brill's Companion to Greek and Latin Pastoral*, Leiden, 235–62.
Fantuzzi, M. and Hunter, R. L. (2004), *Tradition and Innovation in Hellenistic Poetry*, Cambridge.
Farrell, J. (1991), *Vergil's Georgics and the Traditions of Ancient Epic. The Art of Allusion in Literary History*, New York.
— (1992), 'Dialogue of Genres in Ovid's 'Lovesong of Polyphemus' (*Metamorphoses* 13.719–897)', in: *AJPh* 113, 235–68.
Farrington, B. (1963), 'Polemical Allusions to the *De Rerum Natura* of Lucretius in the Works of Vergil', in: L. Varcl and R. F. Willetts (eds.), *Geras. Studies Presented to George Thomson on the Occasion of his 60th Birthday*, Prague, 87–94.
Fear, A. T. (1993), 'Polar Bears in Antiquity?', in: *LCM* 18, 43–5.
— (1994), '*Laus Neronis*: The Seventh *Eclogue* of Calpurnius Siculus', in: *Prometheus* 20, 269–77.
Fedeli, P. (1980), *Sesto Properzio. Il Primo Libro Delle Elegie*, Florence.
— (1985), *Properzio: Il Libro Terzo Delle Elegie*, Bari.
— (2005), *Properzio Elegie Libro II Introduzione, Testo e Commento*, Cambridge.
Feeney, D. (2007), *Caesar's Calendar: Ancient Time and the Beginnings of History*, Berkeley.
Ferrara, G. (1905), *Calpurnio Siculo e il Panegirico a Calpurnio Pisone*, Pavia.
Fey-Wickert, B. (2002), *Calpurnius Siculus: Kommentar zur 2. und 3. Ekloge*, Trier.
Fitch, J. G. (1987), *Seneca's Hercules Furens*, Ithaca, NY.
Flores, E. (1996), 'Gli *Astronomica* di Manilio e l' Epicureismo', in: G. Giannantoni and M. Gigante (eds.), *Epicureismo Greco e Romano*, vol. II, Naples, 895–908.
Fordyce, C. J. (2001$^{repr.}$), *Virgil: Aeneid VII–VIII*, London.
Fortenbaugh, W. (1974), 'Menander's *Perikeiromene*: Misfortune, Vehemence, and Polemon', in: *Phoenix* 28, 430–43.
Fowler, A. (1982), *Kinds of Literature. An Introduction to the Theory of Genres and Modes*, Oxford.
Fowler, D. (2002), *Lucretius on Atomic Motion: A Commentary on De Rerum Natura 2.1–332*, Oxford.
Freudenburg, K. (1987), 'Lucretius, Vergil, and the *causa morbi*', in: *Vergilius* 33, 59–74.
Friedrich, W. (1976), *Nachahmung und eigene Gestaltung in der bukolischen Dichtung des Titus Calpurnius Siculus*, Frankfurt am Main.
Fucecchi, M. (2009), 'Ovidio e la Nuova Bucolica di Calpurnio: Osservazioni e Proposte', in: L. Landolfi and R. Oddo (eds.), *Fer Propius Tua Lumina; Giochi Intertestuali nella Poesia di Calpurnio Siculo*, Bologna, 41–65.
Fuchs, H. (1973), 'Zu den Hirtengedichten des Calpurnius Siculus und zu den *Carmina Einsidlensia*', in: *MH* 30, 228–33.
Fugmann, J. (1992), 'Nero oder Severus Alexander? Zur Datierung der *Eklogen* des Calpurnius Siculus', in: *Philologus* 136, 202–7.
Furley, D. (1970), 'Variations on Themes from Empedocles in Lucretius' Proem', in: *BICS* 17, 55–64.
Fuxa, G. (1831), *Egloghe di T. Giunio Calpurnio Siciliano*, Palermo.
Fyntikoglou, V. (2007), Βιργιλίου Βουγονία: Τὸ Ἐπύλλιο τοῦ Ἀρισταίου (Γεωργικῶν IV 281–558), Athens.
Gagliardi, D. (1981), 'Lettura della VI *Egloga* di Calpurnio Siculo', in: *CCC* 2, 37–44.

—— (1984), *Calpurnio Siculo, un 'Minore' di Talento*, Naples.
Gale, M. R. (1994), *Myth and Poetry in Lucretius*, Cambridge.
—— (2000), *Virgil on the Nature of Things: The Georgics, Lucretius and the Didactic Tradition*, Cambridge.
—— (2005), 'Didactic Epic', in: S. Harrison (ed.), *A Companion to Latin Literature*, Malden, Oxford, Chichester, 101–15.
—— (2007), (ed.), *Oxford Readings in Classical Studies: Lucretius*, Oxford.
—— (2007a),'Lucretius and Previous Poetic Traditions', in: S. Gillespie and P. Hardie (eds.), *The Cambridge Companion to Lucretius*, Cambridge, 59–75.
—— (2009), *Lucretius De Rerum Natura V*, Oxford.
Galinsky, G. K. (1965), 'Vergil's Second *Eclogue:* Its Theme and Relation to the *Eclogue* Book', in: *C&M* 26, 161–91.
Garani, M. (2007), *Empedocles Redivivus: Poetry and Analogy in Lucretius*, New York and London.
Garnett, R. (1888), 'On the Date of Calpurnius Siculus', in: *Journal of Philology* 16, 216–9.
Garson, R. W. (1974), 'The *Eclogues* of Calpurnius. A Partial Apology', in: *Latomus* 33, 668–72.
Garthwaite, J. and Martin, B. (2009), 'Visions of Gold: Hopes for the New Age in Calpurnius Siculus' *Eclogues*', in: W. J. Dominik, J. Garthwaite and P. A. Roche (eds.), *Writing Politics in Imperial Rome*, Leiden, 307–22.
Gatz, B. (1967), *Weltalter, goldene Zeit und sinnverwandte Vorstellungen*, Hildesheim.
Giarratano, C. (1930), 'Calpurnio Siculo', in: *Enciclopedia Italiana* 8, 463.
—— (1943), *Calpurnii et Nemesiani Bucolica. Tertium Edidit Einsidlensia Quae Dicuntur Carmina, Iteratis Curis Adiecit C. Giarratano*, Turin.
Gibson, B. (2004), 'Song Contests in Calpurnius Siculus', in: *PVS* 25, 1–14.
—— (2006), *Statius: Silvae 5*, Oxford.
Gibson, R. K. (1997), 'Didactic Poetry as 'Popular' Form: A Study of Imperatival Expressions in Latin Didactic Verse and Prose', in: C. Atherton (ed.), *Form and Content in Didactic Poetry* (= Nottingham Classical Studies 5), Bari, 67–98.
—— (2003), *Ovid: Ars Amatoria, Book 3*, Cambridge.
Glaeser, C. E. (1842), *Calpurnii Siculi Eclogae*, Göttingen.
Gnilka, C. (1974), 'Die Tiere im hölzernen Amphitheater Neros. Wort- und Versinterpolation bei Calpurnius Siculus', in: *WS* 8, 124–53.
Goldberg, S. M. (1980), *The Making of Menander's Comedy*, Berkeley and Los Angeles.
Gomme, A. W. and Sandbach, F. H. (1973), *Menander: A Commentary*, Oxford.
Goold, G. P. (1997), *Manilius Astronomica*, Cambridge, Mass.
Gotoff, H. C. (1967), 'On the Fourth *Eclogue* of Virgil', in: *Philologus* 111, 66–79.
Gowers, E. (1994), 'Persius and the Decoction of Nero', in: J. Elsner and J. Masters (eds.), *Reflections of Nero: Culture, History and Representation*, Chapel Hill, 131–50.
Grant, M. (2004), 'Continuity in Pastoral: Plants and Food in Virgil', in: *PVS* 25, 125–34.
Grant, W. L. (1965), *Neo-Latin Literature and the Pastoral*, Chapel Hill.
Green, S. J. (2004), *Ovid, Fasti I: A Commentary*, Leiden.
—— (2009), 'The Horse and the Serpent: A Vergilian Perspective on the Final *Eclogue* of Calpurnius Siculus', in: *Vergilius* 55, 55–67.
Green, S. J. and Volk, K. (2011), (eds.), *Forgotten Stars. Rediscovering Manilius' Astronomica*, Oxford.
Griffin, M. T. (1984), *Nero: The End of a Dynasty*, London.

Grimal, P. (1978), *Le Lyrisme à Rome*, Paris.
Gustin, R. (1947), 'Le Printemps chez les Poètes Latins', in: *LEC* 15, 323–30.
Halperin, D. M. (1983), *Before Pastoral: Theocritus and the Ancient Tradition of Bucolic Poetry*, New Haven.
Hardie, P. (1986), *Virgil's Aeneid: Cosmos and Imperium*, Oxford.
— (1998), *Virgil*, Oxford.
— (2002), *Ovid's Poetics of Illusion*, Cambridge.
— (2007), 'Lucretius and Later Latin Literature in Antiquity', in: S. Gillespie and P. Hardie (eds.), *The Cambridge Companion to Lucretius*, Cambridge, 111–27.
— (2009), *Lucretian Receptions History, The Sublime, Knowledge*, Cambridge.
Hardie, P. and Moore, H. (2010), (eds.), *Classical Literary Careers and their Reception*, Cambridge.
Harrison, S. J. (2004), 'Virgil's *Corycius Senex* and Nicander's *Georgica: Georgics* 4.116–48', in: M. R. Gale (ed.), *Latin Epic and Didactic Poetry: Genre, Tradition and Individuality*, Swansea, 109–23.
— (2007), *Generic Enrichment in Vergil and Horace*, Oxford.
Haupt, M. (1875), 'De Carminibus Bucolicis Calpurnii et Nemesiani', in: *Mauricii Hauptii Opuscula I*, Leipzig, 358–406.
Henderson, J. (2013), 'The *Carmina Einsidlensia* and Calpurnius Siculus' *Eclogues*', in: E. Buckley and M. T. Dinter (eds.), *A Companion to the Neronian Age*, Malden, Oxford, Chichester, 170–87.
Herrmann, L. (1931), 'Réflexions sur la Comète de Calpurnius', in: *RBPh* 10, 145–53.
— (1952), 'Les Pseudonymes dans les *Bucoliques* de Calpurnius Siculus', in: *Latomus* 11, 27–44.
Heslin, P. J. (1997), 'The Scansion of *Pharsalia*: (Catullus 64.37; Statius, *Achilleid* 1. 152; Calpurnius Siculus 4. 101)', in: *CQ* 47, 588–93.
Heyworth, S. J. and Morwood, J. H. W. (2011), *A Commentary on Propertius Book 3*, Oxford.
Hill, D. E. (1992), *Ovid. Metamorphoses V–VIII*, Warminster.
— (2000), *Ovid. Metamorphoses XIII–XV and Indexes to Metamorphoses I–XV*, Warminster.
Hinds, S. (1987), *The Metamorphosis of Persephone: Ovid and the Self-Conscious Muse*, Cambridge.
— (1998), *Allusion and Intertext. Dynamics of Appropriation in Roman Poetry*, Cambridge.
Hollis, A. S. (1973), 'The *Ars Amatoria* and *Remedia Amoris*', in: J. W. Binns (ed.), *Ovid*, London, 84–115.
— (1977), *Ovid: Ars Amatoria, Book I*, Oxford.
Horsfall, N. M. (1993), 'Cleaning Up Calpurnius', in: *CR* 43, 267–70.
— (1997), 'Criteria for the Dating of Calpurnius Siculus', in: *RFIC* 125, 166–96.
Hubaux, J. (1927), 'Le Vers Initial des *Églogues*: Contribution à l'Histoire du Texte des Bucoliques Latins', in: *RBPh* 6, 603–16.
— (1930), *Les Thèmes Bucoliques dans la Poésie Latine*, Brussels.
— (1930a), 'Sénèque et Calpurnius Siculus', in: *Mélanges Paul Thomas. Receuil de Mémoires Concernant la Philologie Classique*, Bruges, 451–73.
Hubaux, J. and Hicter, M. (1949), 'Le Fouilleur et le Trésor', in: *RIDA* 2, 425–37.
Hubbard, T. K. (1998), *The Pipes of Pan: Intertextuality and Literary Filiation in the Pastoral Tradition from Theocritus to Milton*, Ann Arbor.
Hübner, W. (2006), '*Vir gregis*: Imitations Structurelles de Virgile dans les *Astronomica* de Manilius', in: *Pallas* 72, 137–48.

Hulsenboom, P. (2013), "'Now I Have Forgotten All my Verses': Social Memory in the *Eclogues* of Virgil and Calpurnius Siculus', in: *Language and Literary Studies of Warsaw* 3, 13–28.
Hunter, R. L. (1996), *Theocritus and the Archaeology of Greek Poetry*, Cambridge.
—— (1999), *Theocritus: A Selection (Idylls 1,3,4,6,7,10,11 and 13)*, Cambridge.
—— (2006), *The Shadow of Callimachus: Studies in the Reception of Hellenistic Poetry at Rome*, Cambridge.
Hutchinson, G. (2006), *Propertius Elegies Book IV*, Cambridge.
—— (2013), *Greek to Latin: Frameworks and Contexts for Intertextuality*, Oxford.
Ingalls, W. B. (1971), 'Repetition in Lucretius', in: *Phoenix* 25, 227–36.
Ireland, S. (1992), *Menander: Dyskolos, Samia and Other Plays: A Companion to the Penguin Translation of the Plays of Menander by Norma Miller*, London.
James, S. L. (2012), 'Elegy and New Comedy', in: B. K. Gold (ed.), *A Companion to Roman Love Elegy*, Malden, Oxford, Chichester, 253–68.
Janka, M. (1997), *Ovid Ars Amatoria Buch 2 Kommentar*, Heidelberg.
Janko, R. (1984), *Aristotle on Comedy: Towards a Reconstruction of Poetics II*, Berkeley and Los Angeles.
Jennison, G. (1922), 'Polar Bears at Rome', in: *CR* 36, 73.
—— (1937), *Animals for Show and Pleasure in Ancient Rome*, Manchester.
Jermyn, L. A. S. (1949), 'Virgil's Agricultural Lore', in: *G&R* 18, 49–69.
—— (1951), 'Weather-Signs in Virgil', in: *G&R* 20, 26–37, 49–59.
Joly, D. (1974), 'La Bucolique au Service de l'Empire: Calpurnius Interprète de Virgile', in: *L'Idéologie de l'Impérialisme Romain*, Paris, 42–65.
Karakasis, E. (2005), *Terence and the Language of Roman Comedy*, Cambridge.
—— (2005a), '*Totum ut te faciant, Fabulle, nasum*: Catullus' XIII Reconsidered', in: *Studies in Latin Literature and Roman History* 12, 97–114.
—— (2011), *Song Exchange in Roman Pastoral*, Berlin.
Keen, R. (1985), 'Lucretius and his Reader', in: *Apeiron* 19, 1–10.
Keene, C. H. (1912), Review of Giarratano, C. (1910), *Calpurnii et Nemesiani Bucolica*, Naples, in: *CR* 26, 96–8.
—— (1996[repr.]), *The Eclogues of Calpurnius Siculus and M. Aurelius Olympius Nemesianus*, London.
Kegel-Brinkgreve, E. (1990), *The Echoing Woods: Bucolic and Pastoral from Theocritus to Wordsworth*, Amsterdam.
Keith, A. (2008), *Propertius. Poet of Love and Leisure*, London.
Keller, O. (1963[repr.]), *Die antike Tierwelt*, vol. I, Leipzig.
Kenney, E. J. (1958), '*Nequitiae Poeta*', in: N. I. Herescu (ed.), *Ovidiana: Recherches sur Ovide*, Paris, 201–9.
—— (1983), 'Virgil and the Elegiac Sensibility', in: *ICS* 8, 44–59.
—— (2007), 'Lucretian Texture: Style, Metre and Rhetoric in the *De Rerum Natura*', in: S. Gillespie and P. Hardie (eds.), *The Cambridge Companion to Lucretius*, Cambridge, 92–110.
Kettemann, R. (1977), *Bukolik und Georgik. Studien zu ihrer Affinität bei Vergil und später*, Heidelberg.
Knox, P. E. (1995), *Ovid Heroides Select Epistles*, Cambridge.
Konstan, D. (1995), *Greek Comedy and Ideology*, New York and Oxford.
Korzeniewski, D. (1971), *Hirtengedichte aus neronischer Zeit*, Darmstadt.

— (1972), 'Die *Eklogen* des Calpurnius Siculus als Gedichtbuch', in: *MH* 29, 214–6.
— (1973), 'Zwei bukolische Probleme', in: *Hermes* 101, 499–501.
— (1974), 'Néron et la Sibylle', in: *Latomus* 33, 921–5.
— (1976), 'Zur ersten und siebten *Ekloge* des Calpurnius Siculus', in: *MH* 33, 248–5.
Korzeniowski, G. S. (1998), *Verskolometrie und hexametrische Verskunst römischer Bukoliker*, Göttingen.
Kraffert, H. (1883), *Beiträge zur Kritik und Erklärung lateinischer Autoren*, Aurich.
Krautter, K. (1992), 'Lucan, Calpurnius Siculus und Nero', in: *Philologus* 136, 188–201.
Kromer, G. (1979), 'The Didactic Tradition in Virgil's *Georgics*', in: *Ramus* 8, 7–21.
Kronenberg, L. J. (2000), 'The Poet's Fiction: Virgil's Praise of the Farmer, Philosopher, and Poet at the End of *Georgics* 2', in: *HSPh* 100, 341–60.
Kühner, R. and Stegmann, C. (1962), *Grammatik der lateinischen Sprache, Satzlehre*, Darmstadt.
Küppers, E. (1981), 'Ovids *Ars Amatoria* und *Remedia Amoris* als Lehrdichtungen', in: *ANRW* 2.31.4, 2507–51.
Küppers, J. (1985), 'Die Faunus–Prophezeiung in der 1. *Ekloge* des Calpurnius Siculus', in: *Hermes* 113, 340–61.
— (1989), 'Tityrus in Rom: Bemerkungen zu einem vergilischen Thema und seiner Rezeptionsgeschichte', in: *ICS* 14, 33–47.
La Bua, G. (1999), *L' Inno nella Letteratura Poetica Latina*, San Severo.
— (2010), 'Nota a Calp. *Ecl.* 1, 67s. (e Ov. *Fast.* I 715s.), in: *Eikasmos* 21, 239–45.
La Penna, A. (1962), 'Esiodo nella Cultura e nella Poesia di Virgilio', in: *Hésiode et Son Influence* (*Entretiens Hardt* 7), 213–70.
— (1997), *'Fallit Imago:* Una Polemica di Manilio contro Virgilio e Lucrezio (nota a Manilio IV 306)', in: *Maia* 49, 107–8.
Lamagna, M. (1994), *La Fanciulla Tosata: Testo Critico, Introduzione, Traduzione e Commentario*, Naples.
Lana, I. (1965), *La Poesia nell' Età di Nerone*, Turin.
— (1998), 'Il Principato di Nerone', in: I. Lana and E. V. Maltese (eds.), *Storia della Civiltà Letteraria Greca e Latina*, vol. II, *Dall' Ellenismo all' Età di Traiano*, Turin, 819–33.
Landolfi, L. (1990), 'Manilio e le Ansie dell' Insegnamento: L' *excursus* Metodologico (*Astr.* II, 750–787)', in: *Pan* 10, 27–37.
— (1999), 'OYPANOBATEIN: Manilio, il Volo e la Poesia. Alcune Precisazioni', in: *Prometheus* 25, 151–65.
— (2009), 'L' Effemeride 'Bucolica': Calpurnio Siculo e i Giochi dell' Intertestualità (Saggio di Commento alla V *Ecloga*)', in: L. Landolfi and R. Oddo (eds.), *Fer Propius Tua Lumina; Giochi Intertestuali nella Poesia di Calpurnio Siculo*, Bologna, 89–128.
Langholf, V. (1990), 'Vergil–Allegorese in den *Bucolica* des Calpurnius Siculus', in: *RhM* 133, 350–70.
Lape, S. (2004), *Reproducing Athens: Menander's Comedy, Democratic Culture, and the Hellenistic City*, Princeton.
Latte, K. (1932), 'Randbemerkungen IV', in: *Philologus* 87, 268.
— (1960), *Römische Religionsgeschichte*, Munich.
Leach, E. W. (1964), 'Georgic Imagery in the *Ars Amatoria*', in: *TAPhA* 95, 142–54.
— (1973), 'Corydon Revisited: An Interpretation of the Political *Eclogues* of Calpurnius Siculus', in: *Ramus* 2, 53–97.
— (1974), *Vergil's Eclogues: Landscapes of Experience*, Ithaca, NY.

— (1975), 'Neronian Pastoral and the World of Power', in: A. J. Boyle (ed.), *Ancient Pastoral: Ramus Essays on Greek and Roman Pastoral Poetry*, Berwick, 204–30.
— (1981), '*Georgics* 2 and the Poem', in: *Arethusa* 14, 35–48.
Lenchantin de Gubernatis, M. (1912), 'La Natura in Tito Calpurnio Siculo', in: *Classici e Neolatini* 8, 75–90.
Levi, M. A. (1949), *Nerone e i suoi Tempi*, Milan.
Luck, G. (1983), 'Besuch in Rom', in: P. Händel and W. Meid (eds.), *Festschrift für Robert Muth zum 65. Geburtstag am 1. Januar 1981 dargebracht von Freunden und Kollegen*, Innsbrucker Beiträge zur Kulturwissenschaft 22, Innsbruck, 231–6.
Luiselli, B. (1960), 'Note su Calpurnio Siculo', in: *AFLC* 28, 135–53.
— (1963), '*L'Apocolocyntosis* Senecana e la Prima *Bucolica* di Calpurnio', in: *A&R* 8, 44–52.
Lyne, R.O.A.M. (2003$^{repr.}$), *The Latin Love Poets from Catullus to Horace*, Oxford.
Mackie, N. (1989), 'Urbanity in a Roman Landscape: the *Eclogues* of Calpurnius Siculus', in: *Landscape Research* 14 / 1, 9–14.
Maes, Y. (2008), 'Neronian Literature and the Grotesque', in: *Studies in Latin Literature and Roman History* 14, 313–23.
Magnelli, E. (2006), 'Bucolic Tradition and Poetic Programme in Calpurnius Siculus', in: M. Fantuzzi and Th. Papanghelis (eds.), *Brill's Companion to Greek and Latin Pastoral*, Leiden, 467–77.
Mahr, A. (1964), *Untersuchungen zur Sprache in den Eklogen des Calpurnius Siculus*, Vienna.
Malamud, M. (2009), 'Primitive Politics: Lucan and Petronius', in: W. J. Dominik, J. Garthwaite and P. A. Roche (eds.), *Writing Politics in Imperial Rome*, Leiden, 273–306.
Maltby, R. (2002), *Tibullus: Elegies. Text, Introduction and Commentary*, Cambridge.
Manni, E. (1938), 'Le Legenda dell' Età dell' Oro nella Politica dei Cesari', in: *A&R* 6, 108–20.
Marchiò, M. (1957), 'Un Componimento Georgico sulle Orme di Virgilio: l' *Egloga* V di Calpurnio Siculo', in: *GIF* 10, 301–14.
Martin, B. (1996), 'Calpurnius Siculus' 'New' *Aurea Aetas*', in: *AC* 39, 17–38.
— (2003), 'Calpurnius Siculus: The Ultimate Imperial 'Toady'?', in: A. F. Basson and W. J. Dominik (eds.), *Literature, Art, History: Studies on Classical Antiquity and Tradition in Honour of W. J. Henderson*, Frankfurt am Main, 73–90.
Martirosova, Z. (1999), *Eclogue and Elegy: Intertextual and Intergeneric Dialogue between Vergil's Eclogues and Roman Love Elegy*, Diss., Columbia.
Mayer, R. (1980), 'Calpurnius Siculus: Technique and Date', in: *JRS* 70, 175–6.
— (1982), 'Neronian Classicism', in: *AJPh* 103, 305–18.
— (1990), 'The Epic of Lucretius', in: *PLLS* 6, 35–43.
— (2005), 'Creating a Literature of Information in Rome', in: M. Horster and C. Reitz (eds.), *Wissensvermittlung in dichterischer Gestalt*, Stuttgart, 227–41.
— (2005a), 'The Early Empire: AD 14–68', in: S. J. Harrison (ed.), *A Companion to Latin Literature*, Oxford, 58–68.
— (2006), 'Latin Pastoral after Virgil', in: M. Fantuzzi and Th. Papanghelis (eds.), *Brill's Companion to Greek and Latin Pastoral*, Leiden, 451–66.
— (2012), *Horace: Odes Book I*, Cambridge.
Mazzarino, A. (1983), 'Dittico Calpurniano', in: *NAFM* 1, 401–11.
McKeown, J. C. (1989), *Ovid, Amores, vol. II. A Commentary on Book One*, Leeds.
— (1998), *Ovid, Amores, vol. III. A Commentary on Book Two*, Leeds.

Merfeld, B. (1999), *Panegyrik–Paränese–Parodie? Die Einsiedler Gedichte und Herrscherlob in neronischer Zeit*, Trier.
Merkelbach, R. (1983), 'Zur sechsten *Ekloge* des Calpurnius', in: *RhM* 126, 69–71.
Merone, E. (1967), *Innovazioni Linguistiche in Calpurnio Siculo*, Naples.
Messina, C. (1975), *T. Calpurnio Siculo*, Padua.
Michalopoulos, A. N. (2006), *Ovid Heroides 16 and 17: Introduction, Text and Commentary*, Cambridge.
Miller, J. F. (1992), 'The *Fasti* and Hellenistic Didactic: Ovid's Variant Aetiologies', in: *Arethusa* 25, 11–31.
Mitsis, P. (1993), 'Committing Philosophy on the Reader: Didactic Coercion and Reader Autonomy in *De Rerum Natura*', in: A. Schiesaro, P. Mitsis and J. S. Clay (eds.), *Mega Nepios: Il Destinatario nell' Epos Didascalico / The Addressee in Didactic Epic* (= MD 31), Pisa, 111–28.
Momigliano, A. (1944), 'Literary Chronology of the Neronian Age', in: *CQ* 38, 96–100.
—— (1960), 'Literary Chronology of the Neronian Age', in: A. Momigliano (id.), *Secondo Contributo alla Storia degli Studi Classici*, Rome, 454–61.
Monella, P. (2009), 'Pastori, Patroni, Dèi. Personaggi Politici e loro Inclusione nel Mondo Bucolico (Tibullo, Virgilio, Calpurnio Siculo)', in: L. Landolfi and R. Oddo (eds.), *Fer Propius Tua Lumina; Giochi Intertestuali nella Poesia di Calpurnio Siculo*, Bologna, 67–87.
Montanari-Caldini, R. (1981), 'Virgilio, Manilio e Germanico: Memoria Poetica e Ideologia Imperiale', in: *Cultura e Ideologia da Cicerone a Seneca*, Florence, 71–114.
Morelli, C. (1914), 'Nerone Poeta e i Poeti intorno a Nerone', in: *Athenaeum* 2, 117–52.
Morford, M. (1985), 'Nero's Patronage and Participation in Literature and the Arts', in: *ANRW* 2.32.3, 2003–31.
Murgatroyd, P. (1991), *Tibullus I*, London.
—— (1994), *Tibullus: Elegies II*, Oxford.
Murley, C. (1947), 'Lucretius, *De Rerum Natura*, Viewed as Epic', in: *TAPhA* 78, 336–46.
Mynors, R. A. B. (2003$^{repr.}$), *Virgil: Georgics*, Oxford.
Narducci, E. (1979), *La Provvidenza Crudele. Lucano e la Distruzione dei Miti Augustei*, Pisa.
Navarro-Antolín, F. (1996), *Lygdamus: Corpus Tibullianum III 1–6*, Leiden.
Nelis, D. (2004), 'From Didactic to Epic: *Georgics* 2.458–3.48', in: M. R. Gale (ed.), *Latin Epic and Didactic Poetry: Genre, Tradition and Individuality*, Swansea, 73–107.
Nelson, S. A. (1998), *God and the Land: The Metaphysics of Farming in Hesiod and Vergil*, New York.
Nethercut, W. R. (1973), 'Vergil's *De Rerum Natura*', in: *Ramus* 2, 41–52.
Neuburg, M. (1993), 'Hitch your Wagon to a Star: Manilius and his Two Addressees', in: A. Schiesaro, P. Mitsis and J. S. Clay (eds.), *Mega Nepios: Il Destinatario nell' Epos Didascalico / The Addressee in Didactic Epic* (= MD 31), Pisa, 243–82.
Newlands, C. E. (1987), 'Urban Pastoral. The Seventh *Eclogue* of Calpurnius Siculus', in: *ClAnt* 6, 218–31.
—— (2002), *Statius' Silvae and the Poetics of Empire*, Cambridge.
Newman, J. K. (1967), *The Concept of Vates in Augustan Poetry*, Brussels.
Nisbet, R. G. M. and Hubbard, M. (1970), *A Commentary on Horace: Odes. Book I*, Oxford.
—— (1978), *A Commentary on Horace: Odes. Book 2*, Oxford.
Nisbet, R. G. M. and Rudd, N. (2004), *A Commentary on Horace: Odes. Book 3*, Oxford.
Nisetich, F. (2001), *The Poems of Callimachus*, New York.

Novelli, A. (1980), *Il Linguaggio di Calpurnio Siculo*, Lecce.
Ostrand, K. D. (1984), *Aspects of the Reign of the Emperor Domitian*, Diss., Missouri–Columbia.
Otis, B. (1964), *Virgil. A Study in Civilized Poetry*, Oxford.
— (1970[repr.]), *Ovid as an Epic Poet*, Cambridge.
Otto, A. (1964), *Die Sprichwörter und sprichwörtlichen Redensarten der Römer*, Hildesheim.
Paladini, M. L. (1956), 'Osservazioni a Calpurnio Siculo', in: *Latomus* 15, 330–46, 521–31.
Papanghelis, T. D. (1994), *Ἡ Ποιητικὴ τῶν Ρωμαίων "Νεωτέρων"*, Athens.
— (1995), *Ἀπὸ τὴ Βουκολικὴ Εὐτοπία στὴν Πολιτικὴ Οὐτοπία*, Athens.
— (1999), 'Eros Pastoral and Profane: On Love in Virgil's *Eclogues*', in: S. Morton Braund and R. Mayer (eds.), *Amor:Roma. Love & Latin Literature*, Cambridge, 44–59.
— (2006), 'Friends, Foes, Frames and Fragments: Textuality in Virgil's *Eclogues*', in: M. Fantuzzi and Th. Papanghelis (eds.), *Brill's Companion to Greek and Latin Pastoral*, Leiden, 369–402.
Paratore, E. (1939), 'Spunti Lucreziani nelle *Georgiche*', in: *A&R* 3.7, 177–202.
Paschalis, M. (1996), 'Προφητεία και Εξουσία στη Λατινική Βουκολική Ποίηση της Κλασικής Περιόδου', in: D. I. Kyrtatas (ed.), *Ιεροί Λόγοι: Προφητείες και Μαντείες στην Ιουδαϊκή, την Ελληνική και τη Ρωμαϊκή Αρχαιότητα*, Athens, 135–51.
Pearce, J. B. (1990), *The Eclogues of Calpurnius Siculus*, San Antonio, Texas.
Pearce, T. E. V. (1970), 'A Note on *Ille ego qui quondam...*', in: *CQ* 20, 335–8.
Perkell, C. G. (1989), *The Poet's Truth: A Study of the Poet in Virgil's Georgics*, Berkeley and Los Angeles.
Perrelli, R. (2002), *Commento a Tibullo: Elegie, Libro I*, Soveria Mannelli.
Perutelli, A. (1976), 'Natura Selvatica e Genere Bucolico', in: *ASNP* 6, 763–98.
Piazzi, L. (2007), *P. Ovidii Nasonis Heroidum Epistula VII Dido Aeneae*, Florence.
Pichon, R. (1966), *Index Verborum Amatoriorum*, Hildesheim.
Pinotti, P. (1993), *Remedia Amoris: Introduzione, Testo e Commento*, Bologna.
Pöhlmann, E. (1973), 'Charakteristika des römischen Lehrgedichts', in: *ANRW* 1.3, 813–901.
Postgate, J. P. (1902), 'The Comet of Calpurnius Siculus', in: *CR* 16, 38–40.
— (1905), '*Pharsalia* Nostra', in: *CR* 19, 257–60.
Prestagostini, R. (1984), 'La Rivalità tra Comata e Lacone: una Paideia Disconosciuta (Theocr. 5.35–43, 116–9)', in: *MD* 13, 137–41.
Putnam, M. C. J. (1995), 'Silvia's Stag and Virgilian Ekphrasis', in: *MD* 34, 107–33.
— (1995a), *Virgil's Aeneid: Interpretation and Influence*, Chapel Hill.
— (2010), 'Some Virgilian Unities', in: P. Hardie and H. Moore (eds.), *Classical Literary Careers and their Reception*, Cambridge, 17–38.
Ramorino, L. (1986), 'Influssi Lucreziani nelle *Bucoliche* di Virgilio', in: *CCC* 7, 297–331.
Raynaud, E. (1931), *Poetae Minores*, Paris.
Reed, J. D. (1997), *Bion of Smyrna: The Fragments and the Adonis*, Cambridge.
Reeh, A. (1973), *Interpretationen zu den Astronomica des Manilius mit besonderer Berücksichtigung der philosophischen Partien*, Marburg.
Reeson, J. (2001), *Ovid Heroides 11, 13 & 14 – A Commentary*, Leiden.
Reeve, M. D. (1978), 'The Textual Tradition of Calpurnius and Nemesianus', in: *CQ* 28, 223–38.
Reitz, C. (2013), 'Columella, *De Re Rustica*', in: E. Buckley and M. T. Dinter (eds.), *A Companion to the Neronian Age*, Malden, Oxford, Chichester, 275–87.

Risselada, R. (1993), *Imperatives and Other Directive Expressions in Latin: A Study in the Pragmatics of a Dead Language*, Amsterdam.
Rivoltella, M. (2006), 'Melior Viret Herba Tapetis (Calp. Sic. VI 71): Persistenza ed Evoluzione di un Cliché Figurativo Epicureo', in: *Aevum* 80, 121–3.
Roche, P. (2009), *Lucan, De Bello Civili, Book 1*, Oxford.
Rogers, R. S. (1953), 'The Neronian Comets', in: *TAPhA* 84, 237–49.
Romano, D. (1980–1), 'Nova Spectacula. L' Elogio di Nerone nella VII *Ecloga* di Calpurnio Siculo', in: *AASLP* 40, 241–51.
–– (2002), 'Calpurnio e I Penati. La Chiusa del Vaticinio di Fauno nella 1 *Ecloga*', in: D. Romano (id.), *Tra Antico e Tardoantico*, Palermo, 91–6.
Romano, E. (1978),'Gli Appelli al Lettore negli *Astronomica* di Manilio', in: *Pan* 6, 115–25.
Römer, F. (1994), 'Mode und Methode in der Deutung panegyrischer Dichtung der nachaugusteischen Zeit', in: *Hermes* 122, 95–113.
Rosati, G. (2002), 'Muse and Power in the Poetry of Statius', in: E. Spentzou and D. Fowler (eds.), *Cultivating the Muse: Struggles for Power and Inspiration in Classical Literature*, Oxford, 229–51.
Rosenmeyer, T. G. (1969), *The Green Cabinet. Theocritus and the European Pastoral Lyric*, Berkeley.
Rosivach, V. (1998), *When a Young Man Falls in Love: The Sexual Exploitation of Women in New Comedy*, London and New York.
Ross, D. O. (1975), *Backgrounds to Augustan Poetry: Gallus, Elegy and Rome*, Cambridge.
Ruggeri, E. (2002), 'Calpurnio Siculo e l' Età di Nerone', in: *InvLuc.* 24, 201–43.
Rumpf, L. (1996), *Extremus Labor. Vergils 10. Ekloge und die Poetik der Bukolika*, Göttingen.
Rutherford, R. (1995), 'Authorial Rhetoric in Virgil's *Georgics*', in: D. Innes, H. Hine and C. Pelling (eds.), *Ethics and Rhetoric: Classical Essays for Donald Russell on his Seventy-Fifth Birthday*, Oxford, 19–29.
Salanitro, G. (1975–6), 'Due Note di Filologia Latina', in: *Helikon* 15–6, 481–5.
Salvatore, A. (1949), 'De Laudibus Pisonis cum Panegyrico Messallae atque Calpurni Bucolicis Comparatis', in: *RFIC* 27, 177–90.
Sarpe, G. (1819), *Quaestiones Philologicae*, Progr., Rostock.
Saunders, T. (2008), *Bucolic Ecology: Virgil's Eclogues and the Environmental Literary Tradition*, London.
Sauter, F. (1934), *Der römische Kaiserkult bei Martial und Statius*, Stuttgart and Berlin.
Scarcia, R. (1993), '*Intelligendi aditus*: Aspetti dello Studio Virgiliano di Manilio', in: D. Liuzzi (ed.), *Manilio fra Poesia e Scienza*, Galatina, 127–45.
Schachter, A. (1927), *Der Globus: Seine Entstehung und Verwendung in der Antike*, Leipzig.
Schäfer, A. (2001), *Vergils Eklogen 3 und 7 in der Tradition der lateinischen Streitdichtung*, Frankfurt am Main.
Schäfer, S. (1996), *Das Weltbild der Vergilischen Georgika in seinem Verhältnis zu De Rerum Natura des Lukrez*, Frankfurt.
Scheda, G. (1969), *Studien zur bukolischen Dichtung der neronischen Epoche*, Bonn.
Schenkl, H. (1885), *Calpurnii et Nemesiani Bucolica*, Leipzig.
Schetter, W. (1975), 'Nemesians *Bucolica* und die Anfänge der spätlateinischen Dichtung', in: C. Gnilka and W. Schetter (eds.), *Studien zur Literatur der Spätantike*, Bonn, 1–43.
Schiesaro, A. (1993), 'Il Destinatario Discreto: Funzioni Didascaliche e Progetto Culturale nelle *Georgiche*', in: A. Schiesaro, P. Mitsis and J. S. Clay (eds.), *Mega Nepios: Il Destinatario nell' Epos Didascalico / The Addressee in Didactic Epic* (= MD 31), Pisa, 129–47.

—— (1994), 'The Palingenesis of *De Rerum Natura*', in: *PCPhS* 40, 81–107.
Schiesaro, A., Mitsis, P. and Clay, J. S. (1993), (eds.), *Mega Nepios: Il Destinatario nell' Epos Didascalico / The Addressee in Didactic Epic* (= *MD* 31), Pisa.
Schmid, W. (1953), 'Panegyrik und Bukolik in der neronischen Epoche: Ein Beitrag zur Erklärung der *Carmina Einsidlensia*', in: *BJ* 153, 63–96.
Schmidt, E. A. (1969), 'Hirtenhierarchie in der antiken Bukolik?', in: *Philologus* 113, 183–200.
—— (1972), *Poetische Reflexion: Vergils Bukolik*, Munich.
—— (1998–9), 'Ancient Bucolic Poetry and Later Pastoral Writing: Systematic and Historical Reflections', in: *IJCT* 5, 226–51.
Schröder, B. (1991), *Carmina non quae nemorale resultent: Ein Kommentar zur 4. Ekloge des Calpurnius Siculus*, Frankfurt am Main.
Schubert, C. (1998), *Studien zum Nerobild in der lateinischen Dichtung der Antike*, Stuttgart.
Shackleton-Bailey, D. R. (1978), 'Notes on Minor Latin Poetry', in: *Phoenix* 32, 305–25.
Shotter, D. (2008), *Nero Caesar Augustus: Emperor of Rome*, Harlow.
Simon, Z. L. (2007), '*Frange, puer, calamos*… Bukolische Allegorie, Panegyrik und die Krise des Dichterberufs in der vierten *Ekloge* des T. Calpurnius Siculus', in: *AAntHung* 47, 43–98.
—— (2007a), '"*Sacra Calpurni Vestigia*" Calpurnio Siculo e i Nuovi Percorsi della Bucolica Umanistica nel Secondo Quattrocento', in: *StudUmanistPiceni* 27, 157–76.
—— (2007b), '*Non Vulgare Genus:* Ekphrasis, Literarisches Gedächtnis und Gattungsspezifische Innovation in der sechsten *Ecloge* des T. Calpurnius Siculus', in: *ACD* 43, 57–70.
Skutsch, F. (1897), 'T. Calpurnius Siculus', in: *RE* 3.1, 1401–6.
—— (1905), 'Einsiedlensia Carmina', in: *RE* 5, 2115–6.
Skutsch, O. (1985), *The Annals of Q. Ennius*, Oxford.
Slater, N. W. (1994), 'Calpurnius and the Anxiety of Vergilian Influence: *Eclogue* I', in: *Syllecta Classica* 5, 71–8.
Smith, R. A. (1997), *Poetic Allusion and Poetic Embrace in Ovid and Virgil*, Ann Arbor.
Solodow, J. B. (1988), *The World of Ovid's Metamorphoses*, Chapel Hill.
Soraci, G. (1982), 'Echi Virgiliani in Calpurnio Siculo', in: *Atti del Convegno di Studi Virgiliani, Pescara 23–25 Ottobre 1981*, vol. II, San Gabriele, 114–8.
—— (1997), 'Crocale', in: P. D' Alessandro (ed.), *ΜΟΥΣΑ. Scritti in Onore di G. Morelli*, Edizioni e Saggi Universitari di Filologia Classica. Fuori Sezione 5, Bologna, 315–21.
Spadaro, M. D. (1969), *Sulle Egloghe Politiche di Tito Calpurnio Siculo*, Catania.
Spencer, D. (2005), 'Lucan's Follies: Memory and Ruin in a Civil-War Landscape', in: *G&R* 52, 46–69.
Stanzel, K. H. (1989), 'Bukolische Dreiecksverhältnisse. Zu Calpurnius' und Nemesians zweiter *Ekloge*', in: *WJA* 15, 183–201.
Steudel, M. (1992), *Die Literaturparodie in Ovids Ars Amatoria*, Hildesheim.
Stroh, W. (1999), 'Vom Faunus zum Faun: Theologische Beiträge von Horaz und Ovid', in: W. Schubert (ed.), *Ovid: Werk und Wirkung. Festgabe für Michael von Albrecht zum 65. Geburtstag*, Studien zur klassischen Philologie 100, vol. II, Frankfurt am Main, 559–612.
Sullivan, J. P. (1985), *Literature and Politics in the Age of Nero*, Ithaca, NY.
Summers, W. C. (1920), *The Silver Age of Latin Literature: From Tiberius to Trajan*, London.
Svennung, J. (1935), *Untersuchungen zu Palladius und zur lateinischen Fach- und Volkssprache*, Uppsala.

Taliercio, A. (2010), 'Calpurnio Siculo, *Ecl.* VII e Virgilio: Dialettica Letteraria e Politica', in: *StudRom* 58, 52–74.

Tatum, W. J. (2007), 'The Presocratics in Book 1 of Lucretius' *De Rerum Natura*', in: M. R. Gale (ed.), *Oxford Readings in Classical Studies: Lucretius*, Oxford, 132–45.

Theiler, W. (1956), 'Zu den Einsiedlern Hirtengedichten', in: *SIFC* 27–8, 565–77.

Thibodeau, P. (2011), *Playing the Farmer. Representations of Rural Life in Vergil's Georgics*, Berkeley and Los Angeles.

Thill, A. (1979), *Alter ab illo: Recherches sur l'Imitation dans la Poésie Personelle à l' Époque Augustéenne*, Paris.

Thomas, R. F. (1983), 'Callimachus, the *Victoria Berenices*, and Roman Poetry', in: *CQ* 33, 92–113.

— (1985), 'From *recusatio* to Commitment: The Evolution of the Virgilian Programme', in: *PLLS* 5, 61–73.

— (1987), 'Prose into Poetry: Tradition and Meaning in Virgil's *Georgics*', in *HSPh* 91, 229–60.

— (1988), *Virgil: Georgics*, 2 vols, Cambridge.

— (1993), 'Callimachus back in Rome', in: M. A. Harder, R. F. Regtuit and G. C. Wakker (eds.), *Callimachus*, Groningen, 197–215.

— (1998), 'Virgil's Pindar?', in: P. Knox and C. Foss (eds.), *Style and Tradition: Studies in Honor of Wendell Clausen*, Stuttgart, 99–120.

Toohey, P. (1996), *Epic Lessons: An Introduction to Ancient Didactic Poetry*, London.

Townend, G. B. (1973), 'The Literary Substrata to Juvenal's Satires', in: *JRS* 63, 148–60.

— (1978), 'The Fading of Memmius', in: *CQ* 28, 267–83.

— (1980), 'Calpurnius Siculus and the *Munus Neronis*', in: *JRS* 70, 166–74.

Toynbee, J. M. C. (1942), 'Nero *Artifex:* the *Apocolocyntosis* Reconsidered', in: *CQ* 36, 83–93.

— (1973), *Animals in Roman Life and Art*, Ithaca, NY.

Traglia, A. (1950), *La Flessione Verbale Latina*, Turin.

Traill, A. (2008), *Women and the Comic Plot in Menander*, Cambridge and New York.

Trépanier, S. (2007), 'The Didactic Plot in Lucretius, *De Rerum Natura* and its Empedoclean Model', in: R. W. Sharples and R. Sorabji (eds.), *Greek and Roman Philosophy 100 BC–200 AD*, vol. I, London, 243–82.

Tromaras, L. (2001), *Κάτουλλος. Ο Νεωτερικός Ποιητής της Ρώμης*, Thessaloniki.

Uden, J. (2010), 'The Vanishing Gardens of Priapus', in: *HSPh* 105, 189–219.

Vallat, D. (2006), 'Phénomènes de Réécriture dans l'Onomastique du Genre Bucolique', in: *Interférences Ars Scribendi* 4 (=http://ars-scribendi.enslsh.fr/article.php3?id_article=36&var_affichage=vf).

Vallet, G. (1956), *Calpurnius Siculus. Les Bucoliques*, Paris.

Van Sickle, J. (1992), *A Reading of Virgil's Messianic Eclogue*, New York.

Vance, E. (1981), 'Sylvia's Pet Stag: Wildness and Domesticity in Virgil's *Aeneid*', in: *Arethusa* 14, 127–38.

Ventura, M. S. (2006), 'Reescribiendo a Nerón (Calpurnio Sículo, 1.33–88, Tácito, '*Anales*', 13.4.1–3)', in: *Argos* 30, 121–43.

Verdière, R. (1952), 'À l'Ombre des 'Charmes' d' Einsiedeln', in: *RBPh* 30, 799–804.

— (1954), *T. Calpurnii Siculi De laude Pisonis et Bucolica et M. Annaei Lucani De laude Caesaris Einsiedlensia quae dicuntur carmina*, Brussels.

— (1956–7), 'Sur un Point de Messianisme dans les Synoptiques et chez Calpurnius', in: *RUB* 9, 89–92.

—— (1966), 'La Bucolique Post-Vergilienne', in: *Eos* 56, 161–85.
—— (1968), 'La Date de l'Action de la Première *Bucolique* Calpurnienne', in: *AC* 37, 534–9.
—— (1971), 'Notes de Lecture', in: H. Bardon and R. Verdière (eds.), *Vergiliana. Recherches sur Virgile*, Leiden, 375–85.
—— (1977), 'Qui est le Mélibée des *Bucoliques* de Calpurnius?', in: *RPh* 51, 15–21.
—— (1982), 'Quand le Couchant Aura Vu Derrière lui se Lever des Aurores', in: J. M. Croisille and P. M. Fauchère (eds.), *Neronia. Actes du IIe Colloque de la Société Internationale d'Études Néroniennes*, Adosa, 173–90.
—— (1985), 'Le Genre Bucolique à l'Époque de Néron: les *Bucolica* de T. Calpurnius Siculus et les *Carmina Einsidlensia*. État de la Question et Prospectives', in: *ANRW* 2.32.3, 1845–1924.
—— (1987), 'À Quelle Époque Vécut T. Calpurnius Siculus?', in: *Neronia III, Actes du IIIe Colloque International de la Société Internationale d'Études Néroniennes (Varenna – Juin 1982)*, Rome, 125–38.
—— (1992), 'Calpurnius Siculus et le Culte de la Personnalité', in: *Helmantica* 43, 31–40.
—— (1993), 'Calpurnius, en Fin d'Analyse…', in: *Helmantica* 44, 349–98.
Verity, A. and Hunter, R. L. (2002), *Theocritus. Idylls*, Oxford.
Vinchesi, M. A. (1991), 'La Terza *Ecloga* di Calpurnio Siculo fra Tradizione Bucolica e Tradizione Elegiaca', in: *Prometheus* 17, 259–76.
—— (1992), 'Funzione del Tecnicismo nella Poesia Bucolica di Calpurnio Siculo', in: I. Mazzini (ed.), *Civiltà Materiale e Letteratura nel Mondo Antico*, Università degli Studi di Macerata. Pubblicazioni della Facoltà di Lettere e Filosofia 64: Atti di Convegni 19, Macerata, 149–61.
—— (1996), *Calpurnio Siculo. Egloghe*, Milan.
—— (2002), 'Calpurnio Siculo e i Nuovi Percorsi della Poesia Bucolica', in: L. Castagna and G. Vogt-Spira (eds.), *Pervertere: Ästhetik der Verkehrung. Literatur und Kultur neronischer Zeit und ihre Rezeption*, Beiträge zur Altertumskunde 151, Munich, 139–51.
—— (2008), 'Il *Certamen* Mancato: per un' Analisi Tematica della VI *Egloga* di Calpurnio Siculo', in: P. Arduini, S. Audano, A. Borghini, A. Cavarzere, G. Mazzoli, G. Paduano and A. Russo (eds.), *Studi Offerti ad Alessandro Perutelli*, vol. II, Rome, 543–57.
—— (2009), 'Spigolature Calpurniane', in: L. Landolfi and R. Oddo (eds.), *Fer Propius Tua Lumina; Giochi Intertestuali nella Poesia di Calpurnio Siculo*, Bologna, 143–54.
—— (2009a), 'Tematiche e Modalità Inniche nella IV *Egloga* di Calpurnio Siculo', in: *Paideia* 64, 571–88.
—— (2010), 'Aspetti della Poesia Bucolica di Età Neroniana. Per una Lettura della VII *Egloga* di Calpurnio Siculo', in: *Quaderni di Acme* 120, 137–59.
—— (2012), 'Presenze dell' Elegia Latina nella Poesia Bucolica di Calpurnio Siculo', in: F. Bognini (ed.), *Meminisse iuvat: Studi in Memoria di Violetta de Angelis*, Pisa, 705–21.
—— (2014), *Calpurnii Siculi Eclogae*, Florence.
Volk, K. (1997), '*Cum carmine crescit et annus*: Ovid's *Fasti* and the Poetics of Simultaneity', in: *TAPhA* 127, 287–313.
—— (2001), 'Pious and Impious Approaches to Cosmology in Manilius', in: *MD* 47, 85–117.
—— (2002), *The Poetics of Latin Didactic: Lucretius, Vergil, Ovid, Manilius*, Oxford.
—— (2003), 'Manilius' Solitary Chariot-Ride (*Astronomica* 2.138–40)', in: *CQ* 53, 628–33.
—— (2004), '"Heavenly Steps": Manilius 4.119–121 and its Background', in: R. Boustan and A. Y. Reed (eds.), *Heavenly Realms and Earthly Realities in Late Antique Religions*, Cambridge, 34–46.

—— (2008), *Oxford Readings in Classical Studies: Vergil's Georgics*, Oxford.
—— (2009), *Manilius & his Intellectual Background*, Oxford.
Vozza, P. (1993), 'L' Ars Poetica di Calpurnio–Coridone ed il Giudizio sull' Età Neroniana', in: *BStudLat.* 23, 282–308.
—— (1994), 'Un Silenzio Eloquente (*Quid tacitus...?* Calpurnio *Ecl.* 4.1–4)', in: *BStudLat.* 24, 71–92.
Walter, H. (1988), *Studien zur Hirtendichtung Nemesians*, Stuttgart.
Wendel, C. (1901), *De Nominibus Bucolicis*, Leipzig.
Wendel, H. (1933), *Arkadien im Umkreis bukolischer Dichtung in der Antike und in der französischen Literatur*, Giessen.
White, H. (1999), 'A Singing Contest in Calpurnius Siculus', in: *QUCC* 62, 149–51.
Wilkinson, L. P. (1969), *The Georgics of Virgil: A Critical Survey*, Cambridge.
Williams, G. (1978), *Change and Decline: Roman Literature in the Early Empire*, Berkeley.
Williams, R. D. (1973), *The Aeneid of Vergil: Books 7–12*, Glasgow.
Wilson, A. M. (1985), 'The Prologue to Manilius 1', in: *PLLS* 5, 283–98.
Wimmel, W. (1970), 'Apollo–Paupertas. Zur Symbolik von Berufungsvorgängen bei Properz, Horaz und Calpurnius', in: W. Wimmel (ed.), *Forschungen zur römischen Literatur. Festschrift zum 60. Geburtstag von K. Büchner*, vol. II, Wiesbaden, 291–7.
Wiseman, T. P. (1982), 'Calpurnius Siculus and the Claudian Civil War', in: *JRS* 72, 57–67.
Wistrand, E. (1987), *Felicitas Imperatoria*, Göteborg.

Index Locorum

Aetna
46–7: 106

Afranius
tog. 117 Ribb.³: 131

Antiphanes
fr. 131 K–A: 210

A.P.
7.100: 197 and n. 16
9.136: 167 and n. 54
12.127: 197 and n. 16

Apollonius of Rhodes
1.77: 189
2.65: 17
4.1467: 189
4.1485: 189
4.1497: 189

Apuleius
Met.
5.7.5: 53

Aratus
1: 67 and n. 103, 183
1–18: 183
16–8: 182
460–1: 183
909–87: 62
1036–7: 183

Aristotle
Poet.
1447ᵇ19–20: 158

M. Aurelius Antoninus
Fro. 1.p.180 (68N): 45 and n. 137

Ausonius
Mos.
144: 84

Bion
fr. 3: 95, 215 and n. 97
fr. 9.10: 125
fr. 12: 246
E.A.
19: 199
[2]: 125

Caecilius Statius
com. 66–7 Ribb.³: 135

Callimachus
Aet.
1.13–6 ff. Pf.: 60
1.20 Pf.: 70
1.22–4 Pf.: 81, 203
1.22–8 Pf.: 54
1.25–8 Pf.: 184
2.1–2 Pf.: 203
Ep.
32.1 Pf.: 80
Hymn to Apollo
108 ff.: 54
Hymn to Zeus
52 ff.: 70
Iamb 3: 112
Iamb 12: 112

Calpurnius Siculus
1: 3, 4, 8, 9, 33, 48 and n. 1, 83 and n. 185,
    111, 117, 136, 236, 241, 251
1–3: 3 and n. 8
1.1: 17
1.1–3: 15
1.4: 16, 152, 190
1.4–5: 15, 16
1.4–7: 8
1.5–9: 19, 240
1.6: 8, 20
1.7: 18
1.8: 19, 67 and n. 102
1.8–9: 15
1.8–10: 8
1.8–12: 8, 18

1.9: 16
1.9–10: 8, 18 f., 57
1.10: 19 and n. 21
1.11: 16
1.11–2: 8
1.12: 19
1.13: 20
1.13–5: 25
1.16–7: 21
1.16–8: 21
1.17–8: 8, 17
1.18: 21, 42
1.19: 8, 15, 20
1.20: 15, 24
1.20–1: 8, 22
1.20–3: 22
1.21: 22
1.22–3: 75
1.26: 45 and n. 137
1.26–7: 18
1.28–9: 22
1.29: 22, 52
1.29–30: 107
1.30: 22, 45 and n. 137
1.32: 20
1.33: 30
1.33–88: 15, 43
1.34–7: 24
1.36: 34, 35
1.36–7: 26
1.36–42: 34, 37
1.37–9: 35, 44, 45
1.42: 30, 31, 68 and n. 108
1.42–5: 30
1.42–59: 37
1.43–4: 76 and n. 152
1.44: 33, 46 f. and n. 139, 68
1.45: 1 and n. 1, 33 and n. 91, 37
1.46: 25, 33, 46 f. and n. 139
1.46–7: 8, 25, 28, 43
1.46–57: 28, 37
1.46–59: 34
1.47: 25, 26
1.48: 26
1.49: 1 and n. 1
1.49–50: 28
1.50–1: 27, 41

1.54: 35
1.55: 45
1.55–7: 37
1.57: 44
1.58–9: 37
1.58 f.: 71 and n. 123
1.58–62: 37
1.63–8: 28, 34, 37
1.64: 31
1.65: 28
1.65–6: 28
1.66: 44
1.67–8: 28
1.69–73: 37
1.73: 37 and n. 109
1.74–6: 26, 35
1.77–81: 1 and n. 1
1.77–83: 38, 39
1.80–1: 45
1.82–3: 28, 38
1.84–5: 29
1.84–6: 40, 41
1.84–8: 37, 39
1.85: 29 and n. 67, 44
1.86: 39
1.87–8: 8, 39
1.88: 39
1.91: 112 and n. 99
1.92: 46 f. and n. 139
1.92–3: 41
1.92–4: 15
1.93: 42, 79
1.94: 41, 80
2: 3, 4, 8, 9, 45, 83 and n. 185, 102, 188, 195, 197 and n. 16, 205, 208, 223, 224 and n. 5, 252, 253
2.1: 195
2.1–2: 195
2.1–3: 197
2.2: 196
2.3–4: 195, 213
2.4: 195
2.4–6: 125
2.4–7: 8
2.5: 8, 195, 196
2.6: 54, 196
2.7–8: 196

2.9: 195, 196
2.10: 198
2.10–11: 198
2.10–20: 196
2.11: 198
2.12: 8, 132, 199
2.13: 8
2.13–4: 199
2.15: 200
2.15–20: 8
2.16–7: 200
2.18: 8
2.18–9: 200
2.19: 103
2.19–20: 200
2.21: 8, 216
2.21 ff.: 201
2.24: 202
2.28: 203
2.28–35: 202
2.29: 218 and n. 111
2.30: 203
2.31: 202
2.32–3: 203
2.34–5: 204, 215
2.36: 170, 204
2.36–9: 204
2.37: 8
2.40: 205
2.40–1: 217
2.41: 205, 217
2.42: 205
2.43: 205
2.44: 206, 218 and n. 111
2.44–51: 206
2.47: 206
2.48–51: 206, 215
2.49: 206
2.51: 206
2.52–9: 206
2.52 ff.: 209
2.55: 207
2.56: 9, 207, 217
2.56–9: 218
2.57–9: 8, 208
2.59: 8, 207, 218
2.60: 208, 209

2.60–1: 113, 208
2.60 ff.: 208
2.61: 208, 209
2.62–3: 8, 210, 218 and n. 111
2.62–7: 208
2.64–7: 210
2.65: 210
2.66: 210
2.67: 170
2.68: 8
2.68–71: 210
2.68–75: 208, 210
2.69: 211
2.70: 210
2.71: 211, 218 and n. 111
2.72–3: 8, 212
2.72–5: 210
2.75: 211, 218
2.76: 45, 212 and n. 85
2.76–83: 208, 212
2.77: 212
2.78: 212
2.78–9: 175, 212
2.80: 218
2.80–3: 212
2.83: 218
2.84: 45, 213
2.84–91: 208
2.85: 213 f.
2.87: 214
2.90–1: 214
2.91: 218
2.92: 214
2.93: 186, 214
2.93–4: 81
2.94: 214, 216
2.95: 215
2.96: 216
2.96–7: 81, 214, 215 and n. 99
2.97: 216
2.98: 216
3: 3, 4, 8, 45, 123, 124, 125, 128, 130, 134, 141, 143, 145, 148, 149, 150, 151, 152, 152 f. and n. 138, 153, 208, 211 and n. 77, 213 and n. 89, 252, 253
3.1: 45
3.1–2: 8

3.1–6: 125
3.1–9: 134
3.1–44: 125
3.2–3: 127
3.3: 126, 135
3.4–6: 126
3.7: 126
3.7–8: 126, 207
3.8: 127, 128
3.8–9: 126, 127, 135
3.9: 127
3.10: 127
3.10–2: 127, 128
3.13: 129, 131
3.13–4: 128
3.14: 129, 206
3.15–6: 129
3.15–7: 8, 129
3.16: 8, 129
3.18: 45
3.18–23: 129
3.19: 206
3.19–21: 152
3.20–1: 130
3.22–3: 130
3.23: 130
3.24: 131
3.24 ff.: 131
3.25: 45, 131, 132
3.26–7: 8, 132, 133
3.26–30: 133
3.27: 8
3.28: 133
3.28–30: 133
3.31–2: 134
3.33: 151
3.33–4: 134
3.35: 140
3.36–9: 135
3.37: 135
3.38: 135
3.39: 135
3.42: 135
3.43–4: 75, 136, 136 f. and n. 68
3.45: 137, 139
3.45–7: 137
3.46: 137

3.46–7: 138
3.47: 138
3.48–9: 138
3.50: 138, 139
3.51–4: 139
3.55: 137, 139
3.55–6: 140
3.55–60: 140
3.56–8: 140
3.59–60: 140
3.60: 142
3.61: 213 and n. 89
3.61–2: 141
3.61–3: 213 and n. 89
3.62: 142
3.63: 8, 213 and n. 89
3.63–4: 143
3.63–7: 142
3.63–9: 211 and n. 77
3.64: 8, 143
3.65: 144
3.65–7: 143
3.67: 144
3.68: 206
3.68–9: 144, 145
3.69: 144
3.70–2: 144
3.70–5: 144
3.73–4: 145
3.76–80: 146
3.76–85: 145
3.81: 147
3.81–5: 147
3.82–5: 147
3.86: 149
3.86–91: 147
3.88: 149
3.89–90: 148
3.90: 149
3.93: 149
3.94–5: 149
3.96–8: 134, 150
3.98: 8
4: 3, 4, 48 and n. 1, 67 and n. 103, 82 and n. 184, 83 and n. 185, 102, 111, 113, 117, 170 f. and n. 74, 188, 201, 236, 241, 251
4.1: 50

Index Locorum — **277**

4.1–4: 8, 48 and n. 3, 50 f. and n. 13, 93
4.2: 8, 48, 49 f., 83
4.3: 49, 243
4.3–4: 48
4.5: 49, 51, 52, 53, 84
4.5–6: 10, 24
4.5–8: 31, 51
4.5 ff.: 57
4.7–8: 53
4.8: 53
4.9–10: 54
4.10: 54
4.11: 55, 80 and n. 172
4.12: 50 f. and n. 13, 52
4.12–3: 45, 55
4.14: 55
4.14–5: 55
4.15: 56
4.16: 8, 57
4.16–8: 55
4.17: 55, 57, 67 and n. 102
4.19–20: 8, 83
4.19–21: 57
4.19 ff.: 57
4.20: 57
4.20 f.: 57 and n. 49
4.21: 57, 58
4.23: 58
4.23–8: 95
4.24: 58 and n. 54
4.25–6: 58, 170 f. and n. 74
4.26–7: 58
4.27–8: 59, 83, 84
4.30: 59
4.31–2: 50 f. and n. 13, 61
4.32: 62
4.33: 61
4.33 ff.: 61 and n. 67
4.34: 61
4.35: 8, 61
4.37: 8, 59
4.38: 8, 59 f.
4.38–41: 60 and n. 62
4.39–40: 85
4.39–42: 1 and n. 1
4.39–49: 60
4.39 ff.: 2 and n. 3

4.40: 60 and n. 62
4.43–9: 60 and n. 62
4.46–7: 60
4.52: 24, 50 f. and n. 13
4.53–4: 62
4.53–5: 84
4.53–7: 62 and n. 76
4.54: 62 and n. 76
4.54–5: 62
4.55: 54
4.56–7: 202
4.57: 62 and n. 76
4.59–63: 21, 113, 132, 190, 202
4.59 ff.: 64
4.60: 8
4.60–1: 64, 198
4.60–3: 78
4.61: 54, 64
4.62: 152
4.62–3: 63 f.
4.62 ff.: 216
4.63: 64, 75 and n. 146, 84
4.64: 65 and n. 93, 152
4.65: 65
4.65–6: 64
4.65 ff.: 61 and n. 67
4.66: 83
4.66–7: 65, 198
4.68–9: 65
4.70–2: 54
4.73 ff.: 66
4.74: 66, 83
4.74–5: 55 and n. 34
4.76–7: 66, 84
4.78: 67 and n. 102
4.82: 48, 67 and n. 103, 69 f. and n. 115
4.82–3: 67
4.82 ff.: 61 and n. 67, 69 f. and n. 115
4.83: 69 f. and n. 115, 84
4.84: 68
4.84–6: 61 and n. 67, 68
4.85: 68
4.86: 61 and n. 67, 68
4.87: 1 and n. 1
4.87–8: 68
4.88: 8, 75 and n. 146
4.88–9: 61 and n. 67, 68

4.90: 69
4.90–1: 69
4.91: 85 and n. 200
4.92: 70
4.93: 61 and n. 67
4.94: 50 f. and n. 13, 70
4.95: 70
4.95–8: 8
4.96: 70, 84
4.97–8: 93
4.97–101: 70 f. and n. 122, 71
4.97 ff.: 61 and n. 67
4.100: 61 and n. 67
4.101: 70 f.
4.102: 8
4.102–6: 71, 170, 205
4.103: 71
4.104: 71, 84
4.106: 72
4.107–11: 72
4.108: 93
4.108–9: 73
4.109: 85 and n. 200
4.109–10: 73
4.110–11: 8
4.111: 73, 85 and n. 200, 93
4.112: 112 and n. 99
4.112–6: 72
4.112 ff.: 72
4.114–5: 72
4.115: 84
4.115–6: 72
4.117 ff.: 86
4.118: 74
4.119: 74
4.119–21: 74
4.121: 74
4.122–3: 74
4.122–6: 61 and n. 67
4.123–4: 74
4.124: 85
4.125–6: 75
4.127: 75
4.127–8: 61 and n. 67
4.128–9: 75
4.129: 75 f., 85 and n. 200
4.130–1: 75

4.131: 75, 85 and n. 200
4.132–3: 76
4.132–4: 76 and n. 151
4.132–6: 76
4.133: 8
4.133–4: 76
4.135: 76
4.136: 8
4.137: 33, 68
4.137–8: 76
4.137–41: 31, 76
4.137 ff.: 61 and n. 67
4.139–40: 77
4.141: 77
4.142–4: 77
4.144–5: 61 and n. 67, 77
4.145: 77
4.145–6: 77
4.146: 77
4.147: 52
4.147–8: 199
4.147 ff.: 82
4.148: 78
4.150: 54, 78
4.150–1: 153
4.151: 78, 82 and n. 184, 200
4.152: 78
4.152–5: 79
4.153: 8
4.155–6: 113
4.155 ff.: 79
4.156: 80
4.158–9: 68 and n. 109, 80
4.159: 68 and n. 109
4.160: 54
4.160–3: 17
4.161: 81, 152
4.162: 80 and n. 172
4.163: 81, 152
4.166: 8, 81
4.168: 8, 82, 83, 214
4.168–9: 41 and n. 124
4.169: 82
5: 3, 5, 9, 45, 157 and n. 3, 158, 161, 166 and
    n. 53, 170 f. and n. 74, 173, 175, 181,
    182, 185, 186, 188, 189, 190 and n. 176,
    191, 252, 253

5.1: 166 and n. 53, 186, 189
5.1–2: 125
5.1–16: 186
5.2: 8, 186
5.3: 166 and n. 53, 187, 189
5.3–4: 186
5.4: 166 and n. 53, 189
5.5: 8, 179, 186
5.5–11: 190
5.7: 179, 186, 189
5.8: 179, 187
5.9: 186, 189
5.9–10: 180 f., 187
5.10: 179, 180, 187
5.11: 179, 186, 189
5.12: 179
5.12–3: 179, 186, 189
5.12–6: 167
5.14: 8, 179
5.14–48: 167 f. and n. 58
5.15: 8, 187
5.16: 167, 169, 179, 180
5.16–7: 168
5.16–48: 167 f. and n. 58, 168
5.16–85: 167 f. and n. 58
5.16–119: 182
5.17: 169
5.18: 168, 179, 181
5.19–20: 169
5.20: 8
5.21: 169
5.22–3: 168
5.23: 8, 169
5.24: 170, 179, 180
5.24–5: 170, 205
5.24 ff.: 179
5.25–8: 170
5.26: 179, 180
5.27: 179, 180
5.27–8: 170
5.28: 179, 180, 181
5.29: 8, 180
5.29–30: 170
5.30: 179, 181
5.32: 179, 185 and n. 160
5.32–4: 170
5.32–5: 171

5.32–42: 170
5.33: 171, 179 and n. 128
5.34: 181
5.34–5: 170
5.35: 171
5.36: 179 and n. 128, 180, 181
5.36–8: 170
5.37: 8, 99
5.38: 179, 181
5.39: 181
5.39–42: 171
5.39 ff.: 179
5.40: 8
5.41–2: 171
5.43: 179 and n. 128
5.43–8: 172
5.44: 179
5.45: 172
5.46: 181
5.47–8: 172
5.48: 8
5.49: 173, 174, 185 and n. 160
5.49–52: 172
5.49–55: 173
5.49–65: 167 f. and n. 58
5.49–94: 167 f. and n. 58
5.49–95: 167 f. and n. 58
5.49–101: 167 f. and n. 58
5.51: 179, 180 and n. 138
5.52: 179, 180, 181
5.52–3: 174
5.52–5: 173
5.54: 173
5.55: 173
5.56: 173
5.56–9: 173
5.56–62: 173
5.57: 179, 180 and n. 138
5.58: 179, 180 and n. 138, 181
5.59: 8, 173
5.60–1: 174
5.60–2: 173
5.62: 174, 179, 180
5.62–5: 174
5.63: 181
5.63–5: 173
5.64: 174, 185 and n. 160

5.66: 175
5.66–71: 174
5.66–94: 167 f. and n. 58
5.66–101: 167 f. and n. 58
5.66–103: 167 f. and n. 58
5.66 ff.: 179
5.67: 175, 185 and n. 160
5.68: 8, 174
5.69: 179, 180 and n. 138
5.69–71: 175
5.70: 179, 180 and n. 138
5.70–1: 185 and n. 160
5.72: 185 and n. 160
5.72–3: 179
5.72–82: 174, 175
5.73: 8, 179, 180
5.74: 175
5.74–6: 175
5.77: 176 f.
5.78: 167, 177
5.79: 176, 179, 181
5.80: 181
5.80–1: 179
5.81: 176, 180
5.81–2: 179, 180
5.82–5: 174
5.83: 179, 180
5.84: 8
5.86–8: 176
5.86–94: 167 f. and n. 58, 174
5.88: 177, 185 and n. 160
5.89: 176, 181
5.89–90: 179
5.89 ff.: 179
5.90: 176
5.91: 179, 180, 181
5.91–2: 180
5.92: 177
5.92–4: 176
5.95: 180
5.95–6: 179
5.95–101: 167 f. and n. 58
5.95–105: 167 f. and n. 58
5.95–115: 177
5.95–118: 167 f. and n. 58
5.96: 180
5.96–125: 167 f. and n. 58

5.97: 179 and n. 128
5.98: 179
5.98 ff.: 179
5.99: 177, 185 and n. 160
5.101: 177
5.102: 179, 181
5.102–3: 177, 179
5.102–18: 167 f. and n. 58
5.104: 178, 179, 181
5.104–18: 167 f. and n. 58
5.106: 181
5.106–7: 177
5.106–18: 167 f. and n. 58
5.106 ff.: 179
5.107: 45 and n. 134
5.107–9: 45
5.110: 181, 185 and n. 160, 206
5.111: 179, 181
5.111–2: 177
5.112: 179
5.112–4: 218
5.113: 45, 178, 181, 185 and n. 160
5.116: 178
5.116–8: 177, 178
5.117: 179, 180
5.119: 180, 187
5.120–1: 186, 214
6: 3, 5, 8, 45, 102, 114, 130, 224 and n. 5, 231
    and n. 37, 234, 240 and n. 79, 249, 252
6.1: 89, 225, 226
6.1–2: 225
6.1–5: 226, 227
6.2: 8, 225
6.3: 8, 225, 226
6.3–4: 225
6.3–5: 225
6.4: 225
6.5: 225
6.6: 228 and n. 26
6.6 ff.: 226
6.7: 228, 243 f. and n. 92
6.7–8: 228
6.8: 228
6.9: 229, 246
6.13: 230
6.14–6: 231
6.15: 229

6.16: 231
6.17–8: 232
6.17 ff.: 141
6.18: 228 and n. 26
6.19: 233 and n. 44
6.19–20: 233
6.19 ff.: 233 and n. 44
6.21: 234
6.22: 233 and n. 44
6.23: 233 and n. 44
6.23–4: 233 and n. 44, 234
6.24: 233 and n. 44
6.25–6: 233
6.28: 234
6.29: 234
6.33: 239
6.34: 45, 235, 245, 246
6.35: 236
6.36: 236, 238 and n. 71
6.38: 236, 237 and n. 65, 239
6.41: 236
6.42: 239
6.42–3: 236
6.45: 235 f. and n. 55
6.49–50: 228 and n. 26
6.50: 238
6.51: 228 and n. 26
6.52: 239
6.53–4: 238
6.55: 239
6.56: 238
6.56–7: 239
6.57: 239
6.59: 242
6.60–1: 240
6.60 ff.: 8
6.61: 8
6.62: 241
6.64: 241
6.64–5: 241
6.65: 241
6.66: 240
6.67: 242
6.68–9: 242
6.70: 240 and n. 79, 241
6.70 ff.: 242
6.71: 243

6.72: 243 and n. 89
6.73: 242
6.74: 242
6.75: 228 and n. 26, 242
6.76–8: 244
6.77: 228 and n. 26, 243 f. and n. 92
6.77–8: 228 and n. 26
6.78: 8, 244 and n. 93
6.79 ff.: 243 and n. 91
6.80: 244
6.82–3: 244
6.83–5: 244 and n. 95
6.84–6: 244 and n. 95, 245
6.86: 245
6.86–7: 244 and n. 95
6.87: 247
6.87–8: 244 and n. 95
6.88: 247
6.89: 248
6.89–93: 249
6.90–1: 247 f. and n. 109
6.92: 189
7: 3, 5, 8, 9, 55 and n. 35, 78 and n. 164, 83 and n. 185, 87 and n. 1, 89, 90, 91, 92, 93, 95, 96, 97 and n. 36, 98, 99, 102, 103 and n. 65, 105, 107, 108, 109, 111 and n. 96, 112 and n. 100, 113, 114, 114 f. and n. 105, 115, 117, 118, 119, 226, 236, 241, 251, 253
7.1: 89
7.1–2: 89, 90
7.1–3: 91, 98
7.1–22: 115
7.2: 8, 88, 106
7.2–3: 8
7.3: 8, 88, 107
7.4: 92
7.4–6: 91
7.5: 8, 91, 92
7.5–6: 119
7.6: 33, 68, 88, 91, 106
7.7: 91 and n. 19
7.7 ff.: 92
7.8: 8, 92, 93
7.9: 93, 94
7.9–10: 93
7.9–12: 102

7.10: 8
7.11: 88 and n. 7, 94
7.11–2: 94
7.13–4: 45, 95
7.13–5: 8
7.13–8: 94
7.14: 8
7.14–5: 116
7.16–8: 218
7.17: 2 and n. 3
7.18: 94, 106
7.19–20: 95
7.19–22: 109
7.20: 54, 95, 114
7.20–2: 78 and n. 164, 95
7.21–2: 170
7.23: 97, 105, 106, 109
7.23–4: 105
7.23–56: 97
7.23–72: 97, 115
7.25: 98, 105
7.26–9: 97 and n. 36
7.27: 106
7.28: 104
7.28–9: 97 and n. 36, 113
7.30: 116
7.30–1: 106
7.30–2: 8
7.30–3: 98, 117
7.30–4: 104, 106
7.31: 98
7.34: 98, 106, 116
7.35–6: 104, 116
7.36: 106
7.36–7: 119
7.37 ff.: 88
7.38: 106
7.40–2: 55 and n. 35, 56 and n. 40
7.40–6: 96, 103, 115
7.41: 102, 119
7.43–4: 103
7.44: 103 and n. 66
7.46: 103 and n. 66, 106
7.47: 104, 106, 117, 119
7.47–8: 102, 119
7.48: 103
7.48–53: 106

7.48 ff.: 1 and n. 1
7.49: 106
7.50: 106
7.50–3: 119
7.51: 106, 115
7.51–3: 105
7.53–4: 102, 119
7.53–6: 98
7.54: 116
7.55a: 103 and n. 66
7.56: 98
7.57: 106
7.57–72: 97
7.58: 99, 100 and n. 54
7.59: 99 and n. 48
7.60: 106
7.60–1: 99 f. and n. 50, 104
7.60–3: 99 f. and n. 50
7.61: 116
7.61–2: 99 f. and n. 50
7.61–3: 99, 99 f. and n. 50
7.62–3: 99 f. and n. 50, 104
7.64: 100, 106
7.64–6: 116
7.65: 100 and n. 54
7.65–6: 1 and n. 1, 97 and n. 36, 100, 103
7.66: 104, 106
7.66–7: 101
7.66–8: 100
7.69–70: 116
7.69–71: 101, 116
7.70: 106
7.71–2: 101, 119
7.72: 101 and n. 58, 102
7.73: 108, 119
7.73–4: 114
7.73–5: 109
7.73–84: 115
7.74–5: 31, 114
7.76: 106
7.77: 106
7.78: 109
7.79: 55 and n. 35
7.79–80: 112
7.79–84: 111
7.80: 88, 106
7.80–1: 114

Index Locorum — **283**

7.81: 109 and n. 89, 110, 114
7.81–2: 96
7.82: 106
7.83–4: 112 and n. 98, 119
7.84: 112 and n. 98

Cassiodorus
Inst. Div. Litt.
2.5.10: 84
var.
7.15.3: 217

Cato the Elder
agr.
5.7: 178
10.3: 175
11.4: 175
30: 177
32.1: 206
92: 169
128: 169
151.3: 206

Catullus
8.13–4: 132
14a.19: 106
35: 136
35.17: 21
44.10–5: 106
61: 19
61.34–5: 19
61.194–5: 146
61.206–10: 212
66.13–4: 135
68.5–8: 137
68.55–6: 138
68.68: 139
68.135: 131
68b.135: 229
70.3–4: 127
72.5: 207
76.9: 127
76.19: 137

Celsus
5.26.31: 175
5.28.15.$_B$: 175

Cicero
Arat.
119: 178
Att.
1.15.2: 88
15.4.2: 85 and n. 200
de Or.
2.38.159: 233 and n. 44
Div.
1.13–5: 62
1.21.8 (*poet.* 6.67): 53
2.30.63: 50f. and n. 13
Fin.
4.72: 166
Leg.
2.7.13: 67 and n. 103
N.D.
3.17: 30
Pis.
89: 245
Rep.
2.25–7: 28

Ciris
233: 200
376: 244 and n. 93

CIL
2.2863: 2 and n. 3

Columella
1 *praef.* 32: 204
1.4.5: 116
2.9.14: 147
2.10.1: 147
2.10.26: 206
3.18.1: 206
3.18.4: 169
4.17.3: 177
4.24.4: 116
4.27.5: 177
5.11.1: 205
6 *praef.* 3–4: 204
6.32.2–3: 176
7.2.3: 211
7.3.1: 204
7.3.8: 178

7.3.21: 177
7.3.23–4: 173
7.4.4: 211
7.4.6: 176
7.4.7: 212
7.5.10: 175
7.5.16: 175
7.8: 171
7.9.12: 176
8.5.18: 176
9.9.1: 84
10 *praef.* 3: 203 and n. 42
10.1.1.24: 216
10.80: 168
11.2.14: 176
11.2.41: 206
11.2.60: 177
11.3.9: 174
11.3.13: 212 and n. 85
11.3.52: 115
12.33: 176

Curtius Rufus
4.2.21: 116

Dio Cassius
60.35.1: 38

Dictys Cretensis
3.4: 83

Diomedes
GL 1.482.20–1 Keil: 159, 166
GL 1.482–3 Keil: 159

Dracontius
Rom.
4.*tit.*: 169 and n. 67

Eins. Eclogues
1: 201, 223
1.19–21: 242
1.22–4: 54
1.27: 54
1.32–3: 54
1.41: 166 and n. 53
2: 51 and n. 15

2.1: 51
2.15–6: 210
2.15 ff.: 75
2.21–34: 68 and n. 108
2.22–3: 31
2.23: 76 and n. 152
2.26: 186
2.38: 54

Empedocles
On Nature
B 3: 182
B 4: 182
B 8.1: 183
B 17.1: 183
B 17.16: 183
B 23.11: 182
B 35.1–3: 182
B 38.1: 183
B 62.1–3: 165
B 131: 182

Ennius
Ann.
206–7 Skutsch: 32 and n. 87
263 Skutsch: 239

Euripides
Bacch.
1084–5: 70
Hipp.
215–22: 19

Eustathius
Bas. hex.
2.9 p.884[B]: 217

Fronto
Ep. ad Am.
2.7.1 p. 192 N: 83

Fulgentius
Myth.
praef. p. 7.1 Helm: 83
p. 12.21 Helm: 83

Germanicus
Arat.
1: 67 and n. 103
1–2: 67 and n. 103

Grattius
Cyn.
141: 169
461: 165

[Hegesippus]
3.9.5: 217

Hesiod
Th.
22–3: 203
WD
1–2: 182
10: 161, 183
106–7: 183
286: 183
383 ff.: 167
568: 168
582 ff.: 173
654–62: 182
659: 182

Homer
Il.
20.226 ff.: 239

Horace
Ars
302: 172
Carm.
1.2.41–3: 77
1.2.45: 76
1.6.17 ff.: 243 and n. 87
1.9.15–6: 132
1.12.9–10: 200
1.12.30: 70
1.12.46–8: 38
1.12.57: 77
1.13.8: 230
1.17.1–3: 76 and n. 151
1.17.25–8: 134
1.19.5: 207

1.37.1–4: 76 and n. 149
2.5.5–9: 150
2.8.5–8: 127
2.11.13–7: 50
3.1.2: 73
3.7.7–8: 137
3.9.14: 18
3.10.14: 139
3.18.15–6: 76 and n. 149
3.30.7–8: 198 and n. 19
3.30.13–4: 198 and n. 19
4.2.57–60: 235 f. and n. 55
4.4.43: 218 and n. 111
4.5.16–40: 37
4.15.1–4: 54
C.S.
45: 61
53–68: 37
Epist.
1.1.49: 75 and n. 145
1.7.44–5: 243 and n. 87
2.1.1: 29
2.2.51–2: 80 and n. 171
2.2.177–8: 94
Epod.
1.27–8: 94
14.16: 230
17.3: 112 and n. 99
Serm.
2.2.52: 61
2.3.245: 228
2.6: 79

Hyginus
Fab.
181: 225 and n. 11

Jerome
In Isa.
16.9 f.: 85

Juvenal
7.192: 235 f. and n. 55
8.34–6: 225 and n. 11
11.204: 109
12.39: 245

Laus Pisonis
216–9: 79

Livy
1.18–21: 28
21.22.8–9: 106

Longus
Daphnis and Chloe
1.8.2f.: 167 and n. 54
1.24.4: 133 and n. 48

Lucan
Bellum Civile
1.1–66: 27
1.3: 26
1.5–6: 40
1.12: 27
1.33–45: 37
1.45–6: 77
1.46: 76
1.60–2: 40
2.248: 44
2.604–5: 104
4.589–660: 237 and n. 65
5.153–5: 104
6.507 ff.: 99
9.619: 84

Lucretius
1.10 ff.: 168
1.24: 183
1.24–6: 183
1.50–1: 164, 165
1.51: 164
1.54–61: 164
1.77: 165
1.80–2: 183
1.117–8: 198 and n. 19
1.127–8: 164
1.131: 165
1.137: 183
1.143: 183
1.149: 183
1.205: 164
1.256: 169
1.269: 164

1.370–1: 183
1.377 ff.: 166
1.399: 164
1.402–3: 164
1.450: 164
1.539: 162, 164
1.673: 164
1.714–5: 187f. and n. 171
1.716–33: 159
1.921–50: 183
1.925–30: 198 and n. 19
1.926–7: 183
1.956: 164
1.1018: 187f. and n. 171
1.1103: 187f. and n. 171
2.34–6: 243 and n. 89
2.53: 165
2.55–61: 164
2.62: 165
2.65: 187f. and n. 171
2.66: 165
2.105: 187f. and n. 171
2.109: 187f. and n. 171
2.114: 187f. and n. 171
2.319: 173
2.529: 183
2.532: 187f. and n. 171
2.660: 187
2.731–2: 187f. and n. 171
2.955–6: 187f. and n. 171
2.1023: 164
2.1059–60: 187f. and n. 171
3.10: 187f. and n. 171
3.31 ff.: 164
3.36: 183
3.87–93: 164
3.420: 183
3.582: 165
3.603: 165
4.9: 183
4.24: 183
4.26: 162, 183
4.29–30: 183
4.227: 165
4.577: 165
4.829: 187f. and n. 171
4.1068: 175

4.1170: 165
4.1200: 169
5.1: 183
5.14–5: 75
5.110 ff.: 165
5.446: 187 f. and n. 171
5.461 ff.: 173
5.498–9: 187 f. and n. 171
5.509: 183
5.510: 187 f. and n. 171
5.672–4: 214 and n. 90
5.780–820: 101
5.802: 172
5.823–4: 187 f. and n. 171
5.925–1010: 242
5.948–52: 242
5.951: 242
5.1091: 166
6.35–41: 164
6.43 ff.: 183
6.83: 183
6.84: 183
6.92–5: 183
6.369: 172
6.528–9: 187 f. and n. 171
6.529–30: 187 f. and n. 171
6.937: 183

Luke the Evangelist
8.22–25: 70 f. and n. 122

Macrobius
Sat.
5.19: 244 and n. 93

Manilius
1.1: 184
1.4: 184
1.4–6: 184
1.10: 184
1.13–9: 184
1.23: 184
1.113–4: 184
1.113–7: 184
1.117: 184
1.120: 164
1.194: 163

1.373: 165
1.809 ff.: 165
1.905–26: 39
2.8–11: 184
2.49–59: 184
2.53–9: 184
2.137: 184
2.137–40: 184
2.142: 184
2.183: 174
2.749–87: 163
2.751: 163
2.761: 165
2.767: 184
2.939: 165
3.4: 184
3.36 ff.: 164
3.39: 163
3.41: 184
3.93: 184
3.160 ff.: 164
3.203–5: 166
3.204: 165
4.119: 163
4.121: 184
4.430: 184
4.818: 164
5.1–11: 184
5.27: 184
5.259: 169

Mark the Evangelist
4.35–41: 70 f. and n. 122

Martial
1.49.31: 235 f. and n. 55
2.29.4: 109
5.56: 58 and n. 51
5.65.15–6: 76
8.50.7: 116
8.55.7–12: 64 and n. 80
10.42.3: 218
10.103.7–8: 89
13.4.1: 76
13.96: 236
14.47.1: 207 and n. 57
Sp. 7.1–3: 117

Sp. 21.3–4: 101
Sp. 23.4: 99

Martianus Capella
1.2: 53

Matthew the Evangelist
8.23–27: 70 f. and n. 122

Menander
fr. 791 K–A: 139
Mis.
fr. 4 Arnott: 139
Per.
155–7: 151
177 ff.: 151
340: 133 and n. 51
354 ff.: 151
504 ff.: 151
512 ff.: 152
976 ff.: 151

Menander Rhetor
2.377: 77 and n. 156

Moretum
21–9: 147
120: 18

Moschus
fr. 1.11–3: 50
[3].21: 243
[3].23–4: 200
[3].27–9: 199
[3].46–9: 198

Nemesianus
Ecl.
1.1–2: 241 and n. 81
1.1–8: 105
1.6–7: 206
1.22: 54
1.28–9: 75
1.30–1: 241 and n. 81
1.32–3: 243
1.68: 170, 204
1.72: 50 and n. 10

1.72–4: 59
1.82: 54
1.86–7: 186, 214
1.87: 214
2: 201, 226 and n. 15
2.1–2: 198
2.5: 65
2.14–5: 215
2.15: 54
2.16: 195 and n. 3, 213
2.18: 50 and n. 10
2.29–30: 200
2.35–6: 211 and n. 77
2.37–8: 211 and n. 77
2.49: 69 and n. 114
2.55: 170
2.56: 203
2.70–1: 113, 209
2.74–81: 213 and n. 89
2.77: 213
2.78: 213 and n. 89
2.83: 54
2.88–90: 186, 214
3.2: 186 and n. 163
3.26: 70
3.67–9: 186, 214
4.13: 54
4.19: 215
4.25: 215

Nicander
Ther.
51–4: 176
179–80: 176

Ovid
Am.
1.1.26: 243 and n. 87
1.2.3: 137
1.2.18: 139
1.2.19–20: 135
1.4: 147
1.6.17–8: 134, 138
1.6.67–8: 146
1.7: 151
1.7.1: 144
1.7.28: 135, 144

1.7.47–50: 134
1.7.59: 135
1.8.31–2: 147
1.8.43–4: 132
1.8.85–6: 127
1.9: 135
1.11.7–8: 135
1.15: 56 and n. 41
2.1.3–4: 207
2.1.15: 70
2.4.12: 127, 207
2.4.26: 140
2.5.34–42: 146
2.6.57: 52
2.16.33–40: 139
2.16.45–6: 127
2.17.5: 139
2.17.34: 215
2.18.17: 139
2.19.14: 135
3.1.5: 52
3.1.41: 149
3.3.5–6: 146
3.4.1–8: 126
3.4.43–6: 134 f.
3.5: 150 and n. 127
3.5.17: 129
3.6.25–6: 139
3.6.65: 132
3.11a.2: 149
3.12.16: 215
3.13.11: 83

Ars
1.1–2: 164
1.2: 184
1.17: 163
1.29: 184
1.30: 184
1.30–3: 184
1.35–40: 164, 184
1.50: 165
1.67: 129
1.146: 165
1.161: 165
1.253–4: 184
1.253–6: 165
1.253 ff.: 165

1.263–5: 164
1.263–6: 184
1.264: 163
1.267: 164
1.279: 187
1.375: 166
1.383–5: 135
1.385: 230
1.462: 135
1.503: 164 f.
1.504: 139
1.631–6: 127
1.708: 132
1.711: 230
1.729: 139
1.737: 230
1.771–2: 184
1.772: 164, 184
2.3: 184
2.9–10: 184
2.11: 184
2.105: 165
2.169–71: 134
2.173: 163
2.201: 165
2.273: 163
2.281–6: 135
2.285: 138
2.377–8: 133
2.399: 229
2.412: 135
2.433: 165
2.485: 169
2.493: 184
2.493–4: 184
2.493–508: 54
2.528: 146
2.717: 164
2.745: 163
3.1–2: 165
3.43: 163
3.57: 163
3.57–8: 164
3.59–60: 165
3.67: 165
3.83–98: 166
3.129–30: 164

3.162: 178
3.163–4: 165
3.195: 163
3.315–6: 164
3.342: 184
3.349–50: 165
3.502: 35 and n. 98
3.567–70: 134
3.611: 165
3.621–6: 135
3.667–72: 184
3.699–700: 135
3.723: 82 and n. 183
3.749–50: 166
3.790: 184
Epist.
1.66: 88 and n. 7
2: 125
2.23: 88 and n. 7
2.107–10: 126
2.145–8: 148
3.55: 132
4.14: 135
4.19–20: 127
4.168: 132
5.1: 127
5.5: 130
5.9–10: 131
5.21–5: 136
5.109–10: 127
5.117: 150
5.124: 150
6.117–8: 132
7.4: 130
7.27: 126
7.61: 135
7.149: 132
7.195–6: 148
8.107–10: 137
9.71–2: 237 and n. 65
11.29: 137
12.21: 127
12.25: 127
12.57–8: 126, 137
12.124: 127
12.169–70: 137
12.206: 127

13.119–20: 140
15.44: 140
17.253–60: 135
17.260: 135
18.41: 134
18.118: 139
18.164: 139
20.125: 230
21.60: 139
21.240: 135
[Epist. Sapph.]
137: 19
137–40: 19
181: 64 and n. 88
Fast.
1.13: 46
1.149–50: 170
1.157–8: 168
1.278: 165
1.287–8: 77
1.311–2: 173
1.321: 170
1.616: 29
1.669: 75 and n. 145
2.274: 21
2.457: 202
2.469: 171
2.585: 127
2.853: 168
3.21: 230
3.218: 171
3.284: 170
3.313: 65
3.421–2: 77
3.485: 142
3.553: 132
3.688: 135
3.741: 169
4.125: 169
4.377–86: 103 f.
4.495: 241
4.629–76: 33
4.653 ff.: 15
4.673–6: 33
4.721 ff.: 170, 209
4.723: 209
4.743–6: 210

4.753–4: 177
4.953–4: 69
5.89: 21
5.177: 225 and n. 11
5.371–2: 99
5.699–702: 196
6.126: 230
Ib.
515: 196
Met.
1.89: 30 and n. 75
1.447: 104
1.466: 198 and n. 20
1.520: 243 and n. 87
1.1664–723: 21
1.1689–712: 21
2.54: 65
2.840: 104
2.861: 238 and n. 71
2.864: 238
3.18: 73
3.144: 82 and n. 183
3.216: 21 and n. 32
3.729–30: 178 and n. 121
5.411: 104
6.384: 199
6.392: 199
6.392–4: 199
7.22: 217
7.111: 64 and n. 87
7.354: 198 and n. 20
7.379: 198 and n. 20
8.153: 84
8.253: 198 and n. 20
8.297: 64 and n. 87
8.305: 196
9.64: 106
9.80–1: 64 and n. 87
10.83–4: 245
10.96: 237
10.99: 237
10.110 ff.: 235
10.113: 236
10.114–5: 236
10.118–9: 236
10.123: 236
10.125: 236

10.133: 237 and n. 65
10.150 ff.: 237 and n. 65
10.159: 198 and n. 20
10.644: 104
11.732: 198 and n. 20
11.793: 45 and n. 137
13.719 ff.: 137
13.812–20: 212 and n. 82
13.820: 211
13.821–30: 144
13.831–9: 146
14.108: 65
15.1: 29
15.1–4: 29
15.96: 30 and n. 75
15.787–8: 39
15.868–70: 76
Pont.
2.2.48: 77
Rem.
3: 184
9: 163
17 ff.: 148
32: 146
36: 138
41: 163, 164
43: 163
49–52: 163
55: 163
77: 184
101–2: 165
131: 165
175: 165
217: 165
252: 184
283: 230
287–8: 133
298: 163
361–98: 184
398: 184
407: 184
421: 129
461: 165
487: 166
601: 137
601 ff.: 148
607–8: 163

644: 129
703: 184
715: 184
752: 243 and n. 87
803: 163
813–4: 163
Trist.
2.1.361: 242
2.57: 76
4.10.1: 242
4.10.21–3: 58 and n. 51
5.2.52: 76
5.5.61: 76
5.11.25–6: 76

Palladius
1.35.11: 176
2.16: 176
4.7.1: 177
5.6: 212
6.8: 175, 212
6.9: 171
7.6: 212
11.14.10: 169
12.13: 173
14.155: 218

Paul the Deacon
Fest.
p. 92.2.3 L: 107

Paulinus of Nola
Carm.
27.79: 84

Phaedrus
4.10.2: 44

Philostratus
Epist.
16: 151

Plautus
Amph.
374 ff.: 247
836: 127
1035: 247 f. and n. 109

Asin.
591 ff.: 126
Bacch.
859–60: 133
Cas.
404 ff.: 247
782: 127
859: 127
Cist.
472: 127
522 ff.: 133
Curc.
147–57: 134
Epid.
403: 133
Men.
1007 ff.: 247
Merc.
24–5: 137
824: 131
Mil.
185–94: 127
1050: 132
Pers.
228: 127
231–2: 135
443: 115
809 ff.: 247
Rud.
807 ff.: 247
Stich.
29–30: 88
Truc.
926–7: 133

Pliny the Younger
Ep.
2.5.10: 116

Pliny the Elder
Nat.
2.23.92: 38
2.23.93–4: 38
2.89: 38
7.65: 176
8.21: 97 and n. 36
8.118: 176

8.189: 204
8.217: 99
9.19: 100
10.116: 228
10.195: 176
12.126: 176
13.37: 206
16.53: 176
16.95.1–3: 170
16.141: 85 and n. 200
17.102: 205
17.104: 205
17.156: 206
18.61: 117
19.93.3: 176
19.122: 85 and n. 200
20.147: 83
24.22: 176

POXy 7, 1021: 37 and n. 109

Propertius
1.1.21: 139
1.3.40: 137
1.4.1–4: 139
1.6.9–10: 127
1.6.27–8: 148
1.7.8: 129
1.8a.3–4: 126
1.8b.35: 132
1.10.30: 243 and n. 87
1.12.9: 130
1.15.1: 149
1.15.1–2: 126
1.15.8: 127
1.15.25: 127
1.16.7–8: 146
1.16.23–4: 134
1.16.39–40: 137
1.16.47–8: 138
1.18.15–6: 138
1.18.22: 136
2.1.4: 215
2.1.49: 149
2.1.57–8: 126
2.1.78: 148
2.4.2: 132

2.5.21–4: 133
2.5.30: 139
2.8.11: 126
2.8.14: 134
2.8.15: 139
2.8.17 ff.: 148
2.9a.31–6: 127
2.13.11–2: 136
2.13.35–6: 148
2.15.18–20: 133
2.15.29–30: 127
2.16.25–6: 127
2.16.36: 149
2.18a.7: 132
2.20.4: 129
2.24.18: 149
2.24.21–2: 135
2.30b.23: 131, 229
2.31: 90
2.31.1–2: 90
2.34.73–4: 197 f.
3.1: 198 and n. 19
3.2.3–4: 200
3.3.13–26: 54
3.3.39–40: 238
3.6.5: 135
3.6.23: 139
3.8.8: 134
3.8.28: 139
3.8.29–32: 135
3.9.45: 207
3.15.14: 214 and n. 90
3.21.33: 149
3.25.9: 138
4.1: 90, 118
4.1.19–20: 209
4.1.29: 18
4.1b.73–4: 54
4.1b.133–4: 54
4.2: 22
4.2.11–8: 22
4.2.41–6: 22
4.2.53–4: 23 and n. 41
4.2.59: 22
4.3: 125
4.3.29 ff.: 137
4.4.4: 215

4.4.73–8: 209
4.5: 147
4.5.31: 134
4.5.61: 243f. and n. 92
4.6.1: 73
4.6.9: 207
4.7.31: 127
4.8.75: 129
4.11.60: 33
4.11.91: 131

Quintilianus
Inst.
10.1.46: 67 and n. 103
10.1.46–57: 158
10.1.85–8: 158

Rhetorica ad Herennium
4.16: 233 and n. 44

Seneca the Younger
Apoc.
4: 15, 36 and n. 103
4.1: 31, 37
4.1.15–32: 24
4.1.22 ff.: 119
4.1–3: 37
5.2: 166 and n. 53
5.3: 166 and n. 53
5.4–6.1: 38
6.2: 166 and n. 53
7.4: 37, 166 and n. 53
8.2: 37
10.3–11.2: 37
11.5: 37
12.2–3: 37
13.4–14.2: 37
Ben.
3.7.5: 247f. and n. 109
Br.
4.5: 41
Cl.
1.1.1: 37
1.1.2: 37
1.1.3: 37
1.1.4: 37
1.1.5: 37
1.1.6: 29
1.1.7–8: 37
1.1.7–9: 37
1.3.3: 37
1.5.1–2: 37
1.5.4: 37
1.8.2: 37
1.9.1–1.11.3: 41
1.11.2: 41
1.11.3: 41
1.19.8: 37
1.23: 37
1.26.5: 37
2.1.4: 37
Dial.
11.12.5: 76
Ep.
73.8: 116
86.15: 161
88.22: 101
90.15: 102
107.11: 70
115.4: 73
H.F.
85: 28
H.O.
369: 217
1741: 44
Med.
98: 116
N.Q.
7.17.2: 38
7.21.3: 38 and n. 111
7.29.2–3: 38 and n. 111
[Oct.]
472–91: 41
482: 41
489: 77
Phaedr.
1026: 49
Phoen.
577: 44
Tr.
153: 44

Servius
ad *A.* 2.474: 106

ad *Ecl.* 7.53: 218
Praef. ad *G.* 129.9–12 Thilo: 162 f.

Silius Italicus
3.316: 84
3.626–7: 76
13.200: 84
14.475: 45 and n. 137
15.308: 84

Solinus
1.19: 210
33.11: 116

Statius
Silv.
1.1.105–7: 76
1.1.106: 77
4.2.22: 76
Th.
1.23–4: 77
7.379–80: 104
8.718: 196
8.724–7: 196
8.746: 196
10.535: 84

Suetonius
Aug.
40.5: 109
58: 77
Cl.
13: 37 and n. 109
29: 37 and n. 109
30.2: 166 and n. 53
46: 38
Iul.
81.2: 238 and n. 67
Ner.
6: 16 and n. 7
7: 33 and n. 91
10: 40
10.1: 40
10–11: 37
11.1: 97 and n. 36, 119
11.2: 119
12: 40

12.1: 97, 103
12.2: 97
13: 37
15–7: 37
16: 118
19: 37
25: 40
26.1: 18 and n. 20
30.3: 119
31: 119
31.1: 119
31.2: 87 and n. 2, 102, 119
31.3: 118
32: 118
53: 16 and n. 7, 29 and n. 65
Tib.
1: 29 and n. 67

Tacitus
Ann.
1.11: 29
2.12.12: 50 and n. 9
11.35: 37 and n. 109
12.42: 37 and n. 109
12.58: 32, 33 and n. 91
13.4: 37 and n. 109, 41
13.4–5: 37
13.8.1: 110
13.11: 37
13.28–9: 37
13.31.1: 97, 106
13.31–2: 37
13.51: 37
13.58: 73 and n. 138
14.12: 33 and n. 91
14.28: 37
14.48: 37
14.53: 89
14.55: 37, 41
15.32: 97 and n. 36
15.32.3: 97 and n. 36
15.42: 119
15.42.1: 119
15.43.1–2: 119
16.28: 22 and n. 37
Hist.
4.49.20: 50 and n. 9

Terence
Ad.
120: 134
120–1: 133
170 ff.: 247
476: 133
Andr.
278: 127
865: 238 and n. 67
Eun.
59–61: 135
72: 133
122: 131
219: 137
457: 133
646: 133
715–6: 247
771–816: 134
985: 133
1026–7: 139
Haut.
300–1: 135
Hec.
312: 127
Phorm.
144: 139
551f.: 148

Tertullian
Spect.
3: 117

Theocritus
Ep.
6.1–2: 138 and n. 76
Id.
1: 94, 125, 216
1.1: 57
1.1–2: 215
1.1–3: 54, 95
1.7–8: 241
1.12: 243
1.12–4: 25
1.15: 15
1.19: 196
1.21: 225, 243
1.22–3: 199

1.25–6: 143, 171 and n. 76
1.27–56: 97, 235
1.29–31: 94
1.52–4: 105
1.55: 65
1.71–5: 198
1.77 ff.: 199
1.115: 100
1.128–9: 133
1.134: 232 and n. 41
1.135: 235
1.136: 228
2.40: 133
2.88: 139
2.94–103: 135
2.94 ff.: 135
2.125: 142
3: 7, 131, 137, 140, 148
3.1–5: 25
3.2–5: 130
3.8: 213
3.9: 147
3.10–11: 213
3.19–20: 140
3.21–3: 146
3.24–7: 147
3.34–6: 132
3.38: 225
3.45: 216
3.52–4: 147
4: 88 and n. 7, 115
4.12: 198
4.12–4: 88
4.14: 200
4.26–8: 93
4.45–6: 238
4.45–9: 130
4.50: 240 and n. 78
4.50–3: 126
4.58 ff.: 243f. and n. 92
5: 94, 102, 103, 125, 130, 147, 216, 223, 225, 234, 245, 249
5.1 ff.: 145
5.5–7: 141, 147
5.8–10: 147
5.20 ff.: 233
5.21: 235

5.21–30: 225
5.24: 235
5.29: 228
5.30: 235
5.31–2: 243
5.31–4: 129
5.31 ff.: 19, 239
5.41 ff.: 246
5.44–5: 132
5.48–9: 225
5.50–1: 174
5.58–9: 207 f. and n. 60
5.59: 210
5.60–1: 132
5.60–5: 234
5.61: 225
5.65: 234
5.66–73: 243
5.68–71: 234
5.74: 240 and n. 78
5.78: 21
5.80–3: 203
5.81–3: 209
5.86–7: 212
5.96–7: 146
5.98–9: 175, 212
5.102: 238
5.112: 189
5.116 ff.: 246
5.129: 101
5.133: 146
5.136–7: 228
6: 102, 196, 201, 216
6.3: 213
6.3–4: 195, 243
6.4: 15
6.8: 243
6.17: 142
6.34–40: 141
6.36: 213
6.46: 216
7: 10, 102, 114, 125, 216
7.8–9: 225
7.15–8: 114
7.16: 114
7.17–8: 114
7.21: 15

7.41: 228
7.43–4: 113
7.51: 65 and n. 93, 95
7.88: 225
7.88–9: 60, 132, 243
7.138: 225
7.138–9: 173
7.141: 228
[8]: 58, 102, 196, 216, 223, 225, 249
[8].3: 213
[8].3–4: 195, 213, 225
[8].6–10: 233
[8].6–11: 233
[8].11–2: 233
[8].11–24: 225
[8].13–24: 225
[8].14–5: 235
[8].15–6: 143
[8].18–9: 133
[8].18–24: 235
[8].25–7: 234
[8].28: 213
[8].29: 213
[8].30: 201
[8].41–2: 71
[8].41–8: 73, 139 and n. 83
[8].52: 112
[8].55: 57
[8].56: 211
[8].61: 213
[8].72–3: 142, 213
[8].88: 213
[8].93: 213
[9]: 102, 196, 201, 216, 223, 225
[9].1–2: 242
[9].5–6: 242
[9].11: 101
10: 138
10.10: 138
10.15–6: 133
10.34: 146
11: 7, 137, 140, 152, 208, 226 and n. 16, 252
11.1–3: 215
11.9: 213
11.12–5: 41
11.17: 243
11.17–8: 215

11.21: 150
11.29: 240 and n. 78
11.31–3: 208
11.34–7: 142, 208, 210
11.35–7: 211
11.38: 226
11.38–40: 138, 140, 208
11.40–1: 138, 146, 208, 235
11.41: 100
11.42–9: 208
11.55–6: 140
11.56: 146
11.56–9: 146
11.72 ff.: 144
11.75: 142
11.76: 230
11.80–1: 215
12: 89, 118
12.1: 89
13.64–5: 126
14: 134, 151
14.2: 226
14.35–6: 134
14.43: 134
15: 96, 118
15.1: 226
15.34–5: 96
15.87–8: 96
16.48 ff.: 198 and n. 19
16.88–97: 35
16.99–100: 35
17: 67 and n. 103
18.47–8: 136
[20]: 112
[20].3–4: 209
[20].21 ff.: 213
[20].30: 142
21: 147
22.19: 70
22.137–40: 196
[23]: 138, 149
[23].17: 134
[23].17 ff.: 138
[23].20–1: 148
[23].46–8: 148
[27]: 216
[27].44: 196

Tibullus
1.1.11–24: 172
1.1.11 ff.: 56
1.1.19–20: 210
1.1.23: 210 and n. 68
1.1.31 ff.: 172
1.1.33–44: 172
1.1.35–6: 170, 209
1.1.46: 139
1.1.53 ff.: 172
1.1.55–6: 139
1.1.73–4: 133
1.1.75–6: 135, 207
1.2.14: 146
1.2.31: 134
1.3.25–6: 25
1.3.34: 210
1.3.81: 149
1.4.21–6: 127
1.4.55: 132
1.4.77: 132
1.5.19–20: 130
1.5.40: 139
1.6.5–6: 126
1.6.9: 137
1.6.73: 144
1.6.73–4: 133
1.7: 118
1.7.61–2: 90
1.8.55: 132
1.8.64: 137
1.8.68: 138
1.9.1–2: 127
1.9.19: 149
1.9.40: 149
1.9.51: 207
1.9.53: 147
1.10.1–10: 36
1.10.7–10: 36
1.10.8: 207 f. and n. 60
1.10.15: 210
1.10.25 ff.: 210
1.10.29–32: 36
1.10.45: 35
1.10.45–6: 36
1.10.45–50: 36
1.10.53–6: 135

1.10.59–66: 133
2.1.53–4: 84
2.1.60: 210
2.1.67–8: 238 and n. 70
2.3.83: 139
2.4.1–4: 139
2.4.6: 207
2.4.6–7: 127
2.4.15: 207
2.4.20: 207
2.5: 35
2.5.1–18: 34
2.5.2: 34
2.5.19–22: 35
2.5.20: 210
2.5.38: 99
2.5.42: 210
2.5.65–78: 34
2.5.79–82: 34
2.5.83: 34
2.5.83–90: 34
2.5.87–104: 209
2.5.109–10: 126
2.6.19–20: 148
2.6.34: 129
2.6.45–6: 135
[3].1.15 ff.: 206
[3].2.29–30: 148
[3].3.1 ff.: 206
[3].4.3: 207
[3].4.64: 135
[3].4.66: 139
[3].6.7: 207
[3].6.41–2: 127
[3].7.126: 200
[3].7.161: 74
[4].13.19–20: 127

Valerius Flaccus
1.166: 189
5.304–9: 117
7.66–7: 83

Valerius Maximus
1.pr.1.17: 67 and n. 103

Varro
L.
6.68: 45 and n. 137, 107
Men.
100: 169 and n. 66
rust.
1.1.5: 75
1.36: 206
1.43: 206
2.1.18: 206
2.1.21–3: 175
2.2.4: 204
2.2.10 ff.: 173
2.2.14: 169
2.2.15: 172
2.2.15–7: 206
2.2.17: 171
2.2.18: 211
2.4.8: 169
2.5.14: 178
2.7.8: 176
2.9.4: 45 and n. 137
2.11.3–4: 171
2.11.6–9: 212
2.11.6 ff.: 174
2.11.7: 175
3.9.14: 176
3.10.3: 169
3.12.6: 99

Velleius Paterculus
2.36.2: 166

Vergil
A.
1.155: 104
1.166–8: 242
1.169: 110
1.254–96: 25
1.282: 53
1.286: 26
1.291–6: 8, 25
1.294: 25
1.296: 25
1.490: 235 f. and n. 55
1.666: 112 and n. 99
2.129: 234

2.185: 105 and n. 78
2.203 ff.: 106
2.217: 106
2.474: 106
3.210: 104
3.246: 234
3.392: 144
3.672: 105 and n. 78
4.68: 207 and n. 58
4.441 ff.: 178 and n. 121
4.505: 218 and n. 111
5.21–2: 104
5.285: 144
5.286–9: 104
5.312–3: 104
5.670: 248 and n. 110
6.299–300: 104
6.441: 104
6.792–3: 31
6.792–4: 31
6.809–12: 28
6.817–25: 27
6.826–31: 27
6.833: 27
6.851: 53
7.81–106: 32
7.475–510: 50 f. and n. 13
7.483–510: 237
7.483 ff.: 235
7.488: 236
7.490: 236
7.513: 237
7.514–8: 237
7.607: 104
7.635–6: 237
7.688: 18
7.808–9: 239
8.319–27: 31
8.325: 53
8.523: 104
8.601: 203
8.675–728: 26
8.717: 75 and n. 145
8.717–9: 26
9.44: 234
9.85: 19
9.387: 104

9.575: 196
9.690: 234
10.413: 21
10.727–8: 236
10.876: 234
11.377: 234
11.522–9: 104
11.677–89: 17
11.679–81: 18
12.6–7: 104
12.345: 234
12.480: 234
12.677: 20
12.678: 234
12.942: 236
Ecl.
1: 8, 79, 81 and n. 176, 87, 89, 103, 107, 108, 117, 125
1.1: 60, 76, 90, 174, 186, 225, 243
1.2: 55, 64 and n. 86
1.4: 60, 70, 76, 94, 174, 225
1.4–5: 90
1.5: 59, 60
1.6–7: 53
1.6–10: 33, 87
1.7 ff.: 170
1.7–8: 209, 210
1.8: 81
1.9: 186
1.9–10: 75
1.10: 57 and n. 49
1.12 ff.: 172 and n. 81
1.14: 225
1.18: 53, 109
1.19–25: 88
1.26: 91 and n. 19
1.27 ff.: 87
1.30–5: 128
1.31–5: 95
1.32: 59
1.33: 59
1.34: 59, 170 f. and n. 74, 211 and n. 76
1.36: 91 and n. 19
1.36–8: 128
1.36–9: 87
1.38: 57
1.40–5: 33, 87, 89

1.41: 68
1.42: 33
1.42–3: 209
1.46: 108
1.51: 108, 205 and n. 50
1.51–2: 49
1.51 ff.: 49 and n. 6
1.52: 225
1.53–4: 206
1.56: 57
1.59: 235
1.64–6: 60
1.70: 28
1.70–1: 209
1.75: 70
1.77–8: 206
1.82–3: 41, 186, 214
1.83: 82
2: 5, 17, 55 f. and n. 39, 66 and n. 98, 115, 125, 132, 137, 141, 197 and n. 16, 208, 216, 253
2.1: 133, 197
2.1–5: 55 f. and n. 39
2.3–5: 215
2.4: 55 f. and n. 39
2.4–5: 197
2.6 ff.: 138
2.7–13: 82
2.8–9: 225
2.8–13: 15
2.12–3: 173
2.14–6: 132
2.19–22: 143, 211
2.20: 210
2.20–2: 208
2.21: 211
2.22: 211 and n. 76
2.23–4: 140, 208
2.25: 213
2.25–7: 141, 208
2.26–7: 141
2.28–35: 208
2.28 ff.: 132
2.29: 209, 235
2.30: 62
2.31: 132, 140
2.32–3: 133
2.33: 32
2.36 –8: 21, 113, 132, 190, 202
2.36–55: 208
2.40–4: 132
2.40–55: 146
2.45–6: 146
2.51: 212
2.51–3: 213
2.54–5: 69
2.56: 55, 209
2.60: 69, 142
2.60–1: 55
2.62: 113
2.66–7: 41, 81, 186, 214
2.67: 82
2.68: 128, 207
2.69–73: 144
2.70–2: 81, 214
3: 58, 67 and n. 103, 94, 102, 117, 125, 130, 147, 201, 216, 223, 225, 233 and n. 42, 245, 249, 250
3.3 ff.: 145
3.7: 247
3.8 ff.: 246
3.9: 203
3.10: 189
3.11: 177
3.12: 91
3.16–20: 149
3.20: 149
3.25–6: 133, 147
3.25–7: 227
3.25 ff.: 233
3.26–7: 22 and n. 36, 141
3.27: 233
3.28 f.: 233
3.29: 234
3.29–30: 143, 171 and n. 76
3.29–31: 235
3.29–48: 225
3.31: 225, 226
3.32–4: 143
3.36: 238 and n. 66
3.36–7: 208
3.36–47: 97, 235
3.39: 94
3.45: 65

3.46: 65
3.48: 235
3.49: 20
3.50: 234
3.50–1: 234
3.51: 247
3.52: 21
3.55: 243
3.55–9: 242
3.55 ff.: 195
3.57: 169
3.59: 226
3.60: 67 and n. 103
3.62: 203
3.62–3: 203
3.65: 206
3.68–9: 146
3.73: 41
3.74–5: 101
3.76: 125
3.78: 125
3.82: 101
3.83: 206
3.84: 52, 55
3.84–5: 16
3.92: 61
3.93: 106
3.95: 175
3.107: 125
3.108: 249
3.108–10: 216
3.111: 81, 215 and n. 99
4: 31, 52 and n. 18, 66 and n. 98, 71, 77, 117, 251, 254
4.1: 30, 52
4.1–4: 55 and n. 34
4.2: 52
4.3: 30, 52, 66
4.4: 30
4.6: 30, 76
4.7: 76 f.
4.8: 30
4.9: 30
4.15: 77
4.17: 68, 77
4.18–20: 73
4.20: 65

4.21–2: 71
4.43–4: 71
4.46–7: 77
4.55–7: 65
4.58: 225
5: 17, 52 and n. 18, 71, 72, 94, 102, 113, 114, 117, 148, 189, 201, 216, 240 and n. 79, 251
5.1: 195
5.1 ff.: 19, 240
5.3: 19, 225, 243
5.4: 103
5.5: 225
5.6: 19, 70
5.8: 225
5.9: 225
5.10: 125
5.10–11: 130, 244
5.12: 25, 130
5.13–4: 75
5.13–5: 23, 136
5.15: 225
5.16: 206
5.19: 19, 70, 189, 240 and n. 79
5.20–3: 199
5.25–6: 200
5.25–8: 198
5.26: 238 and n. 67
5.34–5: 204
5.35: 72, 95, 170
5.37: 72
5.40: 225
5.43–4: 148 f.
5.44: 213
5.47: 54, 95
5.49: 189
5.54–5: 91
5.56–80: 38
5.60: 235
5.60–1: 32, 38
5.65–80: 209
5.74–5: 203
5.75: 170
5.79: 75
5.84: 241
5.85: 21, 113, 132, 190, 202
6: 54 and n. 33, 80 and n. 171, 117

6.1: 57, 64
6.1–2: 52
6.1–12: 203
6.1 ff.: 54
6.3–5: 64 and n. 80, 79, 81 f. and n. 179
6.4–5: 81
6.5: 81
6.6–8: 24
6.8: 55
6.11–2: 24
6.12: 24
6.21: 65
6.21–2: 65, 204
6.27–8: 101, 198, 199
6.27–30: 65
6.31: 187 f. and n. 171
6.31–2: 187 f. and n. 171
6.32: 187 f. and n. 171
6.33: 187 f. and n. 171
6.33–4: 187 f. and n. 171
6.34: 187 f. and n. 171
6.36: 187 f. and n. 171
6.39: 187 f. and n. 171
6.40: 187 f. and n. 171
6.45 ff.: 129
6.52: 129, 138
6.53: 15, 16
6.53–4: 129
6.54: 199
6.67–9: 113, 190, 202
6.67–73: 21
6.69–71: 65
6.82: 55
6.84: 59
6.85–6: 41, 143, 186, 214
6.86: 187
7: 17, 94, 102, 115, 125, 201, 216, 223, 225
7.1: 186, 199, 215, 225, 243
7.1–2: 125, 196
7.2–3: 195
7.4–5: 195, 213, 225
7.7: 125
7.7–9: 125
7.9–13: 129
7.10: 225
7.14: 125, 151
7.16: 195, 225

7.17: 57, 253
7.18–9: 226
7.21–2: 203, 204
7.24: 57
7.25–6: 202
7.29–36: 209
7.30: 189, 235
7.33: 210
7.45: 174
7.53–6: 72
7.53–60: 139 and n. 83
7.56: 176
7.59: 125, 245
7.63: 125
7.65: 57
7.67: 245
7.68: 57
8: 102, 117, 153 and n. 140, 216
8.1–4: 196
8.2–3: 200
8.2–4: 65
8.3: 73, 195, 198, 225
8.4: 200
8.13: 63
8.14–5: 173
8.16: 105
8.22: 57, 215
8.22–4: 200
8.29–30: 231
8.33–4: 231
8.34: 231
8.39: 213
8.43–50: 231
8.52–6: 232 and n. 41
8.52 ff.: 232 and n. 41
8.55: 103, 228
8.55–6: 232
8.58: 231, 232 and n. 41
8.58–60: 148, 231, 232 and n. 41
8.71: 106
8.83: 207
8.85–9: 150
9: 50 f. and n. 13, 108, 117, 125, 216, 250
9.4: 35
9.9: 91
9.20: 225
9.23–5: 25, 130, 248

9.36: 228
9.37: 51, 93
9.37–8: 241
9.46: 92
9.46–50: 38, 92
9.47: 92
9.48–9: 38
9.57–8: 200
9.63: 41, 186, 214
9.66: 81
10: 5, 117, 123, 128, 137
10.1: 65 and n. 93, 187, 204
10.8: 59
10.10: 128
10.16: 198
10.21–30: 199
10.24–5: 203
10.28: 128
10.37: 125
10.37–40: 246
10.40: 206
10.41: 125
10.42: 187
10.44–9: 128
10.48–9: 178
10.51: 42, 64 and n. 86
10.52–4: 23
10.53–4: 136
10.69: 214
10.70–1: 243
10.71: 62, 105, 145
10.77: 41, 81, 186, 214
G.
1: 181
1.1–5: 162, 164
1.3–4: 204
1.5: 183
1.7: 75
1.27: 70
1.29: 105 and n. 78
1.40–2: 184
1.43–6: 164
1.45: 74
1.45–6: 164
1.49: 105 and n. 78
1.50 ff.: 165
1.74: 72

1.84: 165
1.92: 19
1.100: 164
1.101: 162
1.104: 165
1.107: 176, 212 and n. 85
1.119: 74
1.147–9: 36
1.154: 72
1.157: 177
1.159: 62
1.167: 164, 165, 167
1.169–75: 164
1.176: 162, 180
1.193: 165
1.204–5: 164
1.210: 162
1.213: 74
1.263: 176
1.272: 190
1.338–50: 75
1.351–92: 62
1.355: 172
1.368: 178
1.406: 198
1.424: 19
1.441–64: 62
1.463–514: 39
1.487–92: 39
1.500: 33
1.503–4: 77
1.506–8: 237
2.1: 164
2.1–2: 184
2.27: 206
2.33–4: 205
2.35: 162, 164
2.36: 162
2.39: 184, 187
2.39–46: 183
2.73–82: 177 and n. 119
2.78–80: 205
2.82: 205
2.103 ff.: 165
2.114: 165
2.176: 159, 162
2.216: 174

2.259–60: 212 and n. 85
2.264: 74
2.288: 166
2.308–9: 172
2.322: 17
2.323 ff.: 168
2.346: 165
2.354: 165
2.365–6: 177
2.380–96: 75
2.380 ff.: 190
2.384: 187
2.393–6: 164
2.400 ff.: 177
2.401–2: 178
2.404: 178
2.407: 206
2.433: 165
2.483–6: 183
2.490: 159
2.490–3: 159
2.490–542: 243 and n. 89
2.493: 159
2.527–31: 75
3: 9, 181, 191
3.1: 170, 204
3.1–2: 184
3.8 ff.: 198 and n. 19
3.17 ff.: 198 and n. 19
3.40–2: 183
3.56–7: 238
3.72 ff.: 238
3.74: 171
3.79–80: 238
3.87–8: 239
3.88: 238
3.100–1: 164
3.110: 165
3.135: 178
3.157–8: 164
3.158: 176
3.176 ff.: 171
3.177: 58
3.284–6: 184
3.288: 162, 178
3.291–3: 184
3.294: 170, 184, 205

3.295: 162
3.295 ff.: 190
3.297 ff.: 178
3.298–9: 178
3.300 ff.: 190
3.301: 85 and n. 200
3.305: 181
3.308–10: 171
3.309: 58, 171
3.309–10: 171
3.311 ff.: 175
3.318 ff.: 172 and n. 82
3.320–1: 177
3.322–3: 168
3.322–6: 173
3.323: 170
3.323–5: 170
3.327: 173
3.327–38: 173
3.327 ff.: 173
3.332–3: 174
3.335: 174
3.335 ff.: 174
3.336–7: 174
3.384 ff.: 175
3.387–90: 175, 204
3.400–2: 58
3.400–3: 171
3.414–5: 176
3.420: 162
3.420–4: 176
3.421: 177
3.435: 174
3.440: 162
3.440 ff.: 175
3.441–3: 178
3.441 ff.: 190
3.448–54: 175
3.448 ff.: 176
3.449: 177
3.453–4: 175
3.480: 198
3.484–5: 177
3.492: 170
3.520–1: 187
4: 181, 203 and n. 42
4.1–2: 184

4.32: 204, 206
4.41: 176
4.51: 165
4.112–5: 206
4.116–48: 184, 203 and n. 42
4.120: 204
4.126: 204
4.146: 50
4.148: 203 and n. 42
4.149: 165

4.179: 201
4.181: 85 and n. 200
4.307: 168
4.425: 19
4.559: 204

Zeno of Verona
Tract.
2.27.2: 85

General Index

a-historical 91
aberration 49, 206
ablative 44, 85, 116, 178, 187f., 217
absence / absent 87f., 92, 94, 128, 139, 199, 214, 233, 247
abstention 144
abstinence 200
Acanthis 228, 243
Achilles 246
Acis 137
Acontius / Cydippe 136
Actium 26
active (*gram.*) 164, 181
address 24, 35, 56, 161–4, 179, 183, 189, 226
addressee 161, 163–5
adjective 25, 44, 52, 60, 65f., 68, 78f., 84, 89–91, 95, 99, 105, 140, 169, 188, 201, 214, 244
adjudicator 249
Adonis 96
adulescens 148, 150
adultery 128
adverb / adverbial 44, 103, 128, 248
adviser 152
adynaton 8, 39, 100, 227, 229, 231f., 235
Aegle 20, 65, 204
Aegon 88, 92f., 145, 245
Aeneas 17, 25–7, 31f., 35, 56, 248
Aeon 31
Aeschinas 134
aestheticism 102, 106f., 109, 141
aesthetics of deviation 23, 124, 251
Aetas Aurea 9, 30, 42, 50, 71, 76, 86, 102, 232
aeternus 77, 86
Aether 30
aetiological elegy 23
affliction 175
African wart-hog 99
age difference / distinction 189, 246
Ageanax 245
aggressive lover 151
agna / us 8, 81, 210f.

agonistic / antagonistic 48, 93, 103, 143, 147, 195, 225, 244, 248, 253
agraffe 96
agrestis 57, 75, 159
agricultural / agriculture 4, 9, 34, 36, 38, 72, 94, 98, 128, 133, 138, 158
Agrippina the Younger 33, 36f.
air 172, 174, 187
Alcimedon 153, 215, 235
Alcippe 151
Alcon 5, 113, 130, 198, 213, 215, 223–5, 227–32, 234, 244
Alconis laudes 130, 244
Alecto 237
Alexandria / Alexandrian 5, 96, 229f.
Alexis 56, 62, 66, 68f., 73, 112, 132, 138f., 141, 144, 146, 197f., 209, 211–3, 230, 246
alienate / alienation 49, 51, 60–2, 82, 127, 131, 138, 209, 215
allegorical / allegory 32, 63, 81, 166, 223
allusive 25, 32, 40, 45
Alphesiboeus 124, 128, 150, 153, 200, 216
altar 170
altercatio / altercation 149, 201
alternate / alternation 225, 242, 249
Amaryllis 59f., 87f., 90, 128, 132, 140, 146, 213
amatory 125, 172
Amazon 18, 35
ambiguity / ambiguous / unambiguous 10, 43, 46f., 112, 123, 189, 251
ammonia 176
amoebaean 195, 197, 201, 206, 212, 215, 219, 224f., 227, 244f., 248
amor 128, 130, 140, 149f., 207, 214, 230, 242, 244f.
amorous 42
Amphion 140
amphitheatre 5, 9, 43, 78, 87f., 90f., 93, 95–8, 101–3, 105–7, 110–2, 117–9
Amyntas 4, 41, 48, 55, 57f., 67–70, 72–6, 81, 85f., 199
Anchises 27, 31

angry father 58
animal 25, 34f., 81, 84, 88, 97, 99–101, 103, 105, 117–9, 125f., 128–30, 138, 142–6, 168, 171f., 174f., 177–9, 185, 190, 198, 210, 225, 227–9, 232, 235, 238
animal and plant comparison 138
anonymous 112, 132, 140, 147f., 161, 163
anti-Callimachean 80, 106
anti-Neoteric 49, 80, 92, 145, 201, 206
anti-Neronian / anti-Neronianism 22, 111
antrum 15f., 19–21, 70, 240f.
Aphrodite 33
Apocolocyntosis 15f., 31, 36f.
apolitical 46, 241
Apollo / Apollonian 3, 5, 8, 15, 24, 34–6, 46, 54, 62, 64, 67f., 72, 79–81, 86, 90, 95, 109f., 112, 119, 199, 201–4, 231, 237, 251
Apollonius of Rhodes 17, 158, 189
apostrophe 129, 208f.
apotheosis 29, 38f., 76f., 235
Appendix Vergiliana 18
appetite 88
apple 87
Aquitanian 90
Aratus 159–61, 163, 182, 246
arbiter 4, 216, 230, 234, 240, 247, 253
arbitrator 249
arbutus 73, 85, 101f.
arcade 102
Arcadian 238
archaic / archaising 88f., 187
archaism 89, 160
architectural 90, 105, 118f.
arena 65, 91f., 99, 101, 103, 105, 107, 117, 119, 251
aretalogy 23, 61
Argonautic / *Argonautica* 17, 189
Argus 21
Ariadne 142
Arion 232
Aristotelian 158
Armenia 110
Ars Grammatica 158
Arsinoe 96

art / artistic 34, 49, 55f., 66, 96, 102, 105, 110, 113, 119, 158, 171, 190, 195, 202f., 205, 251
artifact 94
artificial 101f., 117, 119
artificiality cult 102
Ascanius 236, 248
Asinius Gallus 31
assassination 38f.
Assyrian 54, 78
Astacus 4, 195–8, 200, 203–8, 210, 212–9, 252
Ästhetik der Verkehrung 8, 23
astonish / astonishment 96, 101, 103
Astraea–Dike 30
astrology 159
astronomical 39, 62, 67
Astylus 5, 141, 223f., 226–30, 232–6, 238, 240–8, 250
asyndetic 116
Atlas 28, 67
atypical 48, 226, 240
auditorium 105
Augustan / Augustus 5f., 8, 10, 23, 26, 29, 31–3, 35–41, 45f., 57, 59, 65, 68, 70, 74f., 80, 86, 90, 99, 101, 104, 110, 123f., 229, 248, 251
aurea saecula 31f., 51
authority / personal experience 165, 180
automatism 102
autumn 5, 15f., 167f., 177, 227
avena 42, 55, 64, 72
axle 92, 105

babble 241
bacchic 19, 62
Bacchus 62, 74f., 142
bark 15, 22f., 75, 136
barley 147
basket 62, 105, 144f.
battle 33, 38
Battus 126, 240
beans 147
bear 100, 103, 146
beautiful / beauty 21, 119, 141f., 214, 216, 229, 231f.
bee 162, 200f.

beech / beechen 4, 8, 15 f., 22, 50, 61 f., 91, 136, 207 f., 218
belated / belatedness 163, 198, 217, 226
belittlement of the pastoral opponent 145
Bellona 8, 25 f., 28, 43
bequeathe 16, 114, 185 f., 188, 190, 198, 214
Berenice 96
betrayed lover 137, 142
bickering 130, 141, 145, 227, 233, 244
bird 105, 168, 173, 185, 198, 228
birth 2, 30, 52, 71, 171
birthday 33, 90
bisexual / bisexuality 245, 249
bison 99 f.
bitumen 174–6
bleed 126
blocking character 247
blood / bloodshed / bloody 26, 38 f., 40 f., 76, 126, 170
bloodthirsty customs 103
bloom / blooming 72 f., 86
blows 144, 234, 247
boar 99
bos Indicus 99
branch 177, 206, 218, 225
brand / branding 174, 176, 179
bread 147
breaking-off / rounding-off of lists 165
breast 133
breeze 48
bribed office 37
bride / bridegroom 19, 32, 231
Britain 37, 110
broken heart 139
brooch 96
broom-tree 15, 19
Brundisium 31
Brutium / Bruttian 174, 176
Brutus 27, 38
Bucaeus 133, 138
bucolic 1, 3–9, 15–25, 28–32, 34 f., 38 f., 41–3, 45–8, 50–8, 60, 62, 64–7, 69, 74–6, 78–80, 82 f., 86–95, 98–103, 105, 107–9, 112–5, 117–9, 123–6, 128, 130–3, 136 f., 140 f., 143–6, 149, 152 f., 157, 161, 171, 173–5, 180, 186, 188–91, 195, 199–201, 204 f., 207–9, 213–7, 223–32, 235, 237–41, 243–6, 248–53
bucolic accessory 145
bucolic action 20
bucolic activity 152
bucolic adjudicator 249
bucolic arbiter 230
bucolic celebration 4
bucolic character 16, 21, 41, 114, 141, 186, 189, 216
bucolic circumstances 143
bucolic clothing 251
bucolic community 251
bucolic competitor 94
bucolic connotation 103
bucolic contest 93
bucolic context 20
bucolic convention 25
bucolic corpus 17, 30, 34, 38, 48, 52, 157, 201, 209, 223, 251
bucolic delight 69
bucolic dimension 189
bucolic discourse 34
bucolic disguise 74
bucolic echo 237, 241
bucolic ethics 253
bucolic ethos 223
bucolic experience 100, 214
bucolic figure 83, 89, 114, 133, 152, 157, 189, 249
bucolic flora 8
bucolic frame / framing 15, 117, 191
bucolic genre 17, 38, 53, 55, 78, 103, 117, 230, 239 f., 252
bucolic *genus* 29, 52, 102, 186, 232, 237, 251
bucolic hero 87
bucolic home 89
bucolic idealism 74
bucolic identity 89
bucolic idyll 7
bucolic imagery 200, 238
bucolic interest 24
bucolic intertext 32, 89
bucolic landscape 87, 93, 118, 237
bucolic life 113
bucolic location 8

bucolic love 146, 235
bucolic lover 4, 153
bucolic mantle 21, 24
bucolic marker 86, 199
bucolic mask 9, 31, 114, 152
bucolic match 248
bucolic model 16
bucolic narration / narrative 16, 19, 25, 41, 43, 46
bucolic norm 15, 137, 149, 152, 230, 252
bucolic occupation 90, 144
bucolic oeuvre 204
bucolic order 82
bucolic panegyric 9, 15, 42, 251
bucolic pantheon 109, 199, 240
bucolic paradise 35
bucolic performance 64
bucolic plot 239
bucolic poem / poet / poetics / poetry 3, 6f., 15–7, 20, 23f., 38f., 42f., 46f., 50, 56f., 62, 64f., 76, 80, 87–9, 91, 98, 102, 105, 108, 113, 117, 124, 149, 152f., 161, 186, 188, 207f., 214–6, 226f., 229, 231, 239, 244, 248
bucolic practice 195
bucolic prehistory 17, 189
bucolic present 224
bucolic prize 230
bucolic production 16f.
bucolic prophecy 19
bucolic protagonist 19
bucolic *puella* 25
bucolic quality 22
bucolic realm 69
bucolic scenario 15f., 19f.
bucolic setting 42, 186
bucolic simile 98
bucolic singer 213, 231
bucolic song 19f., 32, 66, 78, 93, 95, 98, 117, 125, 130, 171, 217, 228, 240, 248f., 252
bucolic space 80, 118, 209, 213, 231, 251
bucolic story 238
bucolic strains 52
bucolic task 94, 144
bucolic teacher 132
bucolic text 17, 41, 125, 229, 245, 251

bucolic *topos* 238
bucolic tradition 17, 58, 93, 95, 98f., 102, 130, 136, 195, 217, 227, 251
bucolic trend 79, 92
bucolic value 51, 74, 249
bucolic veneer 252
bucolic work 31f.
bucolic world 23, 25, 34, 53, 94f., 112, 175, 248
bucolisation / bucolise 114, 117, 252
build / building 90, 119
bull 64, 88, 99f., 107, 129, 134, 143, 150, 200, 211, 238
bystander 234, 246

C. Calpurnius Piso 3, 63
Caeculus 18
Caesar 27, 30–3, 38–40, 46, 68, 70–2, 81, 86, 92, 104, 163, 238
caesura 82, 92
Calais 18
calendar 161
calf 150, 211
Callimachean / Callimachus 7, 18, 20f., 23, 32, 49, 54, 56f., 60, 62, 64–6, 78, 80f., 92, 95, 101, 105, 112, 123, 131, 136, 141, 159, 183–5, 187, 198, 201–3, 206, 213, 219, 251
Callimachean–Neoteric 7, 11, 35, 42, 46, 56f., 64, 75, 79f., 92, 95, 102, 105–8, 118, 123, 141, 145, 185, 206, 232, 239, 242
Callimacheanism 7, 187, 202
Callirhoe 131f.
calming of the wind 70
Calpurnius Siculus 1–254
Calpurnius Statura 9, 18
Calvus 7
Camilla 18, 239
Camillus 27, 37
canales 66, 83f.
candida pax 35f.
canere / cantare / cantus 22, 30, 32, 46, 52, 63, 66, 76, 81, 90, 93, 132, 162, 168, 183f., 196, 228, 231, 242
Canthus 5, 157, 166f., 179, 185f., 189–91
cap 18

capella 8, 71, 170
Capitoline 105
captive city 26 f.
carmen 18, 20, 22, 24, 34, 42, 46, 51, 54 f., 64, 73, 81, 83 f., 137 f., 162, 183 f., 203, 214, 225, 232 f., 242
carve 4, 22–4, 136 f.
cassia 146
Cassius 38
catalogue 237
catch-term / word 9 f., 42, 46, 54, 57, 64, 66, 79, 81, 86, 92, 95, 104 f., 118, 145, 185, 202, 206, 213, 219, 232, 239, 242, 251
cattle 179, 189 f., 198
cattle-breeding 162
cattle fertility / prosperity 71
Catullan / Catullus 7, 19, 212, 253
cave 19 f., 25, 240–2
celebrate / celebration / celebratory 4, 35, 52, 69, 75, 104, 118, 209
celestial abode 77
Ceres 36, 74 f., 241
champion 225
chasing off serpents 176
cheese 59, 142, 170 f., 210
cherry 58, 136
chestnut 73, 146, 212 f., 218
chew 129
choral song 75
Chromis 20, 187
cicada 173
Cicero 45, 159
cicuta-playing 58
Cinna 7
circus 97, 104
citational / citationality 205, 253
city 5, 26, 34, 51, 56, 80, 87–92, 94–6, 98, 107–9, 112, 119, 171, 241, 253
civil bloodshed 41
civil conflict 26–8, 40
civil strife 28, 39
civil war 25–7, 34, 37–40
Classical Latin 44, 84 f., 88, 218
Claudian / Claudius 10, 16, 26, 28, 33, 37 f., 59, 110, 166
clause 44, 116, 181, 218

clausula 17, 104, 142, 144, 178, 180, 187, 198, 236–9
clemency / *Clementia* 4, 9, 37, 40 f., 76, 103
Cleopatra 26
close / closing / closure 36, 46, 78, 81 f., 89, 112, 117, 125, 143, 153, 186 f., 214 f., 248, 252
clothes / clothing 96, 152, 251
cloud 172
coarse 140
cohort 37
coin 29, 70
cold 178 f.
colloquial / colloquialism 52, 84 f., 88 f.
coloni 34 f., 162
Columella 63, 157, 166, 168, 176, 203
Comatas 141, 145, 147, 228, 243, 246
comedy / comic 6, 45, 58 f., 95, 123 f., 126–8, 131–5, 137, 139, 147 f., 150–3, 171, 208, 210, 213, 231, 244, 247–50, 252
comet 36, 38–40
compare / comparison 17, 19 f., 29, 37, 50, 52, 78, 89, 98, 103, 117, 138, 140 f., 182, 199 f., 208, 224, 227–9, 236, 251
compete / competing / competition / competitive 94, 102 f., 118, 143, 196
competing animals 103
competitor 94, 118, 132, 228
Compitalia 75
compound 199, 237
comprehensive preparation 179
Concordia 27 f.
confiscation 28, 79, 93
conjunction 44 f.
conjunctive 181, 218
consul 30, 52, 66
contentment with the love of one beloved only 131
contestant 5, 55, 153, 195 f., 201, 206, 208, 215, 217, 223, 225, 228, 230, 232, 240, 242, 248
continuation / continue / continuity / continuous 8, 29, 34, 38, 53, 60, 79, 89, 95 f., 98, 109, 111, 113, 166, 179, 216
continuous monologue 166, 179

convening 93, 103, 118, 125, 138, 186, 196, 225
cool / cooling / coolness 15, 18f., 48–50, 98, 101, 129, 172f., 195
coordination 116
Corpus Tibullianum 74
corruption 37
Corydon 4f., 8f., 15, 17, 19–21, 24f., 41–3, 47–72, 74, 76–80, 82, 84, 86–9, 91–6, 98, 101–3, 105, 107–9, 111–5, 117, 119, 124, 128, 130, 132, 138–44, 146, 152f., 190, 196f., 199, 207, 209, 211f., 216, 226, 230, 246, 251, 253
couched censure 110
count 143
country / country-side 5, 7f., 31, 72, 102, 112, 119, 183, 249, 253
court 59, 112
courting 133, 244
cow / cowherd 33, 88, 134, 143, 150, 196, 225, 235
cricket 105, 107
Crocale / Crotale 4, 197, 206–8, 210–3
crook 130
cross-reference 164, 182
crow 228
cry /crying 70, 138, 231
cryptic 63, 94
cubs 146
cud 129
culpability 135
Cumae 30
cup 94, 106, 153, 215, 218, 235
cutter 177
Cyclops 93, 138, 140–2, 144, 210, 235, 240
cylinder / cylindrical 105, 115, 119
Cynisca 134
Cynthia 135
Cyparissus 236f., 245
cypress 236
Cytherea 33

dactyl / dactylic 25f., 82, 185, 203
Damoetas 21f., 55, 113, 132, 141, 145, 149, 171, 196, 227, 233, 247, 249
Damon 124, 128, 145, 148f., 153, 200, 227, 231–3

dance 70, 76
Daphnis 32, 72, 92, 125, 133, 141f., 148, 150, 153, 167, 186, 204, 207, 213, 216, 233, 235, 238
darling 127, 129, 132f., 142, 152, 246
dative 44, 84, 91, 164, 179, 215, 218
de-bucolisation / de-bucolise 32, 114, 251
De Clementia 36f.
de grege regendo 5, 157
de-pastoralisation / de-pastoralise 32, 46, 123, 251
death / die 16, 36, 41, 60, 72, 147f., 238
Decii 27
deconstruct / deconstruction / deconstructive 78, 91, 94, 100, 102, 118, 188, 196, 251f.
deductio 231
deductum carmen 54, 81
deer 99, 174, 235, 245
default 48, 58, 78, 82
deictic 180f.
deified 32, 53, 72f., 81, 86, 92, 242
deity 30, 32f., 68, 76, 95, 170, 199, 202–4, 240
Delphis 135, 142
Demophoon 125
deponent verb 45
descriptio loci 97
deus iuvenis 33, 47, 81, 87f., 91
dew 172f.
diaeresis 180
dialogue 43, 87, 125, 166, 237, 239, 250, 254
Dichterweihe 16, 65, 189
diction 50, 60, 69f., 83–5, 88f., 94, 115f., 118, 131, 167, 171, 178f., 181, 191, 207, 218f., 252
didactic 9, 62, 67, 157–85, 187f., 190f., 252
didactic intent 160–4, 166f., 173, 179, 188, 191, 252
didactic intra-textual drama 185
didaxis 160, 163, 183, 187, 190
Diomedes 158f.
Diphilos 247
directive expressions 180
discidium 125

disease 175 f., 178
disillusionment 10, 111
distant 49, 60, 112, 172
distressed lover 130, 135, 139, 145
dives amator 147
divine 4, 8 f., 15, 25, 28, 30 f., 33 f., 40, 42, 47, 53, 61, 68, 70 – 3, 75 – 7, 79, 86 – 9, 91, 109 f., 112 – 4, 117, 119, 125, 170, 184, 199, 206, 210, 237
divine emperor 15, 28, 34, 42, 47, 77, 79, 117, 119
divine epiphany / intervention 34, 70, 73, 184
divine *puer* 31, 42
divinum carmen 20
docere 90, 162 f.
docile young age 61
docilis 17, 21, 42, 46, 61
docta puella 136
doctrina 229
doctus 21 f., 42, 136
dog 225, 249
domina 81, 138 f.
Domitian 1
Domus Aurea 119
Donace 113, 198, 211, 213, 215
Dorism 131
Dorylas 216
doves 146
dowry 132
dowry–wife 150
draw 4, 216 f.
dream 129, 150
driving away 174, 180
Drusi 27
Dryad 242
duet 141
dulcis / dulcitas 54, 64, 78 f., 95, 114, 174, 196
dura puella 150

Early Latin 88
earth 29 f., 33, 73, 101, 187
easy virtue 133
echo / echoing 10, 59, 71, 83 f., 215, 237, 241

ecphrasis / ecphrastic 8 f., 43, 94, 97, 106 f., 115 f., 118 f., 197, 233, 235, 238 f., 250 f., 253
efflorescence 72
Egeria 33
egg 98, 231
Einsiedeln Eclogues / poet 4, 51
elder / older 15, 23, 87, 91 f., 103, 113 – 5, 186, 189 f., 216, 244, 246, 252
elegiac 8 f., 18 f., 21, 23 f., 34 f., 42, 56, 64, 88, 108, 123 – 53, 178, 184, 196 – 8, 206 – 9, 211 – 5, 217, 219, 226, 229 – 32, 237, 249 f., 252 f.
elegiac affair 178
elegiac appeal 207 f.
elegiac behaviour 128
elegiac character 135, 198, 211
elegiac code 147
elegiac colouring 129, 132, 197
elegiac connotation 212
elegiac corpus 124, 207, 215
elegiac discourse 35, 123, 125, 128, 130, 132, 138, 141, 153, 197, 207, 215, 230
elegiac disposition 128, 153, 213 f.
elegiac element 253
elegiac ethics 230
elegiac ethos 136, 151
elegiac fascination 128
elegiac feature 9
elegiac genre 23, 129, 131 f., 146, 229, 249
elegiac *genus* 125, 127
elegiac help 206
elegiac heroine 19, 132
elegiac ideal 148
elegiac identity 108
elegiac image / imagery 129, 134 f.
elegiac inclination 128, 133 f., 230
elegiac intertext 211, 230
elegiac intrusion 123, 207
elegiac leaning 153
elegiac love 128, 133, 153
elegiac love–poetry 214
elegiac lover 123, 127, 129, 139, 147 f., 213, 237
elegiac marker 153
elegiac mode 127
elegiac model 24, 212

General Index

elegiac mood 217
elegiac narrative 21, 34, 139, 142
elegiac outlook 207
elegiac passion 127, 215
elegiac pattern 197f.
elegiac plight 131
elegiac poem 136
elegiac poet 23, 108, 123, 128f., 178, 198, 214
elegiac poetry 209
elegiac principles 230
elegiac propensity 144
elegiac provenance 252
elegiac *puella* 146
elegiac quality 252
elegiac realm 206, 208
elegiac record 138
elegiac register 123, 136, 139, 142, 150, 207
elegiac rhetoric 133, 226
elegiac ring 230
elegiac role 135
elegiac sensibility 208, 211, 250
elegiac setting 138, 209
elegiac situation 133, 148
elegiac stance 130
elegiac suitor 209, 211
elegiac syntagm 129
elegiac tactics 206
elegiac teacher 184
elegiac topic 124, 131, 137f.
elegiac *topos* 140
elegiac trait 252
elegiac transformation 212
elegiac trend 209
elegiac triangle 133, 196f., 213, 231, 249
elegiac turn 207
elegiac undertone 88, 128
elegiac value 206, 230, 253
elegiac wording 149, 197
elegiac work 19
elegising 56, 124–8, 130, 132, 135, 138, 141f., 145, 149, 207
elegy 5f., 8, 23, 29, 34–6, 46, 56, 87f., 117f., 123f., 128f., 133–5, 137, 144, 148, 153, 172, 178, 188, 197, 200, 209–11, 213, 230, 252f.
elevated 66, 69, 107f., 113, 252

elk 99
elm 19, 50, 129, 208
empathetic / empathy 87, 164, 179, 200, 237
Empedocles 159, 161, 182
emperor 3–5, 10, 15f., 21, 24–9, 33f., 36f., 39–43, 46f., 53f., 56, 61, 67–74, 76f., 79, 86, 90, 92, 101, 105, 109–14, 117–9, 166, 199, 251
encomiastic 35, 96, 109f., 113, 118
encomium 10, 35, 67, 86, 101, 111, 117f., 136, 251
Ennian / Ennius 32, 239
enrich / enrichment 23, 153, 188, 191, 252f.
enumeration 100f., 184, 188
Enyo 19
epic 6, 8, 11, 17f., 20–7, 29f., 32, 34, 40, 42–6, 50, 53, 56, 63–5, 69f., 77, 81, 95, 97, 104, 109–11, 118, 137, 144, 157–60, 162, 196, 198–200, 202, 211, 228, 231, 234–9, 242f., 248, 250–2
epicising 97, 234, 251, 253
Epicurean 159, 162, 183, 243
epigonal / epigone / epigonic 16f., 124
epigonism 43
epigram 148f.
epigraphic 2, 111
epiphany 70, 73, 184, 203
epistle 4, 8, 125, 130, 153, 237
epistolary / epistolography 88, 148
epos 8, 157f.
epylliac / epyllion 129, 138, 235, 239
equestrian 41
Erichtho 99
Erichthonius 239
eros 8, 88, 231
erotic 4, 8, 23, 25, 107, 112, 123, 125–33, 135–41, 143–51, 197, 206f., 209–13, 215, 219, 229–31, 243, 246, 249
erotic appeal 213
erotic association 125
erotic bliss 206, 229
erotic competitor 132
erotic connotation 150, 212
erotic context 129
erotic counsellor 137
erotic discourse 125

erotic endeavour 149
erotic epistle 8, 130
erotic exclusiveness 131
erotic exclusivity 150, 230
erotic fault 135
erotic favour 139
erotic feeling 211
erotic fickleness 150
erotic frustration 209
erotic gift 145, 147, 210, 212
erotic grief 146
erotic heartlessness 148
erotic involvement 246
erotic jealousy 132
erotic letter 136
erotic loss 129
erotic misery 25
erotic nature 149
erotic pain 23
erotic pallor 138
erotic passion 126, 128
erotic plight 126f., 131, 144, 215
erotic predicament 123, 144
erotic present 212f.
erotic quarrel 129f.
erotic rebuff 230
erotic rejection 112
erotic relationship 151
erotic rival / rivalry 127, 131, 140f., 147, 150, 211, 213, 229
erotic scorn 132
erotic setting 136, 207
erotic sleeplessness 150
erotic sorrow 133
erotic success 211f., 219
erotic triangle 107, 126, 143, 145, 197, 231, 249
erotic trouble 128, 145, 150
erotic violence 150
estate 79, 157
eternal peace 68
ethical dative 164, 179
Etruscan 17, 28
etymological 205
Eunica 112
Evander 31
evening 41, 82, 143, 170, 174, 186f., 214

evict / eviction 35, 209
Evmaras 147
ewe 171, 204, 210f.
excel / excellence / excellent 56, 95, 105, 107, 118, 140, 202, 208f., 216, 228f., 232, 250
excerpt 50, 248
exclusiveness 131, 229
exclusivity 131, 150, 230
exclusus amator 8, 134, 138, 150
exemplum 26, 40
exhort / exhortation 21, 59, 144, 164, 233, 245
external appearance / beauty 118, 141, 214, 228–31
external cause 44
external narrator 55, 195

fagina pocula 94, 97, 208
faginus / fagus 16, 22f., 76, 90–2, 94, 97, 186, 207f., 218
fail / failure 111, 117, 123, 139, 200, 208f., 212
false promises 147
Fama 29
fame / famous 3, 25, 27, 183, 211
farcical 247
farm / farmer / farming 18, 34, 41, 158, 162f., 177, 179f., 188, 190, 237
fate 25, 31
father 15f., 25, 27, 58, 78, 104, 143, 152, 167, 190f.
fauna 8, 33, 99f., 117, 225, 232, 251
Faunus 4, 8, 15f., 18–25, 29f., 32–4, 41, 43, 46f., 76, 107, 136, 170, 199, 204, 251
fawns 146
feed / feeding 100, 177, 179, 206
feet / foot 126, 178, 199
felicitas / felix 37, 68, 108, 114, 119, 159, 197
feminine 115, 243
fennel flower 146
fickleness 127, 148, 150, 172
fiction / fictional 109, 111f., 123, 253f.
field 39, 72, 74, 170, 172, 176, 204, 212, 237
Filippo da Giunta 224

financial 59, 170
first-person speaker 161, 166, 183
fisherman 107, 147
fistula 17, 21, 58, 66, 83, 92, 202, 214, 231
fleece 71, 174, 185, 210, 212
flirting 133
flock 59, 62, 130, 143, 152, 157, 166, 168, 170, 172–4, 176f., 179, 187, 190f., 204, 206, 211, 214, 225, 238
Flora 203f.
flora 8, 16, 33, 50, 101, 117, 238, 251
Florales 97
flower 73, 146, 200f., 226, 238
flute 21, 57, 75, 133, 150, 190, 202f., 225, 235
flute-girl 133, 150
fog 172
fold 145, 168
food / foodstuff 58, 129, 171f., 177, 185
foot (*metre*) 25
Fordicidia 33
forest 8, 88, 100, 215, 242, 244
formalistic 6, 162, 195, 198, 202, 224–7, 244, 253
formosus 90, 148f., 195, 197f., 213
formula 56, 164f., 180, 191, 248
fortuitous meeting 125
fortune 79, 132, 211
fossor 74, 86
foundation narrative 34
fountain 101, 139, 204
fowling 198
fragilis 66, 83, 177, 185, 239
frame / framework / framing 15f., 29f., 35, 42, 52, 55, 87, 102, 117, 119, 125, 130, 141, 147, 161, 186–8, 191, 224, 226f., 245, 248f., 252
frigus 49, 178
frondatio 177, 206
frugality 93
fruit 73, 101, 146, 205, 212f., 218, 232
frustrate / frustration 10, 108, 111, 118, 126, 151, 209
Furor 8, 25, 28
future 26f., 34, 54, 66, 85, 164, 180–3, 218

G. Memmius 162
Galatea 25, 59, 95, 128, 137, 139f., 146, 150, 171, 210f., 235
galerum / galerus 18
Gallan / Gallus 21, 23, 31, 42, 64, 108, 113, 117, 123, 127f., 133, 136, 153, 178, 214
game 75, 88, 93, 98, 103f., 117, 201, 245, 251
garden / gardening 101f., 149, 184, 196, 203, 210, 214f.
gardener 4, 196, 203f., 208, 216f., 219
garment 96, 114, 133
generic 2, 5–10, 20, 23f., 32, 34f., 42f., 45–59, 61f., 64–7, 70–3, 75–7, 79, 81–4, 86, 88–90, 93, 95–8, 103–6, 108–10, 115, 117f., 123–34, 136–8, 142–6, 148f., 152f., 157–63, 166–70, 172–4, 178f., 182–8, 191, 195–201, 203–17, 219, 223–7, 229–33, 235–42, 245, 247–53
generic adhesion 160
generic admixture 23
generic alienation 62
generic allegiance 159, 174, 197
generic alteration 50, 72, 198, 204
generic ambivalence 6, 66, 137, 142, 144, 146, 178, 199, 208, 227, 250
generic anxiety 51, 144
generic aspiration 50, 53, 115, 226
generic asset 161
generic association 123, 211
generic background 208
generic blurriness 232
generic boundary 32, 45f., 153, 188, 219, 252
generic branching out 6, 204, 252
generic category 158
generic change 43, 253
generic character 71, 123, 129, 132, 200, 226
generic characterisation 56
generic code 131, 137, 152f., 167, 186f.
generic colouring 43
generic comprehensiveness 199
generic conduct 248
generic connotation 42
generic consciousness 23

generic constituent   98, 109, 117, 125 f., 157, 251
generic contact   188, 250
generic convention   179
generic coolness   48–50
generic cornerstones   98
generic criterion   166, 182
generic definition   159
generic demand   54, 183
generic demarcation   124, 161
generic descriptive term   129
generic development   81, 253
generic deviation   83, 89, 95, 104, 115, 211
generic dialogue   237, 239, 250
generic direction   86, 201
generic discourse   124
generic dislocation   50
generic disposition   215
generic distanciation   93
generic distancing   20
generic diversification   55, 149, 153, 207
generic diversion   252
generic diversity   129, 178, 214
generic endeavour   115
generic enrichment   153, 252
generic essential   225, 237, 252
generic estrangement   62
generic ethics   226
generic evolution   9, 43, 115
generic experience   223, 227, 229
generic favourite   124, 134, 205
generic feature   110, 160, 162, 182, 184, 186, 188, 235, 247
generic feeling   142, 169
generic flexibility   198
generic fluidity   76, 200, 208, 215
generic forerunner   7
generic form   79
generic formation   5 f., 9, 124, 157, 185, 188, 231
generic framing   161
generic fullness   226
generic function   117, 152
generic gathering   199
generic history   173, 252
generic ideal   59

generic identity   2, 7, 10, 20, 75, 123, 188, 205, 227, 245
generic illusion   183
generic impression   216
generic inclination   24, 126
generic innovation   9, 73, 217
generic interaction   8, 23, 34, 42, 46, 123, 136 f., 144, 153, 172, 178, 187, 199, 236, 252 f.
generic interest   118, 125, 132
generic interface   123, 137, 211
generic interplay   6, 172, 199, 236 f.
generic intrusion   124, 178, 247
generic issue   50, 215
generic key-stone   161
generic landscape   230
generic leaning   145, 213
generic lens   133
generic literary criticism   158
generic literary experience   6
generic location   49
generic marker   6 f., 49, 54, 59, 65, 71, 86, 126, 138, 158, 179, 186, 195, 208, 213, 237
generic meaning   240 f.
generic meta-poetic connotation   35
generic modification   6
generic motif   103, 168
generic movement   8, 77, 136, 152
generic norm   124, 142, 159, 240
generic novelty   43, 47, 83, 86, 118, 207, 216 f., 226 f., 249, 251
generic nuances   124
generic opposition   23
generic option   42
generic orientation   83, 105, 117, 249
generic origin   168, 173
generic outlook   57, 126, 131, 137, 214, 216, 240
generic partiality   24
generic pattern   169, 227
generic patterning   131, 152, 223
generic perspective   23, 35, 131
generic picture   134, 142, 170
generic plan   124
generic poetic form   108

generic point of view   49, 174, 209, 216, 241, 250
generic polyphony   239
generic position   240
generic precept   179
generic preference   46, 130, 136 f.
generic prerequisite   93, 185, 191, 206, 238, 252
generic process   123
generic profile   6 f., 123, 130, 137, 142, 152, 241
generic progress   188
generic propensity   128, 136
generic quality   205
generic re-assessment   86
generic re-evaluation   66, 86, 106, 126, 226
generic re-orientation   86, 118, 153, 205, 208, 227, 235 f., 241, 249
generic realm   128
generic reminiscence   170
generic renewal   251
generic repertoire   6, 242
generic rift   108, 240
generic role   6, 163
generic rule   6, 64, 145, 224
generic sensibilities   86
generic shift   237
generic sign   86, 136, 232
generic standard   160, 166, 188
generic standing   157, 252
generic status   131, 158
generic system   57
generic technique   184
generic tendency   129, 136 f., 248
generic tension   5, 52, 127, 167, 188, 226, 237, 239 f.
generic term   42, 55, 204, 208, 210 f., 237
generic theme   173
generic theory   6
generic touch   23
generic tradition   7, 86, 97, 219, 226
generic transcendence   5, 53, 66 f., 71, 76, 89, 96, 126, 224
generic transcending   61, 110, 145
generic transgression   43, 137
generic transition   81
generic transposition   143, 236

generic trend   123, 148, 215, 233
generic value   231
generic versatility   212, 235
generic zone   6
generically   30, 43, 48 f., 53, 57, 67 f., 75, 78, 85, 89, 104, 119, 124 f., 127 f., 131, 133, 139 f., 142, 146, 152, 178 f., 185, 189, 191, 195, 197, 201 f., 206, 208 – 11, 215, 219, 223, 231, 235, 240 – 2, 244, 250
genitive   91, 187
genius Augusti   75
genre   5 – 7, 17, 19, 23, 29 f., 38, 47 – 53, 55, 58, 61 f., 64, 66 f., 69 f., 73, 75 – 8, 83, 86, 88 f., 95, 97, 103, 108 f., 117, 119, 123 f., 129, 131 – 3, 146, 148, 150, 157 f., 160 – 2, 175, 178, 188, 190 f., 196, 199 f., 207, 212, 215 – 7, 229 f., 237, 239 f., 247, 249 f., 252
gens Calpurnia   2 f.
genus grande   18 f., 21 – 4, 35 f., 42, 45 f., 65, 70, 79 – 81, 97, 104 f., 111, 118, 235 – 8, 242, 251 f.
genus tenue   23 f., 42, 46, 49, 54, 75, 79 – 81, 86, 101, 107, 123, 131, 183 f., 237, 239, 251
georgic   4, 8 f., 20, 23, 58, 62, 72, 74 f., 86, 92, 95, 113, 157 – 60, 167 – 81, 185 – 91, 198 f., 201, 203 – 6, 212, 214 – 7, 219, 237, 252 f.
georgic-didactic propensities   167
georgic-didactic prose   169
gerund   91
gerundive   164, 180
gift   21, 32, 69, 102, 126, 132, 145 – 8, 151, 190, 199, 202, 207 f., 210, 212 f.
girlfriend   145
gleaner   138
glorification / glorify   101, 190
glorious / glory   26 f., 31 f., 118, 202
Glykera   151
go-between   61, 135
goat   5, 8, 125, 143, 145, 149, 167, 169, 171, 174, 186, 190, 225
goatherd   93, 124, 128, 132, 140, 147 f., 153, 231

god   4, 15, 19, 22–5, 32–5, 42, 46, 51, 53f., 57, 59, 61, 67–70, 73, 75–7, 79, 81, 86f., 108–10, 118, 128, 130, 199, 202f., 206f.
goddess   19, 25, 30, 71, 77, 136, 203f.
Golden Age   4, 15, 26, 30–2, 35f., 38, 42, 47, 51–3, 64, 71, 102, 231f., 235, 242
goldfinch   228, 243f.
Gorgo   96
gracilis   62, 105, 145, 214
grass   129, 149, 170, 173, 204, 238, 243
graze / grazing   173, 179, 238
greed / greedy   36, 236
Greek   3, 31–3, 50, 58, 85, 91f., 149, 160, 162, 182, 199, 211f., 226–8, 240f., 243f., 252
Graecising   228f.
green cabinet   10, 28, 38, 41, 48, 53, 56, 62, 69, 78, 87–9, 91f., 94, 101, 115, 117, 123, 132f., 140, 144, 153, 171, 189f., 196, 200, 202, 204, 209, 223, 231f., 235, 241, 245f., 248, 251f.
green community   189
green mallow   61f.
green stuff   177, 179, 185
green tradition   189
grief   88, 146, 204, 237
grievance   59, 189
grotto   70, 102
ground   98, 101, 174, 177
grove   19f., 71, 206
guest-genre   6, 123
guilt   108, 144
guitar   34
gum-resin   174

haedus   8, 62, 143, 225
hair   151, 214, 231
hairy   100
Halesus   21
handsome / handsomeness   141f., 213, 230
hang   87, 98, 147f.
hapax   44, 66, 83, 116, 169, 218
happiness / happy   24, 26, 34, 42, 59, 150
hare   99f., 138, 146
harmonious   98, 149
haste   22

Haupt   1, 3
hayloft   177
hazel   19, 50
heartlessness   148
heat   15, 18, 48, 83, 138, 173, 195, 237
heaven   70, 76
heifer   4, 125f., 129, 143, 150, 171, 211
Helen   136
Hellenising   228f.
Hellenism   116, 229
Hellenistic   158f., 187
hemiepes   169
Hercules   28f., 126, 237
herd / herding   15, 19, 32, 52, 94, 125, 167f., 238
herdsman   4, 55, 58f., 61, 63, 67, 81, 87, 94, 109, 112, 114, 142, 148, 167f., 170–3, 177, 185f., 196, 204, 208f., 213, 216, 223, 228f., 231f., 239, 243f., 248, 250
Hermes   21
Hermesianax   161
Hesiod / Hesiodic   159–63, 167, 182, 203
hexameter / hexametric   24–6, 29, 32, 34, 82, 119, 158, 185, 199, 203, 230, 238
hibiscum   61f., 105, 145
hiems   168, 179
Hieron II of Syracuse   35
hill   68, 98, 130, 200, 237
hippopotamus   100
hircus   8, 169
Hirtius   41
historical   1, 6, 9f., 26, 33, 43, 52, 58, 60, 66, 114, 119, 152, 223
historicising analysis   6
history   20, 23, 29, 31, 51, 60, 91, 114, 149, 166, 173, 186, 197, 216, 241f., 248, 252
holm-oak   186, 199
Homer   158
homoerotic   138, 246
homosexual / homosexuality   67, 197, 224, 245–7
honey   174, 200
hoopoe   228
Horace / Horatian   7, 18, 44f., 76, 188
horizon of expectations   229
horse   5, 111, 228, 238f.

host–generic formation 185
host–genre 6, 108
hostile / hostility 5, 57, 60, 102, 223, 229
hot 15 f., 19, 129, 173
hunger 58, 60
hunt / hunting 32, 100, 118, 235
huntsman 17
husbandry 9, 204
hyacinth 129, 146
Hyblean 64
Hylas 126
hymn / hymnic 34, 54, 61, 70, 90, 113, 201
hypallage 216
hypogeum 101

iambic 75
Iberian 2, 60
iconography 22, 36
Ida 70, 176
Idas 4, 195–8, 200, 202–4, 206–19, 252
ideological / ideology 26, 29, 35 f., 40, 253
Ides of March 38
idyll / 'idyllic' 7, 17, 25, 56, 67, 88 f., 92 f., 96 f., 105, 107, 118, 124, 126, 131–6, 138–43, 148 f., 152, 196 f., 201, 208, 212 f., 215, 226, 233, 235, 240, 243, 245 f., 248, 252
idyllic 17, 50, 52, 241, 249
ilex 50, 129, 186, 199, 240
imagery 52, 58, 60, 62, 65, 71 f., 79, 86, 98, 102, 105–7, 134 f., 138, 140, 145, 150, 168, 177, 182 f., 189, 197–200, 205, 207, 232, 238, 247
imitate / imitation / imitator 1, 7, 25, 27–32, 36, 39, 46, 51, 64 f., 70, 74, 96, 109, 124, 141, 150, 163, 181, 213, 227, 243, 246, 252
impartial / impartiality 234, 243
imperative (*mood*) 164, 167, 180 f.
imperatival 165, 180 f., 187, 191
Imperator 33
imperial 4, 9, 15, 28 f., 36 f., 41 f., 48, 52, 56, 59 f., 68 f., 74, 79 f., 86, 94, 96, 102–4, 110 f., 119, 196
imperium 24, 26, 28, 39, 53
incantation 22
inclines and slopes 98
incompetence 57, 140 f., 233
indicative (*mood*) 164, 181, 218
indifferent lover 148
indulgence 135
infatuation 128
infection 175
infinitive 84, 104, 116
ingens 18, 174, 178, 185
ingratitude / *ingratus* 126 f.
innards 26 f.
innovation / innovative 8 f., 45, 53, 66, 73, 84, 86, 127, 168, 206, 217, 235, 254
inscribe / inscription 23, 44, 75, 136, 148
insect 228
instruct / instruction 5, 161–4, 167, 183–6, 188
instructional 160 f., 165, 180, 185
intellektuelle Proletarier 58
interjectional 129
internal cause 44
intertext 6, 8, 10, 17, 22–4, 26 f., 29, 31 f., 34, 36, 39, 49–53, 55 f., 58, 60, 66 f., 69, 71–3, 77, 79, 82, 87–90, 96, 104, 106, 111, 118, 123, 127 f., 131, 137, 142 f., 146, 152, 167, 176–9, 191, 198, 206, 208–15, 230, 233–6, 238, 240 f., 245, 247–53
intertextual 18, 21, 24, 30, 34 f., 42 f., 45 f., 71, 89, 96, 104, 108 f., 111, 114, 117 f., 123 f., 159 f., 169, 174, 178, 197 f., 201, 213–5, 219, 237, 247, 249, 251 f.
intertextuality 26, 46, 160, 250
intertextually 32, 35 f., 57, 90, 104, 107, 114, 204, 215, 231, 235, 241, 248
intra–textual drama 185
intra–textual dramatic setting 162
intra–textual persona 161
inverse / inversion 6, 49, 79–81, 86, 89, 92, 114, 124, 202, 215, 252
invert 98 f., 102, 113, 116 f., 177, 251
invidia 80
invocation / invoke 4, 61, 67 f., 95, 170, 182, 202 f., 240
Iollas 4, 21, 64, 113, 125–7, 129–32, 134, 136, 141, 149–53, 207, 223, 246, 249
Iulia gens 32 f., 35, 37 f.
iunctura 62, 104, 135, 174, 180, 236

iurgia   130, 244
iustitia   4, 37
iuvenilis / iuvenis / iuventa   33, 47, 61, 68, 81, 87f., 91, 163, 166, 189
ivory   106
ivy   19, 62f., 94, 185

Janus   36
jay   228
jealousy   132f., 151
jewelry   151
joint pursuit   164
journey   87, 90, 107, 182–4
judge / judgement   55, 78, 112, 136, 201, 227, 230, 234, 242–4, 248f.
Julio–Claudian dynasty   26, 38
Junia Aurunculeia   19
juniper   72
Juno   18, 28
Jupiter   25, 67–70, 86, 240
jussive   164, 181

kid   81, 93, 225
king / kingdom   18, 28, 30–3, 60
kiss   140, 209, 211, 245f.
kletic   34
knife   170
knight   97, 113
komast   146
komos   131
Kouretes   70

L. Arruntius Camillus Scribonianus   37
labour   187
Labrax   247
Lachesis   31
Lacon   141, 145, 147, 228, 240, 243, 246
Ladon   17, 21, 42
lamb   143, 145, 171, 204f., 210, 225
lament   4, 199
land confiscation   28, 79, 93
landscape   50, 52, 60f., 70, 87, 90–3, 98f., 102, 118, 126, 128, 171, 174, 186, 230, 237, 249, 254
Laocoon   106, 111
Lares   170, 210
lassa crudelitas   41

late summer   16, 168
lateness   227
Latin   9, 21f., 42–5, 50, 61–3, 75, 78, 84–6, 88f., 100, 112, 115, 125, 158, 160, 167, 184f., 189, 218, 228, 244, 251, 253
Latinus   18, 32
Latium   30f.
laudatory discourse   36, 46
laudes principis   24, 52, 61, 78, 119
laurel   62f., 69, 146
Laus Pisonis   3f.
Lavinia   32
law / legal / legalistic   9, 26, 30, 74, 86, 174, 231
lawn   173
leaf   177f., 202, 205, 215
leafage   177, 179
leaning staff   189
lecture in progress   182
legislation   4, 28, 31, 74
leisure   128, 131, 185, 242
leno / pimp   247
lentus   60, 70, 75f., 88–90, 94
lepus variabilis or *timidus*   99
less pastoral   7, 78, 251
lesson–poem on the go   185
Leuce   25
levis / levitas   57, 149, 181, 185, 202f., 231f., 237
lexical / lexicon   9, 116f.
Liberalia   74
libertas / liberty   59, 87, 112, 128, 153, 171, 229
lily   139, 146, 208
Linus   21, 113
lion   147, 236
liquidus   78f., 141, 180
list   165, 182
literary   5f., 8, 10, 29f., 39, 46f., 53, 58, 61, 63, 73, 75, 77f., 86, 88f., 91, 95, 99, 107, 111f., 124, 153, 158f., 168, 185, 196, 199f., 207, 212, 215, 227, 229, 236, 240, 249–51, 253
literary competence   229
literary criticism   153, 158f.
literary predecessor   159
literary secondariness   227

literary trend 6, 8, 124, 158
Litigium 224
liveliness 200
livestock 34, 185, 190
locus amoenus 8, 15 – 8, 21, 48 – 50, 52, 69, 76, 86, 88, 98 f., 101, 117, 119, 126, 129, 195, 208, 215, 237, 241, 249, 251, 253
locus horridus 99, 126, 241
lone performer / singer 56, 93 f., 102, 118, 138
long life 76
looks 4, 112, 141 f., 224, 228, 230, 232
lop / lopping 177, 179, 185, 206
loss 58, 67, 72, 88, 93, 108, 126, 128 f., 148, 204, 224, 236
loss of temper 224
loud 51, 71
love / lover / beloved 4, 7, 21, 23, 25, 42, 62, 66 – 9, 71, 73, 80, 88, 112, 117 f., 123, 126 – 48, 150 – 3, 159, 163, 168 f., 175, 178, 197 f., 206 f., 209 – 17, 229 – 32, 235, 237, 242 f., 245 – 7, 249
lover's cruelty 88, 134, 148, 231, 237
lowing 88
loyalty 56
Lucan 26 f., 36, 40, 44 – 6, 63 f., 94, 99, 152, 223
Lucania / Lucanian 2, 18, 94, 100
Lucilius 2
Lucretian / Lucretius 52, 101, 159 f., 162 – 5, 167 f., 172 f., 183, 187 f., 242 f.
ludere 57, 75
Ludi Megalenses 104
lupine 147
lustratio 94, 170
luxury 110
Lycidas 4 f., 65, 89, 113 f., 125 – 9, 131, 133 – 45, 147 – 52, 207, 211, 213, 215, 223 f., 226 – 34, 238, 240 – 5, 247 f., 250
Lycopas 234
Lycoris 128, 133, 178
Lycos 134
Lycotas 5, 78, 87 – 9, 91 f., 94 f., 107 – 9, 114 f., 223, 233
lyric poetry 62, 76, 231

Maecenas 79 f., 163 f., 183 f.
maecenatism 59
magnus 54, 65, 90, 130, 187, 195
manifold preparation before undertaking a main task 165
Manilius 39, 159 f., 162 f., 167, 184
manual 167 f., 172, 177
marble 106
marginal 203, 208 f., 248
marigold 146
Mark Antony 26, 31, 33, 38
Mars 5, 45, 109 f., 112, 118
Marsyas 199
Martial 1, 44, 58, 99, 111, 119, 236
martial 19, 28, 118
masculine / masculinity 115, 246
mask 9, 31, 63 f., 114, 152 f., 166, 223, 243
masquerade bucolique 9, 223
material reward 79
materialistic 58 f., 79, 95, 170 f.
materialistic concern 58, 170
materialistic value 95
maturity 17
meadow 70, 170, 173, 238
meal 170
mechanism 52, 87, 101, 105, 119, 154
Medea 231
mediate / mediator 34, 135, 151
medical / medication 174 – 6
meet / meeting 21, 39, 87, 112, 125, 195, 199
Meliboeus 4, 24, 28, 41, 43, 48 – 50, 54 f., 60 – 7, 78 – 81, 83 f., 86, 108 f., 111, 125, 151, 199, 204 f., 209, 251
Memmius 162 f.
memory 65, 93, 241
Menalcas 19 – 23, 32, 55, 62, 72, 80, 113 f., 130, 132, 141, 143, 145, 147, 149, 171, 189, 196, 227, 233, 240, 244, 247, 249
Menander / Menandrian 133, 150 – 2
menial 81, 87, 130, 144, 203 – 5, 248
merae bucolicae 3, 8, 45, 252 f.
Mermnon 132
Messalla 34, 63, 90
Messiah / messianic 31, 71
meta-language / meta-linguistic 6, 11, 42, 47, 49, 81, 86, 91 f., 95, 102, 104 – 7, 113,

152, 185, 189 f., 199, 205, 213, 232, 237, 239, 242, 249
meta-narrative   226
meta-poetic   15–7, 21, 24, 35, 42 f., 46, 91, 95, 101 f., 105–8, 114, 118, 124, 131, 145, 152, 185, 190 f., 205, 213, 217, 232, 237–9, 242, 251–3
metaphor   184
metre / metrical   1, 25 f., 29, 34, 82, 92, 105, 131, 138, 144, 181, 185, 218, 232
Mezentius   236
Micon   5, 157, 166–8, 170, 172, 174, 179, 181 f., 185–91, 223, 249
miles gloriosus   147
military   28, 46, 69, 104, 134, 150
military tribune   104
militia amoris   135
milk / milking   25, 58, 71, 86, 142–5, 170 f., 204, 211 f., 235
milking-pail   170, 211
Milon   88, 138, 245
mime / mimetic   58, 96, 115, 133 f., 138, 142, 158
mime-like   115
Minerva   199
Mnasyllos   20, 187
Mnasyllus   5, 223, 228, 234, 240–3, 247–50
modal   62, 150, 152, 197, 230, 236, 239, 250
mode   6, 19 f., 66, 71, 108, 110, 127, 133, 152, 157 f., 160 f., 167–70, 172 f., 175, 177, 188–91, 204, 237, 252
model reader   229
modification / modify   6, 54, 85, 109, 188, 227, 250, 254
Moeris   35, 51, 93, 108, 241
monarch   27, 37
monetary / money   95, 171
monologue   166, 179
Mopsus   19–21, 23, 72, 113 f., 126–8, 130, 132–4, 136, 140 f., 145, 147–52, 189, 211, 213, 215, 223, 231, 240, 244 f.
mora   201 f.
morning   170, 172 f.
morphology   9, 115, 228
Morson   234
Moschion   151

Moschus   50, 198–200, 239, 243
mountain   8, 79, 238
mud   168 f.
munus   9, 97, 102 f., 147
Musa / Muse   21, 30, 52, 55, 57 f., 61, 81, 113, 136, 182, 202–4, 240, 244
music / musical   4, 15, 21 f., 34, 41 f., 57, 60, 64, 66, 75, 103, 132 f., 140 f., 149, 199, 209, 211, 216, 228–30, 232 f., 241, 246
music restored   75
musical distinction   140
musical excellence   140, 209, 216
musical incompetence   140 f., 233
musical performance   140, 149, 211, 216
musical skill   141, 232 f.
mute listener-student   179
mute worshipper   73
Mutina   33, 41
Myrrhine   151
myrtle   69, 146
mystes   108
mystic   108, 110, 244

Naiad   21, 242
Naias   65
narcissus   146
narrative   3, 8, 17, 20–2, 25, 28 f., 33 f., 38, 41, 43 f., 46, 48, 83, 87, 89 f., 95–8, 102, 105, 107, 109–13, 115, 117–9, 123–6, 128–32, 134, 137–40, 142 f., 148 f., 151 f., 158, 162, 168, 172, 180–2, 184–6, 195, 214, 224, 226 f., 229, 232, 235–7, 239, 242, 245–50, 252
narrative pattern   87, 96
narrative transition   180
natural / naturalness / nature   10, 32, 48, 59, 71–3, 76, 86, 88, 93, 98, 100–2, 110, 118, 139, 161 f., 168, 182 f., 186, 200, 215, 217, 224, 237 f., 240 f., 249
natural sound   48, 86, 98, 215, 240 f., 249
naumachia   100
negotium   24, 205
neighbour / neighbouring   151, 240
Nemesianus   3, 8, 198, 215 f.
nemus   15, 19 f., 206
neo-Callimacheanism   7

General Index

Neoteric / Neotericism 5–7, 10f., 35, 42, 46f., 49, 54, 56f., 60, 64, 75, 79f., 90, 92, 95, 101f., 105–8, 118, 123, 131, 136, 141, 145, 185, 200–2, 206, 210, 213, 219, 229, 231f., 239, 242f., 248, 253f.
Nero / Neronian 1–3, 5, 8–10, 16, 18, 21–4, 26–44, 46f., 50f., 53f., 56, 59–64, 68, 71, 74, 76, 80, 85–8, 90, 92, 95, 97, 99, 101, 103f., 107–14, 117–9, 124, 126, 149, 152, 166, 184, 188, 223, 235, 243, 249, 251
nest 168, 185
New Comedy 123f., 135
new pastoral 20, 42, 71, 92, 114, 189, 206, 216
New Poetry 102
Nicander / Nicandrean 160–2
night / nightfall 25, 90, 131, 137f., 145, 172f., 214, 217
nightingale 228
Nikias 226
noise 39, 93, 186, 215, 224, 241
nominative 244
non-bucolic 18, 89, 96, 123, 126, 131, 134, 137, 139, 147, 196, 226f., 238
non-mimetic 158
non-pastoral 7, 18, 59, 79, 89, 94, 96, 104, 117f., 134–6, 138, 142, 146, 148, 152, 189, 196f., 199, 229, 232, 250, 252
non-reciprocated love 128, 146
noon / noonday 15f., 41, 173, 237
noontide 82, 138, 195
nova spectacula 91f.
novel 42, 49f., 52–4, 57, 83, 86, 107f., 115, 118, 153, 201f., 205, 208, 211, 215, 217–9, 226f., 249, 252
novelty 43f., 47, 83, 86, 118, 183f., 207, 216f., 226f., 249, 251
noverca 249
Numa Pompilius 28f., 33
Nützlichkeit 123
Nyctilus 5, 223–5, 228–32
Nymph 8, 21, 33, 61, 65, 76, 136, 199, 203f., 240, 242, 244
Nysa 128, 148, 231, 250

oak 50, 65, 69, 132, 147f., 173f., 186, 199
oath 127
Octavia 31
Octavian 8, 26, 31, 33, 38, 81, 163
old age 109, 114, 189
Olympic games 88, 93, 245
omen 38, 136, 150
oppositio in imitando 42, 230
orchard 88, 204
order 59, 68, 72, 75, 79, 82, 93, 110, 129, 153, 164, 170, 172, 180, 187, 201, 209, 242
order of appearance 201
Oread 76
Orestes 246
originality 7
Ornytus 4, 9, 15–20, 22, 41f., 80, 152, 190
Orpheus 232, 237, 245
orphic lyre 64
orphic power 198, 200
orphic syndrome 64f., 196, 237
osier 144
otium / otium poeticum 60, 90, 131, 242
oval 106
ovatio 69
Ovid / Ovidian 19, 21, 29f., 33, 35, 39, 45, 52f., 56, 60, 64f., 78, 82, 86, 102, 104f., 127, 129f., 132, 137, 146–8, 150f., 153f., 158–61, 163, 166–8, 170, 184, 191, 198–200, 211f., 230, 236–9
ovile / ovilia 55, 80f., 113
owl 228

P. Quinctilius Varus 24
pagina 22, 24
pain 23, 126, 150
palace / palace trials 37, 77, 96, 119
Palaemon 234, 249
Palatine 68, 90, 110
Pales 71f., 95, 170, 204, 209f.
Pallas 21, 236
pallor 138f.
Pan 8, 21f., 32, 70, 76, 128, 132, 199
panegyric / panegyrical 3, 8–11, 15, 19–21, 23–6, 29, 32–6, 39, 42f., 45–7, 51f., 56f., 61, 66, 69, 71–9, 86, 90, 92,

95 f., 98, 101–7, 109, 112–5, 117 f., 136, 189, 199, 251–4
Pansa   41
pantheon   8, 32, 67 f., 76, 86, 109, 118, 170, 199, 204, 240
Parcae   77
parents   143, 205
Parilia   9, 94, 97, 209 f.
Parthenius   7
Parthian   69, 110
Pasiphae   129, 138
passer–by   22, 234, 242
passing away   72, 204
passive   45, 163 f., 181, 218
'passive'   246 f.
pastime   25
pastoral   2–8, 10, 15–26, 28, 30–2, 34 f., 38 f., 41–3, 45–82, 84–115, 117–9, 123–54, 157, 161, 166 f., 169–75, 177 f., 185–91, 195–217, 219, 223–54
pastoral activity   62, 82, 87, 101, 129, 143, 208
pastoral affair   150
pastoral alienation   131
pastoral animal   100, 117
pastoral antagonist   147
pastoral apprenticeship   132 f.
pastoral art   171, 190
pastoral artifact   94
pastoral asset   148, 174, 242
pastoral assistant   130
pastoral attitude   230
pastoral beaten track   18, 30, 94, 128
pastoral bliss   71
pastoral book   3
pastoral cabinet   113, 197
pastoral calibre   137, 191, 227
pastoral canon   5, 56, 196
pastoral character   4, 17, 41, 55, 87, 103, 112, 118, 130, 141, 196, 228, 252
pastoral closure   186
pastoral coating   202
pastoral code   69, 76, 214
pastoral collection   117
pastoral colouring   55, 89, 99, 186
pastoral community   7, 26, 35, 41, 92, 94, 113, 149, 171, 206, 246

pastoral composition   55, 216
pastoral contestant   223
pastoral context   43
pastoral continuance   89
pastoral continuity   34, 109
pastoral convention   207
pastoral conversation   103, 118
pastoral corpus   74, 86 f., 123, 133, 187, 203, 210, 216
pastoral correctness   197
pastoral cycle   252
pastoral data   6
pastoral deity   95, 204
pastoral *desideratum*   48
pastoral designation   99
pastoral dimension   34
pastoral discourse   6, 23, 127
pastoral dislocation   108, 127, 142, 144 f., 153, 197, 241
pastoral divinity   132
pastoral doings   143
pastoral domain   253
pastoral dwelling   89
pastoral ease   94
pastoral ecphrastic piece   106
pastoral elegy   210
pastoral empathy   200
pastoral ending   187
pastoral enjoyment   98
pastoral environment   60
pastoral epigone   16
pastoral *eros*   231
pastoral ethics   16, 140
pastoral ethos   238
pastoral exchange   225
pastoral exhortation   21
pastoral existence   8, 253
pastoral experience   216
pastoral facade   215
pastoral feature   98
pastoral fellow   128
pastoral festival   74
pastoral figure   67, 85, 87 f., 91, 103, 113 f., 125, 138, 141, 145, 147, 152, 166, 189, 216, 223–5, 231, 233 f., 240 f., 245 f., 248

pastoral form 56, 65, 114, 154, 189, 204 f., 252
pastoral fortune 79
pastoral framing 186, 188, 191
pastoral genre 48 f., 51 f., 66, 78, 97, 117, 119, 123, 200, 217
pastoral *genus* 42, 107, 225, 230 f.
pastoral girl 142
pastoral god / goddess 32, 53, 76, 128, 136, 203
pastoral guest 153
pastoral habit 93, 98, 114, 234
pastoral heritage 7
pastoral history 51, 114, 186, 197
pastoral holdings 79
pastoral home 90
pastoral idea 214
pastoral ideal 42, 51, 59, 65, 73, 95, 230 f.
pastoral idealism 58
pastoral identity 78, 94, 108, 208 f.
pastoral idyll 7, 142
pastoral image 55, 57, 94, 98
pastoral imagery 98
pastoral import 125
pastoral inhabitant 59, 98
pastoral initiation / initiator 113 f.
pastoral instrument 66
pastoral interlocutor 108, 134
pastoral intertext 58, 123, 127 f., 137, 142, 177 f., 210, 212 f., 247
pastoral judge 234
pastoral landscape 61, 70, 90–3, 98 f., 171, 174, 186, 249
pastoral liaison 133
pastoral life 21, 62, 87, 89, 91, 102, 214
pastoral literature 76, 167
pastoral location 76, 199
pastoral love 66, 118, 242
pastoral lover 71, 118, 126, 132, 141 f., 144, 153, 229
pastoral marker 98
pastoral memory 65, 93
pastoral menial task 81
pastoral meta-language 47, 232
pastoral model 5, 92, 131, 137, 152, 169, 200
pastoral moment 73, 251

pastoral music 57, 133, 140
pastoral name 189
pastoral narrative 41, 95, 118 f., 126, 130, 143, 152, 214, 237, 249
pastoral nature 200
pastoral noise 186
pastoral *nomen* 17
pastoral norm 51, 82, 86, 89, 93, 95, 104, 113, 115, 128, 138, 144, 148, 153, 189, 204, 212, 224, 232, 234, 248, 251 f.
pastoral occupation 8, 90, 93 f., 125, 130, 133
pastoral opponent 141, 145, 147, 149
pastoral order 59, 68, 79, 82, 93, 129, 153
pastoral origin 239
pastoral pantheon 32, 68, 86, 109, 118, 170, 199, 204, 240
pastoral past 189, 224
pastoral patterning 227
pastoral pedigree 114, 189, 196
pastoral performance 200, 240
pastoral permanence 34, 89, 108, 112
pastoral pet 236
pastoral pleasure 93
pastoral poem / poet / poetry 2 f., 10, 15–7, 21 f., 24, 30, 35, 42 f., 45 f., 51 f., 55, 57, 59–63, 65, 68, 70 f., 78–82, 87, 89, 91–3, 95 f., 101, 105–7, 113 f., 117 f., 124, 137, 145, 152 f., 167, 186, 190, 201 f., 214 f., 217, 224, 226, 240, 244, 251
pastoral poetics 6, 20 f., 49, 54, 91, 106, 108, 113, 132, 188, 190, 202, 235 f., 242, 251, 254
pastoral posture 243
pastoral practice 223
pastoral precept 230
pastoral predecessor 8, 82, 227
pastoral prehistory 196
pastoral pretension 50
pastoral production 16, 25, 57, 90, 92, 114, 117, 131
pastoral program 157
pastoral property 143
pastoral provenance 77
pastoral qualification 99
pastoral realm 68
pastoral reed 78

pastoral region 142
pastoral register 74
pastoral relaxation 172
pastoral rule 144
pastoral scenario 186, 217, 233, 253
pastoral scene 15
pastoral scenery 196
pastoral session 253
pastoral setting 3, 22, 52, 117f., 145, 201, 204
pastoral shade 8, 48, 57, 90, 173, 186, 225, 237
pastoral sign 57
pastoral simplicity 93
pastoral singer 54, 62, 72, 88, 93, 95, 130, 143, 202, 204, 209, 213
pastoral singing 201, 241, 253
pastoral situation 90
pastoral song 22, 45, 49, 55–7, 59f., 65f., 70, 72, 75, 78f., 90, 93, 95, 98, 101f., 106, 118, 130, 140, 171, 186, 203f., 215, 223, 241, 248
pastoral sorceress 128
pastoral space 28, 42, 48, 51, 53, 56, 58, 60, 62, 69f., 75, 88, 93, 108, 136, 144, 153, 171, 206, 209, 230
pastoral stake 226
pastoral standard 225
pastoral staple 200
pastoral state of affairs 143
pastoral story 125, 186
pastoral subject-matter 80, 130
pastoral succession / successor 7, 113, 152, 190, 202, 216
pastoral symbolism 31
pastoral technique 104
pastoral term 100
pastoral text 123, 131, 152
pastoral topic 153, 251
pastoral *topos* 234, 249
pastoral tradition 6, 8, 10, 15, 17, 19–21, 23–5, 28, 39, 45, 50, 53, 55–9, 61f., 67, 70, 74, 76–8, 100, 103, 105, 108f., 117, 125, 133, 136–9, 143–5, 147, 149, 152f., 170f., 175, 189, 195, 197, 200f., 203f., 207, 212, 215f., 219, 227, 229, 237, 240f., 249, 251f.

pastoral tree 101, 129, 206, 240
pastoral trend 92, 110, 117, 226
pastoral typology 206
pastoral umpire 230, 242, 248
pastoral upheaval 248
pastoral value 48, 56, 59, 72f., 86, 89f., 95, 101, 208, 215, 230, 232, 248, 253
pastoral victory 94
pastoral voice 61, 93
pastoral wealth 94, 118
pastoral work 56, 144, 196
pastoral world 35, 38, 42, 49, 55, 60, 101, 108, 136, 178, 197, 199, 209, 213, 215, 223, 225, 231f., 246, 253
pastoralism 59, 61, 88, 92, 95, 136, 144, 204, 223, 231, 254
pasturage 172
pasture / pasturing 79, 173, 200, 238
Pataikos 151
pater 16, 18, 77, 152, 190
pathetic fallacy 8, 65, 88, 98, 107, 196, 198f., 237
Patroclus 246
patron / *patronus* 4, 15, 41, 48, 63, 79f., 90, 240
patronage 10, 79, 111
patulus 90f., 116, 186
pauper-poet 15
paupertas / poverty 58, 79f., 111–4, 147
Pausanias 161
pax 4, 9, 26, 30, 34–7, 53, 68, 230
pax Augusta 26
peace / peaceful 26, 28, 30f., 34–6, 40, 51f., 68, 71, 75, 77
peacekeeper / peacemaker 27, 37, 71
peculium 59, 74, 128, 171
pedagogue / pederastic 89, 246
pen / penning 94, 170, 172–4, 185
penates 39
penitence 139, 144
perfect (*tense*) 116
Peripatetic 158
Perses 161, 163
Persius 110, 152, 223
persona 10, 17, 53, 159, 161–3, 166, 182, 201, 230
personal authority 180

personal empathy / involvement 164, 179
Perusia 41
Petale 228 f., 235, 242 f., 245 f.
Petasos 228, 238 f.
Philinus 246
Philippi 27 f., 38, 41
Philostratus 151
phocae / vituli marini 100
Phoebus 24, 68 f., 203, 237
Phyllis 125 f., 128 – 36, 138 – 42, 144 f., 147 – 51, 207, 211, 228, 242, 244 f.
pietas / piety 56 f., 208 f.
pignus 226, 234
Pindar 110
pine-tree / *pinus* 8, 16, 18 f., 50, 55, 57, 88, 202, 218
pipe / piping 8, 15, 17, 21, 57, 64, 75, 92, 95, 113, 132 f., 140, 145, 147, 190, 199, 202, 233, 243
Pirithous 246
pitch 174 – 6
pitiless lover 148
pius 32, 56
plait / plaiting 144 f.
plane-tree 50, 86
plant 9, 17, 65, 69, 138, 146, 206
Platonic 158
Plautine / Plautus 85, 132, 247, 249
pledge 95, 143, 201, 224 f., 229, 234 f., 238, 245, 249
plough / ploughman 74, 98, 237
plum 146
plural 44, 85, 112, 164, 179, 187
poculum 94, 97, 107, 207 f., 238
poem 1, 3, 6 f., 9 f., 15 f., 19, 27, 36, 43, 49, 51, 57, 63, 67 f., 71, 76, 86 – 9, 96, 106, 109 f., 114, 117 – 9, 123 – 5, 135 – 8, 142, 150, 153, 157 – 9, 161 – 3, 172, 181 f., 184 – 8, 191, 195 – 7, 199 f., 215, 217, 223 f., 226, 229, 233, 235, 240, 244, 248 f., 252 f.
poet 1 – 3, 7, 9 f., 15, 21, 23, 25 – 7, 29 f., 32 f., 35 – 8, 41 – 3, 45 – 8, 50 f., 55, 58, 60, 62 – 5, 78 – 82, 89 f., 93, 96, 104 f., 108, 111 – 4, 118, 123 f., 128 f., 136 f., 145, 150, 152 f., 157, 159, 161 – 6, 168, 178, 182 – 5, 188, 198 – 201, 214, 224, 226 f., 229, 239, 243, 251, 253
poet of small means 80, 112
poet-teacher 162, 183 f.
poetic / poetical / poetics 3, 5 – 7, 9, 11, 16 – 8, 20 f., 24, 27, 35 f., 41 f., 46 f., 49, 51 – 7, 60, 62, 64 – 6, 70, 75, 78 – 81, 84, 86, 90 – 2, 94 f., 98, 101 – 9, 111, 113 – 5, 117 f., 124, 131 f., 135 – 7, 141, 143, 145, 149, 153, 158 – 64, 166, 182 – 5, 187 – 91, 199 f., 202 – 4, 207 f., 210, 226, 229, 231 f., 235 f., 241 f., 245, 248, 251 – 4
poetic art 102, 105, 113
poetic discourse 35, 46, 92, 95, 98, 102, 105, 107 f., 111, 113, 117, 131, 229, 252
poetic excellence 107, 202
poetic initiation 16, 64, 113, 202 f., 252
poetic purity 141
poetic register 113
poetic self-consciousness 160 f., 182 – 5, 188, 191, 252
poetic simultaneity 160 f., 182 – 5, 188, 191, 252
poetic slenderness 56, 66, 184
poetic succession 16, 64, 190, 202 f.
poetological 16 – 8, 20 f., 23 f., 43, 46 f., 49, 54, 56 f., 60, 62, 64 f., 78 – 81, 86, 91 f., 95, 102 – 4, 106 f., 109, 114, 119, 123, 125, 136, 145, 183 – 5, 187, 189 f., 198, 200 f., 203, 205 – 7, 213, 219, 237, 239, 242, 248
poetry 2, 6, 11, 15 – 7, 20 – 4, 35, 38 f., 42 – 6, 51 f., 54 – 7, 59 – 62, 64, 67, 69 f., 73, 76, 78 – 80, 87 f., 91 f., 95, 101 f., 105 – 7, 113, 117, 119, 123, 136, 145, 149, 153, 157 – 63, 165 – 9, 173, 181 – 8, 190 f., 201 – 3, 206 – 9, 214 – 6, 224, 231, 235, 237, 240, 243 f., 251 – 3
poetry as symptom of or antidote to love 214 f.
polar bear 100, 103
Polemon 151
political / politics 5, 7 – 11, 15 f., 24, 28 – 32, 34 f., 37, 40 f., 43, 46 – 8, 50, 52, 56, 63, 65, 67 f., 70, 73, 75, 79, 81, 86, 92, 107, 111, 119, 136, 149, 166, 236, 241, 251, 253 f.

Pollio 31, 55, 80
Polybotas 133
Polyphemus 25, 131, 137, 139 f., 142, 146, 196, 210 f., 230
Pomona 203
Pompey 27
poor poet 58, 112
poppy 146
populus Romanus 26
portico 90, 119
post–Augustan 86
Post–Classical 9, 42 – 5, 47, 49 f., 53, 83 – 6, 88 f., 115 f., 118, 217 – 9, 251 f.
post–Theocritean 3, 58, 85, 149, 199, 211 f., 246
practical issues 165
praeceptor / *praeceptum* / *praecipere* 162 f., 166, 180, 187, 191
praeceptor amoris 35, 126, 130, 134, 184
Praeneste 18
praesagium 39
praesens deus 57, 68
praeteritio 180, 203
pragmatics 253
praise 1, 3 f., 10, 19, 24, 30, 32 – 4, 36, 41, 46, 51, 53, 64, 69, 72 f., 86, 90, 92, 101, 105, 107, 110, 112, 114, 119, 136, 211, 213, 232, 242, 253
Praxinoa 96
prayer 61
pre–Calpurnian 8, 10, 25, 48 f., 51, 56 – 9, 65 f., 69, 71 – 3, 78, 86, 89, 93 – 5, 97 f., 118, 130 f., 136 f., 139 f., 145, 148, 153, 175, 188, 190, 196, 203, 205, 208 f., 213, 223, 225 f., 232, 234, 241, 252
pre–Vergilian 71, 189
precept 118, 157, 166 f., 170 f., 173 – 9, 185, 189, 230
precious stone 106, 119
pregnant use 95
preposition / prepositional 43 f., 100, 116
present 4, 145 f., 175, 212 f.
prestige 111, 119
priamel 138
pride 210
primus–motif 183 f.

prince / *princeps* 4 f., 9 f., 24, 34 f., 46, 52, 61, 63, 68, 71, 78, 87, 109, 112, 114, 118 f., 254
princeps–motif 63
principatus 16, 28, 36 f., 39 – 41, 59
prize 93 f., 143, 153, 196, 208, 215, 225, 230
profit 58 f., 95, 170 f.
programmatic 15, 30, 45, 47 – 9, 59, 61 f., 64, 70, 75, 80, 107, 117, 125, 143, 145, 190, 197, 199, 201, 208 f., 227, 235, 241, 245, 251
prolixity 96
pronoun 61, 164, 179, 248
propaganda 9, 31, 68, 119
propemptikon 245
Propertian / Propertius 18, 22, 118, 197 f., 215
prophecy / prophet / prophetic 4, 9, 15, 18 – 25, 29 f., 32 – 6, 38, 41, 43 – 6, 107, 202 f.
proscriptions 41
prose 169, 173 – 6, 178, 181, 203, 252
Protagoras 161
protreptic 142
proverbial 94, 103
pruning 144, 177
pseudo–Theocritean 201
Ptolemy 67, 118
public show 92, 109
puella 25, 127, 135 f., 146, 150, 163, 197 f., 213, 215, 226, 238
puer 31 f., 42, 83, 138, 179, 189, 195, 197 f., 215, 225
punish / punishment 28, 129, 145
pure / purely 74, 94, 190, 198, 210, 231, 253
purification / purify 94
purity 25, 60, 78, 80, 141
Pylades 246

quarrel 5, 129 f., 135, 147, 223, 233, 244 f., 248 f.
quasi–hymnic 90
quasi–magic 102
queri 129
questioning–patterns 165

quicksilver 174
quince 146
quindecimviri sacris faciundis 34
quinquennium 2, 5, 26, 28, 31, 36, 38, 111
Quirinus 29

rack 143
rain 62, 172
reaping hook 237
recitation / recite 27, 37, 248
recline 16, 70, 76, 129, 174, 243
reconciliation / reconciliatory 4, 125, 135–7
recusatio 24, 46, 63, 67
red acanthus 65
reed-grass 149
reed-pipe 15, 17, 21, 75
referee 227, 234, 243, 249
refrain 211
regime 1, 5, 10, 50, 109–12
religious 23, 50, 56, 61, 75, 207–9
remorse 151
Remus 28
repeat / repetition / repetitive 7, 59, 64, 86, 127, 130, 163f., 181–3, 188, 198
repentance 4, 144
reproach 202, 233
Republic / Republican 38, 40, 101
res publica 27
respect 73, 91, 246
rhetoric / rhetorical 23, 124, 132f., 139, 143, 180, 226, 233, 235
rhinoceros 99
riddle 249
rival / rivalry 93–5, 102, 112, 126–8, 131f., 134, 136, 140f., 147f., 150f., 211, 213, 229, 243, 245
river 21, 54, 78, 82, 100, 199f., 241
rocky-setting 57
Roman 7, 18, 20f., 24, 26–9, 31, 39–41, 53f., 56, 58, 60, 63, 78f., 86–8, 91f., 97, 100, 106, 112f., 118, 123f., 126, 129, 131, 135f., 139, 147, 149, 153, 158f., 161–3, 183, 187, 201f., 206, 210, 226f., 229, 232, 240f., 247f., 252–4
Roman Callimacheanism 7, 187, 202
Roman New Comedy 124, 135

Rome 8, 26–8, 31–3, 36, 39, 41, 54, 60, 80, 87f., 90f., 93, 102, 107, 110, 112, 117, 119, 183, 229, 232, 248
Romulus 28f., 44
rose 146
rota Vergiliana 17
rural 7, 22, 35f., 41, 101, 107, 119, 209
rus 54, 56, 70, 81, 96, 170, 199, 253
rush 149, 185
rustic / *rusticus* 8, 18, 50, 52, 55f., 69, 71f., 78, 85, 88–90, 98, 107, 109, 111–4, 118, 131, 142, 181, 199, 203f., 208f., 211, 213, 231, 241
rusticitas / rusticity 55f., 112f., 118
Rutulian 236

sacrifice / sacrificial 33, 81, 86, 170, 209f.
safeguard / safety 34, 76, 89
Sannio 247
Sappho 19
satire / satiric / satirist 27, 89, 110, 171
Saturn 29–31
Satyr 8, 199
Scribonia 31
scythe 22
sea 50, 100, 141, 147
sea-leek 174f.
seal 100, 103
second Triumvirate 41
secure / *securitas* / security 4, 8f., 26, 30, 34–9, 44, 49, 51, 53, 57, 68, 73–5, 79, 87, 89, 95, 105, 107f., 111f., 131, 135, 139, 144, 161, 164, 171f., 179, 191, 204, 206f.
self-praise 4
self-presentation 209
self-reflexive 55, 105, 108, 124, 165, 182–4
self-reflexive question 165
semiquinaria 180
senator 37, 41
Seneca / Senecan 15f., 28, 31, 36f., 41, 44, 46f., 63, 166, 223, 247
separate / separation / separator 3, 113, 130, 138, 143, 179, 199
sepulchral 148
sermo amatorius 207, 230
sermo plebeius 45

serpent / serpentine   106, 118, 176 f., 180, 241
servile adulator   10
servitium amoris   139, 150
Servius   162, 178
servus callidus   135
servus fallax   150
set-phrase   165, 180
Severus Alexander   1, 63
sex / sexual / sexuality   25, 131, 144, 153, 169, 197, 229, 233, 243 – 7, 249
Sextus Pompey   41
shade / shadowy / shady   8, 15, 18 – 20, 38, 48 – 50, 55, 57, 59, 76, 82, 90, 98, 101, 129, 132, 173 f., 186, 195, 199, 201, 206, 225, 237
shearing   71, 174 – 6, 179, 212
sheep   5, 8, 71, 82, 99, 145, 167, 170, 190
shepherd   15, 18, 20 – 2, 25, 35, 42, 47, 60, 148, 170 f., 190, 199, 204, 207, 243 f.
Sibylline books / oracles   34 f.
Sicilian / Sicily   2, 41, 211, 244, 248
sidus Iulium / *Caesaris astrum*   38 – 40, 72, 92
silence / silent   39, 50 f., 73, 86, 93, 118, 200, 241, 245, 250
Silenus   20, 65, 187, 204
Silvanus   8, 202 f.
Silvia   235 f.
Simaetha   135, 142
Simichidas   10, 113 f., 245
simile   98, 134, 228, 236
sing / singer / singing   30, 34, 47, 54 – 6, 60, 62, 67, 72, 78 f., 82, 85, 88, 93 – 5, 102, 118, 129 f., 132, 134, 138, 140, 143, 149, 161, 173, 195 f., 200 – 2, 204, 206 – 10, 213, 215 f., 224, 227 f., 230 – 4, 237, 241 – 3, 245, 250, 252 f.
singing match   4 f., 21, 67, 93 f., 102 f., 118, 143, 146, 195 f., 202, 214, 223 – 5, 227 f., 230, 232 – 4, 239, 242 – 4, 248, 251 f.
singular   162, 164, 167, 179, 228
sitting arrangements   111 f.
skin   18, 99, 145, 147, 175
sky   67, 77, 105
slapstick   247, 250
slave   112, 128, 132, 135, 147, 247, 249

sleep   174
sleepless / sleeplessness   8 f., 137 f., 150
slender / slenderness   54, 56 f., 62, 64 – 6, 79, 81, 145, 184, 202 f.
slogan   119
small means   3, 80, 109, 112 f., 118, 147
snake   61, 106, 111, 174, 176, 180
sol / sun   15 – 9, 62, 82, 170, 173 f., 177, 185 f., 214
soldier   35, 37, 133
son   5, 18, 27, 31 f., 34, 157, 162, 166 f., 190 f.
song   4, 15, 19 f., 22 – 4, 32, 36, 41 f., 45, 48 f., 52, 55 – 7, 59 f., 64 – 7, 69 f., 72, 75, 78 f., 90, 92 f., 95, 98, 101 f., 106, 117 f., 123, 125, 128, 130, 132, 134 f., 137 f., 140, 146, 148 – 50, 153, 171, 186, 195 f., 198 – 200, 203 – 6, 214 – 7, 223, 225, 228, 231 f., 240 – 2, 244, 248 f., 252 f.
song about songs   123, 217
song-contest   4, 41, 52, 118, 195 f., 208, 214 – 7, 219, 223, 227, 233, 240, 243 f.
song-exchange   4 f., 8, 21, 48, 55, 61, 67, 69, 82, 93, 102 f., 118, 130, 141, 145, 147, 149, 175, 189, 214, 224 – 6, 233, 235, 240, 242, 244 f., 249 f., 253
song-making   248
song-performance / song-performing   67, 225, 248
sonorous   59, 73, 93, 118, 186
sorceress   124, 128, 150
sorrow   87, 133
Sosias   151
sound / resound   28, 39, 48, 52, 60, 72, 79, 83, 85 f., 98, 200, 215, 240 f., 249
sparsio   101, 119
spectacle / *spectaculum*   89, 91 – 3, 96 f., 100, 118 f.
spectator   101
spellbound tree   73
spendthrift   59, 95, 171
sphere   29
spring   5, 73, 97, 167 – 9, 172, 212
spring (*fons*)   78, 88, 195, 242
squabble / squabbling   242, 247, 249
squanderer spouse / wife   128, 171
stag   5, 224, 235 f., 245

stage mechanisms 101
stake 5, 143, 224–6, 228, 233, 235, 238, 248, 250
stalls 143
stamp 174
State 27–9, 34, 37, 40, 254
Statius 1, 119, 223
statue 22f., 110, 207
steal / stealing 145, 149
step-mother 143
stick 130
Stimicon 93–5, 102, 223, 245
Stoic 30, 163
straw 141, 177f., 233
strawberry 61f.
stream 49, 241
strophe / strophic 4, 67, 69, 71f., 76, 211, 226, 232
structural / structure 3, 22, 26, 29, 61, 87, 105f., 119, 129, 137, 167, 185, 195, 241, 251
student 158, 160–4, 166f., 179f., 182f., 185, 187f., 191, 252
style / stylistic 1, 6, 8, 17f., 20, 30, 43, 46f., 54, 56, 61, 65, 69f., 76, 84, 86, 89, 95, 107, 114, 123f., 126, 129, 131, 137f., 150, 152, 167, 169, 179, 181, 187, 190f., 228f., 233, 243, 251f.
subjunctive 164, 181, 218
substantive 171, 208
succession / successor 7, 16, 64, 67, 98, 113, 150, 152, 190, 201–3, 211, 216
Suetonius 46, 166
suicidal / suicide 4, 147f., 151, 231
sulphur 174f., 177
summary 164, 182
summer 5, 15f., 18, 129, 138, 167f., 172f., 176, 180, 185, 195, 212, 227
sumptuosity / sumptuous 87, 90, 96, 117, 243
superlative 229
surrendered hands 135
sus babirussa 99
swallow 168
swan 228
sweet / sweetness 64, 78, 95, 146, 172, 174, 196, 199, 201

sweet-heart 113, 125, 130, 135, 140, 143, 146, 150f., 212, 231, 235
sylvan 55, 88, 199
sympathetic reaction 87
syntactic / syntax 9, 43f., 91, 116, 178, 229
syntagm 17f., 22, 25f., 29f., 34f., 42, 52f., 60, 65, 77, 80, 88, 94, 104, 116, 127, 129, 162, 165, 169, 172, 174, 179f., 187f., 198, 203, 207, 213, 215–7, 229f., 234, 241
Syracusan / Syracuse 35, 96
Syrinx 21
syrinx 7, 131, 138, 140f., 226

tale within a tale narrative 129
Tarentine / Tarentum 50, 211
Tarpeian peak 105
taurus 8, 64, 88, 99, 107, 143, 200
teach / teacher / teaching 21, 132f., 158, 160–4, 166f., 179, 182–5, 187f., 190f., 204, 246, 252
teacher-disciple bond 190
teacher-pupil relationship 162
teacher-student constellation 160f., 164, 166, 191
teacher-student liaison 161
tears 138
technical 42, 48, 55, 99, 103, 118f., 157, 160f., 163, 167, 169, 171, 173, 175–7, 179, 191, 205f., 212
telescope / telescoping 124, 198, 240
Terence 44, 132, 247, 249
teres 42, 46, 78f., 105, 185, 239
terminus technicus 103, 143, 204, 206, 212, 225, 233
text / textual 1, 3, 6, 17, 22–4, 26f., 29, 35–7, 40f., 43, 45f., 48, 53, 60, 62, 67, 80, 85, 96f., 109, 115, 118f., 123, 125, 128f., 131, 136f., 143f., 148, 150, 152f., 158, 161, 163, 166–8, 171f., 174, 177f., 180, 182, 185, 188, 191, 197, 201f., 204, 224, 228f., 235–7, 239, 244f., 247, 250–3
Thalysia / Thalysian 113f., 245
Thapsus 104
theft / thief / thievery 145, 149, 233
Themis 30

General Index — **333**

Theocritean / Theocritus 2 f., 6 – 8, 10, 16 f., 23, 25, 49 f., 56, 58, 61, 67, 85, 88 f., 92 f., 95 – 7, 105 f., 109, 113, 115, 117 f., 123, 126, 131, 133 – 40, 142 f., 147, 149, 152, 158, 175, 188, 196 – 9, 201, 208, 210 – 2, 215 f., 223, 226, 233 – 5, 240, 243, 245 f., 248, 251 f.
theoretical knowledge 159, 165
Theseus 142, 246
Thestylis 132, 135
thicket 126, 186
thirst 173, 177
thorn / thorny 60, 126, 149
threat / threaten 4, 58, 146 – 8, 151, 213, 244, 247
throne 15 f., 38
thunderbolt 70
Thurii 18
Thyrsis 4, 94, 171, 196, 201, 210, 216, 245
Tibullan / Tibullus 34 – 6, 46, 74, 90, 118, 210
tillage 162
Titus 2
Tityrus 4, 8, 10, 21, 34, 38, 49, 53, 57, 59 – 61, 63 f., 68, 70, 75 f., 78 f., 81, 87 – 91, 94 f., 107 – 9, 112 f., 128 f., 132, 145, 150, 152, 171, 205, 216, 231 f.
toga 53, 109
token resistance of the beloved 249
topos 71, 80, 124, 138, 140, 198, 227, 234, 238, 249
Torquatus 19, 27, 223
town 96, 119
Tractatus Coislinianus 158
tradere 16, 152, 190
traditional pastoral / pastoralism 61, 64, 66, 68 f., 73, 78, 88, 92, 95, 136, 144, 154, 188, 204, 211 f., 232, 250
tragedy / tragic 19, 24, 28, 62, 231, 240
transcend / transcendence / transcending 5, 45 f., 48, 52 f., 57, 61, 66 – 8, 71, 74, 76, 79, 89, 94, 96, 110, 117, 123 f., 126, 144 f., 149, 154, 188, 219, 224, 226
transitional set-phrases 180
translatio imperii 39
transmission 2 f., 105
treatise 160, 167, 173, 176

tree 4, 8, 15 – 7, 19, 22 f., 50, 55, 57, 59, 61 f., 69, 71, 73, 75, 85 f., 88, 90 f., 98, 101 f., 129, 136, 138, 147, 177, 185 f., 195, 199 – 201, 205 – 7, 216, 218, 232, 236 f., 240
trimmer / trimming 174, 177
trip 88, 93
triumph 26 f., 69, 90
Trojan 111, 236, 248
trophy 143
Troy 33
trumpet / trumpeter 28, 75, 237
tunica 109
turtle dove 145 f.
tusks 98
tutorial 185
twin brother 151
twitter 168
typology 93, 118, 158, 206, 249

umpire 5, 67, 196, 199, 201, 216, 223, 225, 230, 234, 242 – 4, 248, 250
un-Callimachean 49, 95, 141
unblemished (*notion of*) 78, 141
Underworld 27, 31
unfamiliar (*notion of*) 49, 205
unknown (*notion of*) 49, 206
unpastoral 7, 61, 74, 131, 138, 144, 149, 171, 197, 201, 206, 226, 229, 231
untrodden paths 184
untrustworthiness 127
(un)willingness-motif 187
urban / *urbanitas* / *urbs* 8, 26, 39, 53 – 9, 62 f., 69, 74, 81 f., 87, 89 – 96, 98, 100, 102 f., 107 – 9, 112, 114 f., 117, 119, 128, 131, 133, 135, 138, 142, 153, 171, 196, 207, 209, 213, 241, 245, 251, 253
utilitas / utility 165, 179
uxor dotata 132

vacca 16, 152, 190
vacuus 242 f.
Valerius Flaccus 189
Valerius Messallinus 34
valley 98, 104
Varro 45, 167, 174, 180
Varro of Atax 159, 178

vates 32, 65, 184
vaticinium 22, 45, 47, 251
vegetation 117, 232
venatio 101, 105, 118
venom / venomous 106
Venus 25
verb / verbal 43–5, 55, 57, 65, 75 f., 81, 91, 103–7, 116, 140, 142, 162–5, 167, 169, 183 f., 190, 207, 218, 238, 242
Vergil / Vergilian 3, 5–8, 10, 16–25, 27 f., 30–5, 38 f., 41–3, 45–7, 49–82, 85–94, 97, 101 f., 104–9, 111–4, 117 f., 123–5, 127–9, 132 f., 136, 138–41, 143–5, 149 f., 152 f., 158–60, 162–4, 166–8, 170–3, 175–8, 180 f., 183 f., 186–90, 196–204, 206–17, 223 f., 226 f., 229–35, 238 f., 241, 243–6, 248 f., 251–4
Vertumnus 22 f.
veteran 35, 104
vetus 35, 91 f., 180
via Latina 90
victim / victimise 56, 134, 170, 226, 247
victor / victorious / victory 26, 38, 63, 94, 104, 135, 202, 214, 217, 227 f., 233 f., 250
viewing 93, 102, 105 f., 108, 112, 117 f.
vigil 146
vigilatum carmen 137 f.
vine / vineyard 52, 144, 208
vintage 15
violence / violent 41, 133 f., 150
violet 146
Virgo 30
visual arts 102
viticulture 162
Vitruvius 118
vituli / aequorei vituli 100, 103, 116
vocabulary 44
voice 24, 52, 55, 61, 77, 93, 138, 140, 223, 228 f., 232
voluntary death 148
Vulgar Latin 45

wakeful / wakefulness 137 f.
wander / wandering 19, 35, 138, 186
war / warrior 18, 25–8, 34, 36–40, 60, 70, 74 f., 109, 236

wasteful wife 59
water / watery 48, 78, 98, 101, 141, 173, 199, 204, 206, 214 f., 241
wax-joined 132 f., 147
wealth 4, 17, 36, 47, 90, 94 f., 106, 110 f., 113, 118, 142 f., 146 f., 211
weapon 26
weather 15, 62, 172, 177
weave / weaving 62, 105, 107, 144 f., 197
wedding 231
weeping 138, 236
Werbende Dichtung 130, 143, 147
Werbung 4, 139, 141, 143
wild 64, 99, 101, 198, 225, 232
willow 105, 129, 185, 206
win / winner 5, 94 f., 112, 130, 138 f., 145, 202, 211 f., 217, 223, 225, 229 f., 235, 243 f.
wind 42, 59, 70, 177, 200
wine 139
winter 5, 73, 167 f., 170, 175, 177, 179 f., 185
wolf-skin 18
wolf-hound 225
wood / wooden / woodland 9, 43, 51 f., 57, 87, 97 f., 100, 105, 177, 199, 208, 218, 242
woods 59 f., 69, 71, 93 f., 98, 100, 113, 132, 140, 142, 172, 177, 231, 243 f.
wool 84, 174 f., 179, 185, 211
wording 52 f., 64, 72, 82, 86, 90, 149, 167, 171, 178, 186, 197–9, 201, 212, 214–6, 219, 229, 233, 238, 247
worship / worshipper 28, 73
wrangling 224
wreath 146, 202
writing 23, 136, 224

yodelling 88
young 4, 8, 15, 23, 33 f., 61, 70, 87 f., 91, 94, 103, 109, 113 f., 135, 142, 148 f., 151, 163, 166, 186, 189–91, 196, 206, 209, 214, 216, 225, 236, 245 f., 251 f.
youngling 143, 170 f.

Zeus 70
zoological 99
zoom out 6, 124, 198, 240

ἀγών 202, 228, 233, 243 f., 249
ἀμοιβαῖον 21
ἀσυχία 91
βουκολιασμὸς 195, 197, 201, 212, 219, 224 f., 227, 244 f., 252
εἰδογραφία 5
θεωρητική 159
κισσύβιον 97, 105, 197, 208, 235

μακαρισμὸς 108 f.
ποίησις παιδευτική 158
πρῶτον λεγόμενον 66
σκίλλα 176
συμπάθεια τῶν ὅλων 199, 237
σφραγὶς 56, 182
ὑφηγητική 158, 167
φιλοπονία 29